The Lost Centuries

By the same author

A SOLDIER WITH THE ARABS

THE STORY OF THE ARAB LEGION

BRITAIN AND THE ARABS

WAR IN THE DESERT

THE GREAT ARAB CONQUESTS

THE EMPIRE OF THE ARABS

THE COURSE OF EMPIRE

THE MIDDLE EAST CRISIS

THE LOST CENTURIES

From the Muslim Empires to the Renaissance of Europe

1145–1453

Lieutenant-General
SIR JOHN GLUBB
K.C.B., C.M.G., D.S.O., O.B.E., M.C.

PRENTICE-HALL INC.
Englewood Cliffs

Printed in Great Britain

Library of Congress Catalog Card Number—67-22280 54072

What means this turmoil among the nations?
Why do the peoples cherish vain dreams?
See how the kings of the earth stand in array,
How the rulers make common cause . . .
Princes, take warning;
Learn your lesson, you that rule the world.
Tremble, and serve the Lord, rejoicing in his presence,
But with awe in your hearts.

Psalm II (Trans. RONALD KNOX)

Cities and Thrones and Powers
Stand in Time's eye,
Almost as long as flowers,
Which daily die:
But, as new buds put forth
To glad new men,
Out of the spent and unconsidered Earth
The Cities rise again.

This season's Daffodil,
She never hears
What change, what chance, what chill,
Cut down last year's;
But with bold countenance,
And knowledge small,
Esteems her seven days continuance
To be perpetual.

RUDYARD KIPLING

Preface

THIS book is the fourth of a series of books, in which my object has been to join the history of Rome to that of the modern world. Roman supremacy lasted from perhaps 150 B.C. to A.D. 180, the date of the death of Marcus Aurelius. However, in spite of intervals of confusion and barbarian invasions, the Western Roman Empire did not finally disappear until A.D. 476.

The Eastern Roman Empire, with its capital in Constantinople, continued in existence and under Justinian (483–565) even made an attempt to reconquer the West. The effort was beyond her power and the Franks, Goths and other barbarians constituted their own kingdoms in Italy, France and Spain.

The Arabs emerged from the Arabian peninsula in 634 and by 712 had conquered an empire extending from Spain and Morocco to modern Pakistan and the borders of China. Europe, cut off from overseas trade, relapsed into a feudal and agricultural society. The Islamic countries remained the dominating powers of the world—omitting distant China—until the tide turned gradually between the twelfth and the fifteenth centuries, the period covered by the present narrative. Thereafter the rise of Europe and subsequently of America is well-known.

* * *

Centuries of war between Muslims and Christians elapsed before Europe achieved the upper hand. The Renaissance followed and the general lines of education in the West were laid down. Religious hostility against Islam was still intense and the memories of the long wars in the Mediterranean were vivid.

Probably as a result of these influences, the principle was generally accepted that a liberal education necessitated a knowledge of Latin and, if possible, of Greek and a fair acquaintance with Roman history from the republic to the first twelve Caesars. Thereafter historical teaching ceased and was resumed, in England at least, at the Norman Conquest in 1066. An interval of eight hundred years was passed over in silence or dismissed in one contemptuous sentence such as "the centuries of barbarian Oriental invasion". Roman civilization was said to have been reborn at the Renaissance and to have grown into modern Western democracy, no debt to Arab or Muslim culture being admitted.

In our own days, ease of travel and the labours of many orientalists and Arabists in Europe and, in recent years, in America have enabled us to form a truer appreciation of the course of history in Western Asia and the Mediterranean from the seventh to the fourteenth centuries. Even, however, if we assume, for the sake of argument, that Roman and now European civilization are superior to any produced by the Arabs or the Persians, it certainly does not follow that the centuries of Muslim predominance should be completely censored from our text-books. For history is a continuous process and one event, whether it be a happy or a tragic one, leads to another. Even, for example, if we continue to insist that the Arabs in Spain were heathen barbarians, there is no doubt that the long religious wars in the peninsula forged the weapon of Spanish chivalry which later conquered America. In spite of these considerations, however, the old taboos and prejudices still survive.

In the immense stretches of time which separate the palaeolithic age from our own, eight centuries have been omitted from our curricula. I am not endeavouring to glorify one race at the expense of another or to prove any pet theory of my own, but I cannot help feeling that the history of our development should be impartial and continuous. My hope is that my four volumes may draw the attention of a few at least of my contemporaries to The Lost Centuries.

J. B. G.

Author's Note

EVERY work which in any way involves Arabic names is liable to involve a controversy over transliteration. There is now a generally accepted method in use among Arabists for transliteration into English. Rightly or wrongly I have not used the modern English method because I have tried to produce one which would help the ordinary reader to pronounce correctly, although knowing no Arabic.

The complexity of Arab titles increased with the decadence of their civilization. Many Muslim princes, during the centuries dealt with in this book, assumed two titles in front of their personal names. The first, which I have called the Throne-name, was taken by a new sultan when he mounted the throne. It took the form of king accompanied by an adjective—The Victorious King, The Just King and so on. The second title was a religious one and embodied the word *deen*, which means religion. Such names were Sword of the Religion, Glory of the Religion, Defender of the Religion.

Thus the names and titles of a sultan might be "The Victorious King, Sword of the Religion, Muhammad the son of Hamdan": Al Malik al Nasir Saif al Deen Muhammad. The confusion is increased by the fact that one writer might refer to this individual as the Victorious—al Nasir—another might call him Saif al Deen and a third might refer to him as Sultan Muhammad. I have tried to use only one name for each person. Where this is the Throne-name I have retained the article al—Al Nasir, Al Aadil—where it is the personal name I have used no article.

The omission of a bibliography in the first three volumes of this series has been criticized and I have accordingly added a brief bibliography to this work, covering all four volumes. The production of a book nowadays seems to be almost as complicated as the preparation of a budget—everything one wants to do would cost too much. The price of books has risen so rapidly that every addition to the length risks raising the price beyond the capacity of the reader.

I have always complained of historians who wrote books full of place names but without maps. I consequently resolved that every place mentioned in my text would be shown on a map, a process which has inevitably increased costs. The same applies to genealogical trees and footnotes. I have tried to compromise on all these requirements. Doubtless some readers would prefer more footnotes and bibliography and fewer maps and genealogical trees or vice versa. I can only crave their indulgence.

I have endeavoured to base the four volumes of this series on the works of the original Arab historians, especially Tabari, Masoodi, Ibn al Athir and Maqrizi. Their histories are extremely lengthy and detailed. For example, one of the works of Ibn al Athir, *Al Kamil fi al Tarikh*, runs into twelve volumes. Thus the work of ploughing through them in the original Arabic has greatly exceeded that of reading all the other books in the bibliography.

A number of lives of the Prophet Muhammad exist in European languages, but after his death in A.D. 632 there are scarcely any histories available in European languages for four hundred and sixty years. Tabari and Masoodi are inevitably our principal sources.

Then, in the 1090s, everything is suddenly changed with the commencement of the Crusades. An extensive literature of the Crusades exists in European languages although the historians in most cases devote little space to the Muslim world, with the exception of Syria and Egypt where the Crusaders were actually operating.

French orientalists have been more active than English in this field and nearly all the Arab historians of the period of the Crusades have been translated into French. Arab historians of North Africa are likewise nearly all obtainable in French. We are profoundly indebted to such great French *savants* as Quatremère, Blochet, Baron de Slane and Lévi-Provençal.

Unfortunately I am able to read rapidly only in English, French and Arabic. Thus many interesting works in Greek, Latin, Persian, Turkish, German and Spanish have been beyond my reach. My life was an active one, spent chiefly in the open air, until I reached the age of fifty-nine, when it appeared to be too late to fill the gaps in my education. As I had learnt Arabic in the course of my duties, however, I decided to base my work on the classical Arab historians, the earliest of whom have not been translated.

I wish again to express my thanks to the Librarian of The School of Oriental and African Studies of the University of London, to the India Office Library at the Commonwealth Relations Office, to the Tunbridge Wells Public Library, to Professor Albert Hourani, Professor of Arabic at Oxford and to Mrs. E. M. Hatt of Faber and Faber Ltd., who introduced me to Ibn al Awam.

I am grateful to the following for permission to quote: the Cardinal Archbishop of Westminster and Burnes and Oates Ltd. for verses from

Ronald Knox's version of the Psalms, to Mrs. Bambridge and Macmillan and Co. Ltd. for verses from "Cities and Thrones and Powers" from *Puck of Pook's Hill* by Rudyard Kipling and to Penguin Books Ltd. for lines from Nevill Coghill's version of *The Canterbury Tales*.

Contents

List of Maps

List of Genealogical Trees

I

War on Two Fronts

There came, more suddenly than we can conceive, a cataclysm—a tidal wave. Four thousand lean Arab spearmen were the vanguard. It will never be explained but we know that there was behind them and filling them with fire, a religion—Islam.

Our people, Christendom, made a last rally of our race for the recovery of Syria from the men of the desert. It is called the "Crusades". That forlorn hope stands vividly in the European mind as a glorious episode of its past. With the end of the thirteenth century that great debate of which Syria had been the field seemed ended. The Christian effort at recovery had failed.

HILAIRE BELLOC, *The Battle Ground* (condensed)

The Seljuqid conquest of 1040–1055 had opened the doors of the country to the nomads. In vain did the chiefs of the Seljuqid race endeavour to close the door behind them, to draw the bolt, and to bar the road to the Turko-Mongol tribes of High Asia. A last great Seljuqid, Sanjar, had tried to arrest the decadence of his family but the heroism of the great sultan wore itself out before difficulties ceaselessly renewed.

RENÉ GROUSSET, *L'Empire des Steppes* (condensed)

I[1]

THE Arabs first appeared on the stage of history as a result of the preaching of Muhammad from A.D. 613 to 632. In the seventh century the world (if we omit India and China) contained two Great Powers—Byzantium, the eastern half of the Roman Empire—and Persia, which included modern Iraq, Iran and Afghanistan. The Arabs were confined to the Arabian Peninsula, between the Red Sea and the Persian Gulf. Most of them were ignorant nomadic tribesmen, who lived in tents in their deserts, and were looked upon with contempt by the Byzantines and Persians, both heirs of ancient civilizations.

Before the death of the Prophet Muhammad, all these ignorant Arabian nomads had—nominally at least—accepted his preaching. A year after his death, they suddenly burst out of their arid peninsula and attacked simultaneously the two Great Powers of the time, Byzantium and Persia.

Within the lifetime of one man, the Persian Empire had ceased to exist and the Arabs had reached the frontiers of China. The Byzantine Empire had meanwhile been driven across the Taurus into Asia Minor. At the same time, the Arabs had swept across North Africa to Morocco, then up through Spain and across the Pyrenees into the south of France. Their triumphant career was finally arrested at Tours, in 732, exactly a hundred years after the death of Muhammad. In the interval they had achieved naval command of the Mediterranean.

The Arabs formed themselves into a great secular empire with its capital at Damascus. Its territories extended from the Atlantic to the borders of China, an area half as large again as that controlled by the Roman Empire in its heyday. The rulers of the empire, known as the khalifs, were derived from the Umaiyid dynasty, the descendants of a cousin of Muhammad. In 750, the Abbasids overthrew the Umaiyids and moved the imperial capital from Damascus to Baghdad.

After the move of the khalifate to Baghdad, Arab imperial power began to decline in the West. Andalus, as the Arabs called Spain, became independent under an Umaiyid prince in 763. In 800, Ifriqiya, corresponding to eastern Algeria and Tunisia, achieved dominion status, followed by independence, annexing also Sicily and southern Italy. The Arabs still dominated the western Mediterranean but as individual states, no longer as one empire.

[1] This chapter contains a summary of the three previous works in this series, *The Great Arab Conquests*, *The Empire of the Arabs* and *The Course of Empire*. It sets the scene for the beginning of the present narrative in 1145.

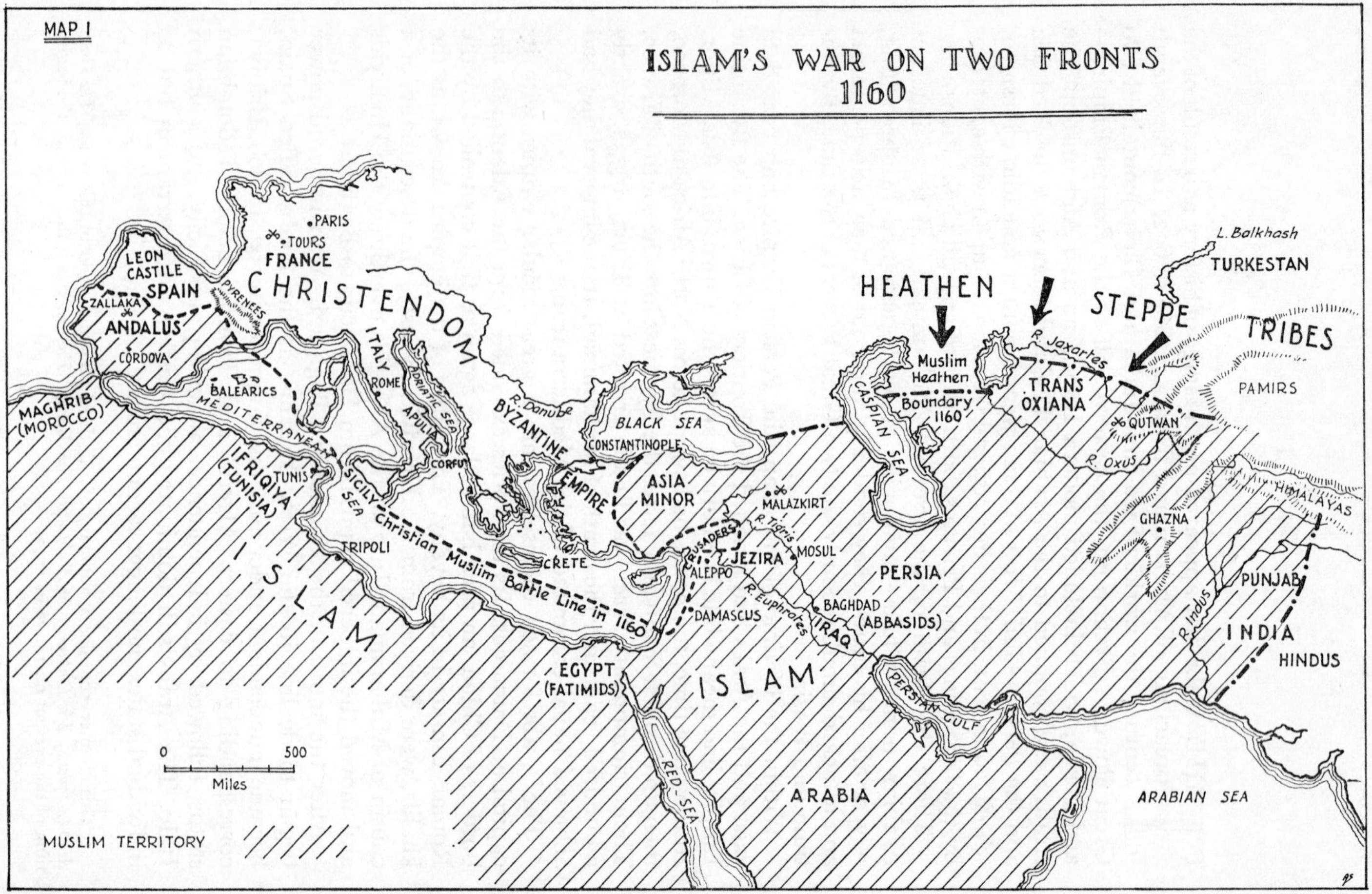
MAP I
ISLAM'S WAR ON TWO FRONTS
1160
PARIS
TOURS
FRANCE
LEON
CASTILE
SPAIN
ZALLAKA
ANDALUS
CORDOVA
PYRENEES
CHRISTENDOM
ITALY
ROME
ADRIATIC SEA
APULIA
CORFU
BALEARICS
MEDITERRANEAN
MAGHRIB
(MOROCCO)
IFRIQIYA
(TUNISIA)
TUNIS
SICILY
SEA
TRIPOLI
Christian Muslim Battle Line in 1160
CRETE
R. Danube
BYZANTINE
EMPIRE
BLACK SEA
CONSTANTINOPLE
ASIA
MINOR
CRUSADERS
ALEPPO
DAMASCUS
MALAZKIRT
R. Tigris
MOSUL
JEZIRA
R. Euphrates
BAGHDAD
(ABBASIDS)
IRAQ
PERSIA
EGYPT
(FATIMIDS)
ISLAM
I S L A M
RED SEA
ARABIA
PERSIAN GULF
CASPIAN SEA
HEATHEN
STEPPE
TRIBES
Muslim
Heathen
Boundary
1160
R. Jaxartes
TRANS
OXIANA
QUTWAN
R. Oxus
L. Balkhash
TURKESTAN
PAMIRS
HIMALAYAS
GHAZNA
PUNJAB
R. Indus
INDIA
HINDUS
ARABIAN SEA
0
500
Miles
MUSLIM TERRITORY

In 821, East Persia and Trans-Oxiana achieved their own governments. Thereafter Persian troops ceased to be entirely reliable and the Baghdad khalifs began increasingly to recruit their regular armies from Turkish slaves, the personnel for which were bought as boys in Turkestan. These soldier slaves were known as Mamlooks and must not be visualized as poor oppressed creatures. On the contrary, they were a highly privileged class, clad in resplendent uniforms, magnificently mounted and often behaving with extreme arrogance towards the "free" Arab population. In 861, these soldier-slaves murdered the Khalif Al Mutawakkil in Baghdad and themselves assumed control of the government.

* * *

The murder of Al Mutawakkil in 861 is a landmark in history, indicating the end of the rule of Muhammad's family as despotic emperors of the world's greatest empire. The Turkish army commanders were able to exercise authority in Iraq but the loyalty of the distant provinces had been to the khalif who, as the Prophet's successor, had enjoyed both religious and political prestige. When the provinces realized that the khalifs were the helpless prisoners of their own mercenaries, they broke away from the empire and military leaders seized power in the provinces and established dynasties. These movements were not primarily dictated by what we know as nationalist sentiment. Rather the collapse of the central imperial authority compelled each province to fend for itself. Perhaps exhausted by its prodigious exploits in the past, the Arab race no longer seemed to possess the vitality or the desire to rule.

Although, however, the loss of their military spirit had deprived the Arabs and the Persians of political domination, they continued to lead the world in science, culture and education, and Arabic remained the language of learning, of science, of philosophy, of poetry and of diplomacy.

* * *

For a hundred years after the murder of Mutawakkil in 861, Persia, Iraq, Arabia and Egypt remained in considerable confusion. In 972, however, a major revolution took place in North Africa. The descendants of Ali, another cousin of the Prophet Muhammad, had long claimed that they, and not the Abbasids or Umaiyids, were the rightful heirs to the khalifate. They were supported in their claim by a considerable proportion of Muslims who were known as the Shiites.

A member of Ali's family assumed the title of khalif, occupied Egypt in 972 and shortly afterwards annexed Syria also. The new dynasty called themselves Fátimids, claiming descent from the Prophet's daughter Fátima.

Following the example of the new ruler in Cairo, the Umaiyid sovereign of Andalus also assumed the title of khalif. There were now, therefore, three khalifs in the field, representing three rival branches of Muhammad's family, the Abbasids, the Umaiyids and the Fatimids, each jealous of the other. The Abbasid Khalif in Baghdad was virtually powerless, but the Fatimid was the active ruler of an empire which included North Africa, Egypt and Syria. The Umaiyid Khalif controlled a wealthy, civilized state in Spain.

* * *

The break-up of the great Arab Empire opened a new era in the history of Europe. For some three centuries, the Muslim world from the Atlantic to Turkestan had presented an impenetrable, monolithic wall to the Christian nations of the West, shutting them off from trade with Africa, Asia or the Far East. Europe, which in Roman times had possessed a wealthy commercial civilization, had reverted to a primitive, agricultural state of society.

But with the division of the Arab Empire between three khalifs, the first cracks appeared in the Arab wall. The Fatimid Khalif regarded the Abbasids as his chief enemies and was willing to conclude trade agreements with Europe. After three centuries of unchallenged Arab command of the sea, Christian ships were able once again to sail the blue waters of the Mediterranean. The relaxation of the Arab blockade resulted in a gradual increase of wealth in Europe and with it a revival of power and culture. After three centuries of Muslim domination, the West began very slowly to recover, while the Arabs were weakened by their internal divisions.

* * *

While the balance of power was thus slowly changing in the Mediterranean, dramatic events were occurring in the East. The vast plains of Central Asia, beyond the north-eastern border of the Arab Empire, stretched for three thousand miles to the Sea of Japan. This immense area was inhabited by nomadic horse tribes whose principal occupation in life was war. Their killing weapon was the bow, which they invariably used on horseback and at full gallop. In 1029, the Ghuzz, a primitive tribe of horse nomads from Central Asia, burst into northern Persia and swept across the country with their tents and flocks, massacring, looting and raping as they went.

In 1055, Tughril Beg the Seljuqid, the chief of these wild tribesmen, occupied Baghdad and the Abbasid Khalif was obliged to recognize his rule. Tughril Beg died in 1063 and was succeeded by his nephew Alp Arslan. Both the Fatimid Khalifs and the Byzantines were alarmed by the military prowess of the Seljuq Turks. Abandoning all idea of Muslim solidarity, the Fatimids of Egypt entered into an agreement with Constantinople. In 1071, however, the Sultan Alp Arslan completely defeated the Byzantine army at Malazkirt and within a few years the Ghuzz had overrun Asia Minor and reached the Bosphorus. The Byzantine Empire seemed to be on the verge of collapse.

In 1071, the year of Malazkirt, the Seljuqs also conquered Syria and Palestine from the Fatimids, whose empire was thereby reduced to Egypt alone, for North Africa had already become independent. The Seljuq Empire now extended from Asia Minor to the Oxus and from the Caspian to the Indian Ocean. The Ghuzz Turkmans had been heathen when they burst into northern Persia but the Seljuq Emperors, Tughril Beg and Alp Arslan had become Muslims. Although their Arab and Persian subjects were highly educated, neither Tughril Beg nor Alp Arslan could read or write. In 1072, Alp Arslan was succeeded by his son Malik Shah, who ruled with justice and vigour, even with glory, from 1072 to 1092.

* * *

Christendom had been fighting a defensive battle against Muslim aggression in the Mediterranean, in France, Spain and Italy, Sicily and Crete, for four centuries. Throughout this period, however, the eastern flank of the long Christian battle front had been firmly held by the Byzantine Empire. But after the Battle of Malazkirt in 1071, the Seljuq armies had reached the Bosphorus. At any moment they might cross into Europe and the long Mediterranean battle front be turned on its eastern flank.

The Byzantine Emperor Alexius appealed to the West for help in the defence of Christendom and in 1095 the pope preached the First Crusade. It is obvious, when we view the Mediterranean front as a whole, that what was required to protect Europe was the recovery of Asia Minor. This done, a defensive front should have been established from the Gulf of Alexandretta to Samsun and it was doubtless something of this kind which Alexius hoped to achieve.

By an unfortunate piece of muddled thinking, however, this simple strategic requirement became confused in the minds of the Western Crusaders with the emotional conception of the liberation of Jerusalem. The popular enthusiasm for religious pilgrimages to the sepulchre of Christ seemed to make it additionally desirable that Jerusalem be under Christian rule. The First Crusade broke through Asia Minor, continued southwards and captured Palestine, but meanwhile the Turks

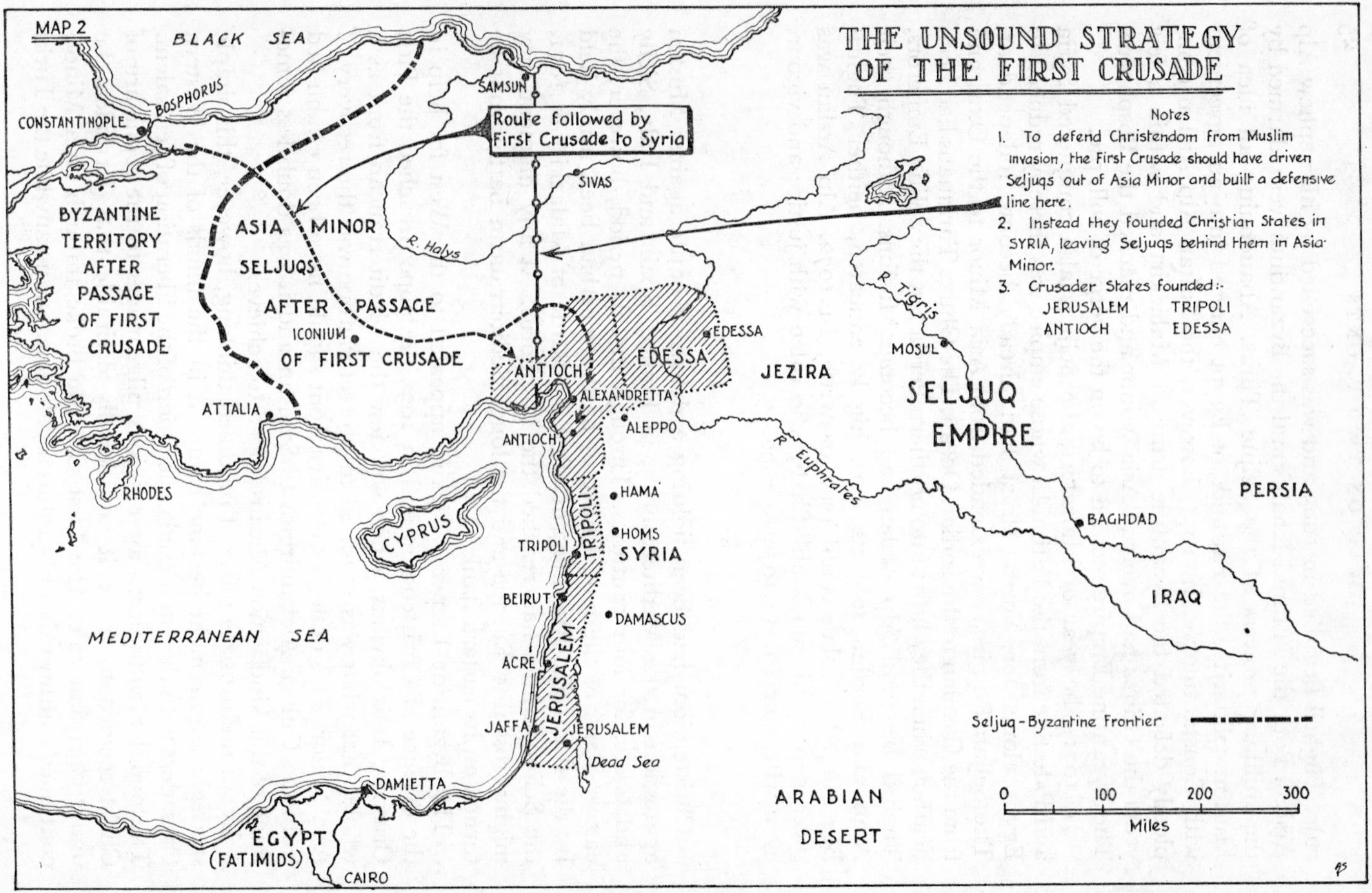
MAP 2
THE UNSOUND STRATEGY OF THE FIRST CRUSADE
Notes
1. To defend Christendom from Muslim invasion, the First Crusade should have driven Seljuqs out of Asia Minor and built a defensive line here.
2. Instead they founded Christian States in SYRIA, leaving Seljuqs behind them in Asia Minor.
3. Crusader States founded:-
JERUSALEM TRIPOLI
ANTIOCH EDESSA
Route followed by First Crusade to Syria
BLACK SEA
BOSPHORUS
CONSTANTINOPLE
SAMSUN
SIVAS
R. Halys
BYZANTINE TERRITORY AFTER PASSAGE OF FIRST CRUSADE
ASIA MINOR
SELJUQS AFTER PASSAGE OF FIRST CRUSADE
ICONIUM
ATTALIA
RHODES
CYPRUS
MEDITERRANEAN SEA
ANTIOCH
EDESSA
ALEXANDRETTA
ALEPPO
HAMA
HOMS
SYRIA
TRIPOLI
BEIRUT
DAMASCUS
ACRE
JAFFA
JERUSALEM
Dead Sea
DAMIETTA
EGYPT
(FATIMIDS)
CAIRO
JEZIRA
R. Tigris
MOSUL
R. Euphrates
SELJUQ EMPIRE
BAGHDAD
PERSIA
IRAQ
ARABIAN DESERT
Seljuq-Byzantine Frontier
0 100 200 300
Miles

re-established their hold on Asia Minor, cutting off the communications of the Crusaders with Europe. The result of this mistake was two-fold. Firstly, the Crusaders were thereafter ultimately bound to fail as they had no land communications with the west and the ships of the twelfth century were incapable of carrying the men and equipment necessary to maintain an army in Syria.

Secondly, the Turks closed up again on the frontiers of the Byzantine Empire, though it is true that the Crusaders, by creating a diversion in Syria and Palestine, succeeded in postponing the invasion of Europe by the Turks for several centuries. When the present volume opens, therefore, the Crusaders held three states on the coasts of the eastern Mediterranean, the Kingdom of Jerusalem, the County of Tripoli and the Princedom of Antioch. The fourth Crusader state, the County of Edessa, had been mostly lost in 1144 immediately before the commencement of the present narrative. A remnant of the County of Edessa west of the Euphrates, however, was still held.

* * *

Arab rule in Spain enjoyed its Golden Age in the tenth century but after 1008 it fell into confusion. Fifty years later, in 1058, King Ferdinand I of Castile and Leon had compelled nearly all the Muslims in Spain to pay him tribute. At this moment, however, a fanatical Berber Muslim sect appeared in the Maghrib (Morocco) under the name of the Murabiteen or Almoravids. In 1086, they crossed to Spain and completely defeated Alfonso VI of Castile at Zallaka (called by the Spaniards Sagrajas) and the Christians were again thrown on the defensive. The Murabits degenerated rapidly and the Christians began to regain their losses when a new Berber sect, the Muwahhideen or Almohades, appeared in Morocco. Under an extremely capable leader, Abdul Mumin, they defeated the Murabits in North Africa and when the present narrative opens, the Muwahhideen were almost ready to intervene decisively in Spain.

* * *

Meanwhile, important events had been taking place in the central Mediterranean. From 827 onwards, the Arabs, coming by sea from Ifriqiya, had conquered Sicily and in 843 they crossed to the mainland and occupied southern Italy. In the second half of the eleventh century, however, the Normans drove the Arabs from southern Italy, and in the twenty years from 1061 to 1081 the Norman Duke Roger conquered Sicily.

In 1134, Roger II of Sicily carried the war against the Muslims over to Africa and by 1150 he was in occupation of the whole African coastline from Tunis to Tripoli. Strategically this conquest was of great importance, for it gave the Sicilian fleet the power to control the narrow waters of the Mediterranean between southern Italy, Sicily and Tunis. Thus, when our narrative opens, the two sides were perhaps equally balanced in Spain, while, in the centre of the battle line, the Normans had seized a long stretch of the coast of North Africa.

* * *

While this was the situation on the five-hundred-year-old battle front on the Mediterranean, the Muslim world was threatened on the east by a far more serious danger. Western historians have concentrated most of their attention on the prolonged Mediterranean struggle which changed the history of Europe, terming it the world struggle or the great debate. Looking back more calmly, we can appreciate that the world did not, even in the twelfth century, consist only of the Mediterranean and that Christianity and Islam were not the two embattled rivals for world leadership but, on the contrary, were cousins, related to one another both by blood and in culture and tradition.

Meanwhile, however, on the vast steppes of Southern Russia (to use modern geographical terms) and in Central Asia, the teeming and savage Turkish and Mongolian tribes were already pressing on the frail eastern defences of Islam. The Seljuqs and their tribesmen, the Ghuzz, had burst through those barriers a century earlier, but in 1145 when our narrative begins, they had become converted and, to some extent at least, absorbed into the body of Islam. Now ever-fresh waves were washing up on the eastern frontiers.

For more than fifty years, from 1105 to his death at the age of seventy-one in 1156, Sanjar, the last great Seljuq Sultan, had devoted his life to the defence of the eastern frontier of Islam against the heathen. In 1141, however, Sanjar had been disastrously defeated and the eastern wall of Islam began to crumble.

When the present volume opens, therefore, Islam is already engaged in a war on two fronts, of which the eastern was to be far the more desperate and disastrous. For a century or more, Islam seemed to be fighting for its very survival between the Christian nations of the West and the Turkish and Mongol hordes of the East.

Perhaps ironically, Islam was ultimately to survive, not by winning the Holy Wars which she alone of the great religions regarded as a pious obligation, but by the peaceful conversion of her conquerors. It is easy to see now that Islam and Christianity were infinitely nearer to one another than either was to the Mongols. Yet such is the tragedy of human history, for men are always swayed by short-sighted jealousies and rivalries, often resulting in wars against those nearest to themselves.

NOTABLE DATES

Preaching of Muhammad	613–632
Arab conquest of Syria, Iraq, Egypt and Persia	636–659
Conquest of Spain and the Punjab	712
Fall of the Umaiyid Khalifs of Damascus Establishment of the Abbasids in Baghdad	750
Murder of Khalif Mutawakkil Abbasids lose political control	861
Umaiyids in Spain assume title of Khalif	929
Establishment of Fatimid Khalifs in Cairo	972
Henceforward there are three rival khalifs, the Abbasid, the Fatimid and the Umaiyid	
Seljuq seizure of Baghdad	1055
Seljuqs defeat Byzantines at Malazkirt	1071
First Crusade	1098–1099
Sultan Sanjar, the last great Seljuq defends the eastern frontier of Islam	1105–1156

II

The Débâcle

The Franks directed their march towards Damascus with their host, estimated at fifty thousand horse and foot. A great multitude joined in the struggle with them, composed of the levies, the death-dealing Turks, the town bands and volunteers. The infidels gained the upper hand over the Muslims. Meanwhile reports reached the Franks of the rapid advance of the Islamic armies. They found no way of escape save to retreat in disorder. The people rejoiced at this mercy which God had bountifully bestowed upon them and to God be praise and thanks.

IBN AL QALÁNISI, *The Damascus Chronicle*
Trans. H. A. R. GIBB (abridged)

The return of the Christian army to Jerusalem was followed by a lasting estrangement between the Latins of Syria and the Latins of the West. Between France and the New France across the sea there was henceforward interposed a veil of misunderstanding, of discontent and of mutual criticism.

RENÉ GROUSSET, *Histoire des Croisades*

II

FROM 1099 until 1144, the Franks had successfully defended their conquests in Syria and Palestine. Their territory had consisted of four states. The Kingdom of Jerusalem was the largest but the Princedom of Antioch and the Counties of Tripoli and Edessa had remained virtually independent, occasionally according suzerainty to the Kingdom of Jerusalem.

The numbers of troops at the disposal of the Crusader states had always been quite inadequate. They had been able to hold their own for forty years solely because the Seljuq Empire was in anarchy. During their years of power, the Seljuq Sultans had established a feudal system in Syria, the Jezira and Iraq, which had been divided up into fiefs for Turkish warlords. These, while acknowledging the supremacy of the sultan, were jealous of one another and were incapable of co-operation if the sultan were too weak to coerce them. Thus, while the sultans were engaged in civil wars in Persia, the Muslims were unable to organize any combined effort against the Franks.

In 1127, however, Zengi, a Mamlook of the Seljuq Sultans, was made Lord of Mosul. Almost immediately he seized Aleppo, defeating the other Turkish lords in the area. It seemed possible that he might be about to achieve Muslim unity in Syria and the Jezira. Damascus, however, the rulers of which were also Mamlooks, repulsed his attacks and concluded a treaty with Jerusalem against him.

On 24th December, 1144, Zengi by a lightning march seized the city of Edessa, reducing the County of Edessa to a small area west of the Euphrates, the first major disaster which the Crusaders had suffered. Two years later, however, Zengi was murdered by his own servants on 14th September, 1146. An ill-conceived attempt by Jocelin II, Count of Edessa, to recover the town was defeated by Zengi's son, Noor al Deen, on 2nd November, 1146.

* * *

The Kings of Jerusalem from 1099 until 1143 had normally been strong enough to command the forces of all the Frankish states in war. Such a recognized leader was essential to military efficiency, for feudal lords, Frankish and Turkish alike, were too jealous to co-operate without an authoritative commander. Unfortunately on 7th November, 1143, King Fulk of Jerusalem had been killed, leaving only a twelve-year-old son, Baldwin III, whose mother Melisinda was made regent.

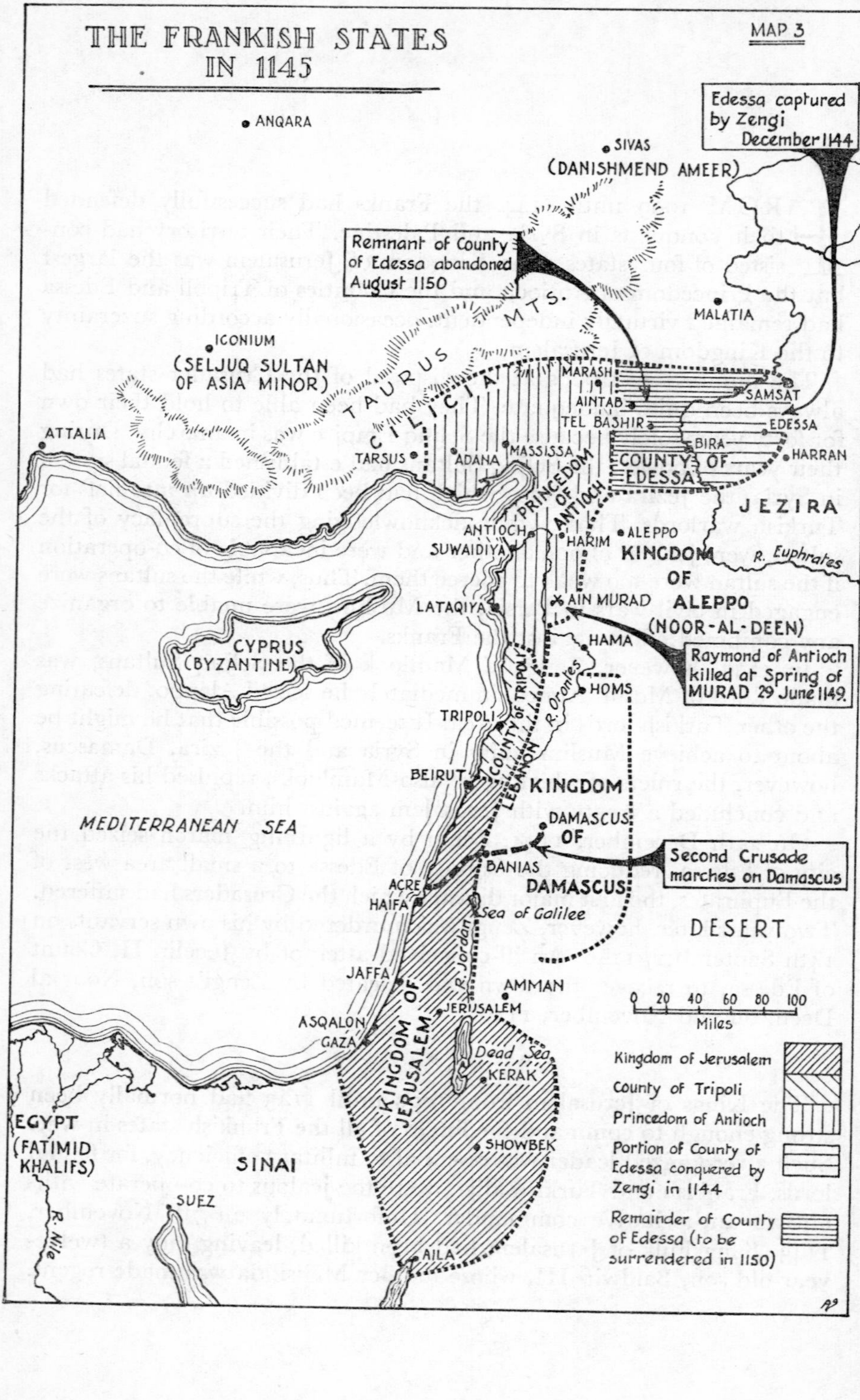
THE FRANKISH STATES IN 1145
MAP 3
Edessa captured by Zengi December 1144
ANQARA
SIVAS
(DANISHMEND AMEER)
Remnant of County of Edessa abandoned August 1150
TAURUS MTS.
MALATIA
ICONIUM
(SELJUQ SULTAN OF ASIA MINOR)
CILICIA
MARASH
SAMSAT
AINTAB
TEL BASHIR
EDESSA
ATTALIA
TARSUS
ADANA
MASSISSA
BIRA
HARRAN
COUNTY OF EDESSA
PRINCEDOM OF ANTIOCH
JEZIRA
ANTIOCH
ALEPPO
SUWAIDIYA
HARIM
KINGDOM OF ALEPPO
R. Euphrates
LATAQIYA
AIN MURAD
(NOOR-AL-DEEN)
CYPRUS (BYZANTINE)
HAMA
Raymond of Antioch killed at Spring of MURAD 29 June 1149.
HOMS
COUNTY of TRIPOLI
R. Orontes
TRIPOLI
LEBANON
BEIRUT
KINGDOM
MEDITERRANEAN SEA
DAMASCUS
OF
Second Crusade marches on Damascus
BANIAS
DAMASCUS
ACRE
HAIFA
Sea of Galilee
DESERT
R. Jordan
JAFFA
AMMAN
0 20 40 60 80 100
Miles
JERUSALEM
ASQALON
GAZA
Dead Sea
KINGDOM OF JERUSALEM
Kingdom of Jerusalem
KERAK
County of Tripoli
Princedom of Antioch
EGYPT
(FATIMID KHALIFS)
Portion of County of Edessa conquered by Zengi in 1144
SHOWBEK
SINAI
SUEZ
Remainder of County of Edessa (to be surrendered in 1150)
R. Nile
AILA

The news of the fall of Edessa fell like a thunderbolt on Western Europe. Louis VII, King of France, was the first ruler to take the cross. Then, on 25th December, 1146, at the Diet of Spiers, the Emperor of Germany, Conrad III of Hohenstaufen, did the same.

With some twenty thousand Germans, he reached Constantinople on 10th September, 1147, after a good deal of looting and disorder on the march. Jealousies and difficulties of protocol immediately arose, for both the Byzantine Emperor Manuel Comnenus and Conrad claimed to be Roman Emperors. The German predilection for plundering civilians also led to friction with the Byzantine authorities.

The Seljuq Sultans of Persia had lost their power but a junior branch of the family had established itself in Asia Minor with its capital at Iconium. Masood, the ruling sultan, was thus in a position to dispute the passage of the Crusaders. Conrad had quarrelled with Manuel Comnenus and was jealous of Louis VII whose army was approaching Constantinople. He accordingly decided to proceed and defeat Sultan Masood without awaiting the French. Had Louis VII, Conrad and Manuel been bigger men, they might have marched together and swept triumphantly across Asia Minor.

The absence of such harmony was vividly illustrated by the fact that Manuel chose this moment to conclude a treaty with Sultan Masood. It would be unjust, however, to charge Manuel with originating schism among Christians, for Roger II, King of Sicily, was at the same time attacking the Byzantine Empire across the Adriatic. Shortly after Conrad left Constantinople, Roger captured the Byzantine island of Corfu.

The headstrong Conrad left Nicaea on 15th October, 1147, intending to follow the road through Iconium which the First Crusade had used. He was carrying only eight days' rations for an estimated march of twenty days through enemy country. He had taken Byzantine guides but on 24th October they mysteriously vanished. The next day near Dorylaeum, as the Germans struggled on in hunger and thirst, they were suddenly attacked by the Seljuq army.

The Turks consisted entirely of mounted archers whose tactics were to gallop round the enemy, pouring arrows into his ranks. When the Germans charged, the Turks simply galloped away, returning to ply them with arrows as soon as the charge petered out. Hungry, thirsty and bewildered, the Germans suffered a total disaster. Conrad arrived back as a fugitive in Nicaea on 3rd November, where his temper was not improved by finding Louis VII with the French army.

When Louis arrived in Constantinople, he heard that the Emperor Manuel had just concluded a twelve-year treaty with the Sultan of Iconium. Warned by the disaster which had befallen the Germans, he

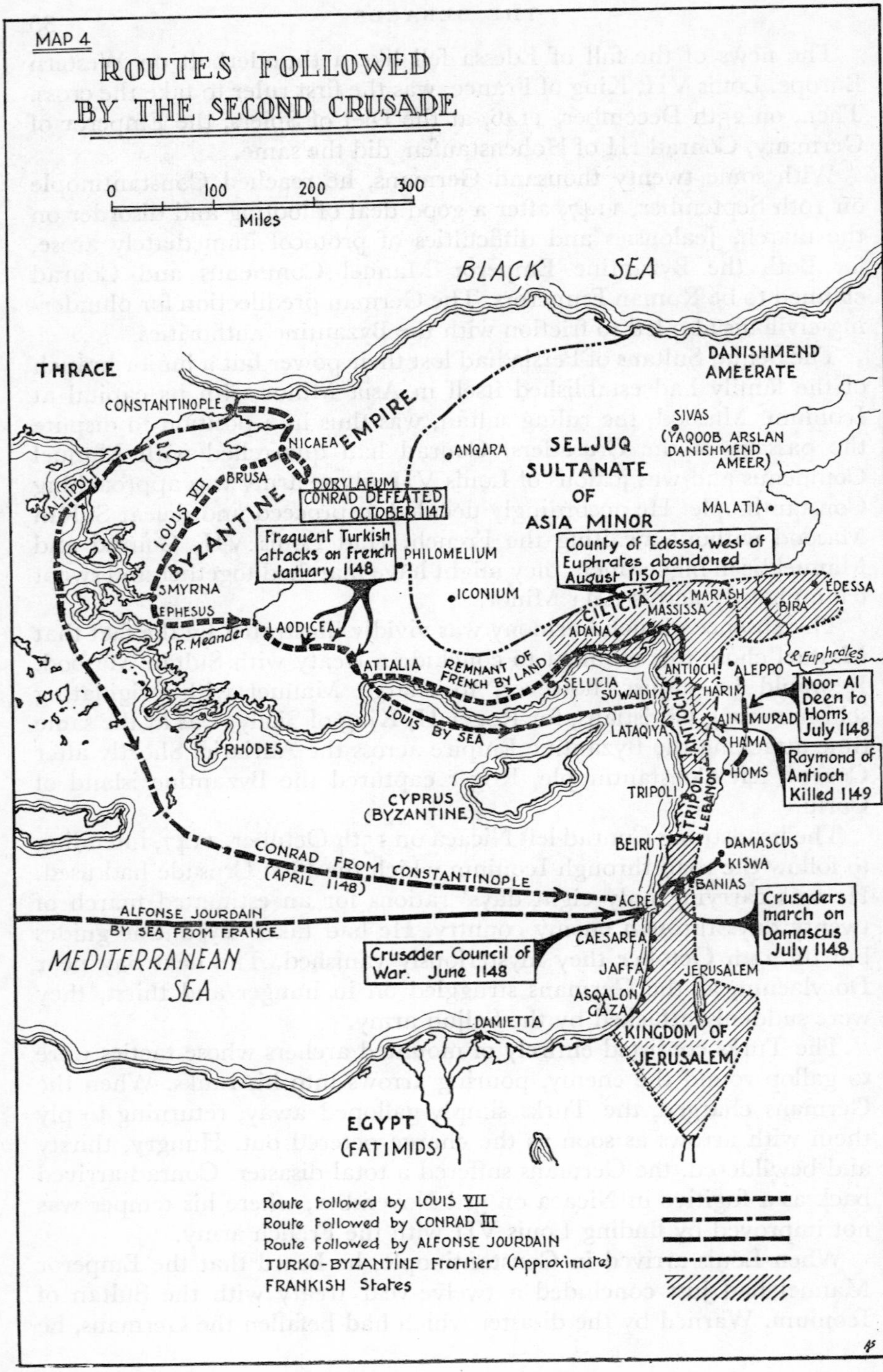
MAP 4
ROUTES FOLLOWED BY THE SECOND CRUSADE
0 100 200 300
Miles
BLACK SEA
THRACE
CONSTANTINOPLE
GALLIPOLI
NICAEA
BRUSA
LOUIS VII
BYZANTINE EMPIRE
DORYLAEUM
CONRAD DEFEATED OCTOBER 1147
ANQARA
DANISHMEND AMEERATE
SIVAS
(YAQOOB ARSLAN DANISHMEND AMEER)
SELJUQ SULTANATE OF ASIA MINOR
MALATIA
Frequent Turkish attacks on French January 1148
PHILOMELIUM
County of Edessa, west of Euphrates abandoned August 1150
SMYRNA
EPHESUS
ICONIUM
MARASH
EDESSA
BIRA
CILICIA
MASSISSA
ADANA
LAODICEA
R. Meander
R. Euphrates
ATTALIA
REMNANT OF FRENCH BY LAND
ANTIOCH
ALEPPO
SELUCIA
SUWAIDIYA
HARIM
Noor Al Deen to Homs July 1148
LOUIS BY SEA
LATAQIYA
AIN MURAD
ANTIOCH
HAMA
RHODES
Raymond of Antioch Killed 1149
HOMS
TRIPOLI
LEBANON
CYPRUS (BYZANTINE)
TRIPOLI
BEIRUT
DAMASCUS
KISWA
CONRAD FROM CONSTANTINOPLE (APRIL 1148)
BANIAS
ACRE
Crusaders march on Damascus July 1148
ALFONSE JOURDAIN BY SEA FROM FRANCE
CAESAREA
MEDITERRANEAN SEA
Crusader Council of War. June 1148
JAFFA
JERUSALEM
ASQALON
GAZA
DAMIETTA
KINGDOM OF JERUSALEM
EGYPT (FATIMIDS)
Route Followed by LOUIS VII
Route Followed by CONRAD III
Route Followed by ALFONSE JOURDAIN
TURKO-BYZANTINE Frontier (Approximate)
FRANKISH States

decided to bypass Seljuq territory and follow the coast, which was dotted with Byzantine fortresses. Passing through Smyrna and Ephesus, he crossed the Meander where, on 1st January, 1148, he was heavily attacked by the Turks, although well inside Byzantine territory. On 6th January, Louis left the Meander valley and marched over bleak mountain ranges to Attalia, where he arrived early in February. Half-starving, struggling through winter storms, under constant Turkish attacks and suffering heavy casualties, the French narrowly escaped a complete catastrophe.

At Attalia, Louis agreed with the Byzantine governor for ships to convey the army to Suwaidiya—or St. Siméon—the port of Antioch where he landed on 19th March, 1148. The ships having been too few to take the army and the many non-combatants and pilgrims, the king had sailed with the knights, abandoning the infantry, who were thereupon heavily attacked by the Turks. The Greeks did nothing to help and in fact the panegyrist of Louis claims that they assisted the Muslims.[1] Eventually more ships appeared and a further contingent embarked. A small remnant of people on foot, whether soldiers or pilgrims, struggled through to Antioch, but the majority were killed or died on the way.

It is fruitless now to endeavour to weigh the relative guilt of the Franks and the Greeks. The former were rough, undisciplined, arrogant and addicted to looting. Yet all the Turkish attacks on the French occurred on Byzantine soil and the Greeks made no effort to help the Crusaders. On the other hand, Manuel was being attacked by King Roger II of Sicily and was threatened with invasion by nomadic tribes north of the Danube, a danger which actually materialized six months later. He could not afford to wage war also against the Sultan of Iconium.

* * *

When Zengi had been murdered on 14th September, 1146, his dominions had been divided between his two sons. Noor al Deen Mahmood seized Aleppo while his brother Saif al Deen Ghazi became King of Mosul. Zengi had been a Turkish slave who only came late in life to Syria, but Noor al Deen had grown up in the Arab countries and could claim to be a native. As capable a soldier as Zengi, he was more civilized, more diplomatic and commanded the respect, perhaps the affection, of the Syrians.

As long as Syria and the Jezira[2] had been held by rival Turkish warlords, the Franks had been able to hold their own but the situation

[1] Odo de Deuil, *Concerning the Expedition of Louis VII in the East.*
[2] For Mosul and the Jezira, see Map 2, page 26.

THE DYNASTY OF ZENGI

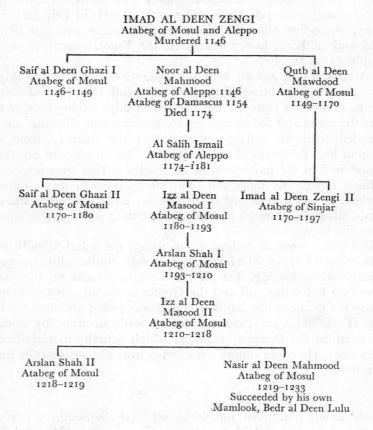

IMAD AL DEEN ZENGI
Atabeg of Mosul and Aleppo
Murdered 1146

- Saif al Deen Ghazi I
  Atabeg of Mosul
  1146–1149

- Noor al Deen Mahmood
  Atabeg of Aleppo 1146
  Atabeg of Damascus 1154
  Died 1174
  - Al Salih Ismail
    Atabeg of Aleppo
    1174–1181

- Qutb al Deen Mawdood
  Atabeg of Mosul
  1149–1170
  - Saif al Deen Ghazi II
    Atabeg of Mosul
    1170–1180
  - Izz al Deen Masood I
    Atabeg of Mosul
    1180–1193
    - Arslan Shah I
      Atabeg of Mosul
      1193–1210
      - Izz al Deen Masood II
        Atabeg of Mosul
        1210–1218
        - Arslan Shah II
          Atabeg of Mosul
          1218–1219
        - Nasir al Deen Mahmood
          Atabeg of Mosul
          1219–1233
          Succeeded by his own Mamlook, Bedr al Deen Lulu
  - Imad al Deen Zengi II
    Atabeg of Sinjar
    1170–1197

NOTE

(1) Turkish warlords often died young, leaving children as their heirs. In these circumstances, a senior army officer was often appointed guardian of the heir with the title of atabeg or father-officer. More often than not, the atabeg usurped the throne and founded a dynasty of atabegs.

(2) Titles were lavishly used at this time. These atabegs were also called kings and sultans.

would be completely changed if Noor al Deen were able to unite the Muslims, a danger which had hitherto been averted by the alliance of the Turkish lord of Damascus with the Franks.

In May 1147, before the Second Crusade set out, the Franks, with unbelievable folly, had invaded the territory of Damascus. The atabeg of the city, Mueen al Deen Anar, had called upon Noor al Deen for help. At the last moment the Franks of Jerusalem had realized their mistake and their alliance with Damascus had been patched up again.

When Louis VII reached Antioch in March 1148, the ruling prince, Raymond of Poitiers, explained to the king that the only danger to the Frankish states lay in the possibility that Noor al Deen might unite the Muslims. The obvious course was for the Crusaders to march on his capital, Aleppo, which was only fifty miles away. Muslim disunity was the *sine qua non* of Frankish survival. It was not a question of whether Edessa or Damascus were a better city to attack. The essential was to eliminate Noor al Deen before he united the Muslims.

Louis VII was unconvinced by this obvious truth and replied obstinately that he had come to defend Jerusalem. Louis' wife, Eleanor of Aquitaine, was the niece of Raymond, Prince of Antioch. She quickly grasped the truth of her uncle's reasoning and tried to persuade the king but Louis resented the co-operation between his wife and Raymond. Eventually Louis marched out of Antioch for Jerusalem, dragging his angry wife with him and without even saying goodbye to Raymond. The latter, a stupid, arrogant man, was so infuriated that he took no further part in the Crusade.

Meanwhile Conrad III had spent the winter in Constantinople where he had become a close friend of Manuel Comnenus. In the spring he sailed for Palestine, reaching Acre on 17th April, 1148. Shortly afterwards more troops arrived from France under Alfonse Jourdain, Count of Toulouse, a son of the original Raymond de Saint-Gilles, who had established the County of Tripoli after the First Crusade. In 1148, the reigning Count of Tripoli, Raymond II, was his great-nephew.[3] Alfonse Jourdain set out for Jerusalem but died suddenly in agony at Caesarea. His son Bertrand, who was with him, accused Raymond of Tripoli of having poisoned him and swore to be revenged. As a result Raymond did not join the Crusade which finally was limited to the Kingdom of Jerusalem alone.

Louis VII arrived in Jerusalem in May 1148. Never before had so great a gathering of kings, nobles and knights been seen in any Crusader state. On 24th June, 1148, a general council assembled at Acre, presided over by Conrad III of Germany, Louis VII of France and Baldwin III of Jerusalem.

[3] At this time both the Prince of Antioch and the Count of Tripoli were called Raymond.

THE NORMAN PRINCELY HOUSE OF ANTIOCH

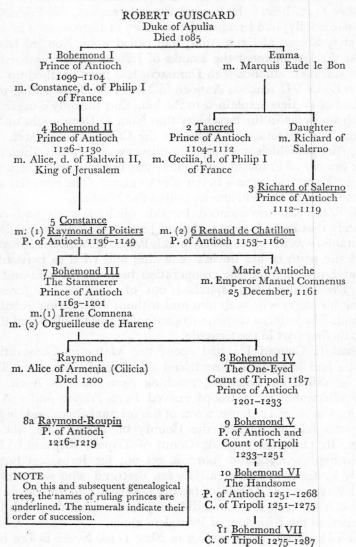

ROBERT GUISCARD
Duke of Apulia
Died 1085

1 Bohemond I
Prince of Antioch
1099–1104
m. Constance, d. of Philip I of France

Emma
m. Marquis Eude le Bon

4 Bohemond II
Prince of Antioch
1126–1130
m. Alice, d. of Baldwin II, King of Jerusalem

2 Tancred
Prince of Antioch
1104–1112
m. Cecilia, d. of Philip I of France

Daughter
m. Richard of Salerno

3 Richard of Salerno
Prince of Antioch
1112–1119

5 Constance
m. (1) Raymond of Poitiers
P. of Antioch 1136–1149
m. (2) 6 Renaud de Châtillon
P. of Antioch 1153–1160

7 Bohemond III
The Stammerer
Prince of Antioch
1163–1201
m. (1) Irene Comnena
m. (2) Orgueilleuse de Harenc

Marie d'Antioche
m. Emperor Manuel Comnenus
25 December, 1161

Raymond
m. Alice of Armenia (Cilicia)
Died 1200

8 Bohemond IV
The One-Eyed
Count of Tripoli 1187
Prince of Antioch
1201–1233

8a Raymond-Roupin
P. of Antioch
1216–1219

9 Bohemond V
P. of Antioch and Count of Tripoli
1233–1251

10 Bohemond VI
The Handsome
P. of Antioch 1251–1268
C. of Tripoli 1251–1275

11 Bohemond VII
C. of Tripoli 1275–1287

NOTE
On this and subsequent genealogical trees, the names of ruling princes are underlined. The numerals indicate their order of succession.

DYNASTY OF TOULOUSE-PROVENCE

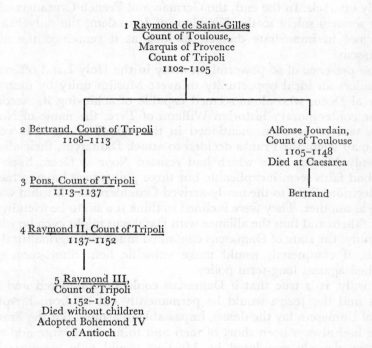

1 Raymond de Saint-Gilles
Count of Toulouse,
Marquis of Provence
Count of Tripoli
1102–1105

2 Bertrand, Count of Tripoli
1108–1113

Alfonse Jourdain,
Count of Toulouse
1105–1148
Died at Caesarea

Bertrand

3 Pons, Count of Tripoli
1113–1137

4 Raymond II, Count of Tripoli
1137–1152

5 Raymond III,
Count of Tripoli
1152–1187
Died without children
Adopted Bohemond IV
of Antioch

NOTE

There was a brief interregnum from 1105 to 1108 during which a cousin, William Jourdain, exercised control. (*The Course of Empire*)

Although the ostensible object of the Crusade was to recover Edessa, Jocelin II, Count of Edessa, was likewise absent. Antioch, Tripoli and the remains of the County of Edessa west of the Euphrates were in imminent danger of invasion by Noor al Deen and could not have been asked to bring their armies to Acre, but their rulers should certainly have been present had they not been prevented by their family quarrels. In the end, the German and French Crusaders offered their services solely to the Kingdom of Jerusalem, the only Frankish state not in immediate danger, as long as it remained the ally of Damascus.

The presence of so powerful an army in the Holy Land offered the Crusaders an ideal opportunity to avert Muslim unity by destroying Noor al Deen, who alone seemed capable of achieving it. According to the contemporary historian William of Tyre, the name of Noor al Deen was never even mentioned in the council at Acre. Incredible as it may seem, the Franks decided to attack Damascus, their ally and the only Muslim state which had resisted Noor al Deen. Such folly and bad faith seem inexplicable but three points may have influenced the decision. First, to the newly-arrived Crusaders, one Muslim was the same as another. They were inclined to think it a sin to be friendly with any of them and thus the alliance with Damascus might even be wicked. Secondly, the state of Damascus contained much rich agricultural land which, if conquered, would make valuable fiefs. Short-term greed weighed against long-term policy.

Thirdly, it is true that if Damascus could be conquered and held, Syria and the Jezira would be permanently cut off from Egypt, for east of Damascus lay the desert, impassable to armies. But the Frankish states had always been short of men and to annex a large additional territory densely populated by Muslims would only accentuate the lack of manpower. There were many older and more prudent men in the Kingdom of Jerusalem who perfectly appreciated the folly of attacking their only Muslim friend. Unfortunately Baldwin III was only seventeen and could not carry much weight against the Emperor and the King of France.

The army marched from Acre through Banias to Kiswa and then turned northwards until, on 24th July, 1148, it reached the belt of gardens south of Damascus. Abaq, the titular Prince of Damascus, was a child and an old Mamlook of the family, Mueen al Deen Anar, was atabeg or regent.

Anar had not expected this insane attack by his friends and was unprepared, but hastily summoned his feudatories to arms. The Crusaders meanwhile pressed on, suffering some casualties in the lanes and orchards which extended two miles south of Damascus. Conrad led a

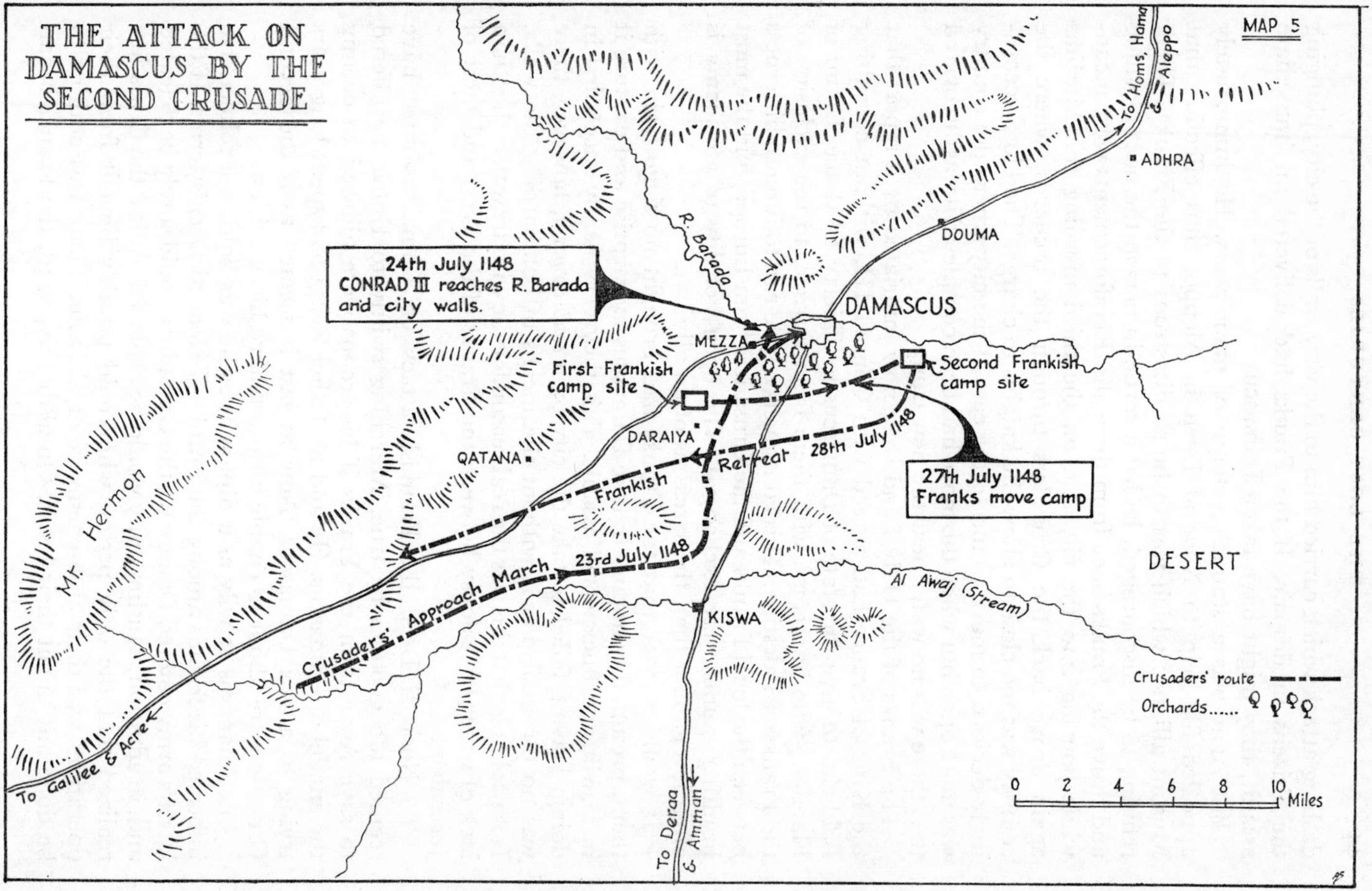
THE ATTACK ON
DAMASCUS BY THE
SECOND CRUSADE
MAP 5
24th July 1148
CONRAD III reaches R. Barada
and city walls.
R. Barada
DAMASCUS
MEZZA
DOUMA
ADHRA
To Homs, Hama & Aleppo
First Frankish
camp site
Second Frankish
camp site
27th July 1148
Franks move camp
DARAIYA
QATANA
Frankish
Retreat 28th July 1148
23rd July 1148
Crusaders' Approach March
Mt. Hermon
KISWA
Al Awaj (Stream)
DESERT
To Galilee & Acre
To Deraa & Amman
Crusaders' route
Orchards......
0
2
4
6
8
10
Miles

dashing attack which carried him to the very walls of the city, plunging the citizens in despair. If the Franks had delivered an immediate assault, they might have taken Damascus.

But Anar was a staunch veteran of many wars. He immediately appealed for help to Noor al Deen in Aleppo, thus effecting that Muslim alliance which was to be so disastrous to the Franks. Then, refusing to be discouraged, he led a sortie in person the next morning and drove the Franks back from the walls. Reinforcements were meanwhile pouring into the city and on the third morning the Muslims again drove back the Crusaders through the orchards, where the country was too close to allow the knights to charge. The kings accordingly decided to move round to the east of the city where the country was more open but when the move had been completed it was discovered that there was no water near the new camp.

The Franks of the Holy Land were now infuriated by a report that the King of France had agreed with Conrad III, without consulting Baldwin, to give the state of Damascus to Thierry D'Alsace, Count of Flanders, who had come with them from Europe, to the exclusion of the Franks of Palestine. This controversy gave rise to intense bitterness between the local Franks and the Crusaders from Europe, and the most insulting taunts were exchanged. The open hostility of an enemy is often less galling than the sarcasms of an ally.

It would appear that the Franks had brought no siege train with them, presumably hoping to take Damascus by surprise and capture it in a swift and unexpected assault. This they very nearly succeeded in doing. Having failed to take the city by a *coup de main*, however, there was no use besieging it without the means of bombarding the walls. It is probable that this was the real reason for the withdrawal, rather than lack of water or jealousy between the Franks of the West and those of Jerusalem.

To Noor al Deen the Frankish attack on Damascus must have seemed too good to be true. Marching swiftly to Homs, he offered to save Anar from the Franks if his troops were allowed to occupy the citadel of Damascus. He and his father Zengi had spent long years trying to annex Damascus. Now at last it seemed as if the Second Crusade were about to enable him to realize his ambition.

But Anar was as wily as a diplomat as he was bold as a soldier. He informed his friends among the Franks of Noor al Deen's terms. If the latter's army entered Damascus, the Crusaders would surely be defeated and, in addition, Muslim unity would be achieved. At last the Crusaders realized that the only person who could possibly benefit from their operations was their arch-enemy Noor al Deen. There was nothing to be done but to cut their losses. On 28th July, 1148, the Franks began their retreat, hotly pursued by the triumphant army of Damascus, losing heavy casualties and most of their baggage before they re-entered their own territory. The siege of Damascus had lasted only five days but its historical consequences were to be profound and enduring.

The Western Crusaders and the Franks of the Holy Land blamed each other for the débâcle. Not only were the kings and nobles filled with mutual hate but even the men-at-arms and the camp-followers exchanged bitter and contemptuous taunts. For forty years the West was to disinterest itself entirely in the Crusader states. When at last a new Western Crusade was to land in Palestine, it was to be already too late—the Kingdom of Jerusalem had ceased to exist. Anar was the only hero of the campaign. Not only had he, by a combination of bold fighting and skilled diplomacy, defeated an emperor and two kings but he had saved the precarious independence of Damascus from Noor al Deen. Rarely if ever in history has an alliance of two Great Powers met with so humiliating a disaster, in five short days without even fighting a battle.

On 8th September, 1148, Conrad sailed from Acre, stopping to see Manuel Comnenus at Constantinople. While the Crusaders had been in the East, Roger II of Sicily had invaded the Byzantine Empire. As Conrad was already on bad terms with Roger he concluded a treaty with Manuel against him. Louis VII remained in Palestine until after Easter 1149, when he sailed to Italy. Meeting King Roger II at Potenza, he signed a treaty with him against Conrad and Manuel. Thus the first result of the Second Crusade was to divide Europe into hostile military alliances.

* * *

While the Kingdom of Jerusalem was suffering these disasters, Raymond of Antioch had quarrelled with Jocelin II, the unworthy count of what was left of the County of Edessa. To spite Raymond, Jocelin made a separate truce with Noor al Deen, at the very moment when the latter's troops were laying waste the territory of Antioch.

In May 1149, Noor al Deen invaded the Principality of Antioch. Raymond, instead of calling on Tripoli and Jerusalem for help, set out with four hundred[4] knights and a thousand foot, to meet Noor al Deen with six thousand horse. On 29th June, 1149, at the Spring of Murad near Afamiya, the army of Antioch woke up to find itself completely surrounded. A few fled but the majority fought on until they were exterminated. At the last Raymond alone was left alive. He stood

[4] Runciman, in *History of the Crusades*, says four thousand. Abu Shama in *Two Gardens* says four hundred, which seems undoubtedly correct. H. A. R. Gibb in his translation of Ibn al Qalanisi has four thousand.

at bay, striking down all who approached him, until, by a concerted charge from every direction at once, he was overrun and killed. A stupid, headstrong man, he had done much harm to the Frankish cause though he was brave in battle and died a hero's death. His head and his right arm, which had slain so many Muslims, were sent to the khalif in Baghdad.

"He was," writes Ibn al Qalanisi, the chronicler of Damascus, "one of the most famous of the Franks for his bravery, his vigour and his stature. He was especially famous for the fear which he inspired, his arrogance and his ferocity."

Noor al Deen exploited his victory by marching through the territory of Antioch to the port of Suwaidiya. It was the first time he had ever seen the sea. From the day of his birth, the Franks had held the whole coast. In August 1149, he made a truce with Antioch, for he was not ready to besiege the city. He fixed the frontier on the Orontes and left a garrison at Harim, only twenty-five miles east of Antioch.

* * *

Before 1148, the Muslims had hesitated to attack the Franks too vigorously for fear of provoking a new Crusade. Now that the Crusade had come and had ended in fiasco, Noor al Deen felt that he had nothing to fear. Other Muslim leaders hastened to share in the loot. Sultan Masood of Iconium, at peace with the Byzantines, crossed the Taurus, took Marash and advanced to Tel Bashir (Turbessel), the new capital of the Count of Edessa. Ibn Ortoq, the Turkish prince of Mardin, also crossed the Euphrates. On 4th May, 1150, Jocelin II, Count of Edessa, in spite of his separate peace, was captured by Noor al Deen. He died some ten years later, still in prison in Aleppo. In the summer of 1150, Baldwin III arrived in Antioch and made peace with Noor al Deen, but the principality was reduced to a narrow strip of coastal plain.

After the capture of Jocelin II, Manuel Comnenus offered to buy the remnant of the County of Edessa, namely Tel Bashir (Turbessel), Samsat, Aintab and Bira (Birejik).[5] The Franks accepted and decided to evacuate the area. The disappearance of Raymond of Antioch and of Jocelin II had left their two young widows as rulers. The whole responsibility for the disintegrating Frankish States fell on King Baldwin III of Jerusalem, now a youth of eighteen. Leading the combined armies of Jerusalem and Tripoli, he arrived to cover the withdrawal. The inhabitants, mostly Armenians and Syrian Christians, insisted on accompanying the Crusaders and the civilian refugees formed a long and pitiful convoy of men, women and children. The Franks had for fifty years held the County of Edessa and almost all the refugees must

[5] Map 3, page 34.

have been born under Crusader rule. Many were in tears at leaving the only homes they had ever known. With their poor possessions slung on donkeys and camels, they provided one of the most tragic sights produced by war.

It was August 1150. Wrapped in a cloud of dust, the piteous caravan trudged across the plain beneath the scorching sun. Soon Noor al Deen's army appeared. Unlike the dashing and haughty chivalry of France, the Frankish troops in the Holy Land formed a steady, veteran army. King Baldwin III with a party of knights led the march. Behind him stretched the long column of refugees, on foot, in carts or clinging to their pack animals. Two detachments of the army of Antioch covered the right and left flanks. The rearguard consisted of the bulk of the army, commanded by Raymond II, Count of Tripoli,[6] and Humphrey of Toron, constable of the Kingdom of Jerusalem.

All day long in sweltering heat, the Turkish horse-archers galloped up and down parallel to the column pouring their arrows into the helpless mass. There could be no question of charging out across the plain to chase them away. The army marched shoulder to shoulder, never breaking rank. We even read of Frankish archers walking along backwards, arrow on bowstring, their faces towards the horse-archers galloping ceaselessly past.

As for the refugees, they could only plod on beneath the pitiless sun, breathing in the clouds of dust. The loads on some of the pack animals were so stuck full of arrows that they looked like gigantic hedgehogs.

Towards the evening of the second day in this long running fight, when Humphrey of Toron led a sortie against the enemy, a Turkish horseman called to him, "The Ameer So-and-so sends his compliments," naming a Muslim officer who was a friend of Humphrey. "He says you need not worry. We'll all be going back tonight as we're out of rations." Soon afterwards the column lagered for the night. When day dawned there was not a Turk to be seen across the widespread plain.

It was unfortunate that, owing to the low standard of education among Turks and Franks, many of the historians were clerics who thought it incumbent on them to curse "unbelievers". Such incidents as that described in the previous paragraph suggest that the knights were more tolerant. These anecdotes also explain the suspicions of newly-arrived Crusaders from Europe, who accused the native Franks of fraternizing with the enemy.

Manuel Comnenus, who was still at war with Roger II of Sicily, was unable to defend the remnants of the County of Edessa, which he had bought. Within a year it was all occupied by the Muslims. Such

[6] I remind the reader again that this was Raymond of Tripoli—Raymond of Antioch had been killed.

was the end of one of the original four Frankish states, "such fine country, so full of timber, of running water, of broad plains and arable fields, which had formerly easily maintained five hundred knights". It is well to remember that, under a feudal economy, land was the only means of maintaining an army. The loss of the County of Edessa meant the loss of a division of troops.

Early in 1152, Raymond II of Tripoli was assassinated by Ismailis, a fanatical Muslim sect established in the mountains not far from the city.[7] He left a son, Raymond III, who was only twelve years old. His widow, the Princess Hodierne, became regent.

Under the feudal system, the barons taxed and judged their tenants and raised troops. Thus the king had few administrative duties, his principal rôle being to command in war, a task which female regents could not perform. With Hodierne as regent of Tripoli and Constance as regent of Antioch, all military responsibility devolved on Baldwin III who was only nineteen. The early death of their male children and the general infertility of the Franks in the Holy Land was one of their principal problems, due presumably to a climate against which their ancestors had not developed immunities.

Constance of Antioch was only twenty-two, with a son, Bohemond III, who was a child. Her remarriage to an experienced soldier might have provided a prince for Antioch but she resolutely rejected all suitors, including a near relative of the Byzantine Emperor. Then suddenly, in April 1153, she fell in love with and married a penniless knight newly come from France, who thereby became Prince of Antioch. Renaud de Châtillon was handsome, recklessly brave and an utterly unscrupulous adventurer. An infamous ruler and a disastrous statesman, he was to play a leading rôle in the destruction of the Franks.

Although the Muslims were only twenty-five miles from Antioch, he began his career by attacking the Armenians of Cilicia, who were in revolt against Manuel Comnenus. Then suddenly reversing his policy, in the spring of 1156, he raided Cyprus, captured John Comnenus, a nephew of the emperor, and brutally plundered the whole island.

* * *

Anar, the veteran atabeg of Damascus, had died on 28th August, 1149, the year after his defeat of the Second Crusade, and the weakly Prince Abaq assumed control. The old alliance with the Franks was renewed but the friendly feelings of the Damascenes had been alienated.

Noor al Deen was a skilful politician and a strong ruler whose orders were obeyed. He was also of the same religion as the people of Damascus. He opened an ostensibly affectionate correspondence with Abaq

[7] For an account of the Ismaili Assassins, see *The Course of Empire*.

while secretly sending agents to subvert the Damascus army and to bribe the town guard, at the same time cutting off supplies from the city. On 18th April, 1154, Noor al Deen suddenly threw off the mask and marched on Damascus, which he reached on the 25th, the town guard opening the gates. The long struggle of Damascus to retain its independence was over, and the development which the Franks most dreaded had come to pass.

In October 1157, however, Noor al Deen fell ill and seemed to be dying. Sending for his brother Nusrat al Deen, he appointed him governor of Aleppo. A Kurdish soldier of fortune, Asad al Deen Shirkuh, was made responsible for Damascus. So near death did Noor al Deen appear that his own soldiers looted his tents.

Six months later, however, he was convalescent. When he seemed to be dying, his brother Nusrat al Deen had conspired to seize the throne but Shirkuh the Kurd and his brother Ayoub had remained steadfastly loyal to their apparently dying master. When he recovered, it was to be in them that he placed his confidence, a development which was to change history.

* * *

The disastrous Second Crusade had deprived the Franks of all hope of aid from the West. The only possible remaining source of help was Byzantium. Baldwin III, a statesman beyond his years, sent Humphrey of Toron on an embassy to Constantinople. His first task was to disown the brutal raid on Cyprus by Renaud de Châtillon. Humphrey returned bringing with him the emperor's niece, the beautiful Theodora Comnena, as a bride for the king. Baldwin III was twenty-seven and Theodora only thirteen but already a famous beauty, tall and graceful, with a pink and white complexion and masses of shining golden hair. Baldwin fell deeply in love and they were married in September 1158.

In October, the Emperor Manuel arrived in Cilicia with a great army. Disowned by Baldwin, Renaud de Châtillon was seized with panic. Accompanied by the Bishop of Lataqiya, he went humbly, barefooted and bareheaded, to the emperor's camp near Massissa. Manuel, surrounded by a large company of nobles and people, was seated on his imperial throne. The invader of Cyprus prostrated himself before the emperor, who left him for some time lying prone in the dust. He was then obliged to acknowledge the suzerainty of Manuel and to admit a Byzantine garrison into the citadel of Antioch.

Soon after Renaud's humiliation, Baldwin III arrived to greet the emperor, who was now his uncle by marriage. He made an excellent impression even on the sophisticated Byzantine courtiers, for he was handsome, courtly and wise beyond his years. He showed mature statesmanship by actively reconciling the Franks, the Armenians and the Byzantines with one another.

After wintering in Cilicia, the emperor, on 12th April, 1159, made a state entry into Antioch. Clad in the purple imperial mantle, stiff with gold and precious stones, he rode into the city. Renaud de Châtillon and other Frankish lords walked humbly beside his horse, holding his bridle or his stirrups. On either side marched the Varangian Guard, some of them English volunteers, armed with battleaxes. The King of Jerusalem, on horseback but unarmed, rode behind the emperor. Preceded by trumpets, cymbals and drums, the imperial procession passed through the streets, which had been gaily decorated with awnings, carpets, flowers and greenery.

On his arrival at the palace, Manuel was able to enjoy the luxury of a bath, a custom to which, William of Tyre informs us, the Byzantines were addicted. Eight days of feasting, hunting and tournaments ensued, the emperor distributing lavish gifts and large sums of money. The Franks did not greatly relish the emperor's suzerainty over Antioch but they hoped that Manuel would help them to destroy the ever-increasing power of Noor al Deen.

At last, in May 1159, the great combined army set out to attack Aleppo. When only twenty-five miles from that city, however, it was met by a deputation from Noor al Deen asking for peace and offering in return the release of several thousand Christian prisoners. Without consulting the Franks, the emperor immediately agreed. In June 1159, Manuel returned to Constantinople. After all the fraternization and the processions, the Franks had profited nothing. "The Greeks," a Frankish writer bitterly remarked, "are more fond of bravado than of serious fighting." Yet, in spite of these sneers, there was no doubt that Noor al Deen had been terrified. Manuel could doubtless, had he wished, have recovered a part of the Frankish territory recently lost, as the price of peace.

Chalandon, in his history of the Comneni,[8] attributes Manuel's action to calculated high policy. The emperor knew that the Franks had acknowledged his suzerainty because they were afraid of Noor al Deen. If the latter had been destroyed, the Franks, no longer afraid, would have denounced Byzantine sovereignty. As a result, Manuel saw his advantage in keeping the Crusaders and Noor al Deen nicely balanced. Yet Manuel's conduct seems to have been a good deal less than straightforward, for he must have been fully aware that the Franks expected him to fight, which he actually had no intention of doing. The fact is that Manuel and the Franks of Outremer[9] viewed

[8] Chalandon, *Les Comnènes*.

[9] Outremer, meaning Overseas, was the collective term used for all Frankish states in the Eastern Mediterranean.

the situation from different angles. To the Franks the defence of Jerusalem was a duty imposed upon all Christians. Manuel was in pursuit of world empire and sought to make use of all foreign states, irrespective of their religion, to achieve his object.

Three months after his return to Constantinople, Manuel marched against Qilij Arslan II, who had succeeded Masood as Sultan of Iconium.[10] The object of his Antioch campaign became immediately apparent. To support him he summoned the Franks of Antioch and the Armenians of Cilicia, both of whom had acknowledged his suzerainty. His new ally Noor al Deen attacked his fellow Muslim Qilij Arslan from the east as did also Yaqoub Arslan, the Danishmend Ameer of Sivas. Entirely surrounded by enemies conjured up by Manuel's skilful diplomacy, Qilij Arslan II in the autumn of 1161 sued for peace and acknowledged Byzantine suzerainty. In 1162, he was obliged to visit Constantinople as a humble satellite of the empire.

The idea of a universal emperor had, in Roman times, been as widely acknowledged as the idea of the United Nations and a World Government has been today. In the twelfth century some of this mystique inspired Manuel Comnenus. For many years he seemed to be progressing steadily in extending his suzerainty alike over Europe and Asia. But his successes were achieved by political legerdemain rather than by strength. In the long run, empire can only exist where it is supported by adequate military and financial resources. In the end Manuel's ephemeral Roman Empire was to collapse like a house of cards.

Meanwhile in 1161 Manuel, at the height of his glory, sent an embassy to Antioch to ask Princess Constance for the hand of her daughter Marie, whom he had presumably seen the year before. The young princess sailed from Antioch and was married to the emperor on 25th December, 1161, in Santa Sophia. "She was more than beautiful," wrote a Greek panegyrist,[11] "so beautiful that all the tales of Aphrodite with her lovely smile, Juno and her white arms, Helen with her graceful neck and charming little feet—all the fair dames of antiquity whom men for their beauty had ranked with the goddesses—all seemed but an idle tale compared to Marie of Antioch."

* * *

In November 1160, his suzerain Manuel Comnenus being safely back in Constantinople, Renaud de Châtillon attempted to raid the flocks of a number of Armenians and Syrian Christians with whom he was at peace. But he was intercepted by a Muslim force, unhorsed and carried off to prison in Aleppo. There, to the relief alike of friend and

[10] Genealogical tree, page 168. [11] Diehl, *Figures Byzantines*, quoted by Grousset.

foe, he was to lie for sixteen years. In 1163, however, the young Bohemond III came of age and was acclaimed Prince of Antioch.

Baldwin III, King of Jerusalem, died in Beirut on 10th February, 1162, at the age of thirty-three, an event which produced universal mourning among Christians and Muslims alike. When it was suggested to Noor al Deen that he seize the opportunity to invade the Frankish states, he nobly replied that it would be disgraceful to do so, as the Christians were to be pitied at the loss of so gallant a prince.

Although still young he had shown remarkable statesmanship. Unlike many of his violent and irascible subjects, he was able to take a broad view of the situation and to appreciate the necessity of the Byzantine alliance. He was cool and brave in battle. Pitted against the formidable Noor al Deen, he won as many battles as he lost. In the south, he captured Asqalon and garrisoned Gaza. His courtesy and charm and his engaging manners were such that he captivated alike the Emperor Manuel and the Muslim peasants of Palestine. In an age of violent jealousies and passions, he was wise and self-controlled beyond his years. Had he lived to middle age, the history of Outremer might have been different.

NOTABLE DATES

Fall of Edessa	24th December, 1144
Arrival of Conrad III of Hohenstaufen at Constantinople	10th September, 1147
Arrival of Louis VII at Constantinople	5th October, 1147
Defeat of Conrad at Dorylaeum	25th October, 1147
Repulse of the Turks by Louis VII on the Meander	1st January, 1148
Arrival of Louis VII at Antioch	19th March, 1148
Arrival of the Second Crusade outside Damascus	24th July, 1148
Conrad sails from Acre	8th September, 1148
Death of Raymond of Antioch at the Spring of Murad	29th June, 1149
Death of Mueen al Deen Anar, atabeg of Damascus	28th August, 1149
Abandonment of the remnant of the County of Edessa	August 1150
Assassination of Raymond II of Tripoli	Spring 1152
Capture of Damascus by Noor al Deen	25th April, 1154
State entry of Manuel Comnenus into Antioch	12th April, 1159

The Sultan of Iconium, Qilij Arslan II, acknowledges Byzantine suzerainty	Autumn 1161
Marriage of Marie of Antioch to Manuel Comnenus	25th December, 1161
Death of Baldwin III, King of Jerusalem	10th February, 1162

PERSONALITIES

Louis VII, King of France
Eleanor of Aquitaine, his wife
Conrad III of Hohenstaufen, Emperor of Germany
Raymond of Poitiers, Prince of Antioch
Constance of Antioch, his wife
Marie of Antioch, their daughter, married to Manuel Comnenus
Renaud de Châtillon, second husband of Constance
Jocelin II, Count of Edessa
Raymond II, Count of Tripoli
Melisinda, Queen Mother of Jerusalem
Baldwin III, King of Jerusalem, her son

Muslims

Noor al Deen Mahmood, the son of Zengi
Mueen al Deen Anar, atabeg of Damascus
Masood, Seljuq Sultan of Iconium
Qilij Arslan II
Yaqoub Arslan, the Danishmend Ameer of Sivas

III

The Struggle for Egypt
1160–1174

"And the heart of Egypt shall melt in the midst of it. And I will set the Egyptians against the Egyptians: and they shall fight every one against his brother, and every one against his neighbour. . . . And the spirit of Egypt shall fail in the midst thereof; and I will destroy the council thereof . . . and the Egyptians will I give over into the hand of a cruel lord; and a fierce king shall rule over them. . . . Woe to them that go down to Egypt for help.

Isaiah XIX, 1 to 4, and XXXI, 1

Egypt is the most important country in the world.

NAPOLEON BONAPARTE

III

IN 1162, Baldwin III was succeeded on the throne of Jerusalem by his brother Amaury.[1] The change of king coincided with a new phase in politics—the struggle for Egypt.

After two hundred years of rule, the Fatimid Khalifs had become completely decadent. In 1149, the Khalif Hafidh had died after a reign of nineteen years, constantly disturbed by riots and civil war. The real rulers of Egypt, however, were the wazeers or chief ministers who wielded all the power, while the khalifs lived in seclusion in magnificent palaces surrounded by an aura of sanctity but deprived of all authority. The khalifs being powerless, the wazeerate was seized by the most powerful commander, a situation which produced an endless succession of coups d'état. "The wazeerate of Egypt," writes Ibn al Athir,[2] "belonged to whoever had the power to take it. The wazeers behaved like kings. Scarcely anyone became wazeer of Egypt except by war, murder or similar means."

The Khalif Hafidh had been succeeded in 1149 by his son Dhafir, who appointed Sulaiman ibn Maisal his wazeer, but the governor of Alexandria, Ali ibn al Salar, marched on Cairo, killed Ibn Maisal and made himself wazeer. In April 1153, however, Ibn al Salar was assassinated by Abbas ibn Temeen, his stepson whom he had brought up, and who became wazeer in his place. Nasr, the son of Abbas, was a close personal friend of the Khalif Dhafir, who was twenty-one.

At the khalif's suggestion, Nasr agreed to murder his own father, the Wazeer Abbas. On second thoughts, however, he decided to reverse the process and to aid his father to kill the khalif. In April 1154, the Khalif Dhafir was murdered at night when paying a private visit to Nasr and the body was secretly buried. The next morning the Wazeer Abbas, who had arranged the crime and whose son had committed it, arrived at the palace at the usual time to see the khalif, but the latter could not be found. In a dramatic act, Abbas first pretended consternation and then fury. Accusing the khalif's two brothers of murdering him, he ordered their instant decapitation in his presence.

He then loudly proclaimed the accession of Dhafir's five-year-old son, Faiz. With incredible callousness the cold-blooded Abbas picked

[1] Baldwin and Amaury were the sons of Fulk of Anjou, King of Jerusalem. Fulk, by an earlier marriage, had had a son called Geoffrey Plantagenet, the father of Henry II, King of England. Thus the kings of England and of Jerusalem were cousins. See Genealogical Tree, page 60.

[2] Ibn al Athir, *Al Kamil fi al Tarikh.*

FATIMID KHALIFS OF EGYPT

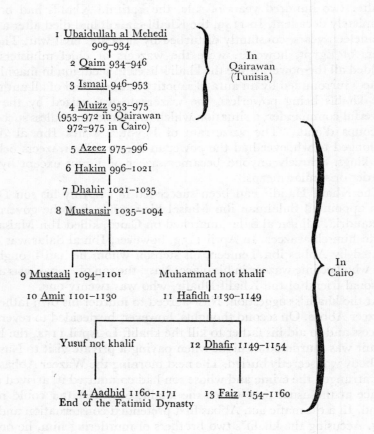

In Qairawan (Tunisia):

1 Ubaidullah al Mehedi 909–934

2 Qaim 934–946

3 Ismail 946–953

4 Muizz 953–975 (953–972 in Qairawan 972–975 in Cairo)

In Cairo:

5 Azeez 975–996

6 Hakim 996–1021

7 Dhahir 1021–1035

8 Mustansir 1035–1094

9 Mustaali 1094–1101 — Muhammad not khalif

10 Amir 1101–1130 — 11 Hafidh 1130–1149

Yusuf not khalif — 12 Dhafir 1149–1154

14 Aadhid 1160–1171 — 13 Faiz 1154–1160

End of the Fatimid Dynasty

up the child, whose father and two uncles he had just butchered, and placing him on his shoulder carried him to the throne with every sign of loyalty and tender affection. The unhappy infant suffered such a shock in witnessing the decapitation of his two uncles that he became subject to fits and was thereafter nicknamed the Screamer.

But this orgy of bloody murders was too much even for the decadent Fatimid court. The ladies of the palace cut off their long hair and sent it to Talaia ibn Ruzzik, the governor of upper Egypt. Roused by this romantic appeal, Ibn Ruzzik, preceded by the long tresses of the royal ladies borne at the ends of lances, marched on Cairo and made himself wazeer in June 1154. (This was the year in which Noor al Deen took Damascus.)

In July 1160, however, the child Khalif Faiz died. Ibn Ruzzik replaced him by his cousin Aadhid, a boy of nine, whom he married to his own daughter. These precautions, however, were in vain for, in September 1161, Ibn Ruzzik was himself assassinated. His son succeeded him as wazeer but, in December 1162, a provincial governor, Shawar[3] al Saadi, marched on Cairo and made himself wazeer. (King Baldwin III had died on 10th February, 1162.) Shawar was a wealthy Egyptian but not a soldier, and in August 1163 an Arab officer by the name of Dhirgham al Lakhmi overthrew Shawar who, however, escaped to Syria and took refuge with Noor al Deen. After a massacre of notables and officers, Dhirgham assumed the wazeerate. Caught in this unending succession of bloody coups d'état, Egypt was indeed in a tragic predicament.[4]

* * *

Amaury[5] had been crowned King of Jerusalem in the Church of the Holy Sepulchre on 18th February, 1162. He was twenty-seven years old, short in stature but with a handsome face and fair hair and beard. Unlike the earlier unlettered Crusaders, both Baldwin and Amaury were well-educated, Amaury being something of a legal scholar. He was quick to appreciate the significance of the Egyptian situation. The united Muslims of Syria and the Jezira were already stronger than the Franks. The Egyptians were poor fighters but their country was extremely rich. Whichever side obtained possession of Egypt would be the victor in Palestine. The chaotic situation in Cairo tempted Amaury to intervene. In September 1163, he invaded Egypt, defeated the wazeer Dhirgham and laid siege to Bilbeis, but the Nile

[3] The accent is on the first syllable, as in the English word shower.
[4] Ibn al Athir, *Al Kamil*; Maqrizi, *Ittiadh al Hunafá*; Usama ibn Munqidh, *Reminiscences*.
[5] The English form of the name is Amalric.

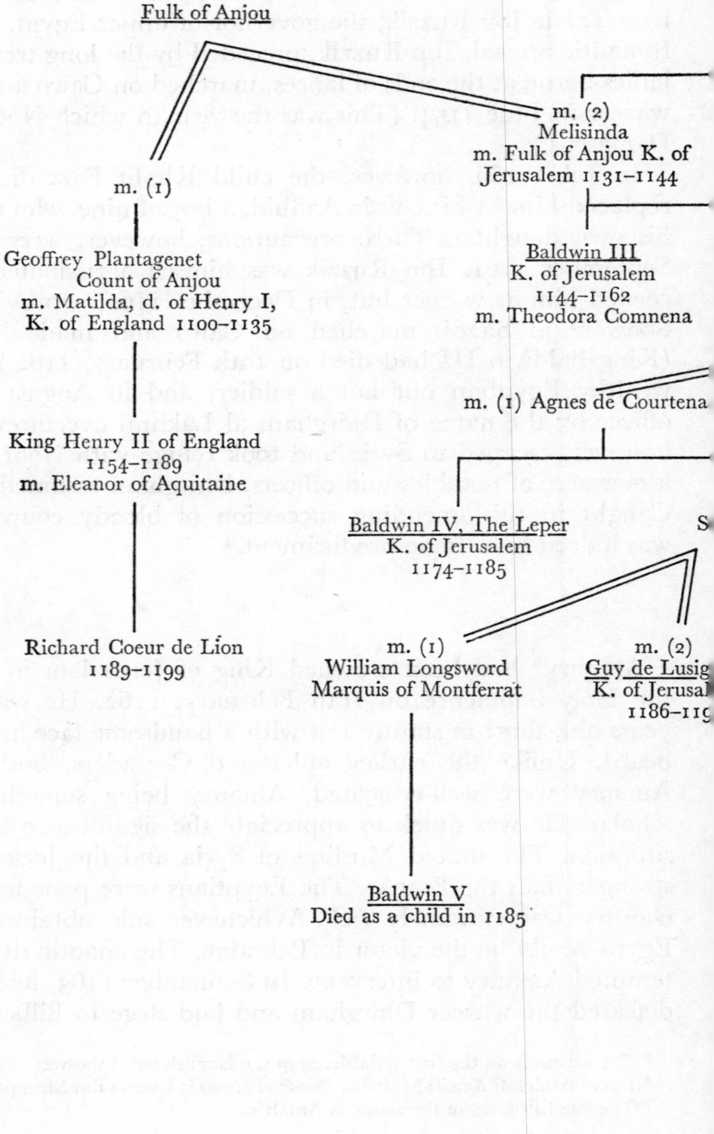
Fulk of Anjou
m. (1)
Geoffrey Plantagenet
Count of Anjou
m. Matilda, d. of Henry I,
K. of England 1100–1135
King Henry II of England
1154–1189
m. Eleanor of Aquitaine
Richard Coeur de Lion
1189–1199
m. (2)
Melisinda
m. Fulk of Anjou K. of
Jerusalem 1131–1144
Baldwin III
K. of Jerusalem
1144–1162
m. Theodora Comnena
m. (1) Agnes de Courtena
Baldwin IV, The Leper
K. of Jerusalem
1174–1185
m. (1)
William Longsword
Marquis of Montferrat
m. (2)
Guy de Lusig
K. of Jerusal
1186–119
Baldwin V
Died as a child in 1185

THE ROYAL HOUSE OF JERUSALEM, 1100-1225
(and their relationship to the English Royal Family)

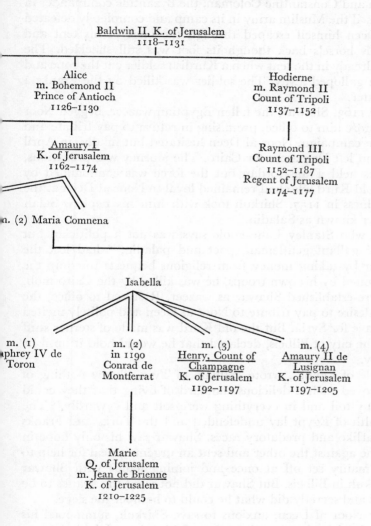

Baldwin II, K. of Jerusalem
1118–1131

Alice
m. Bohemond II
Prince of Antioch
1126–1130

Hodierne
m. Raymond II
Count of Tripoli
1137–1152

Amaury I
K. of Jerusalem
1162–1174

Raymond III
Count of Tripoli
1152–1187
Regent of Jerusalem
1174–1177

n. (2) Maria Comnena

Isabella

m. (1)
phrey IV de
Toron

m. (2)
in 1190
Conrad de
Montferrat

m. (3)
Henry, Count of
Champagne
K. of Jerusalem
1192–1197

m. (4)
Amaury II de
Lusignan
K. of Jerusalem
1197–1205

Marie
Q. of Jerusalem
m. Jean de Brienne
K. of Jerusalem
1210–1225

floods obliged him to withdraw. Returning to Jerusalem, he wrote to Louis VII to ask for help.

In the hope of compelling Amaury to return from Egypt, Noor al Deen had meanwhile attacked Husn al Akrad, the famous castle of Crac des Chevaliers. Raymond III of Tripoli, supported by Bohemond III of Antioch and Constantine Coloman, the Byzantine commander in Cilicia, surprised the Muslim army in its camp and completely defeated it. Noor al Deen himself escaped through the back of his tent and jumped on his horse's back though its foot was still shackled. The Franks were already in the tent when a Kurdish soldier cut the rope and Noor al Deen galloped away. The soldier was killed by the Franks a few seconds later.

In October 1163, Shawar, the fallen Egyptian wazeer, begged Noor al Deen to restore him to office, promising in return to pay tribute and the cost of the campaign. Noor al Deen hesitated but finally, in April 1164, a column left Damascus for Cairo. The journey was precarious, for the Franks held Trans-Jordan but the force was commanded by Shirkuh, the old Kurd who had remained loyal to Noor al Deen at the time of his illness in 1157. Shirkuh took with him his nephew Salah al Deen, better known as Saladin.

Dhirgham, who Stanley Lane-Poole says was not a politician but "a brave and gallant gentleman, poet and paladin,"[6] had lost the khalif's favour by taking money from religious bequests to equip the army. Abandoned by his own troops, he was killed by the Cairo mob, and Shirkuh re-established Shawar as wazeer. Restored to office, the latter felt no desire to pay tribute to Noor al Deen and politely invited Shirkuh to leave for Syria. But the old Kurd was made of sterner stuff and, seizing the city of Bilbeis, declared that he would hold it until he got the money.

"The people of Egypt", wrote William of Tyre, "knew nothing of arms and enjoyed such a delicious standard of living that they could not endure any toil and in everything were soft and cowardly." The immense wealth of Egypt lay undefended and the Turks and Franks alike were warlike and predatory races. Shawar saw his only hope in playing off one against the other and sent an urgent appeal for help to Jerusalem. Amaury set off at once and joining hands with Shawar besieged Shirkuh in Bilbeis. But Shawar did not want the Franks to be too victorious and secretly did what he could to hamper the siege.

Meanwhile Noor al Deen, anxious to save Shirkuh, summoned his brother Mawdood,[7] who was the ruler of Mosul, and laid siege to Harim, the key to Antioch, which had so often changed hands. Supported by Constantine Coloman, the Byzantine commander in Cilicia,

[6] Stanley Lane-Poole, *The Story of Cairo.* [7] Genealogical tree, page 38.

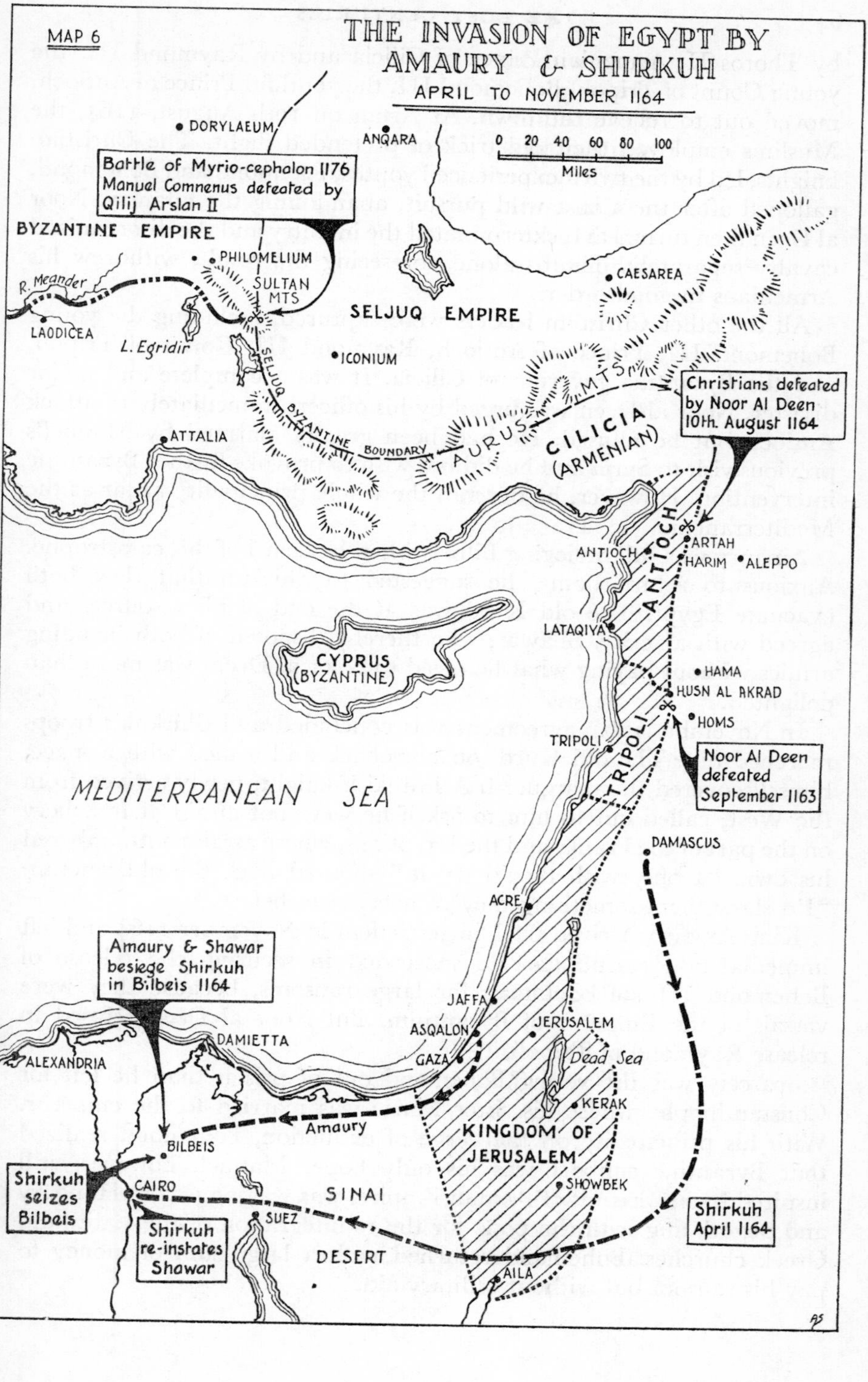
MAP 6
THE INVASION OF EGYPT BY AMAURY & SHIRKUH
APRIL TO NOVEMBER 1164
0 20 40 60 80 100
Miles
DORYLAEUM
ANQARA
Battle of Myrio-cephalon 1176
Manuel Comnenus defeated by
Qilij Arslan II
BYZANTINE EMPIRE
PHILOMELIUM
R. Meander
SULTAN MTS
LAODICEA
L. Egridir
SELJUQ EMPIRE
CAESAREA
ICONIUM
SELJUQ BYZANTINE BOUNDARY
TAURUS MTS
Christians defeated
by Noor Al Deen
10th. August 1164
ATTALIA
CILICIA
(ARMENIAN)
ANTIOCH
ARTAH
HARIM
ALEPPO
LATAQIYA
CYPRUS
(BYZANTINE)
HAMA
HUSN AL AKRAD
HOMS
TRIPOLI
Noor Al Deen
defeated
September 1163
MEDITERRANEAN SEA
DAMASCUS
ACRE
Amaury & Shawar
besiege Shirkuh
in Bilbeis 1164
JAFFA
ASQALON
JERUSALEM
DAMIETTA
ALEXANDRIA
GAZA
Dead Sea
KERAK
Amaury
KINGDOM OF
JERUSALEM
BILBEIS
Shirkuh
seizes
Bilbeis
CAIRO
SINAI
SHOWBEK
Shirkuh
April 1164
SUEZ
Shirkuh
re-instates
Shawar
DESERT
AILA
AS

by Thoros II, Armenian Prince of Cilicia and by Raymond III, the young Count of Tripoli, Bohemond III, the youthful Prince of Antioch, moved out to relieve the town. At Artah on 10th August, 1164, the Muslims employed their old trick of pretended flight. The Christian knights, led by the two inexperienced youths, Raymond and Bohemond, galloped after them in a wild pursuit, abandoning the infantry. Noor al Deen then turned and exterminated the infantry and the disorganized cavalry separately. Thoros alone, foreseeing the result, withdrew his Armenians in good order.

All the other Christian leaders were captured, including the young Bohemond III, Prince of Antioch, Raymond III, Count of Tripoli, and the Byzantine governor of Cilicia. It was a complete and major disaster. Noor al Deen was urged by his officers immediately to attack Antioch but he refused. He had been greatly alarmed by Manuel's previous visit to Syria and he did not wish to provoke further Byzantine intervention. However, he overran the whole principality as far as the Mediterranean.

Amaury was still besieging Bilbeis when he heard of this catastrophe. Anxious to return home, he suggested to Shirkuh that they both evacuate Egypt. The old Kurd was at the end of his resources and agreed with alacrity. Shawar, who thereby disposed of both invading armies without paying what he owed to Noor al Deen, was more than delighted.

In November 1164, agreement was concluded and Shirkuh's troops marched out. The old Kurd, on horseback and armed with a mace, himself covered the rearguard. A Frankish knight, newly arrived from the West, called out to him to ask if he were not afraid of treachery on the part of the Franks and the Egyptians, whose armies outnumbered his own. "I only wish they'd try it," shouted back the old veteran. "I'd show them something they've never seen before."

King Amaury arrived back in Jerusalem in November 1164 and left immediately for Antioch. He succeeded in securing the release of Bohemond III and Coloman for large ransoms, because they were vassals of the Emperor of Byzantium. But Noor al Deen refused to release Raymond of Tripoli.

Scarcely was the young Bohemond out of prison than he left for Constantinople, where his sister Marie was married to the emperor. With his principality on the verge of extinction, Bohemond realized that Byzantine support was his only hope. Manuel, however, still inspired by his dreams of Roman Empire, was waging war in Hungary and negotiating with the pope for the re-integration of the Latin and Greek churches. Bohemond returned with a large sum of money to pay his ransom but without military aid.

As has already been explained, Frankish soldiers in the twelfth century were paid in land and not in money. Within the Principality of Antioch, there was no longer enough land to maintain an army. In these circumstances, Bohemond III was obliged to hand over an increasing number of fortresses to the military orders, the Hospitallers and the Templars.

A monastic order dedicated to John the Baptist had existed in Jerusalem before the Crusades, to care for sick and needy pilgrims. In 1120, the Hospitallers became military, though the nursing tradition also remained. The Templars, on the other hand, were from their foundation purely combatant and were founded in 1119 to protect poor pilgrims on the robber-infested roads of Palestine. Also called "The Poor Knights of Christ", they were dedicated "to fight with a pure mind for the supreme and true King".

Unfortunately the two orders were often to introduce one more anarchic element into the chaotic Frankish states. They acknowledged no superior but the pope and thus constituted two private armies which refused to accept orders from the local rulers or bishops. Often they were hostile to one another. But both orders soon became rich owing to pious donations in the West and were thus able to provide armies in Outremer without paying them in grants of land. Consequently, as the territories of the Frankish states contracted, the rulers were obliged to hand over more and more fortresses to the military orders, which garrisoned them without cost to the local princes.

* * *

Noor al Deen, still dreading Byzantine intervention, continued to act cautiously but Shirkuh was anxious only to return to Egypt. In January 1167, Noor al Deen consented and the old Kurd left with two thousand cavalry. Shawar immediately appealed to King Amaury and, on 30th January, the Frankish army left Asqalon.

Shawar met the king at Bilbeis and promised to pay the Franks four hundred thousand gold bezants if they remained in Egypt until Shirkuh left. Shawar, when in difficulties, was always lavish in promises to pay. (He had still not paid Noor al Deen.) Amaury sent Hugh of Caesarea to obtain the khalif's ratification of the terms.

William of Tyre gives a full account of Hugh's visit to the khalif. The knight followed Shawar through the long corridors and splendid courtyards where gold-overlaid roof-beams were supported on marble columns. Jets of sparkling water shot high into the air from golden pipes and brightly coloured tropical birds flitted from branch to branch of the shrubs in the courts. The entrances to the palace were guarded by detachments of the khalif's Sudanese guards.

At length Shawar and his Christian visitors reached the inner apartments, guarded by many groups of armed men, glittering with gold and silver. They entered a hall divided in the centre from wall to wall by an immense curtain, woven of gold thread and many-coloured silks and sparkling with jewels. Laying aside his sword, the wazeer prostrated himself three times before the curtain. Suddenly, with a dramatic sweep, the curtains were drawn back revealing the Khalif Aadhid, a languid youth of sixteen, seated high on a golden throne glittering with precious stones. Shawar begged the khalif's agreement to the treaty with the Franks to which Aadhid graciously assented, though Hugh roused the indignation of the courtiers by insisting on shaking hands with the khalif.

Shirkuh, meanwhile, had crossed the Nile above Cairo and camped on the west bank facing the city, opposite the Frankish army. For nearly a month the two armies faced one another across the river. Then, early in March 1167, Shirkuh suddenly marched southwards up the Nile. The allies immediately set out in pursuit. So anxious was the young Amaury to overtake the enemy that he abandoned the Frankish infantry and pressed on with only three hundred and seventy-five knights and the Egyptian cavalry.

Shirkuh and his two thousand cavalry were six hundred miles from Damascus. The country population of Egypt was hostile. A defeat would mean annihilation. Even the stout old Kurd felt that it would be best to recross the Nile and to make for home. Only two voices were raised in favour of battle. The first was that of a Turkish mamlook, Sharf al Deen Burghash. "Those who fear death, wounds or captivity," he cried, "are not fit to serve kings. Let them become fellaheen or stay at home with their women." The second voice was that of Shirkuh's own nephew, Salah al Deen Yusuf—our Saladin.

Stirred by these bold speeches, Shirkuh on 18th March, 1167, decided to stand and fight. He chose a piece of ground made uneven by sandy hummocks and difficult for a charge of knights. The place was known as Babain or Two Gates. He placed Saladin in the centre with orders to flee when charged by the Franks. He then posted himself with his main strength on a flank.

Everything happened as the old veteran had foreseen. The Franks charged impetuously in the centre and pursued Saladin off the field, leaving Shirkuh to destroy the Egyptians. When the king returned with his knights, his allies had disappeared. Amaury returned to Cairo to his former position.

Nearly all the Muslim victories over the Franks were obtained by a simulated flight. In earlier times under stronger kings such as Baldwin I, it had been possible to control the barons. At any period of history,

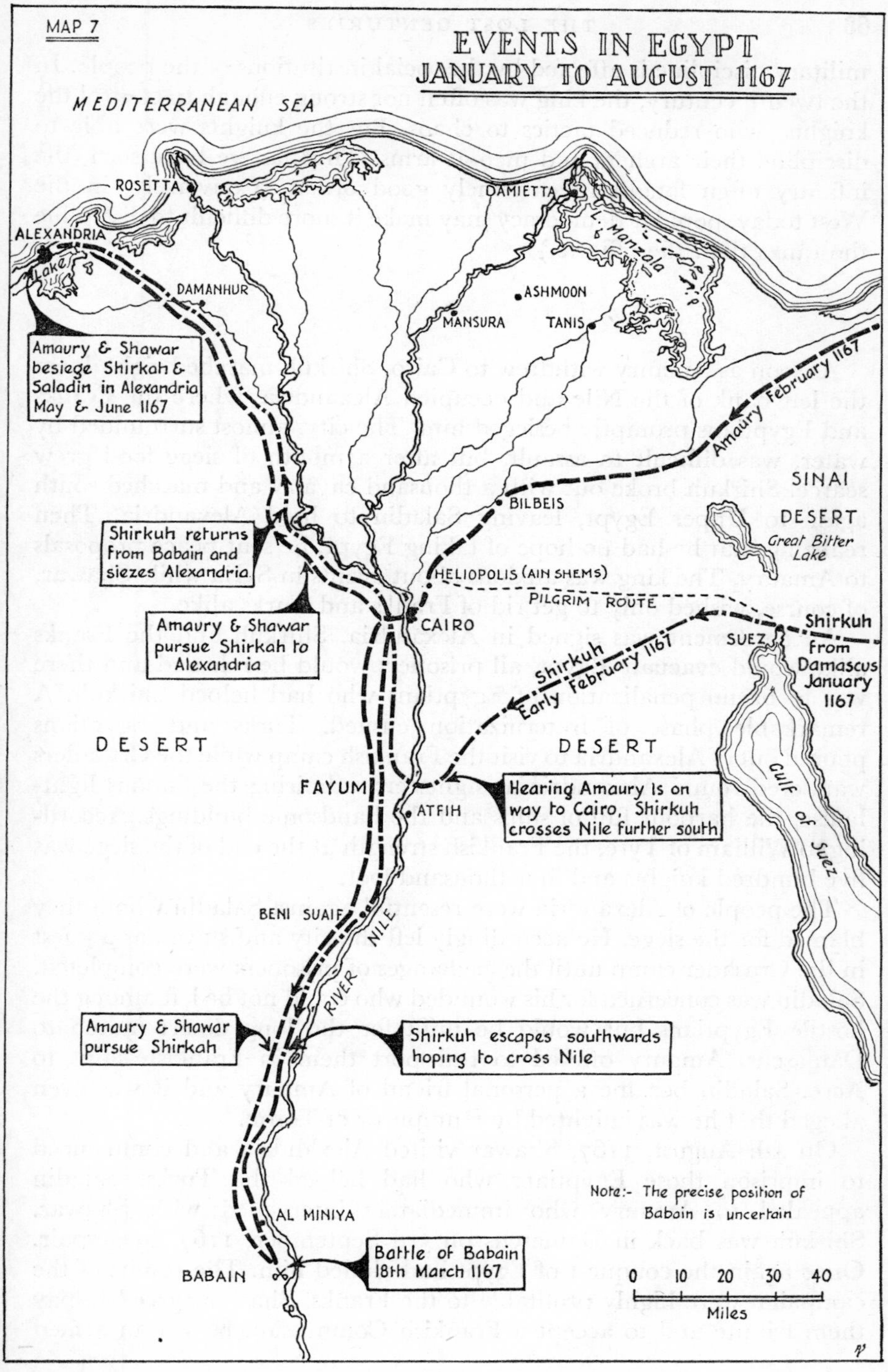
MAP 7
EVENTS IN EGYPT
JANUARY TO AUGUST 1167
MEDITERRANEAN SEA
ROSETTA
DAMIETTA
ALEXANDRIA
Lake
L. Manzala
DAMANHUR
ASHMOON
MANSURA
TANIS
Amaury & Shawar besiege Shirkah & Saladin in Alexandria May & June 1167
Amaury February 1167
SINAI DESERT
BILBEIS
Great Bitter Lake
Shirkuh returns from Babain and siezes Alexandria
HELIOPOLIS (AIN SHEMS)
PILGRIM ROUTE
CAIRO
Amaury & Shawar pursue Shirkah to Alexandria
SUEZ
Shirkuh From Damascus January 1167
Shirkuh Early February 1167
DESERT
DESERT
FAYUM
ATFIH
Hearing Amaury is on way to Cairo, Shirkuh crosses Nile further south
Gulf of Suez
BENI SUAIF
RIVER NILE
Amaury & Shawar pursue Shirkah
Shirkuh escapes southwards hoping to cross Nile
Note:- The precise position of Babain is uncertain
AL MINIYA
Battle of Babain 18th March 1167
BABAIN
0 10 20 30 40
Miles

military discipline is affected by the social institutions of the people. In the twelfth century, the king was often not strong enough to control the knights, who reduced tactics to chaos. But the knights were able to discipline their archers and men-at-arms. Thus, as we have seen, the infantry often fought in extremely good order. (Conversely, in the West today, popular democracy may make it more difficult to discipline the ranks than the officers.)

* * *

As soon as Amaury withdrew to Cairo, Shirkuh marched right down the left bank of the Nile and occupied Alexandria, where the Franks and Egyptians promptly besieged him. The city, almost surrounded by water, was difficult to assault, but after a month of siege food grew scarce. Shirkuh broke out with a thousand cavalry and marched south again to Upper Egypt, leaving Saladin to hold Alexandria. Then realizing that he had no hope of taking Egypt, he sent peace proposals to Amaury. The king was anxious about events in Syria while Shawar, of course, wished only to get rid of Franks and Turks alike.

An agreement was signed in Alexandria. Shirkuh and the Franks alike would evacuate Egypt, all prisoners would be released and there was to be no penalization of Egyptians who had helped Shirkuh. A remarkable phase of fraternization ensued. Turks and Egyptians poured out of Alexandria to visit the Frankish camp while the Crusaders wandered round Alexandria as sightseers, admiring the famous lighthouse, the harbour full of ships and the handsome buildings. According to William of Tyre, the Frankish strength at the end of the siege was five hundred knights and four thousand foot.

The people of Alexandria were resentful against Saladin whom they blamed for the siege. He accordingly left the city and stayed as a guest in the Crusader camp until the exchanges of prisoners were completed. Saladin was concerned for his wounded who could not be left among the hostile Egyptians but would be unfit for the long desert march to Damascus. Amaury offered to transport them in Frankish ships to Acre. Saladin became a personal friend of Amaury and it was even alleged that he was knighted by Humphrey of Toron.

On 4th August, 1167, Shawar visited Alexandria and commenced to imprison those Egyptians who had helped the Turks. Saladin appealed to Amaury who immediately intervened with Shawar. Shirkuh was back in Damascus on 3rd September, 1167, in despair. Once again the conquest of Egypt had eluded him. The results of the campaign were highly profitable to the Franks. Shawar agreed to pay them tribute and to accept a Frankish Commissioner with an armed escort in Cairo. This measure proved their undoing. They had come as allies but they remained as masters.

Some of the barons urged Amaury to write to the kings of the West to come and occupy Egypt but he rejected the proposal as a breach of the treaty which he had signed. He had shown himself a courteous and honourable adversary. "Never," writes Ibn al Athir, "had the Franks had so brave, so cunning or so intelligent a king." On 20th August, 1167, the Frankish army arrived back in Asqalon. On 29th August, Amaury was married at Tyre to Maria Comnena, grand-niece of the Emperor Manuel.

* * *

Early in 1168, Manuel proposed a joint Franko-Byzantine conquest of Egypt and a treaty, negotiated by our historian, William of Tyre, was signed in Constantinople in September 1168. Meanwhile Shawar had grown tired of the presence of an arrogant Frankish commissioner in Cairo—an early example of European tactlessness towards Egyptians. Hoping once again to play off the two parties against each other, he sent his son to negotiate with Noor al Deen.

The barons and the Hospitallers urged the king to anticipate the Muslims by himself re-invading Egypt. Amaury refused to break his faith but, in a Grand Council in Jerusalem, the plan was pressed more urgently, only the Templars refusing. Unfortunately William, Count of Nevers, with a well-equipped force, had landed shortly before from France and exerted all his influence on the side of the war party. Indifferent to diplomacy, he wished to fight unbelievers.

The King of Jerusalem was not an autocrat. His appointment was elective and in the council he was only the first among his peers. Amaury, still a young man, was unable to resist the demands of the barons and gave his unwilling consent. "The king had no good reason for fighting the Egyptians contrary to the agreement which he had ratified on oath," writes William of Tyre, "for they relied on our people . . . who did not perjure themselves after pledging their faith."

The army of Jerusalem left Asqalon on 20th October, 1168, for Bilbeis. Shawar sent an emissary to meet the king and protest at the breach of trust. It is, however, to be noted that Abu Shama[8] does seem to suggest that Shawar had actually reached an agreement with Noor al Deen with the object of himself denouncing the treaty. There is no denying, however, that it was the king who actually broke it.

The Frankish action caused a wave of indignation throughout Egypt and Bilbeis offered resistance. On 4th November, 1168, the Franks took the town and, with incredible folly, plundered it and

[8] Abu Shama, *Two Gardens*.

massacred many of the inhabitants. Ibn al Athir notes that, if the Franks had behaved generously at Bilbeis, they could immediately have taken Cairo, where they had many sympathizers. But there was no inducement to surrender if massacre were to be the result.

The king, who had been compelled against his wishes to engage in the campaign, remained half-hearted. Instead of marching instantly on Cairo, he endeavoured to mitigate the sufferings of Bilbeis. A few days later, however, the Frankish fleet sailed across Lake Manzala and took Tanis, killing many of the inhabitants. In the twelfth century, cities which resisted could legitimately be sacked. Thus the looting of Bilbeis and Tanis were political blunders rather than military crimes.

The king had embarked unwillingly on the campaign and still sought a way to escape from it. He sent a message to Shawar that he would retire in return for a cash payment. By a speedy move Cairo could have been taken but these hesitations were fatal. Suddenly news arrived that Shirkuh was coming.

When he heard of the new Frank invasion, Noor al Deen decided to take strong action. He gave Shirkuh eight thousand cavalry in addition to the army of Damascus. This time there was to be no mistake. Saladin did not wish to go and Shirkuh was obliged to appeal to Noor al Deen to issue an order. "Pack your bags, young man," he said to his nephew when the order came. "We have to hurry." History would have been different if Saladin's excuses had been accepted.

As soon as Shawar heard of Shirkuh's approach, he warned Amaury. The Franks at first considered marching to meet him but the old Kurd's forced marches were famous and he reached Cairo before he could be intercepted. On the former campaign, the Franks had been welcomed as the protectors of Egypt from the Turks. Now Shirkuh was hailed as the saviour of the country from the Franks. This time Shirkuh's army was far more numerous than that of Amaury and the Egyptians were on his side. On 2nd January, 1169, the Franks left Bilbeis and withdrew to Palestine.

* * *

On 8th January, 1169, Shirkuh made his entry into Cairo and was soon in control. The Fatimid Khalifs had long been accustomed to civil wars between rival leaders, on the conclusion of which they appointed the winner to be wazeer. Shirkuh paid the boy Khalif Aadhid several visits during which he allegedly secured his approval to the elimination of Shawar. The old Egyptian had hitherto survived by balancing the Turks against the Franks. Now the Turks held Cairo with an overwhelming army. In one form or another they were to remain for seven hundred years.

Shawar and Shirkuh frequently exchanged "amicable" visits, each seeking some means to destroy his "ally". Shirkuh was content to wait but the youthful Saladin pressed his uncle to act. On 19th January, 1169, Shawar rode out as usual to Shirkuh's camp, accompanied by an escort with drums and trumpets playing and colours flying. He was met by Saladin who told him that his uncle had gone to visit the tomb of the Imam Shafei and suggested that they ride over to join him. When Shawar agreed they rode off together, stirrup to stirrup. Saladin's escort also joined the party.

Suddenly Saladin leaned over from the saddle, seized Shawar by the collar and dragged him from his horse. At the same moment, Saladin's escort fell upon that of Shawar and dispersed it. Shawar was taken to Shirkuh's camp, where his head was cut off and sent to the khalif. Aadhid replied by sending a wazeer's robes to Shirkuh. The latter immediately garrisoned the citadel with his Turkmans. The old Kurd had achieved his ambition. Sixty years old, he was short, fat, one-eyed and ugly but a great fighter and a voracious eater, especially of meat. On 23rd March, 1169, he was seized with colic and died soon afterwards.

The unexpected death of Shirkuh might well have created anarchy, for several senior officers aspired to the command. Saladin, who was only thirty-one, was one of the youngest candidates. Thinking perhaps that a young man would be easy to handle, the officials of the Fatimid court supported him. Being a diplomat as well as a strong personality, Saladin secured his own appointment as wazeer without bloodshed.

To the Muslims, every man from the West was a Frank, were he French, English, German, or Italian. The western historians by referring to all the peoples of Syria, Iraq or Egypt as Saracens missed many important factors. These countries were in reality inhabited by races of extremely varied origins. The Arabs were Semitic, the Turks resembled the Mongol type, the Egyptians were partly African, the Kurds are believed to be of Aryan origin. It is, therefore, of interest to note that, in the struggle for power in which Saladin was victorious, he appealed to his fellow Kurds in the army not to allow the command to pass to the Turks.

The Egyptians were now chiefly concerned with how to get rid of the Damascus army, and their thoughts turned towards the Franks. A messenger was intercepted leaving Cairo with a letter sewn in his sandal appealing to Amaury for help. Saladin caused the official who had written the letter to be instantly beheaded. All the khalif's entourage were changed and replaced by Turks whom Saladin could trust. One of his own slaves was made chamberlain of the palace.

These arbitrary measures did not pass unopposed. On 23rd August,

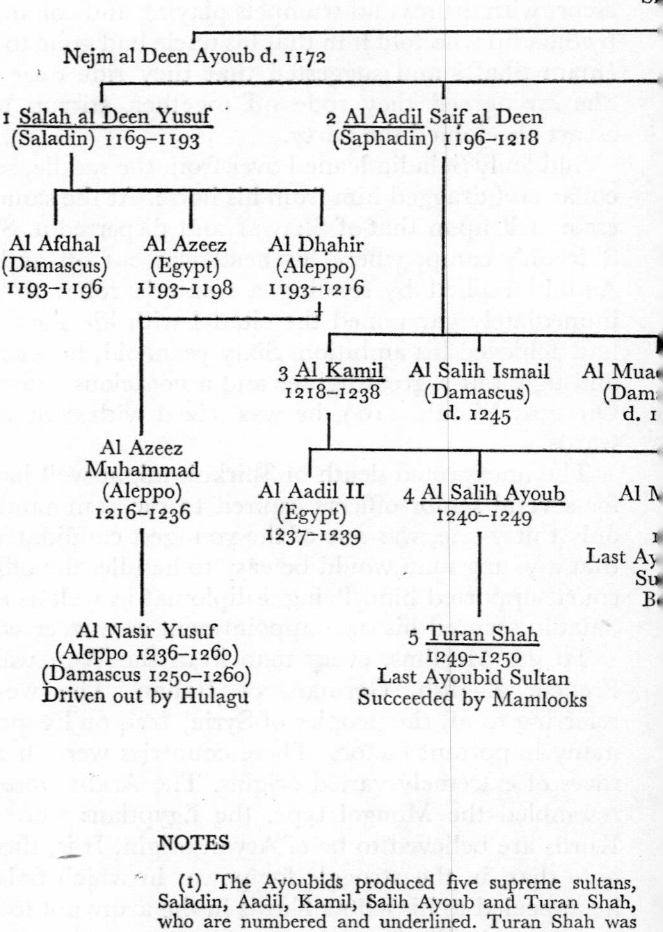

NOTES

(1) The Ayoubids produced five supreme sultans, Saladin, Aadil, Kamil, Salih Ayoub and Turan Shah, who are numbered and underlined. Turan Shah was succeeded by the Mamlooks, Aibek and Spray of Pearls.

(2) After that Nasir Yusuf ruled Syria for ten years till driven out by Hulagu.

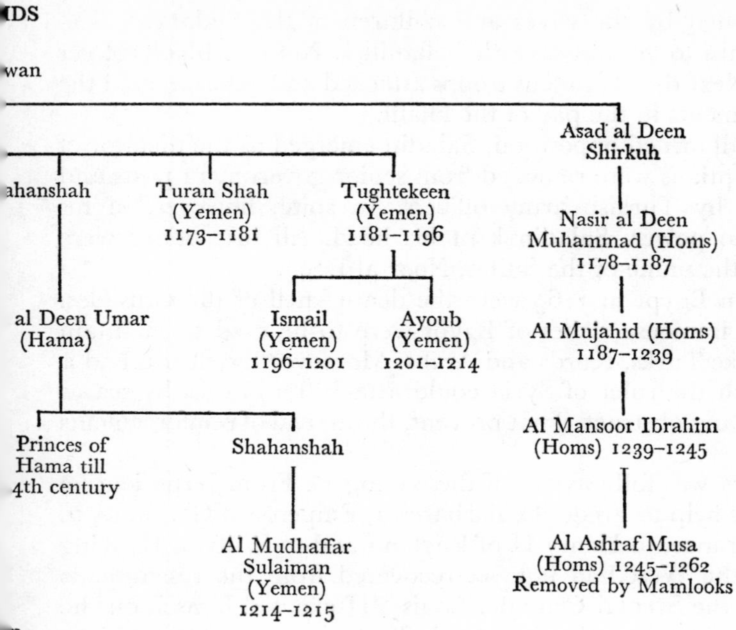

(3) Ayoubid rule in the Yemen had already ended in 1228.

(4) The descendants of Shirkuh remained princes of Homs till 1262.

(5) Thereafter the only Ayoubid princes to survive were the rulers of Hama, who remained until 1340, latterly as governors under the Mamlooks.

1169, the khalif's Sudanese troops mutinied and a desperate battle was joined between them and the Turks. Finally the latter set fire to the quarters inhabited by the wives and children of the Sudanese, who broke their ranks to go and save their families. Not one black soldier was left alive. Next the Damascus troops attacked and exterminated the Armenian regiments in the pay of the khalif.

Freed from all armed opposition, Saladin emerged as the dictator of Egypt. All Egyptians were removed from senior government posts and were replaced by Turkish army officers. In spite, however, of his meteoric rise to power, Saladin kept his head. All his actions were carried out in the name of the Sultan Noor al Deen.

The events in Egypt in 1169 were the death knell of the Crusades. Thereafter the immense riches of Egypt were to be used to maintain armies of warlike Turks, Kurds and Arabs. Moreover Egypt still had a fleet with which the ruler of Syria could attack the Franks by sea as well as by land and obstruct, if not prevent, the arrival of reinforcements from the West.

King Amaury was fully aware of these dangers. From Jerusalem he sent appeals for help to Frederick Barbarossa, Emperor of Germany, to Louis VII of France, to Henry II of England and to William II, King of Sicily. But the West had not yet recovered from the resentments engendered by the Second Crusade. Louis VII excused himself on the grounds that he feared an English attack. Barbarossa was engaged in a struggle with the pope and the Italian republics. The King of Sicily was at war with the Byzantine Emperor. Amaury's delegates returned to report that there was no hope of aid from the West.

The Emperor Manuel, however, had been alarmed by the Syrian[9] occupation of Egypt and decided to assist the Franks to reconquer that country. On 8th July, 1169, his fleet cleared the Dardanelles, but when the flotilla arrived at Acre Amaury was not ready. He wished to strengthen the frontier against Noor al Deen before leaving. Thus surprise was lost and Saladin had ample time to prepare. Moreover the Byzantine fleet had only three months' rations which were almost finished before they left Acre.

The Frankish army eventually left Asqalon on 16th October and met the Byzantine fleet at Damietta on 27th.

Several days were wasted pitching tents. Saladin had expected an attack on Bilbeis. If the Franks had attacked immediately, they might have taken Damietta by a *coup de main*. During the delay, the Muslim army was able to move from Bilbeis to Damietta.

The Byzantines had already finished their rations. The Franks still

[9] The use of the words Syria and Egypt seems unavoidable but we may remember that their rulers were not henceforward native Syrians or Egyptians but Turkish conquerors.

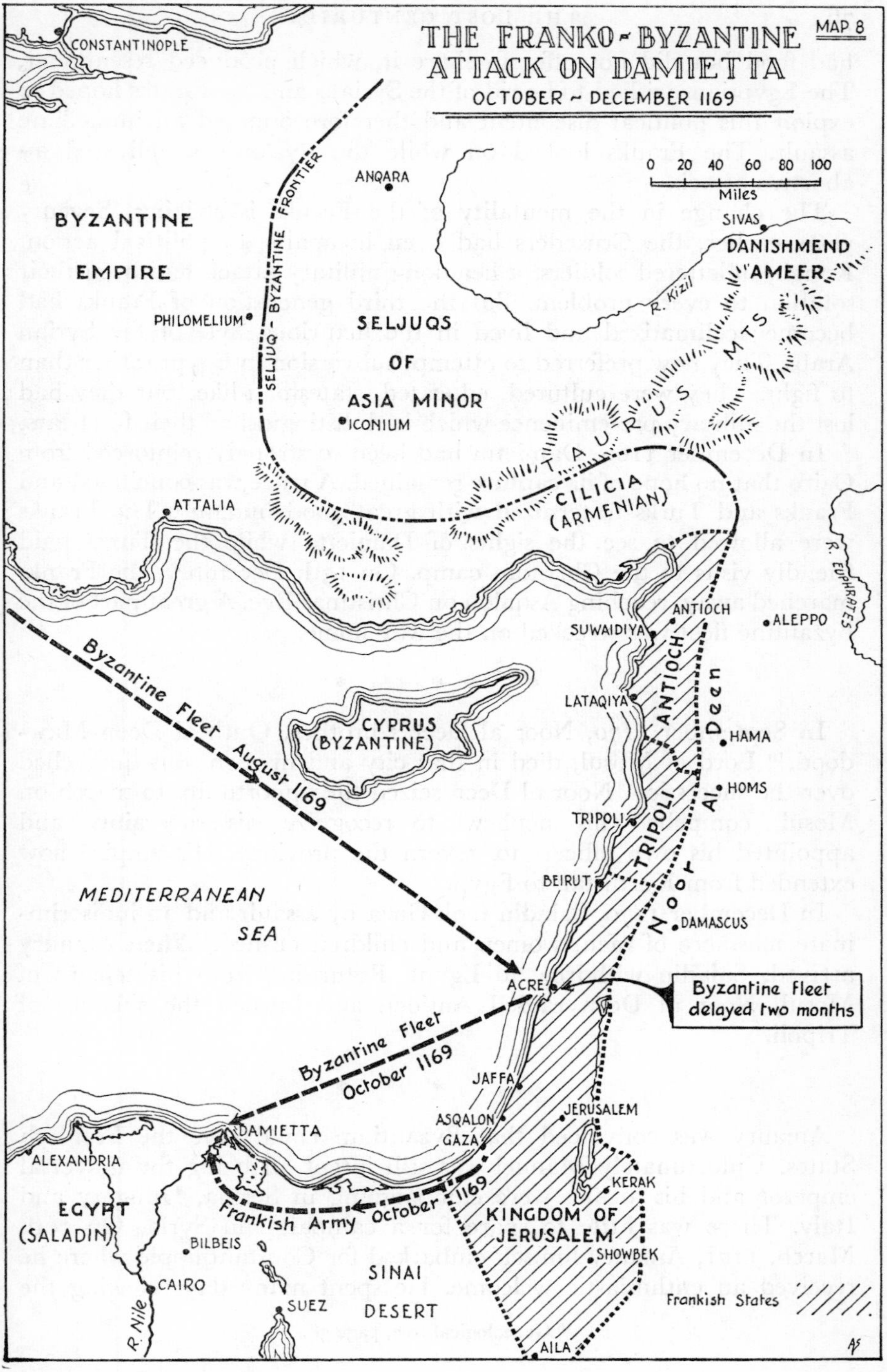

MAP 8
THE FRANKO-BYZANTINE ATTACK ON DAMIETTA
OCTOBER - DECEMBER 1169
0 20 40 60 80 100
Miles
CONSTANTINOPLE
ANQARA
SIVAS
BYZANTINE EMPIRE
SELJUQ - BYZANTINE FRONTIER
DANISHMEND AMEER
R. Kizil
PHILOMELIUM
SELJUQS OF ASIA MINOR
ICONIUM
TAURUS MTS
CILICIA (ARMENIAN)
ATTALIA
R. EUPHRATES
ANTIOCH
SUWAIDIYA
ALEPPO
Byzantine Fleet August 1169
CYPRUS (BYZANTINE)
LATAQIYA
HAMA
HOMS
TRIPOLI
Noor Al Deen
BEIRUT
DAMASCUS
MEDITERRANEAN SEA
ACRE
Byzantine fleet delayed two months
Byzantine Fleet October 1169
JAFFA
ASQALON
JERUSALEM
GAZA
DAMIETTA
ALEXANDRIA
KERAK
EGYPT (SALADIN)
Frankish Army October 1169
KINGDOM OF JERUSALEM
BILBEIS
SHOWBEK
CAIRO
SINAI DESERT
SUEZ
R. Nile
Frankish States
AILA
AS

had food but did not offer to share it, which produced resentment. The Egyptians wished to be rid of the Syrians and the Franks hoped to exploit this political discontent and therefore opposed an immediate assault. The Franks looked on while the Byzantines delivered an abortive attack.

The change in the mentality of the Franks is striking. Seventy years earlier, the Crusaders had been incapable of political action. Rough, unlettered soldiers, a headlong military attack had been their solution to every problem. But the third generation of Franks had become acclimatized and lived in the luxurious style of the Syrian Arabs. They now preferred to attempt subversion in Egypt rather than to fight. They were cultured, educated, statesman-like, but they had lost the military pre-eminence which had distinguished their forebears.

In December 1169, Damietta had been so strongly reinforced from Cairo that no hope of its capture remained. A truce was concluded and Franks and Turks fraternized with great good humour. The Franks were allowed to see the sights of Damietta while the Turks paid friendly visits to the Christian camp. On 13th December, the Franks marched away, reaching Asqalon on Christmas Eve. A great part of the Byzantine fleet was wrecked on the way home.

* * *

In September 1170, Noor al Deen's brother, Qutb al Deen Mawdood,[10] Lord of Mosul, died in that city and his two sons quarrelled over the succession. Noor al Deen seized the opportunity to march on Mosul, compelled his nephews to recognize his suzerainty and appointed his own officers to govern the province. His empire now extended from Kurdistan to Egypt.

In December 1170, Saladin took Gaza by assault and an indiscriminate massacre of men, women and children ensued. When Amaury arrived, Saladin withdrew to Egypt. Returning from his seizure of Mosul, Noor al Deen raided Antioch and burned the suburbs of Tripoli.

* * *

Amaury was convinced that Byzantium could save the Frankish States. Unfortunately Manuel was still intent on being the universal emperor and his armies were campaigning in Serbia, Hungary and Italy. There was little to spare for a campaign in Syria. On 10th March, 1171, Amaury himself embarked for Constantinople where he received an enthusiastic welcome. He spent many days viewing the

[10] Genealogical tree, page 38.

beauties and the historical monuments of the city, for he was well-read and interested in history.

The Franks of the Holy Land now found it easier to get on with the Byzantines and even with the Muslims of Syria than with their European cousins, for in many respects the mentality of the Eastern Mediterranean transcends the boundaries of religion. The king re-embarked for Syria on 15th June, 1171.

* * *

Of the two great divisions of Islam, it will be remembered that the Fatimid Khalifs were Shiites, whereas Noor al Deen, Saladin and the people of Syria and the Jezira were Sunnis. In 1171, Noor al Deen wrote to Saladin, instructing him to abolish the Fatimid khalifate and to bring Egypt back to the Sunni faith. On 10th September, 1171, public prayers were read in Cairo for the Sunni khalif in Baghdad instead of for the Fatimids. Aadhid, the last Shiite khalif, was already unconscious and died three days later unaware that Egypt had changed allegiance. Some reports state that Aadhid died of illness, others that he was murdered by Saladin's brother or that he killed himself.

Saladin was now virtually King of Egypt and seized the immense wealth of the Fatimids, perhaps the richest dynasty in the world. Noor al Deen was becoming jealous of his lieutenant and, in the autumn of 1171, commenced preparations to invade Egypt and to remove him from his post. A conference of the senior officers of the army was called in Cairo and Saladin explained the situation. A few young officers replied that if Noor al Deen came, they would resist him in arms. At this moment, Ayoub, Saladin's father, leaped to his feet and exclaimed, "I declare before God that if Noor al Deen comes we will all fall prostrate and kiss the ground. Egypt is his. If he told us to cut off your head, we would do so."

When the council had dispersed, Ayoub rebuked his son for a fool. "Why expose your secret thoughts before all the officers?" he demanded. "Now they will all write to Noor al Deen and tell him what you said. Your only chance is to send him a letter yourself and this is what you will write. 'I have heard that my lord proposes to visit this country. There is no need for him to go to such trouble. Let my lord send a messenger who can tie a rope round my neck and lead me unresisting to my lord.' " Noor al Deen was placated by this obsequious missive and cancelled the preparations for the expedition.

Nevertheless two years later, in 1173, Noor al Deen's jealousy was roused once more. Plans for a joint attack on the Franks were prepared by him but Saladin was no longer in a hurry to conquer the Franks, who were keeping Noor al Deen occupied in Syria. If the Franks were eliminated, the sultan would be free to invade Egypt. In the same year, Saladin sent his brother Turan Shah with an army to occupy the Yemen, apparently as a refuge for the family if Noor al Deen were to occupy Egypt.

Early in 1174, a Shiite-Fatimid plot was hatched in Egypt. The conspirators wrote to King Amaury and to William II, King of Sicily. But in April Saladin discovered the plot, which was quickly suppressed with torture and crucifixion. When the Sicilian fleet appeared off Alexandria in August, the conspiracy had ended four months before. The slowness of communications in the twelfth century made it impossible to co-ordinate distant operations.

Early in 1174, relations between Noor al Deen and Saladin were again approaching a crisis and the outbreak of civil war appeared to be imminent, when, on 15th May, 1174, Noor al Deen died suddenly in Damascus. He left a son Al Salih,[11] who was only eleven years of age. Immediately the unity of Syria and the Jezira was jeopardized. Damascus, Aleppo and Mosul were seized by rival ameers, jealous of one another. The Ameer of Damascus made an independent agreement with Jerusalem according to the traditional policy of the city before the Second Crusade. Hostilities appeared to be imminent between the ameers of Aleppo and Mosul.

This almost instantaneous disintegration revealed the fragility of the new Muslim unity, which only the authority of some great personality could maintain. Noor al Deen had been not only a competent soldier but a revered character. He was a painstaking administrator and a man of deep piety. Particularly after his serious illness in 1157, he lived a simple, almost an ascetic life. He gave much of his wealth to pious foundations and spent a great part of his time in religious exercises. He was an ardent advocate of Muslim Sunni orthodoxy, which he promoted, partly by the suppression of the Shiites and partly by the foundation of orthodox colleges and religious institutions. He roused a new spirit of religious enthusiasm among Syrian Muslims, thereby facilitating unity and reviving the war spirit. His successor Saladin imitated and profited from these policies.

Allied to the Byzantine Emperor and the King of Sicily, while the grumblings of Shiite revolt persisted in Egypt, King Amaury glimpsed for a moment the possibility of recovering, from a Syria in anarchy, the losses which the Franks had suffered at the hands of Noor al Deen and his father Zengi. These hopes were to prove illusory for, on 11th July, 1174, King Amaury himself died in Jerusalem at the age of thirty-eight. The loss was to prove irreparable.

11 His title was Malik al Salih Ismail.

NOTABLE DATES

Death of the Fatimid Khalif Hafidh	1149
Succession of coups d'état in Egypt	1149 to 1163
Death of Baldwin III of Jerusalem	10th February, 1162
First Frankish invasion of Egypt	September 1163
Noor al Deen defeated at Husn al Akrad	Autumn 1163
Invasion of Egypt by Shirkuh	April 1164
Armies of Tripoli and Antioch completely defeated at Artah	10th August, 1164
Shirkuh and King Amaury both evacuate Egypt	November 1164
Shirkuh and Amaury return to Egypt	January 1167
Shirkuh and Amaury again agree to evacuate Egypt	August 1167
Amaury again invades Egypt and takes Bilbeis	Oct.-Nov. 1168
Amaury evacuates Egypt Shirkuh seizes Cairo	January 1169
Death of Shirkuh Saladin seizes Egypt	23rd March, 1169
Death of Noor al Deen	15th May, 1174
Death of King Amaury	11th July, 1174

PERSONALITIES

Muslims

Noor al Deen Mahmood, the son of Zengi
Shirkuh, Ayoub — brothers and Kurdish mercenary commanders
Saladin, the son of Ayoub
Aadhid, the last Fatimid (Shiite) Khalif of Egypt

Franks of Outremer

Baldwin III, King of Jerusalem
Amaury I, King of Jerusalem, brother of Baldwin
Raymond III, Count of Tripoli
Bohemond III, Prince of Antioch
Thoros II, Armenian Prince of Cicilia

Byzantines

The Emperor Manuel Comnenus

IV

The Fall of the Kingdom
1174–1189

The tragedy of Raymond was the tragedy of all the Frankish colonists of the second and third generation, who . . . were ready to become part of the oriental world but were forced by the fanaticism of their newly-come western cousins to take sides; and in the end they could not but take sides with fellow-Christians.

STEVEN RUNCIMAN, *A History of The Crusades*

Jerusalem, if I forget thee,
Perish the skill of my right hand.
Let my tongue stick fast to the roof of my mouth
If I cease to remember thee,
If I love not Jerusalem
Dearer than heart's content.

Psalm CXXXVII (Trans. RONALD KNOX)

F

IV

FOR a short time at the beginning of 1174, when Noor al Deen was preparing to invade Egypt, Saladin's future had seemed highly precarious. Then suddenly, within the space of three months, the dangers threatening him vanished. Noor al Deen and King Amaury were dead, each leaving a child as his heir.

Baldwin IV, the heir to the Kingdom of Jerusalem, was thirteen years old, serious, brave, handsome and extremely intelligent. Our historian William of Tyre had been his tutor and Baldwin IV was the best educated of all the Kings of Jerusalem. But already a curious lack of sensation had affected his arms. Soon the cause was all too plain—he was a leper.

After an initial struggle for power, Raymond III, Count of Tripoli, was made regent, an eminently suitable choice. He was the king's nearest male relative, his mother having been the sister of Baldwin's grandmother.[1] He was also Prince of Galilee, having married the heiress of that province. Taken prisoner by Noor al Deen at Artah in 1164, he had spent eight years in confinement in Aleppo. He was well-read, spoke fluent Arabic and was familiar with Islam. Thirty-four years old, he was tall and lean, with a large nose and a long beard. In character he was cold, unemotional, free from pride, wise and moderate.

Meanwhile Malik al Salih, the eleven-year-old son of Noor al Deen, had made his capital in Aleppo. This had been the headquarters of Noor al Deen before his seizure of Damascus, and its people were deeply attached to the Zengids. The Damascenes, however, were determined not to be subject to Aleppo[2] and wrote to invite Saladin.

Leaving his brother, Malik al Aadil, as viceroy of Egypt, Saladin entered Damascus unopposed on 26th November, 1174. He at first professed to be the servant of the young Al Salih and to have come to supervise his education. He courted popularity in Damascus, distributing large sums of money. He then marched northward and, on 9th December, occupied Homs after a ten-day siege. Hama surrendered and, on 30th December, 1174, he laid siege to Aleppo.

The young King Al Salih rode weeping into the centre of the city, appealing for the support of the people, who responded with enthusiasm. The government of Aleppo determined to resist and sent requests

[1] Genealogical tree, page 60.

[2] The rivalry between Aleppo and Damascus exists to this day.

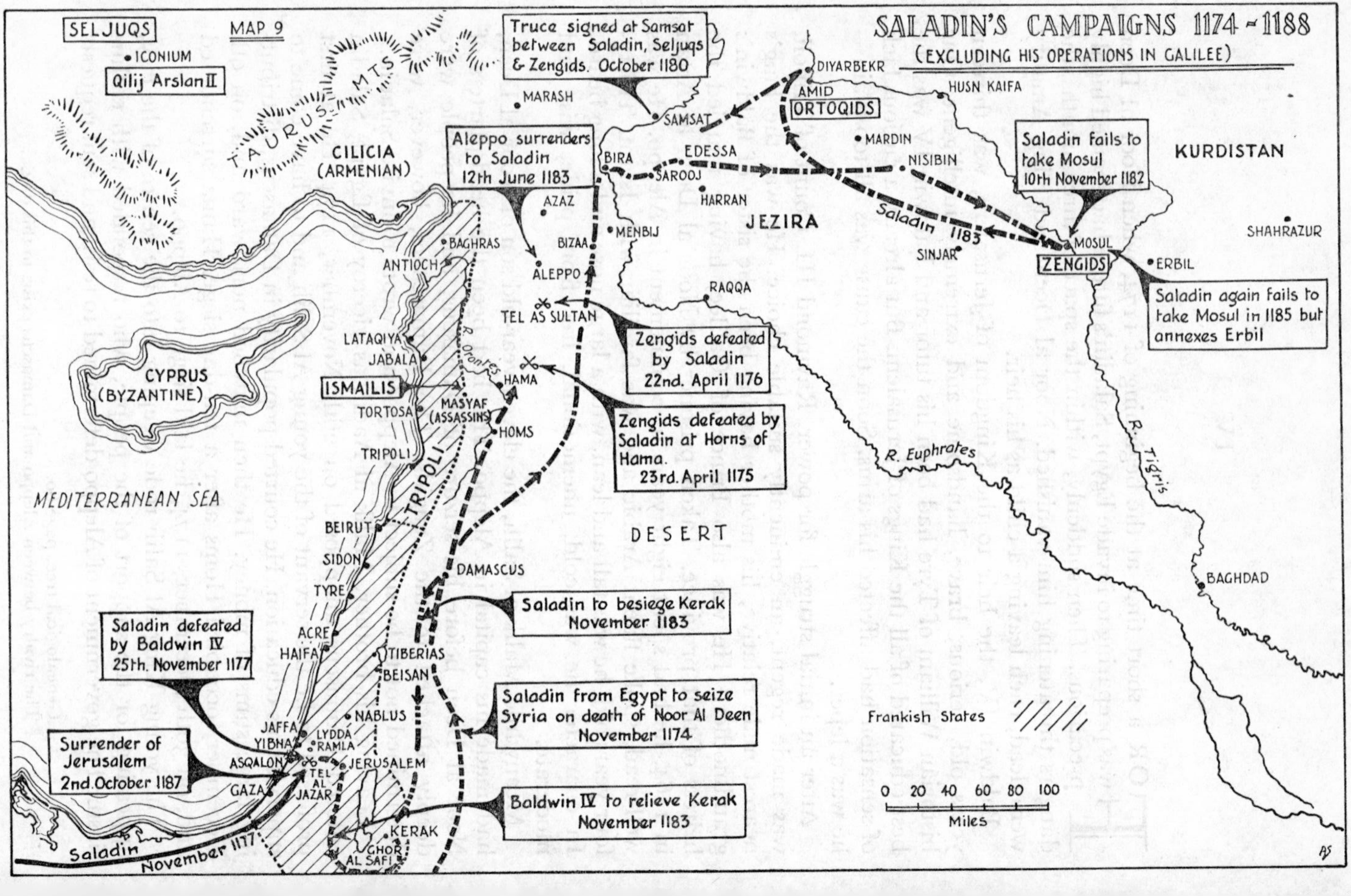
SALADIN'S CAMPAIGNS 1174 – 1188
(EXCLUDING HIS OPERATIONS IN GALILEE)
MAP 9
SELJUQS
ICONIUM
Qilij Arslan II
TAURUS MTS
CILICIA (ARMENIAN)
MARASH
Truce signed at Samsat between Saladin, Seljuqs & Zengids. October 1180
SAMSAT
DIYARBEKR
AMID
ORTOQIDS
HUSN KAIFA
MARDIN
NISIBIN
Saladin fails to take Mosul 10th November 1182
KURDISTAN
Aleppo surrenders to Saladin 12th June 1183
BIRA
EDESSA
SAROOJ
HARRAN
JEZIRA
Saladin 1183
SINJAR
MOSUL
ZENGIDS
ERBIL
SHAHRAZUR
Saladin again fails to take Mosul in 1185 but annexes Erbil
AZAZ
MENBIJ
BIZAA
BAGHRAS
ANTIOCH
ALEPPO
RAQQA
TEL AS SULTAN
Zengids defeated by Saladin 22nd. April 1176
LATAQIYA
JABALA
R. Orontes
CYPRUS (BYZANTINE)
ISMAILIS
HAMA
TORTOSA
MASYAF (ASSASSINS)
HOMS
Zengids defeated by Saladin at Horns of Hama. 23rd. April 1175
R. Euphrates
R. Tigris
TRIPOLI
MEDITERRANEAN SEA
BEIRUT
DESERT
SIDON
DAMASCUS
TYRE
BAGHDAD
Saladin to besiege Kerak November 1183
Saladin defeated by Baldwin IV 25th. November 1177
ACRE
HAIFA
TIBERIAS
BEISAN
Saladin from Egypt to seize Syria on death of Noor Al Deen November 1174
Frankish States
NABLUS
JAFFA
LYDDA
YIBNA
RAMLA
Surrender of Jerusalem 2nd. October 1187
ASQALON
TEL AL JAZAR
JERUSALEM
GAZA
0 20 40 60 80 100
Miles
Baldwin IV to relieve Kerak November 1183
KERAK
GHOR AL SAFI
Saladin
November 1177

for help to the Ismailis and to Raymond of Tripoli. The Ismailis despatched a party to assassinate Saladin but the attempt miscarried. Raymond made a successful diversion by attacking Homs, compelling Saladin to raise the siege of Aleppo and march southwards, whereupon Raymond slipped back to Tripoli.

In gratitude, the government of Aleppo released Renaud de Châtillon who, it will be remembered, had been taken prisoner in 1160 and had been fourteen years in confinement. His wife, Constance of Antioch, was dead and her son by Raymond of Poitiers—Bohemond III—was Prince of Antioch, but Renaud soon made himself Lord of Kerak by marrying the heiress of that fortress.

The Zengids held not only Aleppo but also Mosul. Saif al Deen Ghazi II, a cousin of Al Salih, was Prince of Mosul and early in 1175 sent his army to support Aleppo.[3] On 23rd April, 1175, a battle was fought at the Horns of Hama in which Saladin was victorious, after which Aleppo agreed to a truce. Thereupon Saladin, abandoning the pretence of loyalty to Al Salih, declared himself King of Egypt and Syria.

In the spring of 1176, however, the Zengids again took the field but were once more defeated by Saladin on 22nd April, 1176, at Tel al Sultan, twenty miles south of Aleppo, which the victor besieged for the second time. But after a month of fruitless attacks, peace was concluded on 29th July, 1176.

Saladin disliked sieges and when faced with a strong city, he normally avoided it, preferring to isolate it by capturing the smaller towns all around it. He had failed to take Aleppo but had cut its communications with the Jezira and Mosul, other Zengid centres, by seizing Bizaa, Menbij and Azaz. When peace was signed, a little girl, the sister of King Al Salih, went to Saladin's camp, where the latter received her kindly and asked what she wanted. "The fortress of Azaz," replied the child boldly and Saladin immediately agreed.

The incident is of interest because for the victor in a battle to give back part of the loot to the ladies is an age-old Arab tribal custom, which I myself often witnessed in the 1920s. Many different races were mingled in Syria in the twelfth century. Nomadic Arab tribes still occupied the desert, the towns were inhabited by a population half Arab, half pre-Islamic Syrian, while the rulers, such as the Zengids, were Turks.

Saladin, however, was a Kurd, a nation which, for six centuries, had shared in that Perso-Arab civilization which led the world. The influence of Arab chivalry on Saladin, in contrast to the Turks, will more than once be noticeable. Indeed his biographer, Baha al Deen,[4]

[3] Genealogical tree, page 38.
[4] Baha al Deen ibn Sheddad, *Al Nuwadir al Sultaniya*.

says definitely that the Turks would never obey the Kurds nor the Kurds the Turks. Baha al Deen had been born in Mosul and died in Aleppo and thus the modern Western reader would call him an Arab. But as we shall frequently see in this narrative, the word Arab in the twelfth century had reverted to its meaning of bedouin or nomad.

These Arabs still maintained their ancient customs which differed considerably from those of the city-dwellers of Syria and their predominantly Turkish rulers. For some reason or other, these chivalrous customs appealed particularly to Saladin. "He was well acquainted with the pedigrees of the old Arabs and with the details of their battles: he knew all their adventures. Thus in conversation with him, people always heard things which they could never have learned from others." This statement shows the evident enthusiasm of Saladin for Arabs and also the complete estrangement which had grown up between them and their Turkish military rulers. In government circles no one knew these Arab customs except Saladin himself.

In another passage, Baha al Deen, who was the sultan's chaplain for five years, describes how he used to sit in public to receive complaints. This extremely ancient custom survived until our own times in the Arabian peninsula. Every prince or local governor would sit in an open hall or tent or in the square of a town, to receive petitioners in person. Thereby all had access to him without the intervention of junior officials, guards or sentries.[5]

In a similar manner, we are told, Saladin gave lavish gifts to all who visited him and no one could ever do so without being obliged to stay for a meal, with the result that the sultan never acquired any private wealth—conduct typical of the ideal Arab prince in the days of their golden age. To make sure once more of the sultan's predilection for Arab tribesmen, Baha al Deen tells us, in describing a military operation, that he sent Arabs to carry it out "because he trusted them".

* * *

Having frightened the Zengids into acquiescence in his supremacy, Saladin turned to revenge himself on their allies, the Ismaili Assassins and the Franks. First he besieged Masyaf, the stronghold of Sinan, the Assassin Grand Master. One night in his tent, however, Saladin woke to find a dagger stuck in his pillow and a note threatening more drastic action.[6] Greatly alarmed, he wrote to ask pardon from Sinan—the Old Man of the Mountain, the Franks called him—and raised the siege.

[5] When I lived with bedouin tribes, I too was always expected to sit in public for a certain time every day to ensure that I should be accessible to rich and poor alike.

[6] I knew an Arab who performed a similar feat against a Druze chieftain with whom he had a feud, although the Druze lived in a stone castle amid his relatives.

He never again molested the Ismailis. In September 1176, he returned to Egypt.

* * *

The Emperor Manuel Comnenus had ruled in Constantinople for forty-three years. In a life of tireless activity, he had immensely increased the territory, prestige and influence of the empire. He had waged wars in Asia Minor, Syria, Egypt, Hungary, Serbia and Italy. We have already seen how Noor al Deen had feared him. Yet, in spite of all his glory, the frontier of Qilij Arslan II, the Seljuq Sultan of Iconium, was still only two hundred miles from Constantinople. In the summer of 1176, Manuel made up his mind to end his glorious career by eliminating the Seljuq Sultanate of Iconium.

Collecting a large and well-equipped army, he advanced up the valley of the Meander. On 17th September, 1176, the army entered the long pass of Myrio-cephalon through the Sultan Mountains.[7] The Turks had occupied the mountain slopes on either side but allowed the advanced guard to pass through unmolested. When the long trains of wagons were half-way through the defile they attacked the column from both sides. In the narrow pass the wagons could not turn but completely blocked the road. The fighting troops could not deploy. In a moment of panic, Manuel lost his head. Instead of rallying the troops, he himself fled, followed by the remnants of his army, which had been almost annihilated. Qilij Arslan II, with surprising generosity, granted peace to the emperor on the field of battle.

As had happened a hundred years before at Malazkirt, the Byzantine army had ceased to exist. Manuel lived four years longer, a pathetic, broken figure. He was so crushed by the disaster that he never again showed the least sign of pleasure. The Frankish states had constantly quarrelled with the Byzantines but the prestige of the empire had been the best guarantee of their survival. Constantinople never recovered from the disaster of Myrio-cephalon.

* * *

In 1177, Baldwin IV came of age and Raymond III of Tripoli ceased to be regent. But the king's leprosy was growing worse and it was essential to provide an heir. As his sister Sibylla was still unmarried, the solution seemed to be to find for her a husband who would make a competent king.

The rivalries of the local barons made it impossible to choose such a husband in Outremer. In 1175, Baldwin had sent an invitation to William Long-Sword, eldest son of the Marquis of Montferrat, to

[7] Map 6, page 63.

come and marry his sister. The choice appeared to be judicious. Gallant, brave and handsome, William was the cousin of both the Emperor Frederick Barbarossa and of Louis VII of France. Tall, frank and outspoken, he seemed likely to prove a strong leader. He landed at Sidon in October 1176. Forty days later, he was married to the Princess Sibylla. Within three months he died of malignant malaria. In 1177, Sibylla gave birth to a son, who was to be King Baldwin V.

In September 1177, Philippe d'Alsace, Count of Flanders, landed at Acre with a splendid force of knights and men-at-arms. The House of Flanders had often rendered brilliant services in the Crusades. A Byzantine fleet, sent by Manuel Comnenus to join in a new attack on Egypt, was lying off Acre. The command was offered to Philippe, for the little leper king was too weak to go. Much to the disgust of the king and the nobles, Philippe excused himself. The Byzantine fleet sailed for home and the campaign was abandoned.

* * *

Saladin, as we have seen, had returned to Cairo in September 1176, the month of Myrio-cephalon. He remained there for more than a year, a great part of which was devoted to building work in Cairo. First of all, he commenced the building of the citadel which still so impressively dominates the city. He also ordered the commencement of work to surround Cairo with walls. The Spanish Arab traveller, Ibn Jubair, who visited Cairo in April, 1183, tells us that all the workmen were Frankish prisoners, "whose numbers were beyond computation".[8]

Leaving Cairo early in November 1177 and by-passing Gaza, held by a small force of Templars, Saladin reached Asqalon with twenty-five thousand men. The little leper king, with less than five hundred knights, was just able to throw himself into Asqalon before the arrival of the enemy. Unwilling as usual to spend time in a siege, the sultan left a small force to mask the town and pressed on. There were no Frankish troops between him and Jerusalem.[9] Marching in fancied security, the Muslims scattered far and wide across the fertile plains, plundering and burning. With perhaps unwonted cruelty, Saladin ordered the decapitation of all prisoners.

The young king acted with extraordinary speed and decision. Summoning the eighty Templars who garrisoned Gaza to abandon the fortress and join him, he broke out of Asqalon and rode rapidly up the coast to Yibna—the Ibelin of the Crusaders—whence he turned east until he reached a point ten or eleven miles south of Lydda. As they rode, the Franks could see the long olumns of smoke rising into the air, where the enemy was burning the towns and villages of the coastal plain.

[8] Muhammad ibn Jubair, *Travels,* trans. R. J. C. Broadhurst. [9] Map 9, page 84.

On the morning of 25th November, 1177, the Muslim army was crossing a gully near Tel al Jazar (called by the Franks Montgisard) when Baldwin IV suddenly charged straight into their midst with his knights. The surprise was complete, for Saladin imagined the little king to be shut up in Asqalon. The Muslims had, the day before, burned the church of St. George at Lydda, and many of the combatants swore that they saw St. George himself, mounted on a white horse, leading their charge against the unbelievers.

Soon the whole Muslim army was fleeing in panic with the sole exception of Saladin's bodyguard, a thousand Mamlooks all dressed in yellow tunics, who enabled Saladin to escape, though most of them were killed in doing so. The remainder of the Muslim army fled in utter confusion back to Egypt. The victory was as complete as it was unexpected.

* * *

In 1180, a feud had arisen between Qilij Arslan of Iconium and the Ortoqid Prince of Husn Kaifa. Saladin decided to intervene and in May 1180, after signing a two-year truce with the Franks, he marched northwards. On 2nd October, 1180, a general two-year truce was signed at Samsat on the Euphrates, including also the Zengids of Mosul and the Armenian Prince of Cilicia.

* * *

Meanwhile Baldwin's leprosy was growing worse and it was apparent that he could not long survive. The heir to the throne was Sibylla's three-year-old son by William of Montferrat. If Baldwin IV died, an adult king would be needed until the child grew up. Amaury de Lusignan, a knight who had come to Palestine some years before, had recently been made constable of the kingdom on the death in battle of old Humphrey of Toron. Amaury now paid a visit to France and brought back a brother called Guy, whom he presented to Sibylla, Baldwin's sister, who declared her intention to marry him. Guy was young and good-looking but weak, vain and frivolous. The dying king protested but his mother Agnes persuaded him. At Easter 1180, Guy and Sibylla were married.

Before he came to the throne, King Amaury, the father of Baldwin the Leper, had been married to Agnes de Courtenay, daughter of Jocelin II, Count of Edessa, who had died in prison in Aleppo.[10] Amaury had been obliged to divorce Agnes when he became king, after she had given birth to Baldwin and Sibylla.

The kingdom now split into two factions. One party consisted of

[10] Genealogical tree, page 60.

Agnes, the Queen Mother, her daughter Sibylla and her son-in-law Guy, the Templars and, in general, the knights newly arrived from France, including Renaud de Châtillon, now Lord of Kerak. The other faction was composed of the native barons of Outremer, some already the third and fourth generation born in the kingdom. The mentality of these early settlers had come to resemble that of the people of the land and they had many Muslim friends.

The chances of survival of the Franks were further reduced in 1180 by the death of Manuel Comnenus, leaving as heir his eleven-year-old son, Alexius II. With the West indifferent, no hope of external support for Outremer remained.

It was the aggressiveness of the new arrivals from France which chiefly made the existence of the Frankish states objectionable to the Muslims. The barons of Outremer were in a dilemma. Feeling themselves too weak to survive, they appealed for help from the West but the volunteers who answered their appeal involved them in war. Had they been able to prevent the arrival of warlike pilgrims from the West, the native Franks might conceivably have lived on in peace with the Muslims. Tension between the advocates of co-existence and those of total war had existed for many years but had been restrained under strong kings. Now with a dying leper on the throne, the schism grew more violent and bitter.

King Baldwin's leprosy was spreading and he had now lost the use of his hands and feet and was almost blind. His mother and his sister Sibylla persuaded him to appoint Guy de Lusignan as regent in spite of the opposition of the barons of Outremer. Guy was obviously incompetent and party strife had destroyed unity, but the kingdom was in desperate need of peace. Fortunately for the Christians Saladin was also anxious for peace, for there were internal tensions in the Muslim camp also.

In Egypt the Shiites still hoped for a Fatimid restoration and were ready to co-operate with the Franks to secure it. Qilij Arslan II of Iconium, the Ortoqids and the Zengids in the Jezira, though cowed for the moment, would all take up arms against Saladin once more if he suffered a defeat at the hands of the Franks. Moreover, within his own family his many brothers, sons and nephews were already eyeing one another jealously.

The elevation of Guy to the regency had placed power in the hands of the men newly come from France. Of these the worst was the bandit-adventurer Renaud de Châtillon, once Prince of Antioch, now Lord of Kerak. In the summer of 1181, during the truce with Saladin, he had marched to Teima and seized a large pilgrim caravan, travelling securely from Damascus to Mecca. The loot was enormous.

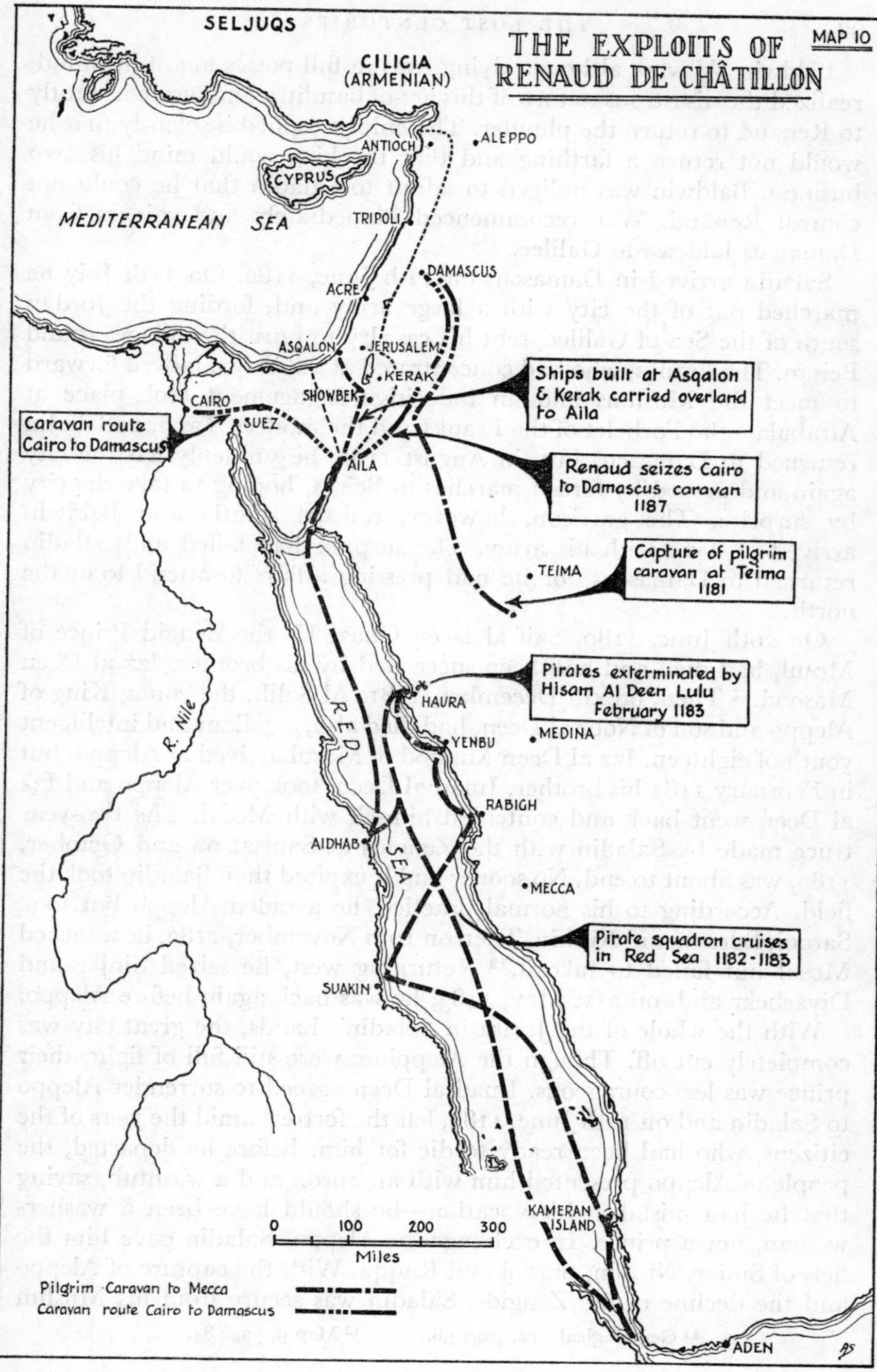
THE EXPLOITS OF
RENAUD DE CHÂTILLON
MAP 10
SELJUQS
CILICIA
(ARMENIAN)
ANTIOCH
ALEPPO
CYPRUS
MEDITERRANEAN SEA
TRIPOLI
DAMASCUS
ACRE
ASQALON
JERUSALEM
KERAK
SHOWBEK
CAIRO
SUEZ
AILA
Ships built at Asqalon & Kerak carried overland to Aila
Caravan route Cairo to Damascus
Renaud seizes Cairo to Damascus caravan 1187
Capture of pilgrim caravan at Teima 1181
TEIMA
Pirates exterminated by Hisam Al Deen Lulu February 1183
HAURA
YENBU
MEDINA
R. Nile
RED SEA
RABIGH
AIDHAB
MECCA
Pirate squadron cruises in Red Sea 1182-1183
SUAKIN
KAMERAN ISLAND
ADEN
0 100 200 300
Miles
Pilgrim Caravan to Mecca
Caravan route Cairo to Damascus

Baldwin IV who, although dying, was in full possession of his mind, realized the disastrous nature of this act of banditry and wrote instantly to Renaud to return the plunder. The culprit replied insolently that he would not return a farthing and that the king could mind his own business. Baldwin was obliged to admit to Saladin that he could not control Renaud. War recommenced immediately and raiders from Damascus laid waste Galilee.

Saladin arrived in Damascus on 12th June, 1182. On 11th July he marched out of the city with a large army and, fording the Jordan south of the Sea of Galilee, sent his cavalry to burn the villages round Beisan. The Franks, who had concentrated at Saffuriya, moved forward to meet the Muslims and an indecisive engagement took place at Afrabala—the Forbelet of the Franks and the modern Taiyiba. Saladin returned to Damascus but, in August 1182, he suddenly left the city again and moved by forced marches to Beirut, hoping to take the city by surprise. The garrison, however, resisted stoutly and Baldwin arrived at Tyre with his army. The surprise had failed and Saladin returned to Damascus, for he had pressing affairs to attend to in the north.

On 20th June, 1180, Saif al Deen Ghazi II, the Zengid Prince of Mosul, had died and had been succeeded by his brother, Izz al Deen Masood.[11] Then, on 4th December, 1181, Al Salih, the young King of Aleppo and son of Noor al Deen, had died also, a gallant and intelligent youth of eighteen. Izz al Deen Masood of Mosul arrived at Aleppo, but in February 1182 his brother, Imad al Deen, took over Aleppo and Izz al Deen went back and contented himself with Mosul. The two-year truce made by Saladin with the Zengids at Samsat on 2nd October, 1180, was about to end. No sooner had it expired than Saladin took the field. According to his normal practice, he avoided Aleppo but took Sarooj, Edessa, and Nisibin. Then on 10th November, 1182, he attacked Mosul but failed to take it.[12] Returning west, he seized Sinjar and Diyarbekr and, on 21st May, 1183, he was back again before Aleppo.

With the whole of the Jezira in Saladin's hands, the great city was completely cut off. Though the Aleppines were still full of fight, their prince was less courageous. Imad al Deen agreed to surrender Aleppo to Saladin and on 12th June, 1183, left the fortress amid the jeers of the citizens, who had been ready to die for him. Before he departed, the people of Aleppo presented him with an apron and a washtub, saying that he had mistaken his vocation—he should have been a washerwoman, not a prince. In exchange for Aleppo, Saladin gave him the fiefs of Sinjar, Nisibin, Sarooj and Raqqa. With the capture of Aleppo and the decline of the Zengids, Saladin was secure from his Muslim

[11] Genealogical tree, page 38. [12] Map 9, page 84.

rivals and was free to revenge himself on the Franks. On 24th August, 1183, he was back in Damascus.

Although his treachery and violence had already more than once placed the kingdom in jeopardy, Renaud de Châtillon was anything but repentant and had meanwhile embarked on an enterprise even more insane than his march to Teima. In the autumn of 1182, while Saladin was away in the Jezira, he decided to launch a battle fleet on the Red Sea. His ships were built, some at Asqalon, some at Kerak itself, and were transported on camel-back to Aila, the modern Aqaba. Saladin had occupied Aila in 1175 but Renaud blockaded the Muslims in their castle while he launched his sixteen ships, on which he loaded several hundred knights and men-at-arms. Renaud did not sail with the fleet. The fact that Aila, though blockaded, was held by the Muslims meant that the expedition had little hope of ever returning, for they had no home port.

The first port of call was Aidhab, some two hundred and fifty miles north of the modern Port Sudan. After plundering the town, they marched inland and seized a caravan. They then crossed to the Arabian shore and plundered Haura, Yenbo and Rabigh. Then back to the African side, they raided Suakin, Kameran Island and other ports. One Arab writer alleges they even reached Aden.

The Red Sea had been an Arab lake for five hundred years and was completely unknown to the Franks. Their reckless courage can be compared only to that of the Spanish conquistadors in Central America. There were no Muslim warships in these waters because no one had ever dreamed of an enemy fleet appearing there, but the ships carrying the rich eastern trade from China and India sailed up the Red Sea from Aden to Egypt. Great was the consternation among the merchants of Cairo and Alexandria at the news of the infidel pirate fleet which was in undisputed control of the Red Sea. Moreover, blasphemous rumours were circulating to the effect that Renaud had sworn to exhume and burn the body of the Prophet, which lay buried in Medina. The raiders did indeed march inland to within a day's journey of the city.

Meanwhile Saladin's brother, Malik al Aadil, the Viceroy of Egypt, acted promptly. As there were no Muslim warships in the Red Sea, the necessary galleys had to be built in Egypt and launched. Special crews, we are told, were recruited from the Maghrib—probably from modern Algeria—for Muslim fleets had for centuries dominated the Mediterranean. Several months had elapsed before the flotilla put to sea under the command of Husam al Deen Lulu. They came up with the Franks at Haura in February 1183. Saladin had himself given orders that every one of the Franks was to be put to death. After a bitter fight on land, the majority were killed, a few only being taken to Mecca, Medina and Cairo to be decapitated in public.

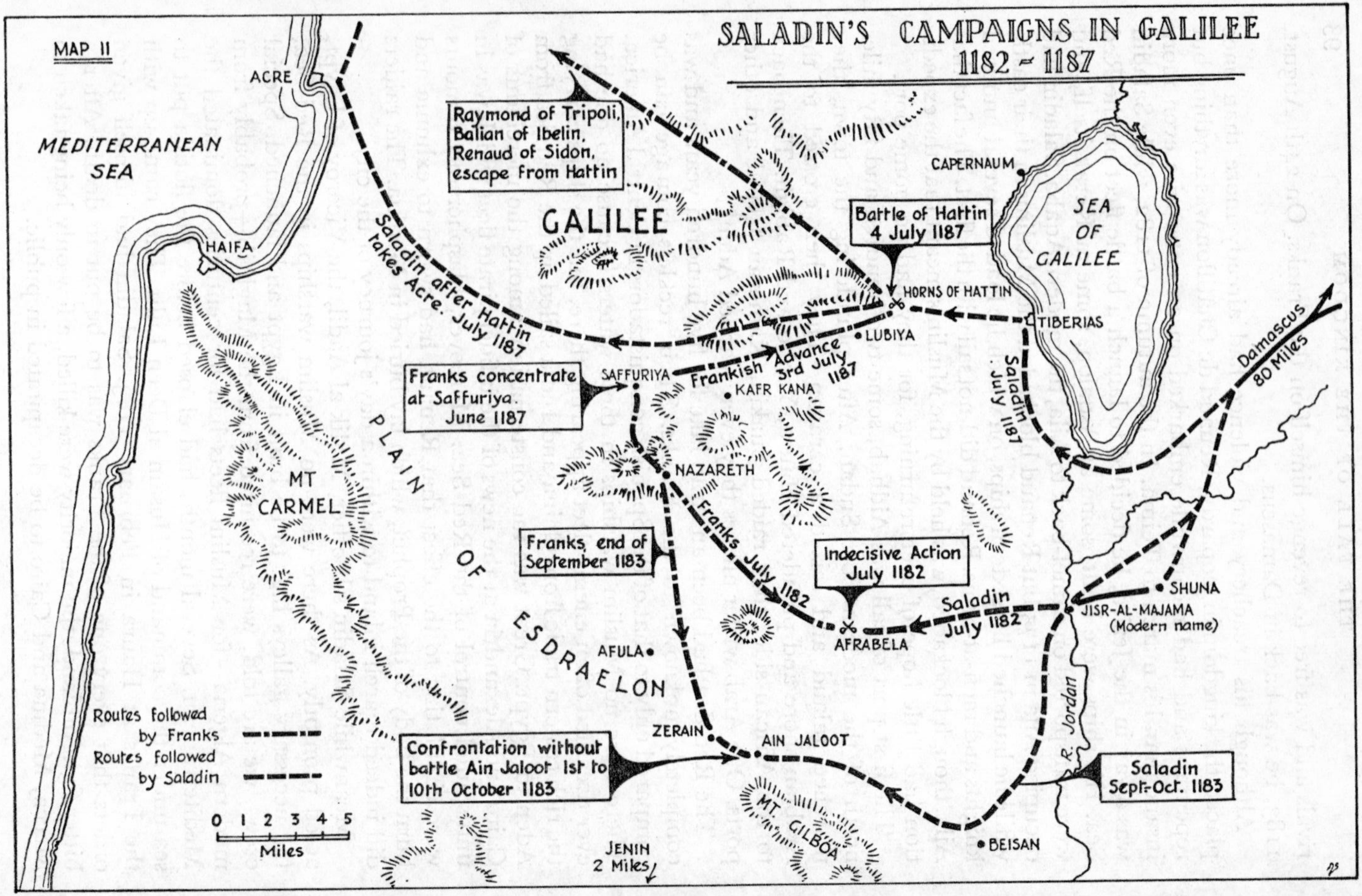
SALADIN'S CAMPAIGNS IN GALILEE 1182 – 1187
MAP 11
MEDITERRANEAN SEA
ACRE
HAIFA
MT CARMEL
PLAIN OF ESDRAELON
GALILEE
Raymond of Tripoli, Balian of Ibelin, Renaud of Sidon, escape from Hattin
Saladin after Hattin takes Acre. July 1187
Franks concentrate at Saffuriya. June 1187
SAFFURIYA
Frankish Advance 3rd July 1187
KAFR KANA
LUBIYA
HORNS OF HATTIN
Battle of Hattin 4 July 1187
CAPERNAUM
SEA OF GALILEE
TIBERIAS
Saladin July 1187
Damascus 80 Miles
NAZARETH
Franks July 1182
Franks, end of September 1183
Indecisive Action July 1182
AFRABELA
Saladin July 1182
SHUNA
JISR-AL-MAJAMA (Modern name)
R. Jordan
AFULA
ZERAIN
AIN JALOOT
Confrontation without battle Ain Jaloot 1st to 10th October 1183
Saladin Sept-Oct. 1183
MT. GILBOA
BEISAN
JENIN 2 Miles
Routes followed by Franks
Routes followed by Saladin
0 1 2 3 4 5
Miles

While the Red Sea venture may surprise us by its reckless courage, it sealed the fate of the Kingdom of Jerusalem. Whereas Saladin might well have acquiesced in the existence on the Mediterranean seaboard of a state controlled by the native barons already half Levantines, the newly-arrived Franks like Renaud de Châtillon seemed to be intent on convincing the Muslims that their lives, their property and their religion would never be secure until these mad dogs had been exterminated.

* * *

Saladin, who had returned to Damascus from the Jezira in August 1183, left the city again on 17th September, and camped on 28th September at Shuna, twenty miles south-south-east of Tiberias.

Next day he forded the Jordan at the place where the Jisr al Mejama bridge stands today, burned Beisan and marched up the plain of Esdraelon—Marj ibn Aamir in Arabic—to Ain Jaloot or Goliath's Spring, while his cavalry rode on and burned Zerain and Jenin.[13]

The Franks, who had concentrated at Saffuriya, marched southeastward until the two advanced guards clashed in a sharp skirmish. The Frankish infantry, however, marching shoulder to shoulder, could not be broken up. The knights, covered by the steady ranks of the infantry, did not engage. The Franks then pitched camp and surrounded themselves with a ditch.

For eighty-four years the Crusaders had clung to the coast of Asia with a few thousand troops. Lack of men had always been their problem. Whenever a battle was expected, all the available man-power was mobilized, including even the garrisons of cities and castles. If such an army were defeated, another could not be raised to replace it. The whole kingdom would be lost. The Muslim situation was the exact reverse. Their man-power was unlimited. If one army were destroyed, another could be recruited in its place.

For eighty years, therefore, the Crusaders had repeatedly applied the same strategy. When a major invasion took place, they collected all the men available, marched to the vicinity of the invading army, but refused battle. Their presence pinned down the Muslim army until the approach of winter compelled the enemy to withdraw. The campaign of 1183 was of this nature. The Franks sought to pin down Saladin's army without risking a battle, until winter should come or until other operations should oblige the Muslims to withdraw.

Nevertheless, the native barons, led by Raymond III of Tripoli, on this occasion only maintained their traditional strategy with

[13] Map 11, page 94. Zerain is the biblical Jezreel, the city of Ahab and Jezebel and Naboth's vineyard.

difficulty, for the king was dying, Guy had no control and the Templars and the Crusaders from France loudly demanded battle. At length Saladin abandoned the campaign. On 14th October, 1183, he was back in Damascus.

* * *

The Red Sea expedition had emphasized the importance of Kerak and Shobek, the castles which threatened communications between Syria and Egypt. In November 1183, Saladin marched on Kerak, his brother Malik al Aadil coming up to join him there with the army of Egypt.

When the Muslims arrived, the wedding festivities were being celebrated for the marriage of Humphrey IV of Toron with Isabella, daughter of King Amaury by his second wife, Maria Comnena. The Lady of Kerak, Etiennette de Milly, had previously been married to Humphrey III of Toron and Humphrey IV was thus her son. (Etiennette was the heiress of Kerak, Renaud being only her consort.) When Saladin's tents were pitched, Etiennette is said to have sent out bread, meat and other delicacies, with a friendly message to Saladin inviting him to join in the feast in memory of old times. It is possible that she may have known him when she was married to Humphrey of Toron who, as we have seen, had many Muslim friends, and who may have knighted Saladin outside Alexandria. Saladin is said in return to have enquired in which tower the bridal chamber was situated and to have sent a crier through his army forbidding anyone to shoot against the tower in question.

The dying king determined to save Kerak. The army marched from Jerusalem round the southern end of the Dead Sea by the modern Ghor al Safi, carrying Baldwin with them on a litter. On 4th December, 1183, Saladin raised the siege without waiting for a battle. In July 1184 he again attacked Kerak, bombarding it with fourteen mangonels, but again raised the siege on the approach of the Jerusalem army.

A year after the king's appointment of Guy de Lusignan as regent, Baldwin IV revoked his decision, as a result of Guy's obvious incapacity. In a fit of temper Guy retired to Asqalon and announced his refusal any longer to obey the king. On 23rd March, 1183, the infant Baldwin V, the son of Sibylla by William Long-Sword,[14] was proclaimed heir to the throne. Meanwhile the dying king resumed authority.

Early in 1185, Baldwin IV summoned a grand council to his bedside. Baldwin V was consecrated king and Raymond III of Tripoli was made regent. If Baldwin V died before the age of ten, Raymond was to

[14] Genealogical tree, page 60.

remain regent until the Kings of France and England and the Emperor of Germany nominated a successor. Guy was not to be eligible for the regency. The Patriarch Heraclius and the newly-elected Grand Master of the Templars, Gerard de Ridefort, a personal enemy of Raymond, were among those who swore to observe these terms.

In March 1185, at the age of twenty-four, the leper king was released from the agony of his tortured life. Blind, paralysed and often with a high fever, he had fought to the last to check the intrigues which divided the kingdom. History has immortalized Godfrey de Bouillon, Saladin and Richard Coeur de Lion, but the Crusades produced no greater hero than this dauntless little leper.

Raymond of Tripoli assumed the regency and called a grand council. Peace was the only hope of survival and a four-year truce was concluded with Saladin, who, as we have seen, had other anxieties.

In the summer of 1185, after concluding this truce, Saladin marched northwards and laid siege for the third time to the Zengid city of Mosul, again in vain. Hearing that the Ortoqid Prince Soqman II had died, he seized his city of Amid. Then suddenly he fell ill and lay between life and death at Harran. The possibility of his early decease set his relatives intriguing but in January 1186 he recovered. He made peace with Izz al Deen the Zengid, leaving him Mosul, but annexed Erbil and Shahrazur beyond the city. As usual, when faced with a great city, he first captured the lesser towns around it, thereby cutting it off. He was a patient statesman rather than a dashing soldier.[15]

Back in Damascus in the summer of 1186, Saladin consulted his brother Al Aadil regarding the family rivalries. Al Aadil was sent back as viceroy in Egypt, accompanied by Saladin's son, Malik al Azeez Othman.

* * *

The Kingdom of Jerusalem was gradually regaining stability when, in August or September 1186, the nine-year-old Baldwin V suddenly died at Acre. Both Raymond of Tripoli and Jocelin III, titular Count of Edessa, were present. Jocelin somehow persuaded Raymond not to accompany the corpse of the little king to Jerusalem for burial, but to go to Galilee until the High Court could assemble and appoint him regent.

No sooner had he gone than Guy's party acted swiftly. Guy and Sibylla rode from Asqalon to Jerusalem. Supported by Queen Agnes, the mother of Sibylla, and by Jocelin, Guy was crowned King of Jerusalem by the Patriarch Heraclius. Renaud de Châtillon came with his levies to support him and the Templars, under their Grand

[15] Map 9, page 84.

Master, Gerard de Ridefort, also declared for Guy. It is true that the Patriarch Heraclius, Gerard de Ridefort and Renaud de Châtillon had sworn to observe the will of Baldwin excluding Guy, but perjury made no difference to such intriguers. Raymond and the native barons, finding themselves outwitted, gathered at Nablus, but they were already too late. Guy had been crowned.

Saladin was anxious to continue the truce and, even with so weak a king as Guy, all might have been well. It was Renaud de Châtillon who was to precipitate the catastrophe. Early in 1187, he seized a rich caravan travelling from Cairo to Damascus and imprisoned all the personnel in the dungeons of Kerak. As Renaud had himself sworn to observe the truce, his action was perjury as well as treachery.

Saladin did not immediately declare war but wrote to Renaud to demand the return of the loot. King Guy, alarmed, begged his principal partisan to comply. To both Renaud replied insolently that he would return nothing. On receiving this answer, Saladin gave way to a fury in which he swore that he would kill Renaud with his own hand. Determined finally to exterminate the Franks of the Kingdom of Jerusalem, he summoned the troops from Egypt and his feudatories from Aleppo and the Jezira, while, with diplomatic dexterity, he made a separate truce with Bohemond of Antioch to prevent his reinforcing Guy.

At this moment of supreme crisis, unbelievable as it may appear, Guy summoned his troops to attack not Saladin but Raymond who, although the sultan was already mobilizing to invade the kingdom, appealed to Saladin for support. The insane intensity of hatred between the two rival parties of Franks was to entail the loss of the kingdom. At the last moment, Guy and Raymond were outwardly reconciled and the Frankish army was ordered to concentrate at Saffuriya. Saladin crossed the frontier on 30th June, 1187, and laid siege to Tiberias on 2nd July. On the same day, King Guy called a council of war at Saffuriya.[16]

News had just arrived that Raymond's wife was besieged in Tiberias, and several voices demanded an immediate advance. Raymond himself spoke last. He pointed out that Tiberias belonged to him and that it was his wife who was besieged there. Saladin, he said, was strongly established with the lake behind him. Between Saffuriya and the Muslim army lay fifteen miles of hilly country without water. The infantry could not cross this space beneath a flaming July sun. Even the horses could not be watered. The only possible course, he emphasized, was to let Saladin take Tiberias. When autumn came, he would have to withdraw and the town could be reoccupied. "It is better to lose

[16] Map 11, page 94.

Tiberias," he concluded, "than to lose the whole country. For if we advance from here, all is lost." It was the traditional Crusader strategy. Mobilize, watch, but avoid battle until winter ends the campaign.

Renaud and Gerard de Ridefort replied sarcastically that Raymond was a notorious traitor and of course wanted to help his Muslim friends. The native barons, however, agreed with Raymond and the council broke up resolved to remain at Saffuriya. After the council dispersed, however, Gerard de Ridefort crept back alone to the king's tent. All his life Guy had never been able to make up his mind. Gerard made him reverse the decision and order an immediate call to arms. At dawn on 3rd July, the army marched out.

Morale was already shaken, for most men believed that they were going to their death. When Saladin heard that the Franks were coming, he cried joyfully, "That is exactly what we want." He had only attacked Tiberias to draw them across this waterless tract. In the evening the Franks, after a scorching day on the dusty, treeless hills, reached Lubiya.[17] The infantry were exhausted and mad with thirst. It was decided to pass the night there—without water. The troops lay awake all night, tortured by thirst and constantly disturbed by guerilla attacks.

When dawn broke, the Franks saw that they were already surrounded. The Muslims set fire to the dry grass and a hot east wind blew the smoke and crackling flames into the faces of the infantry who, overcome with exhaustion, were overrun early in the battle. The knights rallied round the royal standard on two little hills known as the Horns of Hattin. They delivered charge after charge which once or twice seemed to be about to drive the enemy back. Raymond of Tripoli, Balian of Ibelin, Renaud of Sidon and a few other native barons with their followers fought their way out. Guy seems to have lost his head or he could presumably have done the same.

Eventually the three men responsible for the disaster, King Guy, Renaud de Châtillon and Gerard de Ridefort, were taken prisoners and led to Saladin's tent. The sultan, with chivalrous courtesy, invited Guy to sit beside himself and offered him a drink of rose-water cooled with the ice of Hermon. Guy drank deeply and then passed the bowl to Renaud, but Saladin exclaimed immediately, "You gave that man to drink, not I." "For it is one of the noble customs of the Arabs," writes Baha al Deen, "that a prisoner's life is safe if he has eaten or drunk." This sentence, incidentally, is worthy of notice. When Baha al Deen wrote his biography of Saladin, he was living in Aleppo, among Arabic-speaking Syrians.

If these people had thought of themselves as Arabs, observing Arab customs, it would not have been necessary for him to tell them what

[17] Map 11, page 94.

were the customs of the Arabs. Yet when explaining the customs of these people to his readers he seems to assume that they know that Saladin followed these customs. When asked why Saladin behaved in this manner, it was sufficient answer to say, "because such is the custom of the Arabs".

In an angry voice, Saladin denounced the many acts of treachery and brigandage which Renaud had committed in times of peace. "Such is the way of kings," replied the robber baron insolently. With a cry of fury, the sultan drew his sword and slashed at Renaud, fracturing his shoulder. His guards stepped quickly forward and cut off the knight's head at the very feet of the trembling Guy. "Kings do not kill kings," said Saladin reassuringly, "but that man had over-stepped all bounds."

The courtesy of Saladin is well-known but it was reserved for nobles. Perhaps half the rank and file of the Franks had been killed and the remainder were sold into slavery. The sultan, however, ordered that all the Templars and Hospitallers be beheaded in cold blood on the field. For this purpose a number of pious Muslim jurists were allowed each to strike off the head of a prisoner.

* * *

The Franks had never been more than a small military caste, the bulk of the population of their states consisting of Muslims or of Syrian or Armenian Christians. Almost the whole of the male Frankish population called up for the campaign had been exterminated. The morning after the battle the sultan accepted the surrender of Tiberias and chivalrously provided an escort to convey the countess and her suite in safety to Tripoli. (In 1912, a battle took place at Jumaima in Arabia between the tribal confederations of Shammar and Aneiza. Shammar were victorious and captured the Aneiza camp, including the tent and family of their chief, Ibn Hadhdhal. The Shammar prince, Ibn Rasheed, immediately provided an escort to convey the ladies of his defeated enemy's family to safety.)

Saladin realized that the fall of the kingdom might provoke a new Crusade and saw that the first essential was to seize the Mediterranean ports where such an expedition could land. He immediately marched on Acre. Jocelin III of Edessa, whose political manœuvres had gained Guy his throne, was in command at Acre. Better at intrigue than in battle, he surrendered the city without a fight, in spite of the loud protests of the people. Saladin's brother, Al Aadil, Viceroy of Egypt, at the same time invaded Palestine from the south. Jaffa was taken by storm and all the inhabitants killed or sold into slavery, regardless of age or sex.

Our historian Ibn al Athir was at the time living in Aleppo and bought a Frankish girl and her baby son. He was touched one day to find her in tears. "I cannot help crying when I think what has happened to us," she sobbed. "I had six brothers who were all killed and a husband and two sisters but I have no idea what has become of them." Our good historian, long occupied with the actions of princes, raises the curtain for a moment on the poignant tragedy of an ordinary woman.

Meanwhile the Muslims were rapidly taking over the towns of Outremer, denuded of garrisons. Saladin attempted to take Tyre but, finding it well defended, he passed on with his usual dislike of difficult sieges. On 29th July, 1187, he accepted the surrender of Sidon and on 6th August that of Beirut.

On 20th September, 1187, the sultan laid siege to Jerusalem, which was vigorously defended by Balian of Ibelin, one of the leading barons of Outremer and a personal friend of Saladin. He had escaped from Hattin with Raymond and had obtained safe-conduct from Saladin to come to Jerusalem to fetch Queen Maria Comnena, whom he had married after the death of King Amaury. When he reached the holy city, the inhabitants begged him to take command, which would have been contrary to the conditions of Saladin's safe-conduct. Balian, however, wrote to ask Saladin's permission to defend the city. The sultan agreed, at the same time permitting Maria Comnena to leave Jerusalem with her suite and to take refuge in Tyre.

Meanwhile Saladin was pounding the defences of Jerusalem with twelve heavy mangonels, while his sappers were driving mines beneath the walls. (The Muslims were always more expert than the Franks at mining.) Eventually Balian requested an interview with Saladin at which he offered to surrender, if the defenders were allowed to go free. The sultan replied that he would have agreed if the city had surrendered without fighting but that now he would only accept unconditional surrender.

Balian replied with spirit, "If we see death to be inevitable, we shall first kill our women and children, burn our houses and property and destroy the Muslim holy places. Then we shall kill the five thousand Muslim prisoners we hold and finally we shall make a sortie in which every one of us will kill several of your soldiers before we die covered with glory."

Eventually Saladin agreed on condition that ten gold bezants be paid for every man, five for a woman and one for a child. Balian replied that these terms would save the rich but that there were twenty thousand poor Christians who could not pay. Saladin promised to release them all for a hundred thousand gold bezants but Balian could not raise such a sum. Eventually thirty thousand bezants were collected, seven thousand poor were ransomed and fourteen thousand were carried away into slavery. Saladin entered Jerusalem on 2nd October, 1187.

In the end a further thousand prisoners were released without ransom at the request of al Aadil, Saladin's brother, and five hundred for the sake of Balian. It is an Arab custom, when a legal debt has been proved, to remit parts of it at the request of distinguished men present, a point of interest as showing once again the effect of Arab customs on Saladin, as opposed to Turkish methods.

European historians have contrasted the terms accorded by Saladin with the massacre which marked the capture of Jerusalem by the First Crusade eighty-eight years before. The principal explanation lies undoubtedly in the fact that the Arabs in 1187 were a civilized people, while the Franks in 1099 were not. There were, however, other reasons which may also have influenced Saladin. Further fighting would have resulted in the death of many more Muslims and in the partial destruction of the city, which was holy to the Muslims as well as to the Christians. Moreover, many of Saladin's troops were unpaid feudal levies already anxious to go home. Time was also of value, for there was the possibility of the arrival of a Crusade from the West before all the fortresses of Outremer had been conquered. The Christians in Jerusalem were largely women, for whose ransom Saladin received a large sum of money and the city with its treasures undamaged. Savages in the heat of battle kill everything but Saladin was sufficiently civilized to weigh the pros and cons.

Saladin had not always been compassionate. We saw him before the battle of Tel al Jazar send his cavalry to burn the countryside and kill all prisoners. He had personally killed Shawar and had caused the Fatimid partisans in Cairo to be tortured, blinded and crucified. These statements are made by Muslim, not by Christian, historians. It is impossible now confidently to analyse the psychology of men who lived eight centuries ago, and, in any case, the same man may one day be cruel and another day pitiful. It is pleasant at least to read of the chivalrous relations between Saladin and Balian.

On 15th November, 1187, Saladin returned to the siege of Tyre. Meanwhile, however, on 14th July, 1187, ten days after Hattin, Conrad of Montferrat, the brother of William Long-Sword, Sibylla's first husband, had landed at Tyre with a company of knights and had taken command of the defence.

Tyre was joined to the mainland only by a narrow isthmus and as a result Saladin could not bring his superior numbers to bear. Ten Egyptian galleys arrived to blockade the city from the sea. On the night of 30th December, 1187, the Franks attacked the Egyptian ships in the dark, capturing five, while the other five ran ashore. This little action proved to be of great importance, for it allowed the subsequent safe arrival of Frankish reinforcements. With his usual distaste for sieges, Saladin again left Tyre, and on New Year's Day, 1188, he released his feudal levies who were clamouring to go home. Shortly before, Raymond III of Tripoli had died without heir, bequeathing his county to a son of Bohemond III of Antioch.

Not until 1st July, 1188, did the contingents of Aleppo, Sinjar and Mosul return to the war. Still neglecting Tyre, Saladin continued to clear the coast. Tortosa was burnt to the ground. Jabala fell on 15th July and Lataqiya on the 20th. Then followed the castles on the Orontes and Baghras north of Antioch. In the autumn the feudal contingents were again released. In November 1188, Kerak surrendered. Not until 21st March, 1189, did the sultan return to Damascus. On 6th April, 1189, the Pisan fleet anchored off Tyre. The Third Crusade had begun.

NOTABLE DATES

Death of Noor al Deen	15th May, 1174
Death of King Amaury	11th July, 1174
Entry of Saladin into Damascus	26th November, 1174
Defeat of the Zengids by Saladin at the Horns of Hama	23rd April, 1175
Battle of Myrio-cephalon. Byzantines defeated	17th September, 1176
Baldwin IV comes of age	1177
Battle of Tel al Jazar (Montgisard)	25th November, 1177
Princess Sibylla marries Guy de Lusignan	Easter 1180
Renaud seizes caravan near Teima	Summer 1181
Saladin occupies Aleppo	12th June, 1183
Renaud's Red Sea raid	1182–1183
Death of Baldwin IV, the Leper	March 1185
Death of nine-year-old Baldwin V	August 1186
Guy de Lusignan crowned king	September 1186
Capture of Cairo caravan by Renaud de Châtillon	Spring 1187
Battle of Hattin	4th July, 1187
Landing of Conrad of Montferrat at Tyre	14th July, 1187
Capture of Jerusalem by Saladin	2nd October, 1187
Saladin fails to take Tyre	December 1187
Saladin takes Tortosa, Lataqiya and the Orontes valley	Summer 1188
Pisan fleet reaches Tyre	6th April, 1189

PERSONALITIES

Muslims

Noor al Deen Mahmood, son of Zengi
Malik as Salih Ismail, son of Noor al Deen
Saif al Deen Ghazi II
Izz al Deen Mahmood
Imad al Deen Zengi II
} Nephews of Noor al Deen, the Mosul branch of the family.
Saladin, the son of Ayoub
Malik al Aadil, the brother of Saladin

Kings of Jerusalem

Amaury I, son of King Fulk
Baldwin IV, the Leper, son of Amaury
Baldwin V, son of Sibylla, sister of Baldwin IV
Guy de Lusignan

Other Franks

Raymond III, Count of Tripoli
Bohemond III, Prince of Antioch
Renaud de Châtillon, Prince of Antioch, then Lord of Kerak
Jocelin III, titular Count of Edessa
Conrad de Montferrat
Balian of Ibelin

V

The Battle for the Mediterranean

1150–1200

It is admitted today that Muslim Spain represented for Mediterranean Europe a source of refined civilization, of a luxurious and ordered life, an academy of fine manners and good taste. Let us not forget that many precious stuffs, jewels and works of art which adorned the chapels or filled the chests of the ladies of feudal society came from Andalus or even from Persia or Iraq . . . Feudal society copied Arab hairstyles, clothing, ivories, jewels. Why not then also their poetry and romance?
LÉVI-PROVENÇAL, *The Arab Poetry of Spain and the poetry of Mediaeval Europe*

A feutra for the world, and worldlings base.
I speak of Africa and golden joys.

SHAKESPEARE, *King Henry IV*

V

WE have already described[1] the situation in the western Mediterranean when the present narrative opens. In the Maghrib, a new Berber sect, the Muwahhids (better known in Europe as the Almohades), had replaced the Murabits. Ibn Toumert, the founder of the Muwahhids, was dead but had been succeeded by an extremely capable khalif, Abdul Mumin ibn Ali.

In Ifriqiya, Roger II, the Norman King of Sicily, had seized the African coast from Tunis to Tripoli, thereby enabling him largely to control navigation in the narrow waters between Italy, Sicily and Tunis. In Spain the Murabits had in 1086 defeated Alfonso VI of Castile and thrown the Christians on the defensive. With the disintegration of Murabit rule, however, the Christians in 1150 were again advancing.

Abdul Mumin began his operations by counter-attacking the Norman penetration of the centre of the Muslim battle line. In 1159, he marched out of Marakish[2] and along the coast of the Mediterranean, his fleet keeping pace with his army. Entering Tunis and Sousse unopposed, he besieged the Normans in Mehediya. On 22nd January, 1160, King Roger signed a peace with Abdul Mumin and evacuated North Africa. For the first time, the African coast from the Atlantic to Tripoli was united under one native Berber rule.

The twenty-eight years of civil war in the Maghrib caused by the seizure of power by the Muwahhids from the Murabits had led, among the Muslims in Andalus, to a confusion of which the Christians were not slow to take advantage. By 1150, King Alfonso VII was already threatening Cordova. As soon as Abdul Mumin had driven the Normans of Sicily from Ifriqiya, he turned his attention to the situation in Spain. An army of thirty thousand Muwahhids landed at Algeciras and were welcomed by the Muslims of Andalus. Seville and Malaga were quickly occupied. The eastern half of Andalus was held by independent Muslim princes of various kinds, notably a certain Ibn Mardanish who was supported by Castile, who hoped to see a ding-dong Muslim civil war between them and the Muwahhids.

Almeria, the greatest port in Andalus, had been taken ten years before by the Count of Barcelona but was now retaken by the Muwahhids. Cordova was occupied and in the great mosque, still standing today, Abdul Mumin was proclaimed Muslim ruler of Spain. In 1162, Granada was taken by storm. On the west, Badajoz was also garrisoned

[1] Page 27.

[2] The accent is on the second syllable, Marákish, and not Marakeesh.

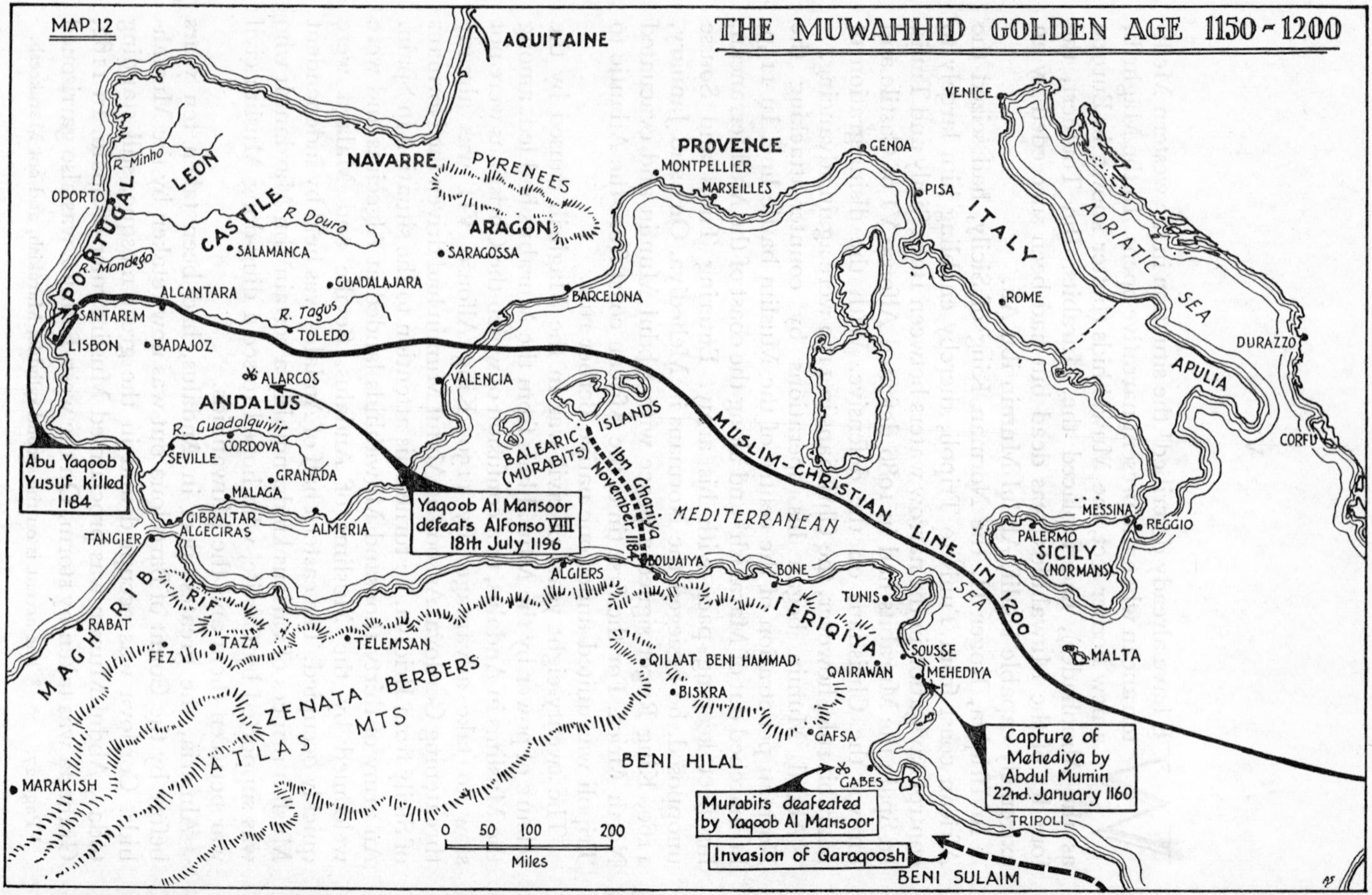
MAP 12
THE MUWAHHID GOLDEN AGE 1150-1200
AQUITAINE
NAVARRE
PYRENEES
ARAGON
PROVENCE
MONTPELLIER
MARSEILLES
GENOA
PISA
VENICE
ITALY
ADRIATIC SEA
ROME
APULIA
DURAZZO
CORFU
MESSINA
REGGIO
PALERMO
SICILY (NORMANS)
MALTA
R. Minho
OPORTO
LEON
PORTUGAL
CASTILE
R. Douro
SALAMANCA
R. Mondego
SARAGOSSA
GUADALAJARA
ALCANTARA
R. Tagus
TOLEDO
SANTAREM
LISBON
BADAJOZ
BARCELONA
VALENCIA
ALARCOS
ANDALUS
R. Guadalquivir
CORDOVA
SEVILLE
GRANADA
MALAGA
GIBRALTAR
ALGECIRAS
ALMERIA
TANGIER
Abu Yaqoob Yusuf killed 1184
Yaqoob Al Mansoor defeats Alfonso VIII 18th July 1196
BALEARIC ISLANDS (MURABITS)
Ibn Ghaniya November 1184
MUSLIM-CHRISTIAN LINE IN 1200
MEDITERRANEAN SEA
ALGIERS
BOUJAIYA
BONE
TUNIS
IFRIQIYA
SOUSSE
MEHEDIYA
QAIRAWAN
MAGHRIB
RIF
RABAT
FEZ
TAZA
TELEMSAN
QILAAT BENI HAMMAD
BISKRA
GAFSA
ZENATA BERBERS
ATLAS MTS
BENI HILAL
MARAKISH
GABES
Capture of Mehediya by Abdul Mumin 22nd. January 1160
Murabits deafeated by Yaqoob Al Mansoor
TRIPOLI
Invasion of Qaraqoosh
BENI SULAIM
0 50 100 200
Miles

by the Muwahhids. In May 1163, when raising a fresh army in Africa, Abdul Mumin died at Rabat, a city which he himself had largely built and which is the capital of Morocco today.

Abdul Mumin had been a fierce and successful fighter. He devoted much attention to his navy and his fleets sailed the Western Mediterranean unopposed. Although he reconquered most of Andalus, the effect of yet more wars was to reduce even further the wealth and civilization of this lovely land which, a hundred and fifty years before, had led the western world in science and culture.

He had been a statesman and an administrator as well as a soldier. He had carried out a complete survey of the Muwahhid Empire extending from the Atlantic to the borders of Egypt and had based upon it a revised system of taxation. He had beautified the imperial capital of Marakish, where his palace was surrounded by gardens and fountains.

Politically, however, the ultimate results of Abdul Mumin's policy were of questionable benefit. In the years 1050 to 1054, nearly a century before his time, the Arab nomadic tribes of Beni Hilal and Beni Sulaim, newly arrived from Arabia, had invaded North Africa,[3] and had overthrown the government of Ifriqiya and spread disorder and anarchy in the area. When Abdul Mumin annexed Ifriqiya to the Muwahhid Empire, he had experienced trouble with the nomad lawlessness of these Arab tribes, but had been impressed with their martial qualities.

He consequently devised a plan by which he hoped to kill two birds with one stone, by transferring the nomadic Beni Hilal from Ifriqiya to the western Maghrib, that is to say Morocco. Here he gave them a privileged position and allotted them tax-free lands which they cultivated with slaves. In return for these favours, he employed them for military service, and to strengthen his armies for the operations in Spain. In the same manner, he settled Beni Abdul Wad, a nomadic Berber tribe of the Zenata group, in the vicinity of Telemsan. These measures, useful at first to recruit the Muwahhid army, were to create many problems in the future.

The original constitution of the Muwahhid state had been strictly equalitarian with no suggestion of hereditary rule. Abdul Mumin was no relation of the Muwahhid mehedi, Ibn Toumert, and was not even of the same tribe. When Abdul Mumin came to power, one of the founders of the sect, Abu Hafas Umar, had been named as his successor, but the khalif[4] had later changed his mind, and nominated his second

[3] *The Course of Empire.*

[4] Khalif merely means successor. Abdul Mumin adopted the title for himself, as successor to the mehedi, Ibn Toumert.

THE AL MUWAHHIDEEN SULTANS, THE DESCENDANTS OF ABDUL MUMIN

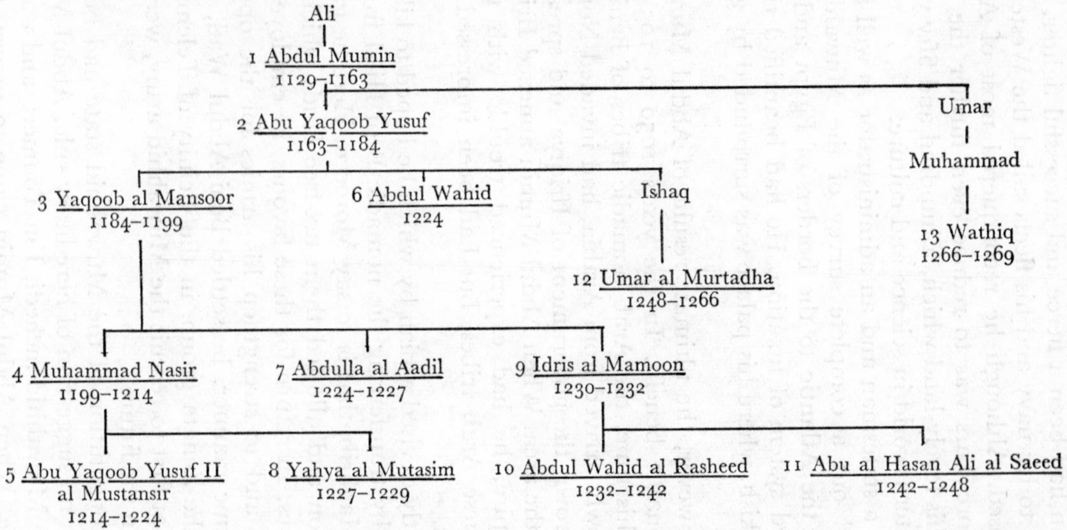

NOTES

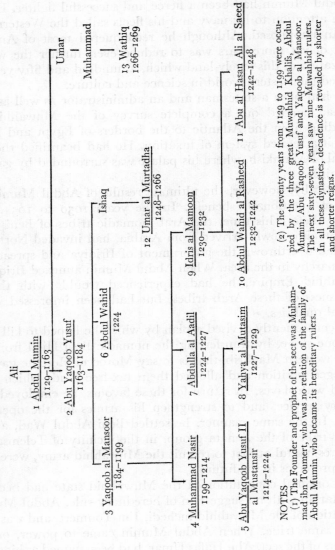

(1) The Founder and prophet of the sect was Muhammad ibn Toumert, who was no relation of the family of Abdul Mumin who became its hereditary rulers.

(2) The seventy years from 1129 to 1199 were occupied by the three great Muwahhid Khalifs, Abdul Mumin, Abu Yaqoob Yusuf and Yaqoob al Mansoor. The next sixty-seven years saw nine Muwahhid rulers. In all these dynasties, decadence is revealed by shorter and shorter reigns.

son Abu Yaqoob Yusuf as his heir. The descendants of Abu Hafas were later to found a rival dynasty in Tunis.

The Muwahhid constitution allowed for two consultative bodies, the Council of Ten and the Council of Fifty. The Ten were the original close companions of Ibn Toumert, the Fifty presumably notables of lesser importance. Such councils are of rare occurrence in Muslim history, where power is normally limited to one man.

* * *

In 1095, Count Henry of Burgundy was on a crusade against the Muslims in Spain, where he married a natural daughter of Alfonso VI, the King of Leon. The county of Portucalia, a small territory round the present town of Oporto, was given him as his wife's dowry. When Count Henry died in 1112, his territory extended from the River Minho in the north to the Mondego in the south.

His son, Alfonso I of Portugal, crossed the Mondego and made war on the Muslims, during the period of their weakness while the Murabits and the Muwahhids were engaged in civil war in Morocco. On 15th March, 1147, he carried Santarem by assault and on 24th October of the same year he took Lisbon, assisted by a party of English and Flemish crusaders.

* * *

As soon as he was firmly established as khalif, Abu Yaqoob Yusuf placed himself at the head of his father's army, consisting chiefly of nomadic tribesmen, and crossed to Spain. Establishing his headquarters in Seville, he took Alcantara and ravaged the Tagus valley down to the very gates of Lisbon which, as we have seen, had been taken by Portugal a few years before. After a year in Seville, Yusuf returned to the Maghrib where the Berber tribes were giving trouble, but his army continued to consolidate its hold and, by 1172, the whole of Andalus was in the hands of the Muwahhids.

The Khalif Yusuf spent the greater part of his twenty-one-year reign in Africa. In 1184, he landed once again in Spain with a large army and laid siege to Santarem. A sudden sortie by the besieged took the khalif by surprise and killed him before his army could defend him. He was forty-six years old and had reigned from 1163 to 1184.

According to Al Marakishi, Abu Yaqoob Yusuf was of a light complexion, with black hair. Tall in stature, with a strong, clear voice, he was courteous and affable. His clear and active intellect had made him an expert in Arab grammar, philology and history. He was interested in science and had considerable knowledge of medicine. His favourite subject, however, was philosophy and he delighted to engage in learned discussions on the works of Plato and Aristotle and the Arab philosophers. The learned Ibn Bajja, long famous in Europe as Avempace, lived at his court as did also the equally well-known philosopher Ibn Tufail.

Abu Yaqoob Yusuf had been a just, liberal, devout and magnanimous ruler. Although he spent little of his time in Seville, he yet carried out there many architectural works, most famous of which is the Giralda tower, still standing today. He built an aqueduct to carry water to Seville, erected dykes to contain the flood waters of the Guadalquivir, and improved the quays and warehouses along the river front. He also added materially to the fortifications of Gibraltar.

In Africa, his activities were constructive and benevolent, and his administration efficient. The roads were free from robbers, justice was impartially administered and judges were selected from pious and honest men.

Muhammad ibn Jubair, one of the most famous of mediaeval voyagers, an Arab of Syrian extraction born in Valencia, has an interesting passage in his famous book of travels. Complaining of the exactions of the authorities at Jidda in the Hejaz, he writes, "May God soon . . . purify this place by relieving the Muslims of these destructive schismatics with the swords of the Almohades (Muwahhids), the defenders of the faith, God's confederates, possessing righteousness and truth. Let it be absolutely certain and beyond doubt established that there is no Islam except in the Maghrib. There is no justice, right or religion in His sight except with the Almohades—may God render them powerful. . . . There remains nothing but the happy prospect of an Almohade conquest of these lands."[5] This enthusiastic tribute to the pious rule of the Muwahhid government was written during the reign of the Khalif Abu Yaqoob Yusuf and is all the more striking in that Ibn Jubair was a man of moderate views and a Spanish Arab, not a Berber.

It was during the reign of Abu Yaqoob Yusuf in the Maghrib that Saladin seized power in Egypt in 1169. The Ayoubids and the Muwahhids eyed one another with some suspicion. A force of Turkmans under a certain Qaraqoosh invaded Tripoli and Ifriqiya from Egypt. These people were from the Ayoubid army in Cairo. Saladin does not appear to have actively supported the campaign of his lieutenant in Africa, but neither did he recall him. He may well have thought it useful to keep the Muwahhids busy with a rebellion in Tunisia to prevent their aspiring to the annexation of Egypt, a conjecture which seems to be confirmed by the fact that Ibn Jubair, writing in Egypt in 1183, alleges that many people there were ready to welcome a Muwahhid

[5] *The Travels of Ibn Jubair*, translated by R. J. C. Broadhurst.

invasion. In 1180, the Tunisian situation was so troublesome that Abu Yaqoob Yusuf was obliged to come in person and stormed the town of Gafsa, which was in the hands of the rebels.

The Khalif Yusuf was succeeded by his twenty-five-year-old son Yaqoob, who assumed the title of Mansoor. He inaugurated his reign by pardoning convicts in prison, a Muslim tradition still followed today in some Arab countries.

It will be remembered that Spain and the Maghrib had previously been ruled by the Murabits, a Berber sect which had originated among the nomads of the Sahara. When the Muwahhids had conquered Andalus, many of the Murabits had fled to the Balearic Islands, where they formed their own government. No sooner did they hear of the death of the Muwahhid Khalif Yusuf than they determined to make a bid to recover the empire. On 13th November, 1184, Ali ibn Ghaniya landed near Boujaiya with four thousand veiled men from the Balearics.[6] Many of the local tribes, Sanhaja Berbers and Beni Hilal Arabs, joined the invaders. Qaraqoosh and the Turkmans did the same and their combined forces quickly took Algiers and Qilaat Beni Hammad. The Beni Sulaim Arab nomads from Tripoli threw in their lot with the rebels who enjoyed the support of the Ayoubids in Egypt. Even the Abbasid Khalif in Baghdad declared for them, for the Muwahhid sect was heretical and Yaqoob al Mansoor had ventured to call himself khalif. Just as, during the Middle Ages, the popes often urged their allies to attack other Christians, so the Prince of the Faithful sought to promote orthodoxy by encouraging Muslims to fight one another.

Yaqoob al Mansoor himself marched to Ifriqiya, defeated Ibn Ghaniya and Qaraqoosh near Gabes, and compelled them to retire to Tripoli, where, however, their armies remained in being.

Meanwhile Alfonso VIII of Castile was continuing the war against the Muslims of Andalus. On 18th July, 1196, Yaqoob al Mansoor encountered Alfonso VIII at Alarcos near Ciudad Real. Alfonso had chosen his position with care on the crest of an ascending slope, both flanks being covered by ravines. The Christians began the battle. Eight thousand knights in full armour charged the centre of the Muslim line. Twice their attack was repulsed but on the third attempt they broke through the Muslim centre. Having pierced the enemy's line, however, their ranks were disordered and the knights themselves too wild with excitement to re-form. The Muslims closed the gap behind them and fresh units of archers surrounded the crowd of exhausted horsemen, pouring in on them a pitiless rain of arrows.

Meanwhile the remainder of the Muwahhid army advanced on the

[6] In the Saharan tribes, as is still the case with the Touaregs in that area, the men veiled while the women went with their faces uncovered.

THE KINGS OF CASTILE

1126–1312

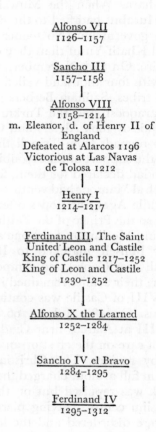

Alfonso VII
1126–1157

|

Sancho III
1157–1158

|

Alfonso VIII
1158–1214
m. Eleanor, d. of Henry II of England
Defeated at Alarcos 1196
Victorious at Las Navas de Tolosa 1212

|

Henry I
1214–1217

|

Ferdinand III, The Saint
United Leon and Castile
King of Castile 1217–1252
King of Leon and Castile 1230–1252

|

Alfonso X the Learned
1252–1284

|

Sancho IV el Bravo
1284–1295

|

Ferdinand IV
1295–1312

Christian infantry, now deprived of cavalry support. The Castilians were utterly routed, only a few panic-stricken fugitives finding asylum in the neighbouring mountains. Twenty thousand Christian prisoners were released by Yaqoob without ransom.

The respective systems of tactics employed by Christians and Muslims were much the same in Spain as in Syria. Frankish knights were so completely covered in armour that they could nearly always break through the Muslim line in a charge. The Arabs, Turks and Berbers were more lightly armoured, presumably for climatic reasons, heavy armour being extremely exhausting in the African heat. As a result, the Muslims relied on their archery and on mobility, turning the flanks or attacking the enemy's rear. Part of the Frankish tactics, however, especially in France itself, may be attributed to the structure of society. The haughty French nobility regarded their own infantry with contempt and abandoned them to destruction without compunction. In Palestine, on the other hand, where war was deadly earnest and social barriers less rigid, we have seen the Franks at times produce a splendid, steady infantry.

Both the Murabits and the Muwahhids had, on several occasions, inflicted crushing tactical defeats on the Spaniards but they never exploited their victories in such a manner as to achieve a politically favourable settlement. This may probably have been due to the fact that the Berbers and the Arab nomads such as Beni Hilal were natives of Africa. To them Andalus was a colony which they were bound to defend but it was not their mother country. As a result, they were content to repulse a Christian invasion but they always failed to pursue a defeated enemy and to achieve final victory.

After Alarcos, all Christian Spain was at the mercy of Yaqoob al Mansoor. The army of Castile had been destroyed, Navarre was ready to swear fealty as a vassal of Yaqoob, Aragon, divided by internal intrigues, was helpless. Portugal alone stood at bay and refused to communicate with the victors. If Yaqoob had marched into Castile, he might well have made himself master of the peninsula. In 1197, the year after Alarcos, Guadalajara and Salamanca were stormed and destroyed but the Muslims behaved rather as raiders than as conquerors. Then Yaqoob returned to Africa.

The reason for the departure of the Muwahhid Khalif before reaching a settlement in Spain was the recrudescence of trouble in Ifriqiya. As soon as Yaqoob al Mansoor crossed into Spain, Ibn Ghaniya advanced once more into Tunisia, rapidly capturing Biskra, Qairawan, Mehediya, Tunis and Bone. By 1203, the Murabits, who in 1148 seemed to have been entirely exterminated by the Muwahhids, were again in possession of an extensive territory stretching from Bone to Tripoli. Ibn Ghaniya was supported by the Ayoubids who thereby, while fighting the Franks in Syria, were at the same time helping the Christians in Spain by raising up enemies against the Muwahhids.

Yaqoob al Mansoor would probably have got the better of all his enemies had he not suddenly died in 1199 at the age of forty. His reign of fifteen years was the Golden Age of Muwahhid rule. His campaigns in Spain, culminating in his great victory at Alarcos, were in general successful. There were no rebellions in the Maghrib. The only serious trouble in North Africa was that caused by Beni Ghaniya in Ifriqiya, but it must not be forgotten that Tunis is a thousand miles from Rabat, as far as Warsaw from London. The campaigns in Spain and Ifriqiya were only interludes in the progress of wealth, culture and ordered administration.

The Muwahhid movement, when founded by Ibn Toumert, had been strictly puritan. When the first sectaries occupied cities containing splendid mosques, decorated by other Muslim dynasties with beautiful marbles, glazed tiles, gilding or stucco, they hastened to daub over all the decorations with white-wash, as the Protestants were later on to do in Europe with the churches which they inherited. Under Yaqoob al Mansoor, however, the Muwahhids themselves erected fine buildings. The new city of Rabat, built round an old monastery fortress, was designed in massive proportions.

Yet these gratifying signs of civilization were in fact only the forerunners of impending collapse. For it was the ascetic and dedicated simplicity of the first Muwahhids which had made them victorious over their enemies. Military defeat was to follow as soon as their stern puritanism gave way to art, culture and luxury.

The Muwahhid Empire under Abdul Mumin, Abu Yaqoob Yusuf and his son Yaqoob al Mansoor had enjoyed seventy-eight years of real glory. Cultured princes, resident in Seville as much as in Africa, patrons of Ibn Rushd—the famous Averroes—and of his fellow-philosopher Ibn Tufail, architects of magnificent buildings, ever victorious in war, Abdul Mumin, his son and his grandson, had been worthy of an imperial throne.

Yaqoob was succeeded in 1199 by his son Muhammad al Nasir, a shy and silent youth of eighteen years of age. Thereafter Muwahhid power was to fall into rapid decline.

* * *

It may reasonably be claimed that the Arabs laid the foundations of modern science, for they were particularly distinguished in the field of mathematics. They invented logarithms, trigonometry and algebra and were pre-eminent in astronomy, chemistry and medicine. Their contribution to the literature, the poetry and the romance of the West is no less basic than their achievements in mathematics. There is little doubt, for example, that they were the inventors of rhymed verse, which was unknown to the Greeks and the Romans. By the fourteenth century, rhyme had become the almost universal poetic form in the West.

It was from the Arabs of Spain that the troubadours of Provence obtained the idea of spiritual or courtly love. Their poems in celebration of romantic love were exactly copied from the Arabic, both in the metre used and also in the conventional plots describing the relations between the lover and his mistress. Lévi-Provençal[7] produces evidence to show that William VIII, Duke of Aquitaine, the first troubadour of Provence, spoke Arabic well.

It is easy to appreciate the passion with which mediaeval Europe mimicked Arab civilization when we see today the equal assiduity with which the peoples of Asia and Africa copy everything Western. Such imitation does not involve any affection for the nations which are imitated. Today Asian nationalists hostile to Europe are the most anxious to import Western manners. In the same way, the Provençal and Spanish Christians passed their lives in fighting the Arabs of Andalus, while at the same time imitating them as closely as they could.

"It is not rash to deduce," writes Lévi-Provençal, "that, from the ninth century onwards, the fashions of Muslim Seville, Cordova, Toledo and Saragossa penetrated and dominated the little Christian courts of the north." The nobles of western Europe were full of martial virtues but they were also coarse and brutal and lived under primitive conditions. It was from the Arabs of Spain that they acquired politeness, courtesy in social relations and respect for women. It was from them that they learned the art of gracious living, of courtly splendour and of relative domestic comfort.

"The part played by Arab influence in the formation, in the Middle Ages, of two sentiments characteristic of the nobility of Christendom has not yet been appreciated. The sentiments referred to were chivalry and courtly love. For this purpose, Spain served as a bridge. When the provinces of central Spain returned to the bosom of Christendom, these influences asserted themselves with increasing force."[8]

The reader may be surprised to hear that the Arabs taught Europe respect for women. The contrast between the mediaeval and the modern Western treatment of women does not consist in the change from servitude to freedom but in the emphasis laid on the difference rather than the likeness between the sexes. The mediaeval man learned

[7] Lévi-Provençal, *Poésie Arabe d'Espagne et Poésie d'Europe Mediaevale.*
[8] Lévi-Provençal, *Le rôle spirituel de l'Espagne musulmane.*

from the Arabs to conceive the ideal of womanhood as a complete contrast to his own character. The romantic lover, far from being an autocrat, was bound to render complete obedience to his mistress.

Recent trends in the West tend to make the sexes resemble one another. Women wear trousers, cut short their hair and engage in the same professions as men. Where once they commanded deference, even adoration, they are now jostled and pushed by men who formerly bowed before them as the embodiments of virtue and beauty. Curiously enough, in the tenth century, women in Baghdad also went through a phase of entering the professions and competing with men. But the movement seems to have been shortlived, possibly because the next stage of decadence involved a breakdown in public security. Women may be the intellectual equals of men but they are physically handicapped in an age of violence. But this very weakness rouses again the chivalry of men, for to them woman is most irresistible when she is weakest.

* * *

The South of France did not acquire only its poetry from the Muslims of Spain but also its learning. The university of Montpellier was famous, many of the professors being Arabs or Jews. In the thirteenth century, the study of anatomy by the dissection of human corpses was introduced to the university by Arab professors, two hundred years before it was permitted in the university of Paris. The invasions of Andalus by the Murabits and the Muwahhids, with their puritan fanaticism, gave rise to an emigratian of Arab scholars, scientists and philosophers, many of them professors from the universities of Cordova or Seville. In the South of France in the thirteenth century well-educated people found it essential to know Arabic which was still the language of learning, only later at the Renaissance to be replaced by Latin. It was in Arabic that the Greek philosophers were studied at Montpellier, as also were Averroes, Avicenna, Rhazes and other famous Muslim authorities.

The proximity of Andalus influenced western Europe just as, in our times, French culture has penetrated North Africa. Many day-to-day Arab customs were adopted in the South of France. The doors of the castles stood open all day to admit passers-by as guests, a custom followed in Arabia down to our own times. At meals, choice morsels of meat were placed before an honoured guest, a practice observed by Arab tribesmen to this day. Hawking, jousting and chess, amusements brought by the Arabs to Spain, were zealously pursued in France.

* * *

"Cleanliness after godliness" our grandfathers used to say but such was not always the European attitude. One of the criticisms occasionally voiced by unsympathetic Westerners who visit the Middle East today is that many Arabs seem to be dirty. They would be better, they say, if they had a bath more frequently. It is amusing to notice that, in Spain and Syria, Arab authors complain of the Franks in identical words—"They rarely if ever have a bath." Indeed, after the eviction of the Arabs from Spain, a Christian king ordered the destruction of all baths as remnants of heathenism.

A Muslim lady in the Middle Ages spent a whole day at the baths, perhaps as often as once a week. She would arrive in the early morning borne in a litter or, if she came of a middle-class family, riding a donkey and escorted by a eunuch. After undressing, she would lie for perhaps two hours in the sweating room, during which the attendants would wash her body and her hair with gentle care.

Before noon a eunuch would arrive from the house with a cold lunch, after which an hour's gossip with her fellow bathers would permit an exchange of views on the efficacy of their respective cosmetics. By then it would be time to return to the serious business of the day. The next stage would normally be the dyeing of the hair. Most of the ladies would probably have black hair, which would be rinsed carefully lock by lock in henna, giving a bronze gloss to their long shining tresses. Some, however, whose hair was of different colours, would have it dyed according to taste.

All superfluous hair was then removed from the body by the use of various pastes, leaving the skin everywhere soft and supple, after which the nails would be treated by the manicurist till they shone like polished gems. The long hours already spent in such tiring labours would by this time have exhausted the fragile devotees of beauty and a break for refreshment and relaxation would have become essential. The eunuchs meanwhile had returned with trays of sweetmeats and preserved fruits, the consumption of which would offer another occasion for intimate gossip.

The climax of the long day's operations was in the infinitely delicate make-up of the face, which was first massaged gently by an attendant with the tips of her fingers. Next all superfluous hairs were plucked with patient care, for the depilatory pastes were reserved for the body only. The eyebrows were then painted and the eyes made to appear larger by the minutely delicate application of kohl, or antimony put on with a tiny ivory stick. The complexion was then adjusted, if desired, by a soupçon of rouge on the cheeks. Then, resuming her clothes, our fair lady mounted the litter with which her eunuchs were waiting at the door. Exhausted by her hard day's work, she was borne home to her house, languid, painted, perfumed from head to foot, but contented and happy in the certitude of her own beauty.[9]

[9] Aly Mazahéri, *La Vie Quotidienne des Musulmans au Moyen Age.*

NOTABLE DATES

Defeat of the Murabits by the Muwahhids Capture of Marakish	1148
Capture of Mehediya by the Muwahhids	22nd January, 1160
Death of Abdul Mumin Accession of Abu Yaqoob Yusuf	May 1163
Death of Abu Yaqoob Yusuf at Santarem Accession of Yaqoob al Mansoor	1184
Landing of Ali ibn Ghaniya in Boujaiya	13th November, 1184
Murabit rebellion in Ifriqiya	1184–1199
Defeat of Alfonso VIII of Castile at Alarcos	18th July, 1196
Death of Yaqoob al Mansoor Succession of Muhammad al Nasir	1199

PERSONALITIES

The Muwahhids (Almohades)

Muhammad ibn Toumert, the Mehedi, founder of the sect	1121–1129
Abdul Mumin ibn Ali	1129–1163
Abu Yaqoob Yusuf	1163–1184
Yaqoob al Mansoor	1184–1199
Muhammad al Nasir	1199–1213

Ali ibn Ghaniya, Murabit rebel against Muwahhids
Abu Hafas Umar, founder member of the Muwahhids
Qaraqoosh, Turkman leader, sent by the Ayoubids to Tunis to oppose Muwahhids

Christians
Alfonso VIII, King of Castile
Count Henry of Burgundy, founder of Portugal
Alfonso I of Portugal, his son.

VI

Lion Heart
1187–1192

In what goes to make a hero, Richard's vices, his anger, his . . . cruelty, count for as much as his chivalric virtues: . . . his qualities were more than life-size. It is here that . . . the secret of his lasting fame still lies. He would not be bound down by the chains of the average, the mediocre and the reasonable and died because the merely possible was not enough for him.

JOHN HARVEY, *The Plantagenets*

Never did any man behold
One so clear-sighted or so bold
Or better tried in noble deeds,
Always prepared to meet all needs;
Such is his courage and his might.
Lords, 'tis no idle talk I write.

AMBROISE, *The Crusade of Richard Lion Heart*
(Eng. trans. MERTON J. HUBERT)

He had the valour of Hector, the magnanimity of Achilles and was equal to Alexander, and not inferior to Roland in valour. The liberality of Titus was his . . . the eloquence of Nestor and the prudence of Ulysses. A man who never knew defeat, impatient of an injury and impelled irresistibly to vindicate his rights. Success made him better fitted for action, for fortune ever favours the bold. He was far superior to all others both in moral goodness and in strength and memorable for prowess in battle.

GEOFFREY DE VINSAUF, *Itinerary of King Richard*

VI

THE fall of Jerusalem had caused consternation in Europe. As usual it was the pope who took the lead in urging a new crusade. Unfortunately Philippe Auguste, King of France, was at war with Henry II of England and time was needed to make peace. The first monarch to answer the call, therefore, was the German Emperor, Frederick Barbarossa, who left Ratisbon on 11th May, 1189.

In Asia Minor, the Sultan of Iconium, Qilij Arslan II,[1] the victor of Myrio-cephalon, was pressing on the frontiers of Byzantium and the Emperor Isaac II Angelus had just concluded a treaty with Saladin against him. As a result, the approach of Barbarossa, marching to fight Saladin, was by no means welcome in Constantinople. After considerable friction and some fighting, Frederick wisely avoided the city and, in March 1190, crossed at Gallipoli[2] and marched on Iconium. Qilij Arslan II was probably ready to allow the Germans to pass but Muslim feeling was too strong for him. On 18th May, 1190, a half-hearted battle took place and the Germans captured Iconium by assault.

Co-operation, however, was then established and Barbarossa marched on to Seleucia, where the Crusaders were to enter the dominions of Leo II, the Armenian ruler of Cilicia. The German army, well-disciplined and some forty thousand strong, was already almost on the frontier of Syria. Saladin had been kept informed by his ally the Emperor Isaac II of the march of the Germans and was deeply alarmed for other contingents of Franks were arriving at Tyre, threatening the Muslims with a double invasion. Then, at this moment of crisis, on 10th June, 1190, Frederick Barbarossa was accidentally drowned in a river near Seleucia. Ibn al Athir admits that, but for the death of Barbarossa, the Muslims would have lost both Syria and Egypt.

Although the emperor had been accompanied by two of his sons, Frederick and Philip, neither was able to control the situation and the German army disintegrated. In October 1190, Frederick reached Acre by sea with a mere remnant of the army.

* * *

At the end of the summer of 1188, Saladin released Guy de Lusignan, his brother Amaury and the Grand Master of the Templars, Gerard de Ridefort, after Guy had sworn not again to fight the Muslims. Guy

[1] Genealogical tree, page 168. [2] Map 4, page 36.

rode down to Tyre but Conrad de Montferrat, who had repulsed the attacks of Saladin, refused to admit him. The native Franks of Outremer were deeply embittered against Guy, to whom they rightly attributed the loss of the kingdom. Guy was obliged to take refuge in Tripoli, where two hundred knights from Sicily had landed and had saved the city.

In the summer of 1189, this weak and irresolute man suddenly made a desperate resolve. On 20th August, 1189, in violation of his oath not to fight again, he marched southwards with a small heterogeneous force including the two hundred knights from Sicily. His avowed intention was to take Acre, one of the most formidable fortresses in the country. The tiny army marched along the seashore, accompanied by the Pisan and Sicilian fleets, which hugged the land, ready to take off survivors in the event of a disaster.

Arriving outside Acre on 28th August, the Franks dug themselves in on a mound called Tel al Fukhar, lying about a thousand yards east of the city. Saladin could easily have destroyed Guy's tiny army on the march but he delayed, besieging the castle of Beaufort, east of Sidon. He did not arrive before Acre until 29th August, 1189, by which time the Franks had dug themselves in. On 1st September, a large fleet arrived off Acre, bringing ten thousand men, mostly infantry, from Flanders and Denmark, just the troops needed for siege warfare. Presumably Guy was aware of the near approach of these reinforcements when he set out on his precarious march.

Meanwhile Saladin's army had taken up a position from Ayadiya, through Berwa and Qaisan to Dawuq. On 15th September, he sent a column down the seashore from the north with reinforcements and supplies for Acre. On 18th September, the sultan attempted to storm the Frankish position at Tel al Fukhar but was repulsed. Six days later, another Christian fleet arrived, carrying further French and German troops and giving the Franks complete command of the sea.

The Franks had now received sufficient reinforcements to make it appear possible for them to take the offensive. On 4th October, 1189, they made a general attack towards the east which at first met with considerable success, even enabling them to occupy Saladin's headquarters at Ayadiya. But the infantry then began to loot and a Muslim counter-attack from the south nearly cut them off from their trenches, and caused them heavy casualties during their withdrawal. Gerard de Ridefort, Grand Master of the Templars, the man largely responsible for the disaster of Hattin, was killed. So heavy were the casualties in this battle that, on 15th October, 1189, Saladin moved his camp to Kharruba to avoid the stench of decaying corpses.

The Franks meanwhile had completed their line with a breastwork and ditch extending from sea to sea. Both armies now settled down to

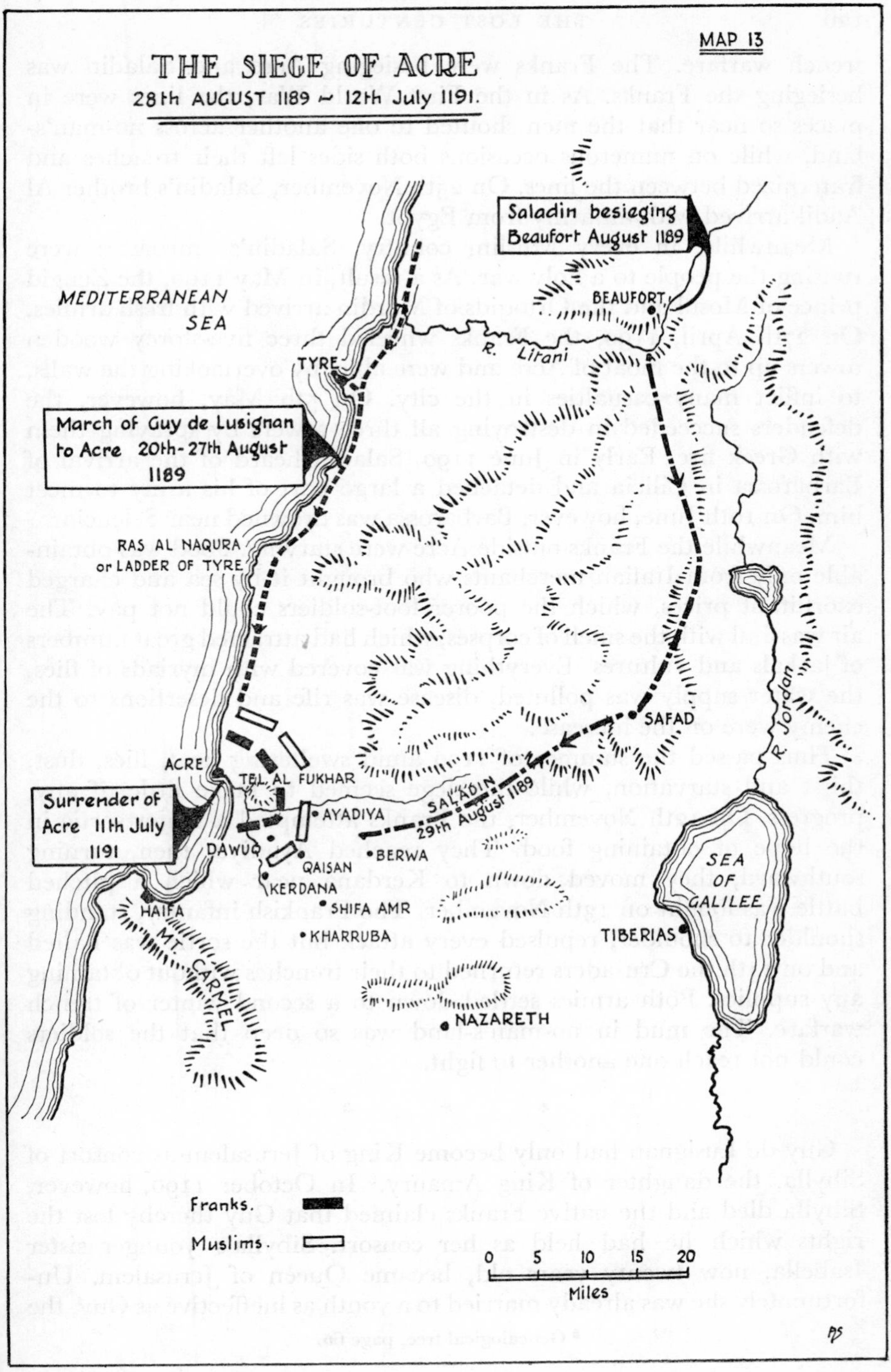
MAP 13
THE SIEGE OF ACRE
28th AUGUST 1189 ~ 12th July 1191.
Saladin besieging Beaufort August 1189
MEDITERRANEAN SEA
BEAUFORT
R. Litani
TYRE
March of Guy de Lusignan to Acre 20th-27th August 1189
RAS AL NAQURA or LADDER OF TYRE
R. Jordan
SAFAD
ACRE
TEL AL FUKHAR
SALADIN 29th August 1189
Surrender of Acre 11th July 1191
AYADIYA
DAWUQ
BERWA
QAISAN
KERDANA
SHIFA AMR
HAIFA
KHARRUBA
MT. CARMEL
SEA OF GALILEE
TIBERIAS
NAZARETH
Franks.
Muslims.
0 5 10 15 20
Miles

trench warfare. The Franks were besieging Acre and Saladin was besieging the Franks. As in the First World War, the lines were in places so near that the men shouted to one another across no-man's-land, while on numerous occasions both sides left their trenches and fraternized between the lines. On 25th November, Saladin's brother Al Aadil arrived with an army from Egypt.

Meanwhile, in every Muslim country, Saladin's emissaries were rousing the people to a holy war. As a result, in May 1190, the Zengid prince of Mosul and the Ortoqids of Mardin arrived with fresh armies. On 27th April, 1190, the Franks wheeled three five-storey wooden towers up to the moat of Acre and were able, by overlooking the walls, to inflict many casualties in the city. On 5th May, however, the defenders succeeded in destroying all three towers by spraying them with Greek fire. Early in June 1190, Saladin heard of the arrival of Barbarossa in Cilicia and detached a large part of his army to meet him. On 10th June, however, Barbarossa was drowned near Seleucia.

Meanwhile the Franks outside Acre were starving. Food was obtainable only from Italian merchants who brought it by sea and charged exorbitant prices, which the poorer foot-soldiers could not pay. The air was foul with the smell of corpses, which had attracted great numbers of jackals and vultures. Everything was covered with myriads of flies, the water supply was polluted, disease was rife and desertions to the enemy were on the increase.

Thus passed the summer of 1190 amid sweltering heat, flies, dust, thirst and starvation, while the siege seemed to make little, if any, progress. On 12th November, the Franks attempted a major sortie in the hope of obtaining food. They reached Ayadiya, then, turning southward, they moved down to Kerdana near which a pitched battle was fought on 13th November. The Frankish infantry, standing shoulder to shoulder, repulsed every attack but the sortie was halted and on 14th the Crusaders returned to their trenches without obtaining any supplies. Both armies settled down to a second winter of trench warfare. The mud in no-man's-land was so deep that the soldiers could not reach one another to fight.

* * *

Guy de Lusignan had only become King of Jerusalem as consort of Sibylla, the daughter of King Amaury.[3] In October 1190, however, Sibylla died and the native Franks claimed that Guy thereby lost the rights which he had held as her consort. Sibylla's younger sister Isabella, now twenty years old, became Queen of Jerusalem. Unfortunately she was already married to a youth as ineffective as Guy, the

[3] Genealogical tree, page 60.

last Humphrey de Toron, feeble descendant of a great family. The marriage was annulled on the grounds that Isabella had been married at the age of eight, too young to give her legal consent. Baldwin, the Archbishop of Canterbury, who was with the army, refused to countenance this dubious transaction but he died on 19th November, 1190. On 24th November, Isabella was married anew to Conrad of Montferrat, a fine soldier and a commanding personality who, by repulsing Saladin from Tyre, had saved the remnant of the kingdom.

The result was, however, that, at the height of a desperate war, there were now two rival Kings of Jerusalem. Guy's supporters claimed that, although originally only the consort of Sibylla, he had in fact been crowned and that the sacrament was still valid. Conrad's party, on the other hand, pointed out that Isabella was now queen and that Conrad, as her consort, had become king.

* * *

It will be remembered that, on the Second Crusade, Louis VII of France had quarrelled violently with his wife Eleanor. When they returned to France, their marriage had been annulled and, in May 1152, Eleanor had married Henry of Anjou, who, in October 1154, had been crowned Henry II, King of England.

Eleanor was the heiress of William X, Duke of Aquitaine, whose grandfather and father had introduced Arabic poetry and Arab romantic love to southern France. In 1164, Eleanor had quarrelled with Henry II and had retired to her own court of Aquitaine, famous for its troubadours and courts of love. In 1172, her son Richard had been installed Duke of Aquitaine at the age of fifteen. Richard was a man of splendid appearance, tall, his head held high, with a handsome face and chestnut hair. Well-educated, a poet and a musician, he always gave a straight, bold answer and never broke his word. In 1183, however, his cruel suppression of a plot in Aquitaine revealed a hard streak in his nature.

The news of the disastrous Battle of Hattin reached France in October 1187. The next day, stirred by a genuinely noble outburst of emotion, Richard took the cross. Meanwhile the pope had appealed to both Henry II and Philippe Auguste, King of France, to make peace and go on a crusade. Henry, however, died on 6th July, 1189, and Richard was crowned at Westminster on 3rd September. Soon afterwards, on 16th March, 1190, he made peace with Philippe Auguste and the two kings set out together, reaching Messina, where they decided to winter, in September 1190. The siege of Acre had already been in progress for a year.

In March 1191, Queen Eleanor came to Reggio on the Straits of

Messina, bringing with her Berengaria of Navarre, whom Richard was to marry, a maid more accomplished than beautiful, as Richard of Devizes says rather unkindly. On 10th April, the English fleet sailed from Messina for Acre. As a result of a storm off Cyprus, however, three English ships took refuge at Limassol, one of them carrying Joan, Richard's sister, widow of William II, King of Sicily, and Berengaria of Navarre.[4]

In Constantinople the dynasty of the Comneni had been overthrown in 1185 and Isaac II Angelus had been raised to the purple.[5] Isaac Comnenus, a prince of the fallen dynasty, had seized Cyprus and declared himself independent. On 6th May, 1191, Richard landed at Limassol, as a result of the equivocal conduct of Isaac towards the stranded English ships. Marching rapidly to Larnaca, Famagusta and Nicosia, he defeated Isaac on 21st May, took him prisoner and annexed the whole island. On 12th May, he had married Berengaria at Limassol.

The seizure of Cyprus was a major, though unpremeditated, victory for the Franks. For three centuries, it was to provide them with maritime bases in the eastern Mediterranean, secure from attack by the numerically superior Muslim armies on the mainland. Richard was a serious student of war but we do not know whether he realized the strategic value of his conquest. It is possible that he did so for, while he was engaged in his brief struggle with Isaac Comnenus, he was visited by Guy de Lusignan and the leaders of his party. They must have told him that the Franks were starving outside Acre. The possession of a fertile island a hundred miles off the coast of Syria would have solved their supply problems.

* * *

Meanwhile the King of France had landed outside Acre on 20th April, 1191. His arrival raised the flagging spirits of the Franks, who redoubled the intensity of the bombardment and began to fill in the ditch. On 8th June, Richard landed amid great rejoicing. As the long period of trench warfare neared the final climax, Saladin moved back his headquarters to Ayadiya. On 5th June, the French attempted an assault but as soon as they moved up to the walls of Acre, Saladin attacked the Frankish lines from the east.

The arrival of the French and English fleets had given the Franks command of the sea. Saladin had foreseen this danger while the kings were still in Messina and had appealed for naval reinforcements to Yaqoob al Mansoor, the Muwahhid Khalif. Saladin's embassy had reached Marakish on 18th January, 1191, but evoked no response. As

[4] Map 21, page 198.
[5] An account of the overthrow of the Comneni is given in the next chapter.

we have already seen, Saladin had previously been stirring up trouble for the Muwahhids in Tunis.

On 16th June and again on 2nd July, the French tried to assault the walls of Acre but Richard was ill, the English did not co-operate and the attacks were repulsed. On 11th July, the English, led by the Earl of Leicester and the Bishop of Salisbury, reached the top of the breach and almost broke into the town. As they fell back, the defenders called to them from the walls asking for terms. Richard was already in touch with Saladin but the Crusaders demanded the restoration of the kingdom as it had been before Hattin and Saladin refused. Eventually, however, the garrison came to terms with Conrad of Montferrat and Saladin was confronted with a *fait accompli*. The lives of the garrison would be spared for a ransom of two hundred thousand gold dinars, two thousand five hundred Christian prisoners would be released and the True Cross captured at Hattin would be returned. Acre surrendered on 11th July, 1191.

Scarcely had Acre been taken over than the rivalry between Guy de Lusignan and Conrad of Montferrat broke out again. More than half of France owed feudal allegiance to the Crown of England and the Lusignan family were feudatories of Richard. As a result the English and the Templars supported Guy, while the French and the native Franks favoured Conrad. At a grand council held on 27th and 28th July, 1191, it was decided to divide the kingdom in half, Guy having Acre and the south while Conrad retained Tyre and the north. Guy would retain the royal title until his death after which it would pass to Conrad and Isabella and their descendants. Conrad thereupon left the army and withdrew to Tyre. Unity of command was abandoned before the war was won.

On 1st August, 1191, Philippe Auguste embarked for France. Richard was a more successful soldier and the King of France was not prepared to play second fiddle. The greater part of the French army, however, remained in the Holy Land under Hugh III, Duke of Burgundy.

On 20th August, the Muslim prisoners from Acre to the number of some two thousand seven hundred were collected in the plain east of the town and, by Richard's order, were put to death. Some modern English writers have cried in horror that this massacre leaves an indelible stain on the fame of Richard, especially when contrasted with the chivalry of Saladin. In so far as this aspect is concerned, we have seen Saladin performing similar actions. He massacred the adherents of the Fatimids in Cairo. Before the Battle of Tel al Jazar, he ordered that all prisoners taken were to be killed. After Hattin, he caused all Templar and Hospitaller prisoners to be decapitated in cold blood. Baha al Deen mentions casually two anecdotes which occurred during the siege of Acre. In one case, Saladin happened to see a party of Muslims bringing in a Frankish prisoner and ordered them to cut off his head at once.

On another occasion, Baha al Deen describes how forty-five Frankish prisoners were brought in. "The sultan's younger sons asked his permission to kill these prisoners, which he forbade them to do." Baha al Deen was surprised and begged the sultan to tell him the reason for the refusal. Saladin replied, "They shall not become accustomed in their youth to the shedding of blood and laugh at it, for they as yet know no difference between a Muslim and an infidel." It may be noted that Baha al Deen was himself not a soldier but a man of religion, yet he was surprised that Saladin did not allow his sons to kill these prisoners with their own hands. The sultan's explanation is, not that prisoners should not be killed, but that young boys should not be their executioners lest, growing callous, they might some day kill Muslims in the same way. Baha al Deen does not tell us whether the prisoners were spared or merely killed by soldiers instead of by the sultan's younger sons.

At this distance of time and in the entirely different mental atmosphere in which we live, it is impossible accurately to appreciate the thoughts and motives of men in the twelfth century. It seems probable, however, that, during the siege of Acre, prisoners taken in battle were frequently killed in cold blood by both sides. Yet there are innumerable proofs that Saladin was a constant exponent of Arab acts of chivalry which appeal to us most strongly.

The Arab of the desert, from whom these customs were originally derived, was an individualist. His ambition was to achieve personal glory by the performance of fantastic deeds of courage or of generosity. To win a fortress after a bitter struggle and then hand it back at the request of a girl, as Saladin had done with Malik as Salih at Aleppo,[6] was the kind of *beau geste* which delighted the Arabs. The dramatic bravado of the Arabs, however, was not soft or sentimental and it went hand-in-hand with endless fightings and killings. Chivalry came to Europe from the Arabs but it was Christianity which added to it the gentleness of the perfect knight, as meek as is a maid. The fact that Saladin was not shocked seems to be proved by the courtly relations established between him and Richard in the ensuing months.

Modern writers are apt to state, rather contemptuously, that life was cheap in the Middle Ages. It is conceivable that this may have been due to the fact that both Muslims and Christians believed in a future and eternal life, in comparison with which a few years more or less in this

[6] Page 85.

troubled world made little difference. Only to those who disbelieve in a future life does the destruction of this one appear the worst injury which can be inflicted.

More serious would be the charge that Richard broke his word, especially as Saladin was punctilious in keeping his promises. On this subject opinions seem to be divided. Maqrizi states that negotiations for the exchange of prisoners broke down and the Franks killed them all, but he makes no charge of broken faith. Baha al Deen says that a dispute arose when the time came for the Muslims to hand over the first instalment. He claims that Saladin had prepared the amount of money needed, though the Franks claimed that the conditions regarding the return of prisoners had not been fully carried out. However, the Franks asked for the instalment to be handed over but Saladin refused to pay it, unless the Muslim prisoners were first sent back, offering to give hostages for the payment of the remaining instalments. The original agreement between Conrad and the garrison of Acre does not seem to have included such a clause and the Franks refused.

Baha al Deen continues: "When the King of England saw that the sultan was making some delay in the fulfilment of the conditions, he acted treacherously with regard to the Muslim prisoners." Baha al Deen adds that Richard had promised the Muslims of Acre (presumably verbally as it was not in the agreement) that, if Saladin did not fulfil the conditions, they would become slaves, not that they would be killed. This phrase suggests that Baha al Deen meant that Richard "acted treacherously" in breaking a verbal promise made to the prisoners, not to Saladin, with whom no agreement had been concluded, for the surrender had been negotiated direct by Conrad with the garrison of Acre. It may incidentally be remembered at this point that Richard had already shown a cruel streak in his character in the suppression of the rebellion in Aquitaine.

Finally we may ask ourselves why Richard killed them, thereby losing two hundred thousand gold dinars, the release of two thousand five hundred Christian prisoners who would have joined his army and the recovery of the True Cross, which would have earned him glory in every Christian country. Mere love of bloodshed would scarcely have caused him to throw away such valuable assets, for Richard was an efficient and practical professional soldier.

Two explanations may be worth consideration. First, nearly six weeks had passed since the surrender of Acre during which the army had been lying idle. It was already 20th August and in two months the campaigning season would be over. A hundred miles of marching and fighting still separated the Crusaders from Jerusalem, which Richard hoped to capture before the winter. It seems possible that the king thought that Saladin was playing for time till the winter rains put an end to operations, a strategy repeatedly used with success by the Franks in the past.

Moreover, time was in general more important to the Crusaders than to Saladin, whose soldiers were in their own country. The French and English were more than two thousand miles from home. The King of France had already gone. Another winter outside Acre might mean the abandonment of the Crusade. Yet as long as the Muslim prisoners remained under guard in their camp, the Franks could neither fight nor march. Their operations were paralysed.

The second possibility is that Richard was anxious to show that he was a man to be feared, a subject to which we shall refer again later.

* * *

As soon as the Franks had regained their mobility by disposing of the prisoners, they set out on 25th August, 1191, to march southwards. They were immediately attacked by Saladin's brother Al Aadil but the attack was repulsed. Under Richard's command, the Crusader army was extremely well ordered and disciplined. It is alleged that the king had stated that any infantryman who fled in battle would have a foot amputated.

The march followed the seashore, the fleet, carrying rations and stores, keeping pace with the troops. The infantry provided the left flank guard throughout the whole length of the column, marching shoulder to shoulder and armed with cross-bows. A party of mounted knights formed the advanced guard and another mounted unit brought up the rear. The remainder of the knights rode in the centre of the army, covered by the infantry. On the right, between the cavalry and the sea, marched other infantry units which were "resting". The infantry changed over every day between those on the left flank who were in continual action with the enemy and those on the right who could "march at ease".

The column was under continuous attack from front, left flank and rear by two types of enemy. First, by Turkman horse-archers who came at full gallop, discharged their arrows and then wheeled away. Secondly, by Arab bedouins brought from the desert, lean, agile men on foot, dodging from cover to cover and shooting their arrows with deadly effect. Neither category attempted to close. Their object was to inflict casualties, particularly to kill horses, for the offensive power of the Franks lay in their cavalry.

On 7th September, 1191, the column was approaching Arsoof when large numbers of the enemy appeared in front, on the left and in the rear. Clouds of Turkmans attacked at full gallop to the sound of

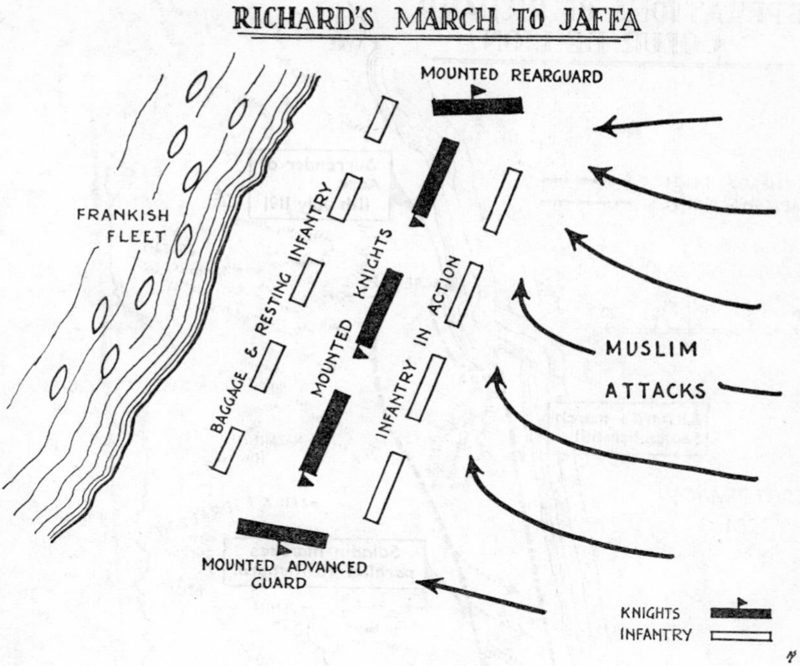

trumpets and the usual continual rolls of drums—so many drums that no other sound could be heard. Even claps of thunder would have been inaudible, said one who was present. A dense cloud of dust enveloped the whole column, sweltering beneath the summer sun. At the same time came large numbers of Arab bedouins and Sudanese on foot, all pouring arrows into the columns. Many horses were being killed, the heat was intense and there was no drinking water to be had until the column could reach Arsoof.

But Richard was in his element. The Grand Master of the Hospitallers, who was commanding the rearguard, galloped up and said, "We can't hold on. We are losing all our horses." "You'll *have* to hold on a bit longer, Master," replied Richard. "I can't do everything at once." The king was organizing a mounted charge which was to come in from a flank and exterminate the Muslim army. But the knights would wait no longer. One or two charged out of the ranks and then the whole of the cavalry followed straight at the enemy.

"Then the Frank cavalry formed up in a mass," writes Baha al Deen who was with Saladin, "and decided to charge. I saw these knights all formed up, surrounded by their infantry. They raised their lances, gave a great shout, the line of the infantry opened to let them

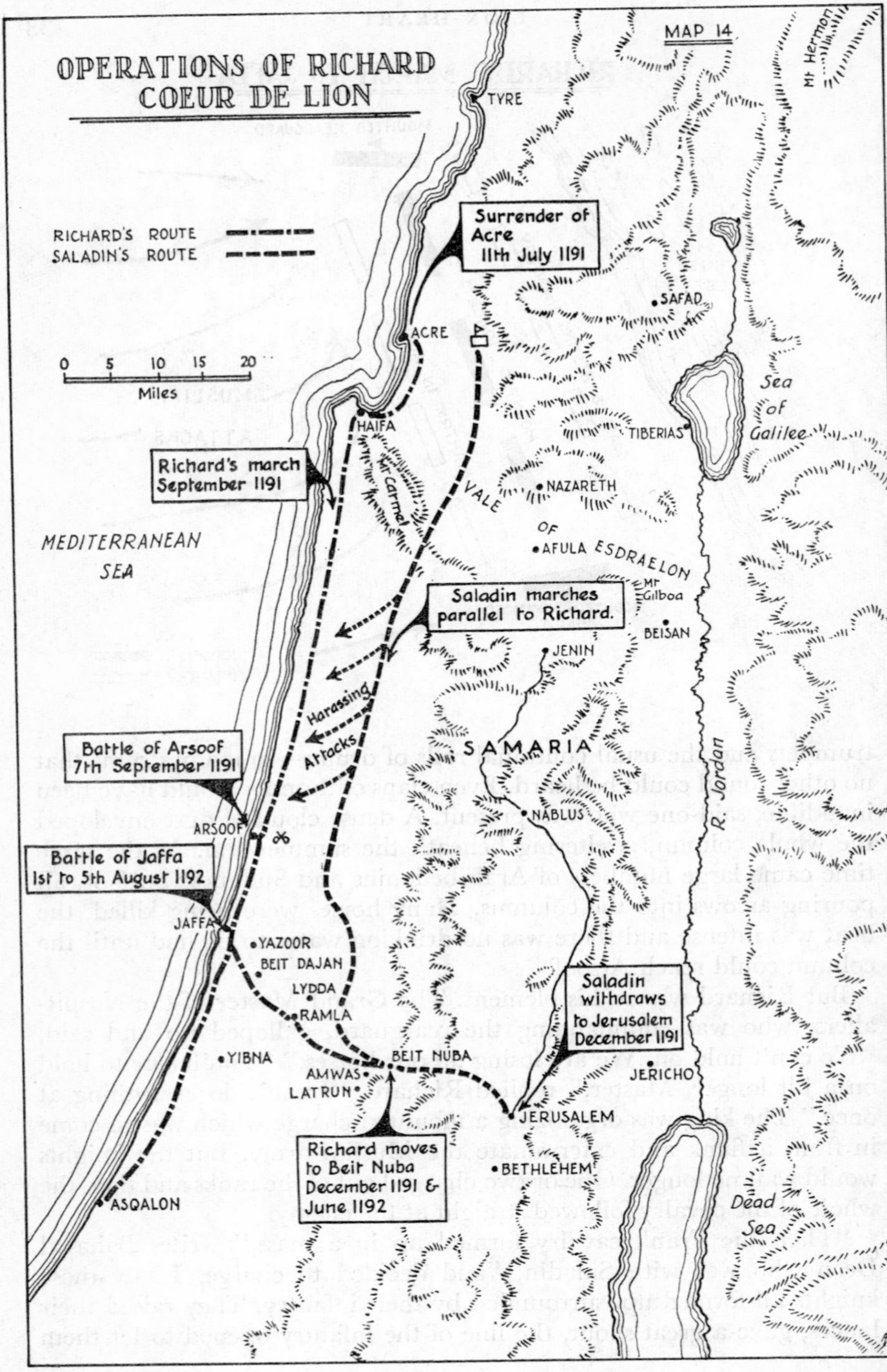
MAP 14
OPERATIONS OF RICHARD
COEUR DE LION
RICHARD'S ROUTE
SALADIN'S ROUTE
0 5 10 15 20
Miles
Mt Hermon
TYRE
Surrender of Acre 11th July 1191
SAFAD
ACRE
Sea of Galilee
HAIFA
TIBERIAS
Richard's march September 1191
Mt Carmel
VALE OF ESDRAELON
NAZARETH
MEDITERRANEAN SEA
AFULA
Mt Gilboa
Saladin marches parallel to Richard.
BEISAN
JENIN
Harassing Attacks
SAMARIA
R. Jordan
Battle of Arsoof 7th September 1191
NABLUS
ARSOOF
Battle of Jaffa 1st to 5th August 1192
JAFFA
YAZOOR
BEIT DAJAN
LYDDA
Saladin withdraws to Jerusalem December 1191
RAMLA
YIBNA
BEIT NUBA
AMWAS
JERICHO
LATRUN
JERUSALEM
Richard moves to Beit Nuba December 1191 & June 1192
BETHLEHEM
ASQALON
Dead Sea

through and they charged out in every direction. Everything on our side was thrown into complete rout."

"These brave men," says Ambroise,[7] "attacked the Turks with so much vigour that every one of them killed his man, drove his lance through his body and lifted him out of the saddle. The Turks were completely taken aback for our men struck them like a thunderbolt amid a great cloud of dust. All the foot archers, who had been causing us such losses, had their heads slashed off."

When Richard saw that the charge had started, he abandoned his attempt to organize a turning movement, clapped spurs to his horse, took the lead and soon strewed the field with dead Turks. When the charge reached the hills, he checked it and rallied the knights, aware of the danger of wild pursuits which had so often led to the defeat of the Franks. Saladin, who had been watching from a hill, kept his head. Ordering his drums to beat, he rallied a part of the fugitives. When Richard led the knights back, Saladin sent men to harass their withdrawal. Richard, however, turned on them, chased them away and rejoined the column.

The sultan, who had just received a large reinforcement of Turkmans, had hoped to make the day a second Hattin. "God alone knows the intensity of anguish which filled his heart after this battle," writes Baha al Deen. This was the first open battle of the Third Crusade and the Muslims had been utterly defeated. After Arsoof they would not again challenge the Franks to a general action.

As Richard continued his march southward, Saladin wished to hold Asqalon but his commanders refused, remembering his massacre of the prisoners at Acre.[8] This interesting admission suggests that Richard's ruthlessness may have been calculated to produce just such a result. As his army would no longer face Richard in the field nor hold a fortress against him, Saladin decided to adopt a scorched earth policy.

Jaffa had already been destroyed. Urgent orders were now sent to evacuate the population of Asqalon. Once more a pathetic convoy of refugees, carrying a few hastily collected possessions, set out weeping to find refuge where they could. The Christians of Edessa had suffered the same fate forty years before. Having razed Asqalon, Saladin now destroyed Lydda and Ramla also.

Richard halted in Jaffa and spent two months, from 10th September to 31st October, 1191, rebuilding the fortress. He needed a firm base on the sea for the advance on Jerusalem. On 31st October, the Franks advanced from Jaffa and built a fort at Beit Dajan. Thence they moved

[7] Ambroise, *Histoire de la Guerre Sainte*. Ambroise was an Anglo-Norman poet, a follower of Richard.

[8] Ibn al Athir, *Al Kamil*. Baha al Deen, *Nuwadir*.

to Ramla, Saladin being at Latrun. On 8th December, 1191, Richard advanced to Latrun and Beit Nuba, while Saladin retreated up the steep, rocky Judaean hills to Jerusalem, of which he set his army to repair the fortifications. On 22nd December, a fresh Muslim army arrived from Egypt.

By this time the winter gales and rain had come and many men and horses fell sick and died. Richard was now able to study the problem of an advance on Jerusalem. The main factors were as follows:

(1) If the Crusaders fought their way up the Judaean mountains and laid siege to Jerusalem, Saladin, avoiding battle, would place his army between them and Jaffa. As had happened at Acre, the Franks would besiege Jerusalem and Saladin would besiege the Franks. At Acre, however, the Crusaders could still receive supplies and reinforcements by sea. If they were besieging Jerusalem, they could receive neither. Unless they could take the city by an immediate assault, they would have to withdraw again when supplies ran low.

(2) The Franks relied in battle on the shock of their armoured knights on galloping horses. But the country between Latrun and Jerusalem consisted of steep rocky hillsides, divided by narrow ravines and spurs of naked rock. The tracks leading up the valleys were commanded by rough, boulder-strewn ridges from which arrows, javelins and rocks could be poured down on the column. It was essentially infantry country, in which neither cavalry nor armour could be used.

The history of armour and regular armies which met with disaster in these Judaean mountains, is a long one. When the Children of Israel first occupied Canaan, they were light and nimble nomads like Saladin's bedouins, but the coastal plains were held by a settled and more civilized people with fighting vehicles. "And the Lord was with Judah; and he drave out the inhabitants of the mountain; but could not drive out the inhabitants of the valley, because they had chariots of iron."[9]

At the outbreak of the Jewish rebellion against Rome, which was to end in the destruction of Jerusalem by Titus in A.D. 70, a Roman army was virtually exterminated by the nimble Jewish guerillas on the very track from Jerusalem to Beit Nuba which the Crusaders would have been obliged to follow. When Titus ultimately came to avenge this disaster, his troops were already holding Amwas and Beit Nuba, but he did not attempt to force his way up the mountains to Jerusalem. He made a long détour to where the mountains peter out into the Vale of Esdraelon and marched southwards through Samaria down the ridge of the mountain range.

[9] Judges I, 19.

My own memories of the track from Beit Nuba to Jerusalem are vivid for, in 1948, the Israeli army tried to climb these mountains. It attacked Latrun with tanks but was repulsed by the Arab Legion. Thus the Israelis were stopped by the line Latrun–Amwas–Beit Nuba, precisely where Richard was stopped by Saladin.

(3) For Richard to climb the Judaean Mountains with his small army relying on armoured shock action was, therefore, not really a military proposition. The native Franks, the Templars and the Hospitallers, however, produced a third argument. There was no use retaking Jerusalem, they said, if the Crusaders then sailed away to Europe. The remnant of Franks who would remain in the Holy Land would be unable to hold it.

In the light of our knowledge of the ground today, we can therefore conclude that Richard's refusal to go farther was correct. On 13th January, 1192, the army evacuated Beit Nuba and Latrun and returned to Jaffa.

* * *

The Crusaders were still divided into two jealous factions, Richard, the English and Guy de Lusignan on one side, the Duke of Burgundy, the French and Conrad of Montferrat on the other. Grousset[10] suggests that Philippe Auguste may have told the Duke of Burgundy, whom he left in command of the French, not to allow Richard to take Jerusalem, lest his glory outshine that of the King of France. As soon, however, as Richard made known his decision not to march on Jerusalem, the French denounced this act of treachery and declared that the city could easily have been captured. The Duke of Burgundy and the French army abandoned Richard in Jaffa and marched back to Acre. At the end of January, 1192, Richard occupied and rebuilt Asqalon, working with his own hands with the masons. He was always solicitous for the welfare of his men and ready to share in all their toils and discomfort.

During the winter, the rivalry between Guy and Conrad became increasingly bitter. The Duke of Burgundy joined Conrad at Tyre. The two even attempted to capture Acre which belonged to Guy, while Conrad sent several embassies to Saladin, offering to conclude a treaty with him. Meanwhile the Genoese declared for Conrad, the Pisans for Guy. These endless feuds went far to destroy any hopes of a Frankish victory.

In April 1192, however, news reached Richard of the increasing confusion in England owing to the attempts of his brother John to usurp the royal authority. Anxious to return home, he summoned the

[10] Grousset, *Histoire des Croisades*.

native Franks to choose themselves a king. When they unanimously chose Conrad, Richard was obliged to agree. A few days later, however, on 28th April, 1192, Conrad was assassinated in Tyre by the Ismailis with whom he had a dispute. The native Franks immediately acclaimed Henry II of Champagne, who was nephew of both Richard and Philippe Auguste. (See genealogical tree on the opposite page.)

In order to legitimize Henry of Champagne as King of Jerusalem, he was obliged to marry Isabella, the daughter of King Amaury and the widow of Conrad, by whom she was pregnant. She gave birth to Marie, who was to become Queen of Jerusalem in 1205 and who was to marry Jean de Brienne in 1210.[11]

In 1191, Richard had sold Cyprus to the Templars for a hundred thousand ducats but, in April 1192, as a result of a rising in Nicosia, the Templars returned the island to the king. The Franks had just rejected Guy as their king, so, on 5th May, 1192, Richard gave him Cyprus on condition of his paying back the price to the Templars. The Lusignans were to rule Cyprus for nearly three centuries.

* * *

Ever since the siege of Acre, Richard had kept up correspondence with Saladin and had met the sultan's brother Al Aadil. After his defeat at Arsoof, Saladin had seemed willing to consider the surrender of Jerusalem, perhaps only to gain time. On 20th October, 1191, Richard had suggested the marriage of his sister Joan to Al Aadil, on condition that the couple rule jointly over the Kingdom of Jerusalem. Saladin and Al Aadil seemed willing to consider the idea but Joan refused to marry a Muslim. Some Western historians have regarded this offer as a joke but it need not have been ridiculous. Muslims were permitted to marry Christian women and Joan would have joined Al Aadil's haram. Byzantine emperors had on several occasions given their women to non-Christians for political reasons. Joan's refusal to be one of several wives is more comprehensible. Richard's subsequent naïve suggestion that Al Aadil become a Christian was scarcely practical.

On 8th November, 1191, when Richard was at Yazoor, a formal meeting took place between him and Al Aadil. Tents were pitched by both sides and hospitality was exchanged. Al Aadil and Richard became personal friends and a general relaxation of hatreds ensued. Relations between Franks and Muslims were permanently improved and were to remain courteous and chivalrous until the fall of the Ayoubid dynasty. It seems reasonable to attribute the ease of Richard's relations with Saladin and Al Aadil to his upbringing at the court of Aquitaine where

[11] Genealogical tree, page 60.

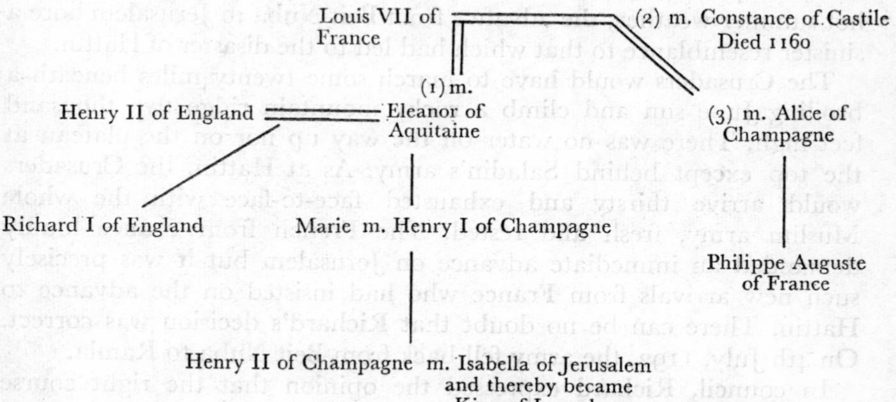

NOTE: Eleanor of Aquitaine first married Louis VII and had a daughter Marie. They were then divorced and Eleanor married Henry II of England and had Richard—Louis married Constance of Castile and then Alice of Champagne, who gave birth to Philippe Auguste.

Arab poetry and Arab manners had been introduced by his ancestors, William VIII and William IX. It is true that the native Franks had also entered into courteous relations with Saladin, but they constituted the third and fourth generation born in Palestine and were admittedly partly arabicized.

* * *

Henry of Champagne the new king, and the French army under the Duke of Burgundy rejoined Richard at Asqalon on 24th May, 1192. On 11th June, the army camped once more at Beit Nuba. For the second time, the question whether to march on Jerusalem was discussed. In the hot summer weather, the advance from Beit Nuba to Jerusalem bore a sinister resemblance to that which had led to the disaster of Hattin.

The Crusaders would have to march some twenty miles beneath a broiling June sun and climb a rocky mountain ridge two thousand feet high. There was no water on the way up nor on the plateau at the top except behind Saladin's army. As at Hattin, the Crusaders would arrive thirsty and exhausted face-to-face with the whole Muslim army, fresh and rested. The French from France loudly demanded an immediate advance on Jerusalem but it was precisely such new arrivals from France who had insisted on the advance to Hattin. There can be no doubt that Richard's decision was correct. On 4th July, 1192, the army fell back from Beit Nuba to Ramla.

In council, Richard expressed the opinion that the right course would be to invade Egypt, a view which was remembered and acted upon many years later. Perhaps in furtherance of such a project, he made agreements with the bedouin tribes of Sinai. The admiration felt for him by Muslims is shown by the fact that a number of Saladin's Mamlooks deserted to him. Richard formed himself a bodyguard of three hundred of them.

Richard now proposed the establishment of a Frankish kingdom under the suzerainty of Saladin. The Jezira and Persia were in anarchy and Saladin seems to have actually contemplated expansion to the east. If he had been freed from war with the Crusaders and even more if they had marched with him, he might well have succeeded. A Frankish-Muslim Empire might, moreover, have saved the world from the terrible scourge of the Mongol invasions and have resulted in a better understanding between Islam and Christianity down to our own times.

The two monarchs were now on the verge of agreement. "Since you trust us with such trust," wrote Saladin to Richard, "and as one good turn deserves another, the sultan grants you the church of the Resurrection and he will share the rest of the country with you." On 19th July, 1192, however, negotiations broke down. Saladin demanded the destruction of Asqalon, Richard insisted on its retention. His obstinacy may have been due to the fact that he had already decided that the Holy Land could only be securely maintained if Egypt were separated from Syria. Saladin, who had united them, was equally convinced that his power rested on their union. Both saw the fortress of Asqalon as their connecting link. The negotiations having failed, Richard marched away northwards. The Franks had recovered the sea coast from Sidon to Asqalon but the Muslim garrison of Beirut separated them from Tripoli and Antioch. Thus the problem of Beirut to the Christians was like that of Asqalon to the Muslims, a fortress separating their two territories. Richard decided to take Beirut before sailing for home.

No sooner had Richard gone north than on 27th July Saladin suddenly threw himself on Jaffa with his whole army. The small Frankish garrison resisted heroically but, after five days, the town was carried by storm, though the citadel still held out. Richard was in Acre when news came of Saladin's attack on Jaffa. Collecting what men he could in a hurry and commandeering some Genoese and Pisan galleys, the king set off down the coast. At dawn on 1st August, 1192, the garrison of the citadel had already opened negotiations for surrender, when Richard's little fleet appeared.

Jaffa is an awkward place to land but Richard was in a hurry. Without his armour, with his shield hung round his neck and a battle-axe in his hand, he jumped overboard and waded ashore. Driving the Muslims from the beach, he chased them through the streets which were swarming with Saladin's soldiers. Striking down the surprised Muslims right and left, he drove them out of the town. Then, joining hands with the garrison of the citadel, he swept out of the gates and attacked and captured Saladin's camp, the sultan being obliged to take to flight. "No man ever fought such a battle, not even Roland at Roncesvaux," sang Ambroise, the minstrel.

Richard said laughingly to the Muslim prisoners, "Saladin is a great sultan. Why did he run away? I did not come to fight. Look, I have no armour on, not even my boots." Saladin rallied his men at Yazoor and his spies soon reported to him that Richard had hardly any men at all and no horses. Four days later, Saladin returned with his army and attacked Jaffa at dawn on 5th August, 1192. Richard had formed up his little army of a few hundred men without horses. Kneeling on one knee behind their shields, with the butts of their lances stuck in the ground, they presented a solid hedge of points to the enemy. Behind the pikemen stood the cross-bowmen ready to shoot. In this solid formation, the Franks repulsed charge after charge. "The bravery of the Franks was such," says Baha al Deen, "that our men were discouraged."

When the Muslim attacks died out, Richard mounted a sorry horse which he had found and himself attacked the enemy, chasing all before him. This was indeed his finest hour. The Muslims stood in front of him at a respectful distance. If he advanced, they fled before him. When he stopped, they too stood and stared. "The King of England," writes Baha al Deen, "lance in hand, rode along the whole length of our army, and not one of our soldiers left the ranks to attack him." In the middle of the battle, a Mamlook had emerged from the Muslim ranks, leading a spare horse sent by Saladin[12] with a message to the effect that "it was not proper that the king should have to fight on so wretched a mount" and begging him to accept a better one. At length, stuck all over with arrows like a porcupine, Richard rode back to his own lines. The battle had lasted all day of 5th August. In the evening the Muslims withdrew to Yazoor and the next day to Latrun. In this epic battle, we do not know whether to admire more the heroic exploits of Richard or the extraordinary chivalry of Saladin. After the fighting the sultan sent the king a present of fresh fruit and cold drinks, chilled with the snows of Mount Hermon.

Peace was signed on 2nd and 3rd September, 1192. The Franks received the coast from north of Tyre to south of Jaffa. Asqalon was neutralized. Lydda and Ramla were divided in half between the Muslims and the Franks. Tripoli and Antioch were included in the same treaty. The agreement included a clause permitting the Christians freely to perform the pilgrimage to Jerusalem without obstruction or the payment of any dues or customs. On 9th October, 1192, Richard embarked for home with the greater part of the Crusaders.

* * *

When the Third Crusade set out, the Kingdom of Jerusalem had ceased to exist. Richard's Crusade, although he did not take Jerusalem, re-established the Frankish states so effectively that they were to last another hundred years. He also added to them the Kingdom of Cyprus. From the religious angle, arrangements had been made for freedom of Christian pilgrimage to Jerusalem. The West, moreover, benefited greatly from the continued existence of Outremer from which wealth, civilization and culture spread throughout Christendom. These material and cultural benefits were increased by Richard's establishment of friendly and courteous relations between Muslims and Christians.

It is remarkable how many Western historians still maintain the mental outlook of the twelfth century and agree that Richard's Crusade was a failure because he did not take Jerusalem. Grousset, in his great *Histoire des Croisades*, published in 1936, says that "the sole object of the

[12] It is curious that Baha al Deen, always anxious to recount Saladin's noble gestures, does not mention this affair. But Baha al Deen was not present at this battle.

Crusade was to take Jerusalem". As the native Franks pointed out at the time, even if it had been taken, they could not have held it once the Crusaders had re-embarked for the West.

NOTABLE DATES

Battle of Hattin	1187
Departure of Barbarossa's Crusade from Germany	May 1189
Arrival of Guy de Lusignan before Acre	28th August, 1189
Drowning of Frederick Barbarossa	10th June, 1190
Death of Sibylla, Queen of Jerusalem	October 1190
Marriage of Isabella, Queen of Jerusalem, to Conrad de Montferrat	24th November, 1190
Annexation of Cyprus by Richard	21st May, 1191
Surrender of Acre	11th July, 1191
Battle of Arsoof	7th September, 1191
First Advance to Latrun	December 1191
Assassination of Conrad de Montferrat Henry of Champagne becomes King of Jerusalem	28th April, 1192
Second Advance to Latrun	June 1192
Battle of Jaffa	1st–5th August, 1192
Signature of Peace	3rd September, 1192
Richard sails for home	9th October, 1192

PERSONALITIES

Muslims

Saladin

Al Aadil, his brother

Franks

Guy de Lusignan Conrad de Montferrat	Rival Kings of Jerusalem

Henry of Champagne, King of Jerusalem

Sibylla, Isabella, her sister	Queens of Jerusalem

Crusaders

Richard I, Coeur de Lion

Philippe Auguste, King of France

Duke of Burgundy, Commander of the French army after the departure of Philippe Auguste.

VII

The Queen of Cities

1200–1221

At the first view it should seem that the wealth of Constantinople was only transferred from one nation to another; and that the loss and sorrow of the Greeks is exactly balanced by the joy and advantage of the Latins. But in the miserable account of war, the gain is never equivalent to the loss, the pleasure to the pain.

GIBBON, *Decline and Fall of the Roman Empire*

Saladin was a very good Saracen, for he was large-minded and charitable, of a pitiful heart and of great kindness.

Gestes des Chiprois

A monarch whose majestic air
Fills all the range of sight, whose care
Fills all the regions everywhere;
Who such a watch doth keep
That, save where he doth set his lance
In rest to check the foe's advance,
His eye with bright and piercing glance
Knows neither rest nor sleep.

BAHA AL DEEN ZUHAIR, *Panegyric on Sultan Aadil*
Trans. by STANLEY LANE POOLE in *A History of Egypt in the Middle Ages*

VII

WE left the Byzantine Empire on the occasion of the death of Manuel Comnenus on 24th September, 1180. The brilliant emperor was succeeded by a son eleven years old, Alexius II Comnenus, under the guardianship of that lovely Marie of Antioch whom the poetic Greeks had compared to Helen and Aphrodite. Manuel had introduced many Latins[1] to Constantinople where their arrogance had made them hated. The popular resentment now broke out in riots against the regency of the Latin Empress Marie.

Andronicus Comnenus was a cousin of the late emperor. A man of brilliant parts but infamous morals, he had spent his life in wild and amorous adventures. Now, already sixty-three, he saw an opportunity to seize the throne. In 1182, he marched on the capital, demanding the dethronement of the child Alexius II and the relegation of Marie of Antioch to a convent. His revolt was the signal for a popular rising in Constantinople against the Franks, all such as failed to take refuge on Italian ships being mercilessly slaughtered. The papal legate was beheaded and his head tied to the tail of a dog, which was chased through the streets.

Andronicus Comnenus made his triumphal entry into Constantinople in September 1182. The lovely Marie of Antioch was strangled and the child Emperor Alexius II was murdered in his bed. Most of the senior officials were dismissed and replaced by creatures of Andronicus who, in September 1184, was crowned emperor in Santa Sophia. Possessed of a brilliant intellect, the new ruler introduced many useful administrative reforms. But he was also a man of sadistic cruelty. Posing as a friend of the common people, he embarked on a campaign of tortures and executions against the aristocracy.

Meanwhile the massacre of the Latins in Constantinople had not passed unnoticed. Resentment against Byzantium had been growing in the West ever since the First Crusade, ninety years before. The Normans of Sicily had always been especially hostile. On 11th June, 1185, an army sailed from Messina and landed at Durazzo. On 24th August, the Sicilians took Salonica and prepared to march on Constantinople.

Panic and revolt began to spread in the capital. Andronicus had ordered the arrest, among others, of a certain noble, Isaac Angelus. But Isaac killed the man sent to apprehend him and fled for sanctuary to Santa Sophia. The incident touched off a new rising. Andronicus

[1] West Europeans, called by the Muslims Franks, were named Latins by the Greeks.

fled but was arrested, subjected to the most atrocious tortures and eventually torn to pieces by the mob after sufferings too horrible to describe. On 12th September, 1185, Isaac Angelus was proclaimed emperor. It was at this time that Isaac Comnenus declared himself the independent ruler of Cyprus, a position from which he was evicted by Richard I of England. Isaac Angelus was successful in driving out the Norman Sicilian invaders. But he had become emperor by a pure coincidence, possessing no qualifications and being himself stupid, vulgar and lazy. Seeing the empire in confusion, the Serbs, Bulgars and Wallachians invaded Thrace in 1187, the year of Hattin.

In 1190, the march of the Emperor Frederick Barbarossa across Byzantine territory nearly caused the fall of Isaac. Barbarossa, openly hostile, encouraged the Serbs and the Bulgars, while Isaac, as already related in the previous chapter, concluded a treaty with Saladin. The angry Barbarossa wrote to his son Henry, soon to be the Emperor Henry VI, to prepare for war against Byzantium. In April 1195, however, Alexius Angelus, the brother of Isaac, led a military *coup d'état* in which the emperor was overthrown, imprisoned and blinded by his heartless brother.

Alexius III Angelus was even more incompetent than his brother Isaac. Disorders broke out everywhere and the Seljuq Sultan of Iconium captured several Byzantine places in Asia Minor. Both Venice and

THE COMNENI

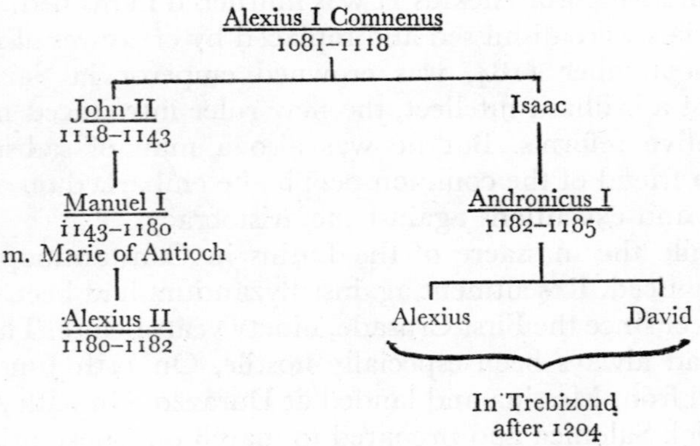

THE ANGELI

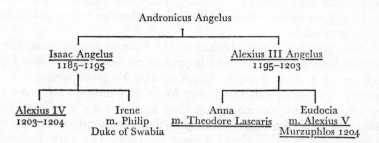

- Andronicus Angelus
  - Isaac Angelus, 1185–1195
    - Alexius IV, 1203–1204
    - Irene, m. Philip, Duke of Swabia
  - Alexius III Angelus, 1195–1203
    - Anna, m. Theodore Lascaris
    - Eudocia, m. Alexius V Murzuphlos 1204

THE HOHENSTAUFENS

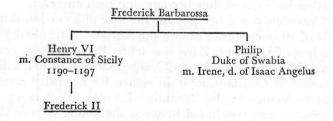

- Frederick Barbarossa
  - Henry VI, m. Constance of Sicily, 1190–1197
    - Frederick II
  - Philip, Duke of Swabia, m. Irene, d. of Isaac Angelus

Genoa were hostile as was also Emperor Henry VI, the son of Barbarossa, who was contemplating the conquest of Constantinople and the proclamation of himself as sole Roman Emperor—the old dream. His marriage to Constance, the heiress of the Norman throne of Sicily, had already made him ruler of Germany, Italy and Sicily. On 28th September, 1197, however, Henry VI died at Messina when preparing to lead a new crusade.

On 8th January, 1198, Innocent III became pope, took Henry's infant son Frederick II under his protection and gave orders for the preaching of a new crusade. None of the kings of western Europe answered Innocent's call but many lords and knights took the cross. They assembled at Venice where they agreed with the Doge Enrico Dandolo for Venetian ships to transport them to Egypt, according to the plan propounded by Richard Coeur de Lion. On 14th September, Boniface de Montferrat was elected to command the expedition.

At this stage, various rivalries began to appear. Europe was divided by the contest for power between the papacy and the Hohenstaufen Emperors. Innocent III was supporting Otto IV of Brunswick, a Guelph,[2] as a candidate to the empire, in opposition to the Hohenstaufens. In September 1202, Philip of Swabia, the Hohenstaufen claimant, arrived in Venice. Philip was the brother of the Emperor Henry VI, who had just died. He had married Irene, the daughter of Isaac Angelus, and Isaac's young son Alexius, escaping from Constantinople when his father was dethroned, had taken refuge with his sister and now arrived in Venice with his brother-in-law, Philip of Swabia. Boniface de Montferrat was a supporter of the Hohenstaufens and Philip of Swabia suggested to him that the crusade, on its way to Egypt, call in at Constantinople and place his brother-in-law on the throne.

The Fourth Crusade had become the plaything of politics. The pope wished it to attack Egypt. Philip of Swabia, the enemy of the papacy, wished to use it to instal his brother-in-law in Constantinople. If Philip were then elected German Emperor, he could claim suzerainty over his young brother-in-law and thus become universal emperor.

As the Crusaders could not pay for the hire of Venetian ships, they agreed first of all to capture Zara on the Adriatic, a revolted Venetian colony, in lieu of payment. Zara was taken by assault on 12th November, 1202. Meanwhile the Doge of Venice had agreed to the diversion of the Crusade to Constantinople in return for extensive commercial concessions to Venice in the Byzantine Empire. In January 1203, a secret agreement was concluded between the young Alexius Angelus, the Doge of Venice and Boniface de Montferrat.

2 The supporters of the Hohenstaufens were called Ghibellines, those of their rivals, Guelphs.

On 23rd June, 1203, the fleet appeared off Constantinople. On 17th July, Alexius III Angelus fled and on 1st August the blind Isaac Angelus re-ascended the throne in association with his son Alexius IV. The city was once again thronged with Latins in spite of the resentment of the Greeks. On 5th February, 1204, Alexius Ducas, nicknamed Murzuphlos, a son-in-law of Alexius III, led a revolt, Isaac Angelus was thrown back into prison, Alexius IV, the brother-in-law of Philip of Swabia, was strangled, all Latins were driven from the city and Murzuphlos assumed the title of Alexius V.

The Crusaders and the Venetians found themselves ignominiously ejected from the city—their plan for maintaining a puppet emperor on the throne had miscarried. They were obliged either to go home or to fight. In March 1204, the Doge of Venice, who was still with the Crusade, signed a treaty with the Crusaders, according to which the city and its plunder, and indeed the whole Byzantine Empire, was to be divided between them. A committee of six Crusaders and six Venetians would elect an emperor.

For nearly nine centuries, the mighty walls of Constantinople had withstood every assault, the undaunted defender of Christendom against the Muslims. On 9th April, 1204, the Crusaders launched their attack on the walls. On the 12th, the city was carried. "To the sound of trumpets and waving their drawn swords," writes the contemporary Byzantine historian Nicetas, "the Latins began to plunder the houses and the churches. I do not know how to tell of the iniquities committed by these scoundrels. . . . They smashed the altar of Santa Sophia and divided the fragments between them. They violated all the women, particularly those most worthy of respect. . . . The whole city was nothing but despair, tears, crying and groans."

Before its sack, Villehardouin had recorded his impressions of Constantinople. "The Crusaders," he writes, "could never have believed that so rich a city could exist in the whole world until they saw these sumptuous palaces and these great churches and the length and breadth of this city, the Queen of the World." Constantinople had been indeed the Queen of Cities, the inviolate imperial capital, repulsing every greedy attacker. Not only the wealth but the art, the treasures, the buildings, the learning and the culture of nine centuries lay stored behind those walls. The destruction of so much which would have been of priceless value to humanity has been called the greatest crime in history. Our next chapter will show that such a phrase is an exaggeration—there is much worse to come—but it was nevertheless a disastrous tragedy.

On 9th May, 1204, Baldwin, Count of Flanders, was proclaimed the first Latin Emperor of Constantinople. Three eighths of the city and the empire, including the most valuable islands and harbours, were annexed by Venice, whose merchants henceforward enjoyed a virtual monopoly to the detriment of her rivals, Genoa and Pisa. The Venetian podestá, or proconsul, in Constantinople held court like an emperor.

Baldwin, who had neither the money nor the administrative staff to rule an empire, was obliged to distribute his territory in fiefs. Boniface de Montferrat obtained Macedonia with his capital at Salonica, where he had himself crowned king. The empire was then divided into a patchwork of fiefs between the Venetians and the Franks. The situation remained chaotic, for many Greek nobles profited by the confusion to carve out independent principalities for themselves.

Meanwhile Theodore Lascaris, who, like Murzuphlos, was also a son-in-law of Alexius III, provided a rallying-point for the Greeks by setting up a new Byzantine capital at Nicaea, only sixty miles from Constantinople. Further east, Alexius and David Comnenus, descendants of Andronicus Comnenus, established another Greek Empire at Trebizond, with its territory extending from Sinope to Georgia. Protected on the south by ranges of mountains, Trebizond was long to remain an island of Greek culture and language in an often hostile Asia.

In 1204, the Byzantine Empire seemed to have been destroyed for ever. In fact, however, it was to rise Phoenix-like from its ashes and to endure with patient pertinacity for another two hundred years.

* * *

In November 1192, after signing peace with the Franks, Saladin made a state entry into Damascus. According to Ibn al Athir, he was considering a campaign to add Persia to his empire, though he wished first to re-visit Egypt and make the pilgrimage to Mecca. But man proposes in vain when God disposes. On 3rd March, 1193, he died in Damascus after an illness of only twelve days. He was fifty-seven years old and had ruled for twenty-two years since the death of Aadhid, the last Fatimid Khalif.

Saladin had been greatly loved by his subjects. He had been entirely devoid of arrogance and was very close to the common people. Although courageous in battle, he was not a conspicuously great soldier. He owed his success to the magnetism of his own personality and to his patient and conciliatory policy rather than to his military victories. He was chivalrous, dignified, generous, compassionate, sincerely religious and never broke his pledged word. Yet he could be brutal and ruthless, particularly in his early life. He had murdered Shawar in Egypt and had killed Renaud de Châtillon when a disarmed prisoner. On several occasions he had ordered the execution of all Frankish

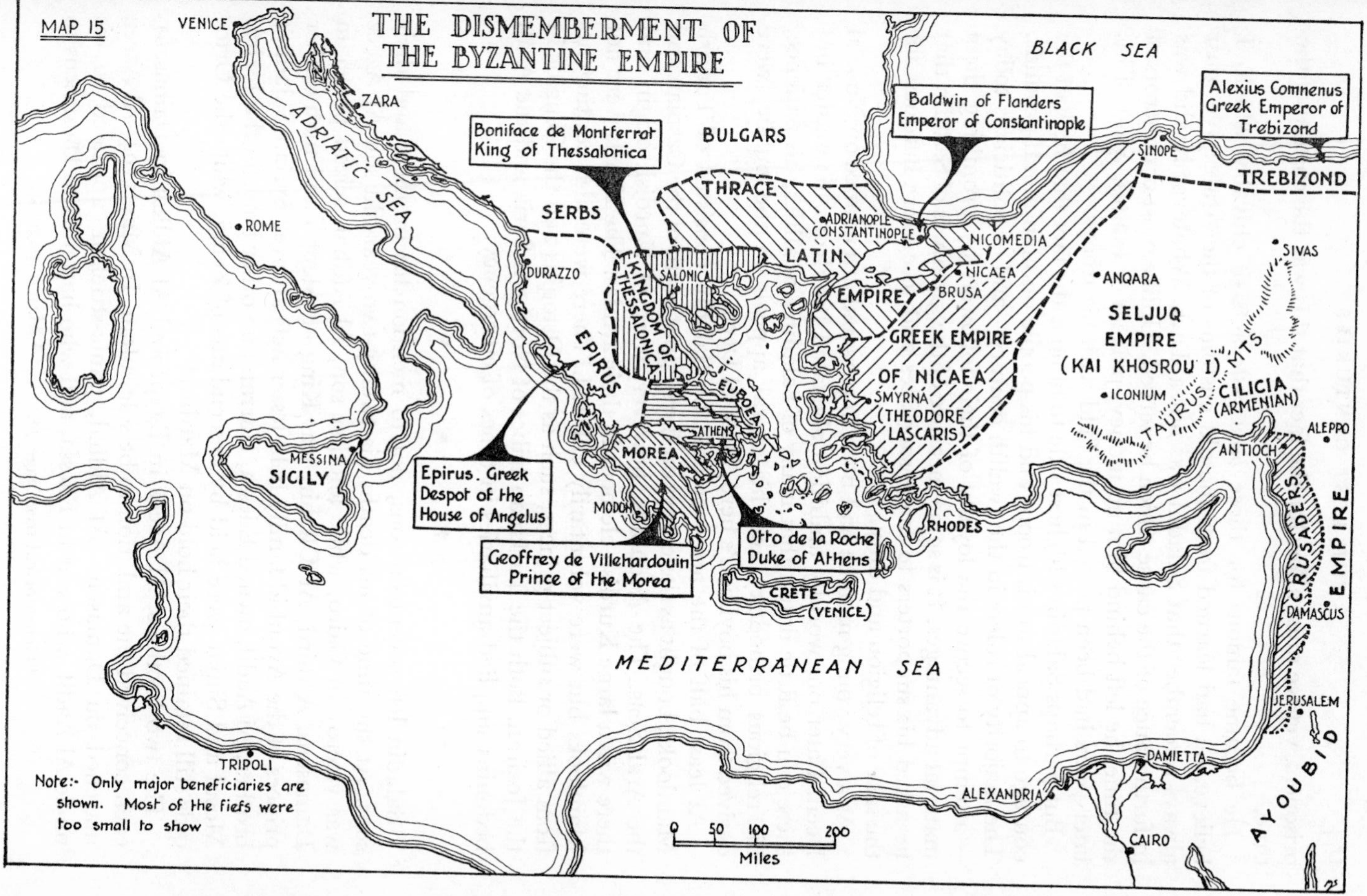
MAP 15
THE DISMEMBERMENT OF
THE BYZANTINE EMPIRE
VENICE
ZARA
ADRIATIC SEA
ROME
BLACK SEA
Baldwin of Flanders
Emperor of Constantinople
Alexius Comnenus
Greek Emperor of
Trebizond
Boniface de Montferrat
King of Thessalonica
BULGARS
SINOPE
TREBIZOND
THRACE
SERBS
ADRIANOPLE
CONSTANTINOPLE
NICOMEDIA
LATIN
EMPIRE
NICAEA
BRUSA
SIVAS
ANQARA
DURAZZO
SALONICA
KINGDOM OF THESSALONICA
SELJUQ
EMPIRE
(KAI KHOSROU I)
GREEK EMPIRE
OF NICAEA
EPIRUS
EUBOEA
SMYRNA
(THEODORE
LASCARIS)
ICONIUM
TAURUS MTS
CILICIA
(ARMENIAN)
ALEPPO
ATHENS
MOREA
ANTIOCH
MESSINA
SICILY
Epirus. Greek
Despot of the
House of Angelus
MODON
RHODES
CRUSADERS
Otto de la Roche
Duke of Athens
Geoffrey de Villehardouin
Prince of the Morea
CRETE
(VENICE)
EMPIRE
DAMASCUS
MEDITERRANEAN SEA
JERUSALEM
AYOUBID
DAMIETTA
TRIPOLI
ALEXANDRIA
Note:- Only major beneficiaries are
shown. Most of the fiefs were
too small to show
0 50 100 200
Miles
CAIRO

prisoners, yet we must allow for the fact that this was the custom of the time.

He became famous for those *beau geste* acts of chivalry which, I believe, he had learned from the old customs of the Arabs. We must always remember that Saladin was not a Turk. Whatever he did was in furtherance of the cause which he served. Unlike most conquerors of the time, he left behind him no money, palaces or estates. Most of his later years had been passed in the field with his troops.

But perhaps Saladin's highest title to fame is the fact that he had the courage to appeal to his troops and his people on high moral grounds. The majority of rulers in the twelfth century—and of politicians today—attempt to secure the loyalty of their followers by promising them material advantages. It is some measure of the greatness of Saladin that he asked his supporters to make sacrifices and to endure hardness for the sake of religion and duty.

As a very young man he had been in personal attendance on Noor al Deen. Later on, worldly ambition alienated him from his master but there can be little doubt that many of Saladin's qualities, his patience, his religious orthodoxy and his moral appeals to the public, were derived from his boyhood's hero, Noor al Deen.

At least half of the army created by Saladin consisted of Turkish Mamlooks, bought as slave boys on the steppes north of the Caspian and the Aral Seas. The Ayoubids, however, were of Kurdish origin and there was a large Kurdish element in their armies. The Kurds were not Mamlooks but were voluntarily enlisted. There were also contingents from allied or subject princes, such as the Ortoqids and the Zengids in the Jezirah. Both the Turkman tribes of Northern Syria and the Arab bedouins supplied auxiliaries in times of emergency.

* * *

Saladin left seventeen sons, not to mention his brothers and their sons. At the time of his death, his twenty-two-year-old son Al Azeez was viceroy in Cairo, while another son, Al Afdhal, seized power in Damascus. A third, Al Dhahir, was King of Aleppo and many other princes of the Ayoubid family held lesser fiefs all over Syria.[3] Saladin's brother, Al Aadil, owned Edessa, Harran and other lands in the Jezira. Mosul and Sinjar were held by descendants of Zengi, while the Ortoqids still retained their hold on Mardin.[4]

The two brothers, Al Azeez in Egypt and Al Afdhal in Damascus, each conceived the ambition to be sole sultan. In May 1194, Al Azeez marched on Damascus. Al Afdhal, panic-stricken, appealed to his uncle Al Aadil, who was in Edessa, and who hastened to Damascus to

[3] Genealogical tree, page 72. [4] Map 9, page 84.

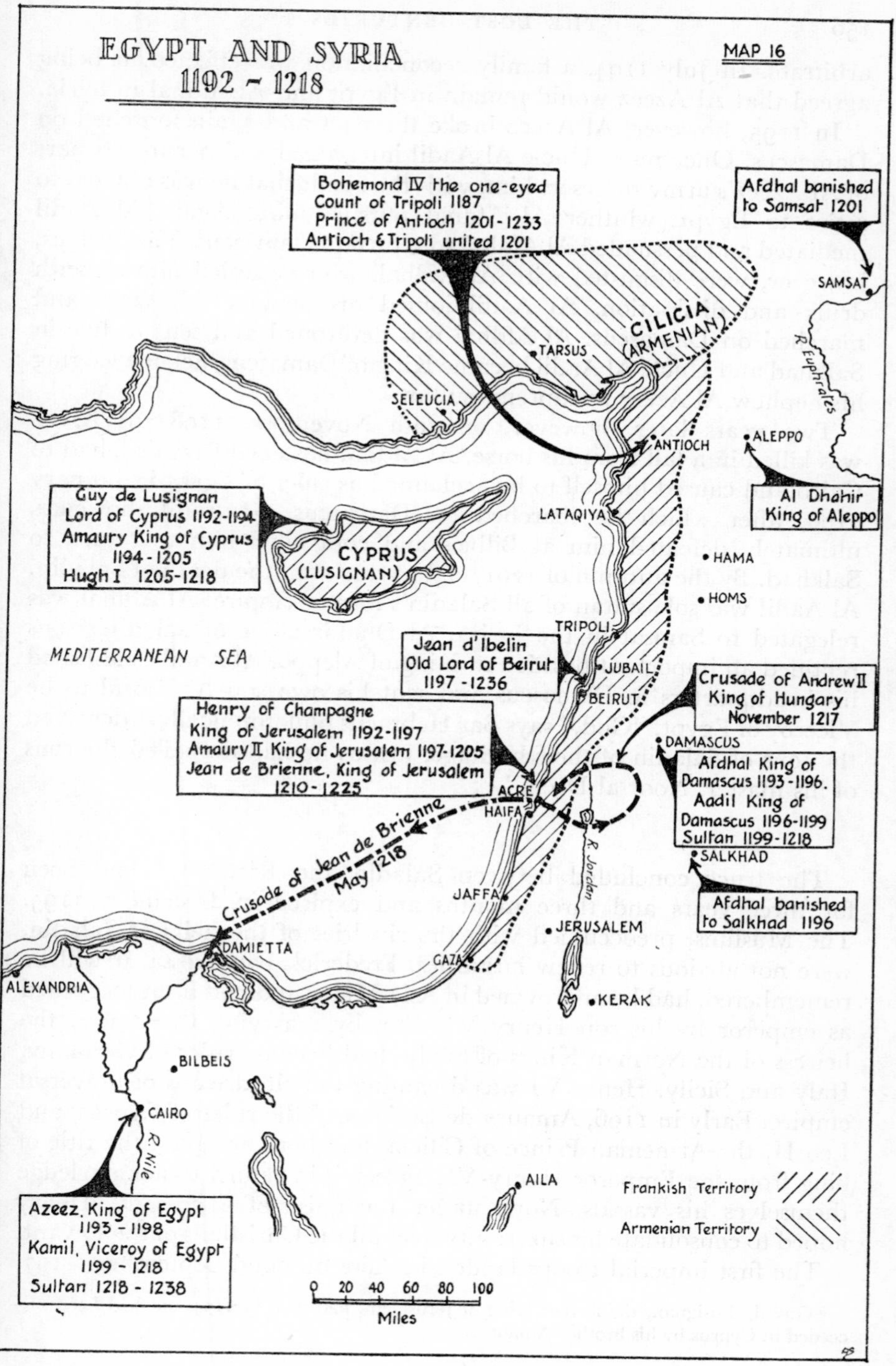

EGYPT AND SYRIA
1192 – 1218
MAP 16
Bohemond IV the one-eyed
Count of Tripoli 1187
Prince of Antioch 1201-1233
Antioch & Tripoli united 1201
Afdhal banished
to Samsat 1201
SAMSAT
CILICIA
(ARMENIAN)
TARSUS
SELEUCIA
R. Euphrates
ANTIOCH
ALEPPO
Al Dhahir
King of Aleppo
Guy de Lusignan
Lord of Cyprus 1192-1194
Amaury King of Cyprus
1194-1205
Hugh I 1205-1218
CYPRUS
(LUSIGNAN)
LATAQIYA
HAMA
HOMS
TRIPOLI
MEDITERRANEAN SEA
Jean d'Ibelin
Old Lord of Beirut
1197-1236
JUBAIL
BEIRUT
Crusade of Andrew II
King of Hungary
November 1217
Henry of Champagne
King of Jerusalem 1192-1197
Amaury II King of Jerusalem 1197-1205
Jean de Brienne, King of Jerusalem
1210-1225
DAMASCUS
Afdhal King of
Damascus 1193-1196.
Aadil King of
Damascus 1196-1199
Sultan 1199-1218
ACRE
HAIFA
Crusade of Jean de Brienne
May 1218
R. Jordan
SALKHAD
Afdhal banished
to Salkhad 1196
JAFFA
JERUSALEM
DAMIETTA
GAZA
KERAK
ALEXANDRIA
BILBEIS
CAIRO
R. Nile
AILA
Frankish Territory
Armenian Territory
Azeez, King of Egypt
1193-1198
Kamil, Viceroy of Egypt
1199-1218
Sultan 1218-1238
0 20 40 60 80 100
Miles

arbitrate. In July 1194, a family reconciliation was effected, it being agreed that Al Azeez would remain in Egypt and Al Afdhal in Syria.

In 1195, however, Al Azeez broke the pact and again marched on Damascus. Once more Uncle Al Aadil intervened and persuaded part of Al Azeez's army to desert him, with the result that he was obliged to retire to Egypt, whither Al Afdhal pursued him. Again Al Aadil mediated and persuaded Al Afdhal to return to Damascus. The Syrians, however, were disgusted with Al Afdhal, who occupied himself with drink and dissipation. Al Aadil joined his nephew Al Azeez and marched on Damascus. Al Afdhal was dethroned and sent to live in Salkhad and Uncle Al Aadil became King of Damascus, acknowledging his nephew Al Azeez as supreme sultan.

Two years later, however, on 29th November, 1198, Al Azeez was killed in a fall from his horse. Al Afdhal hastened from Salkhad to Cairo and caused himself to be acclaimed as ruler of Egypt in January 1199, after which he marched on Damascus. Al Aadil, however, ultimately defeated him at Bilbeis and compelled him to return to Salkhad. By the autumn of 1201, eight years after the death of Saladin, Al Aadil was sole sultan of all Saladin's former empire. Al Afdhal was relegated to Samsat in the Jezira. Al Dhahir alone of Saladin's sons retained an important position as King of Aleppo. Al Aadil established his headquarters in Damascus and sent his own son Al Kamil to be Viceroy of Egypt. "God," says Bar Hebraeus philosophically, "deprived the sons of Saladin of their heritage, just as he had despoiled the sons of his master, Noor al Deen."

* * *

The truce concluded between Saladin and Richard I had been for three years and three months and expired in December 1195. The Muslims, preoccupied with the rivalries of the heirs of Saladin, were not anxious to renew hostilities. Frederick Barbarossa, it will be remembered, had been drowned in Asia Minor and had been succeeded as emperor by his son Henry VI who, by marrying Constance, the heiress of the Norman Kings of Sicily, had become ruler of Germany, Italy and Sicily. Henry VI was dreaming the old dreams of universal empire. Early in 1196, Amaury de Lusignan,[5] the ruler of Cyprus, and Leo II, the Armenian Prince of Cilicia, had both accepted the title of king from the Emperor Henry VI, agreeing in return to acknowledge themselves his vassals. Now, under the guise of a crusade, Henry hoped to consolidate his suzerainty over all the Christians of the Levant.

The first imperial troops landed in Acre on 22nd September, 1197,

[5] Guy de Lusignan, the former King of Jerusalem, had died in 1194 and had been succeeded in Cyprus by his brother Amaury.

and, without even informing the King of Jerusalem, broke the truce by a raid into Muslim territory. Al Aadil, who, as we have seen, was now King of Damascus though not yet sole sultan, retaliated with a quick move in which he captured Jaffa. A few days later, the King of Jerusalem, Henry of Champagne, was killed by a fall from a balcony in Acre. With a new war commencing, the Kingdom of Jerusalem was again without a king.

Isabella, the daughter of Amaury I, although still only twenty-six years old, was fated to be the instrument used to appoint successive Kings of Jerusalem. Married to the middle-aged Conrad de Montferrat to enable him to be crowned, her hand had then been the means of conveying the kingdom to Henry of Champagne. Amaury de Lusignan, the new King of Cyprus, was now judged the best man available and Isabella was accordingly married to him.[6] Crossing to Acre, he inaugurated his reign by the capture of Beirut. Jean d'Ibelin, later to be known as the "Old Lord of Beirut", was given the fief. These were but preliminary skirmishes in anticipation of the arrival of the Emperor Henry VI and his crusading army. Early in 1198, however, news came of the emperor's death. The imperial troops re-embarked for Italy and the anticipated crusade petered out.

King Amaury II of Jerusalem and Cyprus hastened to re-open negotiations with Al Aadil and a new treaty was signed on 1st July, 1198. It was similar to that concluded between Saladin and Richard except that Al Aadil recognized the Frankish acquisition of Beirut and Jubail, a notable gain which once more joined the Kingdom of Jerusalem to the County of Tripoli. In November 1198, owing to the accidental death of Al Azeez the son of Saladin in Egypt, Al Aadil had become sole sultan of Egypt and Syria. He and Amaury II were both moderate and experienced men and did all in their power to restrain the hotheads of both sides.

* * *

Raymond III of Tripoli, who had given such sage advice to Guy de Lusignan before Hattin, died in the autumn of 1187, a few months after that battle, leaving no heir. He had consequently bequeathed his County of Tripoli to Bohemond IV, the second son of Bohemond III, Prince of Antioch.[7] Raymond of Antioch, the eldest son of Bohemond III, died before his father. He had been married to Alice, the daughter of Roupin III, Armenian Prince of Cilicia, and had left by her a young son called Raymond-Roupin.

On the death of Bohemond III in 1201, Raymond-Roupin was the legal heir but his uncle Bohemond IV seized the throne of Antioch.

[6] Genealogical tree, page 60. [7] Genealogical tree, pages 40 and 41.

The Armenians supported Raymond-Roupin, the Franks declared for Bohemond IV and a long civil war began involving Tripoli, Antioch and Cilicia. Bohemond IV, known as the One-Eyed, held Antioch from 1201 to 1216. On 14th February, 1216, however, when Bohemond was away in Tripoli, Raymond-Roupin was crowned Prince of Antioch in the cathedral of the city, and Bohemond was left with only Tripoli. The Templars had been supporters of Bohemond, with the result that the Hospitallers gave their allegiance to Raymond-Roupin. But the latter failed eventually to please either the Franks or the Armenians, and three years later in 1219, Bohemond the One-Eyed regained Antioch, while Raymond-Roupin was obliged to escape by night and gallop *ventre à terre* for Cilicia.

The effect of these parochial disputes was to leave the Kingdom of Jerusalem to defend itself alone, unaided by the contingents of Tripoli, Antioch or Armenian Cilicia. Bohemond the One-Eyed retained the thrones of Antioch and Tripoli until his death in 1233 but there was little or no co-operation between him and the Kingdoms of Jerusalem or Cyprus.

* * *

Before passing on to the narrative of the Fifth Crusade, a short digression may be made to describe the army created by the Ayoubids, which was to dominate the Levant for the ensuing three centuries. In 1200, when Al Aadil had become sole sultan, the Ayoubid army consisted almost entirely of foreigners. Virtually no Egyptians or Syrians were recruited as combatant troops, but they filled most of the administrative posts and also supplied the qadhis and imams, the equivalent of our army chaplains. In general, however, regular combatant units were recruited from Mamlooks or soldier-slaves from the nomadic horse-tribes of the steppes. It was not essential for them to belong to any given tribe or race and, later on, Mongols from farther east were accepted. When purchased, the boys were heathen but they were obliged to profess Islam when they were engaged.

Words are often inadequate to express the ideas of an age other than our own and "Mamlook" is a case in point. The word slaves conveys to us a picture of unwilling victims, chained together in gangs beneath the supervisor's whip. But the word Mamlook was not used for African or other domestic slaves, who were known as abeed or ghulman. It is obvious, moreover, that tens of thousands of young men of the most warlike races on earth could not have been controlled, if they had not themselves wished to serve. In fact, military service in the armies of Egypt or Syria must have offered a dazzling career to the boys of the primitive nomadic tribes. Every Mamlook had a marshal's baton in his knapsack, perhaps even the sceptre of a sultan. There were no distinctions of class or race and many Mamlooks rose to be powerful and wealthy ameers. Perhaps the slave merchant who visited the steppes was looked upon as little more than a travel agent who conveyed his young charges from the bleak and arid plains of the north to the warmth, the wealth and the luxury of Syria and Egypt.

Mamlooks imported as boys were subjected to a long and rigorous training and every effort was made to ensure that their whole lives would be devoted to their military service. The system was indeed largely based on comradeship, the spirit which above all else makes tolerable the lives of soldiers and enables them to bear their hardships and dangers. The morale of the Mamlook regiments was extremely high and doubtless the vast majority of the boys were soon fired by enthusiasm for their units. As soon as they had qualified as trained soldiers, they were legally freed, so that the status of slaves was in practice only a manner of enforcing rigid discipline during the years of training.

The freed Mamlook, however, was bound to continue to serve his master and was known by his name or title. In fact, Mamlooks appear to have nearly always been loyal to their owners and frequently died to defend them. The disadvantage of the system was that this loyalty was to the master alone and not to the state. If an ameer rebelled, his Mamlooks rebelled with him. If his master died, the Mamlook was not bound in loyalty to his successor. In the event of war or emergency, the sultan not only commanded his own Mamlooks but called upon the other Ayoubid princes to join him, each with his private Mamlooks.

This military system seems to us so extraordinary and so confusing that we can scarcely believe that it ever existed. Yet in fact, this organization produced, for some two centuries, the finest army in the world and made Egypt a great power, though the Egyptians were not eligible to serve in their own armed forces.

* * *

King Amaury II and Sultan Al Aadil maintained peace on the frontier, though not without difficulty, and concluded a new five-year truce in September 1204. Unfortunately Amaury II died on 1st April, 1205. Unlike his weak brother Guy, Amaury de Lusignan had governed with firmness and prudence and had succeeded in maintaining his authority alike over the barons of Outremer and the bellicose crusaders from the West. With his death, the crowns of Cyprus and Jerusalem were again separated.

By his first marriage with a woman of the Ibelin family Amaury had a son, now ten years old, who became King of Cyprus as Hugh I.[8]

[8] Genealogical tree, page 204.

Amaury's second wife Isabella, Queen of Jerusalem, died soon after him, leaving a thirteen-year-old daughter Marie, whom she had had by Conrad of Montferrat. This young girl now became Queen of Jerusalem. Jean d'Ibelin, "The Old Lord of Beirut", a veteran knight as wise as he was brave and courteous, was chosen as regent.

In 1208, Marie would reach the age of seventeen and it would be necessary to find for her a husband who would be an efficient King of Jerusalem. A deputation was sent for this purpose to Philippe Auguste, King of France, who selected Jean de Brienne, an impecunious member of a noble family of Champagne, already sixty years old.[9] He landed at Acre on 13th September, 1210, and was married the next day to his young bride.

The Templars, the same rash hotheads as at Hattin, had meanwhile succeeded in terminating the truce, but Jean de Brienne was able to renew it from 1212 to 1217. Whether or not the young Marie was pleased with her sexagenarian husband history has not troubled to relate, but Jean soon proved himself a wise and capable king. Marie died in childbirth in 1212, after giving birth to a girl who was christened Isabella, but is more generally known as Yolanda.

At the Lateran Council on 11th November, 1215, the great Pope Innocent III expressed his unshakeable resolve to send out another crusade. Though he died on 16th January, 1216, the first volunteers of the new Crusade began to disembark at Acre in September 1217. Soon afterwards arrived Andrew II, King of Hungary, who, indifferent to the views of Jean de Brienne, set out immediately to fight the infidels. The Crusaders crossed the Jordan on 10th November, 1217, and advanced on Damascus. Turning back westwards from a point thirty miles south of the city, they recrossed the Jordan north of the Sea of Galilee and returned to Acre laden with plunder. Soon after completing this useless border foray, the King of Hungary returned to Europe.

Meanwhile, however, fresh Crusaders were still arriving. Haphazard raids into Syria were obviously of no value but the Christians enjoyed the great advantage that the Italian navies held complete command of the sea. Jean de Brienne decided to invade Egypt, the plan proposed by Richard I. The fleet sailed on 24th May, 1218, from Acre and two days later entered the Nile opposite Damietta. Jean de Brienne was unanimously accepted as sole commander.

The Muslims had blocked the entrance of the Nile by a chain stretched across the river, one end of which was in Damietta, while the other was covered by a fort on an island close to the west bank. Al Kamil, the Viceroy of Egypt, Al Aadil's eldest son, arrived with the

[9] Genealogical tree, page 203.

army of Egypt and camped a short way upstream of Damietta at Adliya.

On 24th August, 1218, after three months of siege operations, the Franks took the fort on the west bank and were able to cut the chain, but Al Kamil immediately closed the Nile again by sinking a number of ships in the fairway. The Franks retaliated by redigging an old canal and diverting the Nile. We are inclined to picture the Crusades in terms of knights charging in shining armour. The facts were different. The siege of Acre had involved two years of trench warfare, disease, flies and hunger amid the stench of unburied corpses. The campaign of Jean de Brienne against Damietta was to result in three years of similar operations, consisting largely of digging in water-logged soil beneath the scorching Egyptian sun.

Meanwhile, on 31st August, 1218, the old Sultan Al Aadil had died in Damascus at the age of seventy-six. While he lacked something of the magnetism of his brother Saladin, he had been an equally patient statesman, tolerant, wise and generous. A personal friend of Richard I, he had tried to preserve peace with the Franks although ready to strike back when any of them rashly attempted to renew hostilities. By his wisdom and patience, he had kept the empire in peace and prosperity for eighteen years. He was succeeded by his son Al Kamil, who was in the Muslim camp outside Damietta.

Jean de Brienne had at first been the universally obeyed commander but, in September 1218, the papal legate, Cardinal Pelagius, arrived and immediately demanded to be recognized as commander-in-chief.

Heavy fighting developed on 9th October, 1218. Al Kamil, throwing a bridge over the Nile opposite Adliya, attacked the Frankish camp, which was strongly entrenched. A force of infantry described as "Arabs", the exact nature of which is not known, actually carried the trenches and broke into the camp. But they were hemmed in with their backs to the river by a Frankish counter-attack and almost exterminated.

On 4th February, 1219, Al Kamil discovered a plot in his own army to dethrone him. As a result, he withdrew in some confusion to Ashmoon, thirty miles south-west of Damietta and the Franks were able to occupy Adliya unopposed. A few days later, Al Muadhdham, Kamil's brother, arrived with loyal reinforcements from Syria and the mutiny was suppressed. The Muslims returned and camped at Fariskoor. The Franks were now able to attack the walls of Damietta by land from their camp on the east bank but they themselves were besieged between Kamil and Damietta as the Third Crusade had been between Saladin and Acre.

Al Kamil and Al Muadhdham, however, were still torn by anxieties, not only regarding the operations before Damietta but concerning the

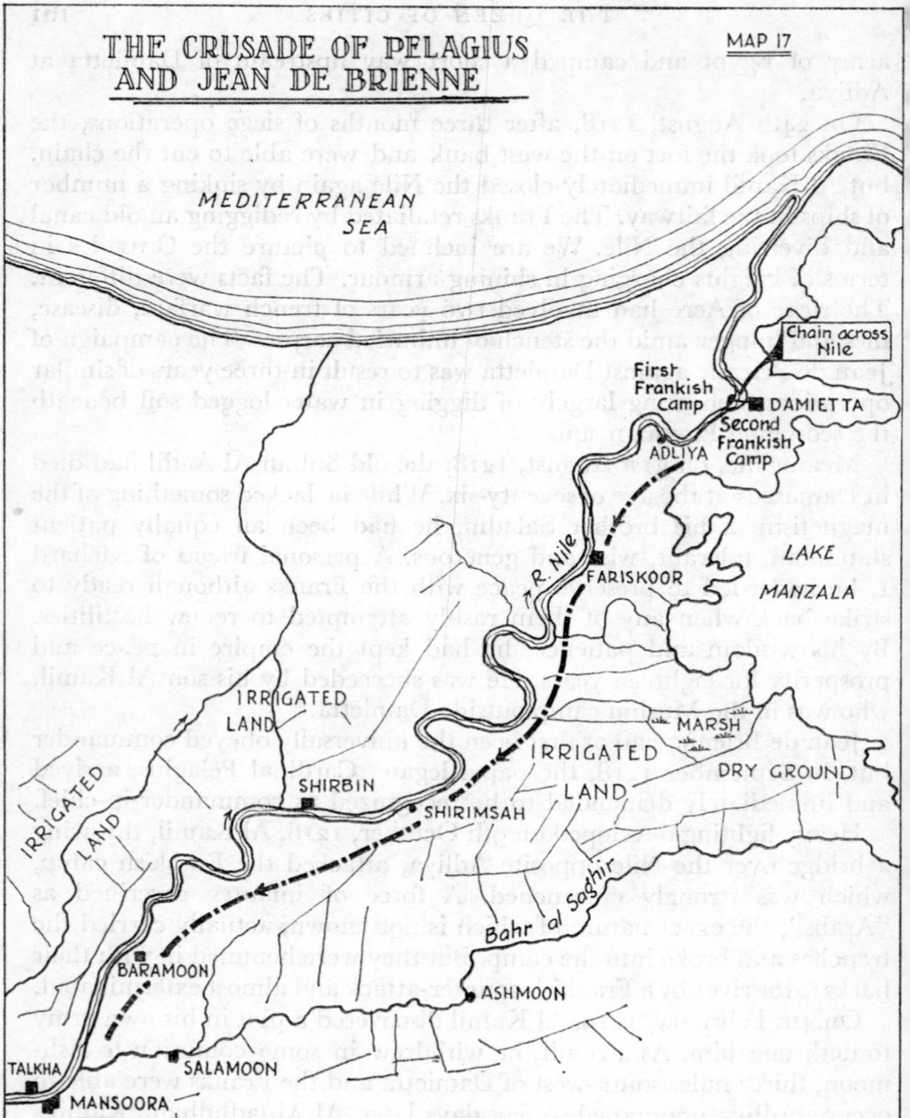
THE CRUSADE OF PELAGIUS AND JEAN DE BRIENNE
MAP 17
MEDITERRANEAN SEA
Chain across Nile
First Frankish Camp
DAMIETTA
Second Frankish Camp
ADLIYA
R. Nile
FARISKOOR
LAKE MANZALA
IRRIGATED LAND
MARSH
IRRIGATED LAND
DRY GROUND
IRRIGATED LAND
SHIRBIN
SHIRIMSAH
Bahr al Saghir
BARAMOON
ASHMOON
TALKHA
SALAMOON
MANSOORA
Kamil's Camp
FRANKISH ADVANCE
0 1 2 3 4 5 10
Miles

fate of the whole empire. The Seljuq sultan of Iconium, Kai Kaus I,[10] had been threatening Aleppo. In the Jezira, Al Ashraf, the brother of Al Kamil and Al Muadhdham, was assuming increasing independence. As a result, in February 1219, Al Kamil decided to open negotiations. He offered to cede the Kingdom of Jerusalem as it had been before Hattin but excluding Trans-Jordan, in return for the evacuation of Egypt. Meanwhile Al Muadhdham, as a corollary, gave orders, in March 1219, for the destruction of the walls of Jerusalem, so that, if the Franks reoccupied it, they would be unable to defend it. A panic among the Muslims of Jerusalem ensued, many fleeing from the city to Damascus or to Kerak.

Jean de Brienne and the Franks of Outremer suddenly found complete victory within their grasp. Incredible as it may appear, the papal legate, Cardinal Pelagius, a hard, arrogant and fanatical Spaniard, categorically rejected the offer. Moreover, the Templars and the Hospitallers, who owed allegiance to the pope alone, supported the cardinal's stand. It is true that, had the terms been accepted, the Franks might not have had the men or the money to defend the kingdom but such considerations should have been discussed before beginning the Crusade. The ostensible object had been to recover Jerusalem, but when it was offered to the Crusaders, they refused it.

On 29th August, 1219, a virtual mutiny broke out in the Frankish camp. The infantry, worn out by the endless toils of trench warfare which always fall to their lot, demanded to be led to a general attack on the sultan's camp at Fariskoor. The Templars, rash as ever, took the lead, Jean de Brienne and the native barons protesting in vain. The infantry and the Templars set out of their own accord and, indeed, at first succeeded in driving back the Muslims. But the enemy returned to the attack, the infantry fell into disorder and Pelagius tried in vain to take command. The infantry were saved from extermination by Jean de Brienne, who checked the pursuing Muslims till the fugitives were back in camp.

Hoping that this disaster would have changed the Frankish attitude, Al Kamil repeated his offer of the cession of the Kingdom of Jerusalem but his delegates were received by the cardinal who rejected all negotiation and warned them not to return.

The modern reader may be surprised at the power of the papal legate but it may be remembered that, ever since the First Crusade, it was the popes who had organized every reinforcement for Outremer. Quite apart from religious scruples, to alienate the pope might well appear impolitic. In September 1219, an English contingent reached the camp, including William Long-Sword, Earl of Salisbury, Rudolf,

[10] Genealogical tree, page 168.

Earl of Chester, William of Arundel and Sussex, and also a fresh French party. Then, at last, after an eighteen-months siege, Damietta was captured on 5th November, 1219. Kamil fell back thirty miles to Talkha and Mansoora.

The Franks were in a strong position in Damietta from which, having command of the sea, they could not be dislodged. This success, however, only made Pelagius more intransigent. On 29th March, 1220, Jean de Brienne, pleading the Armenian-Frankish civil war in Antioch already described, sailed back to Acre. For over a year, the cardinal ruled Damietta like a king. Then in June 1221, he decided to march on Cairo and wrote to summon Jean de Brienne from Acre. On 7th July, 1221, Jean landed once again at Damietta, hoping to dissuade Pelagius from his intention.

But when King Jean argued against a further advance, Pelagius denounced him as a traitor. A German contingent had recently arrived and reported that the Emperor Frederick II, the young son of Henry VI and Constance of Sicily, would soon follow with a great army. Al Kamil once more renewed his offers of the return of Jerusalem and a thirty-year peace but Pelagius returned only an abrupt refusal. On 18th July, 1221, the Franks marched southwards down the narrow strip of land between the Nile and Lake Manzala, reaching Shirimsah unopposed. The cardinal's intention to march on Cairo had been known for several months. Al Kamil had summoned reinforcements from Syria and the Jezira and now lay at Mansoora with a large army.

On 24th July, 1221, the Franks reached the narrow spit of land between the Nile and the Bahr al Saghir, immediately opposite Al Kamil. But no battle ensued. It was the season of the rise of the Nile and the Bahr al Saghir was unfordable. The Muslims opened the sluices and the Crusaders suddenly found themselves knee-deep in water. There was nothing for it but to retreat. With incredible exertions, slipping and falling in the mud, the Franks struggled back to Baramoon, but the banks of the Nile had now been cut and deeper, swift-flowing streams surrounded them. In a moment, the whole crusade collapsed in disaster, while the cardinal, suddenly panic-stricken, begged Jean de Brienne to save him.

There was nothing for it but to send a delegate to Al Kamil to ask him to allow the Crusaders to evacuate Egypt unmolested. There were voices raised in the Muslim camp demanding the extermination of the Franks but Al Kamil, as moderate as Saladin and Al Aadil, refused. The Crusaders were to hand over Damietta and leave Egypt. All prisoners on both sides would be released and an eight-year truce would be signed. There were no penalty clauses but the Frankish leaders were to remain in Al Kamil's camp till Damietta was surrendered.

The dykes were closed and the Crusaders were rescued and supplied with food. Jean de Brienne spent several days as a guest in the sultan's camp and became a personal friend of Al Kamil, as Richard had been of his father Al Aadil. "The people whose sons and daughters, brothers and sisters, we had killed, whose substance we had plundered and whom we had driven naked from their homes, now saved us with their food when we were dying of hunger and assisted us with many kindnesses when we were completely in their power," writes one who was present.[11] Before embarking for Acre, Jean de Brienne signed an eight-year truce with Al Kamil.

* * *

There had been at least one real Christian at the siege of Damietta. St. Francis of Assisi had landed at the Frankish camp and had asked the permission of the papal legate to cross to the Muslim army. Pelagius washed his hands of the whole affair and Francis, with one other brother, walked across no-man's-land and was roughly seized by the Muslim outposts. Eventually, however, he obtained an audience of Al Kamil and preached before him on several occasions.

The Sultan was impressed by the loving simplicity of the *poverello* and, it is alleged, invited him to remain at his court. Francis replied that he would willingly do so if Al Kamil and his men were converted. Finally he suggested that a great fire be lit and that he throw himself into it on condition that, if he emerged unscathed, the Muslims would acknowledge Christ. The sultan refused such a test but when he sent Francis back, he asked him to pray for him "that he might come to know the true faith".

* * *

Preoccupied with the Crusades and the Mediterranean, we have too long neglected eastern Islam and a number of other states to which only occasional reference has been made in the narrative.

The home of the Armenians was in Greater Armenia south of the Caucasus. After the defeat of the Byzantines by the Seljuqs at Malazkirt in 1071, however, the Turkmans overran Armenia and many Armenian refugees escaped to Cilicia, where they set up an Armenian state. In 1100, Thoros I became Prince of Cilicia. In 1129, he was succeeded by his brother Leo I, who married a niece of the Emperor John Comnenus. Their greatest ruler was Leo II, who became Prince of Cilicia in 1187 (the year of Hattin) and king in 1196. He married the daughter of Amaury II de Lusignan, King of Jerusalem and Cyprus. Leo II died in 1219 at the height of his glory, leaving no son, but his

[11] Oliver of Cologne, one of the principal leaders of the German contingent.

daughter married an Armenian lord, Haithum of Lamprun, making him thereby King Haithum I of Cilicia.

* * *

Between 1050 and 1075, the senior branch of the Seljuqs had established an immense empire from the Oxus to the Bosphorus. In 1079, however, Sulaiman ibn Qutlumish, of a junior branch of the Seljuqs, made himself independent in Asia Minor, where his descendants were to rule for two hundred and twenty-one years. Sivas was at first held by the rival dynasty of the Danishmends, but between 1170 and 1175 they were defeated and removed by the Seljuqs. We have already seen how Qilij Arslan II destroyed the Byzantines at Myrio-cephalon in 1176.

When the Latins seized Constantinople in 1204, Kai Khosrou I took advantage of the confusion to move his frontier westwards to Dorylaeum and the Meander.[12] From 1175 to 1240 was the Golden Age of the Seljuqs of Asia Minor. The country was prosperous as a result of active commerce with Persia and the West, and the exploitation of its own mineral resources.

The ruling classes had become cultured and spoke Persian and the names taken by the sultans were those of pre-Islamic Persian heroes. Although Persia was at the time in political confusion, literary activity was at a high level, producing famous poets like Saadi and Nizami and mystics such as Abdul Qadir Qailani and Jalal al Deen Rumi. The surviving ruins of their buildings still testify to the artistic and technical skill of the Seljuqs of Asia Minor.

Although the Seljuq state in 1200 was rich and cultured, the stability of the country was constantly threatened by the influx from the east of wild Turkman tribes who refused to be integrated into so civilized a community.

* * *

After the death of Sultan Sanjar in 1156, Seljuq rule in Persia collapsed. The atabeg Ildegiz, a former Seljuq Mamlook, founded an independent dynasty in Adharbaijan.

The governors of Khuwarizm were likewise former Mamlooks of the Seljuqs. In 1194, Tukush, the Shah of Khuwarizm, killed Tughril III, the last Seljuq, and made himself ruler of all Persia. Tukush died in 1200, leaving his son, Ala al Deen Muhammad, as ruler of Persia.

East of the Oxus, Trans-Oxiana and Turkestan were ruled by the Qara Khitai dynasty, who were Buddhists, though their subjects in Trans-Oxiana were Muslims.

[12] Map 15, page 153.

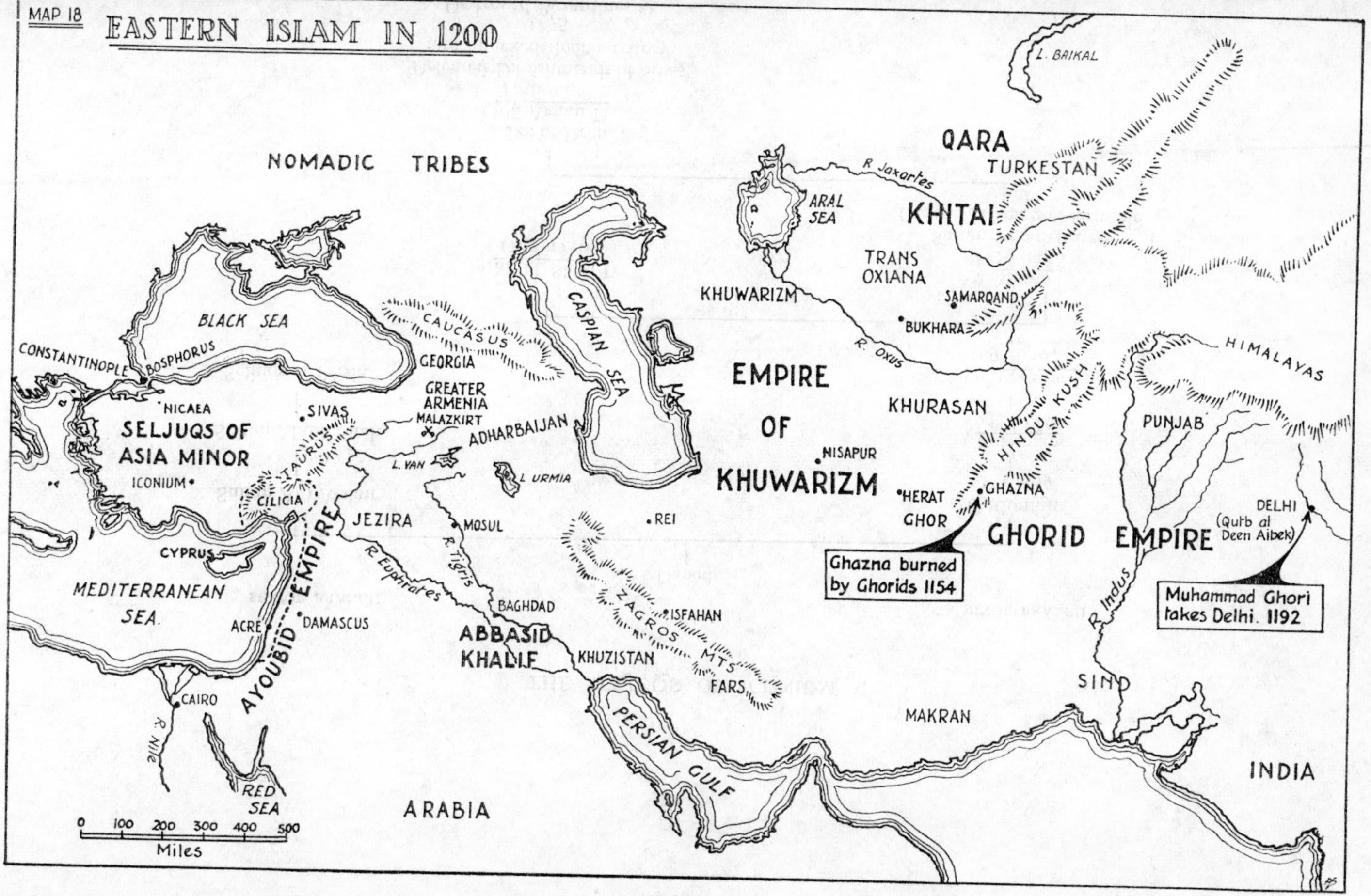
MAP 18
EASTERN ISLAM IN 1200
NOMADIC TRIBES
QARA
TURKESTAN
KHITAI
L. BAIKAL
R. Jaxartes
ARAL SEA
TRANS OXIANA
SAMARQAND
BUKHARA
KHUWARIZM
R. Oxus
BLACK SEA
CAUCASUS
CASPIAN SEA
CONSTANTINOPLE
BOSPHORUS
GEORGIA
GREATER ARMENIA
MALAZKIRT
NICAEA
SIVAS
SELJUQS OF ASIA MINOR
TAURUS
ADHARBAIJAN
L. VAN
L. URMIA
ICONIUM
CILICIA
EMPIRE OF KHUWARIZM
KHURASAN
NISAPUR
HERAT
GHOR
GHAZNA
HINDU KUSH
HIMALAYAS
PUNJAB
DELHI
(Qutb al Deen Aibek)
GHORID EMPIRE
Ghazna burned by Ghorids 1154
Muhammad Ghori takes Delhi. 1192
R. Indus
SIND
JEZIRA
MOSUL
R. Tigris
R. Euphrates
REI
CYPRUS
MEDITERRANEAN SEA
AYOUBID EMPIRE
ACRE
DAMASCUS
BAGHDAD
ISFAHAN
ZAGROS MTS
ABBASID KHALIF
KHUZISTAN
FARS
CAIRO
R. Nile
RED SEA
PERSIAN GULF
MAKRAN
INDIA
ARABIA
0 100 200 300 400 500
Miles

THE SELJUQS OF ICONIUM

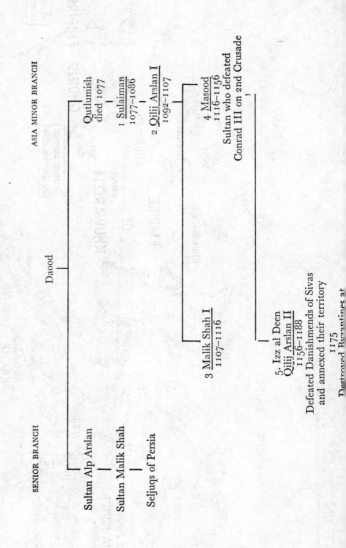

Daood

SENIOR BRANCH

Sultan Alp Arslan

Sultan Malik Shah

Seljuqs of Persia

ASIA MINOR BRANCH

Qutlumish
died 1077

1 Sulaiman
1077–1086

2 Qilij Arslan I
1092–1107

3 Malik Shah I
1107–1116

4 Masood
1116–1156
Sultan who defeated
Conrad III on 2nd Crusade

5. Izz al Deen
Qilij Arslan II
1156–1188
Defeated Danishmends of Sivas
and annexed their territory
1175
Destroyed Byzantines at

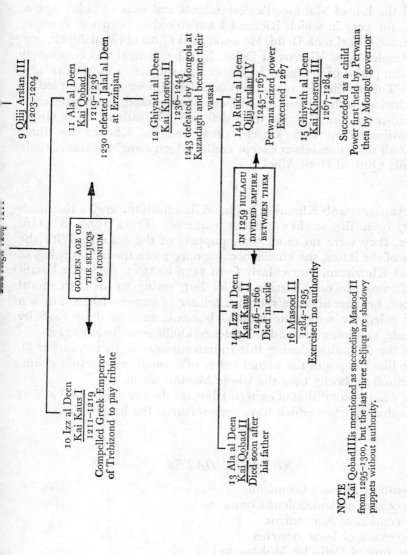

9 Qilij Arslan III
1203–1204

10 Izz al Deen
Kai Kaus I
1211–1219
Compelled Greek Emperor
of Trebizond to pay tribute

GOLDEN AGE OF
THE SELJUQS
OF ICONIUM

11 Ala al Deen
Kai Qobad I
1219–1236
1230 defeated Jalal al Deen
at Erzinjan

12 Ghiyath al Deen
Kai Khosrou II
1236–1245
1243 defeated by Mongols at
Kuzadagh and became their
vassal

13 Ala al Deen
Kai Qobad II
Died soon after
his father

14a Izz al Deen
Kai Kaus II
1246–1260
Died in exile

IN 1259 HULAGU
DIVIDED EMPIRE
BETWEEN THEM

14b Rukn al Deen
Qilij Arslan IV
1245–1267
Perwana seized power
Executed 1267

16 Masood II
1284–1295
Exercised no authority

15 Ghiyath al Deen
Kai Khosrou III
1267–1284
Succeeded as a child
Power first held by Perwana
then by Mongol governor

NOTE
Kai Qobad III is mentioned as succeeding Masood II from 1295–1300, but the last three Seljuqs are shadowy puppets without authority.

In south-east Persia, modern Afghanistan, an empire had been built up between 1000 and 1030 by the great Mahmood of Ghazna, consisting of south-east Persia and the Punjab. In 1173, however, the Ghorids, a family of tribal chiefs from Ghor, between Ghazna and Herat, defeated the last of Mahmood's descendants and annexed his empire. In 1192, the year in which Richard I embarked to return to Europe, Muhammad Ghori took Delhi. He appointed Qutb al Deen Aibek, one of his Mamlooks, as Viceroy of Delhi. In 1202, Bengal was conquered and all the plains of northern India became subject to the Ghorids.

When Tukush died in 1200, however, the Ghorids were tempted to try conclusions with his son, Ala al Deen Muhammad, the Khuwarizm Shah. However, the Ghorids were defeated, Ghiyath al Deen Ghori was assassinated on 15th March, 1203, and the Khuwarizm Shah annexed all their dominions except India, which remained under their Mamlook, Qutb al Deen Aibek.

* * *

The Abbasid Arab Khalifs of Baghdad had until the end of the ninth century, been the world's greatest emperors. From 1050 to 1156, however, they were no more than puppets of the Seljuqs. With the collapse of the latter, the khalifs became once more the actual rulers of Iraq and Khuzistan. Particularly from 1179 to 1225, the great Khalif Al Nasir was not only a strong ruler but, owing to his high moral character, became also the religious arbiter of eastern Islam. His son Dhahir ruled for only nine months but was succeeded in 1226 by Mustansir, another great and enlightened khalif who died in 1242.

Thus the Abbasids, during this Indian summer from 1156 to 1258, became like the popes the actual rulers of a small state, while claiming spiritual authority over the whole Muslim world.

Such was the condition of eastern Islam on the eve of one of the most catastrophic disasters which have ever tortured the human race.

NOTABLE DATES

Death of Manuel Comnenus	1180
Accession of Andronicus Comnenus	1182
Execution of Andronicus Accession of Isaac Angelus	1185
Capture of Delhi by Muhammad Ghori	1192
Death of Saladin	3rd March, 1193
Tughril III, last Seljuq Sultan of Persia, killed by Khuwarizm Shah	24th April, 1194

Death of Henry of Champagne, King of Jerusalem; Election of Amaury de Lusignan	1197
Accession of Muhammad Khuwarizm Shah	1199
Elevation of Al Aadil to be sole sultan	1201
Latin Capture of Constantinople	12th April, 1204
Fall of the Ghorid dynasty	1206
Coronation of Jean de Brienne as King of Jerusalem	14th September, 1210
Fifth Crusade reaches Damietta	26th May, 1218
Death of Sultan Al Aadil	31st August, 1218
Capture of Damietta	5th November, 1219
Fifth Crusade meets with disaster	July 1221

PERSONALITIES

Ayoubids

Saladin	1169–1193
Al Azeez, son of Saladin (Egypt only)	1193–1198
Al Afdhal, son of Saladin (Damascus only)	1193–1196
Al Aadil, brother of Saladin, supreme sultan (1196–1200 in Damascus only)	1200–1218
Al Kamil, son of Al Aadil	1218–1238

The Shahs of Khuwarizm

Anushtikeen, a Mamlook of the great Seljuq Sultan Malik Shah	1077–1097
Qutb al Deen Muhammad, son of Anushtikeen	1097–1127
Atsiz, son of Qutb al Deen (contemporary of Sultan Sanjar)	1127–1156
Il Arslan (these were Shahs of Khuwarizm only)	1156–1172
Tukush, son of Il Arslan	1172–1200
Ala al Deen Muhammad (conquered all Persia)	1200–1220
Jalal al Deen Mangubirdi	1220–1231

The Ghorids

Izz al Deen Hasan, a tribal chief of Ghor	
Saif al Deen Suri	1148–1149
Ala al Deen Husain (captured and burned Ghazna)	1149–1161
Ghiyath al Deen Muhammad, Sultan of South East Persia	1163–1203
Shihab al Deen Muhammad (the great Muhammad Ghori, Conqueror of Delhi)	1175–1206

The Indian Summer of the Abbasids

Al Muqtafi	1135–1160
Al Mustadhi	1160–1179
Al Nasir il Deen Allah	1179–1225
Al Dhahir	1225–1226
Al Mustansir	1226–1242
Al Mustasim	1242–1258

Byzantine Emperors

Manuel I Comnenus	1143–1180
Alexius II Comnenus	1180–1182
Andronicus I Comnenus	1182–1185
Isaac Angelus	1185–1195
Alexius III Angelus	1195–1203
Isaac Angelus (2nd reign) in association with his son Alexius IV	1203–1204
Alexius V Murzuphlos	1204
Baldwin of Flanders	1204–1205
Henry of Flanders	1205–1216
Theodore Lascaris (in Nicaea)	1204–1222

Leaders of the Fourth Crusade

Enrico Dandolo, Doge of Venice
Boniface de Montferrat, Commander of the Fourth Crusade, then King of Macedonia.

Kings of Jerusalem

Conrad de Montferrat
Henry of Champagne
Amaury de Lusignan
} Married Isabella, Queen of Jerusalem

Jean de Brienne, married Marie, daughter of Isabella
Jean d'Ibelin, "The Old Lord of Beirut", Regent for Marie before her marriage to Jean de Brienne.

VIII

The Conqueror of the World

It is but little more than eight score years since all Tartary was in subjection and servage to other nations about; for they were but herdsmen and did nothing but keep beasts and lead them to pastures. . . . Now it befell that of the first lineage succeeded an old worthy man, that was not rich, who was called Changuys. . . . And they chose him to be their emperor. And he commanded them presently to make them ready and to follow his banner. And after this the Chan put in subjection all the lands about him.

Sir John Maundeville

Tchinguiz Khan owed his triumphs to the force of his will, to the resources of his genius and to the indiscriminate use . . . of deceit and treachery. The destruction he wrought spread terror far and wide and deprived the peoples attacked of the courage to defend themselves. Never did a conqueror carry his contempt for humanity to such extremes.

Baron d'Ohsson, *History of the Mongols*

I looked for some to take pity, but there was none. *Psalm LXIX, 20*

He left the name at which the world grew pale,
To point a moral, or adorn a tale.

Samuel Johnson, *The Vanity of Human Wishes*

VIII

IN the twelfth century, Central Asia from the Volga to the Kingan Mountains was inhabited by nomad horse-breeding tribes. Those in the western half of these vast steppes were known as Turks, while farther east lived the Mongols and the Tatars.[1] It is difficult exactly to define the difference between these groups, for the tribes themselves had not thought of such classifications. When the Mongols became famous under Jenghis Khan, they were known in Europe as Tatars, but called themselves Turks, though they appear in reality to have been mostly Mongols.

The principal Turkish tribes were the Qipchaqs, Qanqalis, Qarluqs, Uighurs and Kirghiz. Many Turks lived in fixed settlements, some having long been engaged in mining metals in the Altai Mountains. A considerable proportion of the Uighurs were merchants and caravaners.

The Mongols were the most primitive of the three groups. Their tribes included the Naimans, Keraits, Uirats, Merkits and Jalair and extended from the Altai Mountains to Lake Baikal, east of which lay the Tatars. The Mongols rarely if ever tasted bread, fruit or vegetables but lived almost entirely on the milk and meat of their cattle, sheep and horses, though they were ready also to eat dead dogs, cats, rats or any carrion. Many were so poor that they dressed in the skins of dogs. Their stirrups were of wood, iron stirrups being the sign of a great chief.

Thickset, with slanting eyes, prominent cheekbones, olive complexion and sparse beard, their chief occupation was war, the women being as hardy as the men. Both sexes were greatly addicted to drunkenness. As they never washed themselves or their clothes, their persons emitted a strong rancid odour. In religion they were Shamanists or animists, believing in the existence of great numbers of spirits, though they worshipped a single supreme deity in the form of the Blue Sky.

In the Golden Age of the Arab Empire in the ninth century, many Turks had entered it as slaves while, in the eleventh century, the Ghuzz Turks conquered Persia, and established the Seljuq Empire. With the decline of the Seljuqs, minor Turkish dynasties had seized power.

While, however, the Turks in the Arab countries became civilized, the nomads of the steppes remained unchanged in their way of life.

[1] Tatars is the correct spelling. In Greek mythology, however, Tartarus was hell. The word Tatar may have become Tartar in the West to imply that its bearers were fiends.

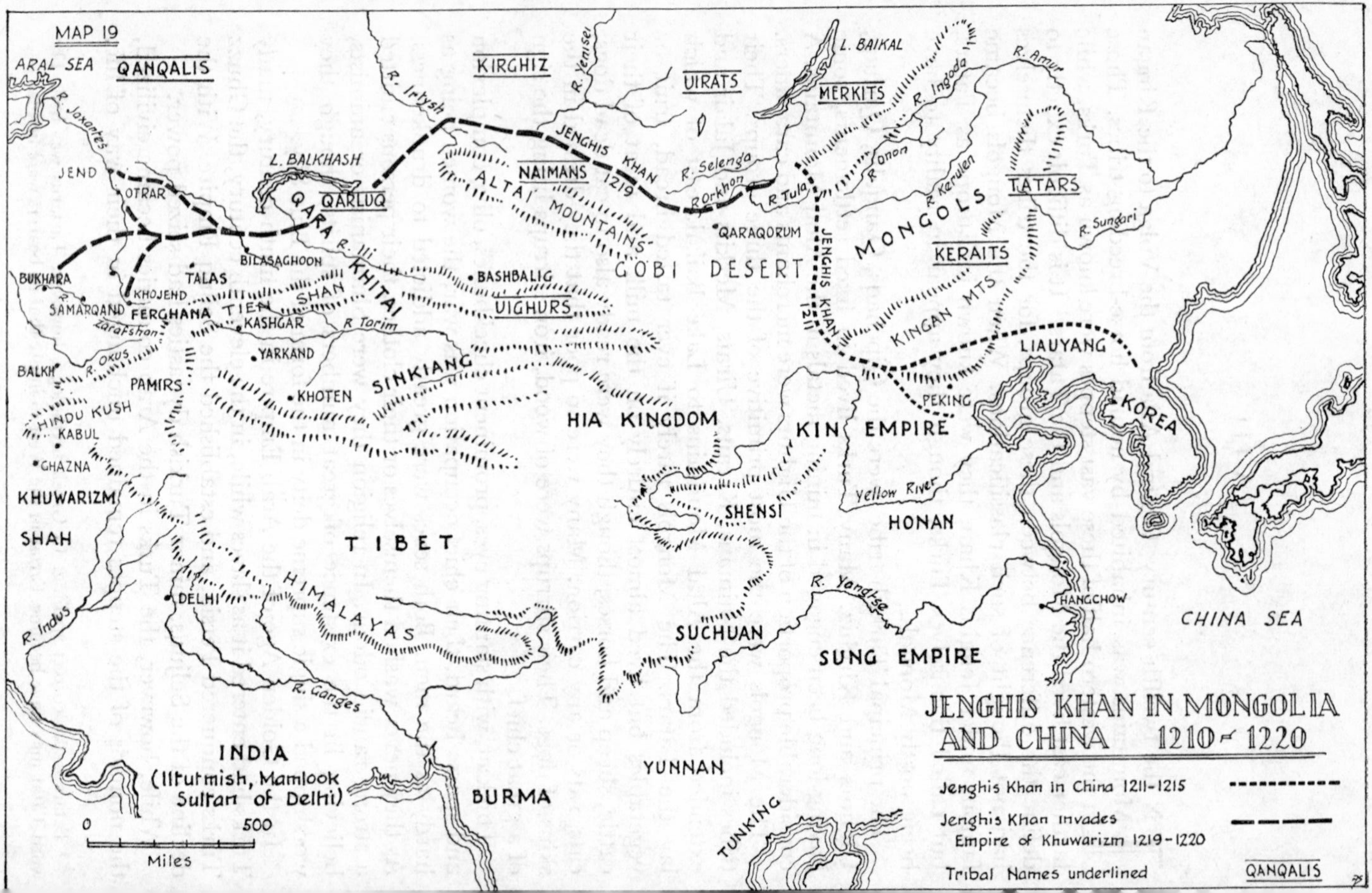
MAP 19
JENGHIS KHAN IN MONGOLIA
AND CHINA 1210-1220
Jenghis Khan in China 1211-1215
Jenghis Khan invades
Empire of Khuwarizm 1219-1220
Tribal Names underlined
QANQALIS
ARAL SEA
QANQALIS
KIRGHIZ
UIRATS
MERKITS
L. BAIKAL
R. Amur
R. Ingoda
R. Irtysh
R. Yenisei
R. Jaxartes
JEND
OTRAR
L. BALKHASH
QARLUQ
QARA KHITAI
R. Ili
JENGHIS KHAN 1219
NAIMANS
ALTAI MOUNTAINS
R. Selenga
R. Orkhon
R. Tula
R. Onon
R. Kerulen
TATARS
R. Sungari
MONGOLS
KERAITS
QARAQORUM
GOBI DESERT
JENGHIS KHAN 1211
KINGAN MTS
LIAUYANG
PEKING
KOREA
BUKHARA
SAMARQAND
Zarafshan
KHOJEND
TALAS
BILASAGHOON
FERGHANA
TIEN SHAN
KASHGAR
R. Tarim
BASHBALIG
UIGHURS
YARKAND
BALKH
R. Oxus
PAMIRS
KHOTEN
SINKIANG
HINDU KUSH
KABUL
GHAZNA
KHUWARIZM SHAH
HIA KINGDOM
KIN EMPIRE
Yellow River
SHENSI
HONAN
TIBET
HIMALAYAS
DELHI
R. Indus
R. Ganges
R. Yangtse
HANGCHOW
CHINA SEA
SUCHUAN
SUNG EMPIRE
INDIA
(Iltutmish, Mamlook
Sultan of Delhi)
BURMA
YUNNAN
TUNKING
0
500
Miles

Those near the borders of the Arab Empire became Muslims, those still on the steppes remained animists.

* * *

The Chinese Empire, the oldest in the world, had been frequently conquered by the steppe tribes. From 907 onwards, the Celestial Empire was ruled by the Khitan but, in 1114, they were replaced by the Kin or Golden Tatars. A fugitive member of the Khitan dynasty, Yeliu (or Prince) Tashi escaped to Turkestan, where he founded a new dynasty called the Qara Khitai. In 1141, Yeliu Tashi defeated Sultan Sanjar, the last great Seljuqid, and annexed Trans-Oxiana.

Politically, therefore, at the end of the twelfth century, we find the Khuwarizm Shah west of the Oxus, the Qara Khitai from the Oxus to the Altai, the Mongols without a government and the northern half of China ruled by the Kin Tatar Emperors of Peking.

* * *

The Mongols were unendingly engaged in savage and brutal tribal wars in which poison, treachery, torture and rape were freely employed. Yissugei, a Mongol leader who had distinguished himself in wars with the Tatars, died in 1175, leaving a thirteen-year-old son called Temujin.

Yissugei had been the chief of several thousand families, a task too great for a boy of thirteen, and Temujin was deserted by all except his near relatives. He spent the next thirty years in a savage struggle to retrieve his father's position. A ruthless fighter, he was also capable of winning devotion. "Temujin will take the coat off his back and give it away," said one of his men. "He keeps his men obedient but he sees that they are well fed." In 1206, a quriltai or tribal council assembled near the source of the River Onon and acclaimed him leader of all the Mongols with the title of Jenghis Khan or the Mighty Lord. He was forty-four years old.

Though he had united the Mongols, to keep them together was no easy task. The Hia Kingdom was a peaceful state south of the Gobi and the years 1207 to 1209 were occupied in plundering it. Already in 1207 Jenghis Khan had received the submission of the Kirghiz and then that of the Uighurs, both Turkic peoples.

In 1211, Jenghis Khan set out to invade the Kin Empire of China. The Mongol army, surprisingly well organized, was divided into units of ten, a hundred, a thousand and ten thousand, and consisted solely of cavalry. Each man was equipped with a bow, an axe, a sword and a lance and was protected by breast-and-back-plates and a helmet, made of leather hardened with lacquer. Flocks of animals accompanied the army for food.

China, unlike Mongolia, did not consist of immense plains which could be crossed at the gallop. The countryside was intersected by great rivers and dotted with fortified cities. The Mongols developed new techniques with surprising facility. Early in 1214, the Kin Emperor sued for peace, and the Mongol conqueror set out for home, laden with an immense booty in gold, silk, horses, cattle and slaves of both sexes. Moukouli, a distinguished Mongol commander, was left in China with an army. Soon after the departure of Jenghis Khan, fighting broke out once more. Moukouli occupied Liauyang and Korea and in 1215, captured the Kin capital, Peking.

Events in China are beyond the scope of this book. Thus much has been included in order to trace the development of the Mongol power, now to be directed against the Muslims. Jenghis Khan arrived back on the River Kerulen in the spring of 1216.

* * *

The Uighur submission to Jenghis Khan in 1209 had carried his border up to that of the Qara Khitai, the ruler of which was Yeliu Chiloucou. In 1212, however, the Qara Khitai Empire was attacked by the Khuwarizm Shah and collapsed. When Jenghis Khan returned from China in 1216, he found the Khuwarizm Shah his neighbour north of the Tien Shan.

During the winter of 1217 to 1218, Jenghis Khan sent a delegation to Muhammad, the Khuwarizm Shah, to conclude peace but added the phrase, "I will look upon you as my dearest son." As the relation between suzerain and vassal was often likened to that of father and son, it is possible that the message really meant, "acknowledge my suzerainty if you desire peace". It was a fateful moment in history. The Mongols and Tatars had hitherto occupied themselves on the borders of China. From Trans-Oxiana to the Atlantic, Muslim civilization led the world. Europe, barely emerging from the Dark Ages, had as yet little to offer. The fragile border between Jenghis Khan and the Khuwarizm Shah marked the boundary between the world of Islam and that of the steppe nomads.

Muhammad, the Khuwarizm Shah, resented the phrase in which Jenghis Khan called him his son, but nevertheless replied amicably. Shortly afterwards a caravan from Mongolia reached Otrar on the Jaxartes. The governor of the town reported to the Khuwarizm Shah his suspicion that the party included Mongol spies. Accounts of the ensuing incident, which was to prove a milestone in history as vital as the murder of Archduke Franz Ferdinand at Sarajevo in 1914, are contradictory. Muhammad al Nessawi, a Persian hostile to the Mongols, alleges that the governor of Otrar was told merely to keep the men under observation. Rasheed al Deen,[2] writing from the Mongol side, states that the Khuwarizm Shah ordered their execution. The fact remains that the caravan was looted and the men with it were killed.

Jenghis Khan may have been dubious of the wisdom of attacking Khuwarizm, for he was unfamiliar with the Muslim world, or on the other hand, he may have been trying to pick a quarrel. In either case the Khuwarizm Shah, whose head had been turned by his easy victories over the Ghorids and the Qara Khitai, seems to have been quite willing to fight.

* * *

Although in 1218, the Empire of Khuwarizm covered a large area, much of it had only been conquered in the previous twenty years and the people had not had time to acquire any loyalty to the régime. Tukush, the father of Muhammad, had married the daughter of the chief of the Qanqalis, wild Turkish nomads north of the Aral Sea. These tribesmen, who formed the greater part of the army, plundered and oppressed the settled population. The Empire of Khuwarizm had grown so quickly that the shahs engaged adult Qipchaqs and Qanqalis in their armies. They do not appear to have had a technique for buying Mamlooks as boys and training them themselves.

Jenghis Khan moved to the Irtysh valley, where he passed the summer of 1219 to fatten the horses. The Mongols did not feed their horses on grain, of which they had none even for themselves. Two years of grazing were sometimes necessary to make the army really mobile.

The Khuwarizm Shah decided not to risk an open battle and distributed his army in garrisons in his walled towns. He seems to have thought that the Mongols, being nomads, would merely raid the open country and then withdraw with their loot, not appreciating that they had learned siege warfare in China. In fact, his unenterprising attitude demoralized his own troops before war began.

Late in 1219, Jenghis Khan advanced towards the Jaxartes. His eldest son, Juji, was sent off with a column to besiege Jend. Another column, under his second and third sons, Jagatai and Ogotai, attacked Otrar, while a third detachment marched on Khojend. In February 1220, Jenghis Khan with the main army crossed the Jaxartes and marched straight on Bukhara. The garrison, consisting of Qanqali mercenaries, decided to abandon the city and cut its way out but was surrounded and exterminated to a man.

Next morning a deputation of notables emerged from the gates and surrendered to Jenghis Khan, who immediately mounted and rode into Bukhara with his guards. Coming to the great mosque, he asked if it were

[2] Rasheed al Deen, *Jamai Tuvarikh.*

the king's palace. On being told that it was the house of God, he mounted the steps and called to his followers, "The hay is cut. Give fodder to your horses," perhaps a pre-arranged signal that looting could begin.

Meanwhile Jenghis Khan and the chiefs had assembled in the great mosque where a drunken orgy ensued. Qorans were pulled from their boxes and trampled under foot, the boxes being used as mangers for the horses, which the qadhis and imams were ordered to hold. Drunkenness was one of the besetting sins of the Mongols. Soon the drunken savages were staggering round the mosque, the marble floor of which was covered with pools of wine and spirits. Women were then dragged in and a general debauch ensued. The venerable imams stood looking on in silent terror at the desecration of their place of worship.

Meanwhile the civil population had been ordered to assemble outside the walls to enable the conquerors to plunder the city unhindered. Orders were then given for the distribution of the people as slaves to various Mongol units. Most of the women were raped but a number of Muslims succeeded in killing their wives and daughters and themselves to escape such a fate. The city was then set on fire. Tens of thousands of people were massacred and their bodies left unburied.

Bukhara had been a great and ancient city, enriched by its situation on the main caravan route from China. But the golden age of Bukhara had been from 900 to 999, during which period it had been the centre of a brilliant efflorescence of Muslim civilization. Its streets had been crowded with poets, historians, doctors and scientists, while its libraries, museums and colleges almost rivalled those of Baghdad itself. Ibn Sina, known in Europe as Avicenna, had worked in the royal library. Firdausi, one of the greatest of Persian poets, composed his early works in Bukhara. Here also Al Razi wrote his great book on medicine, destined to be used for centuries as a text-book in Europe. All this great cultural heritage, the accumulated intellectual wealth of centuries, was obliterated in plunder, rape, bloodshed and arson.

Leaving the smoking ruins of Bukhara, the Mongols marched up the lovely valley of the Zarafshan, filled with gardens, orchards, fields and country villas, driving before them gangs of young men whom they had taken as slaves. Outside Samarqand the army was joined by the three other columns which had captured the towns on the Jaxartes, killing all the inhabitants.

Samarqand in 1220 was one of the richest commercial cities in the world. The Qanqali mercenaries, who constituted most of the garrison, offered to surrender and join the Mongol army. Jenghis Khan agreed to enlist them and they marched out of Samarqand with their families, leaving the citizens to their fate. Twenty-four hours later they were surrounded by the Mongol army and killed to the last man.

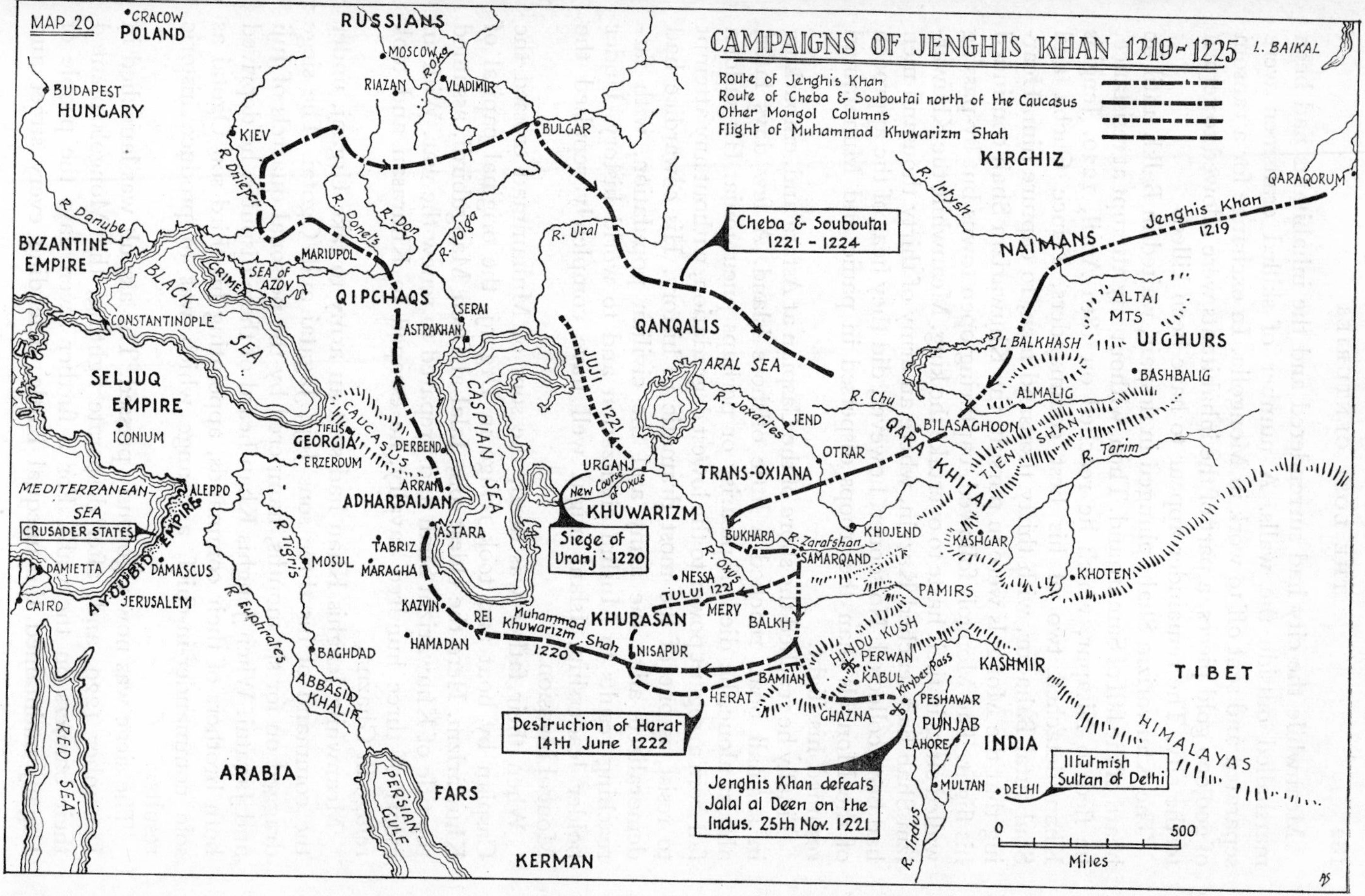
MAP 20
CAMPAIGNS OF JENGHIS KHAN 1219–1225
Route of Jenghis Khan
Route of Cheba & Souboutai north of the Caucasus
Other Mongol Columns
Flight of Muhammad Khuwarizm Shah
Cheba & Souboutai 1221 - 1224
Siege of Uranj 1220
Destruction of Herat 14th June 1222
Jenghis Khan defeats Jalal al Deen on the Indus. 25th Nov. 1221
Iltutmish Sultan of Delhi
Jenghis Khan 1219
JUJI 1221
TULUI 1221
Muhammad Khuwarizm Shah 1220
L. BAIKAL
CRACOW
POLAND
RUSSIANS
MOSCOW
RIAZAN
VLADIMIR
R. Oka
BUDAPEST
HUNGARY
KIEV
BULGAR
KIRGHIZ
QARAQORUM
R. Irtysh
R. Dnieper
R. Donets
R. Don
R. Volga
R. Ural
R. Danube
NAIMANS
BYZANTINE EMPIRE
MARIUPOL
SEA of AZOV
CRIMEA
BLACK SEA
QIPCHAQS
SERAI
ASTRAKHAN
QANQALIS
ALTAI MTS
UIGHURS
L. BALKHASH
BASHBALIG
CONSTANTINOPLE
SELJUQ EMPIRE
ICONIUM
CAUCASUS
TIFLIS
GEORGIA
DERBEND
ERZERDUM
CASPIAN SEA
ARAL SEA
R. Jaxartes
JEND
R. Chu
ALMALIG
BILASAGHOON
QARA KHITAI
TIEN SHAN
R. Tarim
OTRAR
TRANS-OXIANA
URGANJ
New Course of Oxus
KHUWARIZM
ARRAN
ADHARBAIJAN
MEDITERRANEAN SEA
ALEPPO
CRUSADER STATES
AYOUBID EMPIRE
ASTARA
TABRIZ
MARAGHA
MOSUL
R. Tigris
BUKHARA
R. Zarafshan
SAMARQAND
KHOJEND
KASHGAR
KHOTEN
R. Oxus
NESSA
MERV
BALKH
PAMIRS
DAMIETTA
DAMASCUS
CAIRO
JERUSALEM
R. Euphrates
KAZVIN
REI
KHURASAN
HAMADAN
NISAPUR
HINDU KUSH
PERWAN
KABUL
Khyber Pass
KASHMIR
TIBET
BAGHDAD
ABBASID KHALIF
BAMIAN
HERAT
GHAZNA
PESHAWAR
PUNJAB
LAHORE
INDIA
HIMALAYAS
RED SEA
ARABIA
PERSIAN GULF
FARS
MULTAN
DELHI
R. Indus
KERMAN
0
500
Miles

Meanwhile the city had surrendered and the inhabitants had been marshalled outside the walls. A number of skilled craftsmen were separated and sent off to work in Mongolia. In exchange for a ransom of 200,000 gold pieces, a part of the inhabitants were allowed to return to the city. The remainder appear to have been killed.

The Khuwarizm Shah, plunged in despair, waited in Balkh until he heard of the fall of Samarqand. Then, without any attempt at resistance, he fled to Nisapur, which he reached on 18th April, 1220. Jenghis Khan detached two of his best commanders, Prince Cheba and Souboutai Bahadur, with thirty thousand men, to capture him. Hearing that the Mongols were in pursuit, the Khuwarizm Shah continued his flight. The Mongols followed, capturing open towns but by-passing walled cities in their haste to overtake the king. Meanwhile the Khuwarizm Shah had reached Kazvin, where an army of thirty thousand men had been collected. No sooner, however, did they hear of the approach of the Mongols than the troops dispersed in panic and Muhammad resumed his flight.

Finally he reached the shore of the Caspian at Astara and, embarking in a small boat, reached a little offshore island. A few days later, almost alone, he died of pleurisy or perhaps pneumonia. His sudden fall from arrogant power to the lowest degradation, without any attempt to resist, is one of the most dramatic in history. His cowardice had demoralized alike the army and the civilian population, with far-reaching results to Muslim civilization and to world history. Under bolder leadership, Islam might well have completely repulsed the Mongol invasion.

When their father was dead, the sons of Muhammad crossed the Caspian by boat and took refuge in Urganj, the original capital of Khuwarizm. Here the eldest son, Jalal al Deen Mangubirdi, assumed the title of Khuwarizm Shah and prepared to renew the war. With an escort of three hundred cavalry, he escaped to Khurasan and took refuge in Ghazna.

Meanwhile Jenghis Khan had sent an army to take Urganj, under the command of his three sons Juji, Jagatai and Ogotai. The siege dragged on for six months, hampered by the personal quarrels of Juji and Jagatai. When Jenghis Khan heard of these disputes, he deprived both brothers of their commands, appointing his third son Ogotai as sole commander-in-chief, a change which was to produce historic results.

The siege was now vigorously pressed. The assault was launched in December 1220, and, after desperate fighting, the Mongols planted their banners on the walls. For a further seven days the people of Urganj maintained the unequal battle, defending every street and every house. Eventually a handful of survivors surrendered. These were as usual collected outside the walls. Then, with swords, spears, spades, bows and arrows, the Mongols slashed and battered the lives out of the helpless prisoners. The city was then looted and the banks of the Oxus were cut so that its waters flowed over the ruins. In the process the river changed its course, eventually discharging into the Caspian whereas it formerly fell into the Aral Sea.

Khuwarizm had long been wealthy and civilized. Urganj lay on an important trade route from Samarqand to Astrakhan and thence to Eastern Europe. The Oxus, like the Nile, after flowing for some distance through desert, spread into a wide and fertile delta before falling into the Aral Sea. The country had been famous for its theologians, professors and scientists. Here logarithms are said to have been invented, the word being a corruption of the name Khuwarizmi. Now city and countryside were alike reduced to an uninhabited desert.

While Urganj was under siege, Jenghis Khan was camped near Samarqand. Meanwhile his fourth son Tului laid waste Khurasan, then one of the most civilized countries in the world. On 25th February, 1221, Tului reached Merv, the capital of the province. There was no resistance and the inhabitants passively obeyed the order to assemble on the plain outside the city, where all were butchered. According to Ibn al Athir, seven hundred thousand corpses were counted.[3]

As the Mongols approached Merv, a small group of Turkmans camped in the vicinity hastily struck their tents and moved away to the west. Eighty years later, the chief of this clan founded what was later to become the Ottoman Empire.

Tului took Nisapur in April 1221. According to the historian Mirkhond, one million seven hundred and forty-seven thousand people were killed in this city, famous for its colleges, libraries and scholars. Nisapur was razed to the ground, ploughed over and sown with barley. To ensure that nothing of the city survived, even the cats and dogs were killed. After Nisapur Tului attacked Herat, which resisted for eight days. For some reason, the Mongols then accepted its surrender, only twelve thousand people being put to death. Its turn was to come later.

In the spring of 1221, while Tului was ruining Khurasan, Jenghis Khan advanced on the ancient and wealthy city of Balkh. He was met by a deputation of notables, bearing rich gifts and asking to do him homage. In spite of their submission, however, the unresisting inhabitants were massacred and the city was left a heap of smoking rubble.

To record the long list of sieges and massacres in 1221 would be

[3] It is of course never advisable to rely entirely on the round numbers given by mediaeval historians.

wearisome. At every town the same procedure was followed. On reaching a walled city, the Mongols immediately surrounded it completely with an earth rampart and ditch, which were often completed in twenty-four hours by the numerous gangs of slave-prisoners whom they brought with them. Then the batteries of catapults and mangonels were quickly erected. Barbarian invasions were frequent in the ancient world but the more civilized defenders were usually able to hold their cities because they possessed more scientific weapons. With the Mongols, however, the reverse was the case, for their "artillery" was always more powerful than that of the Persians and they had learned siege warfare in China. In some cases they brought Chinese sappers and "gunners" with them. Thus the walls were soon breached and the prisoners were then obliged to fill in the moat, to work battering rams against the gates and to lead the assault up the breaches. The Mongols were thus able to conquer strongly defended cities with only light casualties to themselves, the heaviest losses being borne by the prisoners.

When the city was taken, the inhabitants were marshalled outside the walls for killing, the city being then looted, demolished and burnt. However thoroughly this was done, a small number of people would survive by hiding in the cellars. A few days later, these miserable wretches would scratch their way out from beneath the rubble. To avoid such a possibility, a detachment of cavalry would be sent back after some days with orders to surprise the ruined town at dawn and kill any survivors whom they found.

Juji, the eldest son of Jenghis Khan, had separated from the others after the siege of Urganj and had moved to the steppes north of the Aral Sea. Still sore over his quarrel with his brother Jagatai, he was henceforward to play a lone hand. Moving south from Balkh, Jenghis Khan and his sons Jagatai and Ogotai laid siege to Bamian in the Hindu Kush, in the attack on which a grandson of the Conqueror was killed by an arrow. In a cold fury, Jenghis Khan ordered that Bamian and all that was in it be exterminated. The inhabitants were killed as a matter of routine but in Bamian dogs, cats, mules, donkeys, hens and everything alive was slaughtered, vegetation was destroyed and the trees cut down. A hundred years later Bamian and the surrounding country were still an uninhabited wilderness.

* * *

The escape from Urganj of Jalal al Deen, the new Khuwarizm Shah, and his arrival at Ghazna have already been mentioned. He received a loyal welcome and was soon at the head of an army. Jenghis Khan, who was attacking Bamian, had posted a covering force of some thirty thousand men to hold the southern entrances to the passes through the Hindu Kush, to protect him from Jalal al Deen. The latter, however, advanced and, in a two-day battle at Perwan, defeated the covering force, thereby winning the first victory over the Mongols in Persia.

Jenghis Khan, having obliterated Bamian, marched southwards to avenge the Mongol defeat and Jalal al Deen's somewhat heterodox force melted away. The Khuwarizm Shah was obliged to beat a hasty retreat through the Khyber Pass with the Mongols hot on his tracks. Reaching the banks of the Indus some sixty miles south of Peshawar on the evening of 24th November, 1221, Jalal al Deen decided to cross the next day. In the night, however, the Mongol army arrived. At dawn the Muslims found themselves with their backs to the river, facing the greatly superior Mongol army drawn up in a crescent with its two points on the river bank on either flank of the Khuwarizmi army.

Again and again Jalal al Deen charged furiously into the Mongol ranks but by midday it had become obvious that the Muslims could resist no longer. Mounting a fresh horse, the Khuwarizm Shah led another desperate charge, momentarily compelling the Mongols to give ground. Then suddenly wheeling his horse, he clapped spurs to its flanks and galloped straight for the bank of the Indus, throwing off his breastplate as he rode. The bank was twenty feet high and Jalal al Deen and his horse with a wild splash leaped into the river. His shield on his back and still carrying his standard in his hand, he and his horse swam the mighty Indus beneath the eyes of the Mongol army. Jenghis Khan himself galloped to the river bank in time to see Jalal al Deen emerge on the other shore. Turning to his sons, he told them that so brave a feat of arms was one which they would do well to imitate.

* * *

We have already seen that the dynasty of Ghor had overthrown the Ghaznavids and had made itself master of northern India.[4] In 1206, however, Muhammad Ghori had been assassinated leaving no sons, the Mamlook commanders of his army had seized power and the Ghorid dynasty had ceased to exist. A former slave, Qutb al Deen Aibek, had ruled for four years but, in 1211, he had died while playing polo at Lahore. Iltutmish, a Turkman slave, was chosen to succeed him. When Jalal al Deen swum the Indus in November 1221, Iltutmish had already been ten years Sultan of Delhi.

Jenghis Khan sent two columns to pursue the Khuwarizm Shah but, failing to locate him, they plundered Multan and Lahore and returned through the Khyber Pass to Ghazna. Meanwhile Jalal al Deen had appealed for help to Iltutmish but the sultan made his excuses, having

[4] Page 170.

no desire to draw down the vengeance of the Mongols upon India. Jalal al Deen remained in the Punjab where we shall shortly hear of him again.

* * *

The Mongols, who were at home on the icy plains of Central Asia, feared hot climates. In the spring of 1222, Jenghis Khan returned to Khurasan. Anticipating that Jalal al Deen would come back, he utterly destroyed Ghazna, killing all the inhabitants.

When Jalal al Deen had defeated the Mongols in the Hindu Kush, the people of Herat, thinking that the tide had turned, had raised the standard of revolt. Jenghis Khan, on his return from India, sent an army to punish them. The citizens defended themselves for six months with the frantic courage of despair. Contemporary historians allege that when Herat was ultimately taken on 14th June, 1222, one million six hundred thousand people were massacred.[5]

Jenghis Khan spent the summer of 1222 in the Hindu Kush. The following winter the World Conqueror decided to return to Mongolia. The army was accompanied by immense numbers of slave prisoners. Considering that these men would not be needed in Mongolia, he caused several tens of thousands of them to be butchered, an operation which was completed in twenty-four hours.

The summer months of 1223 were passed in camps north of the Hindu Kush, resting the horses. In the autumn the march northwards was resumed. The countryside was virtually uninhabited, for the Mongols would not permit the people to grow grain crops. They themselves lived on meat and milk and needed only grass not grain. Balkh had been destroyed two years before but a detachment was sent to search out and kill any survivors.

The army then crossed the Oxus and camped near Bukhara, whence Jenghis Khan summoned Muslim religious teachers to explain to him their religion, of which he was graciously pleased to express his approval, except for the pilgrimage to Mecca. "Men can pray to God equally well anywhere in the world," he remarked. Having appointed governors to rule Persia, he crossed the Jaxartes and pitched his camp on the banks of the Onon in February 1225, after an absence of seven years.

* * *

It will be remembered that, after the fall of Samarqand in 1220, Jenghis Khan sent a force of thirty thousand cavalry under Cheba and

[5] The apparently large numbers of killed in these towns may be due to the fact that the villagers in the surrounding country fled to the city for refuge.

Souboutai to pursue Muhammad the Khuwarizm Shah, but that the latter died on an island in the Caspian. The two commanders found themselves in Adharbaijan without an objective.

Early in 1221 they took Kazvin, where the people fought them with knives in the streets until forty thousand Muslims had been killed. In February 1221, they carried massacre and devastation through the Christian Kingdom of Georgia. Returning to Adharbaijan, they took Meragha, all the inhabitants being killed. Ibn al Athir states that an inhabitant of Meragha told him that he saw a single Mongol kill more than a hundred people, who stood unresisting as if mesmerized. Thence the two commanders marched to Hamadan, which they destroyed, killing everyone. In October 1221, for the second time they raided Georgia. Wherever they went they assembled all the women, raped them and then cut their throats. Then passing through the pass of Derbend they emerged into what is now southern Russia but was then the home of the Qipchaq Turks.

The Qipchaqs withdrew westwards and appealed to the Russians whose border then lay on the River Oka, two hundred miles south-east of Moscow. In the thirteenth century, Russia was divided into a number of principalities, under the suzerainty of Grand Duke Jaroslav of Novgorod. The Russians decided to march against the invaders and assembled at Mariupol in the Ukraine. But their efforts lacked co-ordination. Mitislav, Prince of Galitsch, attacked the Mongols single-handed and was completely defeated. The Prince of Kiev and his men resisted for three days but then asked for terms. No sooner did they surrender than all were killed. The Russians offered no further resistance. All over the immense plains of the Dnieper and the Don basins, the country was laid waste and the inhabitants, who everywhere humbly craved for mercy, were ruthlessly massacred.

In the autumn of 1223, Cheba and Souboutai marched northwards and destroyed the wealthy city of Bulgar. They then turned southwards and rejoined Jenghis Khan in 1224 north of the Jaxartes, after an absence from the main army of nearly four years, during which they had marched some nine thousand miles and had conquered West Persia, Georgia and a part of Russia. They had only fought two or three battles, one engagement being sufficient to conquer each country.

The savage cruelty of the Mongols had paralysed all opposition. "Victor and vanquished can never become friends," the Mongol dictum alleged. "The only safety for a conqueror is the complete extermination of the defeated." "These Tatars," wrote Ibn al Athir at the time, "have done things utterly unparalleled in ancient or modern times. Coming from China, they penetrated in less than a year to Iraq and Armenia. May God send a defender to the Muslims for never since the Prophet have they suffered such disasters. On the one hand the Tatars have devastated Trans-Oxiana, Khurasan, Iraq and Adharbaijan. On the other a second enemy, the Franks, have invaded Egypt and seized Damietta,[6] from which the Muslims are unable to evict them."

"In the Muslim countries devastated by Jenghis Khan," wrote the Persian historian,[7] "not one in a thousand of the inhabitants survived . . . If from now until the day of the Resurrection, nothing hindered the natural increase of the population, it could never reach one tenth of its density before the Mongol conquest."

* * *

Repeated messages had been sent to Juji, the eldest son of Jenghis Khan, to report to his father but he remained camped north of the Caspian, pleading illness. Concluding that he was insubordinate, the Conqueror assembled an army to march against him when news came that he was dead.

Juji and his family had become estranged since his quarrel with Jagatai at Urganj. His descendants were for several centuries to rule, in the steppes north of the Caspian, a separate Mongol Empire which counted Russia as a vassal state.

* * *

After resting for a few months in Mongolia, Jenghis Khan decided to return to the Far East. In February 1226, he again devastated the Hia Kingdom. "Only one or two per cent of the people escaped with their lives," writes the Chinese historian Kang-mou.[8] On 18th August, 1227, however, the World Conqueror suddenly died at the age of sixty-six after an illness of only eight days.

* * *

Before Jenghis Khan, the Mongols had been one of the poorest races in Central Asia. They were natural soldiers, but the hardihood of nomads is usually rendered ineffective by their indiscipline. The most extraordinary feat of the World Conqueror was his imposition of an iron discipline on this unpromising material. "A very different picture," remarks Ala al Deen,[9] "from what we see elsewhere. With us, as soon as a slave, himself bought for cash, has ten horses in his stable, his

[6] This was the Crusade of Jean de Brienne, who held Damietta from 1218 to 1221, as related in the preceding chapter.

[7] Ala al Deen al Juwaini, *History of the Conqueror of the World*.

[8] Quoted by d'Ohsson, *History of the Mongols*.

[9] Ala al Deen al Juwaini, *History of the Conqueror of the World*.

owner is obliged to speak to him with circumspection." The disasters suffered by Islam at the hands of the Mongols may indeed be largely attributed to the indiscipline of soldier-slaves. Magnificent fighters, the Turkish Mamlooks were ever ready to assassinate their rulers, to wage wars against one another or to go over to the enemy.

The Conqueror and his Mongols are chiefly remembered for the savagery of their butcheries. We cannot now fully understand the reasons which impelled Jenghis Khan to exterminate whole nations with such thoroughness. To terrorize their enemies into abandoning resistance is comprehensible but this objective would not explain the trouble taken to slaughter the handful of starving wretches who had survived the destruction of some great city.

Nomads are inclined to despise townsmen who lie warm in bed at night. Living lives of intense hardship, they pride themselves on their endurance. Our ideas of over-crowding are purely relative. I knew an old bedouin in Arabia who, camping alone, complained of over-crowding in the desert. If, at night, he saw far away the tiny flicker of a distant camp-fire, he would strike his tent at dawn and set out across the endless pale blue ridges to some distant valley where there was no reminder of the hateful proximity of other men. Some people on the other hand, are happy to live in a tiny room in a skyscraper. To an old-timer, a hundred miles away was a near neighbour. To Jenghis Khan the rich cities and smiling countryside of Khurasan may have seemed no more than an overpopulated slum.

Yet there was also an element of sadism in the Mongols, who invented innumerable ways of killing. Some of their victims, bound hand and foot, were used as targets for their archery. Some were cut in half, some were suffocated by having earth pushed down their throats, some were trampled to death by horses.

"What is the greatest happiness in life?" Jenghis Khan once asked a group of his intimates. "To go hunting on a spring morning, mounted on a beautiful horse, carrying on your wrist a good hawk and watching it seize its prey," replied one of the party. "No," answered the Conqueror, "the greatest pleasure in life is to defeat your enemies, to chase them before you, to rob them of their wealth, to see those dear to them bathed in tears, to ride their horses and to clasp to your breast their wives and daughters."

He was indifferent to civil administration. His governors ruled the conquered provinces in a cruel and arrogant manner, extorting oppressive levies and taxes from the starving survivors of the conquered peoples. The culture, industries, educational standards and prosperity of much of the conquered territory have not recovered to this day.

Jenghis Khan drew up laws for the governance of his people, though they may have been merely the traditional customs of the Mongols. Death was the penalty for homicide, for a soldier deserting his unit, for cattle theft or adultery, for three times allowing prisoners-of-war to escape and for harbouring runaway slaves. It was forbidden to wash in running water or ever to wash clothes, plates or kitchen utensils. To kill an animal for food, it had to be laid on its back and its heart torn out.

The extent of the rule of the Great Khan from Peking to Asia Minor and Hungary may have temporarily facilitated trade between the Far East and Europe by caravans across Central Asia. Unfortunately from this point of view, the unity of the Mongol Empire was to be shortlived.

As we approach the hour of our death, the affairs of this world become increasingly unimportant. In his old age, Jenghis Khan seems to have been worried by doubts and fears. He questioned Muslim and Christian doctors on their faiths and asked them to intercede with God on his behalf. He summoned Chang Chun, a Taoist hermit, from China to Persia to tell him the secret of life. His doubts seem never to have been set at rest, for he died without professing any religion.

NOTABLE DATES

Conquest of Chinese Empire by the Kin Tatars	1114
Establishment of Qara Khitai Empire by Yeliu Tashi	1123–1130
Birth of Temujin	1162
Temujin, chief of all the Mongols, renamed Jenghis Khan	1206
Jenghis Khan invades China	1211
Submission of the Kin Emperor	1214
Mongol capture of Peking	1215
Fall of Bukhara	February 1220
Fall of Samarqand	April 1220
Destruction of Urganj	December 1220
Destruction of Merv	February 1221
Destruction of Nisapur	April 1221
Destruction of Balkh	Spring 1221
Battle of Perwan	Summer 1221
Defeat of Jalal al Deen on the Indus	25th November, 1221
Devastation of Russia by Cheba and Souboutai	1222–1224
Destruction of Ghazna and Herat	Spring 1222
Return of Jenghis Khan to Mongolia	February 1225
Death of Jenghis Khan	18th August, 1227

PERSONALITIES

Jenghis Khan
Juji, Jagatai, Ogotai, Tului — his sons
Moukouli, Cheba, Souboutai — Mongol commanders
Yeliu Chiloucou last ruler of the Qara Khitai
Ala al Deen Muhammad the Khuwarizm Shah
Jalal al Deen his son
Iltutmish Turkish Sultan of Delhi

IX

Al Kamil and the Infidel Emperor

Frederick was . . . fluent in six languages, French, German, Italian, Latin, Greek and Arabic. He was well versed in philosophy, in the sciences, in medicine and natural history and well informed about other countries. His conversation, when he chose, was fascinating. But, for all his brilliance, he was not likeable. He was cruel, selfish, and sly, unreliable as a friend and unforgiving as an enemy. His indulgence in erotic pleasures of every sort shocked even the easy standards of Outremer. STEVEN RUNCIMAN, *History of the Crusades*

Everyone admits how praiseworthy it is in a prince to keep faith . . . Nevertheless our experience has been that those princes who have done great things have held good faith of little account, and have known how to circumvent the intellect of men by craft, and in the end have overcome those who have relied upon their word . . . Therefore a wise lord cannot, nor ought he to, keep faith when such observance may be turned against him . . . But it is necessary to be a great pretender and dissembler; and men are so simple and so subject to present necessities, that he who seeks to deceive will always find someone who will allow himself to be deceived.

NICOLO MACHIAVELLI, *The Prince*

IX

HAVING carried forward the history of the Mongol invasions up to the death of Jenghis Khan in 1227, we must now return to the Crusaders and to Egypt, where we left Sultan Kamil on the throne after the surrender of Jean de Brienne in 1220. Before doing so, however, we must introduce the Emperor Frederick II Hohenstaufen who is about to step on to the stage.

* * *

For many years the papacy had been engaged in a bitter struggle with the emperor for supreme power. This rivalry was accentuated in 1187—the year of Hattin—when the Emperor Frederick Barbarossa proposed to marry his son Henry to Constance of Sicily. That island had been conquered by the Norman Count Roger I between 1060 and 1088. His son, King Roger II, had ruled from 1103 to 1154 and had bequeathed the throne to his son William I. William II became king in 1166 and married Joan, the sister of Richard Coeur de Lion, who, as we have seen, took her on his crusade.

In 1187, William II had no children and the heir presumptive was his Aunt Constance. If she married Henry of Hohenstaufen and William II died childless, Sicily would be united to the German Empire and the Papal dominions would be no more than a small enclave in the empire. To prevent such a union, Pope Clement III was ready to excommunicate Barbarossa. But while matters were in this state, the West was shocked by the news of Hattin and the fall of the Kingdom of Jerusalem. Clement III preached a new Crusade, Barbarossa himself took the cross and set out for the Holy Land but, as we have already seen, was drowned in Cilicia. His son became the Emperor Henry VI, having meanwhile married Constance.

In 1189, King William II of Sicily died childless and Constance became queen. The union of Sicily to the empire seemed inevitable. The Sicilians, however, who under their Norman kings had been a great and independent nation, had no wish to become a mere appanage of the empire. They hastily elected Tancred, an illegitimate grandson of Roger II, to be their king. In 1194, however, after a reign of five years, Tancred died. The Emperor Henry VI seized the opportunity, crossed into Sicily with a German army and caused himself and Constance to be crowned in Palermo. The same year Constance gave birth to a son who was named Frederick.

THE NORMAN KINGS OF SICILY

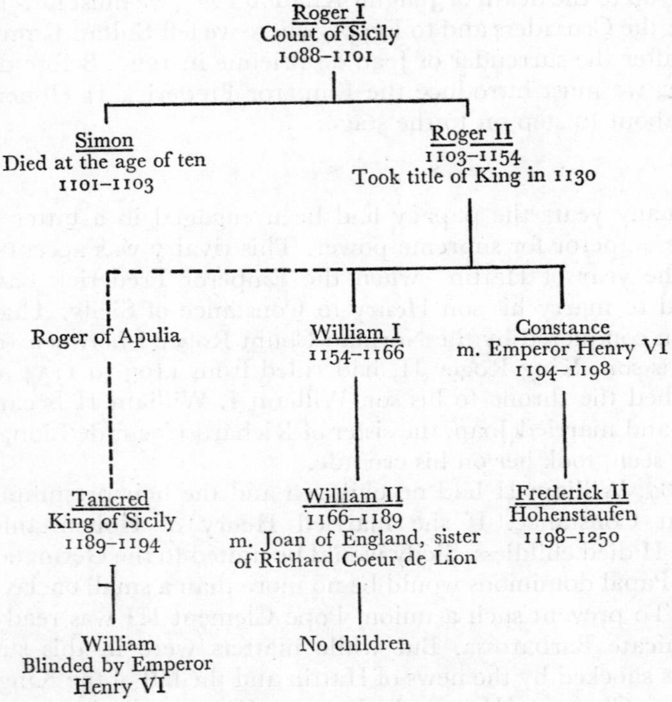

NOTE
Illegitimate descent is shown with a dotted line.

The Arabs had ruled Sicily for more than two hundred years until it was conquered by the Normans. In 1194, a large part of the population still consisted of Muslims. The court of Palermo had inherited the culture and refinement of the Arabs and was the most sophisticated in Europe. The Emperor Henry VI, removing all the money he could lay hands on, returned to Germany, leaving Constance to rule Sicily. Next year, however, the Sicilians rebelled but Henry returned and quelled the revolt with sadistic cruelty, blinding Tancred's infant son William.

Thereupon Henry VI decided to go on a crusade and sent his army ahead to Acre, where we have already noted its arrival during the reign of Amaury II. Before he could embark to follow it, he died in Italy, leaving his son Frederick only three years old. His death gave the papacy an opportunity once more to separate Sicily from Germany. The succession to the empire was elective and the pope supported Otto IV of Brunswick, a rival to the Hohenstaufens, thereby plunging Germany into many years of civil war.

Sicily at first seemed to be more fortunate, Constance being the daughter of their own Norman kings. On 27th November, 1198, however, Constance died, leaving her infant son Frederick as a ward of the pope. The island was immediately torn by a bitter struggle between the Germans left by Henry VI on the one hand and the pope and the Sicilians on the other.

The Norman conquest of Sicily had not been savage like the Christian reconquista in Spain. Indeed the Norman kings had adapted themselves so thoroughly to Arab culture that they had been called the baptized sultans. The most remarkable achievement of the Norman kings, however, was the extraordinary racial and religious co-operation over which they presided. The basic culture of Sicily had been Greek and Byzantine. On this was superimposed for two centuries Muslim-Arab religion and civilization. The influence of Italy was strong and the new rulers were Normans. The Roman and Orthodox Churches lived side by side with Islam, and Greek, Italian, Arabic and French were spoken with equal facility.

So internationally-minded a country was able to trade equally with Europe, Asia and North Africa and the island was extremely wealthy. King Roger had also made Sicily a world centre of learning where Muslims and Christians worked amicably together. The standard of living was Arab, as superior to that of twelfth-century Europe as is that of the West to the Arab standard today. The beautiful palaces of Palermo with their gardens, fountains, running streams and colonnaded piazzas were compared by eastern visitors to the luxurious courts of Baghdad, Cairo and Cordova. The royal entourage included many Arab scientists, poets and musicians. From them Frederick learned to

CYPRUS

MAP 21

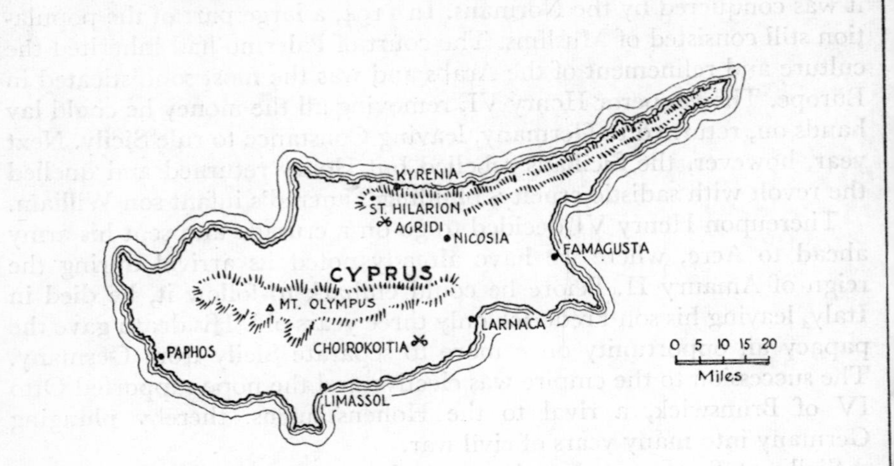

MAP 22

THE MEDITERRANEAN IN 1225

To show the encirclement of the Papal Territory by the Union of The Empire and Sicily. (Sicily included Southern Italy)

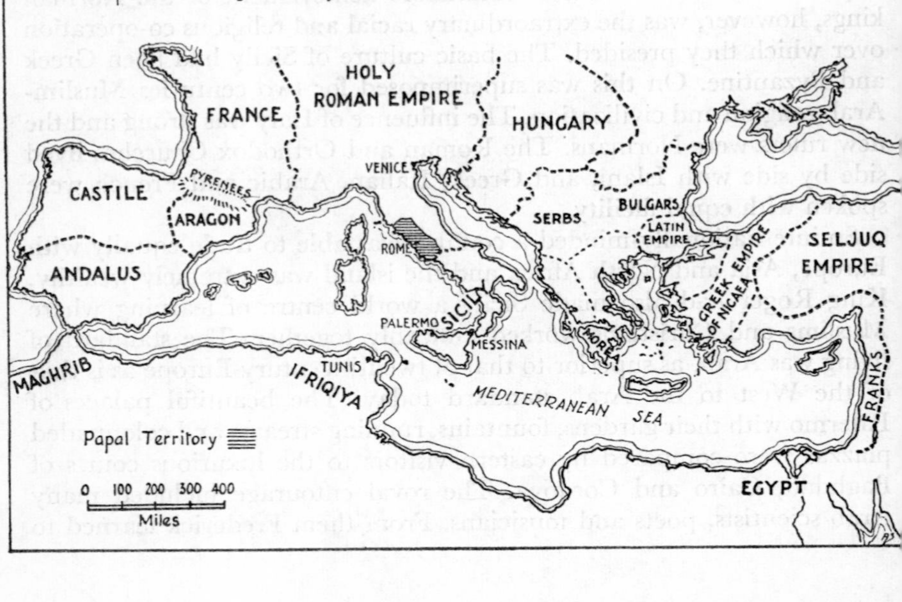

speak fluent Arabic and acquired a devotion to learning which was to last all his life.

Left to his own devices, the boy became an omnivorous reader, an accomplished horseman and a passionate lover of animals, of birds and of beautiful scenery. Long years afterwards in Acre, in one of his irreverent moods, he once remarked that God cannot ever have seen Sicily or he would not have chosen Palestine as His Holy Land. Frederick acquired an affection for the Arabs and the native Sicilians but a strong dislike for the Germans. He possessed a burning spirit, unresting energy and an extreme impatience of restraint.

On 26th December, 1208, he attained his majority at the age of fourteen. Nine months later he was married to Constance of Aragon, a bride chosen for him by the pope. Constance was twenty-four and was already the widow of the King of Hungary. Brought up in Aragon and in Provence, she was familiar with the background of Arab learning and poetry which she found in Sicily.

For fourteen years since the death of Henry VI Germany had been torn by civil wars. In 1212, when Frederick was eighteen, delegates from the Ghibelline party came to offer him the empire. Innocent III was in a dilemma, for the election of Frederick would once more unite Germany and Sicily. At length the pope consented on condition that Frederick abandon the crown of Sicily and swear allegiance to the papacy. In February 1212, Frederick did homage to Innocent III in Rome and rode on to Germany, where he arrived a complete stranger. But Innocent excommunicated Otto IV, who had not proved sufficiently submissive, and Frederick gained the empire with the help of the church. He was to be emperor for thirty-eight years, only nine of which he was to spend in Germany.

In July 1215, at the age of twenty-one, he was crowned at Aix-la-Chapelle, seated on the throne of Charlemagne, and suddenly announced his intention to take the Cross. In 1220, he left Germany to be crowned again as emperor in Rome on 22nd November, amid extraordinary pomp and magnificence. (From November 1219 to September 1221, Jean de Brienne was holding Damietta and Jenghis Khan was conquering Persia.) In Rome, Frederick renewed his vows to go on a crusade and not to reunite the crowns of Germany and Sicily, Henry, his infant son by Constance of Aragon, being declared King of Sicily. Frederick then rode on happily to his beloved Sicily, of which in theory he was no longer king.

Tradition relates that St. Francis of Assisi, returning from Egypt, visited Frederick in Sicily. The emperor arranged for a beautiful courtesan to be introduced into the saint's bedroom at night, while he himself watched through a spyhole. (Frederick was an emperor but

THE

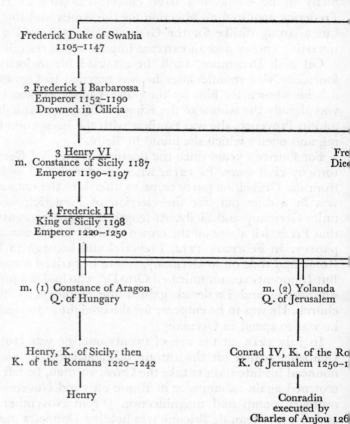

Fre

Frederick Duke of Swabia
1105–1147

2 Frederick I Barbarossa
Emperor 1152–1190
Drowned in Cilicia

3 Henry VI
m. Constance of Sicily 1187
Emperor 1190–1197

Fre
Die

4 Frederick II
King of Sicily 1198
Emperor 1220–1250

m. (1) Constance of Aragon
Q. of Hungary

m. (2) Yolanda
Q. of Jerusalem

Henry, K. of Sicily, then
K. of the Romans 1220–1242

Conrad IV, K. of the Ro
K. of Jerusalem 1250–1

Henry

Conradin
executed by
Charles of Anjou 126

NOTES

(1) German Emperors are numbered and underlined.

(2) Some of them were de facto emperors but were technically only kings, not having received an imperial coronation.

FENS

abia

1 Conrad III
King of Germany 1138–1152
of the Second Crusade

abia
1191

Philip Duke of Swabia
m. Irene, d. of Isaac II Angelus

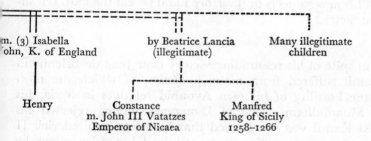

m. (3) Isabella
ohn, K. of England

by Beatrice Lancia
(illegitimate)

Many illegitimate
children

Henry

Constance
m. John III Vatatzes
Emperor of Nicaea

Manfred
King of Sicily
1258–1266

(3) Succession to the empire was elective not hereditary. The Welf or Guelph family were rivals of the Hohenstaufens for the empire. Between Henry VI and Frederick II, the emperor was Otto IV, a Welf (1197–1218).

he was far from being a gentleman.) According to the tradition, the saint drove the woman from his room "with fire". Frederick was impressed. He had never met a real saint before.

After his disastrous crusade, Jean de Brienne came to Rome. He had become King of Jerusalem in 1210 by marrying Marie, the heiress of the kingdom. Marie, however, had died in 1212 leaving a baby daughter Yolanda, now eleven years old. Frederick's wife, Constance of Aragon, had meanwhile died also and the pope now approved of the marriage of the emperor to Yolanda of Jerusalem. At a meeting with the pope on 23rd March, 1223, in the presence of Jean de Brienne, Frederick pledged himself to marry Yolanda and to go on pilgrimage. Two years later Yolanda was married to Frederick in the cathedral of Brindisi on 9th November, 1225, with great pomp.

Once the ceremony was over, Frederick scarcely looked at his bride again, though he amused himself by seducing one of her maids of honour. Jean de Brienne had believed that the wedding would bring the whole strength of the empire to rescue Outremer. On the very day of the marriage, however, Frederick told him brutally that he was no longer needed, thereby depriving Outremer of its leader. Meanwhile the emperor added King of Jerusalem to his imperial titles. Frederick's cynical conduct throughout this affair almost passes belief. The cruelty of his behaviour to his fourteen-year-old bride and his indifference to the welfare of his new subjects in the Holy Land reveal the hard selfishness of his character.

* * *

In Cairo, in spite of his resounding victory over Jean de Brienne in 1221, Al Kamil suffered from many anxieties, of which the most serious was the hostility of his own Ayoubid relatives in Syria, his brother, Al Muadhdham, King of Damascus, having rejected his suzerainty. Al Kamil was so alarmed that he wrote to Frederick II in the autumn of 1226, suggesting that, as titular King of Jerusalem, he pay a visit to Acre. Early in 1227 Frederick in his turn sent an embassy to Cairo. In the autumn of 1227, Al Kamil sent another embassy to Frederick. The ambassador sent by Al Kamil to Sicily on both occasions was Fakhr al Deen ibn al Shaikh who became so intimate with Frederick II that the emperor not only knighted him but gave him leave to bear the Hohenstaufen arms.

Pope Honorius III, a benevolent old man, died on 18th March, 1227, and was succeeded by the more energetic Gregory IX. Frederick, who had been postponing his crusade ever since his coronation in 1215, had finally pledged himself to go in August 1227. Large numbers of Crusaders accordingly assembled in southern Italy, where, however,

THE LAST HEIRS OF JERUSALEM

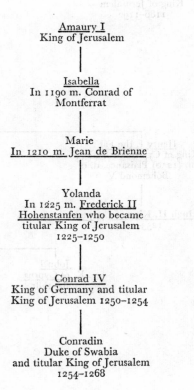

Amaury I
King of Jerusalem

|

Isabella
In 1190 m. Conrad of Montferrat

|

Marie
In 1210 m. Jean de Brienne

|

Yolanda
In 1225 m. Frederick II Hohenstanfen who became titular King of Jerusalem
1225–1250

|

Conrad IV
King of Germany and titular King of Jerusalem 1250–1254

|

Conradin
Duke of Swabia
and titular King of Jerusalem
1254–1268

THE LUS

Hugh VIII de L
Comte de la M

Guy
m. Sibylla, d. of Amaury I
King of Jerusalem
1186–1192

Henry I, the Fat
King of Cyprus 1218–1253
m. (1250) Plaisance, d. of
Bohemond V

Hugh II, King of Cyprus
1253–1267

Marie

John I
K. of Cyprus
1284–1285

Henry II
K. of Cyprus
1285–1324
Last King of Jerusalem
1286–1291

A

ASTY OF CYPRUS

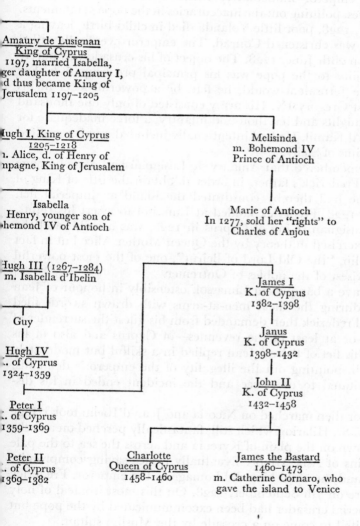

Amaury de Lusignan
King of Cyprus
1197, married Isabella,
ger daughter of Amaury I,
d thus became King of
Jerusalem 1197–1205

Iugh I, King of Cyprus
1205–1218
1. Alice, d. of Henry of
npagne, King of Jerusalem

Melisinda
m. Bohemond IV
Prince of Antioch

Isabella
Henry, younger son of
hemond IV of Antioch

Marie of Antioch
In 1277, sold her "rights" to
Charles of Anjou

Iugh III (1267–1284)
m. Isabella d'Ibelin

Guy

Hugh IV
.. of Cyprus
1324–1359

Peter I
.. of Cyprus
1359–1369

Peter II
.. of Cyprus
1369–1382

James I
K. of Cyprus
1382–1398

Janus
K. of Cyprus
1398–1432

John II
K. of Cyprus
1432–1458

Charlotte
Queen of Cyprus
1458–1460

James the Bastard
1460–1473
m. Catherine Cornaro, who
gave the island to Venice

they were attacked by an epidemic. None the less, on 9th September, 1227, the emperor set sail but himself developed the illness and put back to port. Gregory IX immediately pronounced his excommunication and issued an encyclical condemning his conduct—unnecessarily harsh and arbitrary actions in view of the fact that Frederick really had been ill. The emperor immediately issued a circular letter to all Christian princes, pointing out the inaccuracies in the pope's statements.

On 4th May, 1228, poor little Yolanda died in child-birth, leaving a baby boy who was christened Conrad. The emperor eventually sailed from Brindisi on 28th June, 1228. The object of his crusade was purely political. Hostility to the pope was his principal preoccupation. For him to capture Jerusalem would, he felt, be a powerful asset in his struggle against Gregory IX. His army consisted of only one thousand five hundred knights and ten thousand infantry, a force inadequate for a war against Al Kamil. He had intentionally included a unit recruited from the Muslims of Sicily.

It will be remembered that Amaury de Lusignan had done homage to Henry VI, Frederick's father, in order to obtain the title of King of Cyprus, but he had thereby constituted the island an imperial fief. On 21st July, 1228, Frederick landed at Limassol to assert his rights. Henry I de Lusignan, King of Cyprus in 1228, was a child, and the regency was exercised in theory by the Queen Mother Alice but in fact by Jean d'Ibelin, "the Old Lord of Beirut", one of the most powerful but also the wisest of the nobles of Outremer.

Frederick gave a banquet in Limassol, ostensibly in honour of Jean d'Ibelin but during the meal men-at-arms with drawn swords filed into the hall. Frederick then demanded from his guest the surrender of the regency—or at least of the revenues—of Cyprus and also of his possession of his fief of Beirut. Jean replied in a skilful but moderately worded speech, pointing out the illegality of the emperor's demands. Frederick hesitated to use force and the incident ended in his discomfiture.

The emperor then marched on Nicosia and Jean d'Ibelin took refuge in the castle of St. Hilarion which still, fantastically perched on a rocky crag, looks down on the plain of Kyrenia and across the sea to the pale blue mountains of Asia Minor. Eventually a face-saving compromise was reached and the child king did homage to the emperor. Frederick landed at Acre on 7th September, 1228. On this most ironical of holy wars, the imperial crusader had been excommunicated by the pope but had been invited to come on a crusade by the Muslim sultan.

Meanwhile, however, on 12th November, 1227, Al Muadhdham had died and the cause of Al Kamil's invitation to Frederick had disappeared. Al Muadhdham had been brave, generous, cultured and popular and had been a dangerous rival to Al Kamil. His son, Malik al Nasir Daood,[1] was a youth of twenty-one with whom the sultan believed himself competent to deal. He decided to march on Damascus and was already in Palestine when Frederick landed at Acre on 7th September, 1228.

The emperor's arrival at a time when Al Kamil's situation was so much improved placed the sultan in a quandary. Frederick immediately wrote to him, pointing out that he had come at his request and consequently that he could not possibly accept less than Al Kamil had offered to Jean de Brienne who had come as an enemy. The sultan, however, was no longer in need of the emperor's help. Messengers came and went without result between Acre and Al Kamil's camp at Tel al Ajool.

Frederick decided that only a threat of action would clinch an agreement. Accordingly, with some courage, he set out to march southwards down the coast towards Gaza. The Templars and Hospitallers had at first refused to serve with an excommunicated monarch but they eventually overtook him north of Arsoof, appreciating that Al Kamil's army was in a position to exterminate Frederick's small force, Early in November 1228, the emperor's little army reached Jaffa, which it hastily placed in a state of defence.

Perhaps Frederick's march impressed Al Kamil. At the same time, Al Nasir Daood, the son of Muadhdham, was besieged in Damascus by Al Ashraf, another brother of Al Kamil.[2] After five months of bargaining, an agreement between the sultan and the emperor was finally signed on 18th February, 1229. Its terms were as follows:

(1) Jerusalem was to be handed over to the Franks on condition that they did not rebuild the walls, which had been razed. The villages around Jerualem and the temple area inside the city would, however, be retained by the Muslims.
(2) The villages on the coastal plain between Acre and Jaffa would belong to the Christians and also a line of villages from Lydda to Jerusalem, forming a corridor to the Holy City.[3]
(3) Farther north the Franks recovered Nazareth and Saffuriya and the whole territory of Sidon, previously shared with the Muslims.

The agreement, which was largely negotiated through Fakhr al Deen, whom Frederick had knighted in Sicily, also included a ten-year truce.

These were substantial gains obtained without striking a blow. The

[1] Genealogical tree, page 216. [2] Genealogical tree, page 216.
[3] This solution is extremely interesting as resembling the present de facto situation in which Israel holds the coastal plain and a corridor to Jerusalem.

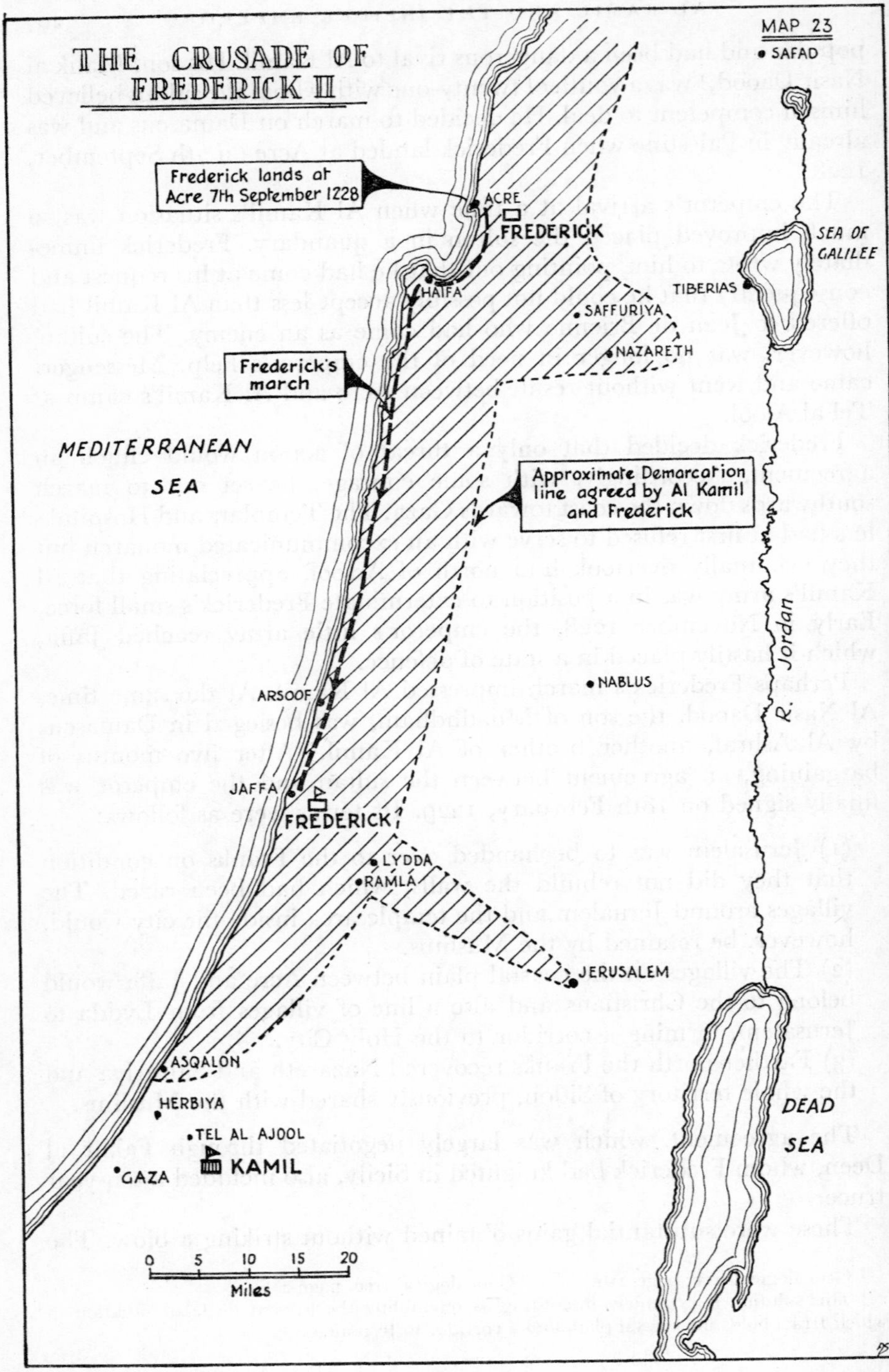
THE CRUSADE OF FREDERICK II
MAP 23
SAFAD
Frederick lands at Acre 7th September 1228
ACRE
FREDERICK
SEA OF GALILEE
HAIFA
TIBERIAS
SAFFURIYA
NAZARETH
Frederick's march
MEDITERRANEAN SEA
Approximate Demarcation line agreed by Al Kamil and Frederick
R. Jordan
NABLUS
ARSOOF
JAFFA
FREDERICK
LYDDA
RAMLA
JERUSALEM
ASQALON
HERBIYA
DEAD SEA
TEL AL AJOOL
KAMIL
GAZA
0 5 10 15 20
Miles

mutual sympathy and toleration shown by Al Kamil and Frederick II seem indeed to be centuries away from the fanaticisms of the Turkmans and the First Crusade, a hundred and fifty years earlier. The Ayoubids had set a remarkable example in enlightenment and toleration, perhaps due to the fact that they were Arabicized Kurds and thus, unlike the Turkmans, the heirs of an ancient civilization. The policy of mutual respect had indeed been inaugurated by Richard Coeur de Lion, who had been brought up in Aquitaine where Arab influence was strong, while Frederick had himself grown up among the Muslims of Sicily.

Both Al Kamil and Frederick II were furiously attacked by their co-religionists. The Franks of Outremer would have nothing to do with Frederick. The Muslim world bitterly denounced Al Kamil for his concessions regarding Jerusalem. Before sailing for Italy, Frederick II visited Jerusalem on 17th March 1229. The Latin Patriarch forbade the Christian clergy to recognize him, with the result that the emperor crowned himself King of Jerusalem in the Church of the Holy Sepulchre in the absence of any priests.

To avoid disturbing the emperor's slumbers, the qadhi had forbidden the muedhdhins to give the dawn call to prayer, but Frederick expressed his regret at not hearing them. Maqrizi praises Frederick warmly, adding that he was well-versed in mathematics, physics and engineering, a remarkable feature in a Frank, most of whom were uneducated. Not all Muslims, however, were impressed by Frederick. Physically his appearance was not regal, for he was small in stature, short-sighted, had reddish hair and was clean-shaven, whereas Muslims considered a beard to be a chief ornament of manhood. The emperor is said to have learned from the Arabs the use of the hood for hawks. On returning to Sicily he wrote a book on falconry.

The barons and people of Outremer had not been consulted by Frederick when he made his agreement with the sultan. The witnesses to the treaty had been the German Grand Master of the Teutonic Order and the Bishops of Winchester and Exeter, who were with the Crusade. Some of the barons saw that the weakness of Frederick's retrocession of Jerusalem was the fact that the city could not be defended. The walls had been razed and the surrounding villages were Muslim. Its retention would depend firstly on the amity of the sultan and secondly on Al Kamil's continuance in power. Frederick with his acute intelligence must have been aware of these weaknesses but perhaps he did not care. He wished to be able to claim that he had won back Jerusalem in order merely to gain support in his struggle against the pope. Gregory IX, on the other hand, continued to behave rather as a lay politician than as a Christian, refusing all compromise with the emperor and even sending Jean de Brienne with a papal army to invade Apulia.

Frederick II re-embarked at Acre on 1st May, 1229, amid painful scenes. Aware of his unpopularity, he left his quarters at dawn to go down to the harbour but a crowd quickly collected and he was pelted with stones and offal in the streets. Landing in Cyprus, he appointed a regency council of five barons, all bitter opponents of Jean d'Ibelin.

Frederick had secured valuable concessions for the Franks and had further contributed to the reduction of fanaticism between the two religions, but he had disastrously divided the Franks into rival factions. A brilliant intellectual and a subtle diplomat, his ideas were in many ways in advance of his times. Yet he was also narrow, brutal, vindictive and treacherous—a man entirely wanting in human kindness. He alienated the Franks of Outremer when he could easily have won them.

Before sailing, he established an Italian garrison in Acre to hold the town against the barons of the kingdom. When, in the summer of 1230, he became temporarily reconciled with Gregory IX, he sent a fresh army from Italy to the Holy Land, to fight not the Muslims but the Franks. The commander of this force, Marshal Filanghieri, was nominated imperial legate in Outremer. Repulsed from Cyprus, he sailed on to Syria where he seized Beirut, the personal fief of Jean d'Ibelin. Thence, marching southward, Filanghieri occupied Sidon, Tyre and Acre also.[4]

On 2nd May, 1232, Filanghieri defeated the Ibelin party north of Acre then, embarking hastily, he landed in Cyprus and occupied the island, the young King Henry I being with the Ibelins in Syria. Many Frankish lords in Cyprus fled from their homes and lived with their families in caves in the mountains. Frederick had indeed made peace with the Muslims but had sown a bitter civil war between the Franks. Fortunately, in the opinion of the chivalrous Al Kamil, the Kingdom of Jerusalem belonged to his friend Frederick and he did not take advantage of the anarchy among the Christians.

On 30th May, 1232, Jean d'Ibelin sailed from Sidon, took Famagusta and marched on Nicosia. Filanghieri abandoned the capital, intending to retire to Kyrenia, but the Old Lord of Beirut overtook the imperialists on 15th June at Agridi between the two towns and inflicted on them a severe defeat. Filanghieri and his army held out in the fortress of Kyrenia from June 1232 to 3rd April, 1233, when they abandoned Cyprus and returned to their base in Tyre.

Jean d'Ibelin, the Old Lord of Beirut, died in 1236. A man of remarkable dignity, wisdom and moderation, as well versed in law

[4] Map 25, page 214.

as in war, he was for many years the uncrowned king alike of the Kingdom of Jerusalem and of Cyprus. With his death anarchy returned to the Franks of Outremer.

In spite of the violence and bloodshed of the Middle Ages, legal forms were treated with respect under the feudal system. Frederick II died in 1250, his son Conrad IV was titular King of Jerusalem until 1254 and his grandson Conradin from 1254 to 1268. Thus from 1228 to 1268, a period of forty years, the Hohenstaufens remained titular Kings of Jerusalem. None of these three rulers did anything for Outremer, yet their legal title through Yolanda being valid, no other king could mount the throne. Jerusalem—or rather Acre—a kingdom without a king, sank into increasing anarchy. Every baron fought for his own interest alone. The military orders, the Templars, the Hospitallers and the Teutonic Order, were as hostile to one another as to the Muslims. The Genoese, Venetians and Pisans, intent only on commercial rivalry, opposed one another with intrigues or even in battle. It was fortunate for the Franks that during these years, the Muslims also were in constant fear, weakness and danger.

* * *

We left Jalal al Deen Khuwarizm Shah after his escape across the Indus, enlisting soldiers in the Punjab.[5] In 1224, the news that Jenghis Khan was returning to Mongolia emboldened him to attempt the recovery of his throne. Crossing the desert of Makran with four thousand men, he easily took Shiraz and Isfahan, the Mongols having left no troops in West Persia. In 1225 he occupied Adharbaijan, establishing his capital in Tabriz. Thence, in 1225 and 1226, he raided the Christian Kingdom of Georgia, taking and looting Tiflis on 9th March, 1226, destroying all the churches.

Jalal al Deen had thus reconstituted a considerable empire west of the Salt Desert. It is true that Khuwarizm and Khurasan were depopulated deserts, but West Persia had suffered far less from the Mongols. There was, however, no guarantee that the invaders would not return and Jalal al Deen proposed an alliance with Ala al Deen Kai Qobad I, the Sultan of Iconium,[6] but the negotiations broke down.

During the years 1228 and 1229, while Frederick II was in Palestine, Jalal al Deen Khuwarizam Shah remained in Adharbaijan, living the life of a robber baron. He neither consolidated his empire nor allied himself with his fellow-Muslims against a possible return of the Mongols. His outlook was that of a mere freebooter and, in 1228, he again devastated Georgia. At the end of 1229, with incredible folly, he laid

[5] Page 186. [6] Genealogical tree, page 168.

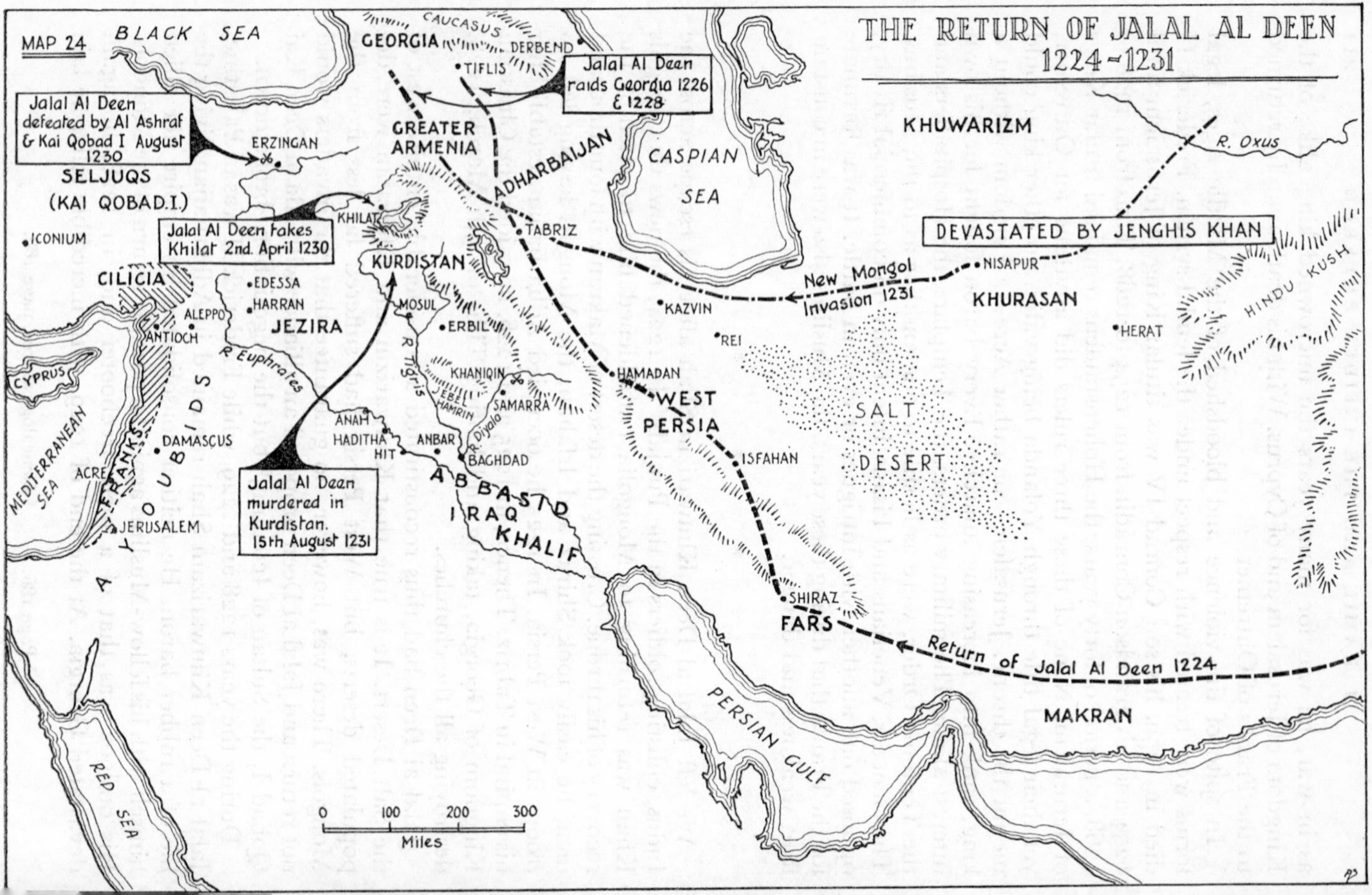
MAP 24
THE RETURN OF JALAL AL DEEN
1224–1231
BLACK SEA
CAUCASUS
GEORGIA
DERBEND
TIFLIS
Jalal Al Deen raids Georgia 1226 & 1228
Jalal Al Deen defeated by Al Ashraf & Kai Qobad I August 1230
ERZINGAN
GREATER ARMENIA
ADHARBAIJAN
CASPIAN
SEA
KHUWARIZM
R. Oxus
SELJUQS
(KAI QOBAD.I.)
KHILAT
TABRIZ
DEVASTATED BY JENGHIS KHAN
ICONIUM
Jalal Al Deen takes Khilat 2nd. April 1230
KURDISTAN
NISAPUR
New Mongol Invasion 1231
CILICIA
EDESSA
HARRAN
MOSUL
KAZVIN
KHURASAN
HINDU KUSH
ALEPPO
ANTIOCH
JEZIRA
ERBIL
REI
HERAT
R Euphrates
R Tigris
CYPRUS
KHANIQIN
JEBEL HAMRIN
HAMADAN
WEST
PERSIA
SAMARRA
SALT
DESERT
R. Diyala
ANAH
HADITHA
HIT
ANBAR
BAGHDAD
ISFAHAN
DAMASCUS
MEDITERRANEAN SEA
ACRE
FRANKS
AYOUBIDS
JERUSALEM
Jalal Al Deen murdered in Kurdistan. 15th August 1231
ABBASID
IRAQ
KHALIF
SHIRAZ
FARS
Return of Jalal Al Deen 1224
MAKRAN
PERSIAN GULF
RED SEA
0 100 200 300
Miles

siege to Khilat, which belonged to Al Ashraf, the brother of Sultan Al Kamil, and took it on 2nd April, 1230.

This wanton aggression provoked an immediate alliance between Al Ashraf and Kai Qobad I, Sultan of Iconium, and their allied armies defeated Jalal al Deen at Erzingan on 10th August, 1230, and drove him back to Adharbaijan. In the winter of 1230 to 1231, however, a new Mongol army suddenly appeared in Adharbaijan. Jalal al Deen's troops dispersed and he himself was murdered, on 15th August, 1231, in the Kurdish mountains when fleeing from the invaders. In the course of 1231, the Mongols occupied all Adharbaijan and Greater Armenia. Thus ended the dynasty of the Khuwarizm Shahs who, after starting as slaves of the Seljuq Sultans, had for a few brief years built up an empire and had then as quickly lost it.

Jalal al Deen possessed the faults and the virtues of a Turkman trooper. Physically brave, living on plunder, he went to bed drunk every night. Lacking in political sense, he spent his years of power attacking his fellow Muslims instead of building up an alliance against the Mongols. From the return of Jenghis Khan to Mongolia in 1225 until the arrival of the new Mongol army to fight Jalal al Deen in 1231, the Muslim rulers had enjoyed a respite of six years in which to unite to oppose further Tatar invasions. Far from profiting therefrom, they merely continued to fight each other.

Meanwhile the Ayoubid princes in Syria were again in revolt against Al Kamil. Profiting by these quarrels, the Sultan of Iconium, Kai Qobad I, seized Edessa and Harran. In 1236, Al Kamil retook them both and left his eldest son Malik al Salih Ayoub as governor of the Jezira.

In 1237, however, another brother of Al Kamil, Al Salih Ismail,[7] rebelled in Damascus. The weary Al Kamil set out once more and, on 6th January, 1238, took Damascus, giving Baalbek to Al Salih Ismail in lieu of the capital. Meanwhile the Mongols had taken and destroyed Erbil,[8] in Northern Iraq, a town belonging to the Khalif Mustansir, who appealed to Al Kamil for troops, in case the Mongols should attack Baghdad.

On 8th March, 1238, Sultan Al Kamil died at the age of sixty. He had been a great ruler, a skilful politician, an enlightened and painstaking administrator. He disliked bloodshed and always sought to negotiate rather than to fight, but throughout his reign he was harassed by family revolts, particularly by his own brothers Al Muadhdham, Al Ashraf and Al Salih Ismail. Yet perhaps his most remarkable quality

[7] Al Kamil's son Ayoub and his brother Ismail both had the throne name Malik al Salih. I have called them Al Salih Ayoub and Al Salih Ismail.

[8] Map 24, page 212.

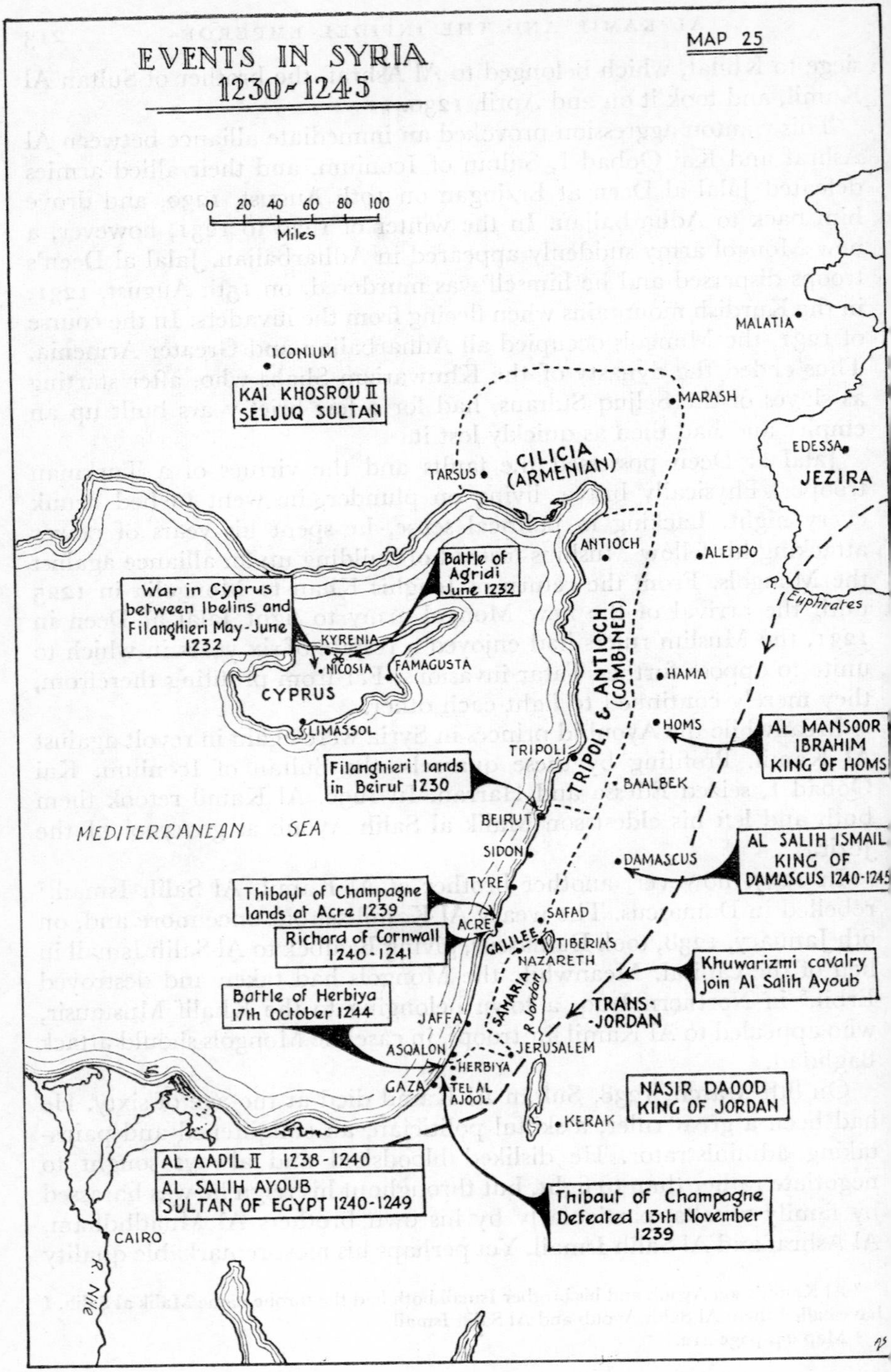
EVENTS IN SYRIA
1230-1245
MAP 25
0 20 40 60 80 100
Miles
ICONIUM
KAI KHOSROU II
SELJUQ SULTAN
MALATIA
MARASH
EDESSA
JEZIRA
TARSUS
CILICIA
(ARMENIAN)
ANTIOCH
ALEPPO
R. Euphrates
Battle of
Agridi
June 1232
War in Cyprus
between Ibelins and
Filanghieri May-June
1232
KYRENIA
NICOSIA
FAMAGUSTA
CYPRUS
LIMASSOL
TRIPOLI & ANTIOCH
(COMBINED)
HAMA
HOMS
AL MANSOOR
IBRAHIM
KING OF HOMS
TRIPOLI
Filanghieri lands
in Beirut 1230
BAALBEK
BEIRUT
MEDITERRANEAN SEA
SIDON
AL SALIH ISMAIL
KING OF
DAMASCUS 1240-1245
DAMASCUS
TYRE
Thibaut of Champagne
lands at Acre 1239
SAFAD
ACRE
Richard of Cornwall
1240-1241
GALILEE
TIBERIAS
NAZARETH
Khuwarizmi cavalry
join Al Salih Ayoub
Battle of Herbiya
17th October 1244
SAMARIA
R. Jordan
TRANS-
-JORDAN
JAFFA
ASQALON
JERUSALEM
HERBIYA
GAZA
TEL AL
AJOOL
NASIR DAOOD
KING OF JORDAN
KERAK
AL AADIL II 1238-1240
AL SALIH AYOUB
SULTAN OF EGYPT 1240-1249
Thibaut of Champagne
Defeated 13th November
1239
CAIRO
R. Nile

was his religious toleration. Frederick was tolerant of religious differences because he was an agnostic, but Kamil was tolerant though a pious Muslim. In accordance with the oft-repeated pattern, the Ayoubids produced three great monarchs and then an anarchy of rival princes. Yet few dynasties in history can boast of three greater rulers than Saladin, Al Aadil and Al Kamil.

Al Kamil had been displeased with his eldest son Al Salih Ayoub and had exiled him by making him governor of the Jezira. He nominated his second son Al Aadil II as sultan although he was only eighteen. In Syria pandemonium broke out between the many rival Ayoubid princes. In 1239, a year after Al Kamil's death, his eldest son Al Salih Ayoub seized Damascus, only to be evicted by his uncle, Al Salih Ismail, who maintained himself in the Syrian capital from 1240 to 1245.

Meanwhile the ten-year truce concluded between Frederick and Al Kamil had expired and, in 1239, Gregory IX had preached a new crusade. On 1st September, 1239, Thibaut IV, Count of Champagne and King of Navarre, landed in Acre with between one thousand and fifteen hundred knights. No sooner did Al Nasir Daood, the son of Al Muadhdham, hear of the landing than, assuming the truce to be broken, he seized Jerusalem. The weakness of Frederick's settlement was thus revealed—Jerusalem could not be defended, although its governor at this time was a representative of the emperor.

In November 1239, therefore, the situation was as follows—Thibaut and his small force were in Acre. Al Aadil II, second son of Al Kamil, was Sultan of Egypt. Al Nasir Daood was King of Transjordan, to which he now added Jerusalem and Samaria. Al Kamil's brother Al Salih Ismail held Damascus from which he had driven Al Kamil's eldest son, Al Salih Ayoub.

The Crusade of Thibaut of Champagne was anarchic in the manner of the undisciplined French chivalry of the time. The French nobles were jealous of one another and unwilling to obey Thibaut. On 2nd November, the Crusaders set out to attack Gaza but on the 13th of the month they met with a crushing defeat north of that town, losing a thousand killed and six hundred prisoners.

Meanwhile in Cairo, Aadil II was passing his time in frivolous amusements. In two years he had frittered away eight million dinars left in the treasury by the careful Al Kamil. On 31st May, 1240, he was arrested by the senior officers of the army and confined in the citadel where, eight years later, he was quietly strangled. The officers then invited Al Kamil's eldest son Al Salih Ayoub to mount the throne. He entered Cairo on 19th June, 1240, and was proclaimed sultan, a position he was to occupy for nine turbulent years.

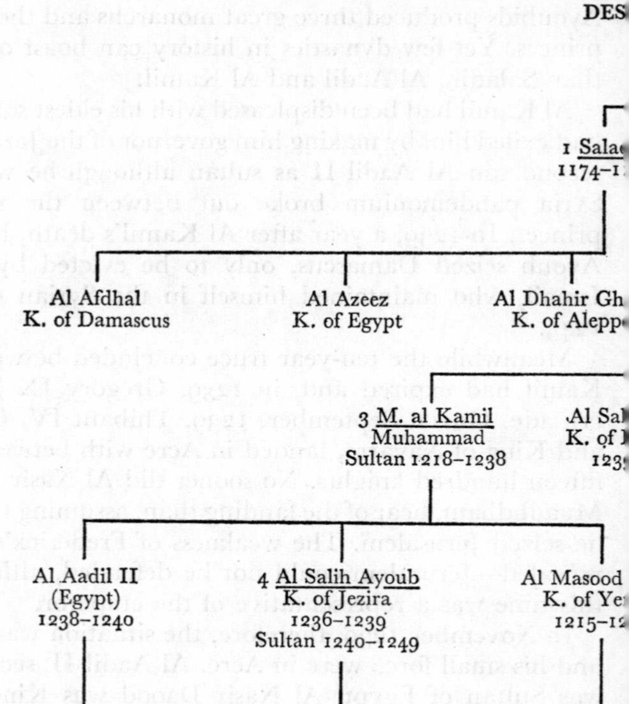

DES
1 Sala
1174–1
Al Afdhal
K. of Damascus
Al Azeez
K. of Egypt
Al Dhahir Gh
K. of Alepp
3 M. al Kamil
Muhammad
Sultan 1218–1238
Al Sal
K. of
123
Al Aadil II
(Egypt)
1238–1240
4 Al Salih Ayoub
K. of Jezira
1236–1239
Sultan 1240–1249
Al Masood
K. of Ye
1215–12
Al Mughith Umar
K. of Transjordan
1249–1263
5 Al Muadhdham
Turanshah
Sultan 1249–1250
Last Ayoubid Sultan
Salah al Dee
Al Ashraf
Child Sultan
1250–12
(under Aibek an
Pearls)

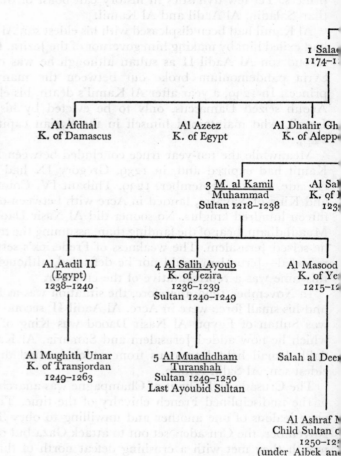

AL AADIL

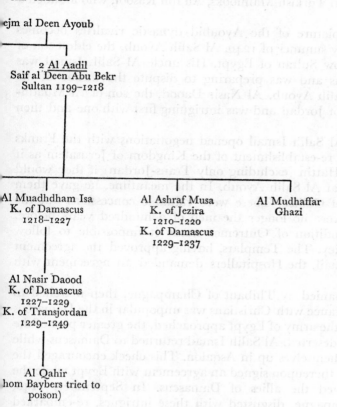

ejm al Deen Ayoub

2 Al Aadil
Saif al Deen Abu Bekr
Sultan 1199–1218

Al Muadhdham Isa
K. of Damascus
1218–1227

Al Ashraf Musa
K. of Jezira
1210–1220
K. of Damascus
1229–1237

Al Mudhaffar
Ghazi

Al Nasir Daood
K. of Damascus
1227–1229
K. of Transjordan
1229–1249

Al Qahir
hom Baybers tried to
poison)

NOTE

Men who became supreme sultan are underlined. It will be noted that with effect from 1199, the sultanate passed down the family of Al Aadil and the sons of Saladin never became sultans.

The once-glorious Ayoubid dynasty seemed to be everywhere in decline. Al Masood, the third son of Al Kamil, had been King of the Yemen from 1215 to 1228 but on his death the family was overthrown by one of their own Turkish Mamlooks, Ali ibn Rasool, who founded a new dynasty.[9]

The confused picture of the Ayoubid dynastic rivalries becomes clearer in the early summer of 1240. Al Salih Ayoub, the eldest son of Al Kamil, was now Sultan of Egypt. His uncle Al Salih Ismail was King of Damascus and was preparing to dispute the throne of the empire with Al Salih Ayoub. Al Nasir Daood, the son of Al Muadhdham, was King of Jordan and was intriguing first with one and then with the other.

At this stage, Al Salih Ismail opened negotiations with the Franks offering them the re-establishment of the Kingdom of Jerusalem as it had been before Hattin (excluding only Trans-Jordan) if they would assist him to defeat Al Salih Ayoub. In the meantime, he gave them Safad and part of Galilee. These were valuable concessions but the Franks of 1240 were no longer the men of a hundred years before. The anarchic condition of Outremer made it impossible to follow any coherent policy. The Templars, having approved the agreement with Al Salih Ismail, the Hospitallers demanded an agreement with Egypt.

Ismail, accompanied by Thibaut of Champagne, then marched to Gaza but this alliance with Christians was unpopular in the Damascus army. As soon as the army of Egypt approached, the greater part of the Damascus troops deserted. Al Salih Ismail returned to Damascus while the Franks shut themselves up in Asqalon. This check encouraged the Hospitallers, who thereupon signed an agreement with Egypt while the Templars remained the allies of Damascus. In September, 1240, Thibaut of Champagne, disgusted with these intrigues, re-embarked for France.

On 11th October, 1240, Richard, Earl of Cornwall, the brother of Henry III, King of England, landed in Acre with a body of crusaders. He was immediately canvassed by both Templars and Hospitallers to join their rival factions. "In the Holy Land," wrote Richard bitterly, "peace has been replaced by discord, unity by division, concord by hatred. The orders of brothers, formerly constituted to defend their common mother, now, swollen with pride by their excessive wealth, quarrel in her very bosom."[10]

Sickened by factional intrigue, Richard went to Asqalon and

[9] It will be remembered that Saladin had seized the Yemen in 1173 when he was afraid of Noor al Deen. Page 78.

[10] Matthew Paris, *Chronica Majora*, quoted by Grousset, *Histoire des Croisades*.

helped to rebuild the fortifications which were finished in March 1241. When a delegation from Sultan Al Salih Ayoub of Egypt visited him, he countersigned the peace concluded with him, as a result of which he obtained further territorial concessions including Tiberias and the release of all Frankish prisoners. A general relaxation of tension ensued.

In 1240–1241, an embassy from Frederick II came from Sicily to Cairo, where it was received with full military honours and remained for the winter as guests of the sultan. After the death of Yolanda, Frederick II had married Isabella, sister of Henry III and of Richard of Cornwall. The fact that he was brother-in-law of Frederick had enhanced Richard's prestige and enabled him to obtain favourable terms for the Franks from the sultan.

Much of the stabilization of the situation had been due to Richard, a wise and moderate man who had refused to be drawn into party intrigues. Simon de Montfort, later to be leader of the barons' war in England, had been one of his companions. No sooner did Richard sail from Acre on 3rd May, 1241, than confusion returned.

On 5th April, 1243, Conrad of Hohenstaufen, the son of Frederick II by Yolanda, attained his majority and became the legitimate King of Jerusalem, superseding his father who, since Yolanda's death, had merely been regent for his son. Marshal Filanghieri attempted, with the help of the Hospitallers, to seize Acre by a coup d'état. It failed and he was recalled by Frederick in disgrace.

The legalistically-minded barons of Acre recognized Conrad as king but, as he was not present to exercise his right, they elected Alice, the dowager Queen of Cyprus, as regent on his behalf—a legal manœuvre to free themselves from Frederick. In fact, Alice exercised no authority and Acre was governed by a commune.

These legal formalities completed, Balian d'Ibelin, the son of the Old Lord of Beirut, on 12th June, 1243, retook Tyre from the imperialists and the emperor Frederick's control disappeared from Outremer. The extreme legalism of the Franks of Outremer in 1243 is of great interest, for it was and still is, a quality typical of the Syrian peoples, who are acute and enthusiastic lawyers. The first Franks had relied on force, not on legal forms. A century and a half in Outremer had thus infused into the native Franks the qualities of the Syrians.

In June 1244, the Templars regained influence and revived the treaty with Al Salih Ismail of Damascus. Al Mansoor Ibrahim, the King of Homs, a great-grandson of Shirkuh, came to Acre on behalf of Ismail and was given a triumphal reception, the streets being carpeted and decorated with silk and cloth of gold. The new alliance directed against Al Salih Ayoub of Egypt consisted of his uncle Al Salih Ismail,

King of Damascus, Al Mansoor Ibrahim, King of Homs and Al Nasir Daood, King of Trans-Jordan,[11] and the Franks of Acre.

It will be remembered that Jalal al Deen Khuwarizm Shah had been defeated and killed in August 1231. His army, left without a commander and unable to return to Khuwarizm which had been occupied by the Mongols, drifted into the Jezira where it lived by plunder. In 1241, Sultan Al Salih Ayoub in Cairo, seeing himself threatened by the alliance of the Ayoubid princes of Syria with the Franks, invited the Khuwarizmis to join him. Ten thousand cavalry accepted the offer and marched from the Jezira to Gaza, overrunning Jerusalem on the way, killing seven thousand Franks in the city and enslaving their women.

On 17th October, 1244, a pitched battle was fought at Herbiya—called by the Franks La Forbie—north of Gaza, between Sultan Al Salih Ayoub's army and the Khuwarizmis on one side and the Ayoubids of Syria and the Franks on the other. The Khuwarizmis first defeated the Syrians, then swinging round, encircled the whole Frankish army, which was almost exterminated. Of three hundred and twelve Templars engaged, only thirty-six survived. Of three hundred and twenty-five Hospitallers, there were left only twenty-six. The Teutonic Order had only three survivors, while a contingent of knights from Cyprus was killed to the last man. Grousset calls the Battle of Herbiya "a second Hattin". It is noticeable that both the disasters at Hattin and at Herbiya were due to the recklessness of the Templars.

On 2nd October, 1245, after the victory at Herbiya, Sultan Al Salih Ayoub took Damascus, thereby reconstituting a single Ayoubid Empire from Egypt to the Jezira. In the summer of 1247, Al Salih Ayoub sent an army commanded by Fakhr al Deen, whom Frederick II had once knighted in Sicily, and retook Asqalon and Tiberias which had been given to the Franks by Al Salih Ismail.

* * *

It will be noted that in the activities described in this chapter, the Franks of Acre and Cyprus have alone been involved. Bohemond V, Prince of Antioch and Count of Tripoli, had disassociated himself from the Acre government. He was a weak ruler who customarily lived in Tripoli, neglecting Antioch. He was succeeded in 1251 by his son, Bohemond VI.

* * *

It will be remembered that the army of the Sultan of Egypt consisted principally of Mamlooks, mostly Turks, with no emotional loyalty to the dynasty or to the country. The increasing weakness of the Ayoubids

[11] Genealogical trees, pages 72 and 216.

tempted the Mamlooks to revolt. To secure his position, Al Salih Ayoub raised a new force of soldier-slaves, whom he quartered in a fortress on the Island of Raudha in the Nile opposite Cairo. Under the title of the Bahri or River Mamlooks, this force was to play a striking rôle in history.[12]

Al Salih Ayoub was of a morose disposition and distrusted his relatives of the Ayoubid family and the Kurdish troops on whom his dynasty had relied in the past. His River Mamlooks were, therefore, intended largely as personal lifeguards for himself. He may thus have been partly responsible for the system under which Mamlooks owed only personal loyalty to their master and not to the state. This principle was to become a marked feature of the Mamlook system.

The Ayoubid princes of Aleppo and Hama rebelled again in 1247. Wearily Al Salih Ayoub toiled back once more to Damascus. He was already ill, probably of tuberculosis of the lungs, and was carried in a litter. In the summer of 1248, his army laid siege to Homs. In May 1249, however, information reached Damascus that a new crusade was about to land in Egypt. Hastily patching up a peace with the rebels in Syria, Al Salih Ayoub, still carried in a litter, hurried back to Egypt.

NOTABLE DATES

Death of William II of Sicily Accession of Tancred	1189
Death of Tancred Emperor Henry VI joins Sicily to the Empire	1194
Coronation of Frederick II at Aix-la-Chapelle Frederick takes the Cross	July 1215
Frederick marries Yolanda of Jerusalem	9th November, 1225
Al Muadhdham, brother of Al Kamil, rebels in Damascus Al Kamil invites Frederick II to land in Acre	1226
Death of Al Muadhdham	12th November, 1227
Frederick lands at Acre	7th September, 1228
Treaty signed between Frederick and Kamil	18th February, 1229

[12] Professor Mustafa Ziada, however, states that the name Bahri was not derived from their barracks on the Nile but from the fact that they were recruited from beyond the sea. Bahr in Arabic properly means sea, though in Egypt it is used also for river.

Frederick re-embarks from Acre	1st May, 1229
Jalal al Deen Khuwarizm Shah takes Khilat	2nd April, 1230
Death of Jalal al Deen	15th August, 1231
Death of Sultan Al Kamil	8th March, 1238
Al Salih Ismail, brother of Kamil, King of Damascus	1240–1245
Al Salih Ayoub proclaimed Sultan of Egypt	19th June, 1240
Visit of Richard, Earl of Cornwall	11th October, 1240 to 3rd May, 1241
Battle of Herbiya, Franks utterly defeated	17th October, 1244
Capture of Damascus by Sultan Al Salih Ayoub Ayoubid Empire re-united	1245

PERSONALITIES

The Holy Roman Empire

Frederick I Barbarossa Hohenstaufen	1152–1190
Henry VI Hohenstaufen	1190–1197
Otto IV of Brunswick	1197–1218
Frederick II Hohenstaufen	1220–1250
Conrad IV Hohenstaufen	1250–1254

Ayoubid Sultans of Egypt

Al Kamil	1218–1238
Al Aadil II	1238–1240
Al Salih Ayoub	1240–1249

OTHER PERSONALITIES

Al Muadhdham Al Salih Ismail	Rebel brothers of Al Kamil
Al Nasir Daood	son of Al Muadhdham
Jean d'Ibelin	"the Old Lord of Beirut"
Marshal Filanghieri	Imperial Viceroy
Thibaut IV	Count of Champagne
Richard	Earl of Cornwall
Bohemond V	Prince of Antioch and Count of Tripoli

X

The Royal Saint

1244–1259

The Crusade of Louis of France was perhaps the only expedition since the days of Godfrey de Bouillon that deserved the name of a Holy War. It was led by a saintly hero, . . . "whose whole life was a prayer, his whole aim to do God's will"; a king whose high and noble character inspired universal trust and reverence; a leader whose courage and endurance rested on the sanctions of faith as well as on the obligations of knightly honour.

STANLEY LANE-POOLE, *A History of Egypt in the Middle Ages*

This holy man, King St. Louis, loved and feared God during his life above all things. The holy king loved truth so much that, even to the Saracens and infidels, although they were his enemies, he would never lie or break his word in anything he had promised them . . . He loved everyone who, with uprightness of heart, feared and loved God.

JEAN, SIEUR DE JOINVILLE, *Memoirs of Louis IX*

Whoever loves to work for virtuous ends,
Public and private, and who most intends
To do what deeds of gentleness he can,
Take him to be the greatest gentleman.
Christ wills we take our gentleness from him,
Not from a wealth of ancestry long dim.

CHAUCER, *Canterbury Tales*
(Done into modern English by
NEVILL COGHILL)

X

IMMEDIATELY after the disastrous Battle of Herbiya on 17th October, 1244, the Latin Patriarch of Jerusalem had sent a delegate to Europe, urging the necessity of a new Crusade. It so happened that, in December 1244, Louis IX of France lay desperately ill and vowed that, if he recovered, he would take the Cross.

The appeal received from the Patriarch of Jerusalem was read before a council held at Lyons in July 1245. Germany and Italy were in anarchy as a result of the struggle between the pope and Frederick II. The King of France alone answered the appeal. He set sail for Cyprus on 25th August, 1248, from Aigues-Mortes, sixty miles west of Marseilles. His army was purely French. Frederick II, protesting publicly his hopes for the success of the expedition, secretly kept the Sultan of Egypt informed of the strength and objectives of the Crusade.

Louis IX was a hero among men. He was of a pure and simple piety, brave, unselfish, temperate, courteous and generous. He always spoke the truth and never broke his word, either to a Muslim or a Christian. Though at times quick-tempered, he was kind and cheerful in manner and was famed for his courage in battle. He fasted constantly, listened avidly to sermons, heard mass twice a day, often rising at midnight to pray in his chapel. He constantly visited hospitals and personally nursed the patients, while he daily fed over a hundred paupers. He was canonized in 1297 and is best known to history as Saint Louis. He was accompanied on his Crusade by his three brothers, the Counts of Artois, Poitiers and Anjou.

The Crusaders landed on 17th September, 1248, at Limassol in Cyprus, which had been chosen as an advanced base. Here they delayed for nine months, eventually setting sail for Egypt on 1st June, 1249. The reason for the long delay is not entirely clear. It is said that Louis wished to sail direct from France to Egypt but that the Franks of Outremer insisted on a meeting in Cyprus to unite the armies and to concert a plan of campaign. By the time these tasks had been completed, it was already winter and the sea-crossing was thought risky. The long delay had two disadvantages. It sacrificed any hope of surprise and it used up a great part of the supplies which the king had brought with him. Moreover, while Louis was in Cyprus waiting to embark, fighting broke out in Acre between the Pisans and the Genoese, at a time when the sea crossing to Egypt could only be carried out with the aid of their combined fleets.

A hundred and twenty large ships had been collected to transport the army, not counting the galleys, which were the warships escorting the convoy. The total strength may have been some twenty thousand men of which two thousand eight hundred knights with their men at arms and five thousand archers were French from France. The remainder were principally from Palestine and Cyprus, with four hundred knights under Guillaume de Villehardouin, Prince of the Morea, from the Latin Empire of Constantinople, and an English contingent under the Earl of Salisbury.

Like Jean de Brienne, Louis IX landed on the west bank of the Nile opposite Damietta, on 5th June, 1249. Sultan Al Salih Ayoub, now in an advanced state of tuberculosis with a large fistula in his leg in addition to his lung trouble, had arrived in April at Ashmoon. When the Frankish fleet came in sight, the Muslim army was drawn up on the west bank of the Nile opposite Damietta. As soon as the Franks began to land, they were charged by the Mamlook cavalry. "When we saw them coming," writes Joinville, "we fixed the butt-ends of our lances in the sand, with the points toward the enemy, and stood up our shields in front of us. When they saw the lines of points directed at the stomachs of their horses they turned back."

The galley of Jean d'Ibelin, the son of the "Old Lord of Beirut", painted within and without and propelled by three hundred oars, came flying across the water, trumpets blowing and drums beating and ran up on the sandy beach, the knights leaping out and taking position beside those of France. The remainder of the Franks, some jumping into the sea up to their waists, came splashing ashore to join in the mêlée. After heavy fighting the Muslims withdrew and, the same night, crossed the river by a bridge of boats to the east bank and by-passing Damietta, fell back to the south, omitting to destroy the bridge. The people of Damietta, seeing themselves abandoned by the army, fled in the clothes they stood up in.

Next morning, 6th June, 1249, the Franks entered Damietta unopposed. In view of the fact that Jean de Brienne had besieged Damietta for eighteen months, the Sixth Crusade seemed to have commenced auspiciously indeed. But now fresh delays occurred. The annual rise of the Nile would shortly begin and it would thereafter be impossible to move in the Delta. There was nothing for it but to wait until the floods subsided in October.

Meanwhile the dying Sultan Al Salih displayed a fierce and feverish energy. A great army was concentrated at Mansoora, stores accumulated and defences constructed, while the leaders who had

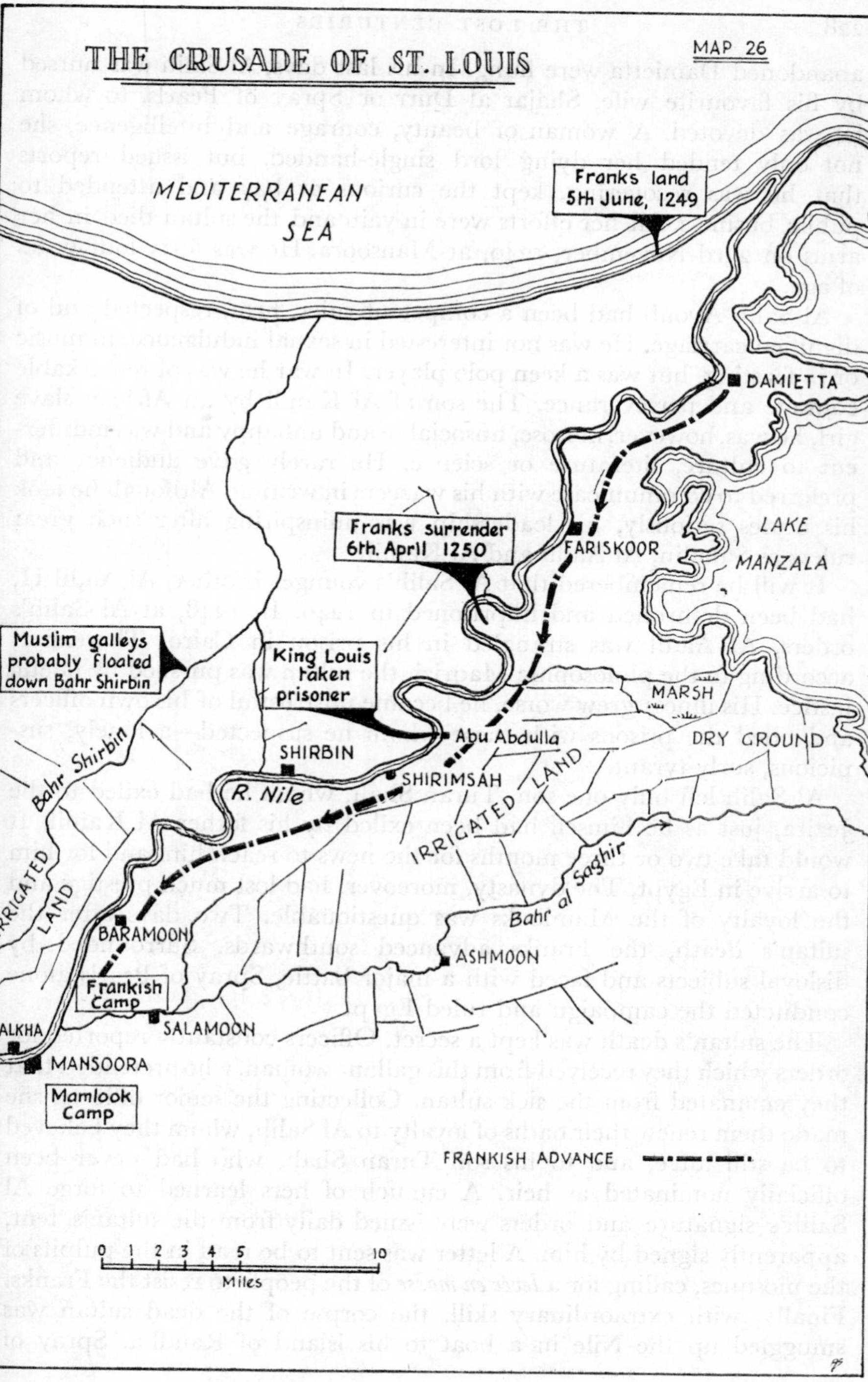
THE CRUSADE OF ST. LOUIS
MAP 26
MEDITERRANEAN
SEA
Franks land
5th June, 1249
DAMIETTA
LAKE
MANZALA
FARISKOOR
Franks surrender
6th. April 1250
Muslim galleys
probably floated
down Bahr Shirbin
King Louis
taken
prisoner
MARSH
DRY GROUND
Abu Abdulla
SHIRBIN
SHIRIMSAH
Bahr Shirbin
R. Nile
IRRIGATED LAND
IRRIGATED
LAND
Bahr al Saghir
BARAMOON
ASHMOON
Frankish
Camp
SALAMOON
TALKHA
MANSOORA
Mamlook
Camp
FRANKISH ADVANCE
0 1 2 3 4 5 10
Miles

abandoned Damietta were hung. In his last days, Al Salih was nursed by his favourite wife, Shajar al Durr or Spray of Pearls, to whom he was devoted. A woman of beauty, courage and intelligence, she not only tended her dying lord single-handed, but issued reports that he was recovering, kept the curious at bay and attended to public business. All her efforts were in vain and the sultan died in her arms on 23rd November, 1249, at Mansoora. He was forty-four years of age.

Al Salih Ayoub had been a competent ruler, firm, respected and of dignified carriage. He was not interested in sexual indulgence, in music or in feasting, but was a keen polo player. In war he was of remarkable courage and perseverance. The son of Al Kamil by an African slave girl, he was, however, morose, unsociable and unhappy and was indifferent to culture, literature or science. He rarely gave audience and preferred to communicate with his wazeers in writing. Although he took his duties seriously, his leadership was uninspiring after such great rulers as Saladin, Al Aadil and Al Kamil.

It will be remembered that Al Salih's younger brother, Al Aadil II, had been dethroned and imprisoned in 1240. In 1248, at Al Salih's orders, Al Aadil was strangled in his prison in Cairo. Thereafter, according to the philosophic Maqrizi, the sultan was pursued by poetic justice. His illness grew worse, he became mistrustful of his own officers and filled the prisons with those whom he suspected—a lonely, suspicious, surly tyrant.

Al Salih left only one son, Turan Shah, whom he had exiled to the Jezira, just as he himself had been exiled by his father Al Kamil. It would take two or three months for the news to reach him and for him to arrive in Egypt. The dynasty, moreover, had lost much prestige and the loyalty of the Mamlooks was questionable. Two days after the sultan's death, the Franks advanced southwards. Surrounded by disloyal subjects and faced with a major battle, Spray of Pearls alone conducted the campaign and ruled Egypt.

The sultan's death was kept a secret. Officers constantly reported for orders which they received from this gallant woman, who pretended that they emanated from the sick sultan. Collecting the senior officers, she made them renew their oaths of loyalty to Al Salih, whom they believed to be still alive, and to his son Turan Shah, who had never been officially nominated as heir. A eunuch of hers learned to forge Al Salih's signature and orders were issued daily from the sultan's tent, apparently signed by him. A letter was sent to be read in the pulpits of the mosques, calling for a *levée en masse* of the people to resist the Franks. Finally, with extraordinary skill, the corpse of the dead sultan was smuggled up the Nile in a boat to his island of Raudha. Spray of

Pearls, still smiling, continued to hand out orders to the army over the sultan's counterfeit signature.

* * *

Meanwhile on 25th November, 1249, the Franks moved slowly southwards from Damietta and on 21st December, 1249, camped on the bank of the Bahr al Saghir[1] channel opposite Mansoora, where they erected mangonels and began to bombard the Muslim camp. The Mamlooks replied by launching earthenware barrels filled with liquid fire. These "shells", thrown by catapults, broke on landing and the fire covered everything in the vicinity. By this means they destroyed the Frankish engines. The two armies faced one another across the Bahr al Saghir, neither of them able to cross.

On 5th February, 1250, however, a local inhabitant showed the Franks a ford across the Bahr al Saghir, near the village of Salamoon. During the night of 7th to 8th February, the army began to cross at the ford, which proved a slow and difficult operation, the current being strong and the banks high and slippery. The plan of battle had been carefully co-ordinated and the king had especially urged all concerned to observe discipline, keep closed up and not embark on private adventures.

In spite of these orders, the Comte d'Artois, who crossed first with the advanced guard, no sooner reached the south bank than he clapped spurs to his horse and galloped off for Mansoora. The Templars, who formed part of the advanced guard, and William Long-Sword, Earl of Salisbury, expostulated, but when the Comte d'Artois galloped away they thought it their duty to follow. The main body was only just beginning to cross the ford.

The Muslims were completely surprised and thrown into utter confusion. Fakhr al Deen, the commander-in-chief, the former friend of Frederick II, was in his bath and was quickly killed. The knights not only burst through the Muslim camp but even galloped into the streets of Mansoora. If the whole Frankish army had delivered this attack united and in battle order, the Muslims would have been destroyed. But after a short time, they perceived that the Franks were only a few scattered horsemen. A certain Baybers, surnamed the Bunduqdari and later to become famous, counter-attacked at the head of the River Mamlooks. The Comte d'Artois was killed. Many knights were caught in the narrow streets of Mansoora, which the inhabitants hastily barricaded to cut off their retreat. Of two hundred and ninety Templars who had followed the Comte d'Artois only five returned alive.

[1] Bahr al Saghir means the small channel, as opposed to the main Nile, which went on to Damietta. The nearest pronunciation for English people is Bahher az Zareer.

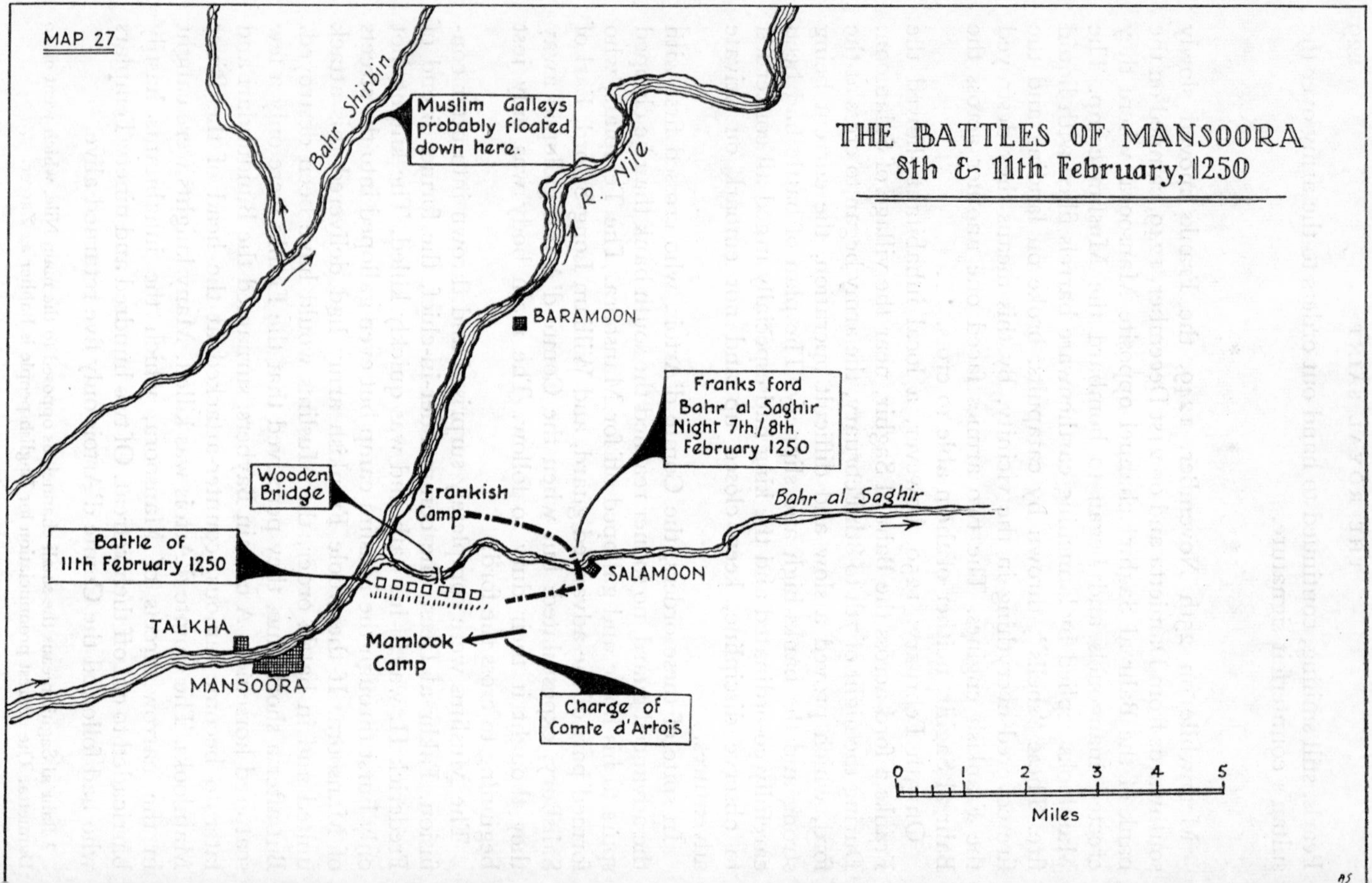
MAP 27
THE BATTLES OF MANSOORA
8th & 11th February, 1250
Bahr Shirbin
Muslim Galleys probably floated down here.
R. Nile
BARAMOON
Franks ford Bahr al Saghir Night 7th/8th. February 1250
Bahr al Saghir
Wooden Bridge
Frankish Camp
Battle of 11th February 1250
SALAMOON
TALKHA
MANSOORA
Mamlook Camp
Charge of Comte d'Artois
0 1 2 3 4 5
Miles

Having thus exterminated the Frankish advanced guard, the Mamlooks, now formed in order of battle and in a high state of exhilaration, advanced against the king. Only half the French army was as yet across the ford and the situation was extremely precarious. The Mamlooks, with the usual Turkish tactics, galloped up and shot their arrows into the Frankish cavalry, then wheeled away while others took their place. The French cross-bowmen were infantry and were still on the north bank, the ford having proved impassable for men on foot. The king, however, stood firm and kept his head under constant attack until the evening, when, an improvised wooden bridge having been thrown across the Bahr al Saghir, the French bowmen were able to cross. The Muslims then withdrew into Mansoora and the Franks occupied their former camp.

The Frankish army was now in a critical situation. The main body of the army, divided into seven battles or battalions, was drawn up on the south bank of the Bahr al Saghir with its back to the river. On the other bank, the old camp was guarded by infantry under the Duke of Burgundy. The two camps were joined by a frail wooden bridge. On the 11th February, 1250, the Muslims launched a full-scale attack on the seven battles south of the river, but after a day of desperate fighting the assault was repulsed. On 28th February, Turan Shah, the new sultan, reached Mansoora, Spray of Pearls surrendered her authority and the death of Al Salih was announced.

The Franks could probably still have withdrawn to Damietta, which they could have held indefinitely, and which might have been eventually exchanged for some concessions in Palestine. But Louis would not consider a retreat. Meanwhile the whole battlefield was strewn with dead bodies, which also blocked the flow of the Bahr al Saghir. Dysentery and fever spread rapidly in the Christian camp. Nearly all the horses were dead and the armoured knights fought on foot.

The Franks had hitherto received their supplies by ship up the Nile from Damietta. Turan Shah now had a number of galleys carried overland on the west bank and launched on the Nile apparently in the vicinity of Shirbin. On 16th March, 1250, thirty-two Frankish vessels, coming up the Nile laden with supplies, were captured. Altogether some eighty supply ships were taken or sunk by the Muslim galleys. The Crusader army outside Mansoora, in addition to dysentery, scurvy and epidemics,[2] found itself starving. After holding on south of the Bahr al Saghir for six weeks, Louis was at last obliged to retreat.

By a remarkable military *tour de force*, the army succeeded in recrossing the Bahr al Saghir over one precarious bridge in spite of

[2] Grousset says that typhus had appeared.

continuous attacks. The barons begged Louis IX to take the best of the surviving horses and escape to Damietta but the king refused to leave his men. On 5th April began the slow and painful retreat along the right bank of the Nile. In close formation, dragging the sick with them, surrounded and harassed day and night by the now triumphant Muslims, the little column battled its way to Shirimsah, nearly half-way to Damietta, Louis himself being so weak from dysentery that he could not mount his horse.

In the small hamlet of Abu Abdulla the king, unable to stand any longer, was laid in a little hovel, apparently dying. He had insisted on remaining with the rearguard, though he might previously have escaped. Sir Philip de Montfort was sent by the king to the sultan to negotiate a truce, while Gaultier de Châtillon, who commanded the rearguard, and Sir Geoffrey de Sergines, sword in hand, defended the hut in which the king was lying. At this moment, a sergeant by the name of Marcel, called out, "Sir knights, surrender. The king orders you to do so." Thereupon the ameer with whom Sir Philip was negotiating cried out that there was no need for a truce, for the army had surrendered.[3]

On 6th April, 1250, between Shirimsah and Fariskoor, the Crusaders surrendered. If the king had not collapsed from illness, says Joinville, probably rightly, he would have got the column back to Damietta. Some reports state that, before the surrender, the king and his entourage of five hundred were promised their lives. Louis was put in chains and taken back to Mansoora. The greater part of the Franks were massacred in cold blood immediately after the surrender. Thereafter three or four hundred were beheaded each night—treatment very different from that accorded by Al Kamil to Jean de Brienne.

Louis was ordered to sign an agreement surrendering all the Frankish possessions in Palestine and Syria and, when he replied that he had no power to do so, he was threatened with torture. He only replied, "I am your prisoner. Do with me as you wish." The fact that Frederick II, the friend of the Sultans of Egypt, was the titular King of Jerusalem, made it difficult for the Muslims to press the point. Eventually the king's ransom was fixed at a million gold besants.

* * *

The late Sultan Al Salih had, in his lifetime, refused to nominate his son Turan Shah as his heir, and his hesitation now proved itself justified. Turan Shah was behaving like a fool. He had quarrelled with Spray of Pearls, though it was she who had enabled him to mount the throne. He had brought some young boon companions with him from

[3] Joinville, *Memoirs of Louis IX, King of France.*

the Jezira and these he now promoted over the veteran commanders of the Mamlooks. He was addicted to drunken orgies and, when in his cups, he boasted of what he would do to these senior officers.

On the 1st May, 1250, while Turan Shah was resting in his pavilion at Fariskoor, Baybers, the officer of the River Mamlooks who had led the counter attack at Mansoora, entered and struck him with his sword. Then, perhaps losing his nerve, he escaped without administering the *coup de grâce*.

Hearing the sultan's cries, some retainers ran to see what had happened and were told by Turan Shah that he had been attacked by a River Mamlook, whose name he did not know. When this report became known, the River Mamlooks realized that, if the sultan lived, he would surely revenge himself upon them. They felt that they had no choice but to kill him. Escaping from his pavilion, Turan Shah took refuge in a wooden tower on the river bank but the Mamlooks gathered round and set it on fire. Breaking away from the tower, the fugitive sultan ran down to the river, crying aloud, "I don't want to be a king. O Muslims, will none of you protect me?" Wading into the Nile, he endeavoured to swim to the farther bank but was overtaken and killed in the water, no finger being raised in his defence. Thus ignominiously ended the dynasty of the great Saladin.

Joinville, with a number of other noble prisoners, was imprisoned in a galley on the river and witnessed the whole incident. A party of excited Mamlooks boarded the galley carrying battleaxes and shouting that they had come to kill the prisoners. Among the Franks was a solitary monk, to whom many of the knights, expecting instant death, knelt and made their confession and from whom they received absolution. The Muslim army was in a state of revolutionary chaos. The Mamlooks, however, went down to Damietta where they massacred all the Frankish sick and wounded.

Returning from Damietta, the mutineers again raised a clamour to kill King Louis and the prisoners, but eventually the enormous ransom which the king had undertaken to pay convinced them that it would be more profitable to spare their lives. The money was handed over by weight, each ten thousand gold pieces being weighed together. Sir Philip de Montfort watched the weighing on behalf of the king. At length, after two days of continuous work, the counting was over and the Mamlook ameers declared themselves satisfied.

Philip de Montfort returned and reported to the king, informing him at the same time that the Muslims had actually made a mistake and had received ten thousand pieces too few. Louis, replying angrily that he had sworn to pay the sum agreed upon, insisted on informing the ameers and on paying a further ten thousand. It is not surprising that some of the Mamlooks were alleged to have remarked that it was a pity that they could not have had Louis instead of Turan Shah as their sultan.

On 7th May, 1250, King Louis IX set sail from Damietta for Acre. Twelve thousand men and ten women are alleged to have been released after the payment of the ransom. The remainder had died of various epidemics, been killed in action or massacred in cold blood, except for such as adopted Islam and disappeared into the population of Egypt.

The original idea put forward by Richard Cœur de Lion and later by Jean de Brienne had been to seize Damietta or Alexandria and hold them in pledge until the Muslims handed over Jerusalem. This strategy would have succeeded at the time of Jean de Brienne, if it had not been for the folly of the papal legate. But whereas the idea of seizing Alexandria or Damietta as a pledge went near to succeeding, the invasion of Egypt and the capture of Cairo was an entirely different proposition.

The Franks had command of the sea and could easily maintain themselves in Damietta. Cairo, on the other hand, was a hundred miles inland, the delta was densely populated, the inhabitants hostile and the country, flooded for several months a year and intersected by canals and rivers, was highly unsuitable for the Frankish tactics of a charge of armoured knights. For the Crusaders to march a hundred miles across such country and keep their communications open was an impossibility.

Confusion seems to have arisen unperceived between the plan of holding Damietta as a pawn and that of marching on Cairo. If the original plan had been to march on Cairo, it would have been better to by-pass the delta, land on the site of Port Said or to the west of Alexandria and march across the desert.[4] We have no means of knowing whether such plans were ever discussed and, if so, why they were rejected.

On the field of battle, the Franks were equally matched with the Muslims, or perhaps superior to them, except for the indiscipline of the knights who were inclined to charge off, abandoning the infantry. Yet, as appeared when Richard Cœur de Lion was in command, with a strong leader they could fight splendidly.

It was in the field of staff organization that their failure was so lamentable. A complete absence of any intelligence system or of any careful thought devoted to planning is noticeable on every campaign. Bogged down above their knees in mud and water opposite Mansoora, the Franks of Outremer must have known that only thirty miles away there was dry, gravelly desert where horses could gallop at full speed for miles. More surprising still, after the disaster to Jean de Brienne, was the fact that Saint Louis attempted exactly to repeat the same plan.

[4] Map 7, page 67.

It is, however, essential to remember that the Franks were operating overseas. Their normal wars in France, Italy or Germany did not necessitate much intelligence organization. The geography and the climate were familiar, the languages spoken were known and the armies could live on the country. Thus lack of staff intelligence, the factor which repeatedly caused the defeat of the Franks, was no problem to the Muslims, who were always fighting in their own country. The technical abilities of the two sides could only have been closely compared if the Muslims had sent an army by sea to land in France.

Louis remained four years in Acre, from May 1250 to April 1254. Ironically enough, the titular King of Jerusalem was the Emperor Frederick II, who died on 13th December, 1250. Louis had no legal standing in Acre but his personality and prestige served to check the anarchic disintegration of the Frankish states as long as he was present. Eventually, however, in April 1254 he was obliged to set sail for France, where his long absence had reduced the country to confusion.

* * *

Great were the rejoicings in Cairo on receipt of the news of the departure of the Franks. Spray of Pearls, to whom the Mamlooks were devoted, was proclaimed Sultana of Egypt and distributed lavish gifts to the troops. The rulers of Egypt were now all Turks, among whom women were very free and often took part in public affairs, with the result that the elevation of Spray of Pearls was easily accepted. Some weeks later, however, a letter was received from the Khalif Mustasim in Baghdad in which he informed the rulers of Egypt that the Prophet himself had said, "Unhappy is the nation which is governed by a woman." "If you have no men," added the khalif, "I will send you one."

In face of so strong an expression of disapproval by the Prince of the Faithful, Spray of Pearls married Izz al Deen Aibek, the commander-in-chief, who had been the slave and court taster of her late husband, the Sultan Al Salih Ayoub. To impart a further semblance of legitimacy to the régime, Malik al Ashraf Musa,[5] a six-year-old great-grandson of Al Kamil, was proclaimed joint-sultan with Aibek.

When, however, news reached Damascus of the murder of Turan Shah and the elevation of Spray of Pearls, the Syrian notables refused to recognize her and invited Malik al Nasir Yusuf, King of Aleppo and a great-grandson of Saladin,[6] to mount the throne. Al Nasir entered Damascus unopposed and marched on to seize Egypt. The news of his approach caused consternation in Cairo but the River Mamlooks marched out to oppose him and a confused battle was fought at Abbasa,

[5] Genealogical tree, page 216. [6] Genealogical tree, page 72.

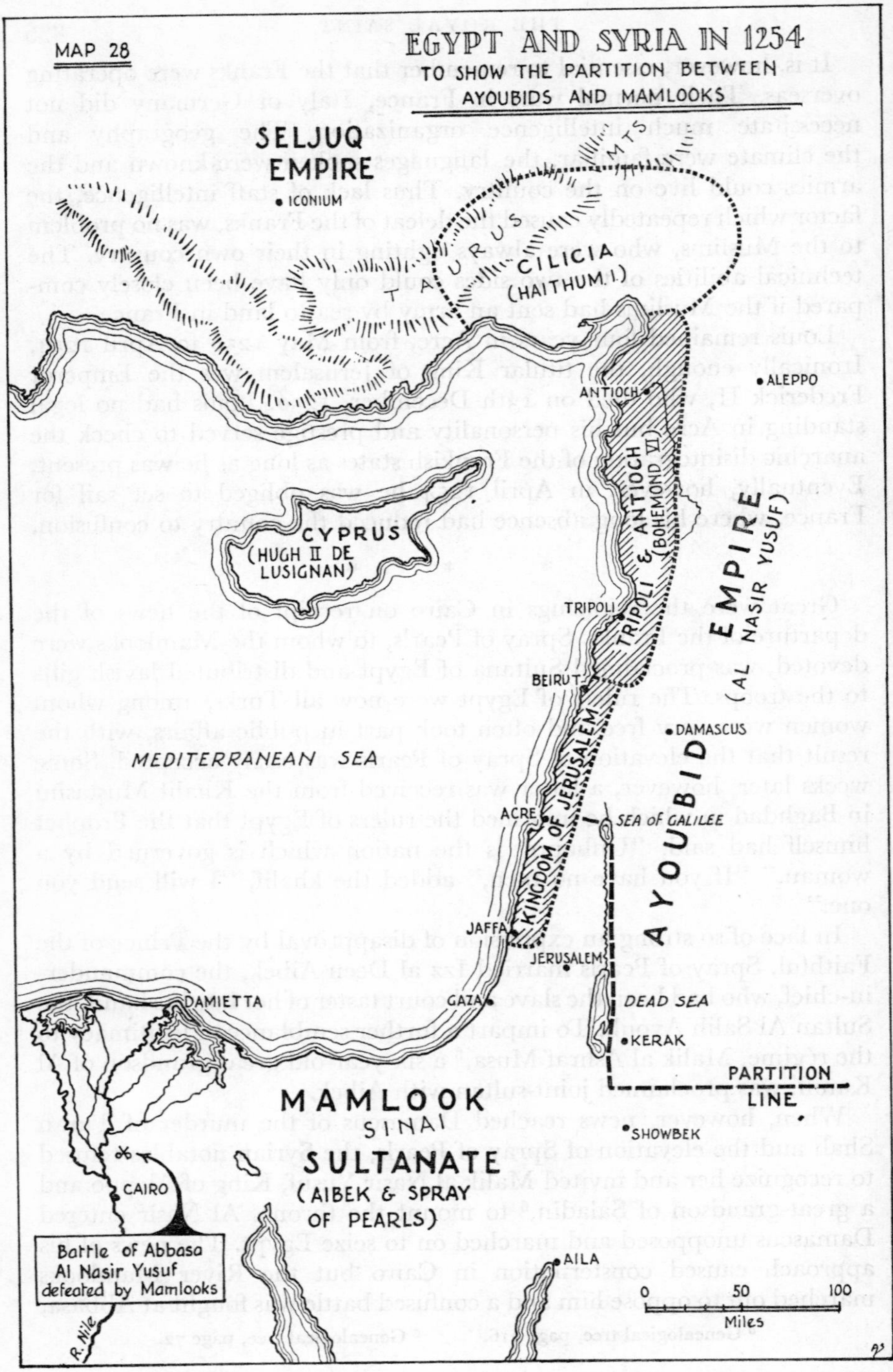

MAP 28

EGYPT AND SYRIA IN 1254
TO SHOW THE PARTITION BETWEEN AYOUBIDS AND MAMLOOKS

north-east of Cairo. Nasir was eventually repulsed and withdrew across Sinai to Palestine. The former Ayoubid Empire was thus divided, Aibek and Spray of Pearls continuing to rule in Egypt, while Al Nasir retained Syria with his capital in Damascus.

But the internal situation in Egypt was far from secure. The River Mamlooks, under their commander Aqtai, had become unbearably arrogant since their defeat of the Crusaders at Mansoora. They terrorized the country, robbing and beating whom they wished and abducting any women they fancied. "If the King of the Franks had taken Cairo, his men would not have behaved so badly," complains Maqrizi.

In 1254, Aibek solved the problem by treachery. Inviting Aqtai, the commander of the River Mamlooks, to a conference in the citadel, he caused him to be seized and murdered and immediately arrested many of the River Mamlooks before they could recover themselves. The remainder fled, many of them to Al Nasir in Damascus. Shortly afterwards an emissary from the Khalif Mustasim negotiated a peace between Aibek and Al Nasir. Palestine was ceded to Egypt but Al Nasir retained Syria and Trans-Jordan as far south as Kerak.

* * *

Meanwhile all was not well between Aibek and his wife Spray of Pearls. A capable, headstrong and beautiful woman, she had governed Egypt alone during the illness and after the death of Al Salih and again after the murder of Turan Shah. The Khalif Mustasim's remarks on female rule had compelled her to associate Aibek with herself but she had continued to act as if she were the ruler and he merely her escort.

Aibek's attitude was different. He now regarded himself as the ruling sultan. Moreover, when he married Spray of Pearls, she had forced him to divorce his former wife, an incident which still rankled. The River Mamlooks had been devoted to Spray of Pearls but had been executed, imprisoned and driven into exile by Aibek. According to Maqrizi, Aibek decided to have Spray of Pearls murdered. In the interval, he sent a delegate to Bedr al Deen Lulu, the Prince of Mosul, to ask for the hand of his daughter. Lulu had been a Mamlook of the last Zengid ruler of Mosul and had supplanted his masters on the throne.

Meanwhile Aibek was still arresting and imprisoning the remnants of the River Mamlooks. One of these, being led to prison in the citadel, passed beneath the window of Spray of Pearls' apartment, where she was wont to sit. Bowing his head, he said in Turkish—perhaps his escort knew only Arabic—"The Mamlook Aidkeen Bashmaqdar. By God, O Queen, we have committed no crime to deserve arrest. Only when he sent to ask for the hand of the daughter of the Prince of Mosul, we were grieved for your sake. We have served you and your martyred[7] husband, Sultan Al Salih. But when we protested about this Mosul girl, Aibek was angry and has treated us as you see." Spray of Pearls fluttered her handkerchief from the window to show that she had heard.

Thereupon the sultana wrote to Al Nasir, the Ayoubid King of Damascus, informing him that she was going to kill Aibek and that afterwards she would marry him and make him King of Egypt as well as Syria. Nasir, however, fearing a trap, sent no reply. On a day in 1257 Aibek returned from the parade-ground in the evening and rode up to the citadel. Dismounting, he went straight to the bath after the heat and dust of the day. Several of Spray of Pearls' slaves followed him and strangled him in the bathroom.

The next day the Mamlooks of Aibek wished to kill Spray of Pearls but Al Salih's former Mamlooks protected her. However, she was imprisoned in the red tower of the citadel. The son of Aibek by his former wife, whom Spray of Pearls had compelled him to divorce, was declared sultan and the fallen sultana was handed over to the vindictive revenge of her rival, Aibek's first wife, who, assisted by her slave girls, killed her by striking her with their wooden clogs. Her body, almost naked, was thrown from the walls of the citadel into the fosse, where it lay for several days before burial.

Spray of Pearls was one of the most remarkable women in history. It was she who saved Egypt from the Crusade of St. Louis by concealing the death of Sultan Al Salih and for three months ruling Egypt and commanding the army in his name. A woman of beauty and forceful personality, she was not free from female jealousy which refused to tolerate a rival in her husband's bed, even though she hated him.

Aibek had ruled Egypt in association with Spray of Pearls for seven years. He was about sixty years old when he was murdered. He had been cruel, autocratic and tyrannical and, according to Maqrizi, had caused many innocent persons to be killed. However, in those stormy times, he was brave, strong and determined. He set an example of arbitrary exactions and seizures which was imitated by his successors. He could not speak Arabic, the language of his subjects. On the death of Aibek, his son Ali had been accepted as sultan, although he was only fifteen years old. A senior Mamlook commander, Qutuz, was appointed regent. In reality, the idea of heredity was quite foreign to Mamlook rule, under which the strongest and the bravest was regarded as the rightful leader.

Meanwhile, as we shall see in the next chapter, the Mongols on 5th February, 1258, had captured Baghdad. In the spring of 1259

[7] Martyred because he died in a war against non-Muslims.

Nasir, King of Damascus, received a Mongol summons to surrender and appealed to Egypt for help. Qutuz, profiting by the public alarm, declared that a boy could not rule in such a moment of danger. Ali, the son of Aibek, was thrown into prison and, in November 1259, Qutuz was proclaimed sultan.

NOTABLE DATES

Louis IX sails from Aigues-Mortes	25th August, 1248
Louis IX lands at Limassol in Cyprus	17th September, 1248
Louis sails from Cyprus	1st June, 1249
Crusaders seize Damietta	6th June, 1249
Death of Sultan Al Salih	23rd November, 1249
First Battle of Mansoora	8th February, 1250
Second Battle of Mansoora	11th February, 1250
Arrival of Sultan Turan Shah	28th February, 1250
Surrender of Saint Louis	6th April, 1250
Murder of Sultan Turan Shah	1st May, 1250
Aibek the Mamlook and Spray of Pearls rule Egypt Malik al Nasir, King of Syria	1250–1257
Murder of Aibek and Spray of Pearls	1257
Qutuz proclaimed sole Sultan of Egypt	November 1259

PERSONALITIES

Louis IX, King of France
Malik al Salih Ayoub, Sultan
Turan Shah, his son and successor
Izz al Deen Aibek, Spray of Pearls — Rulers of Egypt
Qutuz, Sultan of Egypt
Baybers the Bunduqdari, Mamlook murderer of Turan Shah
Malik al Nasir Yusuf, great-grandson of Saladin, King of Damascus.

XI

Hulagu

Wherever the Mongol hordes passed, civilization perished. They seemed to have no object but purposeless carnage and arson. Baghdad and a little later . . . Aleppo were taken by storm and their inhabitants slaughtered. Nothing was left of these cities but ruins and heaps of ashes.
E. J. DAVIS, *The Invasion of Egypt*

In the track of the Mongols only ruins and human bones are to be seen. Surpassing the most barbarous nations in cruelty, they cut the throats of men, women and children in cold blood. They set fire to the towns and villages, destroy the crops and transform a flourishing countryside into a desert; yet at the same time they are animated neither by hatred nor by vengeance. They scarcely know the names of the peoples whom they exterminate.
BARON D'OHSSON, *Histoire des Mongols*

Their works are works of iniquity and the act of violence is in their hands. Their feet run to evil, and they make haste to shed innocent blood: their thoughts are thoughts of iniquity; wasting and destruction are in their paths. The way of peace they know not.
Isaiah LIX, 6, 7 and 8

XI

BEFORE he died, Jenghis Khan had divided his empire between his four sons. The family of Juji, the eldest, was to rule from north of the Caspian and Aral Seas "as far as the hoofs of Mongol horses had trampled the soil". Jagatai, the second son, received the Uighur country as far west as the Jaxartes, while Ogotai was given the Imil valley. Tului was to inherit the homeland south of Lake Baikal. As a result, Juji's sons became the rulers of the Qipchaq Turks, while the subjects of Jagatai and Ogotai were also mostly Turkish nomads. The majority of the Mongols fell to Tului's share. (See Map 29, page 246.)

Conquered territories not inhabited by nomads, such as China and Persia, were not divided but were retained as imperial dominions under the khaqan or supreme khan, who was also to be the suzerain over his brothers. Jenghis Khan nominated his third son Ogotai to the supreme post. At the death of Jenghis Khan the Mongol army is alleged to have totalled a little over a hundred thousand men, but this did not include the many Turks who now marched with them.

In spite of Jenghis Khan's nomination, a quriltai or tribal council was necessary to confirm the new khaqan in office. This took place in 1229 on the banks of the Kerulen. The same quriltai decreed the despatch of three armies. The first, commanded by Khaqan Ogotai himself, was to complete the conquest of the Kin Empire of North China. The second under Batu, the son of Juji, was to conquer Europe. The third was to deal with Jalal al Deen Khuwarizm Shah who had returned to Persia.

Ogotai led an army to China where he remained until May 1234 when the suicide of the Kin Emperor enabled the Mongols to annex North China, thereby becoming the neighbours of the Sung dynasty of South China. Khaqan Ogotai returned to Mongolia in May 1234 but the following year a fresh army was sent to invade the Sung Empire. The same year, Tului, the fourth son of Jenghis Khan, died of drink, leaving four sons, Mangu, Qubilai, Hulagu and Arikbugha, of whom we shall hear more.

* * *

Meanwhile Batu, the son of Juji, set out to invade Europe. He left in 1236 and so completely razed the city of Bulgar that it has never been rebuilt. In 1237 the Mongols turned westwards and on 21st December they took and destroyed Riazan and then Prousk. All the inhabitants

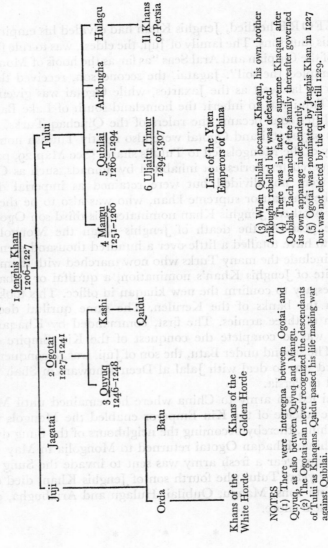

THE KHAQANS OR SUPREME KHANS

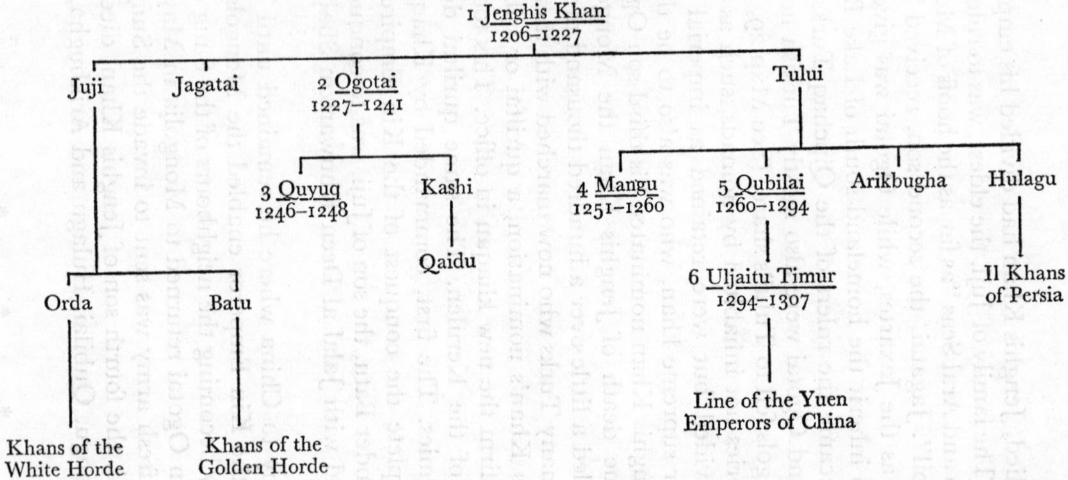

NOTES

(1) There were interregna between Ogotai and Quyuq, as also between Quyuq and Mangu.

(2) The Ogotai clan never recognized the descendants of Tului as Khaqans. Qaidu passed his life making war against Qubilai.

(3) When Qubilai became Khaqan, his own brother Arikbugha rebelled but was defeated.

(4) There was in fact no supreme Khaqan after Qubilai. Each branch of the family thereafter governed its own appanage independently.

(5) Ogotai was nominated by Jenghis Khan in 1227 but was not elected by the quriltai till 1229.

were killed, many being tortured, impaled on stakes, used as archery targets, flayed or roasted alive. Moscow came next, its inhabitants also being exterminated. The next two years were spent ravaging the country between Moscow and the Black Sea. Mongol raids reached Finland and Archangel on the Arctic Ocean, terrified refugees fleeing even as far as Norway.

In December 1240, Kiev was utterly destroyed. In January 1241, the Mongols crossed the Vistula on the ice, driving before them herds of prisoners tied together with ropes. On 12th March, they exterminated the Hungarian army at Mohi, south-east of Budapest. On 24th March, 1241, they took Cracow and then Breslau. Bela IV, King of Hungary, fled to Spalato on the Adriatic, whence he put to sea. A column pursuing him carried fire and sword through what are now Yugo-Slavia and Albania. In May 1241, the detachment turned back northwards through what is now Bulgaria. Batu spent the summer of 1241 in Hungary resting his horses. The Mongols passed the time drinking and amusing themselves with the large numbers of women whom they had captured. Poland and Hungary were virtually depopulated. On 25th December, 1241, they crossed the frozen Danube and one column arrived a few miles from Vienna.

When the Mongols had been a group of tribes south of Lake Baikal, it had been the custom for the tribesmen to collect on the death of the khaqan to elect a successor. This ancient custom was still observed, although their armies were now deployed from Austria to the China Sea. Europe was saved by the timely death of Ogotai, and the withdrawal of the Mongols to choose his successor. Otherwise Batu might well have gone on to conquer Germany, France and Italy, for no army dared to oppose the Mongols.

* * *

It will be remembered that, at Ogotai's inauguration in 1229, the despatch of three armies had been ordered. We have briefly described the campaigns in China and in Europe and must now return to the beginning of Ogotai's reign to record the operations of the Mongol army sent to Persia.

It will be remembered[1] that Jalal al Deen Khuwarizm Shah had left the Punjab in 1224 and had reconquered Persia west of the Salt Desert, while Jenghis Khan was engaged in his last campaign in China. Jalal al Deen had not profited by his six-year respite to build up an army in Adharbaijan. When eventually, after the elevation of Ogotai, a new Mongol army reached Adharbaijan in the winter of 1230 to 1231, Jalal al Deen was unprepared. On the approach of the Mongols his

[1] Page 211.

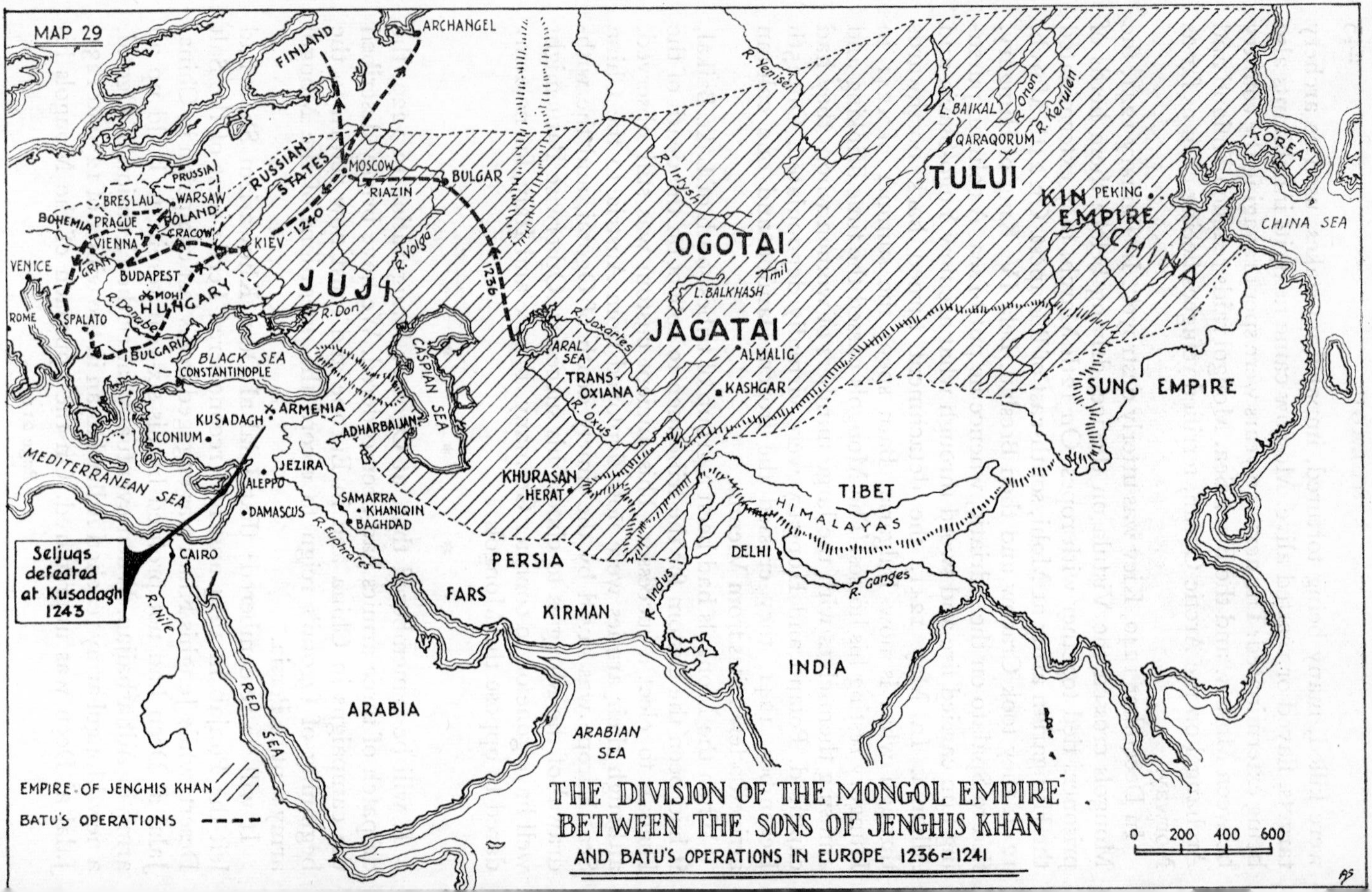
MAP 29
ARCHANGEL
FINLAND
RUSSIAN STATES
PRUSSIA
BRESLAU
WARSAW
POLAND
BOHEMIA
PRAGUE
CRACOW
VIENNA
GRAN
VENICE
BUDAPEST
MOHI
HUNGARY
R. Danube
ROME
SPALATO
BULGARIA
KIEV
1240
MOSCOW
RIAZIN
BULGAR
R. Volga
1236
JUJI
R. Don
BLACK SEA
CONSTANTINOPLE
CASPIAN SEA
KUSADAGH
ARMENIA
ADHARBAIJAN
ICONIUM
MEDITERRANEAN SEA
JEZIRA
ALEPPO
DAMASCUS
SAMARRA
KHANIQIN
BAGHDAD
R. Euphrates
Seljuqs defeated at Kusadagh 1243
CAIRO
R. Nile
RED SEA
ARABIA
PERSIA
FARS
KIRMAN
KHURASAN
HERAT
ARAL SEA
R. Jaxartes
TRANS OXIANA
R. Oxus
JAGATAI
ALMALIG
KASHGAR
L. BALKHASH
Imil
OGOTAI
R. Irtysh
R. Yenisei
L. BAIKAL
R. Onon
R. Kerulen
QARAQORUM
TULUI
KIN EMPIRE
PEKING
CHINA
KOREA
CHINA SEA
SUNG EMPIRE
TIBET
HIMALAYAS
DELHI
R. Ganges
R. Indus
INDIA
ARABIAN SEA
EMPIRE OF JENGHIS KHAN
BATU'S OPERATIONS
0 200 400 600
THE DIVISION OF THE MONGOL EMPIRE BETWEEN THE SONS OF JENGHIS KHAN
AND BATU'S OPERATIONS IN EUROPE 1236–1241

army melted away and the Khuwarizm Shah himself was murdered in the mountains of Kurdistan on 15th August, 1231. Thereafter the Mongols, after consolidating their hold on Adharbaijan, devastated Greater Armenia and the Jezira. As in Russia not a man took the field to oppose them.

In 1237, a Mongol force reached Samarra, only sixty-five miles north of Baghdad. The Khalif Mustansir (1226–1242), however, who had built up a considerable army, defeated them in the Jebel Hamrin but the following year his troops suffered a severe reverse at Khaniqin. With the Mongols in the Jezira, the khalif was now virtually cut off from the Muslims of Syria and Egypt, the desert being impassable to armies. In 1240, a fresh Mongol army devastated Greater Armenia and Georgia. An Armenian delegation went to Mongolia and did homage to Ogotai and the Armenians became Mongol vassals.[2]

* * *

The reign of Ogotai, from 1227 to 1241, had witnessed a continuance of conquests almost as sensational as those of Jenghis Khan himself. The Khaqan, however, passed his life in hunting and drinking. He was the first of the family to build a palace at Qaraqorum but he spent most of his time in camp. He died on 11th December, 1241, at the age of fifty, principally from excess of drink. He had been an easy-going boon companion, indifferent to the business of government, and so generous with money as to be profligate. The countries conquered by the Mongols suffered the worst forms of tyranny and oppression, though in Trans-Oxiana Masood Beg Yalawash, a Muslim, who had been appointed governor, strove to repair some of the ruin left by Jenghis Khan.

In 1242, a Mongol army marched against Ghiyath al Deen Kai Khosru II, the Seljuq Sultan of Asia Minor. A battle was fought at Kusadagh between Erzoroum and Sivas, on 26th June, 1243, in which Kai Khosru II had twenty thousand men, including two thousand Frankish mercenaries from Cyprus. At the first flight of Mongol arrows, however, the Turks fled. The sultan agreed to become a Mongol vassal and to pay an annual tribute of four hundred thousand gold dinars.

In 1244, the Mongols appeared before Aleppo but accepted a large cash indemnity and passed on. In the same year, Bohemond V, Prince of Antioch, received an ultimatum to destroy his defences, pay tribute to the khaqan and send a gift of three thousand young girls. Refusing at first, he subsequently agreed to pay tribute. At the same time, Haithum I, Armenian King of Cilicia, became a Mongol vassal.

[2] Map 29, page 246.

It was not until the spring of 1246, after a five-year interregnum, that Quyuq, the son of Ogotai, was elected khaqan. The immense crowds which assembled at Qaraqorum witnessed to the extent to which fear of the Mongols had spread across the world. In addition to many hundreds of princes of the family of Jenghis Khan, Qaraqorum was crowded with foreign delegations. Rukn al Deen Qilij Arslan IV, the brother of the Seljuq Sultan of Asia Minor, was in attendance as was the brother of the Ayoubid King of Aleppo and the Greek Emperor of Trebizond. There were deputations from the Khalif Mustasim in Baghdad, from the Princes of Mosul, Fars and Kerman and the brother of Haithum I, Armenian King of Cilicia. Yaroslav, the Grand Duke of Russia, came to do homage in person. There were also two monks bearing letters from the pope, one of whom, Carpino, left a narrative of his adventures.

When the time of the election arrived, the members of the quriltai assembled in an immense tent, the poles of which were covered with gold leaf, the walls hung with silk draperies and the floor carpeted with scarlet. Quyuq was duly elected and the assembled princes and the immense crowds on the plain outside prostrated themselves nine times in homage.

When the ambassadors were dismissed, those of the Abbasid Khalif of Baghdad and of the Grand Master of the Ismailis of Alamut were sent back with threats demanding the instant subjection of their masters. The monks presented two letters from the pope, in the first of which His Holiness exhorted the khaqan to become a Christian,[3] in the other he blamed the Mongols for their cruelty. Quyuq Khan himself dictated the reply. "God has commanded my ancestors and myself to exterminate wicked nations," he said. "You ask if I am a Christian. God knows and if the pope wants to know, he had better come and find out."

Louis IX of France was at this time in Cyprus, preparing for his crusade. Imagining the khaqan to be a Christian, he sent him a splendid tent of scarlet cloth fitted up as a chapel, the walls decorated with scenes from the life of Christ. Unfortunately Quyuq accepted the gift as tribute and ordered that the King of France be added to the list of his vassals.

In 1248, after a reign of two years, Quyuq died of drink. He had passed most of his time in dissipation and had left the government to his two ministers, both of them Nestorian Christians.

* * *

Mention has already been made of the resentment nursed by the family of Juji at their exclusion from the succession in favour of Ogotai.

[3] Quyuq's mother was a Nestorian and had in fact brought him up as a Christian.

The early death of Quyuq offered a chance for revenge. Batu, the son of Juji, agreed with the family of Tului to elect Mangu as khaqan. On 1st July, 1251, Mangu was elected by extremely high-handed methods. Descendants of Jagatai and Ogotai who objected were sewn up in felt sacks and trampled to death by horses, for the Mongols entertained a superstition against shedding the blood of princes. Their followers were killed by the forcing of earth and stones down their throats.

Mangu, the grandson of Jenghis Khan, was more thoughtful and less bloodthirsty than his forebears. His mother also had been a Nestorian Christian. He cross-questioned the men of religion—Christians, Muslims, Buddhists, Taoists and Shamanists—and listened to their debates. To another western monk who visited his court, William Rubruquis, he spoke vaguely of completing the conquest of the world, after which universal peace would reign under a single Mongol Emperor. Friar William, who had been sent by Louis IX, had an audience with Mangu, whom he describes as a rather silent man of middle height about forty-five years old. The khaqan was seated on an elevated couch in a tent hung with cloth of gold, and was clad in beautiful furs. A good-looking young woman sat by him, for Mongol women regularly appeared in public with their husbands. A variety of drinks stood on a small table and Mangu first enquired what William would drink. The khaqan himself continued to drink throughout the interview until he became slightly tipsy.

The idea of conquering the world was extremely ancient among the nomads of the steppes. As early as A.D. 568, a Great Khan of the Turks had told a Byzantine envoy that it was time for his people to invade the whole world.[4] Perhaps the fact that their supreme deity was the Blue Sky suggested worldwide ambitions but our knowledge of their religion is scanty. Mangu was concerned to complete the conquest of the world and to establish universal peace. In the west, the immediate enemy was Islam and the khaqan was interested in an understanding with Louis IX, whom he believed to be an enemy of the Muslims. But communications were in practice too slow to allow of military co-operation between France and the Mongols.

The quriltai which elected Mangu in 1251 authorized the despatch of his brother Qubilai with an army to conquer the Sung Empire of South China. Hulagu, another brother, was appointed to lead an army to Persia, Iraq and finally Egypt. A third army was to be sent to India.

Mangu was even interested in administration, not merely in genocide. Shems al Deen Muhammad Kert, of a family connected with the Ghorids who had for a few years ruled East Persia and India, was made

[4] *Chronique de Michel le Syrien* (Fr. trans. Chabot).

governor of Herat, including Merv and Kabul, approximately modern Afghanistan. As governor of Persia, Mangu appointed Arghoon, a Uirat Mongol, one of the first of his race mentioned as a civil administrator. He had been educated by the Uighurs, the most civilized tribe on the steppes. Attempts were made to regulate taxes and to restrain plunder but Arghoon met with bitter opposition from the Mongol princes and commanders. Our Persian historian, Juwaini,[5] was employed under Arghoon. "Mangu," he writes, "was concerned to alleviate the lot of the people, not to increase the wealth of the treasury." Masood Yalawash, the Muslim, was confirmed as governor of Trans-Oxiana, Khuwarizm and Kashgar. His father, Mahmood Yalawash, was sent to administer China.

Hulagu set out for the west in February 1254, in spite of wild blizzards and deep snow, the Mongols being presumably indifferent to cold. The army was accompanied by a thousand Chinese engineers. At Almalig, Hulagu was entertained by the descendants of Jagatai. In the summer of 1255, he camped near Samarqand to rest his horses, while he himself spent forty days in drink and debauchery in a silk and gold tent.

On 2nd January, 1256, Hulagu crossed the Oxus on a bridge of boats and received obsequious delegations from the Seljuqs of Asia Minor and the Princes of Khurasan, Fars and Adharbaijan, bearing splendid gifts. The rest of the winter was passed in drinking and dissipation. In the summer of 1256, the leisurely campaign was continued and the army camped on the slopes of Demavend, north of modern Teheran, whence a summons was sent to Rukn al Deen Khurshah, Grand Master of the Ismailis, to come and do homage.

An immense concentratian of siege engines had been collected and on the 31st October, 1256, the army dispersed in columns to besiege the Ismaili fortresses. On 19th November, 1256, Rukn al Deen Khurshah gave himself up and ordered all Ismaili castles to surrender. As a result ninety Ismaili fortresses capitulated and were demolished. Rukn al Deen Khurshah was sent to Mangu who, however, did not want to see him and arranged for him to be murdered.[6] As soon as the surrender was complete, all the Ismailis were massacred including women and babies at the breast.

In March 1257, Hulagu moved to Hamadan whence he sent an embassy to the Khalif Mustasim demanding his surrender. All other states, he claimed, had capitulated to the Mongols. The khalif must, therefore, demolish the walls of Baghdad and come in person to do homage. The Khalif Mustansir, an active and capable man, had died in 1242 and had been succeeded by his feeble son Mustasim, who left the

[5] Ala al Deen al Juwaini, *History of the Conqueror of the World*.
[6] The Aga Khan today claims descent from Rukn al Deen Khurshah.

THE CAMPAIGNS OF HULAGU

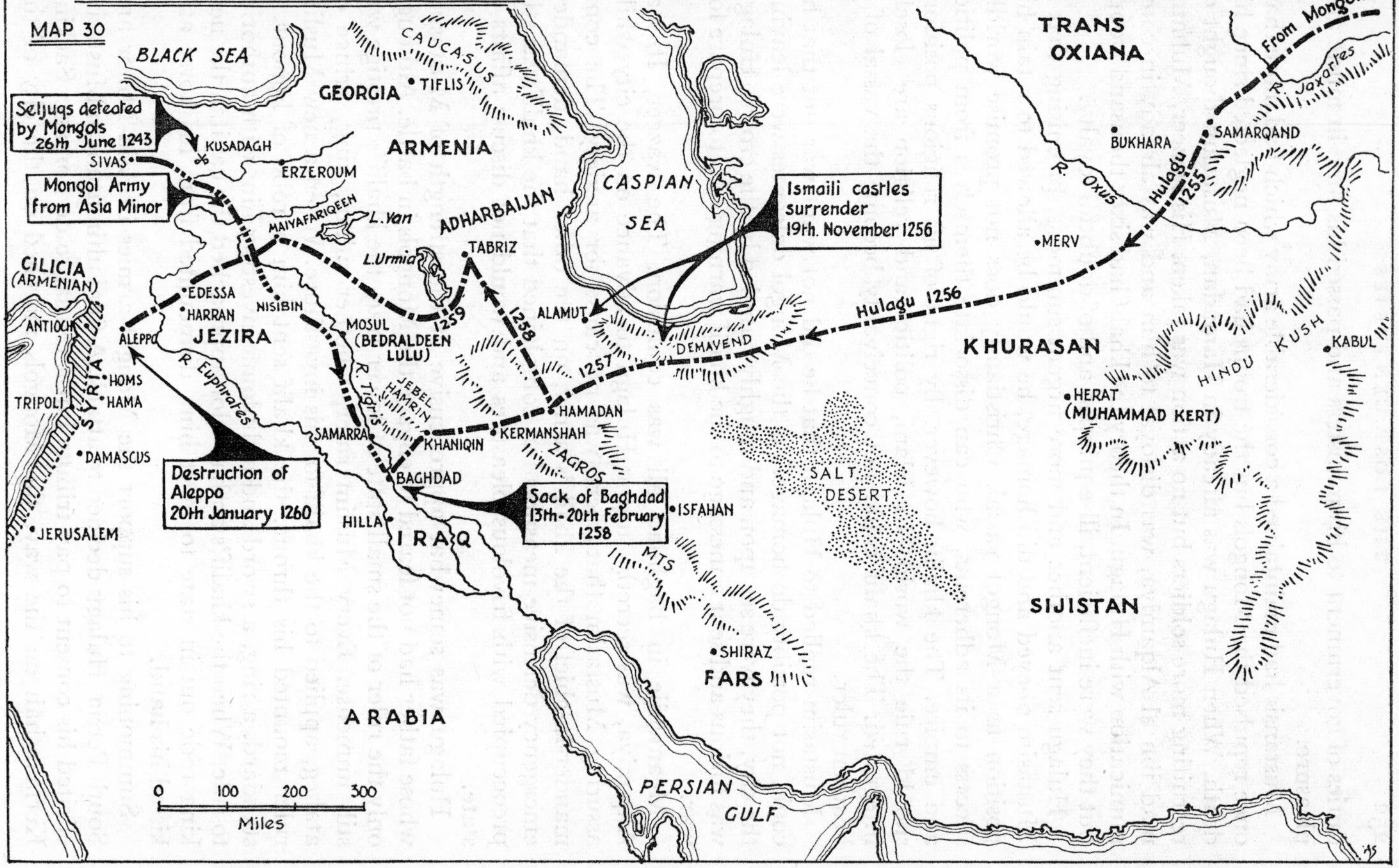

duties of government to his ministers and passed his time in music and pleasure.

Mustansir had maintained a considerable army which had more than once repulsed the Mongols but the troops had been neglected since his death. When Hulagu was already in Hamadan, Mustasim thought of recruiting more soldiers but no action was taken. His wazeer, Muhammad ibn al Alqamiya, was disloyal to him and was already in communication with Hulagu. In theory the khalif had sixty thousand troops but they were inefficient, ill-equipped and of doubtful loyalty.

Hulagu sent another and more urgent summons, promising that if Mustasim obeyed and did homage, he would be allowed to retain his position as a Mongol vassal. Christianity does not promise worldly success to its adherents, who can dissociate themselves from politics and empire. The khalif, however, by right of his religious position, should rule the world. In Islam, politics and religion are closely integrated. The khalif could not conceivably become the vassal of a heathen ruler.

Mustasim replied to Hulagu that he did not want war but that he could not possibly do homage. As the Mongol delegates were leaving the city, they were set upon and roughly handled by the crowd. Hulagu was furious and sent a message to the khalif warning him to prepare for war.

Meanwhile in Baghdad all was confusion. The wazeer, Ibn al Alqamiya, was secretly urging Hulagu to advance on the city while assuring Mustasim that there was no cause for anxiety. The commander-in-chief of the khalif's army, on the other hand, demanded emergency defensive measures but complained that the khalif was still preoccupied with frivolous pleasures and would not discuss affairs of state.

Hulagu was somewhat apprehensive of the strength of Mustasim, whose father had not feared to engage the Mongols in battle. Although only the ruler of the small state of lower Iraq, the khalif's prestige was still immense. Every Muslim ruler, whether sultan, king, prince or atabeg, applied to the khalif for his investiture. When a new Muslim ruler mounted his throne, the khalif sent him a robe of honour, a standard, a ring, a sword and a diploma investing him with authority to rule. When the khalif's ambassador approached the capital, the new king rode out in state to meet him, dismounted from his horse and kissed his hand.

Summoning to his support the Mongol armies in Asia Minor and South Persia, Hulagu decided to attack. A final ultimatum to Mustasim elicited his consent to pay tribute but a refusal to do homage. Sacking Kermanshah on the way, the Mongols marched on the city of the

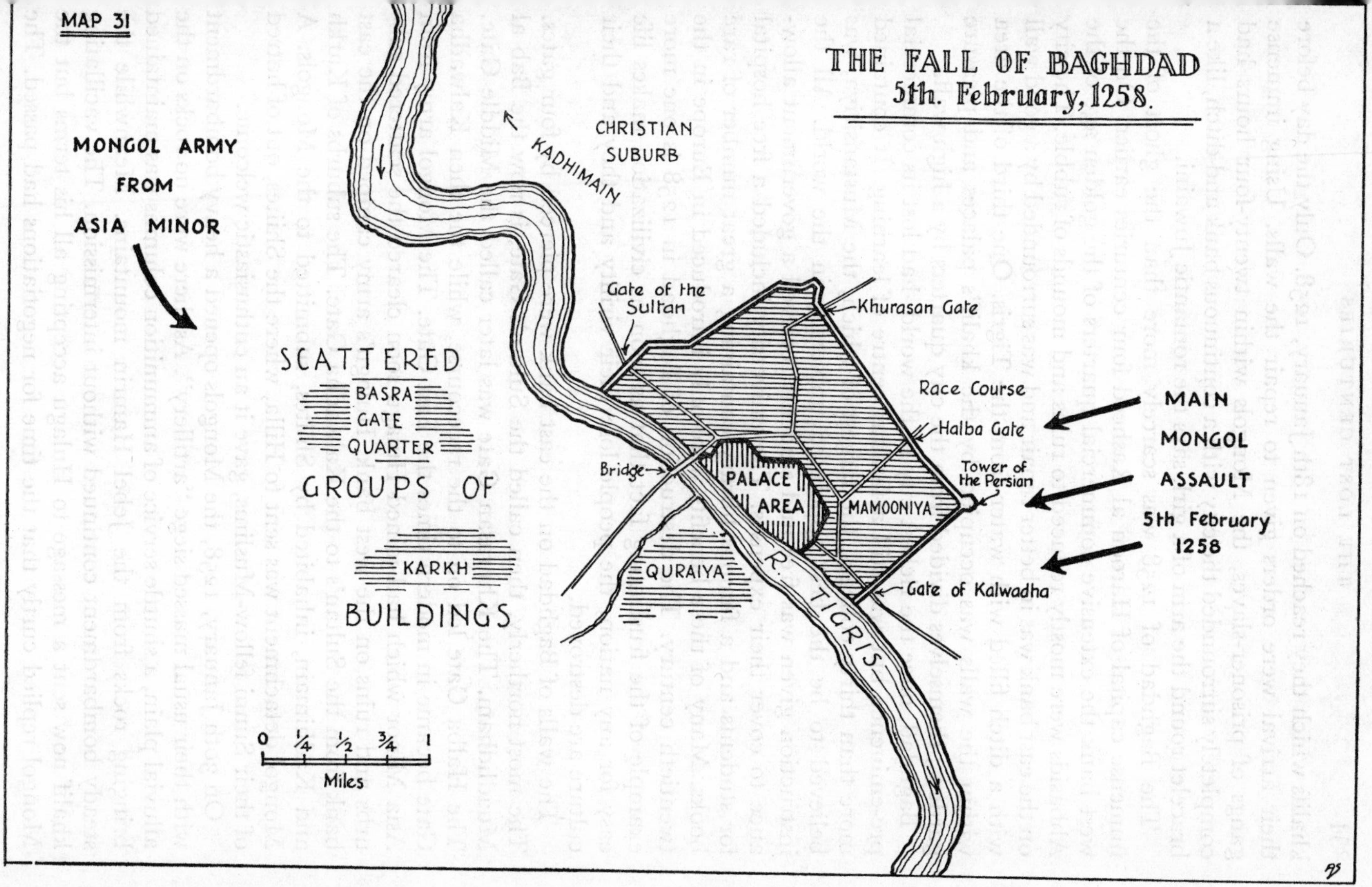
MAP 31
THE FALL OF BAGHDAD
5th. February, 1258.
MONGOL ARMY
FROM
ASIA MINOR
CHRISTIAN
SUBURB
KADHIMAIN
Gate of the
Sultan
Khurasan Gate
Race Course
Halba Gate
Tower of
the Persian
Gate of Kalwadha
MAIN
MONGOL
ASSAULT
5th February
1258
Bridge
PALACE
AREA
MAMOONIYA
QURAIYA
R. TIGRIS
SCATTERED
BASRA
GATE
QUARTER
GROUPS OF
KARKH
BUILDINGS
0 1/4 1/2 3/4 1
Miles

khalifs which they reached on 18th January, 1258. Only the day before their arrival were orders given to repair the walls. Using immense gangs of prisoner-slaves, the Mongols within twenty-four hours had completely surrounded the city with a continuous bank and ditch, like a bracelet round the arm of a girl, says the romantic Juwaini.

The Baghdad of 1258 was scarcely more than the ghost of the immense capital of Haroon al Rasheed four centuries earlier. On the west bank the extensive commercial quarters of the golden age of the Abbasids were mostly reduced to ruins and mounds of rubble. The city on the east bank was in better repair and was surrounded by a good wall with a ditch filled with water from the Tigris. One third of the area within the walls was occupied by the khalif's palaces and pleasure gardens, themselves divided from the city quarters by a high wall.

Baghdad, once the richest city in the world, had lost its commercial pre-eminence but was still a famous centre of learning. It contained more than thirty colleges, the largest of which, the Mustansiriya, was believed to be the best appointed university in the world. All the instruction given was free and students received a government allowance to cover their expenses. The university included a free hospital for students and a famous library containing a great number of rare books. Many of these benefits were only introduced in Europe in the twentieth century. The destruction of Baghdad in 1258 is one more example of the frustrating fact that as soon as civilization makes life easy for any nation, the people lose their virility and they and their culture are destroyed.

The walls of Baghdad on the east bank were pierced by four gates. The most northerly, then called the Sultan's Gate, is now the Bab al Muadhdham. The Khurasan Gate was later called the Middle Gate. The Halba Gate led on to the racecourse, while the then Kalwadha Gate became in modern times the East Gate. The Mongol army from Asia Minor which had joined Hulagu soon cleared the scattered suburbs and ruins on the west bank. Hulagu's army camped on the east bank from the Sultan's to the Kalwadha Gate. The suburbs of Karkh and Kadhimain, inhabited by Shiites, submitted to the Mongols. A Mongol detachment was sent to Hilla, where the Shiites, out of hatred of their Sunni fellow-Muslims, gave it an enthusiastic welcome.

On 30th January, 1258, the Mongols opened a heavy bombardment with their usual massed siege "artillery". As there were no rocks on the alluvial plain, a shuttle service of ammunition columns was maintained bringing rocks from the Jebel Hamrin mountains. Meanwhile the steady bombardment continued without intermission. The vacillating khalif now sent a message to Hulagu accepting all his terms but the Mongol replied curtly that the time for negotiations had passed. The heaviest bombardment was directed against the south-east corner of the walls and by 1st February, the third day of the bombardment, the Persian Tower was in ruins. On 5th February, the Mongols advanced to the assault and mounted the walls on both sides of the Persian Tower. By dawn on 6th February, they held the whole length of the wall from the Racecourse Gate to beyond the Persian Tower and the city lay at their mercy.

Now that all was lost, Mustasim sent deputation after deputation to beg for terms but Hulagu refused to see them. Instead he sent orders for the commander of the khalif's army and the deputy wazeer to report to him and ordered them to withdraw all the khalif's troops from the city. This they succeeded in doing by telling the troops that they were to be allowed to march away to Syria. As soon as the whole army was assembled on the plain outside the walls, the Mongols closed round them and every man was killed. Finally the army commander and the deputy wazeer were killed also. The great city now lay entirely at the mercy of the conqueror without one soldier to defend it.

On Sunday, 10th February, 1258, the Khalif Mustasim with his three sons and about three thousand notables, mostly Muslim religious dignitaries, went out to Hulagu's camp. The conqueror received him politely, enquired after Mustasim's health and requested him to instruct the people to lay down their arms and evacuate the city. The khalif accordingly sent messengers to Baghdad to proclaim that all who wished to save their lives should come out of the city unarmed. As a result, vast crowds of people herded out through the city gates. As soon as they were gathered together on open ground, all were mercilessly butchered. The khalif and his family and suite were then accommodated in tents under armed guard.

The Mongols were magnificently disciplined murderers. In the case of most mediaeval armies, the excited soldiers who mounted the walls of a city in the heat of battle could not be prevented from carrying plunder, murder and rape into the streets. The Mongols were different. Although they mounted the walls on 6th February, the sack of the city did not begin until the thirteenth. For seven days Hulagu's troops stood on the wall looking down at the rich and helpless city at their feet. Such discipline goes far to explain their success.

On the morning of Wednesday, 13th February, 1258, the Mongols entered Baghdad in several columns at different points. Hulagu's mother and his favourite wife, Doquz Khatun, were Nestorian Christians. As a result, the Nestorian Patriarch was permitted to collect a number of his co-religionists in a church where they were protected. All the remainder of the citizens were massacred and the city was systematically plundered and then set on fire.

On the 15th February, Hulagu visited the khalif's palace. He ordered Mustasim to be brought in and said to him ironically, "You are the owner of this house and I am your guest. Let us see what worthy presents you have to offer me." A banquet was served at which Hulagu amused himself by treating Mustasim as his host. The khalif was then obliged to reveal all his treasures of gold, silver, jewels and costly fabrics which had been accumulated by the Abbasids in their five hundred years of power.

A thousand eunuchs and seven hundred women are said to have been found in the palace area, most of them doubtless servants and officials. Mustasim begged earnestly for the ladies on whom "neither sun nor moon had ever shed their rays". Hulagu, like a cat playing with a mouse, agreed that the khalif could retain a hundred women. In the evening Hulagu returned to his camp where the priceless treasures of the Abbasids were stacked all round his tent. The sack and destruction of Baghdad lasted seven days, during which the whole city, including all the mosques, was burned and reduced to ruins. Eight hundred thousand persons are said to have been killed. On 20th February, Hulagu was obliged to strike his camp and march away to avoid the stench of rotting corpses which hung over the city.

For five centuries Baghdad had been the heart of the Muslim world, a city of palaces, of libraries, of mosques and of colleges, of mathematicians, philosophers, poets, historians and theologians. Mounds of smoking rubble from which rose an unbearable stink of decaying flesh now alone marked the site of so much wealth, glory, art, science and learning.

The khalif and his sons were sewn up in sacks and trampled to death by Mongol horses. Mustasim was the thirty-seventh Abbasid Khalif. From the death of the Prophet in 632, the Arab Khalifate had lasted six hundred and twenty-six years. On 17th April, 1258, Hulagu was back in Hamadan where he had left his women and his baggage. Thence he sent a part of the plunder to Mangu Khan in Mongolia announcing his intention of marching on Egypt. At the same time he ordered the building of a castle on an island in Lake Urmia as a repository for the immense wealth which he had acquired.

Amid such scenes of cruelty and carnage, the story of the atabeg of Mosul offers a little light relief. Bedr al Deen Lulu had been a Mamlook of the Zengid princes of Mosul, had ultimately succeeded them and was now eighty years of age. His officers expressed fears for his safety when, after the fall of Baghdad, he was summoned to report to Hulagu. "I hope to soften him," said the old Turk, "in fact I may well take him by the ears."

Received in audience, Lulu laid many priceless gifts at the feet of the khan, finally producing two magnificent gold ear-rings set with enormous pearls. "I wish the khan would allow me to fix them for him," he said ingratiatingly. "Such graciousness would add to the consideration with which I am viewed by my fellow kings and my subjects."

The fierce conqueror having signified his consent, old Lulu took him by the left ear and then by the right and duly attached the ear-rings. As he did so, he glanced for an instant at the members of his staff to show them that he had made good his promise to take the ferocious Mongol by the ears.

* * *

The destruction of Baghdad fell like a thunderbolt on the whole Muslim world. One of those who hastened panic-stricken to pay homage to the conqueror was the Seljuq Sultan of Asia Minor, Kai Kaus II. We must here digress for a moment to bring the history of his dynasty up to date.

The golden age of the Seljuqs of Asia Minor had been, from 1219 to 1234, the reign of Ala al Deen Kai Qobad I, who was succeeded by his son, Ghiyath al Deen Kai Khosrou II. We have seen earlier in this chapter that this sultan had been defeated by the Mongols at Kusadagh on 26th June, 1243 and had become a Mongol vassal. Kai Khosrou II died in 1245 and was succeeded by his eldest son, Izz al Deen Kai Kaus II.[7]

In the following year, however, the Great Khan had ordered the deposition of Kai Kaus II and the elevation of his brother Ala al Deen Kai Qobad II. Soon afterwards Kai Qobad II died and the two surviving brothers, Kai Kaus II and Qilij Arslan IV, fought one another for the throne. In 1254, the two brothers continuing to fight, the Great Khan Mangu ordered the division of the kingdom between them, Kai Kaus II receiving the western half and Qilij Arslan IV the eastern. Kai Kaus II now prostrated himself before Hulagu, to whom he presented a pair of socks on the soles of which his portrait had been painted, imploring the conqueror to place his august feet on the head of his humble slave. To such a pass had fallen those arrogant Turks who had once themselves haughtily dominated the Muslim world.

Hulagu confirmed Mangu's division of the Seljuq dominions but soon afterwards, as a result of an alleged attempt to intrigue with the Mamlook Sultans of Egypt, Kai Kaus II was obliged to flee to Constantinople and died in exile. Qilij Arslan IV remained as nominal ruler but was in reality shorn of all power. The final disappearance of the Seljuq dynasty of Asia Minor will be mentioned in the next chapter.

[7] Genealogical tree, page 168.

Until the death of Kai Qobad I in 1234, the Seljuq Empire of Asia Minor had been a formidable power, which even the Mongols had left alone. As in the case of so many other dynasties, however, fratricidal civil wars had given the Tatars the opportunity to intervene. They never annexed the country or administered it but contented themselves with tribute and periodic violent inroads into Asia Minor. The prestige of the Seljuq dynasty, however, was destroyed and the régime suffered a rapid decline.

* * *

We have already seen that, in 1259, the year after the destruction of Baghdad, Egypt was ruled by the Mamlooks under Sultan Qutuz, while Syria was governed by Al Nasir Yusuf, a great-grandson of Saladin.[8] Al Nasir had sent rich gifts to the Khaqan Mangu, and had received safe conduct from him, but he had not gone in person to do homage. Terrified by the catastrophe of Baghdad, he now sent his son to Hulagu, who was wintering in Tabriz. The deputation returned with a threatening letter from the Mongol conqueror, demanding immediate surrender. "We are not touched by tears or moved by entreaties," wrote Hulagu. "God has erased pity from our hearts. Choose then the safe part and submit before the flames of war are lit. In the wink of an eye your land will become a desert."

On receiving this note, Al Nasir gave way to his indignation. In a written reply he alleged that the Mongols had the characters of devils. "For Muslims," he added, "obedience to God means resistance to you." Mongol conquerors were unaccustomed to the receipt of such letters. On 12th September, 1259, Hulagu marched out of Tabriz. Slaughtering the Hakkiari Kurds on the way, he was joined by contingents from the Christian states of Georgia and Armenian Cilicia, and took the town of Maiyafariqeen. The Ayoubid prince of this little state was done to death by cutting pieces of flesh from his body and stuffing them into his mouth. Hulagu then quickly seized Nisibin, Harran and Edessa, where he went into winter quarters, receiving in audience the Armenian King of Cilicia.

After overrunning the Jezira, Hulagu laid siege to Aleppo, while Homs and Hama sent delegations to do homage. Twenty heavy mangonels opened the bombardment of Aleppo and, after seven days, the city was carried by assault on 20th January, 1260. One hundred thousand young women and children were driven off into slavery, all the remaining inhabitants being massacred and the city razed to the ground. No sooner did Al Nasir hear of the destruction of Aleppo than, on 29th January, 1260, he abandoned Damascus and withdrew

[8] Map 28, page 236.

to Gaza. Scarcely had he gone than a trembling deputation left the city and hastened northwards to the camp of Hulagu, bearing magnificent gifts and the keys of the city gates.

When all Syria and Egypt seemed to be about to meet the fate of Iraq and Persia, the situation was suddenly saved. While Hulagu was still camped near Aleppo, he received news of the death of his brother, the Khaqan Mangu and, according to Mongol custom, marched back towards Mongolia with the greater part of his army. Before leaving he gave the Damascus deputation a document promising their lives to the people of the city. He sent with it two commissioners on his own behalf, one a Mongol and the other a Persian. Kitbugha, a Mongol commander, was left with a body of troops to complete the occupation of Syria. These improvised and conciliatory measures emphasize Hulagu's haste to return to Mongolia, perhaps in the hope of securing his own election as khaqan. In fact, however, he was already too late, for his brother Qubilai had been chosen by a quriltai assembled in the East.

Qubilai, captivated by Chinese civilization, was to found a line of Emperors of China. In Mongolia, Arikbugha, Qubilai's brother, and the clans of Jagatai and Ogotai rejected as illegal the quriltai which had elected Qubilai in China. The families of Jagatai and Ogotai chose as their Great Khan Qaidu Khan, a grandson of Ogotai. He was to pass many years at war with Qubilai. Thereafter the expansion of the Mongols was to come to a halt and their warlike energies were to be turned against one another. Hulagu returned to Tabriz, where he founded the dynasty of the Il Khans but the remnant of Islam was saved.

The Mongols entered Damascus on 1st March, 1260, without a massacre. Their commander, Kitbugha, a Kerait Mongol, was a practising Nestorian Christian. Detachments overran Palestine as far south as Gaza. Hearing that Kitbugha was a Christian, the Franks of the coast sent him friendly deputations.

When Al Nasir in his flight reached the borders of Egypt, Qutuz was alarmed. An adult Ayoubid prince in Cairo would endanger the rule of the Mamlooks. Agents were sent to stir up trouble among the prince's following and to plunder his baggage. Realizing that his presence would be unwelcome in Egypt, he turned east to Trans-Jordan where he was captured by a Mongol detachment and carried a prisoner before Hulagu in Tabriz, where he was subsequently executed.

NOTABLE DATES

Return of Jalal al Deen Khuwarizm Shah to Persia	1226
Ogotai elected khaqan	1229

Defeat and death of Jalal al Deen	1231
Batu's campaign in eastern Europe	1236-1241
Death of Khaqan Ogotai	11th December, 1241
Defeat of Kai Khosrou II at Kusadagh, Seljuqs become Mongol vassals	26th June, 1243
Quyuq elected khaqan	1246
Death of Khaqan Quyuq	1248
Mangu elected khaqan	1st July, 1251
Destruction of Baghdad by Hulagu	6th to 20th February, 1258
Destruction of Aleppo	20th January, 1260
Mongol entry into Damascus	1st March, 1260

PERSONALITIES

Mongol Khaqans

Ogotai, third son of Jenghis Khan
Quyuq, son of Ogotai
Mangu, son of Tului
Qubilai, son of Tului

Other Mongols

Juji, eldest son of Jenghis Khan
Jagatai, second son of Jenghis Khan
Tului, fourth son of Jenghis Khan
Batu, son of Juji
Hulagu, third son of Tului, Il Khan of Persia

Other Princes

Haithum I, Armenian King of Cilicia
Yaroslav, Grand Duke of Russia
The Abbasid Khalif Mustasim
Sultan Qutuz of Egypt
Malik al Nasir Yusuf, King of Damascus

Ghiyath al Deen Kai Khosru II Ala al Deen Kai Qobad II Izz al Deen Kai Kaus II Rukn al Deen Qilij Arslan IV	Seljuq Sultans of Asia Minor

XII

The Spring of Goliath

1250–1277

Baybers was the real founder of the Mamlook Empire. His predecessors had barely and briefly held their power against rivals, revolts and foreign foes. Baybers made himself supreme over all . . . He was the first great Mamlook Sultan and the right man to lay the foundations of the empire.

S. LANE-POOLE, *A History of Egypt in the Middle Ages*

Courage is the thing. All goes if courage goes. J. M. BARRIE

XII

NO sooner had Louis IX sailed from Acre on 24th April, 1254, than the Franks fell once again into anarchy. The strip of coast-line which they still held was divided up between many petty barons, each virtually independent, between the Italian merchant communities competing bitterly against one another, and between the military orders, internationally recruited, each conducting its own foreign policy acknowledging only a vague and distant obedience to the pope. The Frankish states were more than four hundred miles long, but scarcely anywhere as much as thirty miles wide. It is difficult to think of any other country in history with so small a territory and so many rival authorities. In Cyprus, Henry I de Lusignan had died in January 1253, leaving the throne to Hugh II, a baby only a few months old, with the Queen Mother, Plaisance of Antioch, as regent.[1]

Aibek and Spray of Pearls were ruling in Cairo and Al Nasir, the Ayoubid, in Damascus. Jean d'Ibelin, bailiff of the Kingdom of Acre,[2] concluded a ten-year truce with Al Nasir, but the agreement only covered the coast line from Beirut to Arsoof. The Count of Jaffa was not included and raid and counter-raid continued between Jaffa and Jerusalem. In 1256, however, a more general ten-year peace was signed which included both Acre and Jaffa on the Frankish side and Damascus and Cairo on the part of the Muslims. It was at the moment when this treaty was concluded that Hulagu had left Qaraqorum on his expedition to conquer Baghdad and Syria.

The Italian Republics, Venice, Genoa and Pisa, were the only states which maintained fleets in the eastern Mediterranean, and, when united, they were able easily to exercise command of the sea. As long as the Kingdom of Jerusalem had been strongly led by competent kings, the Italian fleets had been willing to play a vital part in defence. But with the disintegration of the Frankish states, each Italian republic devoted itself only to its own commercial interests.

The Venetian and Genoese quarters in Acre were separated by a low mound on which was built a monastery dedicated to St. Saba, which thus overlooked both quarters. One morning in 1256, the Genoese suddenly seized the monastery and invaded the streets of the Venetian quarter. The so-called War of St. Saba had begun. Philippe

[1] Genealogical tree, page 204.

[2] The titular King of Jerusalem was Conradin, the grandson of Frederick II Hohenstaufen, a child far away in Germany.

de Montfort, Lord of Tyre, declared his support for the Genoese, being followed by the Knights Hospitallers. The Venetians were meanwhile assisted by the Pisans and by the formidable Templars and Teutonic knights. The whole kingdom was soon involved in the civil war.

The Venetian Admiral, Lorenzo Tiepolo, broke into the harbour of Acre with the fleet of Venice, effected an armed landing and occupied the monastery of St. Saba, while the Genoese fleet established its base twenty-five miles away in Tyre. In 1258, heavy street fighting still continued in Acre, both Venetians and Genoese erecting mangonels and heavy catapults with which they battered down each other's buildings. While the Franks were thus massacring one another, Hulagu was destroying Baghdad, with the intention of subsequently taking Syria and Palestine also.

Eventually on 24th June, 1258, a major naval battle took place off Acre between the battle-fleets of Genoa and Venice in which the latter was victorious. The Genoese were compelled to evacuate Acre but made up for the loss by transferring their ships, warehouses and business to Tyre. On 7th September, 1264, when the civil war had already been raging for eight years, the Venetian fleet attempted a combined operation to capture and destroy Tyre, but it was repulsed after heavy fighting. According to the Arab historian, Ibn al Furat, the Genoese opened negotiations with the Sultan of Egypt with a view to concerting a joint attack on Acre by the Mamlooks and the Genoese together! Not until 1277, after twenty-one years of fighting, was peace concluded between the Italians, years during which the Mamlooks had been too preoccupied with the Mongol invasions to allow them leisure to capture Tyre or Acre. They were soon to do so, the Franks being too exhausted by their civil wars to be able to resist.

The fratricidal war of St. Saba not only exhausted Outremer but led to the fall of the Latin Empire of Constantinople. It will be remembered that, in 1204, Theodore Lascaris had established at Nicaea a Byzantine imperial government in opposition to the Latin Emperor Baldwin I.

When Theodore Lascaris died in the spring of 1222, he left the Empire of Nicaea a well-established state. Dying without male heirs, he was succeeded by his son-in-law John Vatatzes, who, in a reign of thirty-two years, built a Greek fleet, conquered several islands and invaded Thrace. Meanwhile Boniface de Montferrat, King of Macedonia, had died and a Greek despot Theodore had taken his place. In 1230, the Bulgarians took Adrianople and the Latin Empire continued to shrink. (See Map 15, page 153.)

The Emperor Baldwin I died in 1205, a prisoner in the hands of the Bulgarians. He was succeeded by his brother Henry, an extremely capable ruler, who re-established the prestige of the Latins. When he died in 1216, the crown passed to his brother-in-law Pierre de Courtenai, who also died within a year and was followed first by his widow and then by his incapable son Robert, who with difficulty retained the throne until his death in 1228, leaving an eleven-year-old brother, Baldwin II.

The pope had not originally approved of the diversion of the Fourth Crusade to Constantinople but when the empire was conquered the papacy took it under its protection. Accordingly Gregory IX sent Jean de Brienne, the former King of Jerusalem dismissed by Frederick II, as regent for the child Emperor Baldwin II, giving him the title of emperor also.

In 1235, having plundered Thrace in conjunction with the Bulgarians, John Vatatzes actually attacked the walls of Constantinople. But the veteran Jean de Brienne himself led a sortie which drove off the attackers, while the Venetian fleet defeated that of the Greeks.

On 23rd March, 1237, the Emperor Jean de Brienne died at the age of eighty-nine and the young Baldwin II was left to his own devices. In December 1246, Vatatzes occupied Salonica and, when he died on 3rd November, 1254, he had reconquered nearly all Macedonia and Thrace and was almost ready to lay siege to Constantinople itself. He was succeeded by his son, Theodore II Lascaris, who reigned with mixed success until he died in August 1258, whereupon the commander-in-chief, Michael Palaeologus, seized the throne from John IV Lascaris and was crowned at Nicaea on 1st January, 1259.

It was at this stage that the distant war of St. Saba in Acre sealed the fate of the Latin Empire. It will be remembered that in 1204 Venice had received nearly half the Byzantine Empire in return for the support of her fleet in the capture of Constantinople. She had thereby obtained complete naval command of the Aegean and the Black Sea and had established a commercial monopoly in these waters.

In June 1258, as we have seen, the Venetian fleet gained a victory over the Genoese off Acre. Everywhere defeated by their rivals, the Genoese in 1260 concluded a treaty with Michael Palaeologus for the recapture of Constantinople. In return for the support of the Genoese fleet, Michael promised to drive the Venetians from the re-constituted Greek Empire and to give all their privileges to the Genoese. On 25th July, 1261, the Greeks, assisted by the Genoese, re-occupied Constantinople, Baldwin II escaping by sea. On 15th August, Michael VIII Palaeologus was crowned in St. Sophia and the fifty-seven years of the Latin Empire came to an end.

* * *

When Hulagu had besieged Aleppo in 1260, Bohemond VI of Antioch had gone to the Mongol camp to pay his respects to the conqueror. The politicians of Acre denounced Bohemond for his submission to the Mongols. Hulagu, however, rewarded him by returning to him many fortresses formerly the property of Antioch, which the Muslims had taken in recent years. In the same manner towns conquered by the Muslims were returned to Haithum I, Armenian King of Cilicia. It was even alleged that Hulagu had promised Bohemond and Haithum to return Jerusalem to the Christians. If Mangu had lived a year or two longer this might well have happened and the Mongols might have retained Syria and Palestine, perhaps also Egypt.

When Kitbugha, the Mongol commander left behind by Hulagu in Syria, entered Damascus on 1st March, 1260, he was accompanied by Haithum I, the Armenian King of Cilicia and by Bohemond VI, who was Haithum's son-in-law. As Kitbugha himself was a Nestorian Christian, the Mongol invasion became associated with Christianity in the minds of the Syrians.

At this stage, a certain Julian of Sidon carried out a raid into Syria, of which the government was now Mongol not Muslim. Kitbugha sent his nephew to pursue the raiders but the Mongols were defeated and Kitbugha's nephew was killed. Kitbugha himself then took the field, carried Sidon by assault, killed all the inhabitants whom he could catch and razed the walls.

Soon after, the Templars and Jean II d'Ibelin also raided towards Tiberias but were defeated by the Mongols. If the Franks had been united under a single capable ruler, the death struggle which had begun between the Mongols and the Muslims might well have offered them a priceless opportunity. By whole-heartedly aiding the Mongols, they could have regained much of their former territory if the Mamlooks had been defeated. Conversely, by enthusiastically helping Egypt in this moment of crisis, they might have re-established the friendly relations which existed in Ayoubid days. But the feuds which divided the Franks were so bitter that no concerted policy was possible. If one party favoured the Mongols, the rival faction would attack them. In the end both the Muslims and the Mongols became incensed against the Franks.

* * *

Before leaving Syria for Persia, Hulagu had written a threatening letter to Qutuz, the Mamlook Sultan of Egypt, who assembled his army commanders for a conference. He admitted that the army of Egypt would be no match for Hulagu but when news arrived of the departure of the Mongol conqueror, the Mamlooks decided to fight. One anxiety remained. If all the Franks were to join Kitbugha, the Mongols would be too strong. Qutuz accordingly ordered the mobilization of the Mamlook army and, at the same time, wrote to Acre to ask permission to march across Frankish territory. The people of Acre were incensed against Kitbugha as a result of his sack of Sidon, with the result that they granted Qutuz his request.

The Mamlook ameers were nevertheless reluctant to engage in war with the Mongols and it was only the determination shown by Qutuz which eventually overcame their hesitation. Storming out of the conference room, he shouted, "If no one else will come, I will go and fight the Tatars alone." He then clinched the matter by beheading Hulagu's ambassadors and nailing their heads over the Zuweila Gate of Cairo.

On the 26th July, 1260, the Mamlook advanced guard left Cairo under the command of Baybers the Bunduqdari,[3] the River Mamlook who had led the counter-attack at Mansoora. The River Mamlooks, who had been dispersed under Aibek, had returned to service under Qutuz. The Franks of Acre welcomed the Muslim army and supplied them with rations. Many Franks wished to join the Muslims and fight against the Mongol barbarians, feeling that Muslims and Franks alike were the defenders of civilization against such savages. There was, however, no authority in Acre capable of formulating policy and the Franks ultimately fell between two stools.

From Acre, the Muslims were permitted to march through Frankish territory down the Plain of Esdraelon. Kitbugha, hearing of the Muslim advance, had marched to meet them. Had he secured the alliance of the Franks, he would probably have gained a decisive victory but without allies, the troops left him by Hulagu were heavily outnumbered. Nevertheless Kitbugha was convinced that Mongols were always invincible and advanced straight into the Mamlook army. The battle took place on 3rd September, 1260, at Ain Jaloot—the Spring of Goliath—where the Franks had confronted Saladin in 1183, four years before Hattin.

Qutuz, before advancing to meet the enemy, had delivered a stirring address to the troops, some of whom had even been moved to tears. It may be noticed in this connection that Jenghis Khan's policy of extermination, while it reduced weaker men to paralytic terror, could reinforce the will of the braver. The argument used by Qutuz was based on Tatar savagery. There was no alternative to fighting, he said, except a horrible death for themselves, their wives and their children.

The ever-aggressive Baybers was leading the advanced guard when contact was made with the enemy. Kitbugha charged with so much

[3] The Bunduqdar was the officer charged with the carriage of the sultan's crossbow. Before he had been bought by Sultan Al Salih Ayoub, Baybers had been the mamlook of the Ameer Aidkeen the Bunduqdar, from whom he took this name. Dr. Mustafa Ziada, *Commentary on Maqrizi*.

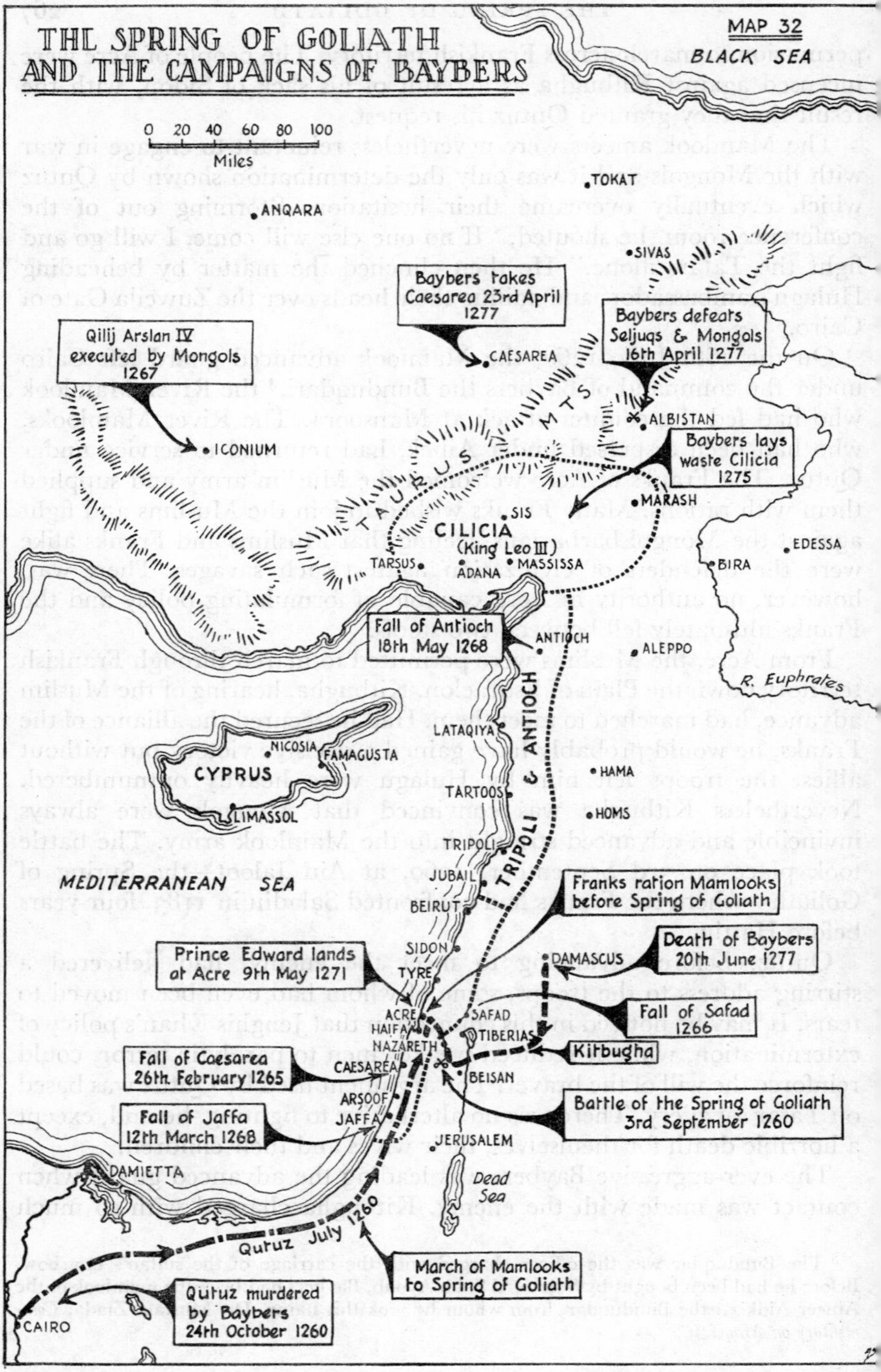
THE SPRING OF GOLIATH
AND THE CAMPAIGNS OF BAYBERS
MAP 32
BLACK SEA
0 20 40 60 80 100
Miles
TOKAT
ANQARA
SIVAS
Baybers takes Caesarea 23rd April 1277
Baybers defeats Seljuqs & Mongols 16th April 1277
Qilij Arslan IV executed by Mongols 1267
CAESAREA
ALBISTAN
TAURUS MTS
ICONIUM
Baybers lays waste Cilicia 1275
MARASH
SIS
CILICIA
(King Leo III)
TARSUS
ADANA
MASSISSA
EDESSA
BIRA
Fall of Antioch 18th May 1268
ANTIOCH
ALEPPO
R. Euphrates
TRIPOLI & ANTIOCH
LATAQIYA
NICOSIA
FAMAGUSTA
CYPRUS
LIMASSOL
HAMA
TARTOOS
HOMS
TRIPOLI
MEDITERRANEAN SEA
JUBAIL
BEIRUT
Franks ration Mamlooks before Spring of Goliath
Death of Baybers 20th June 1277
SIDON
Prince Edward lands at Acre 9th May 1271
DAMASCUS
TYRE
Fall of Safad 1266
ACRE
HAIFA
SAFAD
TIBERIAS
NAZARETH
Kitbugha
Fall of Caesarea 26th February 1265
CAESAREA
BEISAN
ARSOOF
Battle of the Spring of Goliath 3rd September 1260
JAFFA
Fall of Jaffa 12th March 1268
JERUSALEM
DAMIETTA
Dead Sea
Qutuz July 1260
March of Mamlooks to Spring of Goliath
Qutuz murdered by Baybers 24th October 1260
CAIRO

dash that the Mamlook advanced guard was swept away but when the Mongols reached the main body, they found themselves outnumbered. The valley between Mount Gilboa and the hills of Galilee was crowded from side to side and the two flanks of the army of Egypt enveloped and surrounded the Mongols. The air was filled with the weeping and lamentations of the poor villagers, caught between the armies and trying to escape being trampled under foot, while on both sides a loud and continuous roll of drums stirred the martial spirit of the combatants. For a short time it seemed as if the Mongols would break through and the issue hung in the balance. Then Qutuz himself rode to the front, tearing off his helmet so that all could recognize his face. Three times he roared in stentorian tones, "O Muslims!" and then led a desperate counter-charge, which swept the Mongol squadrons from the field.

Kitbugha, performing prodigies of valour, refused to agree to a retreat. "We must die here and that is the end of it," he replied to such a suggestion. "Long life and happiness to the khan." The apparent devotion of such a man almost persuades one that even Hulagu must have possessed some attractive qualities. Kitbugha, undaunted, galloped here and there, rallying one unit after another until his horse was shot under him and he was taken prisoner. His hands tied, he was led before Qutuz. "After overthrowing so many dynasties, you are caught at last you see," cried the victor exultantly. "If you kill me now," replied Kitbugha, "I know that it is God and not you who had decreed my fate. When Hulagu Khan hears of my death, all the country from Adharbaijan to Egypt will be trampled beneath the hoofs of Mongol horses. Ever since I was born I have been a slave of the khan. I am not, like you people, a murderer of my master." The thrust was a shrewd one for these Turkish slave-soldiers had indeed come to power by murdering their masters the Ayoubids and many more Mamlook Sultans were to reach power by assassinating their predecessors. Qutuz, getting the worst of the argument, ordered the head of Kitbugha to be struck off.

The defeat at Ain Jaloot had been for the moment decisive. The remnants of the Mongols recrossed the Euphrates and Sultan Qutuz made a triumphal entry into Damascus. Baybers, whose prowess had done much to win the victory at Ain Jaloot, had hoped as a reward to receive Aleppo from the sultan as a fief. But Qutuz refused his request and the army marched back to Egypt. Baybers was furious and immediately entered into consultations with other commanders to kill Qutuz. On 24th October, 1260, shortly before reaching Cairo, the sultan and his staff made a halt for a day's hunting in the desert. When Qutuz returned to his tent in the evening, Baybers came up to him as if to make a request and, at an agreed signal, stabbed him to death.

The question of his successor had to be decided immediately. "Who killed Qutuz?" Baybers enquired. "Is it not our custom that whoever kills the king has the right to replace him?" The other commanders present were obliged to concede the point and forthwith took the oath of allegiance to Baybers. Qutuz had been sultan for eleven months. The victory of Goliath's Spring must be attributed to his splendid leadership, both in inspiring the Mamlooks to fight and in leading them in battle. Islam, and indeed the whole world, thus owed him a heavy debt, for he saved Egypt from the fate of Baghdad.

Cairo had been decorated to welcome the triumphant return of Qutuz but, the morning after his murder, the town criers were sent through the streets of the city to call, "Ask God's mercy on the soul of the victorious King Qutuz. Pray for the long life of your Sultan Baybers." The public were at first not a little alarmed at this announcement, for Baybers had been one of the River Mamlooks who had formerly so arrogantly oppressed the people and whom Aibek had exiled. However, the morning after his entry into Cairo, the notables and the officers took the oath of allegiance.

Shortly afterwards, Baybers made a triumphal march through the city of Cairo, accompanied by the symbols of royalty. Over his head was held the yellow silk umbrella, surmounted by a gold and silver bird, an article of state pageantry which had been introduced by the Fatimid Khalifs. The Egyptian court now possessed an elaborate tradition of ceremonial, protocol and procedure, evolved by the Fatimids and the Ayoubids over a period of three centuries. On three successive Saturdays in the summer of 1261, the sultan rode in state to play polo, accompanied by the notables and military commanders and preceded by a band of trumpets and drums.

Baybers was to become the greatest of the Mamlook Sultans. He was a Qipchaq Turk but, as he was a big man with blue eyes, his racial origin may well have been mixed. He had been brought up on the steppes and sold as a slave boy in Syria to the Ameer Aidkeen the Bunduqdar. When Sultan al Salih formed the River Mamlooks, he bought Baybers from his owner. He soon rose to prominence in his unit for he had a commanding presence and was brave, full of initiative and completely devoid of scruples.

It was not fear of Baybers, however, which prevented Hulagu from returning to Syria and Egypt, but dissensions within the Golden Family, the descendants of Jenghis Khan. The toleration shown by the World Conqueror to all religions was to prove disastrous to his successors, who each adopted the religion of a conquered country. Qubilai, the new khaqan and Emperor of China, had become a Buddhist. Hulagu was not a Christian, but he was influenced by his wife, a pious

Nestorian, to spare Christians from massacre. Meanwhile Baraka, heir to the inheritance of Juji on the Volga, had adopted Islam.

As a Muslim, Baraka had been deeply incensed by the destruction of Baghdad and the murder of the khalif. His cousin Hulagu had come to be looked upon as the greatest enemy of Islam. Moreover, Baraka, though of course a Mongol, was ruler of the Qipchaqs, Baybers' own people. In 1262, Baraka and Baybers exchanged friendly embassies. In December 1262, Hulagu marched northwards through the Derbend Gates to attack Baraka. The conquest of Syria was halted by this Mongol civil war.

The Great Khan Qubilai, absorbed in the culture and the administration of China, had lost interest in the western provinces and was happy that Persia should be governed by his brother Hulagu, on whom he bestowed the title of Il Khan, which all the descendants of Hulagu were to carry. On the Volga, the inheritance of Juji became known as the Golden Horde.

In the last years of his life, Hulagu consolidated his dominions by annexing Mosul and by absorbing various smaller dynasties in Fars and Kerman. As, in addition, Georgia, Cilicia and the Seljuqs of Asia Minor were his vassals, his dominions extended from the Oxus to within a hundred and fifty miles of Constantinople.

Hulagu died in his camp near Maragha on 8th February, 1265. His devoted Nestorian wife, Doquz Khatun, the protectress of Christians, did not long outlive him. Our historian Bar Hebraeus had been elected head of the Jacobite Christian Church of the East shortly before Hulagu's death. His jurisdiction extended from Cilicia to Adharbaijan, Mosul and Baghdad and he had been received in audience by Hulagu. He was therefore a personal witness of the events of Hulagu's invasions. He refers to the death of Hulagu in the following words: "In 1265, Hulagu, the King of Kings, departed from this world. The wisdom of this man, and his greatness of soul, and his wonderful actions are incomparable. And in the days of summer Doquz Khatun, the believing queen, departed, and great sorrow came to all the Christians throughout the world because of the departure of these two great lights, who made the Christian religion triumphant."[4]

Ala al Deen al Juwaini served under Hulagu in Persia and was thus perhaps obliged to flatter him. It is nevertheless worthy of note that he writes that Hulagu "united in his person all the graces of kingly beneficence and all the wonders of royal kindness". Bar Hebraeus was a Christian but Juwaini was a Muslim and a Persian. Neither of them attempt to deny the facts of the Mongol massacres or their cruel sadism. Both historians wrote while the Mongols were at the height of their power and when, therefore, flattery was essential to survival.

[4] *The Chronography of Bar Hebraeus*. Trans. E. A. Wallis Budge.

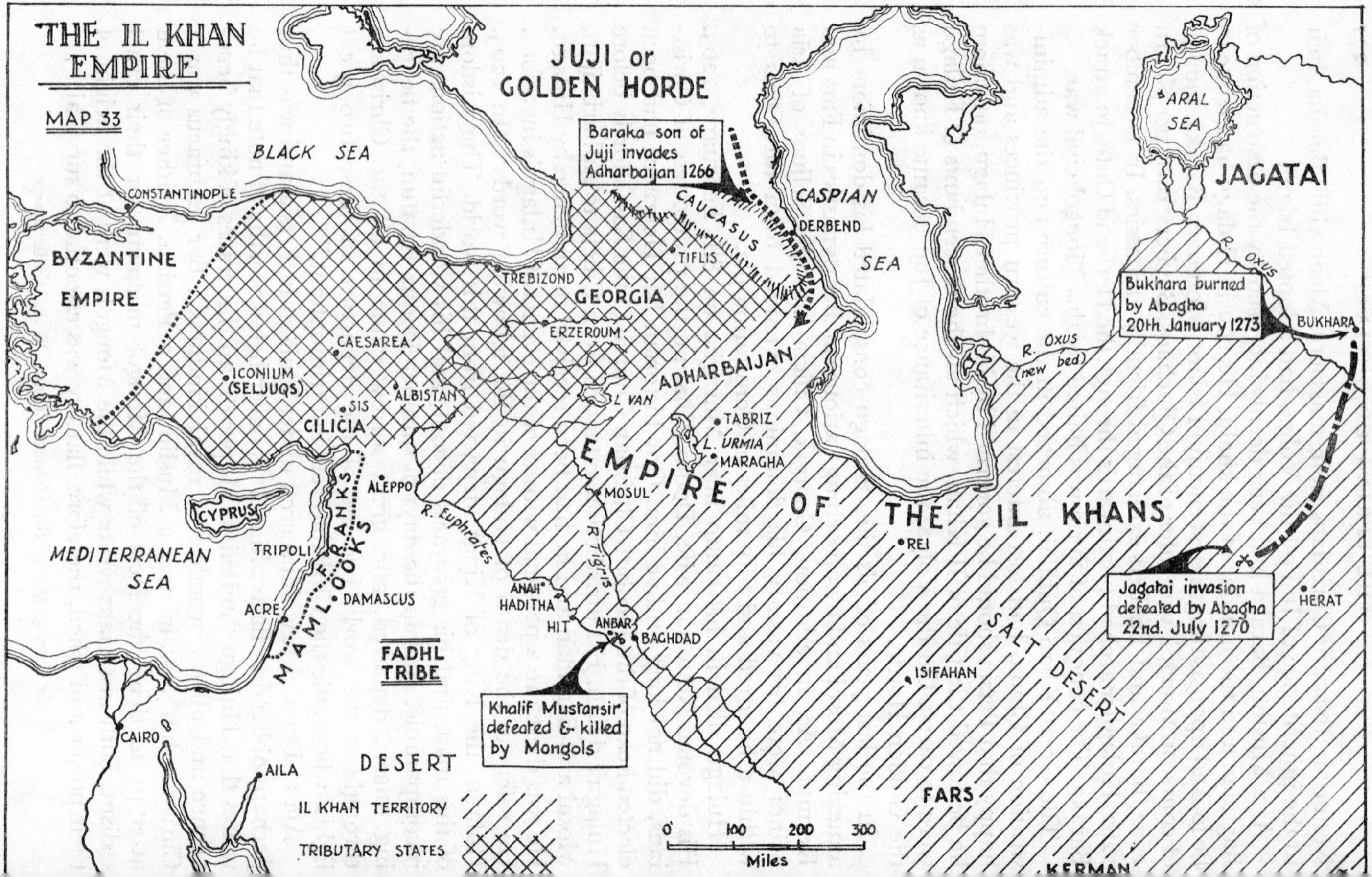
THE IL KHAN EMPIRE
MAP 33
JUJI or GOLDEN HORDE
Baraka son of Juji invades Adharbaijan 1266
BLACK SEA
CASPIAN SEA
ARAL SEA
JAGATAI
CONSTANTINOPLE
BYZANTINE EMPIRE
CAUCASUS
DERBEND
TIFLIS
TREBIZOND
GEORGIA
ERZEROUM
CAESAREA
ICONIUM (SELJUQS)
SIS
ALBISTAN
CILICIA
L. VAN
ADHARBAIJAN
TABRIZ
L. URMIA
MARAGHA
R. OXUS
R. OXUS (new bed)
Bukhara burned by Abagha 20th January 1273
BUKHARA
EMPIRE OF THE IL KHANS
ALEPPO
MOSUL
CYPRUS
MEDITERRANEAN SEA
TRIPOLI
FRANKS
MAMLOOKS
ACRE
DAMASCUS
R. Euphrates
R. Tigris
ANAH
HADITHA
HIT
ANBAR
BAGHDAD
REI
Jagatai invasion defeated by Abagha 22nd. July 1270
HERAT
SALT DESERT
ISIFAHAN
FADHL TRIBE
Khalif Mustansir defeated & killed by Mongols
CAIRO
AILA
DESERT
IL KHAN TERRITORY
TRIBUTARY STATES
0 100 200 300
Miles
FARS
KERMAN

These apparent contradictions, however, may be partly attributed to the policy of the Mongol leaders with whom it was a fixed principle to apply the most extreme savagery towards their enemies. At the same time they endeavoured to retain the loyalty of their supporters by a display of great patriarchal benevolence towards their friends.

On 19th June, 1265, Abagha, the eldest son of Hulagu, was chosen to be Il Khan. Although loyal to the Khaqan Qubilai in distant China, Abagha found himself surrounded by enemies. In 1266, Baraka Khan, the brother of Batu, the son of Juji, passed the Derbend Gates to invade Persia but died on the campaign and his army withdrew. In 1269, however, the Khan of the Jagatai, who had never acquiesced in the elevation of the sons of Tului, invaded Khurasan but, on 22nd July, 1270, he was defeated by Abagha near Herat. The Il Khan crossed the Oxus in retaliation, and on 20th January, 1273, his army took Bukhara, which was plundered and burnt and the inhabitants massacred. Mongol unity, so laboriously achieved by Jenghis Khan, had been completely lost.

* * *

In so far as lay in his power, Hulagu in 1258 had killed all the inhabitants of Baghdad. In 1261, however, soon after the accession of Baybers, an individual arrived in Damascus, accompanied by fifty horsemen of the desert tribe of the Khafaja, claiming to be the uncle of Mustasim. He alleged that he had lain hidden during the massacre and had been living among the nomads of the desert ever since. Baybers, doubtless considering that a puppet Abbasid Khalif would add prestige to his throne, summoned him to Cairo, where he was received in state. A few days later, he was solemnly accepted as Prince of the Faithful with the throne-name of Al Mustansir. The khalifate had been vacant for three and a half years.[5] The sultan accompanied by the khalif then rode in state through the streets, which had been decorated and carpeted. "No tongue," says Maqrizi, "can describe the splendours of that day."

Troops were then enlisted in the name of the khalif who was also given the necessary staff and equipment for an expeditionary force. Baybers accompanied Al Mustansir to Damascus. According to Maqrizi, the sultan had intended to give the khalif a force of ten thousand cavalry but in Damascus it was whispered to him that, if reinstated in Baghdad, the khalif might become too powerful. As a result, the unhappy Al Mustansir was ultimately sent off to reconquer Baghdad with only three hundred cavalry.

The chief of the Fadhl tribe of the Syrian desert joined him with four

[5] Except indeed for the Muwahhid Khalif in Tunis. See page 346.

THE IL KHANS OF PERSIA

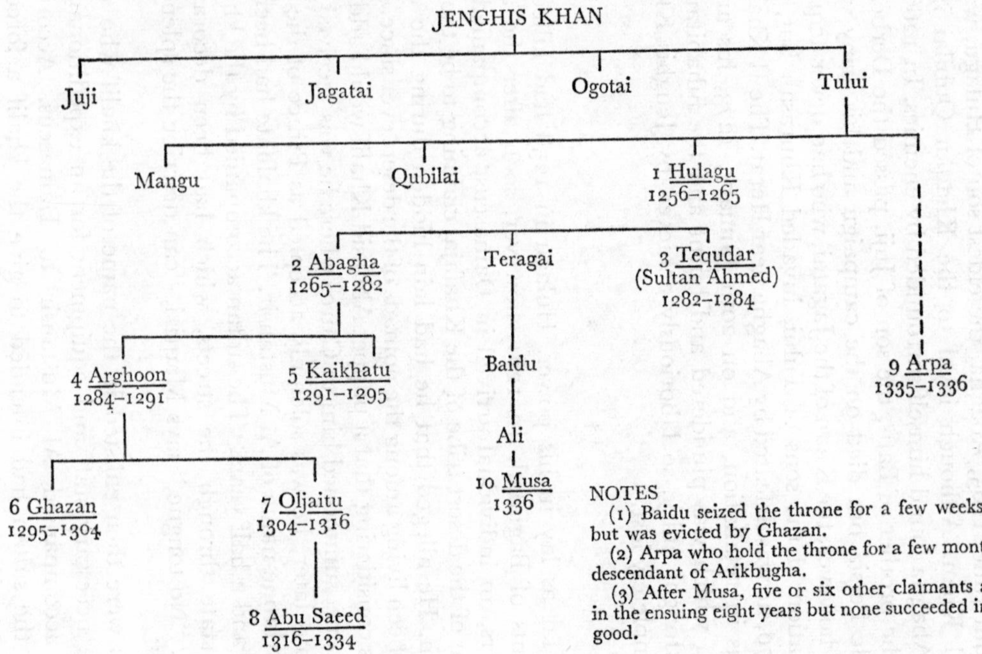

NOTES

(1) Baidu seized the throne for a few weeks in 1295 but was evicted by Ghazan.

(2) Arpa who hold the throne for a few months was a descendant of Arikbugha.

(3) After Musa, five or six other claimants appeared in the ensuing eight years but none succeeded in making good.

hundred Arab horsemen and the party travelled down the west bank of the Euphrates through Anah, Haditha and Hit.[6] At Anbar—near the modern Fellujah—the khalif met a force of Tatars. After a short and sharp encounter, nearly all the khalif's party were killed. Al Mustansir himself was never seen again and was presumably lost among the dead. A certain Ahmed abu Abbas, also a member of the Abbasid family, survived the action and returned to Cairo, where he was made khalif with the title of Al Hakim.

The whole of this affair is difficult to explain. When he first arrived in Cairo, Al Mustansir had been given a royal reception and Baybers spent on him, it was said, a million dinars. The sultan ultimately sent him off to his death with only three hundred men, but why the khalif consented to go with so small a force is difficult to explain.

The Khalif Al Hakim was duly installed in Cairo but later Baybers seems to have decided that it was unwise to have a khalif as well as a sultan in Egypt, and Al Hakim was placed under house arrest in the citadel. For another two hundred and fifty years, there were to be Abbasid Khalifs in Cairo but none of them was ever allowed any authority.

* * *

Although essentially a soldier, Baybers was interested in the administration. In time of famine, he obliged the rich to feed the poor and "many other such acts," records Maqrizi, "in order to win the people's hearts." Whether for religious or political reasons, he sought the rôle of the defender of Islam. Stringent orders were issued against the use of alcohol, against cabaret entertainments and other forms of immorality.

The respective attitudes of Islam and Christianity towards soldiers is one of great interest. To Muslims, war is not only permissible but, in certain circumstances, meritorious. As a result, Muslim soldiers are often extremely pious, a feature which survives to this day. Religious revivals in Islam have frequently been the work of soldiers. In our own times, a military *coup d'état* in a Muslim country is often marked by attempts at moral reform, the closing of night-clubs and the censorship of books and cinema films.

Christians, on the other hand, are always haunted by the fear that war is contrary to the Gospels, yet no government has been able to survive without the power to wage war. The solution for many centuries adopted by Christian nations was to enlist criminals and men of the lowest level of society in their armies. As a result, soldiers acquired the reputation of being brutal and licentious, the very opposite of the Muslim viewpoint.

[6] Map 33, page 272.

These contrasting attitudes are still fertile in misunderstandings between Muslims and Christians. Military intervention in politics or the use of troops in civil disturbances are regarded with resentment in north-west Europe and North America, but in Muslim countries the intervention of the army is often welcomed by the public and soldiers are considered heroes, in contrast to politicians. There was therefore nothing remarkable in the fact that such ruthless soldiers as the Mamlooks should be at the same time religious reformers. We may remark, however, that Baybers, the defender of Islam, was at least twice a murderer and that he himself drank qumiss, the fermented mare's milk of his native steppes, until he was intoxicated.

* * *

Above all, however, Baybers was a soldier. He frequently rode down from the citadel of Cairo to the parade ground to watch the troops exercising. He himself often took a turn and few, if any, of the troopers could handle his lance or shoot his arrows at full gallop with more skill than the sultan himself.

With the Mongols fighting one another, Baybers found himself with a free hand in Syria. The position of the Franks was now hopeless. Their numbers were so far reduced that they could no longer put an army in the field. Various barons and the military orders of knights were distributed round individual castles, none of them strong enough to resist attack by the Mamlook army. Moreover, as there was no field army, a besieged castle could not be relieved. In addition, the owners of the castles recognized no single authority and failed even to co-operate with one another.

Baybers seemed to have acquired the aggressive energy which the Mongols had lost. All the Muslim castles in Syria were supplied and reinforced. The walls of Alexandria were rebuilt and the Damietta channel was blocked, to guard against a fresh crusade against Egypt. The fleet had been neglected since the days of Sultan Al Salih and Baybers gave orders for the building of new ships. The postal services were so improved that a letter could reach Damascus from Cairo in four days. The sultan received reports from all provinces twice a week.

These preliminaries completed, Baybers led his army to Palestine in January 1265, ostensibly to resist an expected Tatar invasion. Suddenly, on the evening of 26th February, 1265, the army was ordered to fall in, made to march all night, and the next morning surprised the Frankish fortress of Caesarea and carried it by assault. The town was levelled with the ground, Baybers himself working with a pickaxe among the soldiers. Another sudden march resulted in the capture of Arsoof, which was also completely destroyed. A board was immediately assembled, consisting of two judges and a treasury official, and the land thus conquered was divided up into fiefs between the officers of the army.

Next year, in the summer of 1266, the sultan was back again at the head of a large army and the whole coastal plain was laid waste from Jaffa to Sidon, in spite of messengers who came out of Jaffa to beg for peace. Then, all of a sudden, the whole army was diverted to Safad. The sultan himself and his staff erected the timber for the mangonels and then stood beside them watching the shooting. Baybers in person was in the front line, promising money and robes of honour to the first to break through the wall. Arab tribes from the desert had been called up to support the troops. Just out of arrow range from the walls, tents were pitched as dressing stations for the wounded, with doctors and surgeons continuously on duty, and food and refreshments were available for the exhausted.

On the fourteenth day of the siege, Safad was still holding out. The besiegers were exhausted and many soldiers remained lying in their tents when their turn came round for duty. But Baybers himself went round from tent to tent. Officers were placed under arrest, soldiers were dragged out of bed, the drums were beaten and the attack was resumed. On the eighteenth day, the garrison surrendered on condition that they evacuate the fortress, carrying neither weapons nor money. In fact, when they left the fortress, they were all treacherously massacred. Baybers then collected his own troops, apologized for the rough way in which he had treated them, thanked them for their labours and distributed among them the money, wealth, and weapons captured in the town.

The extraordinary energy developed by the Mamlook Kingdom under Baybers is shown by the fact that simultaneously with these operations in Palestine, another column this year raided Cilicia, while a third occupied Suakin on the Red Sea, in what is now the Sudan. In the same year, the holy cities of Mecca and Medina acknowledged the suzerainty of Egypt and the nomadic tribes of Beni Sakhr, Beni Lam and Aneiza paid their animal tax in the Hejaz to officials from Cairo.

Again in March 1268, the sultan left Cairo, took Jaffa on 12th March by a surprise assault, razed it to the ground and settled some Turkmans in the area. Then by a sudden swift march he was outside Tripoli, where he ravaged the country, killed all prisoners, levelled all churches. cut down the fruit trees and reduced this earthly paradise to a desert,

When, however, the Lord of Tartoos boldly rode to see him, the sultan thanked him and did not touch his land. Thus each petty baron sought to fend for himself, a situation which made them all harmless to the Muslims. From Tripoli, Baybers rode to the great Muslim cities of

Homs and Hama, where he seemed absorbed in regulations for the prohibition of the sale of wine and for the reform of sexual morality.

Then suddenly, by a forced march, he surprised the great city of Antioch. After four days the walls were scaled on 18th May, 1268. Every man in Antioch was massacred and all the women and children were sold as slaves. The immense wealth of this great city, once the Roman capital of the East and, in 1268, one of the rich depôts of the oriental trade, was distributed among the Mamlook soldiers. Then Antioch was burnt to the ground. It has, to this day, never recovered from Baybers' visitation. If the Mongols were savage, the Mamlooks were not very far behind. A ten-year truce was then concluded with Acre.

The reader finds himself wondering why Baybers did not destroy all the remaining Frankish castles once and for all. It is possible that he was still apprehensive of a new invasion from the West, where St. Louis was reported to be preparing a Crusade. In July 1270, however, Louis attacked Tunis, not Egypt. In the spring of 1271, Baybers seemed to be about to march on Tripoli when he heard of the arrival of Prince Edward of Cornwall, later to be King Edward I of England, who had landed at Acre on 9th May, 1271, with a small force of less than a thousand men. Nevertheless this insignificant detachment from the West sufficed to persuade Baybers to sign a ten-year truce with Tripoli.

Prince Edward wrote to Abagha Khan, the son of Hulagu, to concert a joint invasion of Syria. As a result, in October 1271, a force of some ten thousand Mongols reached the vicinity of Aleppo. Abagha, meanwhile, had been called to resist an invasion of Khurasan by his Jagatai cousins. In consequence, the force sent to Aleppo had been collected from the Mongol garrisons of Asia Minor and was unable to do more than lay waste the surrounding countryside. For some days, Syria was in panic, then the Tatars withdrew northwards once again. Prince Edward's little force in Acre had been too weak to take the field against Baybers.

When Prince Edward had been just over a year in Acre, a ten-year treaty was concluded with his assistance at Caesarea on 22nd May, 1272, between Hugh III, King of Cyprus and titular King of Jerusalem, and Sultan Baybers. The negotiations had been partly conducted by Charles d'Anjou, King of Sicily,[7] who had adopted the policy of friendly relations with Egypt which had previously been initiated by the Hohenstaufens. Nevertheless, Edward of England does seem to have played a useful part in the conclusion of this ten-year truce. On 16th June, 1272, an Ismaili assassin, allegedly sent by Baybers, attempted to murder Prince Edward. It was on this occasion that his wife Eleanor was supposed to have sucked the poison from the wound. Edward re-embarked at Acre on 22nd September, 1272.

7 The story of the seizure of Sicily by Charles d'Anjou is related in Chapter XIV.

As a result of this treaty, Baybers turned his attention to the Armenian Kingdom of Cilicia. During the summer of 1275 he captured and plundered the cities of Massissa, Adana, Tarsus and Sis, the Armenian capital. Sixty thousand Christians were massacred and great numbers of young women and children were carried off as slaves.

* * *

We left the Sultan Qilij Arslan IV as ruler of the Seljuq dominions in Asia Minor after the flight of his brother to Constantinople in 1260.[8] In the ensuing years, the real power in the Seljuq Kingdom was usurped by the wazeer, Mueen al Deen Sulaiman, commonly known as Perwana. In 1267, avid of yet more power, Perwana denounced his master to the Mongols and secured his execution. His three-year-old son, Kai Khosrou III, was raised to the throne but the wazeer Perwana wielded all the power of the government.

At this stage, Perwana invited Baybers to come and conquer Asia Minor and, in February 1277, the sultan left Cairo. On 16th April, 1277, he defeated the Seljuq army assisted by a force of Mongols at Albistan. For some reason, Perwana, though he had invited Baybers, did not join him but fled with the infant sultan to Tokat.

On 23rd April, 1277, Baybers made a triumphal entry into Caesarea, where he held a grand levée, seated on the throne of the Seljuqs. Largesse was scattered in the streets amid a great display of magnificence. A family of local Turkish chieftains, the Qaramans, had been one of the sources of disorder in the disintegrating Seljuqid dominions. Baybers summoned the Ameer Muhammad Qaraman before him and spoke to him in a friendly manner. We shall hear more of the Qaraman ameers in the following pages.

On 9th June, 1277, Baybers was back in Damascus, covered in glory. A certain Ayoubid prince called Malik al Qahir[9] had accompanied the sultan on the campaign and had particularly distinguished himself by his bravery, so that his praise was in every mouth. The sultan was accustomed to monopolize the plaudits of the public and perhaps was jealous. Moreover, he and his commanders had all been slaves of the Ayoubid dynasty and a popular prince of that family might be dangerous.

At a reception in Damascus, Baybers mixed a glass of qumiss for Malik al Qahir whom he invited to join him for a drink. According to Maqrizi, Baybers had put poison in the drink which he had mixed for his guest and then, by accident, drank it himself. The night after this

[8] Genealogical tree, page 168.

[9] He was the son of Al Nasir Daood, formerly King of Transjordan. Genealogical tree, page 216.

reception, the sultan felt unwell and on 20th June, 1277, three days later, he died. He was fifty-five and had reigned for seventeen years.

There is a pleasant story that when Baybers was brought to Syria for sale as a slave boy, he was offered to this Ayoubid prince who, being young, consulted his mother. This perspicacious lady peeped at the new slave from behind a curtain and said to her son, "Don't have anything to do with that one. He has a nasty look in his eyes."

Baybers was an extremely powerful personality. He was brave, hasty, domineering and inspired great fear in the other Mamlook commanders, an essential quality in one who aspired to command so desperate a crew of mercenaries. Unlike the courteous Ayoubids, he enjoyed taunting his defeated enemies. After his victories won over the Franks, he sent insulting and sarcastic letters to their leaders. He was absolutely intrepid, a splendid horseman and was always ready to travel far and fast. One of his peculiarities was his habit of disappearing. On one occasion, when camped at Arsoof in Palestine, he suddenly decided to visit Egypt. Feigning illness in his tent, he slipped out and rode with four attendants to Cairo. Reaching the city on the fourth day, he remained there incognito for forty-eight hours, riding about the streets unrecognized. Five days later, he re-entered his tent at Arsoof at night, emerging next morning saying that he had recovered from his indisposition. Many other such exploits were recounted of him.

According to Maqrizi, Baybers had twelve thousand regular Mamlooks of his own. They were probably mostly of Turkish origin, but some may have been Mongols. Nationalism was not a common emotion in those days. The Mamlooks relied on military pride, *esprit de corps* and a high standard of discipline and efficiency. Their weapon-training text-books, which still exist, were numerous and detailed, their equipment and administration were good, their uniforms splendid.

Baybers' army is alleged to have been four times as numerous at that of the Ayoubids and as a result both Egypt and Syria were very heavily taxed. Yet in spite of the high standard of discipline among junior ranks, Baybers suffered from the common weakness of military dictators. He had risen to power by murdering his predecessor and there was the ever-present possibility that his own subordinates might do the same to him. As a result there are frequent references in contemporary histories to the imprisonment of senior officers for plotting against the sultan.

While Baybers' personal Mamlooks were only twelve thousand, Maqrizi states that he could call on another twelve thousand, but does not specify who these were. There are also casual references to calling up troops in Syria, to contingents brought by subject princes in the north and to the mobilization of the Arab bedouin tribes, who always joined in major campaigns.

Baybers took much trouble to pose as the Muslim hero fighting religious wars, a position greatly facilitated by the fact that his principal enemies were Christians or "heathen" Tatars. His insistence on the fact that religion and morality were essential to victory had its roots far back in Islam, even in Judaism. For the same reason, non-Muslims were often massacred, prisoners of war were beheaded and churches were razed to the ground.

A more attractive side to his character was the manner in which he constantly worked with his soldiers. In every siege and battle he was among the troops, leading a cavalry charge, working the mangonels or swinging a battering-ram against the gates. Baybers was a giant among men, a towering personality, fearless, unresting, inexhaustible, indifferent to luxury or ease. He was also unscrupulous, cunning and pitiless, but he did everything with an exuberance—a panache—which was absent from such gloomier killers as Jenghis Khan and Hulagu.

NOTABLE DATES

Death of John Vatatzes, Emperor of Nicaea	3rd November, 1254
War of St. Saba	1256–1277
Coronation of Michael VIII Palaeologus	1st January, 1259
Entry of Kitbugha into Damascus	1st March, 1260
Battle of the Spring of Goliath	3rd September, 1260
End of the Latin Empire of Constantinople	25th July, 1261
Death of Hulagu	8th February, 1265
Abagha elected Il Khan	19th June, 1265
Capture of Antioch	18th May, 1268
Landing at Acre of Prince Edward of England	9th May, 1271
Signature of ten-year treaty at Caesarea	22nd May, 1272
Baybers' campaign in Asia Minor	February to June 1277
Death of Baybers	20th June, 1277

PERSONALITIES

Mamlook Sultans of Egypt

Qutuz

Baybers the Bunduqdari

Mongols

Qubilai Khaqan, Emperor of China
Hulagu, his brother, Il Khan of Persia
Abagha, son of Hulagu
Baraka Khan, chief of the Golden Horde
Kitbugha, Mongol commander in Syria

Seljuqs of Iconium

Ghiyath al Deen Kai Khosrou II
Izz al Deen Kai Kaus II } his sons
Rukn al Deen Qilij Arslan IV } his sons
Kai Khosrou III, infant son of Qilij Arslan IV
Sulaiman Perwana, the scheming wazeer

Christians

Bohemond VI, Prince of Antioch and Count of Tripoli
Haithum I, Armenian King of Cilicia

Latin Emperors of Constantinople

Baldwin I, Count of Flanders	1204–1205
Henry, his brother	1205–1216
Pierre de Courtenai	1217
Yolanda, widow of Pierre	1217–1219
Robert de Courtenai, son of Pierre	1221–1228
Jean de Brienne, associated with the child Baldwin II	1231–1237
Baldwin II, brother of Robert de Courtenai	1228–1261

Greek Emperors of Nicaea

Theodore I Lascaris	1204–1222
John III Vatatzes	1222–1254
Theodore II Lascaris	1254–1258
John IV Lascaris	1258–1259
Michael VIII Palaeologus (in Nicaea)	1259–1261
(in Constantinople)	1261–1282

XIII

The Reconquista

1200–1250

Historians are beginning to appreciate that Europe after the twelfth century did not reap only material benefits from her victories over Islam. . . . These victories brought her a profit at least equally important by opening her eyes on another world and by broadening most strikingly her intellectual horizon. The scholars of Islam . . . relit a torch which, but for them, might well have been extinguished—that of scientific research. By this means, they opened to Europe the way, the exploration of which was to lead to the Renaissance. LÉVI-PROVENÇAL, *Le Role Spirituel de l'Espagne Musulmane*

Love of flowers was a veritable passion among Spanish Muslims. As they were the greatest botanists in the world, so no other nation approached them in the perfection of their floriculture. The profusion and variety of blossoms of every description were marvellous and enchanting. S. P. SCOTT, *The Moorish Empire in Europe*

It is commonly said among the Greeks that "Africa always offers something new". PLINY

XIII

THE death in 1199 of the great Muwahhid Khalif, Yaqoob al Mansoor, three years after his victory over the Christians at Alarcos, has already been mentioned. His son and successor Muhammad, who assumed the name of Al Nasir, was of the fourth generation from Abdul Mumin and showed those marked signs of decadence which seemed to characterize all the fourth generations of post-Arab conquerors. "His eyes," says a contemporary Arab historian,[1] "were usually modestly directed at the ground; he spoke rarely and with hesitation and was afflicted with a nervous stammer. His character was gentle and little inclined to blood-shed, while his mind was slow to grasp a new subject except after long study."

The victory of Alarcos had temporarily destroyed the power of the Christians of Spain. Muhammad al Nasir profited by the respite to crush the Murabit rebellion in Ifriqiya. The Muwahhid fleet retook Tunis and Yahya Ibn Ghaniya was obliged to take refuge with the tribes of the desert. Muhammad al Nasir decided that only a strong governor could maintain order in Ifriqiya and chose for the post one Abdul Wahid, the son of that Abu Hafas Umar who had been the loyal supporter of Abdul Mumin. The son of Abu Hafas was indeed the man for the task. Yahya Ibn Ghaniya, defeated near Tebessa, took refuge with the nomadic Beni Hilal Arabs and Zenata Berbers south of the Atlas, whence he raided the villagers in the mountains. It will be remembered that the Murabits had emerged from the nomadic tribes of the Sahara, but that the first Muwahhids had been villagers of the Atlas.[2] Thus their dynastic rivalries still represented something of the age-old hostility of the nomad and the cultivator.

All this time, Alfonso VIII of Castile had been diligently preparing to avenge his defeat at Alarcos. Encouraged by the death of Yaqoob al Mansoor in 1199, he broke the seven-year truce to which he had pledged his faith, crossed the border and laid waste the territory of Jaen, north of Granada, with fire and sword. Even the gentle Muhammad al Nasir could not for ever overlook the constant raids of the Castilians and, in February 1211, a large Muslim army was transported by sea to Seville. Alfonso, alarmed at the prospect of retribution, sent desperate appeals for help to the pope, to France and to his fellow monarchs of Christian Spain and Portugal.

But the hand of Yaqoob al Mansoor was no longer on the helm. The

[1] Al Marakishi. [2] Page 113 and *The Course of Empire.*

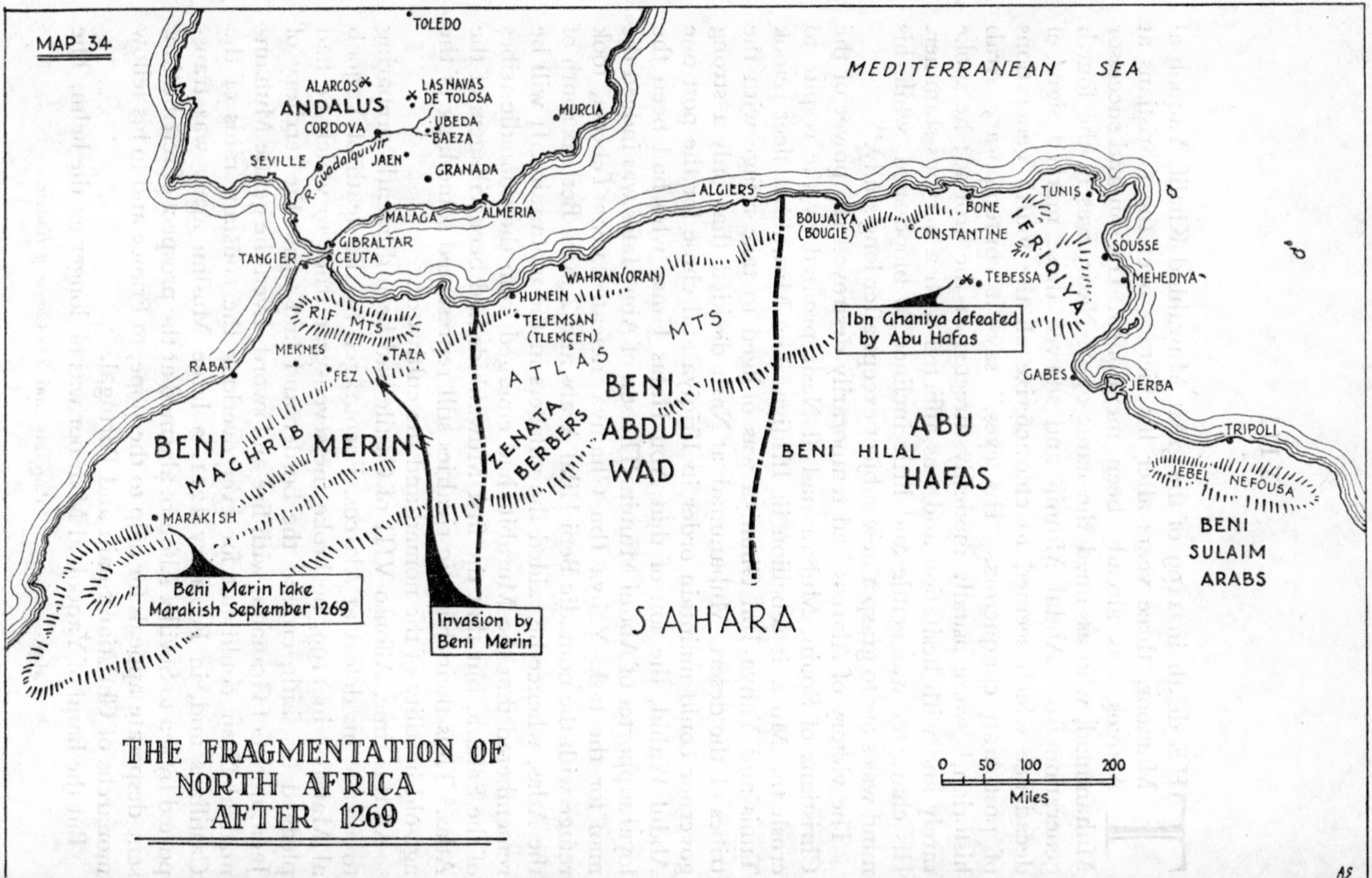

THE FRAGMENTATION OF NORTH AFRICA AFTER 1269

summer of 1211 was wasted in languid operations against a minor castle and the Muslims retired to winter quarters in Andalus without achieving anything. The delay was used by the Christians to build up a great army. The pope preached a crusade against the Muwahhids and, from all western Europe, the faithful, the adventurous and the greedy rallied to the banner of Castile. The Christian forces concentrated in Toledo and, in June 1212, set out to seek the enemy. The final and decisive battle was fought on 16th July, 1212, at Al Uqab, better known in European history as Las Navas de Tolosa.

The battle was long and desperately contested but finally friction between the Berbers of Africa and the Arabs of Andalus seems to have caused the latter to abandon the field and the Muslims were utterly defeated. Orders had been issued to the Christian army that any man who spared the life of one of the enemy would pay for it with his own. (By contrast, after his victory at Alarcos, Yaqoob al Mansoor had released twenty thousand Christian prisoners without ransom.) Many thousands of Muslims were slaughtered in cold blood after King Alfonso's victory. Las Navas de Tolosa was the Waterloo of Arab rule in Spain, exactly five centuries after its conquest by Tariq ibn Zayyad, a period as long as that which divides us from Henry VII, the first Tudor King of England.

The real victim of Las Navas de Tolosa was the refined and cultured civilization of Muslim Andalus, still, even in its decadence, far in advance of both western Europe and of northern Africa. Yet, slowly weakening, it was still to survive for nearly three centuries more in the Arab Kingdom of Granada. Before its final disappearance, it had accomplished its historic rôle of spreading knowledge, refinement, chivalry and romance to the emergent nations of the West.

* * *

The victory of Las Navas de Tolosa not only destroyed Muwahhid rule in Spain, but also raised Castile to pre-eminence among the Christian kingdoms. Three days after the victory, the Christian allies advanced southwards. Baeza had been evacuated by its inhabitants. The great and wealthy city of Ubeda was besieged but the citizens offered to capitulate and to pay a million pieces of gold, if their town were spared. The terms were accepted but when the Spaniards saw the immense wealth of the city, they broke their faith and declared the agreement to be cancelled. In the subsequent sack, sixty thousand Muslims are alleged to have been massacred, the city was stripped bare and then razed to the ground.

The whole of Andalus might have been conquered if Alfonso had pressed on. But the wealth of Ubeda had saved the Muslims. Laden with plunder, the Christians wished only to return home, discipline was relaxed and the victorious army melted away. Alfonso VIII died the year after his great victory, at the age of fifty-nine, and the momentum of the reconquista was lost. The Muslim position could doubtless have been retrieved by a new army from Africa but the gentle Muhammad al Nasir was not the man to face a sea of troubles. Returning hastily to Marakish, he abdicated in favour of his sixteen-year-old son, Yusuf al Mustansir, and died soon afterwards.

Mustansir, a child incapable of the conduct of public affairs, was preoccupied with youthful pleasures. Ifriqiya was securely held by Ibn Abi Hafas, who continued to pay lip-service to the dynasty of Abdul Mumin, but who was now in reality the independent ruler of what we call Tunisia. In the eastern Maghrib around Telemsan, the Abdul Wad clan of Zenata Berbers had seized control. Even the Maghrib itself was invaded by the nomadic Berber tribe of Beni Merin.[3] Mustansir died in 1224 and was succeeded by a certain Abdul Wahid who was strangled a few months later. His successor Aadil was drowned in one of the artificial lakes of the palace in 1227. The Muwahhid power was in complete disintegration.

The throne was now disputed between two rival claimants, Idris al Mamoon, the governor of Seville, on the one hand, and a son of the gentle Muhammad al Nasir on the other. Mamoon solicited and obtained the support of Ferdinand III, King of Castile, surnamed the Saint, who lent him twelve thousand Christian cavalry, with which, in 1230, he was able to cross to North Africa and to capture Marakish. Only thirty-four years had elapsed since, after the Battle of Alarcos, the whole of Christian Spain had been at the feet of Yaqoob al Mansoor.

The Muwahhid Khalif Mamoon was little more than a puppet, placed on the throne of Marakish by Ferdinand the Saint. The decline of the dynasty of Abdul Mumin continued unchecked. In 1232, Mamoon died and was succeeded by his son Rasheed, who, in 1242, was followed by Saeed, a man at last of considerable energy and personality. Meanwhile in 1235, the Beni Abdul Wad Berbers declared themselves independent in Telemsan. Beni Merin were collecting taxes on their own account round Meknes. In Ifriqiya, Abu Zakariya Yahya I in 1236 proclaimed his own independence, annexing Algiers, Boujaiya and Constantine to his territory.

Saeed collected a large army, defeated Beni Merin and marched on Telemsan to bring Beni Abdul Wad to order. After doing so, he was determined to eliminate Yahya abu Hafas also and to re-unite the empire of Abdul Mumin. But when approaching Telemsan he fell into an ambush and was killed. His army retreated on Morocco, where Beni

[3] Pronounced Mereen.

Merin fell upon it and defeated it, subsequently seizing the city of Fez.

Umar al Murtadha was then proclaimed Muwahhid Khalif but he ruled only over the southern half of Morocco, the north being in the hands of Beni Merin. In 1266, he was overthrown by his cousin Abu Dabboos Idris, who seized the throne. In September 1269, however, Beni Merin captured Marakish and the Muwahhid Empire was finally extinguished.

* * *

By his capture of Mehediya in 1160, Abdul Mumin had created a great Berber Empire extending one thousand five hundred miles from Morocco to Tripoli. With the extinction of his dynasty one hundred and nine years later, North Africa broke up into three sectors. The Maghrib, which we call Morocco, was henceforward to be ruled by Beni Merin. The central sector, with the western half of modern Algeria, passed under the control of Beni Abdul Wad, while Ifriqiya acknowledged the rule of Abu Hafas. It is some tribute to the glory of the Muwahhids that, after their fall, no one ever again succeeded in uniting North Africa.

* * *

The Murabits and Muwahhids in the West, the Buwaihids, the Seljuqs and the Ayoubids in the East, had all followed the same course. Each of these "successor states" had been founded by a simple, rough and ready soldier, in some cases illiterate or almost so. His son was better educated but likewise simple, just and manly. The third ruler was cultured, educated, interested in history, literature, poetry, art and philosophy. Under him the dynasty reached its highest point of glory and honour. In the fourth ruler of each dynasty, signs of degeneracy began to appear, accompanied by family quarrels and civil wars.

The fifth generation was, in most cases, quite futile and thereafter rival petty princes disputed the throne until another barbarian invader chased the whole dynasty from the scene. All the barbarian conquerors exhibited many aspects of greatness but once they had acquired Arab culture they degenerated rapidly. This can scarcely have been due to anything inherently evil in that culture itself, for the Arabs had grown up with it for centuries, during which they ruled a great part of the known world.

The conclusion would seem to be that great civilizations belong to those who have given them birth. But when barbarians adopt a mature civilization, it tends to poison instead of nourishing them. In the case of the Arab Empire, the succession of short-term barbarian dynasties was to last for six hundred years until the Ottomans re-united and restored stability to a great part of the area. Throughout these six hundred years, the Arabs, though considerably intermixed with other races, continued to live in the successor states. But they were no longer the masters, for they had abandoned the profession of arms and had become merchants, intellectuals, writers, lawyers or scientists.

The period in which we live, that of the decline of the great civilization of Western Europe, may perhaps be compared to that of the disintegration of the Arab culture which preceded it. Other nations from all over the world are seeking to learn the Western way of life. Will the result be once more to produce a succession of ever-changing groupings until a new, great culture emerges in some part of the world?

* * *

Having followed the course of the Muwahhid Empire until its final extinction in 1269, we must now return once more to Spain. In 1135, seventy-seven years before the Battle of Las Navas de Tolosa, the little land-locked Kingdom of Aragon had become united to Catalonia, thereby acquiring a considerable length of coastline and the great and wealthy port of Barcelona, which maintained its own battle-fleet in the same manner as Genoa, Pisa and Venice.

In 1213, the year after Las Navas de Tolosa, James I, surnamed the Conqueror, had become King of Aragon. The Balearic Islands were still held by the Muslims, but in 1229, James the Conqueror landed in Majorca and captured Palma after a siege of seven weeks, sixty thousand Muslims being massacred and a further thirty thousand carried into slavery. The Balearics were annexed to Aragon.

In 1238, with the aid of an army of French and English crusaders, James I conquered the city of Valencia with its surrounding territory, down to the borders of Murcia. Before his death, he had annexed all the Muslim states on the east side of the peninsula and had raised the once obscure mountain Kingdom of Aragon to the status of an important power. One of the famous heroes of the Middle Ages, he was, in every respect, almost more than life size. In height he towered above other men. His face was handsome, his manners were courtly, his personality charming. He was fearless in battle but compassionate to his subjects. He reigned for no less than sixty-three years, most of which he spent in the conquest of eastern Spain from the Muslims. It is claimed that he knew the whole of the Scriptures by heart and that during his lifetime he founded two thousand churches.

Yet this Christian hero rarely kept faith with Muslims, to whom he was prepared to perjure himself to gain a treacherous advantage, nor did he hesitate to massacre Muslims whenever an opportunity offered. These methods were employed ostensibly in the service of Him who told His followers to love their enemies—a remarkable example of how men obey those precepts of their religion which suit them but fail to notice such as go against their inclinations. In some directions, James the Conqueror seemed even to imitate the hated infidel, for he was cultured and well-educated, a patron of poetry and literature and maintained a numerous establishment of concubines. He died on 7th July, 1276, in Valencia, the city which he had wrested from the Muslims.

* * *

In order to present the career of James I of Aragon, we have departed from strict chronological order and must now return to Ferdinand III, King of Castile, and the aftermath of Las Navas de Tolosa. In 1230, the death of Alfonso IX, King of Leon, had resulted in the final union of Castile and Leon.[4] The new king of the united kingdoms was Ferdinand III, a son of Alfonso IX of Leon by his wife Berengaria, the daughter of Alfonso VIII of Castile. Thereafter the reconquista proceeded more rapidly, Cordova being captured in 1236.

The conquest of Valencia by Aragon in 1238 aroused a tinge of jealousy in Ferdinand III of Castile, who hastened to limit any further expansion by his colleague—or perhaps his rival—by himself occupying Murcia. For a short time, there was some tension between Aragon and Castile but eventually both kings accepted the ancient boundary between Murcia and Valencia as their border.

Returning from his occupation of Murcia in 1246, Ferdinand the Saint invaded the territory of Granada and laid siege to Jaen. The resources of the Ameer of Granada, Muhammad ibn Nasr, surnamed Ibn al Ahmar, were hopelessly inadequate to a single-handed war with Castile. Jaen resisted heroically but the issue could not be long delayed and it was obvious that from Jaen Ferdinand III would march on Granada itself.

Muhammad thereupon made a bold, perhaps even a heroic, decision. Leaving Granada, he rode into Ferdinand's camp and offered to do him homage. The savagery of many recent massacres must have made it seem probable that the King of Castile would seize his visitor and cut off his head. Ferdinand, however, was delighted at the gesture of the ameer and gave him generous terms. His homage was accepted and Muhammad, as a Castilian vassal, was made a member of the Cortes and agreed to pay tribute to Castile and to furnish a contingent of troops when required. By his bold action, he had made possible the survival of the Kingdom of Granada under his descendants, Beni

[4] The number of King Alfonsos in Spain is confusing. This Alfonso IX was King of Leon. The victor of Las Navas de Tolosa was Alfonso VIII of Castile.

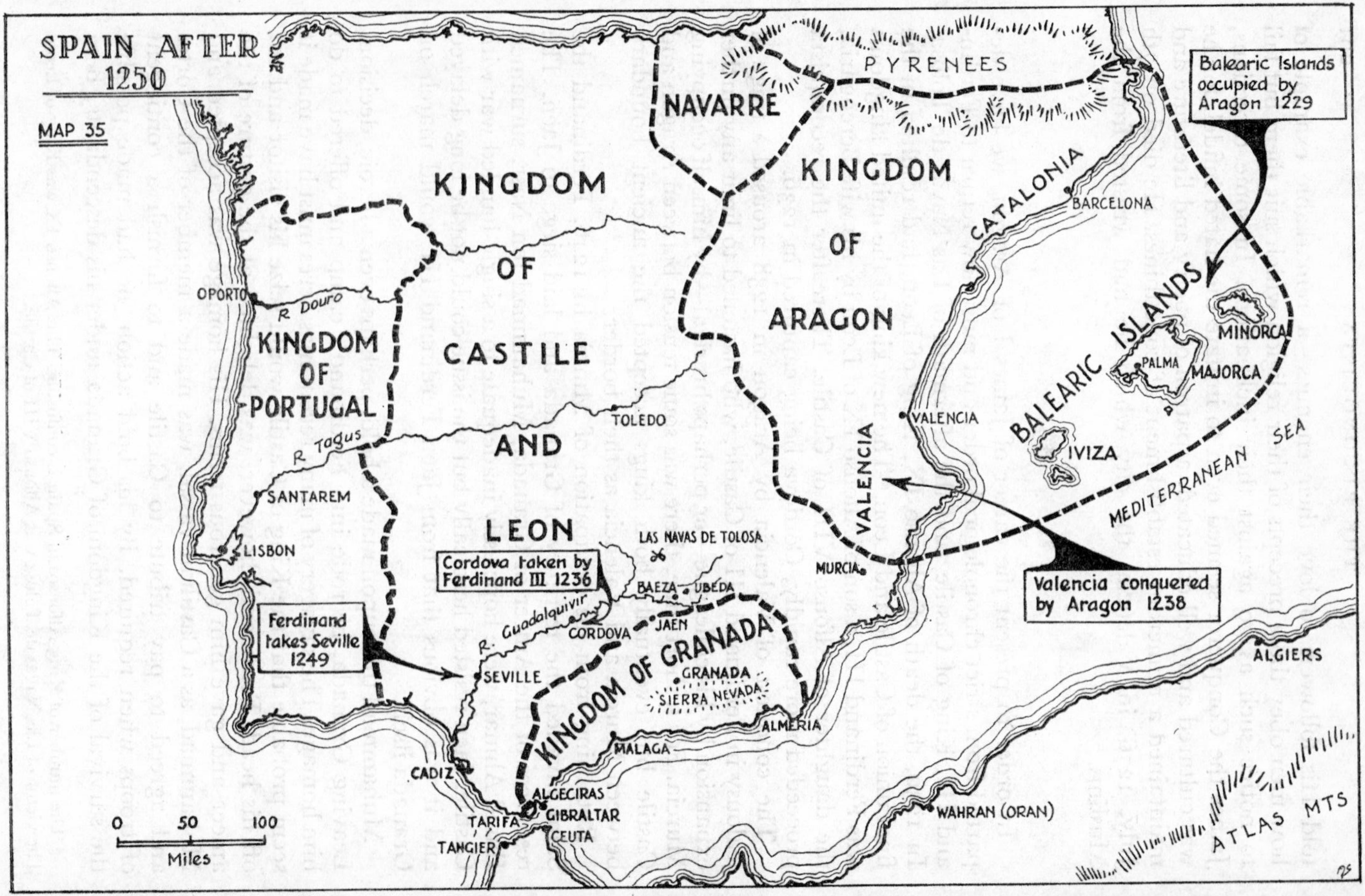
SPAIN AFTER 1250
MAP 35
KINGDOM OF CASTILE AND LEON
KINGDOM OF PORTUGAL
NAVARRE
KINGDOM OF ARAGON
KINGDOM OF GRANADA
PYRENEES
CATALONIA
BARCELONA
VALENCIA
MURCIA
TOLEDO
OPORTO
R. Douro
R. Tagus
SANTAREM
LISBON
LAS NAVAS DE TOLOSA
BAEZA
UBEDA
JAEN
CORDOVA
R. Guadalquivir
SEVILLE
GRANADA
SIERRA NEVADA
ALMERIA
MALAGA
CADIZ
ALGECIRAS
GIBRALTAR
TARIFA
TANGIER
CEUTA
BALEARIC ISLANDS
MINORCA
MAJORCA
PALMA
IVIZA
MEDITERRANEAN SEA
ALGIERS
WAHRAN (ORAN)
ATLAS MTS
Balearic Islands occupied by Aragon 1229
Valencia conquered by Aragon 1238
Cordova taken by Ferdinand III 1236
Ferdinand takes Seville 1249
0 50 100
Miles

Nasr, for a further two hundred and fifty years, during which it was to produce a final flowering of the culture and art of Muslim Andalus. Even today, a visit to the Alhambra enables us for a moment to glimpse something of its loveliness.

Granada having come to terms, the only important objective left to Ferdinand the Saint was Seville, the beautiful city on the Guadalquivir, surrounded for fifty miles in every direction by continuous gardens, villas, orchards and farms. The quays along the Guadalquivir were crowded with ships, the busy streets swarmed with prosperous citizens and with sailors from every port in the Mediterranean. Calling up all his vassals, of whom Muhammad ibn Nasr of Granada was now one, Ferdinand the Saint in 1248 marched on Seville. The lovely and smiling valley of the Guadalquivir was quickly transformed into a desert. The farmhouses were burnt, the fruit trees cut down, the crops trampled underfoot. Seville itself was submerged in a grey fog from the drifting smoke of burning villages.

The fortifications of Seville were extremely formidable and Ferdinand appealed to the pope to proclaim a crusade to assist him to capture this one city alone. Contingents soon came pouring in from all over western Christendom. Assaults, nevertheless, proved vain and the King of Castile was obliged to settle down to a long siege. The whole city was completely surrounded by an earthwork and ditch which cut it off entirely from the outside world. Huts and even houses were erected for the Christian troops, streets of shops sprang up and the besieged city was itself surrounded by another city of booths, tents and buildings.

The siege of Seville was prolonged for no less than seventeen months, after which the Muslim defenders thought it advisable to come to terms before their supplies were exhausted. Ferdinand III was not ungenerous in his response. Those Muslims who desired to emigrate to Africa were permitted to do so with such of their possessions as they could carry. Those who elected to remain were promised the free enjoyment of their religion and their laws.

Great numbers of those who did not migrate to Africa sought refuge in Granada. A marked increase in the wealth and population of that kingdom resulted. Splendid cultivators as they were, the Muslims soon transformed the plains and valleys of Granada into a paradise of fertility. New industries were set up, the mineral resources were more fully exploited and a thriving commerce was maintained with the outside world through the ports of Malaga and Almeria. Thus when all seemed lost, Muslim architecture, refinement, literature, and poetry received unexpectedly a long Indian summer in one of the most lovely provinces in the world, amid the gardens, the palaces and the orchards of Granada, beneath the snow-covered range of the Sierra Nevada.

From 1250 onwards, the peninsula was thus divided between the Kingdom of Aragon, which now included Catalonia, Valencia and the Balearics, and the Kingdom of Castile and Leon, increased by Seville and Cordova. Portugal had assumed approximately the frontiers which it has maintained to this day. Far to the north, the little Kingdom of Navarre still clung to the lower slopes of the Pyrenees, while in the extreme south the lovely mountains and valleys of Granada constituted the last foothold of the Muslims in Spain.

In 1252, Ferdinand the Saint, crowned with glory and honour, was laid to rest with his fathers. He was one of the greatest in the long list of Christian Kings in Spain.

* * *

The historians of the Middle Ages are all too ready to recount the wars and the rivalries of the sultans and the kings of their time, and such are indeed essential if we are to understand the events which produced the world of today. There are moments, however, when we cannot but wish that they would describe more fully the lives of ordinary people. It is therefore a relief to turn to a work composed in the second half of the twelfth century, that is to say at the time of Muwahhid supremacy. It is a book written by an Arab living somewhere between Granada and Seville and which never once mentions war, religion, politics or government. *The Book of Agriculture*, or *Kitab al Felaha*, was the work of Abu Zekeriya Yahya ibn al Awam.

The author seems to have passed his life on a farm which he possessed in the plain of the Guadalquivir. He was presumably well educated, for he quotes classical Greek and Latin authors as well as Arab sources, though he probably read them all in Arabic translations. His attitude to agriculture is extremely technical and he writes at considerable length on the different types of soil and the crops most suitable to each. Wells, water wheels and methods of irrigation are, naturally in a warm climate, discussed at considerable length. The minimum slope for a distributary irrigation channel he considers to be one in two hundred and he describes in detail how to construct one by running a line of levels using an astrolabe and a staff, just as today an engineer would use a theodolite and staff.

The variety of fruits, spices and vegetables used by the Arabs of Andalus, even in these years of rapid decline, indicate a luxurious and sophisticated society. Here are a few only of the vegetables which Ibn al Awam was in the habit of growing on his estate: rice, maize, millet, lentils, peas, haricots, broad beans, chickpeas, artichokes, onions, saffron, madder, chicory, lettuce, cabbage, cauliflower, beetroot, turnips, carrots, radishes, garlic, leeks, parsnips, pimento, cucumber, water-melons, several kinds of sweet melons, gherkins, pumpkins, aubergines, cress, spinach, asparagus, endives, parsley, pepper, chiles, capers and celery. These and many more provided a varied menu for the Muslim gourmet of Andalus.

Arabs have always been fond of perfumes and our author was ready to make many varieties at home. For this purpose he grew wallflowers, lilies, narcissi, roses, violets, citronella, mint, thyme, althaea, acacia, basil, lavender and many other fragrant plants. The commonest scent seems to have been rosewater, which was distilled on a considerable scale and for which roses were extensively cultivated. The perfume of rosewater, we are told, could be varied by redistilling with small quantities of either camphor, sandalwood, saffron, musk, essence of wallflowers or other preparations or by several of them mixed according to taste.

The Arabs, however, did not grow sweet-smelling flowers or plants only in order to make perfumes. They cultivated them also for the fragrance they diffused in the air. "The first gardens that were ever made were in the East," writes a modern author,[5] "and they were gardens of shade, water and perfume." The Song of Solomon is full of the sweet perfumes of gardens:

> "Awake, O north wind; and come thou south;
> blow upon my garden, that the spices thereof
> may flow out."[6]

We are so accustomed to buying our perfumes in bottles that we no longer look to our gardens as sources of fragrance.

Medicinal herbs, special flavourings for food and the preservation of fruit received great attention from the twelfth century Arab gardener. Ibn al Awam gives minute instructions regarding the storage of soft fruits so that they can be eaten fresh, not preserved, at any time of the year. Our modern devotion to tin cans seems to have superseded these pleasant country techniques.

But Ibn al Awam was not a man who farmed only for profit, but was also deeply sensible of beauty. "The house," he says, "should be light and airy and be sited on rising ground so as to enjoy a prospect over the flower garden and the orchards, providing a lovely view restful to the eyes. Moreover, the air will thus be perfumed by the blossoms and the flowers."

By the doors of the house, by fountains or near artificial pools, it is pleasant to plant a scented laurel, myrtle, jasmine, wild cherry or lemon tree. It is sometimes enjoyable to have a large pine tree in the midst of the flower garden, thereby enabling the family to enjoy the

[5] H. L. V. Fletcher, *The Fragrant Garden*. [6] Song of Solomon, IV, 16.

shade in hot weather. An artificial lake is rendered more beautiful if a tree, such as a weeping willow, be grown in the middle of the water, and careful instructions are given how this should be done. In the pleasure garden, arbours and pergolas can be erected and streams of cool, clear water made to run babbling through them. The roses should be grown in a special rose-garden beside the flower garden. The alleyways can be bordered by cypresses.

Our good Arab squire, however, was no idler in perfumed bowers. Farming to him was a serious business. "When hoeing a field," he lays down, "the men should be divided into squads of four, who work down the field in echelon. When using a hoe, the right foot should be advanced. The hoe should not be raised above the head but thrown forward and then brought back."

A foreman employed on the farm must be a just man, well-behaved and of good manners. He must be honest and religious, one who speaks the truth and will be loved by the family. He must be vigilant and rise before dawn, so as to set a good example to the men. He must not lose his temper or indulge in excessive eating or drinking. Every evening, the master and the foreman should walk round together and inspect the work done during the day.

Ibn al Awam loved his trees so much that he studied their psychology with affectionate care. "When a vine is planted near a jujube tree," he assures us, "they feel for one another as a man feels for a beautiful woman. He attaches himself to her, loves her passionately and the breath of one strengthens the other. In the same way if a pomegranate be planted near a myrtle, they conceive a deep affection for one another. Their roots intertwine beneath the ground in a fond embrace and both, if God wills, become more fruitful."

On the other hand, vines, he warns us, cannot endure cabbages. If a cabbage be planted near a vine, the latter will, as it were, turn her back and grow only in the other direction. She will not throw out any new shoots in the direction of the cabbage.[7]

This Arab lord of the manor was a man of quiet piety. He insists that, before beginning to sow any seed, his men must pray, "O God, bestow Thy blessing and Thy compassion on this seed." In spite, however, of his piety and his scientific and meticulous methods, he is not quite free of old wives' tales. "A man of a sad disposition," he cautions us, "should not be used to plant out young date trees. On the contrary, when the men are planting out date palms, they should always be gay and happy, as otherwise the cuttings will not do well."

Even more striking is his system of cautioning barren fruit trees. Two

[7] I have myself agreed with the vine's opinion of cabbage ever since, as a boy, I was at a boarding school in England.

men must approach the guilty tree, one of them carrying an axe. "I want to cut down this tree," he will say in a loud voice. His companion will reply, "O no, don't do that." "Why not?", asks the man with the axe, "it is not bearing any fruit." The second man will then retort, "it will bear fruit next year, I guarantee. If it does not, then you can cut it down." "It often happens," comments our gentle author, "that after such a warning the tree will next year bear a heavy crop."

The exciting thing about this story is that it is one of the parables of Christ.[8] Was this a common saying among Palestine farmers, which Jesus merely used to illustrate his meaning or, conversely, did the parable become so well known that it was interpreted literally and, eleven hundred years later, was believed by the Arabs of Spain?

Yahya ibn al Awam has a good collection of horticultural miscellanea. He alleges, for example, that if perfume be injected into the roots of vines and fruit trees in the autumn, the fruit produced the following summer will be scented. In order to produce a bright yellow rose, he inserted saffron into the roots, while the insertion of indigo resulted in a blue one. His friend, Haj Ahmed of Granada, indeed, used to say that changing the colours of roses by insertions in their roots was so easy as to be mere child's play.

By drawing or writing in ink on apples when still green on the tree, a pattern could be reproduced. When the rest of the apple ripened red, the ink could be washed off and the writing would remain in bright green. Thus "There is no God but God and Muhammad is His Apostle" could be produced in green on a dish of red apples for a party. In a similar manner, young fruit on the tree could be fitted into little cases perforated with a design. The sun shining through the perforations would reproduce the pattern on the skin of the fruit. Or a young fruit inserted in a square box would grow into the shape of the container and cubical pears or apples would result.

About a quarter of our author's work is devoted to livestock, but he would not have been an Arab had he not devoted the longest section of all to horses. His notes are almost identical with those which I learned as a boy in England. Bran-mashes, salt in the manger, water three times a day, vigorous grooming, long slow exercise, rugging up at night, bedding down in the evening and many other routine procedures are unchanged.

Ibn al Awam did not leave it to a groom to look after his horses. "A horseman," he says, "must himself keep his eye on his horse day and night to see how he is doing. He should pick up and examine his feet and his shoes and look him all over. He should never leave this job to anyone else. Remember that a horse cannot complain at what happens to him, tied up as he is like a slave, and condemned to obedience."

[8] Luke XIII, 6–9.

After describing how to train a horse for polo or for the races, we find our gentle author's only reference to public affairs. The section is headed, "Sometimes a horseman has to use weapons, lance, sword and shield," and one seems to detect in his words a sad note of resignation. But, even so, his gentle humour emerges. "Be careful," he enjoins the beginner, "when practising with your sword on horseback, not to cut off your horse's ears or your own right foot."

It is sad to be obliged to take our leave of this simple-hearted country squire with his horses, his flowers and his orchards—a kind of Arab John Evelyn or Izaak Walton in his quiet philosophy—and to return once more to wars, hatreds and massacre.

NOTABLE DATES

Death of Yaqoob al Mansoor Accession of his son, Muhammad al Nasir	1199
Battle of Las Navas de Tolosa	16th July, 1212
Abdication of Muhammad al Nasir Accession of Yusuf al Mustansir	1213
Death of Alfonso VIII of Castile	1214
Capture of Majorca by James the Conqueror, King of Aragon	1229
Union of Castile and Leon under Ferdinand III	1230
Capture of Cordova by Ferdinand III	1236
Capture of Valencia by James I of Aragon	1238
Siege of Jaen by Ferdinand the Saint Granada becomes a vassal of Castile	1246
Capture of Seville by Ferdinand the Saint	1249
Extinction of the Muwahhid Empire	1269
Death of James I, the Conqueror, King of Aragon	1276

PERSONALITIES

Muwahhid Sultans

Yaqoob al Mansoor	1184–1199
Muhammad al Nasir	1199–1213
Yusuf II al Mustansir	1213–1224
Abdul Wahid	1224
Abdulla al Aadil	1224–1227
Yahya al Mutasim	1227–1229
Idris al Mamoon	1230–1232
Abdul Wahid al Rasheed	1232–1242
Ali al Saeed	1242–1248

Umar al Murtadha	1248–1266
Abu Dabboos Idris al Wathiq	1266–1269

Spanish Kings

Alfonso VIII of Castile	1158–1214
Henry I of Castile	1214–1217
Ferdinand III, the Saint, of Castile and Leon	1217–1252
James I of Aragon, the Conqueror	1213–1276

XIV

Mamlooks and Mongols

1277–1290

The ambition of Hulagu and his successors was diverted by . . . a long vicissitude of Syrian wars: their hostility to the Moslems inclined them to unite with the Greeks and the Franks; and their generosity or contempt had offered the kingdom of Anatolia as the reward of an Armenian vassal; the fragments of the Seljukian monarchy were disputed by the emirs who had occupied the cities or the mountains; but they all confessed the supremacy of the khans of Persia; and he often interposed his authority, and sometimes his arms, to check their depredations.

GIBBON, *Decline and Fall of the Roman Empire*

The nature and development of the empire of the Ilkhans in Persia, Mesopotamia and Syria is perhaps the most interesting of all the stories of these Mongol powers, because in this region nomadism really did attempt to stamp a civilized system out of existence . . . The Mongols here did not only burn and massacre; they destroyed the irrigation system that had endured for at least eight thousand years and with that the mother civilization of the Western world came to an end.

H. G. WELLS, *An Outline of History*

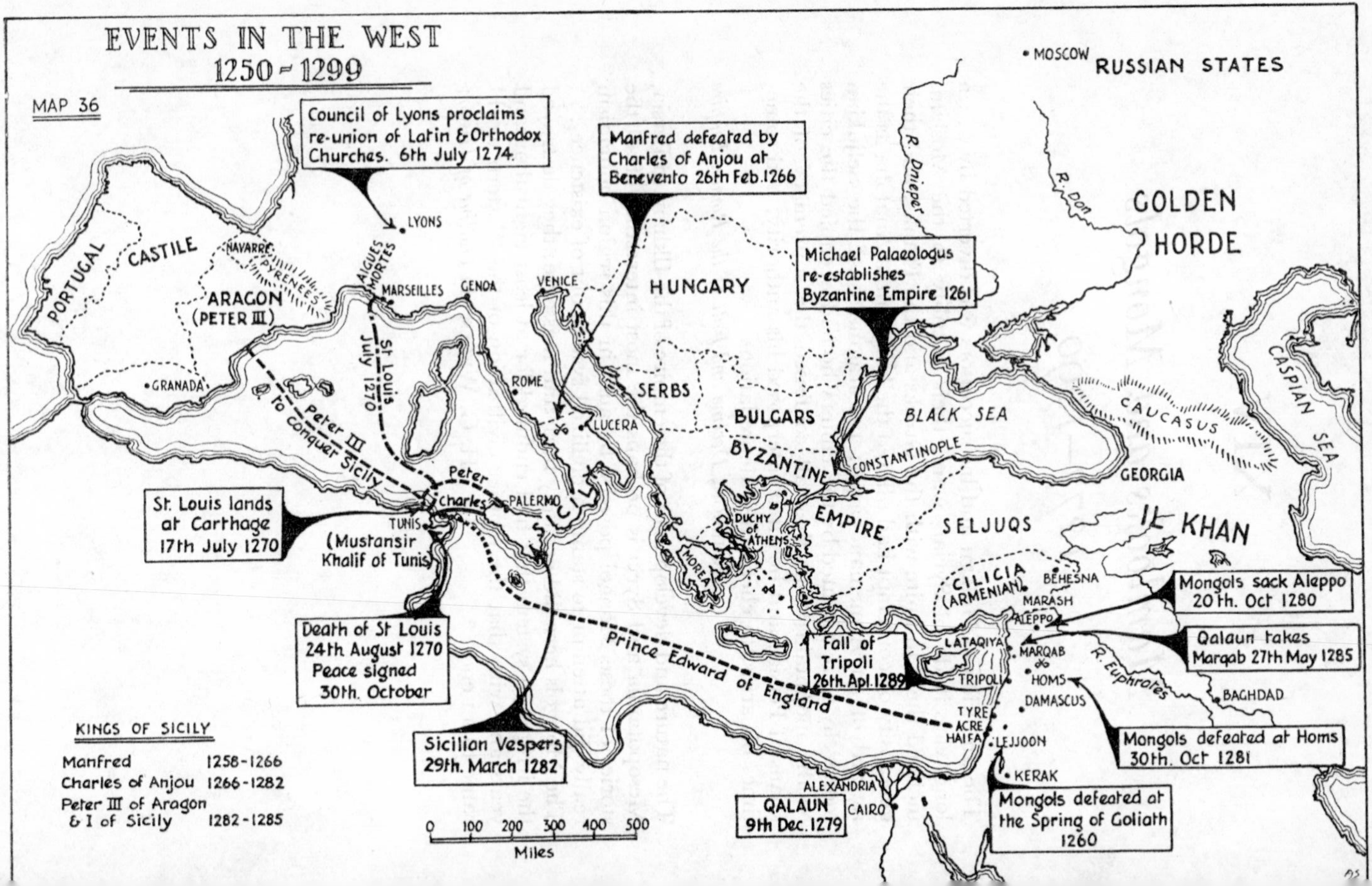

EVENTS IN THE WEST
1250 - 1299
MAP 36
Council of Lyons proclaims re-union of Latin & Orthodox Churches. 6th July 1274.
Manfred defeated by Charles of Anjou at Benevento 26th Feb. 1266
Michael Palaeologus re-establishes Byzantine Empire 1261
MOSCOW
RUSSIAN STATES
R. Dnieper
R. Don
GOLDEN HORDE
CASPIAN SEA
CAUCASUS
GEORGIA
IL KHAN
BLACK SEA
CONSTANTINOPLE
HUNGARY
SERBS
BULGARS
BYZANTINE EMPIRE
SELJUQS
DUCHY of ATHENS
MOREA
CILICIA (ARMENIAN)
BEHESNA
MARASH
ALEPPO
LATAQIYA
MARQAB
HOMS
TRIPOLI
DAMASCUS
TYRE
ACRE
HAIFA
LEJJOON
KERAK
BAGHDAD
R. Euphrates
ALEXANDRIA
CAIRO
PORTUGAL
CASTILE
NAVARRE
PYRENEES
ARAGON (PETER III)
GRANADA
LYONS
AIGUES MORTES
MARSEILLES
GENOA
VENICE
ROME
LUCERA
SICILY
PALERMO
TUNIS
St Louis July 1270
Peter III to conquer Sicily
Peter
Charles
Prince Edward of England
St. Louis lands at Carthage 17th July 1270
(Mustansir Khalif of Tunis)
Death of St Louis 24th August 1270 Peace signed 30th. October
Sicilian Vespers 29th. March 1282
Fall of Tripoli 26th. Apl. 1289
QALAUN 9th Dec. 1279
Mongols sack Aleppo 20th. Oct 1280
Qalaun takes Marqab 27th May 1285
Mongols defeated at Homs 30th. Oct 1281
Mongols defeated at the Spring of Goliath 1260
KINGS OF SICILY
Manfred 1258-1266
Charles of Anjou 1266-1282
Peter III of Aragon & I of Sicily 1282-1285
0 100 200 300 400 500
Miles

XIV

BEFORE continuing the story of the savage duel between the Turkish Mamlooks of Egypt and the Mongols of Persia, a brief note is necessary on contemporary events in Europe.

After the death of Frederick II in December 1250, his son Conrad became King of Sicily and Jerusalem and emperor elect. The papacy, however, was as bitterly hostile as ever to all the Hohenstaufens. In 1254, Conrad died, leaving an infant son, Conradin, in Germany. Frederick II, in his will, had left southern Italy to an illegitimate son called Manfred who, on 10th August, 1258, was crowned King of Sicily in Palermo.[1] Manfred in many ways resembled his father Frederick II, being a free thinker, an enemy of the papacy, intensely ambitious, and intellectually brilliant. He made extensive use of Muslim troops, who were stationed at Lucera in southern Italy.

The papacy was inexorably resolved to destroy the Hohenstaufens but had no army with which to fight Manfred, and thus was obliged to seek some powerful prince to match against him. In June 1263, Charles of Anjou accepted the Sicilian crown. (In Palestine the Mongols had been defeated at the Spring of Goliath in 1260 and Michael VIII Palaeologus had rewon Constantinople in 1261.) Charles of Anjou was a younger brother of St. Louis, but a very different type of man. Hard, clever, ambitious and unscrupulous, he bore little resemblance to a saint. On 26th February, 1266, at Benevento, he defeated and killed Manfred and was crowned Charles I, King of Sicily. In 1268, the youthful Conradin made a bid to recover the Hohenstaufen heritage but was defeated by Charles of Anjou at Tagliacozzo and executed. The popes had finally achieved their ambition of exterminating the Hohenstaufens. On 24th October, 1273, Rudolf I of Habsburg was elected emperor.

In 1269, St. Louis of France, already old, longed to fight one more crusade before he died. It may have been the influence of Charles which persuaded the king to choose Tunis. Louis sailed from Aigues Mortes on 1st July, 1270, and landed on the site of ancient Carthage on 17th July. He did not immediately press the attack, for he was expecting the arrival of Charles with the army and fleet of Sicily. Meanwhile typhoid and dysentery worked havoc in the French army. Charles landed on 24th August, 1270, to be told that Louis had died the same morning.

[1] Genealogical tree, page 200.

On 30th October, peace was signed with Al Mustansir, the Hafsid King of Tunis,[2] in which the latter agreed to pay tribute to Charles and to accord commercial privileges to his subjects. The death of the saint enabled his ambitious brother to use the crusade for purely mundane purposes. A few days after the signature of peace, an English force landed in Tunis under the command of Prince Edward, later to be King Edward I. Disappointed of a crusade in Tunis, Prince Edward sailed on to Acre, where we have already seen him.

Charles of Anjou, King of Sicily, had ambitions to become Latin Emperor of Constantinople, by recapturing the city from Michael VIII Palaeologus. The pope, however, made use of the threat of an Angevin invasion to compel Michael to agree to the reunion of the Latin and Greek Orthodox churches, which was proclaimed at a council held in Lyons on 6th July, 1274. As a result, Gregory X forbade Charles to wage war on Michael.

On 18th March, 1277, a certain Marie[3] of Antioch, a remote descendant of the royal house of Jerusalem, sold her "rights" to the kingdom to Charles of Anjou, who immediately added King of Jerusalem to his titles. On 7th June, 1277, Roger, Count of San Severino, landed at Acre with six galleys, demanding submission to his authority as viceroy of Charles. Hugh III de Lusignan, King of Cyprus, had already been elected King of Jerusalem. The Templars and the Venetians accepted San Severino, the Genoese opposed him. The Kingdom of Jerusalem in 1277 was a hundred miles long but nowhere more than ten miles wide. Charles of Anjou in Sicily inherited the pro-Egyptian policy of Frederick II. Thus Sicily, and, in Outremer, San Severino, the Templars and the Venetians supported an Egyptian alliance, while the Genoese and the Count of Tripoli favoured the Mongols.

We have already seen the expanding ambitions of the Kingdom of Aragon. In July 1276, Peter III, the son of James the Conqueror, became king. This Peter was married to Constance, a daughter of Manfred, the illegitimate son of Frederick II. When Charles of Anjou seized Sicily, Hohenstaufen supporters took refuge with the court of Aragon, where they plotted the overthrow of Charles, who, however, was engrossed in his schemes to be Emperor of Constantinople. Charles pressed the pope to preach a Crusade in support of his attack on the Byzantine Empire. A contemporary Sicilian writer, however, alleged that Charles' cross was not that of Christ but of the impenitent thief—having stolen Sicily, he wished to steal Constantinople.

In April 1282, Charles planned to sail to conquer the Greek Empire

[2] The story of the Hafsid rulers of Tunis is told in Chapter XVI.
[3] Genealogical tree, page 205.

but on 29th March, the people of Sicily rose in revolt and massacred all the French officials and soldiers stationed by Charles in the island —an incident known in history as the Sicilian Vespers. On 30th August, 1282, King Peter of Aragon landed in Sicily and was greeted as a liberator. Hitherto the struggle between the papacy and the emperor had left Europe no strength to intervene in Outremer. The Sicilian Vespers, on 29th March, 1282, gave rise to a hundred and fifty years of war between Anjou and Aragon. Long before its termination, the age of crusading had passed away.

* * *

The death of Baybers on 20th June, 1277, left Egypt without a master. The Mamlook commanders, eyeing one another with jealousy, compromised on the elevation of his eldest son, Malik al Saeed Baraka, an irresponsible youth. In August 1279, however, Baraka was dethroned and sent into exile to Kerak. The Mamlooks offered the empire to the most outstanding of their number, the Ameer Qalaun who, however, urged the elevation of Baybers' second son, Salamish, who was only seven years old. Qalaun accepted the post of regent.

Fearing the jealousy of his brother-officers, Qalaun had adopted this modest attitude to gain time. As regent, he began one by one to arrest his potential rivals or to post them to distant commands, while promoting his own friends to key positions. Then, summoning a council of senior officers, he pointed out the absurdity of confiding power to a child. It was decided to send Salamish to join his brother in Kerak and, on 9th December, 1279, Qalaun was declared sultan. Like Baybers, Qalaun was a Qipchaq Turk, brought to Egypt as a slave and sold to the Sultan Al Salih Ayoub.

Whether from conviction or for political reasons, he assumed a strongly Muslim attitude and immediately ordered the dismissal of all Christians from government service. No sooner had Qalaun been recognized than the Mamlook Viceroy of Damascus, Sonqor al Ashqar, revolted. In April 1280, an army sent from Cairo defeated Sonqor at Kiswa, south of Damascus, whereupon he wrote for help to the Il Khan Abagha. As a result a Tatar army marched on Aleppo in September 1280. The garrison fled to Damascus without offering any resistance and, on 20th October, Aleppo was taken and plundered, the inhabitants being indiscriminately massacred. After laying waste the surrounding country, the Mongols withdrew across the Euphrates.

Emboldened by this unopposed incursion, Abagha decided on a full-scale invasion, the news of which spread terror in Syria. The people of Aleppo and Hama fled to Damascus, while many Damascenes left for

Egypt. At the end of March 1281, Qalaun marched out of Cairo at the head of the army. Alarmed at the possibility of Frankish co-operation with the Mongols, he concluded a ten-year truce on 3rd May with the Templars and the Hospitallers, and on 16th July extended it to include Bohemond of Tripoli. San Severino, the viceroy of Charles of Anjou in Acre, had been instructed to pursue the traditional Sicilian policy of support for Egypt. Being informed of a plot to murder Qalaun, he warned the sultan in time to enable him to arrest the conspirators. On 24th June, 1281, Qalaun also came to an agreement with Sonqor al Ashqar, the Mamlook rebel. The Muslim army then concentrated near Hama.

The Mongols were under the command of Mangu Timur, the brother of Abagha, and were assisted by a considerable force of Armenians under Leo III, King of Cilicia. A pitched battle was fought on 30th October, 1281, near Homs. Early in the battle the Mamlook left wing fled in such confusion that the fugitives reached Damascus without stopping. In the centre, stubborn fighting took place without a decision until Azdemir, a senior Mamlook officer, is alleged to have ridden across no-man's-land, calling out that he was a deserter and wished to speak to Mangu Timur. When led up to the prince, however, he suddenly attacked him, and succeeded in wounding and unhorsing him. Mangu Timur, shaken by his fall, retired from the field, the Muslims seized the opportunity to charge and the Mongols fell back in disorder. The Mamlooks had suffered so heavily that Qalaun made no attempt to pursue. The Armenians with difficulty fought their way back independently to Cilicia.

Meanwhile the fugitives from the Mamlook left wing had announced in Damascus that the Mongols were victorious. A wild panic ensued, the whole population abandoning the city to flee southwards. The news was passed by carrier-pigeon to Cairo where the terrified people crowded into the mosques to implore divine help. After long hours of agonizing suspense, scented pigeons fluttered down on to the Egyptian cotes, for it was the custom to cover the pigeons with perfume when they bore good news. The tidings of the Mongol rout flew from mouth to mouth, weeping was replaced by laughter, the streets were hastily decorated and the public gave themselves up to rejoicing.

Qalaun was back in Damascus on 7th November, 1281, whence he set out for Cairo, where he entered the city in triumph. As he passed Lejjoon, fifteen miles south-east of Haifa, he was greeted by the Count of San Severino, who congratulated him on his victory and presented him with many rich gifts. Not all the Franks, however, wished to conciliate the Mamlooks at the expense of the Mongols. Joseph de Cancy, Prior of the Hospitallers, writing to King Edward I of England, expressed the view that the Mamlook-Mongol wars afforded an excellent opportunity for a new crusade and urged the king to lead it.

* * *

It is noticeable that whereas in the time of Jenghis Khan the Turks were utterly unable to face the Mongols, fifty years later the Mamlooks were nearly always victorious. It seems probable that administrative backing had much to do with the Mamlook victories.

The Mongols had not only reduced the lands they conquered to desert but they continued to treat the surviving inhabitants with extreme brutality. Themselves still uneducated, they depended entirely on Persian officials to collect the revenues. Rasheed al Deen,[4] the historian, himself the prime minister of an Il Khan, describes vividly the humiliating position occupied by educated Persian officials. The wazeer, when speaking to the Il Khan, was obliged to remain throughout the interview on his knees, while at banquets he stood behind the khan's seat to wait upon him. In these circumstances, it is not surprising that the Mongols were ill-served by their Persian officials, that there was rarely any money in the treasury and that the Mongol army was never paid.

In Egypt the Mamlooks, who were scarcely more civilized than the Mongols, were unable themselves to supervise the administration and normally could not speak Arabic. The Egyptians occupied an inferior social position but nevertheless they controlled the administrative services, occupied important positions, were received by the sultan and given robes of honour. Moreover, whereas Persia was ruined, Syria and even more Egypt were wealthy and prosperous. Consequently the Mamlook army was well paid and lavishly equipped. In addition, the sultans laid great emphasis on their rôle as defenders of Islam, with the result that their Egyptian subjects, though not accepted as combatant soldiers, were able as Muslims to share in the glory of Mamlook victories.

* * *

On 29th March, 1282, the Sicilian Vespers—the massacre of the French in Sicily already described—brought an end to the intervention of Charles of Anjou in Outremer and the Count of San Severino sailed for Italy. Charles' interference had been resented by the native Franks but the knowledge that he might intervene had induced caution in the Mamlooks. Now the Muslims realized that Acre no longer had any outside protector.

Two days after the Sicilian Vespers, on 1st April, 1282, Abagha died in Hamadan. He was forty-eight years of age. During the seventeen

[4] Fadhlullah Rasheed al Deen, *Historical Collection*.

years of his reign, he sent several letters to the pope and the Kings of France and England, urging joint operations against the Mamlooks. A letter from Edward I of England to Abagha still survives, thanking the Il Khan for his proposals.

Abagha had named his son Arghoon to succeed him but, on 6th May, 1282, the quriltai nominated Tequdar, Abagha's brother.[5] No sooner had he mounted the throne than he announced his conversion to Islam and assumed the title of Sultan Ahmed. On 25th August, he sent an embassy to Qalaun, informing him of his conversion and seeking an alliance. Qalaun, in a long reply, praised God for Tequdar's conversion but added some caustic references to recent Mongol defeats. Meanwhile Arghoon, the son of Abagha, who had been named by his father as his successor, rebelled against Tequdar but, on 4th May, 1284, was completely defeated and imprisoned by his uncle. When all seemed lost, Arghoon bethought himself of intrigue. "Tequdar," he whispered to the officers detailed to guard him, "is a Muslim and proposes only to promote Muslims. Why should Mongols give up the laws of Jenghis Khan and adopt the Arab religion?" This propaganda met with instant success. Shortly afterwards Tequdar was arrested by his own officers and killed by breaking his back.

Arghoon, recognized as Il Khan, reversed the Islamic policy of his uncle and placed his reliance on Shamanists, Christians, Buddhists and Jews. His first wazeer was a Mongol, a man capable and just, but his position was undermined by intrigue and he was executed on 17th January, 1289, to be succeeded by a Jewish physician. There was scarcely any administration in the Il Khanate. The Mongols lived by plundering the scant remnant of the population which had survived the massacres. Arghoon and his Jewish minister tried, much to the indignation of the Mongol nobles, to substitute regular taxation for uncontrolled looting.

In 1290, Trans-Oxiana was laid waste by Qaidu Khan, the Ogotai claimant to be supreme khan, who was still at war with Qubilai, the emperor of China.[6] The endless Mongol civil wars had saved Syria and Egypt but continued to inflict terrible suffering on Persia and Trans-Oxiana. It was impossible to recognize these once wealthy and civilized countries in the dreary and depopulated deserts ruled by the Il Khans.

There were no hostilities against the Mamlooks during Arghoon's reign of seven years. He died on 7th March, 1291, his Jewish wazeer being murdered while the khan lay on his deathbed.

Arghoon was brave, hardy and intelligent. If three horses were held side by side, he could run up, jump the first two and land astride on the back of the third. Though he had a violent temper, he was normally an

[5] Genealogical tree, page 274. [6] Genealogical tree, page 244.

intelligent and amusing companion. His efforts with the help of his Jewish wazeer to regularize the administration were a civilizing influence. Having arrested the process of Islamization he was denounced by Muslim historians but praised by Christians.

Arghoon had sent four embassies to the pope, to France and to England, outlining serious strategic proposals. In view of the difficulty of shipping horses from Europe, he offered twenty thousand remounts for the use of a new Crusade. If the kings would fix the date of their landing at Acre, the Il Khan promised to be beneath the walls of Damascus on the same day. Only vague protestations of friendship were received in return.

In fact, Philippe le Bel, King of France, had been drawn into the war between Anjou and Aragon following the Sicilian Vespers. The Franks of Syria pinned their hopes on Edward I of England, who had been on a crusade. Edward, however, was involved in wars in Wales and Scotland and could not leave his kingdom.

* * *

It will be remembered that Qalaun, when marching to meet the invasion of Mangu Timur had, in 1281, concluded a ten-year truce with the Franks. Once the Mongols had been defeated, however, Frankish hostility was no longer to be feared. In his *Tashrif al Ayyam*, Ibn Abdul Dhahir, who was Qalaun's Secretary of State, emphasizes that Qalaun was emboldened to act by the internal rivalries in Outremer and by the war between Aragon and Anjou. The succession of the Muslim Tequdar had further reassured the sultan. As a result, in the spring of 1285, he laid siege to the fortress of Marqab, which belonged to the Hospitallers.

The garrison, relying on the ten-year truce, were surprised. On 17th April, 1285, an exceptionally heavy bombardment was opened. The knights offered a spirited resistance until the Muslim miners drove galleries beneath the walls. On 23rd May, one of the main towers fell and the Muslims mounted to the assault. The attack was held but next morning the Hospitallers asked for terms. Qalaun was ready to negotiate. Twenty-five officers of the Hospital were permitted to leave armed and mounted, the remainder evacuated the castle on foot on 27th May, 1285. All reached Tripoli in safety.

The attack on Marqab seems to have been a deliberate infraction of the ten-year truce. There were reasons, however, which impelled Qalaun to commit this breach of faith. The Il Khans were the only serious enemies of the Mamlook state. The Franks would only be dangerous if they joined the Mongols in some future invasion. It was, therefore, advisable to dispose of the Franks while there was a lull in the hostilities with the Tatars.

There was, however, no time to eliminate all the Franks but fortunately for Egypt they were divided against one another. When the truce had been concluded on 3rd May, 1281, Acre and the Templars had favoured friendship with Egypt, while Tripoli and the Hospitallers would have preferred an alliance with the Mongols, but eventually also signed the truce with Egypt. By a swift blow against the Hospitallers and a threat to Tripoli, combined with a show of diplomatic cordiality to the Templars, Qalaun warned the pro-Mongol party and also encouraged Frankish internal rivalries. Finally, in the absence of war with the Mongols, a campaign against the Franks, while involving no risk of defeat, was useful to maintain the sultan's status as the defender of Islam.

* * *

The Hohenstaufens had disappeared, Charles of Anjou was engaged in a deadly war with Aragon, and the West had forgotten Outremer. The barons of the Holy Land fell back on Henry II de Lusignan, King of Cyprus,[7] a sickly youth of fourteen, who was crowned King of Jerusalem in the cathedral of Tyre on 15th August, 1286. In the subsequent festivities, amateur theatricals were held in the palace of the Hospitallers at Acre. "Arthur and the Round Table" was the piece represented, the female parts being taken by some of the younger knights—the last festivities crusader Acre was ever to see.

As though the situation were not already sufficiently precarious, war now broke out between Genoa and Pisa. On 31st May, 1287, the Genoese fleet attacked Acre with a view to killing or capturing all the Pisans and Venetians in the town. While the Italian fleets were locked in battle, the Muslims seized Lataqiya.

On 19th October, 1287, Bohemond VII, Count of Tripoli, died childless and the citizens declared a republic and appealed for help to the Genoese, who sent a fleet to the town. On this, two Frankish merchants went up from Alexandria to Cairo, obtained an audience with Qalaun, and told him that, if Genoa obtained Tripoli as a naval base, she would establish naval command of the eastern Mediterranean and drive all Muslim ships from the sea.

It would be natural to suspect the Pisans or the Venetians of this unsavoury intrigue but a Muslim historian[8] alleges that a disgruntled citizen of Tripoli was the traitor. It is true that Tripoli was still covered by the ten-year truce but the opportunity was too good to be missed for a mere scrap of paper. Mobilizing every available man, Qalaun appeared suddenly beneath the walls of Tripoli in March 1289.

[7] Genealogical tree, page 204. [8] Abu al Mahasin ibn Taghri Birdi.

Frankish reports give the exaggerated figure of forty thousand cavalry and a hundred thousand foot for the Mamlook army.[9] Nineteen mangonels bombarded the walls while one thousand five hundred sappers drove galleries under the fortifications. Tripoli was torn by domestic rivalries until the sultan actually appeared beneath the walls. When the situation became critical, the Venetians began to evacuate by sea but the panic spread to the Genoese who followed suit. Qalaun seized the opportunity to order a general assault and the city was carried on 26th April, 1289.

Tripoli was one of the largest and richest cities on the Mediterranean, comparable perhaps to Marseilles today. In 1289, both the military and the religious spirit of the crusaders had faded and Outremer was principally occupied with commerce. Tripoli was one of the chief harbours for the export of Oriental goods to Europe, a position which it shared with Acre and Alexandria. But it was not only a port, it was also a great industrial city. It contained between three and four thousand looms for the weaving of textiles, particularly pure silk and silk mixed with gold thread, an extremely valuable luxury industry.

Qalaun ordered an indiscriminate massacre. Every man in the city was killed, and the stench of putrefying corpses remained overpowering for several months. The city and harbour were then completely destroyed. Qalaun was still apprehensive of the possibility of a new crusade in co-operation with the Mongols and was anxious to leave no harbours on the coast at which an expeditionary force could land.

As has already been suggested, the Mamlooks were not much inferior to the Tatars in ruthlessness, for they too were Central Asian nomads. One difference between them lay in the fact that the Mamlooks did not kill all the young women and children but carried them off as slaves and concubines. After the fall of Tripoli, Jabala and the other towns in the vicinity were captured without fighting.

It is impossible not to contrast the conduct of the Mamlooks, the self-styled champions of Islam, with that of the first Muslim Arab conquerors in the seventh century. The early Arab armies, commanded by men who had been companions of the Prophet, did not massacre in cold blood. Under them, Christians were safe from molestation on the sole condition of the payment of a poll-tax, though their social position, it is true, was inferior to that of the Muslims.

* * *

In September 1289, Qalaun was back in Cairo after the destruction of Tripoli. The aggressive military spirit of the Mamlooks is illustrated

[9] René Grousset, *Histoire des Croisades*.

by the fact that an expedition was immediately set on foot to invade the Sudan.[10] In November 1289, forty thousand men are alleged to have set out, accompanied by five hundred boats on the Nile, carrying stores, rations, weapons and ammunition.

When the column reached Dongola, the whole population was found to have migrated southwards under the Nubian King. Eventually the refugees were overtaken and some of the inhabitants were brought back to Dongola, though the Nubian King escaped to the south. The Mamlooks then set up a puppet king in Dongola, leaving a garrison to support him, while the main body returned to Cairo.

As soon as the troops withdrew, the legitimate king returned, the Mamlook garrison was driven out and the puppet king was murdered. Shortly afterwards, however, the king wrote to Qalaun offering to pay tribute. This face-saving compromise was accepted and peace was concluded. The Nubians were professing, if somewhat primitive, Christians.

* * *

The fall of Tripoli produced no reaction in the West where attention was riveted on the struggle between Aragon and Anjou. The Armenians of Cilicia, alarmed at the imminent extinction of their Frankish allies, sent a deputation to beg the sultan for peace. Their petition was granted on condition of the surrender of their key frontier fortresses of Marash and Behesna.

Henry II, King of Cyprus and titular King of Jerusalem, did what lay in his power. After the fall of Tripoli, he hastened to Acre and sent a deputation to Qalaun, who was still in Damascus, asking for a renewal of the ten-year-truce. The sultan agreed and Henry II, with a sigh of relief, returned to Cyprus.

Venice alone took positive action. Tripoli had been principally a Genoese port but most of the Venetian business was transacted through Acre. Genoa, meanwhile, made the best of a bad job by concluding a private treaty with Qalaun, giving her valuable commercial advantages in Alexandria. When the Genoese delegation arrived in Cairo, they found embassies already there from the Emperors of Germany and Constantinople. The rulers of Christendom seemed to have already despaired of Outremer and to be jostling one another in an effort to secure the friendship of the victor.

Pope Nicholas IV, however, agreed to support Venice and to preach a crusade. In the summer of 1290, a fleet of twenty galleys sailed from Venice for Acre, bringing the new "Crusaders", almost all of whom were Italians, untrained and undisciplined. The fleet reached Acre

[10] Map 43, page 388.

safely and this disorganized rabble was put on shore. Unfortunately no provision had been made for the payment of the "Crusaders" after landing.

Since the renewal of the ten-year truce, normal business relations had been resumed and Acre was crowded with Arab merchants and commercial caravans. In addition, Arab peasants from neighbouring villages brought their produce for sale in the city.

The Italian crusaders soon became insubordinate, being without pay or occupation. Suddenly, one morning in August 1290, they broke out of the town and proceeded to rob and kill all the Muslim villagers they met. Then, having tasted blood, they poured back into Acre itself, massacring every Arab they could find. The barons and knights, taken unawares, were unable to restore order until many Muslims had been killed. Survivors and the relatives of the dead hastened to complain to the sultan, bearing in their hands the bloodstained garments of the victims. Qalaun was furious and demanded the surrender of the culprits to him for punishment. At a Council held in Acre, Guillaume de Beaujeu, Grand Master of the Temple, demanded their surrender sooner than lose the last outpost in the Levant. The majority of the Council, however, refused and replied to the sultan expressing their regret for the incidents but explaining that the offenders were foreigners, not subjects of Acre.

In October 1290, Qalaun ordered the army to mobilize but, before it was ready to march, he suddenly fell ill and died on 10th November, 1290. He was seventy years old and left three sons and two daughters but only one wife. He had an imposing presence, with broad shoulders and a thick neck, and spoke only Turkish and the Qipchaq dialect, never having troubled to learn Arabic.

His personal Mamlooks are alleged to have been between seven and ten thousand. Uncertain of the loyalty of the River Mamlooks, who had been founded by the Ayoubid Sultan Al Salih, he decided to raise a second force as a check on their power. He accordingly selected some three thousand five hundred Mamlooks of his own and quartered them in the citadel, where they became known as the Burji or Tower Mamlooks. He chose them principally from Circassians of the Caucasus or from the tribes of the Crimea, the River Mamlooks being predominantly Qipchaqs.

Throughout the reign of Qalaun we continue to read of the frequent arrest and imprisonment of senior Mamlook officers, sometimes accompanied by torture. More remarkable still is the fact that, after such treatment, they were sometimes released and re-employed. Perhaps the Mamlooks can best be compared to a ship's company of buccaneers in the Spanish Main. The sultan, like the pirate captain, had risen above his messmates by the greater force, and even ferocity, of his character. His comrades were constantly itching to replace him but respected the alertness which enabled him to crush each plot before its execution.

A fuller description may here be given of the Mamlook military system, surely one of the most extraordinary which ever existed. After their purchase by a sultan or ameer, the boys were put through a severe course of training under strict discipline, involving horsemanship, the use of bow, lance, sword and mace, and also manners and deportment. When the Mamlook boy's training was completed—a process which took several years—he was enlisted in his owner's bodyguards. The great majority of Mamlooks were sultan's or royal Mamlooks. These were divided into two categories:

First were the Mamlooks of the ruling sultan—when an ameer became sultan, he began immediately to buy Mamlooks for his guards until he had acquired several thousand. They were called by their master's throne-name, the Ashrafis, for example, if his title had been Malik al Ashraf, the Salihis if it had been Malik al Salih. The sultan's Mamlooks were united by a very strong *esprit de corps*. A number of them were admitted to positions of confidence close to the sultan. This select group were known as the khassikiya or intimates.

The loyalty of a Mamlook, however, was due to his master in person, not to the state. In practice, Mamlooks seem to have nearly always been loyal to their masters and frequently gave their lives to defend them. If, however, the master died, the Mamlook was not bound to render the same loyalty to his successor.

The second group of royal Mamlooks, therefore, were those of previous sultans. When a sultan died, his Mamlooks were not incorporated in the bodyguard of his successor, but remained as a separate unit of the army, still bearing their deceased master's name, the Nasiris or the Mansooris or whatever it might be. If two or three sultans died in rapid succession, there might be three or four regiments in existence, each the Mamlooks of a former deceased sultan. As time passed, these regiments gradually faded away owing to the death or incapacity of the men.

So much for royal Mamlooks. A third category was that of ameers' Mamlooks. Senior officers were obliged to own a specified number of private Mamlooks of their own who accompanied them in war and thus went to swell the ranks of the regular amy. All Mamlooks were cavalry, highly trained in the use of sword, lance, mace and bow, with which they probably had no equals in the world. Mamlooks would rarely if ever fight on foot.

When recognized as a competent soldier, the Mamlook was legally freed though he was still under an obligation to serve his master. Ibn Hassul[11] states that a Mamlook "would not allow himself to be treated as less than equal to his master in food, drink, dress or riding equipment. He would never deign to perform menial service, such as sweeping or cleaning a dwelling or attending to horses . . . As soon as he was made free, he would not be satisfied with less than . . . command of a regiment".

A fourth category of soldiers was the halaqa. This force consisted largely of the sons of true Mamlooks, born to them in Egypt. These men had never been slaves but had enlisted voluntarily. Not having been born on the steppes, they were somewhat looked down upon by true Mamlooks and could not join regular units. Nevertheless the halaqa seem often to have been more numerous than the Mamlooks. Royal Mamlooks, being a kind of Praetorian Guard, were normally stationed in Cairo in peacetime, while the halaqa seems to have garrisoned Syria and Palestine. At one time, there were said to be twelve thousand soldiers of the halaqa in Damascus and six thousand in Aleppo. In 1315, there were nine thousand halaqa in Egypt. The statistics, however, vary greatly.[12]

In a major emergency, the Turkman and Arab nomadic tribes of Syria were called out, their chiefs being given the honorary rank of ameer. There were also sometimes contingents from tributary princes, though these grew less and less as direct Mamlook rule extended. Mamlook units consisted solely of cavalry but we hear in siege operations of infantry, sappers, naphtha or Greek fire units and, later on, of artillery. As Mamlooks would not fight on foot, it is not clear where these people came from. They were somewhat despised by the Mamlooks and may have been Arabs, Sudanese, or Egyptian-born sons of Mamlooks. They may, however, have been halaqa or else men enlisted for a specific campaign and then discharged. It is unlikely that the Mamlooks would have tolerated the existence of permanent regular military units other than themselves and the halaqa. Moreover, in the frequent *coups d'état* and civil wars in which the Mamlooks fought one another, there is no mention of non-Mamlook units in action.

It is easy to denounce Mamlook ruthlessness, forgetting that they raised Egypt to a Great Power. At the height of their glory, there was probably no emperor more powerful than Baybers or Qalaun and perhaps no army equal to the Mamlooks. Moreover, by halting the terrible devastation of the Mongol conquests, they saved a remnant of that splendid Islamic culture which the Mongols had almost extinguished.

[11] Quoted by Dr. Mustafa Ziada in his chapter on "The Mamluk Sultans", in K. M. Setton, *History of the Crusades*.

[12] A. N. Poliak, *Feudalism in Egypt*.

NOTABLE DATES

Coronation of Charles of Anjou as King of Sicily	1266
Crusade of St. Louis against Tunis	July 1270
Arrival of San Severino, Viceroy of Charles, at Acre	7th June, 1277
Death of Sultan Baybers	20th June, 1277
Elevation of Qalaun to the Sultanate	9th December, 1279
Ten-year truce between Qalaun and the Franks	3rd May, 1281
Defeat of the Mongols near Homs	30th October, 1281
Massacre of the Sicilian Vespers	29th March, 1282
Death of the Il Khan Abagha	1st April, 1282
Tequdar dethroned by Arghoon	May 1284
Capture of Marqab by Qalaun	24th May, 1285
Henry II, King of Cyprus, crowned King of Jerusalem	15th August, 1286
Destruction of Tripoli	26th April, 1289
Italian "Crusaders" land at Acre	Early Summer, 1290
Death of Sultan Qalaun	10th November, 1290
Death of Il Khan Arghoon	7th March, 1291

PERSONALITIES

Sultans of Egypt

Baybers the Bunduqdari	1260–1277
Qalaun	1279–1290

Il Khans

Abagha, son of Hulagu	1265–1282
Tequdar, son of Hulagu	1282–1284
Arghoon, son of Abagha	1284–1291
Qubilai, Mongol Emperor of China	1260–1294
Qaidu, Khan of the Ogotai	

Christian Kings

Conrad IV, son of Frederick II	1250–1254
Manfred, King of Sicily	1258–1266
Charles of Anjou, King of Sicily	1266–1282
Peter III, King of Aragon	1276–1285
King of Sicily	1282–1285

XV

The End of Outremer

1290–1301

The capture of Akka (Acre) by the Egyptians in May 1291 may be appropriately regarded as the end of one chapter and the beginning of another in the history of the Crusades . . . Towards the close of the thirteenth century the Latin possessions in the Holy Land consisted of Tartus, Jubail, Tripoli, Beirut, Sidon, Tyre, Acre and Haifa, strung out along the coast of Syria and Palestine. Both as a trade emporium and as a fortified town, Acre appears to have been greatly superior to the others.

A. S. Atiya, *The Crusade in the Later Middle Ages*

Whatever might be the vices of the Franks, their courage was rekindled by enthusiasm and despair; but they were torn by the discord of seventeen chiefs and overwhelmed on all sides by the powers of the sultan. Gibbon, *Decline and Fall of the Roman Empire*

Ever the mid-space narrowed till closing they mingle and then
Clashed targets together and spears and the fury of armoured men:
Dashed each against other the boss-studded bucklers that strong arms bore:
And the din shrieked up to heaven and roar was swallowed of roar:
And the agony scream and the triumphing shout maddened up evermore
From the slayers and them that they slew and the earth ran streams of gore.

Homer, *The Iliad* (Trans. A. S. Way)

XV

KHALIL, the eldest son of Qalaun, had been nominated as his heir. A deputation from Acre begging for peace having been rejected, the new sultan continued the war preparations commenced by his father. Orders were sent to Syria for the mobilization of all troops. Al Mudhaffar, the King of Hama, the only Ayoubid Prince who still held his fief, was ordered to collect and transport the siege train to the plain outside Acre. On 5th April, 1291, Sultan Khalil arrived with the army of Egypt. Some historians give the strength of his forces as sixty thousand cavalry and one hundred and sixty thousand infantry but such estimates must certainly be exaggerated. In any case his army was ample for the destruction of so weak an enemy. According to Maqrizi, the artillery consisted of ninety-two mangonels, the heaviest siege train ever collected.

The Frankish garrison of Acre consisted of eight hundred knights and fourteen thousand foot, including the recently-arrived Italians—about one tenth of the strength of the attackers. The defences had been divided into sectors. Of these the northernmost was held by the Templars, with the Hospitallers on their right. The central salient with the New Tower was occupied by the knights of Cyprus and Syria, under Amaury, the brother of King Henry II of Cyprus. On his right the knights of the Teutonic Order were responsible. From the Tower of St. Nicolas southwards, stood some French knights and an English detachment under Otto de Grandson, a Swiss employed by Edward I. At their side were the Pisans and the Venetians, above the port. The Genoese, it will be remembered, had made a separate peace with Qalaun after the fall of Tripoli, and did not take part in the defence of Acre.

The bombardment of the walls by Khalil's ninety-two mangonels commenced on 11th April, 1291. On the night of 15th April, by bright moonlight, the Grand Master of the Temple, Guillaume de Beaujeu, supported by Grandson and the English, made a gallant mounted sortie from the Porte St. Lazare. With three hundred knights, they drove in the enemy's outposts and inflicted casualties but they failed to destroy the mangonels which were bombarding the walls.

Another sortie was carried out a few days later from the Porte St. Antoine, by the Hospitallers. This time a moonless night was chosen. At midnight the knights emerged from the gate and rode towards the centre of the Muslim camp. But the Mamlooks were completely prepared, the alarm was sounded, and a large number of torches were

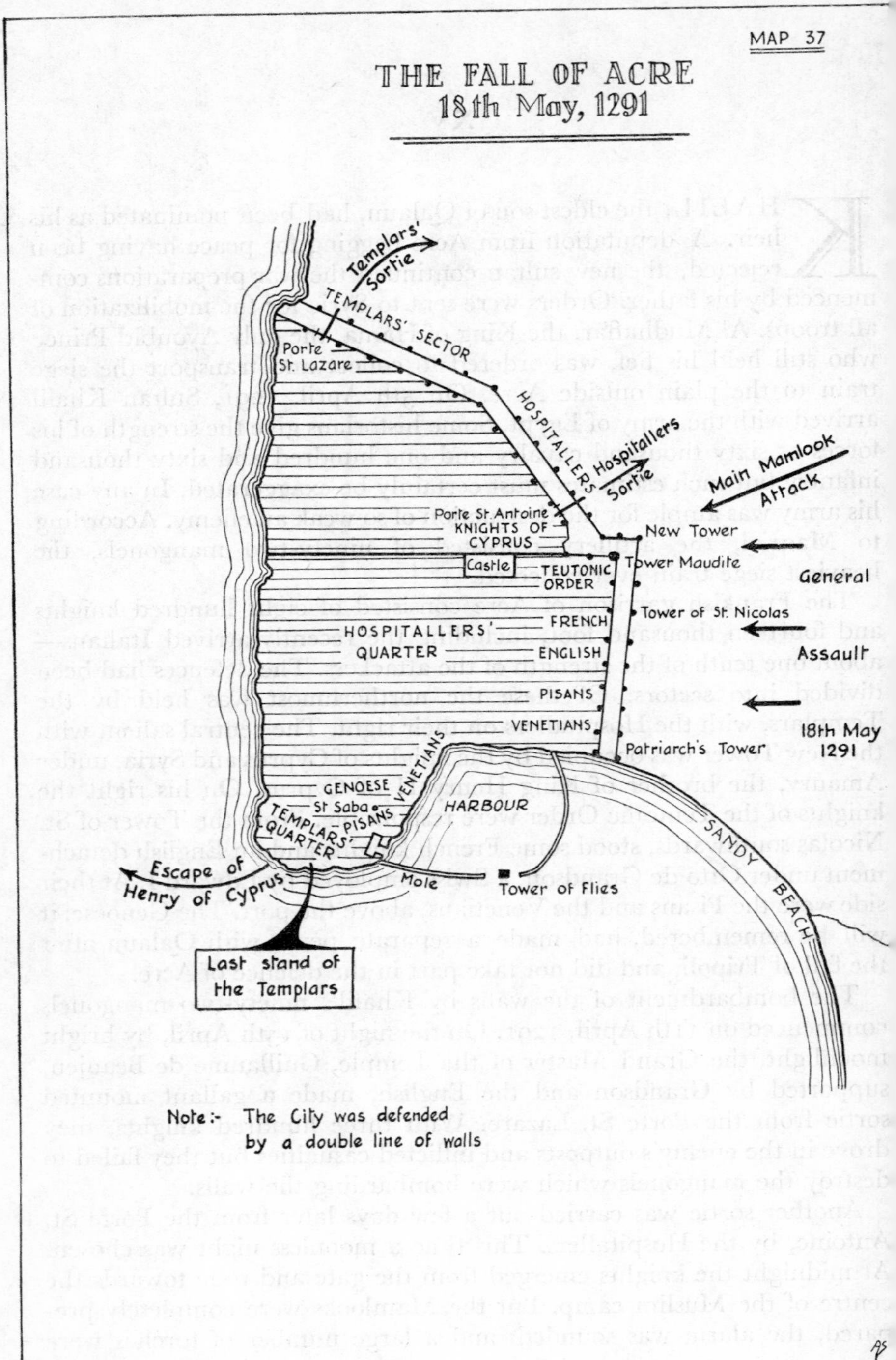
MAP 37
THE FALL OF ACRE
18th May, 1291
Templars' Sortie
TEMPLARS' SECTOR
Porte St. Lazare
HOSPITALLERS
Hospitallers Sortie
Main Mamlook Attack
Porte St. Antoine
KNIGHTS OF CYPRUS
New Tower
Tower Maudite
Castle
TEUTONIC ORDER
General
Tower of St. Nicolas
HOSPITALLERS' QUARTER
FRENCH
ENGLISH
Assault
PISANS
VENETIANS
18th May 1291
Patriarch's Tower
VENETIANS
GENOESE
St Saba
PISANS
HARBOUR
TEMPLARS' QUARTER
SANDY BEACH
Escape of Henry of Cyprus
Mole
Tower of Flies
Last stand of the Templars
Note:- The City was defended by a double line of walls

instantly lighted. Several thousand Mamlooks, ready mounted, immediately charged the Franks, who were forced to withdraw precipitately. The action showed the high standard of discipline and efficiency which prevailed in the Mamlook army.

On 4th May, 1291, Henry II, King of Cyprus, and titular King of Jerusalem, landed in Acre with two hundred horse and five hundred foot. The arrival of this sickly youth at such a moment saved his honour but could not save the city.

Meanwhile the bombardment continued but the sultan relied principally on his sappers. A battalion of a thousand engineers was allotted to the attack of each tower, according to the Patriarch Bar Hebraeus, but the heaviest mining operations were directed against the New Tower. On 15th May, a long stretch of wall collapsed into the ditch. Next morning, 16th May, the Mamlooks carried the New Tower and prepared to attack a wide breach in the inner wall near the Porte St. Antoine. At dawn on 18th May, the sultan launched a general assault on the whole length of the walls from the Porte St. Antoine to the Patriarch's Tower.

It was still dark when the Franks were woken by the "horrible sound"[1] of the Turkish drums, carried on no less than three hundred camels. The Mamlooks advanced in deep columns which overran all opposition. One of these, passing the New Tower, mounted a breach in the inner wall near the Tour Maudite. Before sunrise, the Muslim banners were on the walls. From the Tour Maudite, they extended towards the Porte St. Antoine, where they were held up by the Marshal of the Hospitallers, Mathieu de Clermont. As the Templars further north were holding their own, their Grand Master, Guillaume de Beaujeu, with a handful of knights, hastened to the Porte St. Antoine to support the Hospitallers. The long rivalry between the two orders had done immense harm to Outremer but in death they were not divided.

The Mamlooks were using flame-throwers and, in the heat and smoke, control and liaison were lost. Yet the Templars and the Hospitallers were still holding on at three o'clock in the afternoon when Guillaume de Beaujeu was killed. Soon afterwards the Hospitallers were exterminated and the Muslims poured into the streets. The French knights, with Otto de Grandson and the English, had hitherto successfully held the walls from the Tour St. Nicolas to the sea, but now the Mamlooks were spreading out behind them. Falling back to cover the port, Grandson was able to protect the embarkation of a number of wounded, some of whom reached Cyprus.

Meanwhile terrible scenes were being enacted in the streets of Acre. Women and children, mad with terror, were fleeing hither and thither

[1] Mas Latrie, *Gestes des Chiprois.*

pursued by soldiers. Often one soldier would seize a mother while others would drag away her screaming children, throwing the small babies to the ground to be trampled on by the horses. The total population was said to have been some forty thousand souls. According to Maqrizi, immense numbers of Franks were killed. Ten thousand were said to have been taken prisoner but Sultan Khalil gave orders for the massacre of them all.

In the final débâcle, the surviving Templars took refuge in their castle on the sea. A number of fugitives, some of them women, were able to find asylum with them. These, including the young King Henry of Cyprus, were embarked from the castle on the few remaining boats, while the Templars at the water's edge bade them farewell with a rousing cheer before themselves turning back to die.

The Mamlooks were obliged to recommence siege operations against the Templars' castle. The bombardment was resumed and the sappers tunnelled beneath the walls. Seeing the desperate courage of the defenders, the sultan offered them safe-conduct to Cyprus if they surrendered. The Templars accepted but a party of excited Mamlooks sent to take over the castle began to molest the Christian women. The knights, infuriated, killed the offenders and closed the gate and the savage struggle recommenced.

The handful of Templars resisted the whole Mamlook army for ten days. At last, on 28th May, the Muslims advanced to the assault but the weight of the attacking columns was too great for the building already shaken by the bombardment and undermined by the tunnels of the sappers. As the Mamlooks swarmed into the castle the great building collapsed, burying friend and foe in a common grave.

The walls, towers, churches and public buildings of Acre were laboriously demolished. The remainder of the town was burnt. In the succeeding days, Tyre, Beirut, Athlit, Tortosa and Haifa[2] were evacuated without fighting. Sidon, which also belonged to the Templars, resisted until 14th July, 1291, and was then likewise evacuated. The chapter was closed—there no longer was an Outremer.

* * *

The final loss of Outremer placed the orders of religious knights in a dilemma. The youngest of them, the Teutonic Knights, moved to Germany and devoted their efforts to the conquest and conversion of the heathen of the Baltic. The Hospitallers in 1308 seized Rhodes, whence, and later from Malta, they continued to fight the Muslims. The order had originally been constituted in the Holy Land to nurse sick pilgrims and never lost its medical background. In Britain today,

[2] Map 38, page 327.

the Order of St. John of Jerusalem is closely connected with medical work and is the lineal descendant of the Hospitallers. The order still supports, outside Arab Jerusalem, perhaps the best eye hospital in the Middle East.

The Templars came to a more dramatic end. The order had grown rich and, in 1307, Philippe le Bel, King of France, ordered the confiscation of all its properties—many of the knights were imprisoned, tortured and even burned at the stake.

* * *

The young Sultan Khalil made a triumphant entry into Damascus, the streets of which had been gaily decorated. Thence, returning to Cairo, he received an even more splendid ovation. Soon afterwards he ordered the release of the Abbasid Khalif Al Hakim, who had been under house arrest for thirty years since Sultan Baybers had become suspicious of him. In the middle of April, 1292, the sultan left Cairo for Syria where he captured the fortress of Qilaat al Roum[3] on the Euphrates from a Mongol garrison.

Khalil's reign had begun brilliantly with the final extermination of the Franks, though the victory had in fact been due to the preparations made by his father Qalaun. The young sultan had since shown an arrogance and a petulance which had not endeared him to the senior officers of the army. On 12th December, 1292, Khalil ordered that seven Mamlook ameers, whom he had sent to prison, be brought out and strangled in his presence. Six of them were done to death before his eyes but the seventh, a certain Lajeen, was on the point of suffocation when the bowstring broke. The victim begged for mercy and other officers present joined in the pleas for pardon until the sultan ultimately agreed. The incident was to have a dramatic sequel.

A year later, on 5th December, 1293, when on a hunting trip west of the Nile, Khalil lost his temper with an officer called Baidara. Fearing arrest or assassination, Baidara withdrew, collected a number of other officers and agreed to kill the sultan. A few days later, the hunting expedition came to an end and Khalil sent his escort back to Cairo. He was himself following at his leisure, hawking after birds, when suddenly the conspirators galloped up. Baidara rode straight at the sultan with his sword drawn and slashed him across the arm. Another followed with a swinging blow which broke his shoulder. Then came the Ameer Lajeen who had escaped from strangulation owing to the breaking of the bowstring. "Look, Baidara," he shouted, "the man who would rule Syria and Egypt should strike a blow like this." With these words, he dealt the sultan a swordstroke which made

[3] Map 38, page 327.

him fall from his horse to the ground. At this the remaining conspirators leaped from their saddles and plunged their swords into the body of Khalil.

Baidara immediately seated himself in a nearby tent and accepted the oaths of allegiance of his comrades. Hearing what had occurred, however, another party of officers, led by a certain Ameer Kitbugha galloped after the murderers and, in a brief mounted skirmish, killed Baidara and captured his associates with the exception of Lajeen who had vanished. Khalil was thirty years old and had reigned for just over three years.

Aibek, Qutuz, Baybers and Qalaun had all been tribesmen from the steppes, sold as slaves when young boys. All four had fought their way to the top from the lowest ranks of the Mamlooks and, when sultans, had been able to speak to their troops as one soldier to another. The senior officers of the army still consisted of men of this type, some of the roughest adventurers alive. But Khalil had been brought up a prince. He was intelligent and well-educated but he had not learned the hard way as had these bloodstained veterans. He never consulted them but with youthful arrogance issued his peremptory orders without tact or circumspection.

Hastily gathered together for consultation, the Mamlook ameers, to avoid further schisms, decided to recognize Malik al Nasir Muhammad, the younger brother of the murdered Khalil. The new sultan was only nine years of age and the Ameer Kitbugha was appointed regent. A curious light is thrown on the Mamlook régime by the fact that Kitbugha was a Mongol who had only comparatively recently deserted his compatriots and come over to the Mamlooks. Presumably Mongols, being horse-nomads of the steppes, were accepted by the Mamlooks, although Egyptians, Arabs and even the sons of Mamlooks who were born in Egypt were not admitted to the ranks of pure Mamlook units.

The surviving murderers of Khalil were cruelly tortured and, nailed alive to wooden saddles on the backs of camels, were paraded through the streets of Cairo for several successive days. "Never did Cairo see such days of horror," records Maqrizi, a civilized Egyptian sickened by Mamlook savagery.

Soon, however, the ameers of the successful party fell out. The Tower Mamlooks rose against Kitbugha and a nine-day civil war was fought out in the streets of Cairo before they were suppressed. The streets were deserted, the shops shut and the good citizens lay trembling in their shuttered houses. At last order was restored, the shops were reopened and crowds once more thronged the cheerful streets. When all was quiet, Lajeen, the only survivor of the murderers of Khalil, emerged from hiding and was pardoned.

In November 1294, three hundred personal Mamlooks of Sultan Khalil ran amok through the streets of Cairo till all were killed. The next morning Kitbugha told a conference of senior officers that such disgraceful incidents were due to the fact that Sultan Al Nasir was a child. The army commanders took the hint, the deposition of Al Nasir was approved and Kitbugha was proclaimed sultan on 1st December, 1294. The ten-year-old Al Nasir, who had reigned for one year, was sent into exile in Kerak.

Two years of Kitbugha's reign passed uneventfully. On 20th November, 1296, he left Damascus, where he had been on a visit of inspection, to return to Cairo. Six days later, he camped with his entourage on the coastal plain near Ramla. In the evening, angry words were exchanged between the sultan and one of the ameers.

The officer who had been reprimanded by the sultan consulted his comrades and a group of them, led by Lajeen, decided to kill Kitbugha. Each accompanied by his personal Mamlooks, they marched across the camp in battle order, drums beating and colours flying, to the sultan's tent. Several of Kitbugha's Mamlooks leaped to defend the door of his tent. They were killed to a man but they gained time which allowed the sultan to slip out of the back of the tent, jump on a horse and ride for dear life for Damascus. The mutineers then broke into the sultan's tent but, being unable to find him, immediately swore allegiance to Lajeen, the same whose life had been saved by the breaking of the bowstring.

Meanwhile Kitbugha had shut himself in the citadel of Damascus, whence he sent a message to Lajeen offering his allegiance. The new sultan accepted and appointed him governor of the fortress of Salkhad in what is now called the Jebel Druze. It will be remembered that, when Kitbugha came to power two years earlier, he had pardoned Lajeen for his part in the murder of Sultan Khalil. Such were the vicissitudes of fortune of the Mamlook ameers, one day the central figure in the glittering pageantry of royalty, the next writhing in naked agony nailed to a wooden camel saddle. The power, pomp and luxury of the sultan were dazzling prizes but the stakes were high. Those who gambled must have been men of reckless courage and enterprise.

Since the death of Qalaun six years before, five claimants had accepted oaths of allegiance as sultan. This instability arose partly from the fact that each senior officer kept his own private guard of Mamlooks whom he personally had bought and who were nearly always faithful to the death to their master. When an ameer became sultan, he regarded his brother officers as potential rivals, ready to supplant him at any moment. The sultan thus sought pretexts to arrest and execute them, and to promote his own personal Mamlooks to all important commands. As a result, before swearing allegiance to Lajeen in the camp at Ramla, his fellow-ameers insisted on a special oath by the new sultan. He swore that he would not dispose of them in order to replace them by his own private Mamlooks.

As soon as he reached Cairo as sultan, Lajeen remitted a number of taxes, thereby gaining popularity among the people of Egypt. Although he had killed Sultan Khalil and would have killed Kitbugha, he assumed an extremely religious demeanour, devoting much time to prayer and fasting. In spite, however, of his special oath, he promoted one of his personal Mamlooks to be Viceroy of Egypt. This man proceeded to arrest the senior officers one by one and to replace them with Lajeen's own Mamlooks, exactly as his brother-officers had foreseen.

Having imprisoned the senior officers in Egypt, he prepared to do the same to the commanders in Syria, the most important of whom was Qipchaq, the Viceroy of Damascus. Warned in advance, however, Qipchaq and his friends deserted their posts and went over to the Mongols, where we shall return to them in a few pages.

Dissatisfaction was now widespread among Mamlook officers. One evening Lajeen, who had eaten nothing all day owing to a religious fast, was playing chess with the chief qadhi when several officers came in, saluted and sat down. The sultan, suspecting nothing, made conversation until it was time for the evening prayer. He then rose to say his prayers but, as he did so, one of the officers slashed him with his sword. A few seconds later he had been hacked to pieces. Lajeen had been a man of imposing stature, brave, enterprising and intelligent. He had red hair and blue eyes but his racial origin is not clear. Some said that he was an apostate Crusader.

Anarchy immediately broke out between the various groups of Mamlooks in Cairo. Eventually, to avoid further clashes between rival senior officers, it was decided to recall Al Nasir, the son of Qalaun, who had been previously banished to Kerak. He was now fourteen years old and received an immense ovation when he entered Cairo on 7th February, 1299, to begin his second reign. As he was still a minor, however, a regency was necessary. Regents in the past had often seized the throne for themselves. As a result, two regents were appointed this time, the Ameer Salar, the Viceroy of Egypt, and with him Baybers the Jashnekeer,[4] the mayor of the palace.

* * *

Leaving the young Sultan Al Nasir, in February 1299, commencing his second reign, we must cross the border into Persia, and trace the fortunes of the dynasty of Hulagu in Tabriz.

[4] Jashnekeer was the title of the sultan's taster.

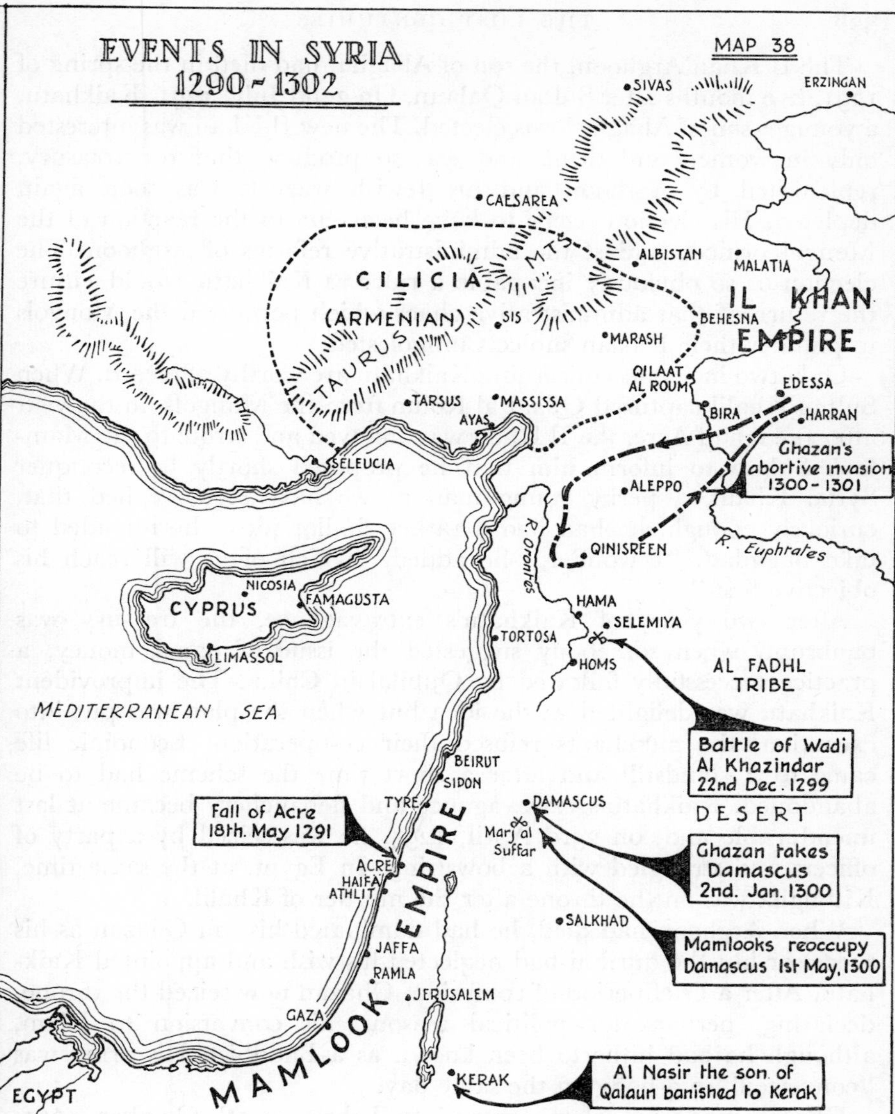
EVENTS IN SYRIA 1290 - 1302
MAP 38
SIVAS
ERZINGAN
CAESAREA
CILICIA (ARMENIAN)
TAURUS MTS
ALBISTAN
MALATIA
IL KHAN EMPIRE
SIS
BEHESNA
MARASH
QILAAT AL ROUM
EDESSA
TARSUS
MASSISSA
AYAS
BIRA
HARRAN
SELEUCIA
Ghazan's abortive invasion 1300 - 1301
ALEPPO
R. Orontes
QINISREEN
R. Euphrates
NICOSIA
FAMAGUSTA
CYPRUS
LIMASSOL
HAMA
SELEMIYA
TORTOSA
HOMS
AL FADHL TRIBE
MEDITERRANEAN SEA
Battle of Wadi Al Khazindar 22nd Dec. 1299
BEIRUT
SIDON
TYRE
DAMASCUS
DESERT
Fall of Acre 18th. May 1291
Marj al Suffar
Ghazan takes Damascus 2nd. Jan. 1300
ACRE
HAIFA
ATHLIT
SALKHAD
Mamlooks reoccupy Damascus 1st May, 1300
JAFFA
RAMLA
JERUSALEM
GAZA
MAMLOOK EMPIRE
KERAK
Al Nasir the son of Qalaun banished to Kerak
EGYPT
SUEZ
AILA
0 20 40 60 80 100
Miles

The Il Khan Arghoon, the son of Abagha, had died in the spring of 1291, five months after Sultan Qalaun. On 22nd July, 1291, Kaikhatu, a younger son of Abagha[5] was elected. The new Il Khan was interested only in women and drink and was so prodigal that the treasury, replenished by Arghoon and his Jewish wazeer, was soon again depleted. His election seems to have been due to the reaction of the Mongol princes against the administrative reforms of Arghoon. The election of so obviously incapable a ruler as Kaikhatu would ensure the return of that administrative chaos which permitted the Mongols to plunder their Persian subjects unmolested.

Only two incidents concerning Kaikhatu are worthy of record. When Sultan Khalil captured Qilaat al Roum from the Mongols, in the year after the fall of Acre, the Il Khan was annoyed and wrote to the Mamlook Sultan to inform him that he proposed shortly to reconquer Syria. Khalil, a perky young man as we have seen, replied that, curiously enough, he had had a rather similar idea—he intended to take Baghdad. "I wonder," he added, "which of us will reach his objective first."

After two years of Kaikhatu's extravagance, the treasury was bankrupt, when somebody suggested the issue of paper money, a practice successfully followed by Qubilai in China. The improvident Kaikhatu was delighted at the idea but when the plan was put into execution, the merchants refused their co-operation. Economic life came to a standstill and after a short time the scheme had to be abandoned. Kaikhatu's extravagance and debauchery became at last unendurable and, on 23rd April, 1295, he was seized by a party of officers and strangled with a bowstring. In Egypt, at the same time, Kitbugha was on the throne after the murder of Khalil.

When Arghoon had died, he had nominated his son Ghazan as his successor but the quriltai had neglected his wish and appointed Kaikhatu. After a brief period of confusion, Ghazan now seized the throne, declaring, perhaps for political reasons, his conversion to Islam, although he had hitherto been known as a Buddhist. His army was "converted" in a body on the same day.

Ghazan made his solemn entry into Tabriz on 5th October, 1295. Whether or not his conversion to Islam had been sincere, he now showed all the enthusiasm of the neophyte. Perhaps, as the Muslims had raised him to the throne, he felt obliged to repay their services. He immediately ordered the destruction of all churches, synagogues and Buddhist temples in the Il Khan dominions. Buddhist priests were to be put to death, Jews and Christians treated with contempt.

Commissioners were sent to the provinces to supervise the demolition

[5] Genealogical tree, page 274.

of churches. Bar Hebraeus, himself a Jacobite patriarch, records that the members of the commissions were open to bribes. The officials who arrived in Erbil in northern Iraq, he states, waited for twenty days in the hope that the local Christians would bring them gold. As none was forthcoming, the churches were razed to the ground. The Mosul Christians, on the other hand, had raised fifteen thousand dinars which they gave to the commissioners, who moved on, leaving the churches untouched.

On 3rd December, 1295, a grand quriltai confirmed the election of Ghazan as Il Khan. He was twenty-four years old and assumed the Muslim name of Sultan Mahmood. Several Mongol princes rebelled, however, alleging that the conversion of the Il Khan to Islam was a betrayal of the traditions of Jenghis Khan. In the first six months of the reign, six princes of the blood and thirty-eight army officers were executed. Meanwhile a Jagatai army once again laid waste Khurasan. Ghazan, however, was young, capable and energetic and was able before long firmly to establish his authority.

On 18th February, 1294, the year before the accession of Ghazan in Tabriz, Qubilai Khaqan, the elder brother of Hulagu, had died in China. He was seventy-eight years old and had been Emperor of China for thirty-four years. Qubilai had been the nominal ruler of the greatest empire the world had ever seen in so far as extent of territory was concerned. It included the whole of China and Korea in the East and extended to the shores of the Adriatic, Poland and Hungary in the West. In fact, however, Qubilai's authority over much of this area was purely nominal and the dynasties of Ogotai and Jagatai were almost always in revolt.

Qubilai, a devoted Buddhist, was tolerant of other religions. An enthusiastic admirer of Chinese civilization, he adopted the elaborate ritual of the court of the Son of Heaven. His rule was benevolent and it is said that thirty thousand poor were daily fed at his expense. State pensions were provided for needy men of letters, for orphans, invalids and cripples. Free hospitals were available for the sick poor.

The descendants of Qubilai were to reign for a further eighty years, being driven from the Celestial Empire in 1370, when a Chinese national revival resulted in the establishment of the Ming dynasty.

* * *

It will be remembered that, in 1298, Qipchaq, the Viceroy of Damascus, and a number of senior Mamlook officers in Syria had deserted to the Mongols, out of fear of arrest by Lajeen. The Il Khan Ghazan gave them an almost royal welcome. After discussing with them the situation in Egypt, he decided that the instability of the régime of

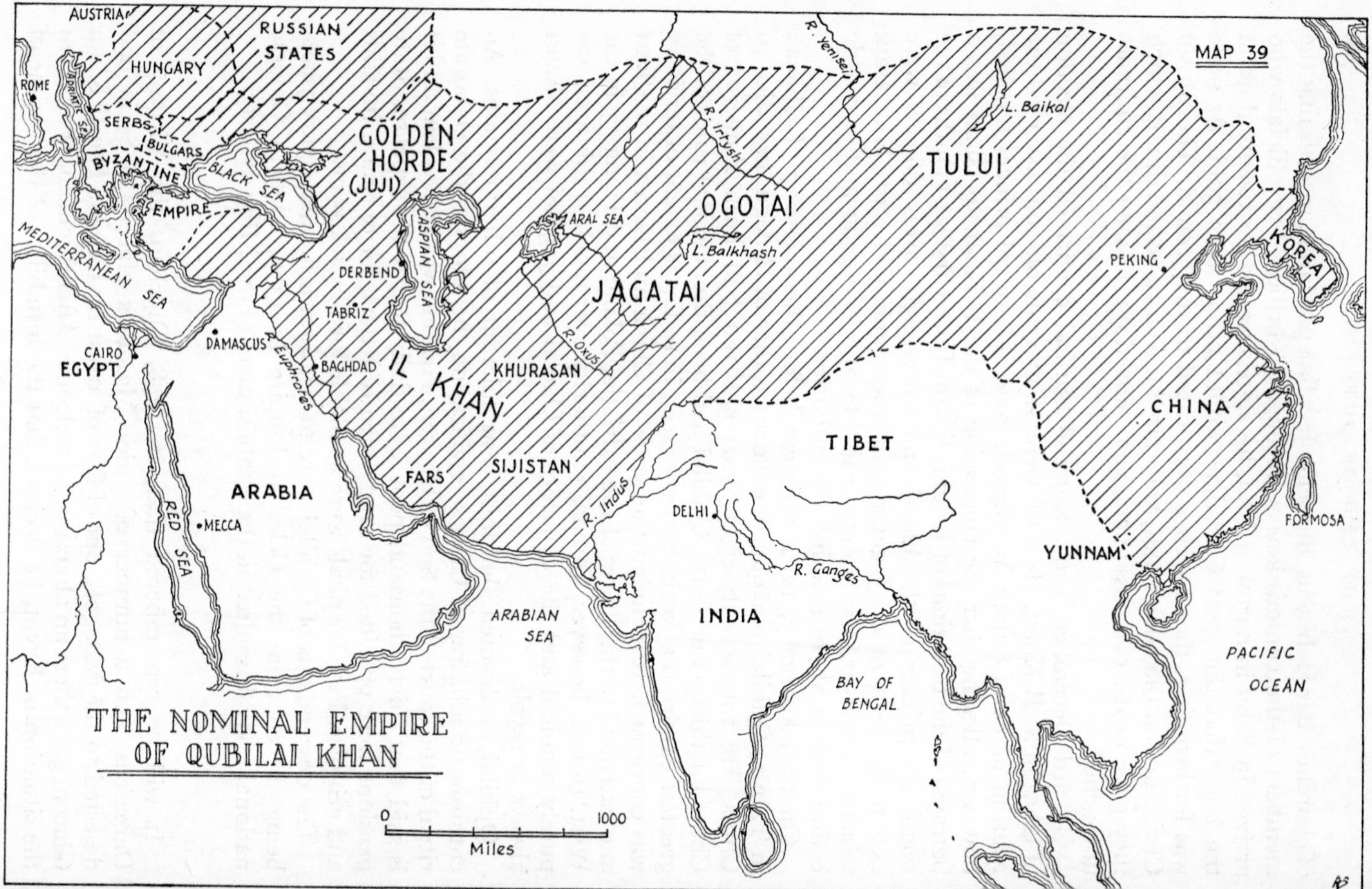
MAP 39
THE NOMINAL EMPIRE OF QUBILAI KHAN
AUSTRIA
RUSSIAN STATES
HUNGARY
ROME
ADRIATIC SEA
SERBS
BULGARS
BYZANTINE EMPIRE
BLACK SEA
GOLDEN HORDE (JUJI)
CASPIAN SEA
DERBEND
TABRIZ
MEDITERRANEAN SEA
DAMASCUS
CAIRO
EGYPT
Euphrates
BAGHDAD
IL KHAN
KHURASAN
FARS
SIJISTAN
ARABIA
RED SEA
MECCA
ARABIAN SEA
ARAL SEA
R. Oxus
JAGATAI
L. Balkhash
OGOTAI
R. Irtysh
R. Yenisei
L. Baikal
TULUI
PEKING
KOREA
CHINA
FORMOSA
YUNNAM
TIBET
R. Indus
DELHI
R. Ganges
INDIA
BAY OF BENGAL
PACIFIC OCEAN
0
1000
Miles

Lajeen offered a good opportunity for an invasion of Syria. A levy of troops was ordered, each man being instructed to bring his arms and equipment, five horses and rations for six months.

Before he could set out, however, Ghazan was obliged to post an army at Derbend against the Golden Horde and another in Khurasan to oppose a possible Jagatai inroad. As usual, the internal rivalries of the Mongols blunted the spearhead of their invasion of Syria. Ghazan left his capital of Tabriz on 16th October, 1299, eight months after the accession of the boy Sultan Al Nasir for his second reign. On 22nd September, 1299, Al Nasir and the Mamlook army had left Cairo to defend Syria. Discipline had been undermined by the mutual jealousy of the two regents and the various Mamlook units had formed themselves into rival factions, supporting either Salar or Baybers.

Meanwhile Ghazan Khan was reported to have crossed the Euphrates with a large force. The Mamlooks passed northwards and camped near Homs. On 20th December, 1299, the Mongol army pitched its tents at Selemiya, a few miles to the east. On 22nd December, the Mamlook army advanced against the enemy, the young Sultan Al Nasir on horseback in front. At ten o'clock in the morning contact was made with the Mongol outposts in Wadi al Khazindar. An order was passed along the line, "Drop your lances. Only swords and maces will be used."

An hour later the Mamlook army was drawn up opposite the Tatars. Isa ibn Mahenna, shaikh of the bedouin Arab Fadhl tribe, was on the right or desert flank, for the Mamlooks always called on the bedouins in time of war. The young sultan was relegated to a place of safety behind the lines. The Ameer Salar, who was in command, rode down the line encouraging the troops. All this time the Mongol army stood motionless.

Eventually the Mamlooks advanced, led by the engineers using flame-throwers, while the cavalry charged with great dash. The Tatars, however, remained immovable, the Mamlook charge lost its momentum and the flame-throwers were extinguished. Ghazan then gave the signal for a general advance. The Mongol counter-attack was led by ten thousand archers on foot, who inflicted terrible casualties, particularly on the horses, many of the cavalry being dismounted. The Tatars then closed with the Mamlooks. For a short time the issue hung in doubt. Then the Mamlooks gave way and their whole army broke up and fled, hotly pursued by the Mongols. In the afternoon Ghazan called off the pursuit, mistakenly it would appear, for Maqrizi says that, if he had not done so, not one Muslim soldier would have survived.

Ghazan's use of his archers is of interest. Originally the nomads of Central Asia, whether Turks or Mongols, had used only cavalry armed with the short bow, shooting at full gallop. Such tactics, irresistible on the steppes, could not be used in the mountains or the rice fields or against the walled cities of China. Their long wars in the Far East had taught the Mongols every branch of the military art and it is in China that we first read of their use of archers on foot.

The interest of the Battle of Wadi al Khazindar, however, is wider. For nine centuries, cavalry had dominated the battlefield. At just about the period we are considering, shooting by men on foot began to challenge cavalry. Ghazan destroyed the Mamlook cavalry with foot archers while, in 1346, forty-six years after the Battle of Wadi al Khazindar, Edward III defeated the French chivalry at Crécy by the same means.

Another remarkable aspect of this battle is the fact that the Mamlooks used Greek fire, in Arabic naft or naphtha. The various mixtures used to produce flame were most commonly employed in sieges, particularly against the Franks. This was due to the fact that the Frankish method of attacking a city was to build high wooden towers, with platforms from which archers could shoot over the walls. Against these methods, the Muslims made extensive use of flame to set fire to the wooden towers. The scarcity of timber in many parts of Outremer meant that the burning of their wooden towers was a serious setback to Frankish siege operations. It is to be noted that the Muslims, owing presumably to this scarcity of timber, relied principally on mining in their sieges, a technique which the Franks never mastered.

Thus the use of fire was directed to burning the enemy's engines rather than to killing men. It is, therefore, surprising at this time to read of two instances of the use of fire against personnel. One was by the columns of infantry ascending the breaches in the walls of Acre, the second in this battle of Wadi al Khazindar. There is no explanation as to whether the flames were discharged through nozzles or thrown in containers which burst on contact. In any case, at the Wadi al Khazindar, the flame attack was a complete failure.

The defeated Mamlook army fled past Damascus and on to Gaza. No sooner did the Damascenes see the panic-stricken state of the troops than they also abandoned everything and fled, many being crushed to death in the struggle to get through the gates. Some scattered in the mountains, others continued their flight to Gaza and Egypt. The Mongols in pursuit carried plunder and death as far as Gaza and Kerak.

On 2nd January, 1300, a Mongol detachment reached Damascus bearing a proclamation from Ghazan with many quotations from the Qoran, promising that there would be no massacre. The Il Khan himself rode into Damascus but the army remained outside, though there was some looting and killing in the surrounding countryside. The

Mongols were accompanied by a contingent of Armenians of Cilicia, who were their tributaries, whose cities had been repeatedly ruined by Mamlook invasions and who now revenged themselves on the Syrians. Damascus was ordered by Ghazan to pay an indemnity of a million dinars, which the city was hard put to it to raise.

When the leading citizens of Damascus came to pay homage to Ghazan, he asked them who he was. They replied, "Shah Ghazan the son of Arghoon Khan, the son of Abagha Khan, the son of Hulagu Khan, the son of Tului, the son of Jenghis Khan." "And who," enquired Ghazan, "is your sultan?" "Malik al Nasir, the son of Qalaun," they replied. "Is that so?" retorted Ghazan, "and whose son was Qalaun?" None of those present could answer, for Qalaun had been bought as an unknown slave boy. The contrast is remarkable between the Mamlooks with no sense of heredity, almost boasting of their slave origin, and the arrogance of the Golden Family, the descendants of Jenghis Khan.

While Ghazan was in Damascus, a report arrived stating that a Jagatai army fifty thousand strong had swept across Khurasan and Sijistan to the borders of Fars. Leaving a garrison of twenty-four thousand men in Syria, Ghazan hastily recrossed the Euphrates on 16th February, 1300. Once again civil wars had arrested the progress of Mongol conquest. Before leaving, Ghazan appointed Qipchaq to be his Viceroy in Damascus, the same post which he had held for the Sultan of Egypt before he deserted to the Il Khan.

After the disaster at Wadi al Khazindar, the Mamlook army reached Cairo in utter disorder. The ameers and the young sultan, however, set themselves energetically to build up a new army. Every available artisan was set to work to make arms. Great numbers of horses and camels were purchased and new and heavier taxes were imposed on the unhappy population.

As soon as Al Nasir heard that Ghazan had returned to Persia, he wrote to Qipchaq to recall him to his loyalty. He and his companions immediately abandoned their posts and rode to Cairo to submit, pleading that they had only deserted out of fear of arrest by Sultan Lajeen. We must, of course, remember when considering the readiness of these officers to change sides that we are not dealing with Persians on one side and Arabs on the other but, on both sides, with a Turko-Mongol military governing class, ruling different subject populations. On 31st March, 1300, Sultan Al Nasir left Cairo with a new army and re-occupied Damascus on 1st May without opposition. Those Syrians accused of having co-operated with the enemy were tortured, crucified, their hands and feet cut off or their eyes put out.

In the autumn of 1300, however, having dealt with the Jagatai invasion, Ghazan decided to return to Syria. The report that the Il Khan was coming back injected new energy into the preparations in Egypt. Further taxes were imposed on the public, arousing fresh resentment. Similar exactions took place in Syria. Refugees from that country continued to arrive in Egypt, driven both by fear of the Mongols and also by poverty, for those who had not been stripped by the Tatars had been ruined by the taxes

In October 1300, the sultan left Cairo with the main body of the army. Meanwhile Ghazan, after once again reducing the province of Aleppo to a desert, turned southwards up the valley of the Orontes. On 19th January, 1301, he reached Qinisreen. The weary Mamlooks, not without misgiving, marched northwards once more. It chanced, however, that the winter was most exceptionally cold and wet. Rain and snow fell unceasingly and Mongols and Mamlooks alike lost nearly all their horses. In February both armies turned back without a battle, leaving General Winter in possession of the field.

* * *

Ghazan was an outstanding commander. The Battle of Wadi al Khazindar had been won by his personal leadership. His failure to conquer Syria was due to the unrelenting hostility of his relatives, the descendants of Jagatai and Juji. Perhaps he also fell between two stools. If, like Jenghis Khan and Hulagu, he had massacred the whole population and razed the cities, he might have struck such terror that all resistance would have been paralysed. But he claimed to be a Muslim and a civilized ruler and therefore ceased to terrify. To maintain control of Syria without the use of terror would have required a garrison strong enough to defeat the Mamlooks while Ghazan was away fighting his Mongol enemies in Persia. For this his resources were inadequate.

NOTABLE DATES

Accession of Khalil the son of Sultan Qalaun	December 1290
Fall of Acre	18th May, 1291
Kaikhatu, son of Abagha Khan, elected Il Khan	22nd July, 1291
Assassination of Sultan Khalil Elevation of Malik al Nasir Muhammad	December 1293
Deposition of Al Nasir Elevation of Kitbugha to the sultanate	1st December, 1294

Assassination of Kaikhatu	23rd April, 1295
Elevation of Ghazan to be Il Khan	3rd December, 1295
Deposition of Kitbugha Elevation of Lajeen to the sultanate	26th November, 1296
Assassination of Lajeen	January 1299
Second Reign of Al Nasir	7th February, 1299
Battle of Wadi al Khazindar Mongols defeat Mamlooks	22nd December, 1299
Capture of Damascus by Ghazan	2nd January, 1300
Abandonment of Ghazan's second invasion of Syria	February 1301

PERSONALITIES

Rulers of Egypt

Sultan Khalil, the son of Qalaun
Malik al Nasir Muhammad, the son of Qalaun
Sultan Kitbugha
Sultan Lajeen
Regent Salar
Regent Baybers the Jashnekeer (The Taster)

Il Khans of Persia

Arghoon Khan, the son of Abagha Khan
Kaikhatu Khan, the son of Abagha Khan
Ghazan Khan, son of Arghoon Khan

SUMMARY OF THE GREAT CRUSADES

Number and Result of Crusade	*Leaders*	*Date*
FIRST		
Jerusalem captured	Bohemond Raymond de St. Gilles Godfrey de Bouillon	1097–1099
SECOND		
Fiasco of attack on Damascus	Louis VII of France Conrad III of Germany	1147–1148

THIRD		
Kingdom of Jerusalem re-established with capital at Acre	Frederick I Barbarossa Philippe Auguste of France Richard I Coeur de Lion	1189–1192
FOURTH		
Constantinople captured	Boniface of Montferrat Baldwin of Flanders The Doge of Venice	1202–1204
FIFTH		
Disaster south of Damietta	Jean de Brienne Cardinal Pelagius	1218–1221
SIXTH		
Frederick II Treaty with Al-Kamil	Frederick II Hohenstaufen	1228–1229
SEVENTH		
Disaster at Mansoora	Saint Louis IX of France	1248–1250
EIGHTH		
Treaty between Charles and the King of Tunis	Saint Louis IX Charles of Anjou	1270

NOTE These are the most famous Crusades to which specific numbers are allotted in European history. In practice, however, war was almost continuous from 1098 to 1291, and Crusaders were constantly coming and going to Outremer throughout these two centuries.

XVI

Sunset in the Maghrib

1250–1492

Dynastic quarrels and political disputes kept the Spanish kingdoms so fully occupied that they did little in the way of resuming the war against the Moors of Granada. On the other hand they developed their commerce and added to their wealth. Thus, even before the marriage of Ferdinand and Isabella, Spain had won a position which prepared her for the part she was about to play. If we reflect that the Spanish people had been tempered by the wars against Islam, we shall have no difficulty in realizing the strength of this new factor which was about to play a part in the life of Europe. HENRI PIRENNE, *A History of Europe* (abridged)

Moors, free and serf, remained in plenty under Christian rule but only one Moslem kingdom . . . was left in Spain, that of the Nasrids of Granada. *The Shorter Cambridge Mediaeval History*

A man has seen nothing until he has seen Granada. *Spanish Proverb*

XVI

WE have already told of the collapse of the Muwahhid Empire and the extermination of the dynasty of Abdul Mumin. For one hundred and nine years, the Muwahhids had ruled the whole of western Islam—Andalus, the Maghrib and Ifriqiya—as a single empire. With the capture of Marakish by the Berber tribe of Beni Merin on 8th September, 1269, the former empire broke up into four independent units. In Spain, the Kingdom of Granada was a nominal, but frequently rebellious, vassal of Castile. In North Africa, the Beni Merin Berbers ruled the Maghrib, the modern Morocco, while the Beni Abdul Wad set up an independent government with its capital at Telemsan in what we would call western Algeria. Ifriqiya, comprising eastern Algeria and the present Tunisia, constituted a third North African state.

We will commence by recounting briefly the history of the North African Muslims from 1269 to 1453 and will then give a short account of the Kingdom of Granada from 1269 until its fall in 1492.

* * *

The history of North Africa for nearly two centuries after 1269 was haunted by the memory of the Muwahhid Empire. Beni Merin, having destroyed the Muwahhids and captured their capital, Marakish, saw themselves as their heirs. Three years after the fall of Marakish, Muhammad II, the King of Granada, appealed for help against Castile. Abu Yusuf Yaqoob, the Beni Merin Sultan, as heir to the Muwahhids, was ready to answer the call. On 16th August, 1275, he crossed the straits of Gibraltar, overran the valley of the Guadalquivir and defeated a Castilian army sent against him. He returned in 1277 and once again laid waste the Guadalquivir valley and the plain of Seville with fire and sword. But whereas the Muwahhids had been statesmen, Beni Merin were tribesmen, who only twenty years before had been tent-dwelling nomads. Their operations in Spain were scarcely more than plundering raids and did little towards achieving political stability.

The King of Castile, Ferdinand the Saint, had died in 1252 and had been succeeded by his son, Alfonso X the Learned. Alfonso, though he is alleged to have regretted not having been present at the Creation, as he would have arranged a better world, was nevertheless unable to arrange the affairs of Castile, where the nobles were in constant revolt.

THE UNION OF CASTILE AND ARAGON

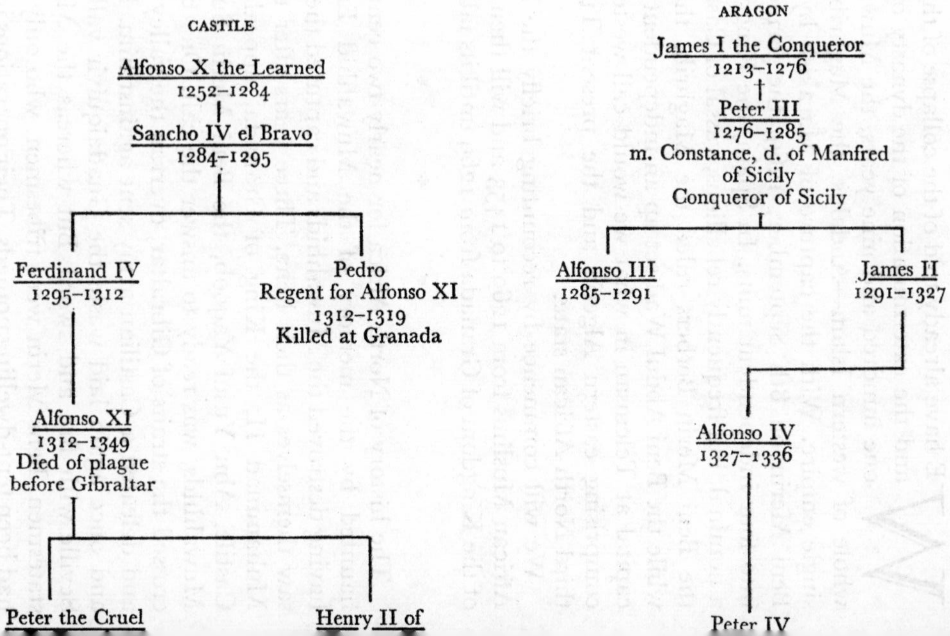
CASTILE
Alfonso X the Learned
1252–1284
Sancho IV el Bravo
1284–1295
Ferdinand IV
1295–1312
Pedro
Regent for Alfonso XI
1312–1319
Killed at Granada
Alfonso XI
1312–1349
Died of plague
before Gibraltar
Peter the Cruel
Henry II of
ARAGON
James I the Conqueror
1213–1276
Peter III
1276–1285
m. Constance, d. of Manfred
of Sicily
Conqueror of Sicily
Alfonso III
1285–1291
James II
1291–1327
Alfonso IV
1327–1336
Peter IV

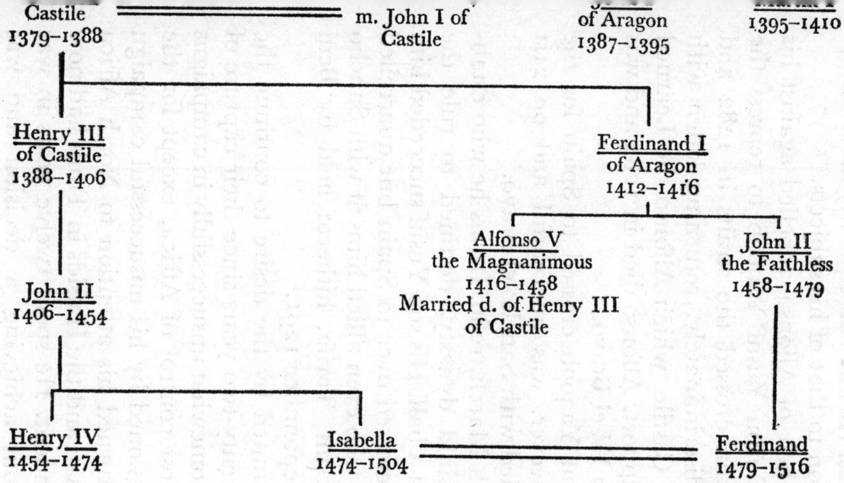

NOTE

It will be noted that both families were descended from John I of Castile.

He was a man dedicated to intellectual pursuits, which earned him little respect from his half-barbaric subjects.

Alfonso's devotion to science and astronomy had resulted in the presence at his court of many Muslim and Jewish professors, the only persons conversant with such studies. He had consequently incurred the opposition of the church in addition to that of his subjects.

Sancho el Bravo, the son and heir of Alfonso, rebelled against his father, who solicited the help of Abu Yusuf Yaqoob to repress the rebellion. The Merinid ruler again crossed the straits in 1282 and plundered Christian territory indiscriminately, returning laden with booty and carrying the crown of Castile, which Alfonso the Learned had pledged to him to gain his support. Alfonso died in 1284 and was succeeded by his rebel son Sancho IV el Bravo.

On 7th April, 1285, Abu Yusuf Yaqoob crossed to Spain for the fourth time. The campaign, however, was uneventful and on 21st October, 1285, peace was concluded with Sancho el Bravo.

Abu Yusuf Yaqoob died on 20th March, 1286. It was he who established the greatness of the Merinid dynasty, destined to rule the Maghrib for a further century and a half. His son Yusuf succeeded him without opposition.[1] In 1291 he crossed over to Spain but quarrelled with Muhammad II of Granada, who even allied himself with Sancho IV against Beni Merin. As a result, Tarifa, hitherto held by Beni Merin, was taken by Castile in September 1291.[2]

Although Beni Merin were haunted by the desire to continue the empire of the Muwahhids, the twenty-two years since their capture of Marakish in 1269 had been spent somewhat unsuccessfully in campaigns in Spain. Meanwhile they had lost control of Africa, except for the Maghrib itself (Morocco). Disillusioned by his unsuccessful campaign in Spain in 1291, Sultan Yusuf turned his attention to North Africa where Beni Abdul Wad in Telemsan and the Hafsids in Tunis had now for some fifty years been independent. He spent twelve years in war against Beni Abdul Wad without achieving a decision and was assassinated in 1307.

Two grandsons, Aamir and Sulaiman, succeeded but both died within two years to be succeeded by their great uncle, Abu Saeed Othman II, who, abandoning imperial ambitions, governed the Maghrib quietly for twenty-one years. Dying on 25th August, 1331, he was succeeded by his son, Abu al Hasan Ali, by whom the task of restoring the boundaries of the Muwahhid Empire was energetically resumed.

Scarcely had he assumed control of the Maghrib than he received an

[1] For genealogical tree of Beni Merin, see page 344.

[2] Map 40, page 347.

urgent appeal from the Sultan of Granada, Muhammad IV, who was hard pressed by Alfonso XI of Castile. Gibraltar had been seized by Castile in 1309 and Abu al Hasan Ali began his intervention in Spain by recapturing the Rock in 1333. Unfortunately Muhammad IV of Granada was killed at Gibraltar and Beni Merin did not move again until seven years later. On 5th April, 1340, the Merinid fleet gained a brilliant victory in the straits over the combined fleets of Castile and Aragon. Having thus made the sea-passage safe, Abu al Hasan Ali sent an army across to Spain, where it joined forces with the army of Granada.

In September 1340, the sultan assumed command of his army at Algeciras. Instead, however, of marching into the enemy's country, he turned aside to besiege the unimportant fortress of Tarifa, thereby allowing the Christians ample time to prepare. Alfonso XI of Castile, reduced at first to despair, was able at length to raise a great army. The church preached a crusade, the Genoese sent a fleet and a large Christian army marched to the relief of Tarifa.

On 30th October, 1340, the two sides fought a pitched battle on the small stream of the Rio Salado, a few miles north of Tarifa. When the battle was at its height, the Christian garrison of Tarifa made a spirited sortie and attacked the Berbers in the rear, throwing them into confusion. The army of Granada succeeded in withdrawing to its own territory but immense numbers of Merinid troops were massacred, the Christians, as usual, giving no quarter. The battle of Rio Salado marked the end of Berber intervention in Spain. Thereafter the Arab Kingdom of Granada was left to defend itself as best it could. Incredible as it may appear, it was to survive alone for another one hundred and fifty years.

The Sultan Abu al Hasan Ali laid the blame for the disaster on the army of Granada and withdrew indignantly to Africa, where he set himself energetically to reconstruct the empire of Abdul Mumin. Let us see what had become of Beni Abdul Wad and of the Hafsids of Tunis during the period of 1269 to 1340 during which the Merinids had been preoccupied with Spain.

* * *

As early as 1207, the Muwahhid Khalif Muhammad al Nasir had appointed Abdul Wahid, the son of Abu Hafas Umar, to be governor of Tunis. Abu Hafas Umar had been a close friend of the founder of the Muwahhid sect, Ibn Toumert. The dynasty of Abdul Mumin was already in rapid decline and ceased to exercise any influence in Tunis where, in 1236, Abu Zakariya Yahya I declared himself independent.

Meanwhile in 1230, he had annexed Boujaiya and Constantine and in 1235 Algiers. The Christian states of the Mediterranean were quick to recognize the shift in the balance of power from Marakish to Tunis.

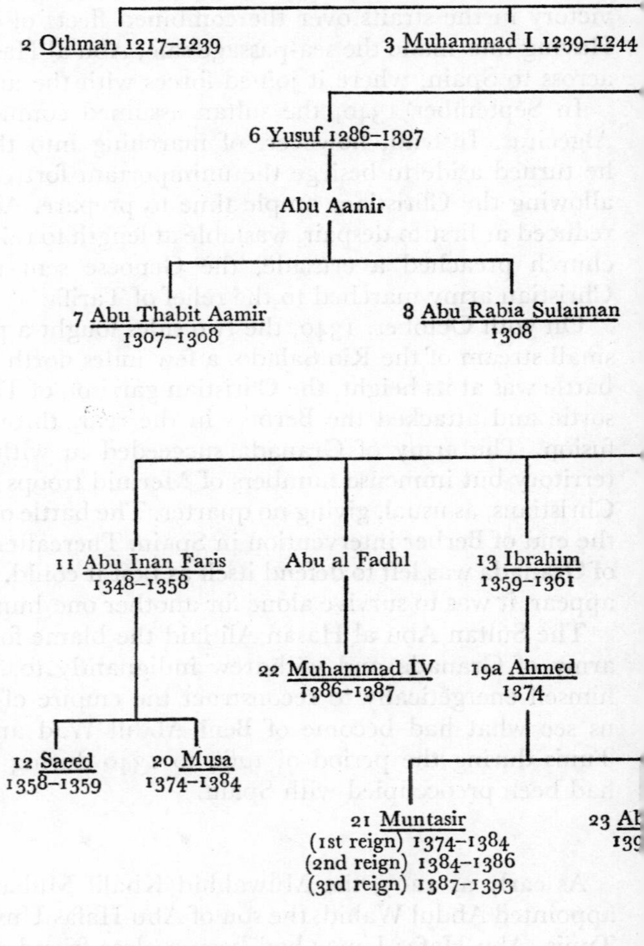
2 Othman 1217–1239
3 Muhammad I 1239–1244
6 Yusuf 1286–1307
Abu Aamir
7 Abu Thabit Aamir
1307–1308
8 Abu Rabia Sulaiman
1308
11 Abu Inan Faris
1348–1358
Abu al Fadhl
13 Ibrahim
1359–1361
22 Muhammad IV
1386–1387
19a Ahmed
1374
12 Saeed
1358–1359
20 Musa
1374–1384
21 Muntasir
(1st reign) 1374–1384
(2nd reign) 1384–1386
(3rd reign) 1387–1393
23 Ab
139

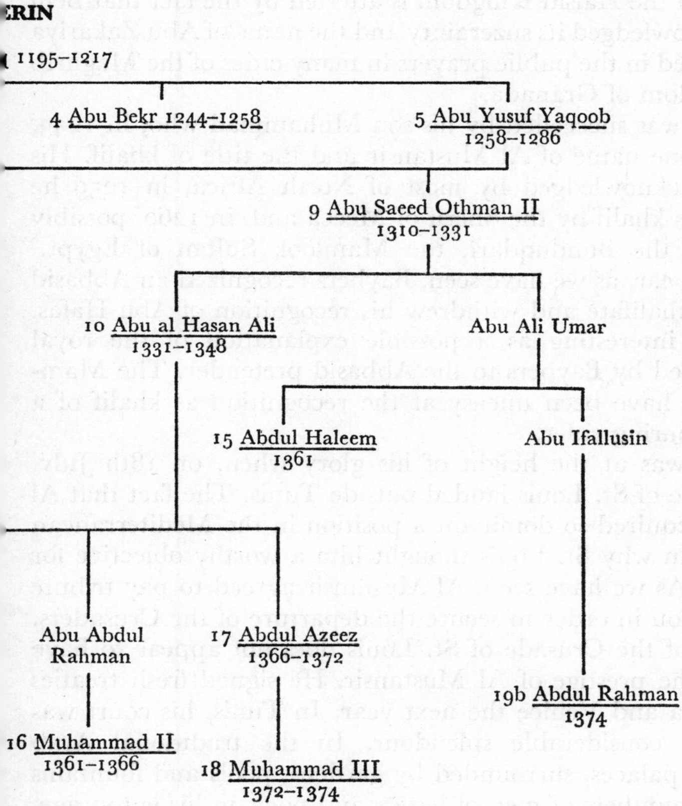

NOTES

(1) Abdul Haqq and his three eldest sons were chiefs of Beni Merin before they conquered the Maghrib.

(2) Abu Yusuf Yaqoob was the first sultan.

(3) From 1258 to 1348, the ninety years of glory, there were five Sultans.

From 1348 to 1393, forty-five years of decadence, there were thirteen rulers.

After 1393, the dynasty was without authority.

In 1231, Venice made a treaty with the Hafsid government, in 1234 Pisa and in 1236 Genoa. In 1239, the Emperor Frederick II appointed a consul in Tunis and Aragon opened diplomatic relations. The growing importance of the Hafsid Kingdom is attested by the fact that Beni Abdul Wad acknowledged its suzerainty and the name of Abu Zakariya Yahya was inserted in the public prayers in many cities of the Maghrib and of the Kingdom of Granada.

Abu Zakariya was succeeded by his son Muhammad who, in 1253, assumed the throne name of Al Mustansir and the title of khalif. His suzerainty was acknowledged by most of North Africa, in 1259 he was recognized as khalif by the Sherif of Mecca and, in 1260, possibly also by Baybers the Bunduqdari, the Mamlook Sultan of Egypt.[3] In the following year, as we have seen, Baybers recognized an Abbasid claimant to the khalifate and withdrew his recognition of Abu Hafas. The incident is interesting as a possible explanation of the royal treatment accorded by Baybers to the Abbasid pretender. The Mamlook Sultan may have been uneasy at the recognition as khalif of a powerful neighbouring ruler.

Al Mustansir was at the height of his glory when, on 18th July, 1270, the Crusade of St. Louis landed outside Tunis. The fact that Al Mustansir had acquired so dominant a position in the Mediterranean goes far to explain why St. Louis thought him a worthy objective for his last crusade. As we have seen, Al Mustansir agreed to pay tribute to Charles of Anjou in order to secure the departure of the Crusaders.

The outcome of the Crusade of St. Louis does not appear to have greatly injured the prestige of Al Mustansir. He signed fresh treaties with Aragon, Pisa and Venice the next year. In Tunis, his court was maintained with considerable splendour. In the traditional Arab pattern, he built palaces, surrounded by gardens, pools and fountains and maintained numbers of men of letters and poets in his entourage. He died of illness on 17th May, 1277, in peace and glory.

As so repeatedly occurred in the histories of the successors of the Arab Empire, the unity of the Hafsid state collapsed with the death of Al Mustansir. The names of the ephemeral rulers who seized and lost power between 1277 and 1370 will be found on the Hafsid genealogical tree.

* * *

We may now perhaps summarize the events of the seventy-one years from the Merinid capture of Marakish in 1269 to the Battle of Rio Salado in 1340. During this period the Merinids had gradually established full control of Morocco but had used all their surplus strength in a series of campaigns in Spain. In Africa, as a result,

[3] It will be remembered that Hulagu took Baghdad and killed the Abbasid Khalif in 1258.

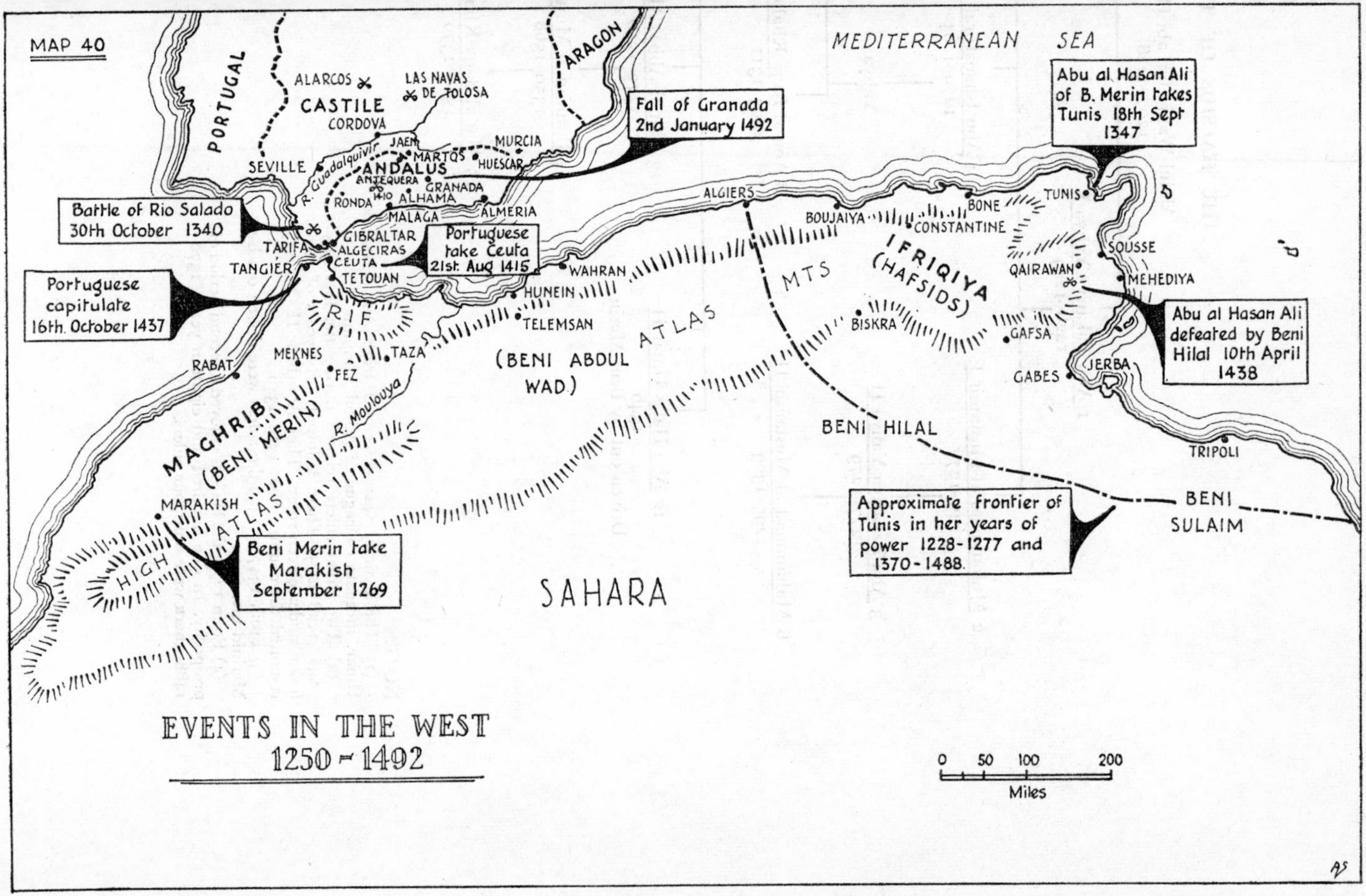

MAP 40
MEDITERRANEAN SEA
PORTUGAL
CASTILE
ARAGON
ALARCOS
LAS NAVAS DE TOLOSA
CORDOVA
JAEN
MARTOS
MURCIA
HUESCAR
SEVILLE
R. Guadalquivir
ANDALUS
ANTEQUERA
GRANADA
ALHAMA
RONDA
MALAGA
ALMERIA
GIBRALTAR
ALGECIRAS
TARIFA
CEUTA
TANGIER
TETOUAN
Fall of Granada 2nd January 1492
Battle of Rio Salado 30th October 1340
Portuguese take Ceuta 21st. Aug 1415
Portuguese capitulate 16th. October 1437
RIF
RABAT
MEKNES
FEZ
TAZA
R. Moulouya
MAGHRIB (BENI MERIN)
MARAKISH
HIGH ATLAS
Beni Merin take Marakish September 1269
WAHRAN
HUNEIN
TELEMSAN
(BENI ABDUL WAD)
ATLAS
ALGIERS
MTS
BOUJAIYA
CONSTANTINE
BONE
TUNIS
IFRIQIYA (HAFSIDS)
BISKRA
GAFSA
QAIRAWAN
SOUSSE
MEHEDIYA
GABES
JERBA
TRIPOLI
Abu al Hasan Ali of B. Merin takes Tunis 18th Sept 1347
Abu al Hasan Ali defeated by Beni Hilal 10th April 1438
BENI HILAL
BENI SULAIM
Approximate frontier of Tunis in her years of power 1228-1277 and 1370-1488
SAHARA
EVENTS IN THE WEST 1250-1492
0 50 100 200
Miles

THE HAFSIDS OF T

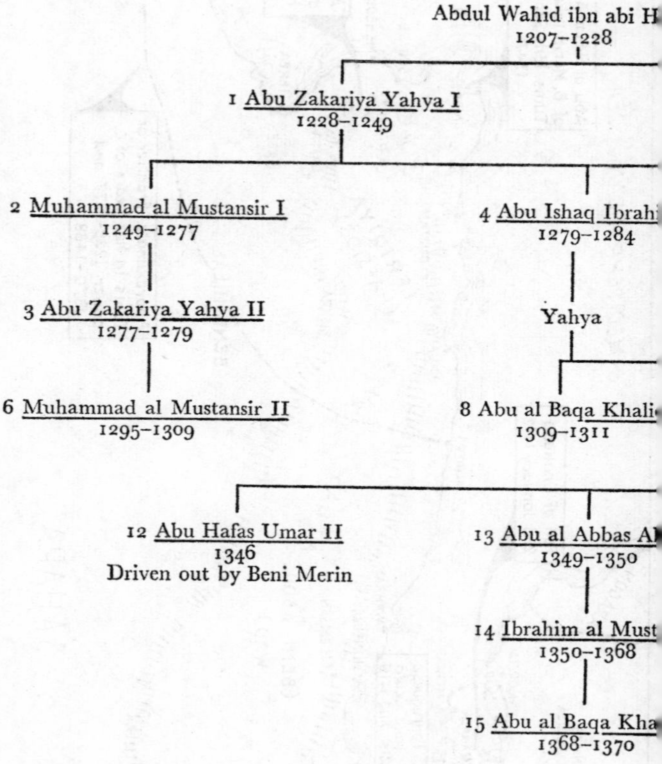

NOTES

(1) The dynasty was descended from Abu Hafas Umar, intimate colleague of Abdul Mumin.

(2) Two great rulers reigned during the first fifty years, 1228–1277. There followed forty years of confusion under eleven rulers. Then Abu Bekr II (No. 11) re-united the country from 1318–1346.

(3) From 1347 to 1349 the rulers were driven out by Merinid invasions.

(4) From 1370, the Hafsids enjoyed a second period of prosperity. In one hundred and eighteen years, 137c–1488, there were only four rulers.

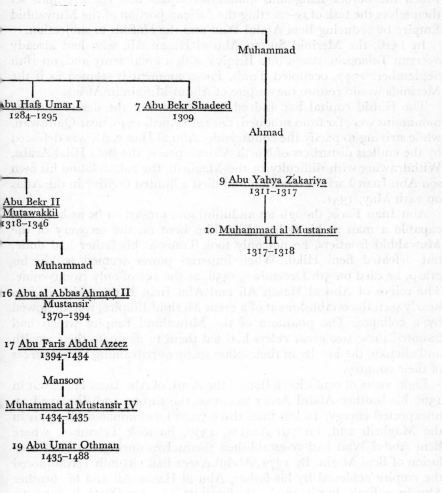

Muhammad

Abu Hafs Umar I
1284–1295

7 Abu Bekr Shadeed
1309

Ahmad

9 Abu Yahya Zakariya
1311–1317

Abu Bekr II
Mutawakkil
1318–1346

10 Muhammad al Mustansir
III
1317–1318

Muhammad

16 Abu al Abbas Ahmad II
Mustansir
1370–1394

17 Abu Faris Abdul Azeez
1394–1434

Mansoor

Muhammad al Mustansir IV
1434–1435

19 Abu Umar Othman
1435–1488

Beni Abdul Wad and the Hafsids of Tunis remained completely independent and indeed, in the case of Tunis, played for nearly a century an important rôle as a Mediterranean power.

In 1340, however, the Battle of Rio Salado inaugurated a new era in which the Berber Kingdoms abandoned Spain and the Merinids set themselves the task of re-creating the African portion of the Muwahhid Empire by reducing Beni Abdul Wad and the Hafsids to subjection.

In 1346, the Merinid Sultan Abu al Hasan Ali, who had already overrun Telemsan, swept into Ifriqiya with a great army and, on 18th September, 1347, occupied Tunis. For a moment it seemed as if the Merinids would restore the empire of Abdul Mumin in Africa.

The Hafsid capital had indeed been taken but the desert and the mountains were far from subdued. On 10th April, 1348, near Qairawan, while striving to pacify the countryside, Abu al Hasan Ali was defeated by the endless disturbers of North African peace, the Beni Hilal Arabs. Withdrawing with difficulty to the Maghrib, the sultan found his own son Abu Inan Faris in rebellion and died a hunted fugitive in the Atlas on 24th May, 1351.

Abu Inan Faris, though an undutiful son, proved to be as bold and capable a man as his father. Like him bent on the recovery of the Muwahhid frontiers, he not only took Tunis as his father had done, but defeated Beni Hilal. When imperial power seemed within his grasp, he died on 5th December, 1358, at the age of only twenty-nine. The reigns of Abu al Hasan Ali and Abu Inan Faris, which had so nearly seen the establishment of a great Merinid Empire, were followed by a collapse. The phantom of the Muwahhid Empire which had haunted these two great rulers had led them to dissipate their wealth and alienate the loyalty of their followers by overstraining the resources of their country.

Eight years of confusion followed the death of Abu Inan Faris, but in 1366 his brother Abdul Azeez mounted the throne and displayed an unexpected energy. In less than three years he eliminated all rivals in the Maghrib and, on 7th August, 1370, he took Telemsan, where Beni Abdul Wad had re-established themselves during the brief confusion of Beni Merin. By 1372, Abdul Azeez had virtually reconquered the empire achieved by his father, Abu al Hasan Ali and his brother Abu Inan Faris, but in the hour of success, on 23rd October, 1372, he too fell ill and died. For the third and last time, the phantom of the reconstructed Muwahhid Empire faded away.

In theory, Beni Merin continued to rule Morocco until 1465. Their power was only really effective for one hundred and fourteen years—from 1258 to 1372. For the remaining ninety-three years of their nominal rule—1372 to 1465—the Maghrib was torn by civil wars, often stimulated by the intrigues of the King of Castile or the Beni Nasr Sultans of Granada.

Beni Merin never achieved the glory or the military power of the Muwahhids. The latter had originated from the settled population. Their mehedi, Ibn Toumert, had studied in Baghdad. His successor, Abdul Mumin, had also been a student. Beni Merin, on the other hand, had stepped straight into the imperial palaces of their predecessors from the ragged tents of the desert. Their tribal outlook unsupported by religious fanaticism had prevented them from attaining the solid military strength of the Muwahhids.

Not only did the Merinids lack the vitalising action of religious fanaticism but they never commanded the whole-hearted support of the settled population which, under the Muwahhids, had produced large armies of solid infantry. Beni Merin derived their troops from their fellow Zenata Berbers and from the Arab bedouins. Both groups, being largely nomadic, were able to put great numbers of cavalry in the field, but their lack of support from the towns and villages is shown by the fact that their crossbowmen were enlisted in Andalus, their archers came from Arabia or Syria, while they also employed one thousand five hundred Turkish cavalry and four thousand Christian mercenaries, who lived in a special quarter in Fez.

Beni Merin power, moreover, was constantly frittered away by dynastic civil wars. The Muwahhids, perhaps owing to their puritan religious origin, had been remarkably free from internal family rivalries. Not that Beni Merin were irreligious—on the contrary, their period of power changed the religious colour of the Maghrib to a pattern which it has retained to this day. But whereas both the Murabits and the Muwahhids had been extremist sects, Beni Merin brought religion back to the general fold of Sunni orthodoxy. The change reduced the energy-generating force of fanaticism but, on the other hand, it united the Maghrib to the main body of Islam.

Their return to orthodoxy may have been assisted by the influx of refugees from Andalus, for the Muslims of Spain had always been orthodox and conservative. The refugees were also useful to an initially ignorant and tribal dynasty, whether as administrators and officials or in the intellectual sphere as poets, professors and scientists. The Merinid period saw the foundation of many colleges and schools, doubtless partly staffed by Andalusian teachers. Particularly were Beni Merin great builders and many of their splendid monuments have survived to our own times.

* * *

The Merinids fell into a rapid decline after 1372, but the Hafsids of Tunis, unexpectedly enough, enjoyed a second long period of glory and prosperity. On 9th November, 1370, Abu al Abbas Ahmed obtained possession of Tunis and reigned over the re-united Hafsid dominions until his death in 1394.

He was followed on the throne of Tunis by his son, Abu Faris Abdul Azeez, who reigned from 1394 to 1434. Revered for his piety and his justice, he extended the frontiers of Ifriqiya to include Tripoli, Gafsa, Biskra and Algiers and virtually re-established the dominant position which Tunis had enjoyed from 1249 to 1277. At his brilliant court he received delegations from the Christian states of the Mediterranean as well as from Granada, from Egypt and from Mecca. In 1424, the Merinids of Fez recognized his suzerainty, while the enfeebled Beni Abdul Wad were little more than his satellites.

Mustansir, the grandson of Abu Faris, died on 16th September, 1435, and was succeeded by his son, Abu Umar Othman, who reigned in peace and glory from 1435 to 1488. It was during his reign, in 1453, that the Ottomans took Constantinople while, four years after his death, Ferdinand and Isabella finally destroyed the Muslim Kingdom of Granada. The Spanish and Ottoman Empires were the two rising powers in the Mediterranean. Between them, the Hafsid Empire of Ifriqiya was eventually to disappear. It had survived in Tunis for three hundred and fifty years during long periods of which it had played the part of one of the great powers of the Mediterranean.

The Arabs had, for five centuries, enjoyed naval command of the Mediterranean but, in the thirteenth century, Europe began to forge ahead in the art of shipbuilding and both their battle and commercial fleets soon outclassed those of the Muslims. Indeed it was their rapid development of firearms and shipbuilding which enabled the Christians to turn the tables on the states of North Africa.

The Hafsids endeavoured to follow the Arab tradition of literary culture and produced a number of authors and historians, the most famous of whom was Ibn Khaldun, on whose great history most of this chapter is based, and who lived for some time in Tunis. The dynasty attempted, not without success, to maintain the ancient civilization which it had inherited but to which it failed to add anything creative.

The Hafsids at first maintained the traditional Muwahhid constitution of the Councils of Ten and of Fifty but their duties seem to have become largely ceremonial. The sultan made use of three wazeers to carry out the actual duties of government. The senior was the Minister for the Army, the second the Minister of Finance and the third the Secretary of State.

The army of Tunis was composed of many different elements, doubtless to guard against plots and dynastic rivalries. The chiefs were largely descendants of the original Muwahhid families, but there were also Ghuzz Turks, whose ancestors had immigrated in the reign of Abdul Mumin. In addition Arabs, Andalusians and Zenata Berbers are mentioned and a regiment of a thousand Mamlook cavalry, purchased as boys in Egypt.

Ifriqiya, more than any other part of Berber North Africa, had been overrun in the eleventh century by the Arab nomads of Beni Hilal and Beni Sulaim, whose presence was responsible for so many disturbances and civil wars. The Hafsids were Berbers but, during their long period of power, Ifriqiya became almost completely arabicized. Only in a few scattered groups of mountains did the Berber language survive and with it the Kharijite Muslim sects which had enjoyed so great a vogue among the Berbers in the ninth and tenth centuries.

* * *

In our account of the varying fortunes of the Hafsid and Merinid Empires frequent mention has been made of Beni Abdul Wad at Telemsan. The tribe, like Beni Merin, originated from the Zenata Berbers, but had been loyal subjects of the Muwahhids who had rewarded them with the governorship of Telemsan.

This town was at the junction of two great highways. One, running north and south, led from Ghana across the Sahara to Telemsan and thence to the seaports of Hunein and Wahran (Oran). The other, leading east and west, ran from Tunis and Algiers through the Taza gap to Fez. At the junction of these great commercial highways, the markets of Telemsan were crowded by the merchants of black Africa and of Europe, of Tunisia and Morocco.

But the central position occupied by Telemsan, commercially so fortunate, was strategically disastrous. For two hundred years, the Merinids and the Hafsids fought one another, backwards and forwards, for the empire of North Africa. The first step in every such campaign was to overrun Telemsan. Again and again the Abdul Wad rulers were obliged to submit, to flee to the mountains or to the desert, or to stand and be killed in battle.

But every time, once the storm had passed, some member of the family would reappear in Telemsan and resume control. In spite of endless misfortunes, the Abdul Wad survived, in ever-increasing weakness, until the *coup de grâce* was administered by the Ottomans in 1554.

* * *

In spite of battles waged in Spain and of frequent piracies at sea, commercial relations between Muslim North Africa and Christian Europe had never been severed. Throughout the fourteenth century, the ships of Venice, Pisa, Genoa, Marseilles and Aragon continued to ply regularly to Ifriqiya and the Maghrib, though Castile and Portugal remained hostile.

There were considerable settlements of European merchants with their warehouses and offices in the ports of North Africa and we have already noted Christian mercenary troops quartered in Marakish and Fez. Commercial activity was even greater in the Hafsid state which largely owed its wealth to the busy ports of Boujaiya, Bone, Gabes, Jerba and of course Tunis. In the latter city, Venice, Pisa, Genoa, Florence and Aragon all maintained prosperous commercial colonies, each controlled by its consul accredited to the Hafsid Khalif. Ifriqiya exported to Europe grain, dates, olive oil, salted fish, textiles, carpets, wool and leather, though this peaceful commerce was at times disturbed by acts of piracy.

Castile and Portugal, however, rejected friendly commercial intercourse, leaning rather to conquest than to trade. In 1399, while the Merinid army was engaged in one of its unending sieges of Telemsan, Henry III of Castile seized Tetouan, massacred most of the inhabitants and carried the remainder into slavery. On 21st August, 1415, the Portuguese seized Ceuta, leaving in it a garrison of two thousand men whom Beni Merin were too weak to evict. On 16th October, 1437, however, a Portuguese army which attempted to take Tangier was obliged to capitulate. In spite of this check, the Portuguese returned and, in the second half of the fifteenth century, established a whole chain of colonies on the coasts of Morocco. The tide had turned. After living for seven centuries in fear of Muslim imperialism, Europe had gone over to the attack in the West.

* * *

Having now briefly sketched the history of Muslim North Africa up to the end of our period in 1453, we must outline the story of the Kingdom of Granada.[4]

In 1246, Muhammad ibn Nasr, the King of Granada,[5] had become a tributary of Castile. By a remarkable mixture of war, diplomacy and intrigue, Granada was to survive for two hundred and fifty years, sometimes paying tribute to Castile, sometimes soliciting the armed assistance of the Merinids, sometimes intriguing with one side or the other in the civil wars of the Spaniards, sometimes embarking on independent wars against Castile.

Muhammad I ibn Nasr, who had become the vassal of Ferdinand the Saint, lived in peace with Castile until his death in 1273, leaving behind him in Granada a strong and prosperous state. Industry and agriculture were thriving, while in every town schools, colleges,

[4] Genealogical tree, page 360. [5] Page 291.

libraries and hospitals perpetuated in miniature that polished and cultured society which had so long set an example of civilization in the West.

In 1275, his son Muhammad II appealed for help to Abu Yusuf Yaqoob, whose resulting invasions of Spain have already been described. Muhammad II was quick to profit by the anarchy of Castile and when he died in 1302, after a reign of twenty-nine years, the boundaries of Granada were firmly held and the state prosperous.

In 1314, the ruling Sultan Nasr (1309–1314) was dethroned by his cousin, Ismail ibn Faraj. The deposed sultan did not hesitate to appeal to Don Pedro, the regent of Castile who, in 1316, inflicted a heavy defeat on the army of Granada. In 1319, the army of Castile appeared in the actual plain of Granada but met with a catastrophic defeat at the hands of the Muslims, Don Pedro being killed. His body was to remain for many years suspended over the gateway of Granada. Ismail ibn Faraj proved a capable Sultan of Granada. He fought several campaigns against Castile, notably one in which he captured Huescar in 1324 by the use of artillery. An exultant poem in Arabic celebrating this triumph has come down to us, beginning:

> "They thought that the thunderbolt dwelt in the sky
> But their thunderbolt struck from the ground . . ."[6]

After the disastrous defeat of the Muslims in 1340 at Rio Salado near Tarifa, Granada was deprived of all hope of Berber support. On 26th March, 1344, Alfonso XI of Castile, assisted by Crusaders from France and England, captured Algeciras after a siege of nineteen months and in 1349 he laid siege to Gibraltar. Plague, however, appeared in the Christian camp and the king was one of the first victims. The curious relations which existed between Castile and Granada are illustrated by the fact that, although the Muslim army was in the field, the sultan immediately agreed to a truce and he and his court politely went into mourning.

Alfonso XI was succeeded by his son, Peter the Cruel (1349–1369), under whom Castile was again torn by civil wars, the disturbances continuing under his half-brother and murderer, Henry of Trastamara (1369–1379). In addition, frequent wars with Portugal, Navarre and Aragon reduced Castile to impotence.

The Nasrid Sultans of Granada were themselves often the victims of dynastic rivalries. On the whole, however, their disputes, palace *coups d'état* rather than civil wars, were less ruinous to their country than were those of Castile. The fact that, of twenty-one Nasrid Sultans of Granada, six were dethroned and subsequently recovered their

[6] Ibn al Khatib, *Al Ihatah fi Akhbar Gharnata.*

authority and one, Muhammad VIII al Mutamassik, was twice deposed and then re-appointed, is enough to prove the precarious nature of their tenure amid these family quarrels.

Muhammad V died in 1391 and was followed by his son Yusuf II. In 1406, however, as a result of an outbreak of mutual raids, Henry III of Castile (1388–1406) decided to conquer Granada but died before he could do so, leaving a child as his heir. The chivalry of Castile was anxious for war, laid waste the country round Ronda and defeated the Muslims in 1410 at Antequera. Peace was, however, re-established and continued throughout the reign of Yusuf III (1407–1417).

The magnanimity and prestige of the sultan were shown by the fact that, on many occasions, rival nobles of Castile asked him to arbitrate in their disputes. At times, when a reconciliation between the hot-headed Castilians proved impossible, the case would be decided by battle in the lists of Granada, the sultan acting as referee. At other times, the lists were occupied by the splendid tournaments of the Muslim knights, who, with reeds for lances, exhibited their equestrian skill without bloodshed beneath the dark eyes of the Arab beauties who watched the exploits of their champions from the galleries. The wealth and luxury of Granada increased rapidly during this Indian summer of prosperity. The farmers and the artisans enjoyed comforts unknown to many of the nobles of Castile. "Of all God's creatures," writes Makkari, "the Andalusians are the most particular regarding the cleanliness of their clothing and their bedding and everything connected therewith." But so high a material standard of living merely increased that decadence which always seems to destroy a peaceable and affluent society.

The chivalry of Spain offered a marked contrast to the Muslims of Granada. Virile, jealous and turbulent, they were far better military material than the graceful and intellectual Arabs. As a result of the Christian conquests, great numbers of Muslims of both sexes were scattered all over Spain as slaves or serfs and were exercising a profound influence on thought and manners. The Spaniards were no longer only fighters. New ideas, new forms of government and new methods of war and navigation were emerging and were, within a hundred years, to create the great empires of Portugal and Spain.

Meanwhile in their fairy castle of the Alhambra, beneath the hot Andalusian sky, while the swallows soared and dived round the battlements overlooking the green ravine below, Beni Nasr revived on a miniature scale the glories of the Umaiyid khalifate of Cordova. In their marble courtyards and their shady gardens, cooled by babbling streams and sparkling fountains, they composed poetry, encouraged literature and listened to soft music. The royal family claimed descent from the Arab tribe of Khazraj, which had been domiciled in Medina during the lifetime of the Prophet. Separated by three thousand five hundred miles and eight centuries from the Arabian tribes of the seventh century, the Arabs of Granada loved to trace their descent from Billi or Abs or the Prophet's Helpers. At the same time new and splendid buildings sprang up in Granada, whose university, colleges and hospitals were far superior to any others in Spain.

* * *

In Castile the death of Henry III ushered in a long struggle between the crown and the nobles under his son John II (1406–1454). The twenty years' reign of John's son, Henry IV, was even more disgraceful. In 1469, however, the marriage of Ferdinand of Aragon with Isabella of Castile at last opened the way to the unity of Christian Spain. Nevertheless, after the death of Henry IV of Castile in 1474, six years of civil war ensued before Ferdinand and Isabella found themselves, in 1480, in undisputed control of Castile and Aragon.

The immediate cause of the fall of Granada, however, was the almost unbelievable folly of the royal family. In 1481, at the precise moment when Christian Spain was united for the first time, the Nasrid Sultan Ali abu al Hasan, known to the Spaniards as Alboacen, not only refused tribute, but actually invaded Christian territory. In 1482, Ferdinand in retaliation captured Al Hamma (Spanish Alhama), a key fortress between Granada and Malaga.

At this critical moment, Muhammad abu Abdulla, the son of Abu al Hasan, rebelled against his father and seized the throne.[7] His mother, jealous of one of the sultan's Christian concubines, had urged her son to this suicidal action. Not only so but Abu Abdulla, called in Spanish history Boabdil, himself marched against the Castilians, was defeated and taken prisoner. His father, Ali abu al Hasan, thereupon re-occupied the throne and ruled until 1485, when he abdicated in favour of his brother, Muhammad XII, surnamed Al Zaghal, who prepared to offer a desperate military resistance.

But Ferdinand and Isabella were skilful politicians. Releasing Abu Abdulla from prison, they supplied him with arms and money to fight his uncle. The foolish youth succeeded in breaking into the city of Granada and the capital itself was the scene of a battle between uncle and nephew. Next year, 1490, the combined armies of Aragon and Castile invaded the kingdom and captured the city of Malaga. The gallant Al Zaghal marched to expel the Christians but was himself attacked from the rear by his nephew, acting in co-operation with the enemy.

In this desperate situation, Al Zaghal abandoned hope and withdrew

[7] Genealogical tree, page 360.

to Telemsan, where he died some years later in destitution. No sooner had Al Zaghal been disposed of than the Catholic Kings turned on their silly dupe, Abu Abdulla, and ordered him to surrender Granada unconditionally, which, however, he refused to do. In the spring of 1491, Ferdinand appeared in the fertile plain of Granada, trampling the crops, cutting down the orchards, burning the villages and killing the inhabitants. The Christians then closely surrounded the city and waited for starvation to do its work. In December 1491, when all food supplies were exhausted, the Muslims agreed to surrender.

The terms offered to them were not ungenerous. The sultan and his officers were to take an oath of allegiance to the Catholic Sovereigns, Abu Abdulla would receive an estate on the southern slopes of the Sierra Nevada and the Muslims would be guaranteed the safety of their lives and possessions and freedom to practise their religion under their own laws. The Castilians entered Granada on 2nd January, 1492, and Arab rule in Spain came to an end seven hundred and eighty years after the conquest of the peninsula by Tariq ibn Zayyad in 712.

A hillock rises on the summit of the long ridge south-west of Granada over which rode a small troop of horsemen and ladies, the family of Muhammad XI Abu Abdulla, the last of the Beni Nasr Sultans. On the summit of this low hill Abu Abdulla drew rein and, gazing for the last time at the lovely city in its green and fertile valley, burst into tears. "You may well weep like a woman," his mother exclaimed bitterly, "over the city which you could not defend like a man."

* * *

Three months later, on 17th April, 1492, at the little town of Santa Fe five miles outside Granada, the Catholic Sovereigns signed the charter which enabled Christopher Columbus to discover America. Spain was thereby launched on that splendid career which led to the discovery and conquest of the New World. How much of the credit for Spanish enthusiasm, heroism and science should be attributed to the Arabs cannot be estimated but it was undoubtedly a notable proportion. In 1497, five years after the fall of Granada, Vasco da Gama sailed round the Cape of Good Hope, making use of an Arab pilot to reach India.

Their Catholic Majesties did not long keep the faith which they had pledged to the Muslims. In 1499, seven years after the surrender, a campaign of forced conversions to Christianity was instituted, under the influence of the queen's confessor, Cardinal Ximenes. In all the long histories of the religious wars, no incidents were more shameful than the perjuries committed by Christian rulers, who had plighted their faith to Muslims—perjuries, alas, too often the result of pressure exercised by popes and cardinals. St. Louis was a shining exception.

The Inquisition then assumed responsibility. The extensive libraries of Granada, packed with priceless books and manuscripts, were burned to the ground. In this frenzy of fanaticism, the Jews suffered the same fate as the Muslims. In the century following the pledge of religious toleration given by Ferdinand and Isabella, three million Muslims are believed to have been executed or banished.

Abu Abdulla at first occupied the estate allotted to him south of the Sierra Nevada but, finding conditions intolerable, he moved to Fez, where he died in 1533. In 1627, when Makkari was writing in Fez his history of Andalus, the descendants of Beni Nasr, he alleges, were counted among the beggars of that city.[8]

NOTABLE DATES

Declaration of Independence by Abu Zakariya the Hafsid in Tunis	1236
Granada becomes a vassal of Castile	1246
First Period of Hafsid supremacy	1228–1277
Period of civil war between Muwahhids and Merinids in Morocco	1220–1269
Capture of Marakish Extinction of Muwahhid Empire Commencement of Beni Merin rule	1269
Crusade of St. Louis against Tunis	1270
Death of Al Mustansir of Tunis Collapse of Hafsid power	1277
Abu Yusuf Yaqoob of Beni Merin invades Spain	1275, 1277, 1282 and 1285
Death of Abu Yusuf Yaqoob Succession of his son Yusuf	1286
Murder of Sultan Yusuf	1307
Defeat of Castilian army outside Granada Death of the Regent Don Pedro	1319
Defeat of Abu al Hasan Ali the Merinid at the Rio Salado End of Berber intervention in Spain	1340
Capture of Tunis by Abu al Hasan Ali the Merinid	1347
Decline of Beni Merin	1372–1465
Second period of Hafsid power in Tunis	1370–1488
Marriage of Ferdinand and Isabella	1469
Fall of Granada	1492

[8] Hitti, *History of the Arabs*.

BENI N

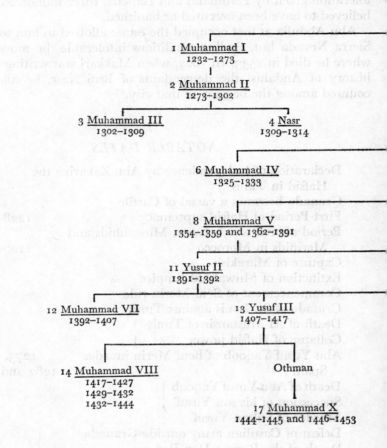

1 Muhammad I
1232–1273

2 Muhammad II
1273–1302

3 Muhammad III
1302–1309

4 Nasr
1309–1314

6 Muhammad IV
1325–1333

8 Muhammad V
1354–1359 and 1362–1391

11 Yusuf II
1391–1392

12 Muhammad VII
1392–1407

13 Yusuf III
1407–1417

14 Muhammad VIII
1417–1427
1429–1432
1432–1444

Othman

17 Muhammad X
1444–1445 and 1446–1453

NOTE

It will be seen once again that the reigns grew sh
as the dynasty became decadent. First hundred y
1232–1333, seven reigns. Second hundred years, 1
1432, twelve reigns. It will be noted that many rei

NADA

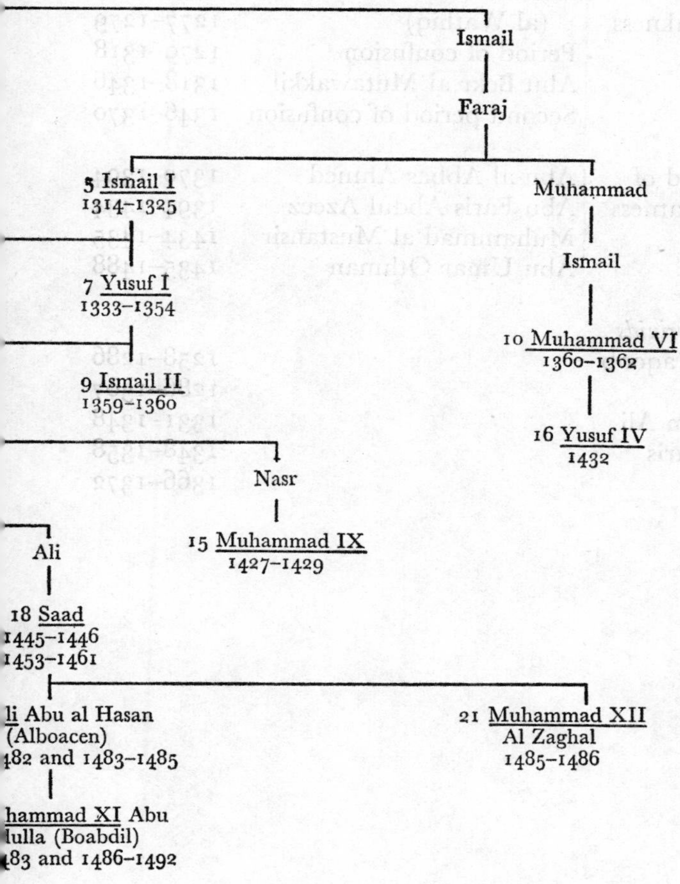

and one three times. This of course indicates
nt upheavals. A sultan is dethroned and another
his place. Then the original one overthrows his
or and returns and so on.

PERSONALITIES

The Hafsids of Tunis

First period of Hafsid greatness	Abu Zakariya Yahya I	1228–1249
	Muhammad al Mustansir	1249–1277
Period of Hafsid weakness	Abu Zakariya Yahya II (al Wathiq)	1277–1279
	Period of confusion	1279–1318
	Abu Bekr al Mutawakkil	1318–1346
	Second period of confusion	1346–1370
Second period of Hafsid greatness	Abu al Abbas Ahmed	1370–1394
	Abu Faris Abdul Azeez	1394–1434
	Muhammad al Mustansir	1434–1435
	Abu Umar Othman	1435–1488

The Great Merinids

Abu Yusuf Yaqoob	1258–1286
Yusuf	1286–1307
Abu al Hasan Ali	1331–1348
Abu Inan Faris	1348–1358
Abdul Azeez	1366–1372

XVII

The Lords of Misrule

1302–1400

O God, the heathen are come into thine inheritance. The dead bodies of thy servants have they given to be meat unto the fowls of the air: and the flesh of thy saints unto the beasts of the land. Their blood have they shed like water and there was no man to bury them. O remember not our old sins but have mercy upon us and that soon, for we are come to great misery. *Psalm LXXIX*

Government, even in its best state, is but a necessary evil; in its worst state, an intolerable one. TOM PAINE, *Common Sense*

After the conquest, the Mongols treated as slaves the feeble débris of the conquered nations and caused to writhe under an execrable tyranny those who had escaped the sword. Their government was the triumph of depravity. The history of the Mongols presents a hideous picture, but being intimately connected with that of several other empires, it is necessary in order to understand the great events of the thirteenth and fourteenth centuries.

BARON D'OHSSON, *History of the Mongols*

XVII

As a result of disturbances in Upper Egypt in 1302, a punitive campaign was undertaken against the Arab tribes of the Upper Nile. Whereas the inhabitants of the Nile delta were probably in general the descendants of the Egyptians of the Pharaohs, nomadic tribes from Arabia proper had at intervals migrated over the Sinai Peninsula and spread themselves over both sides of the Nile farther south.

The Ameers Salar and Baybers, the regents, both accompanied the army, neither trusting the other to act alone. Every male encountered was killed, sixteen thousand of them by disembowelling, while the throats of the remainder were cut. The whole countryside reeked of unburied corpses. The women were carried off as slaves. These operations were not conducted against an enemy government but against the Muslim subjects of Egypt who had been guilty of breaches of the peace.

The vicissitudes of the word Arab are worthy of note. Before Islam, it meant nomadic tribes. For three or four centuries after the great conquests, the word Arab became a glorious appellation to which the many subject nations ardently aspired. By the thirteenth century, it was again a term applied to nomadic tribes as opposed to townsmen. "If an Arab pretended to be a townsman," writes Maqrizi of these operations, "he was told to say the word *daqiq*. If he pronounced it in the Arab way, he was killed." In the twentieth century the name Arab was resuscitated to do duty for townsmen and tribesmen alike.

* * *

In February 1303, the Il Khan Ghazan decided to make another attempt to conquer Syria. This time, however, he did not go in person but sent an army commanded by a certain Qutlugh Shah who, by-passing Damascus, reached Kiswa, a few miles south of the city on 19th April, 1303.[1] Once more panic swept Damascus, many abandoning their homes to hide in the mountains. Those who could not escape spent their days weeping in the mosques and imploring divine protection.

The battle of Marj al Suffar began on the morning of 20th April, 1303, and desperate fighting continued all day without a decision. The young Sultan Al Nasir spent the night on horseback, rallying the stragglers. Mamlook bands of trumpets, cymbals and drums continued to play all night to raise morale.

On the second day the battle was renewed but again without any positive result. The Mongols, who held a ridge of high ground without water, suffered intensely from thirst. The Mamlooks were on lower

[1] Map 38, page 327.

ground but a stream ran through their position. On the third morning the Mongols attacked once again although they were desperately thirsty. Either the Mamlooks were driven back or they deliberately retired, and the Tatars reached the stream. Tormented by thirst, they broke their ranks to drink and the Mamlooks seized the opportunity to deliver a general counter-attack which the disorganized enemy was unable to resist. The victory was complete and the Mongols evacuated Syria in some disorder. The issue had long hung in doubt and the Mongols would probably have been victorious if Ghazan had been present.

Next morning the young Al Nasir rode into Damascus surrounded by an immense crowd consisting of cavalry, of country people, of local notables, of returning refugees and of women and children. Many, with the tears streaming down their cheeks, were crying out praises to God and calling down blessings on the young sultan. The drums were beating, the people crying and the whole scene was one which those who saw it were never to forget.

On 19th June, 1303, the sultan arrived back in Cairo. The city had been splendidly decorated and the streets spread with silk carpets. Large sums of money had been paid for the hire of roofs and windows overlooking the route of the procession. At the head of the parade marched a thousand men holding lances on each of which the head of a Tatar had been transfixed. Next came six hundred Mongol prisoners, each with the severed head of one of his comrades hung round his neck. Behind them in turn were carried the banners and drums captured from the enemy, torn and dragged in the dust.

Ghazan Khan was profoundly distressed by this disaster. A few months later, in October 1303, he fell ill, and died on the evening of 17th May, 1304. The Il Khans were never again to invade Syria.

* * *

Ghazan achieved little success against the Mamlooks but the efforts he devoted to the administration were more effective. Unlike most of his predecessors, who passed their lives in hunting and drinking, he was familiar with every branch of the government. Eighty years of Mongol misrule had reduced Persia and Iraq to a desert. The taxes were farmed out to contractors who extorted four or five times the sums due. In many cases the cultivators, unable to pay, abandoned their lands and became bandits or beggars.

Ghazan's reforms have a surprisingly modern sound. He commenced by ordering a complete survey of each district and an assessment of the taxes due from it. A period was then allowed for appeals which were heard in his own court. When the final assessment was fixed, a master copy of the survey was filed in the capital, after which each taxpayer was notified of his liability and warned not to pay more. For the first time since Jenghis Khan the government took action to repair irrigation canals and land owners were notified that unless they cultivated their farms they would be deprived of them.

Incredible as it may seem, ever since Jenghis Khan the Mongol army had never been paid, but had lived solely on plundering the civil population. Ghazan endeavoured to allocate certain revenues for the regular payment of the troops.

Ghazan's reforms served to highlight the intense misery which had existed since Jenghis Khan, especially when we remember that Persia had been one of the most prosperous and the most cultured nations in the world. Great and wealthy cities had dotted the country, adorned with universities, hospitals, libraries and schools. It is terrifying to think how low a great and civilized nation can fall when it abandons the power to defend itself.

Ghazan's mental versatility was surprising. An enthusiastic astronomer, a keen chemist and botanist, an experienced soldier, he was familiar with every detail of the law, finances and administration of his country. He was an accomplished linguist, and spoke not only his native Mongol but also Arabic, Persian, Indian and Chinese. A keen student of history, he surprised foreign ambassadors by his knowledge of the history of their various countries.

"Young and old," writes Rasheed al Deen, his court physician and historian, "senior and junior officers, obeyed his orders with alacrity. They did this without reluctance because they realized the superiority of his spirit and the wisdom which inspired his actions."

After his conversion he became a genuine Muslim but he soon abandoned religious persecution and returned to the traditional Mongol toleration. In foreign affairs he adhered to the policy of Hulagu, namely hostility to Egypt and friendship with the Christian West. He corresponded with the Byzantine Emperor, Andronicus II Palaeologus, with Philippe le Bel, King of France, and with Edward I, King of England.

In appearance he was a typical Mongol, short and sallow-complexioned. With a will of iron, he could be implacable with his enemies and could use patience and guile to achieve his aims. Yet he had a genuine feeling and sympathy for the common people. The whole country went into mourning for this extraordinary man when he died, and soldiers and civilians alike followed his bier weeping.

* * *

Ghazan's brother, Oljaitu, was elected Il Khan on 21st July, 1304.[2] He appointed Rasheed al Deen, Ghazan's physician, as his wazeer

[2] Genealogical tree, page 274.

with orders to continue the same policies. On 24th July, 1305, Oljaitu laid the foundation of a new capital on the rolling plains of Adharbaijan. He called it Sultaniya, the city of the sultan. In addition to a palace for himself, he built there several mosques, a free hospital and a university in imitation of the former Abbasid institutions in Baghdad, which his great-grandfather Hulagu had taken so much trouble to obliterate. On 14th April, 1306, the wazeer Rasheed al Deen presented to Oljaitu his monumental work entitled *The Historical Collection*,[3] which is still in our hands today.

Unlike Ghazan, Oljaitu was incapable of personally supervising the administration of the finances, a task abandoned by him to the wazeer. This led to desperate intrigues, slanders and bribery between rival Persian aspirants to office and to the resulting wealth.

Oljaitu died on 19th December, 1316, after a reign of twelve years. His death is said to have been caused by indigestion and gout caused by too much eating and drinking, for he was only thirty-six years old. He was generous and good-natured but of rather meagre capacity. He was succeeded by his thirteen-year-old son, Abu Saeed, who was acclaimed Il Khan in April 1317. The Mongol Prince Choban acted as regent. In July 1318, the great historian and wazeer Rasheed al Deen was finally overthrown by his Persian rival, Ali Shah. His overthrow was not accomplished by a popular vote but by persuading the Mongol princes that the wazeer was stealing too much money. His rival, once in office, of course did the same. Rasheed was cut in half at the waist and all his wealth confiscated.

The years 1319 and 1320 were disastrous for Persia owing to droughts, locusts and fresh Jagatai invasions. The Il Khan Abu Saeed, now sixteen years old, summoned the Muslim qadhis to explain the reason for the public misfortunes. The qadhis, who were Persians, doubtless obtained some satisfaction by attributing these disasters to Divine displeasure at the misrule of the Mongols. In atonement for these misdeeds, the young khan ordered the closure of all wine-shops and brothels and the banishment of singing and dancing girls. When the Mamlook Sultan Al Nasir of Egypt, the champion of Islam, heard of these pious actions among the "heathen" Mongols, he hastened to direct that similar measures be adopted in Egypt.

In 1327, the Il Khan Abu Saeed was twenty-three years old but Prince Choban showed no signs of abandoning his authority as regent. In a *coup d'état* planned by the young khan himself, Choban and his two sons were killed and Abu Saeed assumed the reins of government. He was not, however, destined to enjoy peace, for fresh rebellions broke out in 1329 and continued throughout his reign. In the autumn

[3] Rasheed al Deen, *Jama i Tuvarikh.*

of 1334, the young Il Khan fell ill and died on 30th November at the age of thirty. Abu Saeed had been intelligent, generous, well-educated, wrote a beautiful hand, played on the lute and composed music.

As we have seen was the case with so many barbarian successor states, the Il Khans collapsed after the fifth generation from the original conqueror. The founder of the dynasty was Hulagu, the blood-thirsty fighter. Abagha was the second generation, Arghoon the third, a keen administrator, Ghazan the ideal ruler and Abu Saeed, the fifth, well educated and musical, but unable to keep order. The Berber dynasties of Africa followed the same course.

The endless rebellions which followed one another during the seventeen years of the reign of Abu Saeed were not the desperate risings of the conquered Persians, Turks or Armenians. The spirit of these races had been completely crushed. The revolts were all the work of Mongol princes or soldiers whose standards of loyalty and duty had been sapped by a long period of wealth, power and luxury. Their constant rebellions may be contrasted with the attitude of Kitbugha, the Mongol commander killed after the Spring of Goliath, who expressed himself ready to die in carrying out his duty to Hulagu.

Abu Saeed left no children and with him the rule of the Il Khans came to an end. Two shadowy claimants, Arpa and Musa, endeavoured to seize the throne in 1335 and 1336 but without success. Then, for fifty years, Persia, the Jezira and Iraq fell into complete anarchy. The condition of these countries during the fifty years from 1334 to 1384 can perhaps best be described in the words of Baron d'Ohsson.[4] "Rival parties," he writes, "supported the interests of different princes, whom they wished to place upon the throne that they might dominate the country in their name. Intrigue, deceit, perjury, defections, treacheries, bloody encounters between rival hordes who were endlessly slaughtering one another in the interest of ambitious chieftains; the pillaging of the towns, the laying waste of the countryside, the destruction of the products of industry whenever it struggled to produce anything—total war against civilization: these are the outstanding characteristics recorded of these barbarous peoples."

It is perhaps worthy of notice, however, that even during this period, and indeed throughout the duration of the Il Khanate, literary activity continued in Persia. We have seen the same phenomenon among the Arabs of Syria and with those of Andalus under the Berber dynasties. Here also perhaps a pattern emerges. When a great nation falls into decadence, it is conquered by a more virile race, but the original people still for several centuries may retain their cultural pre-eminence although they have become politically a subject race. The fifty years of

[4] Baron d'Ohsson, *A History of the Mongols*.

anarchy which followed the death of Abu Saeed in 1334 were to be terminated by the invasion of Tamerlane in a welter of slaughter and destruction. It is a matter for opinion whether or not such a cure for anarchy was not worse than the disease.

While it would be tedious to recount the endless vicissitudes of the fifty years of Persian confusion from 1335 to 1385, five of the resulting minor dynasties may be briefly mentioned. The most important share of the Il Khan dominions fell to Shaikh Hasan Buzurg, of the Jalair Mongols. From 1336 to 1341, Hasan maintained a succession of three puppet Il Khans but thereafter he ruled in his own name, establishing his capital in Baghdad. In 1356, his son and successor Uwais annexed Adharbaijan, Mosul and a great part of the Jezira, thereby achieving a considerable territory. Uwais died in 1374, leaving Iraq and Adharbaijan to his sons, first Husain, then Ahmed, whom we shall meet again in connection with the invasion of Tamerlane.

During the reign of Abu Saeed, a certain Ameer Muzaffar had been governor of a town in Fars. His son became governor of all Fars and in 1340, after the death of Abu Saeed, declared himself independent and annexed Isfahan. His sons quarrelled among themselves and eventually succumbed to Tamerlane as we shall see below.

The third dynasty was that of the Kerts, who had been princes of Herat in what is now Afghanistan ever since 1245, having weathered the storms of Mongol violence, partly by diplomacy and partly by the reputation of Herat for impregnability. Fakhr al Deen Kert, the ruling prince of the time, had gained the favour of Ghazan. This dynasty also was to be exterminated by Tamerlane in 1381. (See tree, page 377.)

The fourth successor dynasty did not emerge until 1378, forty-two years after the end of the Il Khans. They were a Turkman tribe called the Qara Qoyounlou or Black Sheep, for they bore a black sheep on their war banner. They established their capital in Van. Their most famous chief was Qara Yusuf, or Black Joseph, of whom we shall hear more.

The fifth petty dynasty which arose during the fifty years of anarchy in Persia were likewise Turkmans and were known as the Ak Qoyounlou or White Sheep. Their headquarters were in Diyarbekr and they were at deadly enmity with the Black Sheep.

* * *

We left India in 1223 when Iltutmish, the Mamlook Sultan of Delhi, refused help to Jalal al Deen Khuwarizm Shah, for fear of offending Jenghis Khan, thereby perhaps saving India from the fate of Persia. Iltutmish ruled northern India for twenty-five years from 1211 to 1236. His death was followed by ten years of instability. Eventually,

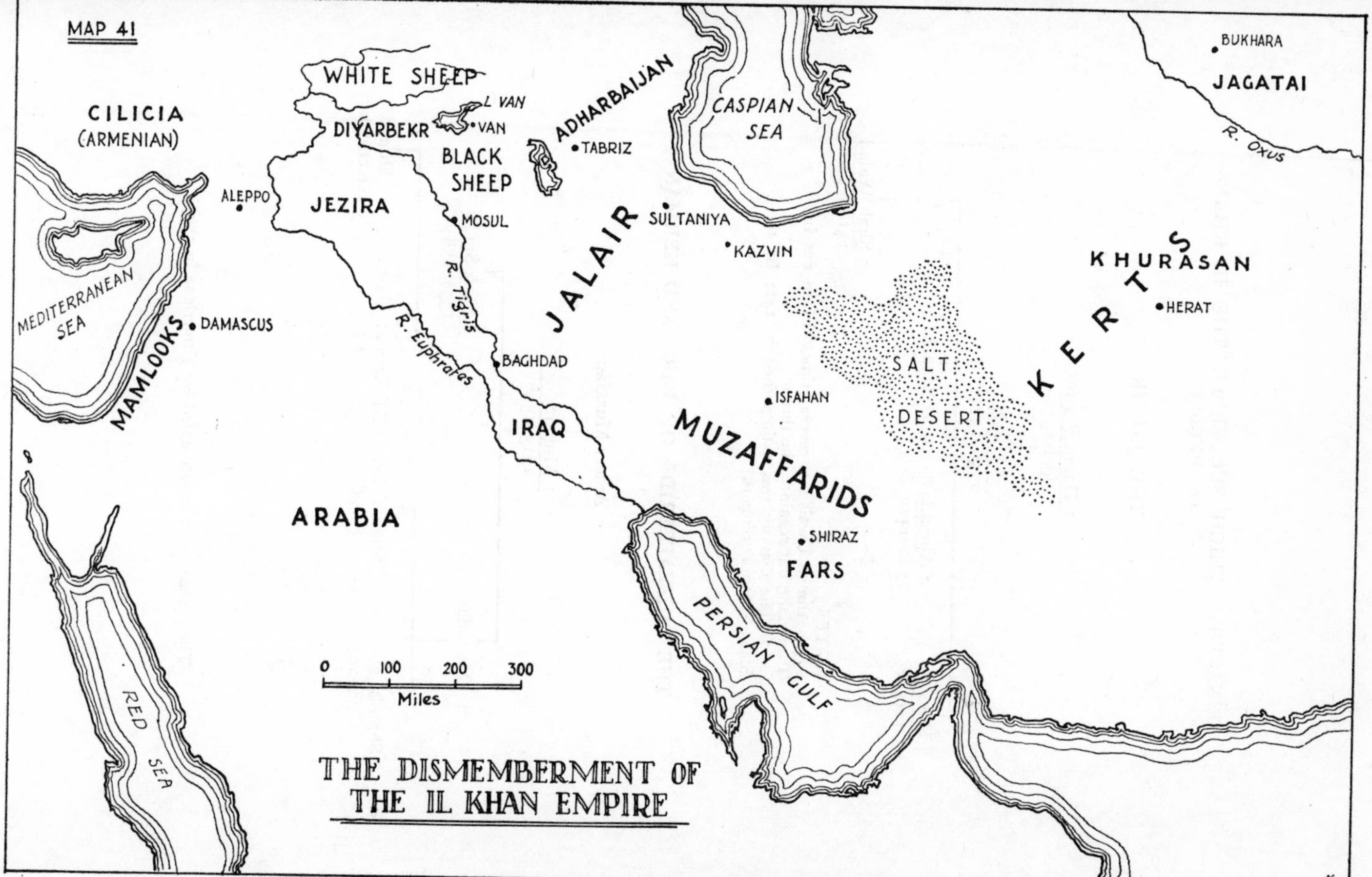
MAP 41
CILICIA
(ARMENIAN)
WHITE SHEEP
L VAN
VAN
DIYARBEKR
BLACK
SHEEP
ADHARBAIJAN
TABRIZ
CASPIAN
SEA
BUKHARA
JAGATAI
R. Oxus
ALEPPO
JEZIRA
MOSUL
JALAIR
SULTANIYA
KAZVIN
KHURASAN
HERAT
KERTS
MEDITERRANEAN
SEA
DAMASCUS
MAMLOOKS
R. Tigris
R. Euphrates
BAGHDAD
SALT
DESERT
ISFAHAN
IRAQ
MUZAFFARIDS
ARABIA
SHIRAZ
FARS
PERSIAN
GULF
RED
SEA
0
100
200
300
Miles
THE DISMEMBERMENT OF
THE IL KHAN EMPIRE

DYNASTIES WHICH SUCCEEDED THE IL KHANS IN PERSIA

THE JALAIR

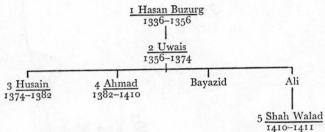

- 1 Hasan Buzurg 1336–1356
  - 2 Uwais 1356–1374
    - 3 Husain 1374–1382
    - 4 Ahmad 1382–1410
    - Bayazid
    - Ali
      - 5 Shah Walad 1410–1411

NOTES

(1) Ahmad Uwais was several times driven out by Tamerlane but regained the throne.

(2) The dynasty was extinguished in 1411 by the Black Sheep Turkmans.

THE MUZZAFFARIDS OF FARS AND KERMAN

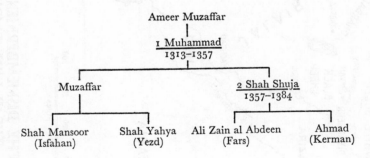

- Ameer Muzaffar
  - 1 Muhammad 1313–1357
    - Muzaffar
      - Shah Mansoor (Isfahan)
      - Shah Yahya (Yezd)
    - 2 Shah Shuja 1357–1384
      - Ali Zain al Abdeen (Fars)
      - Ahmad (Kerman)

The dynasty was exterminated by Tamerlane in 1393.

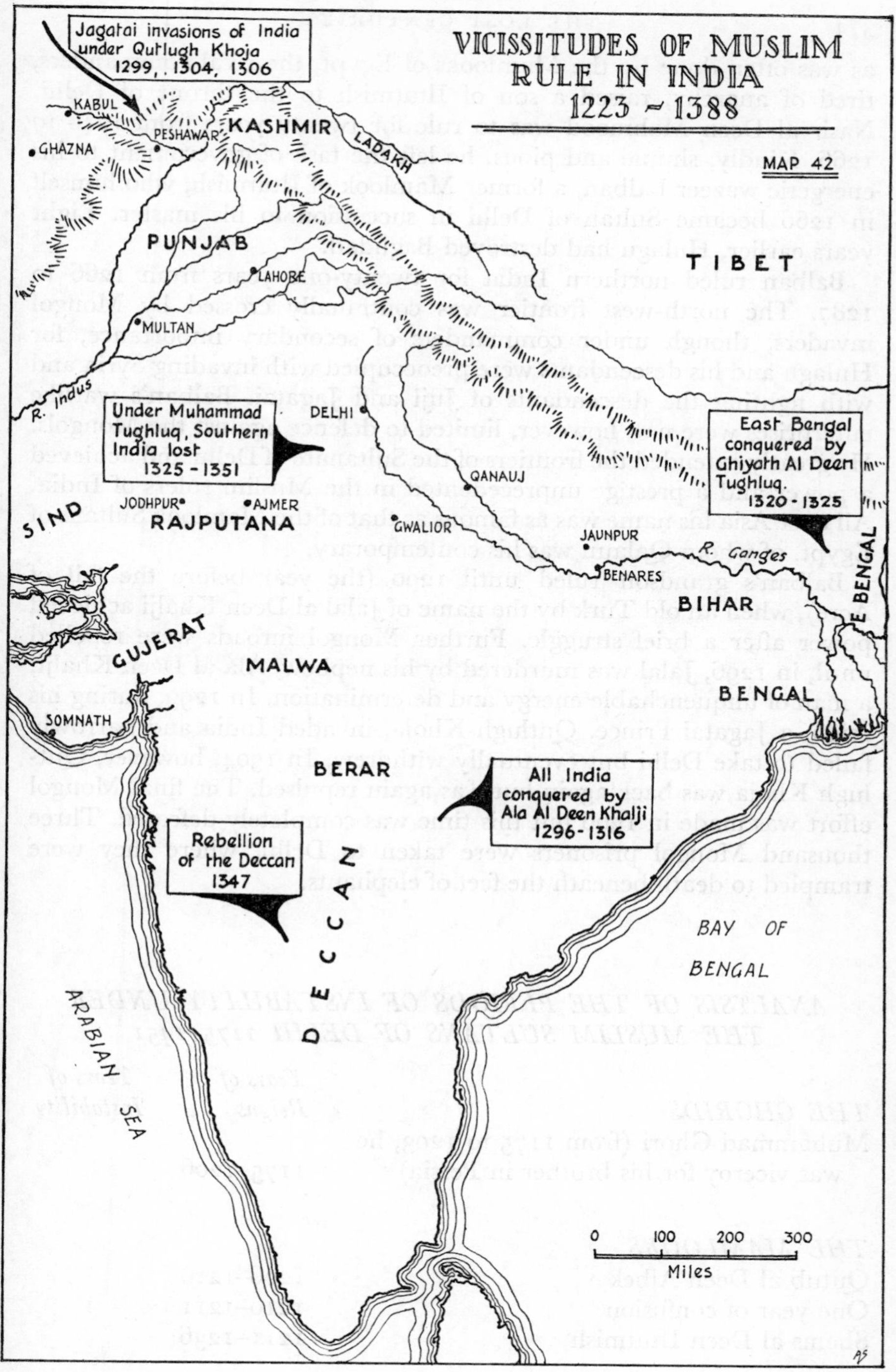
VICISSITUDES OF MUSLIM RULE IN INDIA 1223 – 1388
MAP 42
Jagatai invasions of India under Qutlugh Khoja 1299, 1304, 1306
KABUL
PESHAWAR
GHAZNA
KASHMIR
LADAKH
PUNJAB
LAHORE
MULTAN
R. Indus
TIBET
Under Muhammad Tughluq, Southern India lost 1325 - 1351
DELHI
East Bengal conquered by Ghiyath Al Deen Tughluq. 1320 - 1325
QANAUJ
SIND
JODHPUR
AJMER
RAJPUTANA
GWALIOR
JAUNPUR
R. Ganges
BENARES
E. BENGAL
BIHAR
GUJERAT
MALWA
BENGAL
SOMNATH
BERAR
All India conquered by Ala Al Deen Khalji 1296 - 1316
Rebellion of the Deccan 1347
DECCAN
BAY OF BENGAL
ARABIAN SEA
0
100
200
300
Miles
AS

as was often done by the Mamlooks of Egypt, the rival commanders, tired of anarchy, raised a son of Iltutmish to the throne of Delhi. Nasir al Deen Mahmood was to rule for twenty years from 1246 to 1266. Kindly, simple and pious, he left the task of government to his energetic wazeer Balban, a former Mamlook of Iltutmish, who himself in 1266 became Sultan of Delhi in succession to his master. Eight years earlier, Hulagu had destroyed Baghdad.

Balban ruled northern India for twenty-one years from 1266 to 1287. The north-west frontier was continually crossed by Mongol invaders, though under commanders of secondary importance, for Hulagu and his descendants were preoccupied with invading Syria and with fighting the descendants of Juji and Jagatai. Balban's warlike enterprises were not, however, limited to defence against the Mongols. He greatly extended the frontiers of the Sultanate of Delhi and achieved a power and a prestige unprecedented in the Muslim rulers of India. All over Asia his name was as famous as that of the Mamlook Sultans of Egypt, of whom Qalaun was his contemporary.

Balban's grandson ruled until 1290 (the year before the fall of Acre), when an old Turk by the name of Jalal al Deen Khalji achieved power after a brief struggle. Further Mongol inroads were repelled until, in 1296, Jalal was murdered by his nephew, Ala al Deen Khalji, a man of unquenchable energy and determination. In 1299, during his reign, a Jagatai Prince, Qutlugh Khoja, invaded India and narrowly failed to take Delhi but eventually withdrew. In 1304, however, Qutlugh Khoja was back again but was again repulsed. The final Mongol effort was made in 1306 but this time was completely defeated. Three thousand Mongol prisoners were taken to Delhi, where they were trampled to death beneath the feet of elephants.

ANALYSIS OF THE PERIODS OF INSTABILITY UNDER THE MUSLIM SULTANS OF DELHI 1175–1451

	Years of Reigns	*Years of Instability*
THE GHORIDS		
Muhammad Ghori (from 1175 to 1203, he was viceroy for his brother in Persia)	1175–1206	
THE MAMLOOKS		
Qutub al Deen Aibek	1206–1210	
One year of confusion	1210–1211	1
Shems al Deen Iltutmish	1211–1236	

Rukn al Deen Firuz Shah		1236	
Sultana Raziya	Period of Instability	1236–1239	10
Muizz al Deen Bahram Shah		1239–1241	
Ala al Deen Masood Shah		1242–1246	
Nasir al Deen Mahmood Shah (son of Iltutmish)		1246–1266	
Ghiyath al Deen Balban		1266–1287	
Muizz al Deen Kai Qobad (Grandson of Balban)		1287–1290	3
Period of Instability			
THE KHALJIS			
Jalal al Deen Firuz Shah		1290–1295	
Ala al Deen Muhammad Shah (nephew of Firuz)		1296–1316	
Shihab al Deen Umar Shah (son of Ala al Deen)		1315–1316	
Qutb al Deen Mubarak Shah (son of Ala al Deen)		1316–1320	4
Nasir al Deen Khosrou Shah (servant of Mubarak)		1320	
THE TUGHLUQS			
Ghiyath al Deen Tughluq Shah		1320–1325	
Muhammad Shah Tughluq (son & murderer of Ghiyath al Deen)		1325–1351	
Firuz Shah Tughluq		1351–1388	
Tughluq, Abu Bekr, Muhammad, Iskander	Four years' instability	1388–1392	4
Nasir al Deen Mahmood (grandson of Firuz Shah)		1392–1398	
Invasion of Tamerlane followed by period of anarchy		1398–1399	
Nasir al Deen Mahmood (second reign)		1399–1412	—
			22
THE SAYIDS			
(Arabs of the family of Muhammad)			
Saiyid Khidhr Khan (Tamerlane's nominee)		1414–1421	
The Saiyids continued to rule until 1451			

It was one of the remarkable features of the Mongol conquests that, eighty years after Jenghis Khan, they were still repeatedly attacking both Egypt and India, undeterred by constant lack of success. Many other barbarian conquerors have appeared in these pages but all, on the completion of their conquests, settled down to enjoy the wealth and luxury which they had won. Perhaps the reluctance of the Mongols to become sedentary may be attributed to the fact that in conquering other countries they had simultaneously destroyed them and found themselves starving in a desert of their own creation. Is it possible that Jenghis Khan foresaw this result and deliberately laid waste the conquered countries to ensure that his Mongols remained nomadic and warlike?

Ala al Deen Khalji ruled for twenty years during which he conquered the whole of India. Like Ghazan, his contemporary in Persia, he gave his personal attention to every detail of the administration. He reorganized the system of taxation, regularized the pay of the army, forbade the drinking of alcohol, fixed the prices of foodstuffs and above all maintained public security. He died in January 1316, the year before Abu Saeed became Il Khan. He left the Muslim Empire in India as one of the world's greatest states.

The death of Ala al Deen Khalji was followed by four years of confusion. In 1320, however, Ghiyath al Deen Tughluq became sultan, the authority of Delhi was re-asserted and East Bengal—now East Pakistan—was added to the empire. In 1325, when he had reigned for only five years, he was murdered by his son Muhammad Tughluq, who was to rule for twenty-six years. At the beginning of his reign, he further consolidated his father's vast dominions but in his later years the more distant dependencies began to fall away. He was a man of remarkable intellect yet so erratic as at times to appear mentally unbalanced.

The last years of the reign of Muhammad Tughluq were a period of almost unalloyed misfortune. His cruelty had alienated nearly all his subjects. An insane campaign against Tibet ended in unmitigated disaster. Bengal revolted and declared its independence, after which the whole of southern India broke away and re-established Hindu kings. In 1347, the Deccan rebelled and became an independent kingdom under the Muslim Bahmani dynasty. When Muhammad Tughluq died in 1351, his dominions had been reduced to the Kingdom of Delhi alone.

He was succeeded on the throne by his cousin Firuz Shah Tughluq, the son of a Muslim father and a Rajput princess. Kindly, easy-going and incapable, he gave the Delhi Kingdom thirty-seven years of rest after the violence, restlessness and cruelty of Muhammad Tughluq.

THE KERTS OF HERAT

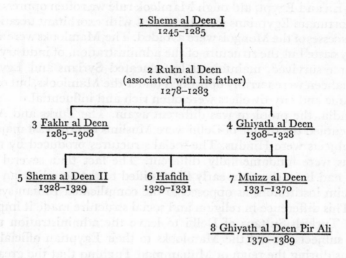

1 Shems al Deen I
1245–1285

2 Rukn al Deen
(associated with his father)
1278–1283

3 Fakhr al Deen
1285–1308

4 Ghiyath al Deen
1308–1328

5 Shems al Deen II
1328–1329

6 Hafidh
1329–1331

7 Muizz al Deen
1331–1370

8 Ghiyath al Deen Pir Ali
1370–1389

The dynasty was exterminated by Tamerlane.

He remitted many of the exorbitant taxes imposed by his predecessor and encouraged agricultural production. But his weakness further reduced the prestige of the throne and, when he died in 1388, the Kingdom of Delhi fell into complete anarchy, offering a tempting bait to Tamerlane, whose invasion of India in 1398 will be related in a later chapter.

* * *

Three main territories had been conquered by the nomads of Central Asia, whether Turks or Mongols, and in each case the result had been different. In Persia, prosperity, culture, civilization itself, had been virtually destroyed and to this day have never recovered.

In Syria and Egypt, although Mamlook rule was often oppressive and the unfortunate Egyptians were burdened with exorbitant taxation, the worst excesses of the Mongols were avoided. The Mamlooks were a ruling military caste but the structure of the administration, of industry and of commerce survived, maintained by educated Syrians and Egyptians. The fellaheen were terribly oppressed under the Mamlooks, but officials, merchants and city-dwellers were often rich and influential.

In India, the problem was different again. The Turks and Afghans who occupied the throne of Delhi were Muslims but the vast majority of their subjects were Hindus. The social structures produced by the two religions were fundamentally different. The fact that several of the sultans had been slaves in early life testified to the equalitarian nature of Muslim institutions as opposed to the complicated Indian system of caste. This difference in religion and social structure made it impossible for the Turkish Sultans of Delhi to leave the administration to their Hindu subjects, as did the Mamlooks to their Egyptian officials.

It was during the reign of Muhammad Tughluq that the great Arab traveller Ibn Battuta visited the court of Delhi. He notes that the officials employed by the Sultan of Delhi were in many cases Muslim Turks, Arabs or Persians. Although the Persians and the Arabs had long since lost their political independence in their own countries, they still retained their educational and cultural pre-eminence and continued to be in demand as administrators and technicians in other countries. In spite of the fact that Muhammad Tughluq was in theory Sultan of all India, the roads, according to Ibn Battuta, were often unsafe owing to the activities of Hindu bandits.

Many of the Turkish Sultans of Delhi, like the Mamlooks of Egypt, were great men and fine soldiers but they failed to establish a stable Muslim régime. Their stormy reigns were passed on the one hand in suppressing rebellions in India, on the other in repulsing Mongol invasions. They may thus have saved India from the fearful devastation which ruined Persia but, owing to the difference of religion, they failed to secure the loyalty and gratitude of their subjects as the Mamlooks succeeded, to a considerable extent, in doing in Egypt and Syria.

* * *

It is curious that, in our own time, a great deal of discussion occurs regarding the political constitutions of different countries, principally as to whether or not they permit the people free expression of their views. The question whether any particular system is capable of raising the most suitable persons to the highest rank in the government rarely gives rise to controversy. Yet a review of the presidents and prime ministers produced in the Western democracies during the last fifty years reveals the fact that, except in occasional moments of crisis, the majority of them have been mediocrities.

In the fourteenth century, three of the greatest empires in the world were ruled by Turko-Mongol nomads from the steppes of Asia. It is interesting to notice the widely differing systems which they adopted in order to solve this problem of the selection of the most capable men to rule.

So great had been the prestige of Jenghis Khan that the rule of his descendants—the Golden Family—was accepted without question for more than a century in every country which he had conquered. Yet, as we have seen, the right of selection was exercised by the grand council or quriltai, which frequently neglected the wishes of the late king. The disadvantages of hereditary rule are obvious; the king's eldest son may be incapable. Curiously enough, it was Europe which adhered to primogeniture and thus risked an incapable monarch. The Arab and the Mongol systems alike mitigated this danger by departing from strict primogeniture and choosing as the new ruler the most capable member of the ruling family. To ensure a suitable ruler, they ran the risk of rival claimants, but these would at least be limited to the small group of the royal family. By not necessarily adhering to primogeniture, they avoided the danger of the succession of an imbecile eldest son.

The Mamlook system offered a complete contrast to that of the Mongols. The Mamlooks were bought as slave-boys and no one was interested in their genealogy. A Mamlook relied on his own efforts for his advancement, with the result that any man who rose to high rank was certain to be a man of outstanding courage and determination. Their military successes, indeed, can doubtless be largely attributed to the fact that every senior officer had fought his way to the top. War is the best military promotion examination.

But the very fact that all senior army officers were men of strong wills made the selection of the sultan all the more difficult. On the death of a ruler, a deadly struggle at times ensued to decide his successor. The advantages of the system can be readily seen in the case of the Mamlooks of Egypt. The principle that the throne belongs to him who can seize it can at times produce a succession of rulers of outstanding quality. No man of weak resolution or vacillating character can survive the gruelling test of such a struggle for power.

The disadvantage of the system lies in the risk of internal violence or even civil war after the death of one sultan before his successor emerges. When this period of disorder lasted only four or five days, the disorganization was no worse than that of a general election. But where the rival claimants were equally matched or when no outstanding personality was apparent, longer periods of disorder or even civil war might result. When such a deadlock appeared likely, the son of the previous sultan was sometimes raised to the throne, a subterfuge intended merely to gain time until the struggle for power enabled the next real sultan to emerge.

The effects of the system are less obvious in the case of the Sultans of Delhi than in that of the Mamlooks of Egypt, owing to the many extraneous factors involved in India. Yet even in the case of Delhi, the periods of anarchy do not appear to have been as long as might have been anticipated. An analysis of the years of instability has been included in the table of the Sultans of Delhi from 1175 to 1398, a period of two hundred and twenty-three years.[5] It would appear that, throughout the whole of this period, only twenty-two years of confusion occurred between reigns. When we remember that Europe suffered some eleven years of major wars in the fifty years from 1914 to 1964, these intervals of anarchy do not appear so outrageous.

These questions are, even today, by no means academic. The rulers of Russia since the revolution, for example, have been chosen by a struggle-for-power method. Probably more than half the executive rulers of the governments of the world today have been chosen by revolution, *coup d'état* or other form of struggle, not by the votes of the public.

It is curious that an age like our own, which rightly regards religious intolerance with dislike, should yet be so intolerant of other political systems. In Britain and the United States, impartial consideration of alternative methods of government is rendered almost impossible by popular prejudices. Even to refer to methods of choosing rulers other than our own is to elicit indignant accusations of communist, fascist, colonialist or other immoral leanings. In such an atmosphere, academic discussion is impossible.

[5] Page 374. The confusion created by Tamerlane after 1398 is not included in this calculation as being due to external invasion, not internal instability.

Human affairs are so intricate that didactic generalizations are always dangerous. While, therefore, we may be satisfied that our own system of government is well fitted to our people at this point of time, it is extremely doubtful whether we are justified in insisting that it is equally suitable to all the nations of the world today.

Historically, the selection of leaders by a struggle-for-power system has a distinguished record. It was the method frequently used in both the Roman and Byzantine Empires, and to some extent under the Arabs and their successors. Again and again in history, it produced splendid rulers who could never have emerged through universal suffrage. There is no Muslim ruler in the world today who has been chosen by universal suffrage, yet many of them are extremely popular.

People living under a Western democratic constitution are perhaps too inclined to believe that rulers who wield personal authority necessarily disregard the wishes of their people. I myself served in a government which included an elected parliament but in which the cabinet could not be brought down by a parliamentary defeat but only by an order from the sovereign. Constitutionally, the king was empowered to retain in office a government which had lost the support of the country. In fact, however, this never occurred for long. As soon as public dissatisfaction became obvious, the ruler dismissed the prime minister and chose another more acceptable to the people.

Ironically enough, under Western democracy, a government which has lost the confidence of the country can survive in power for several years until the constitution makes another election obligatory. Under the system to which I refer, this could not occur. The king would never have risked his popularity by retaining in office for two or three years an administration disliked by his subjects. Thus limited democracy, paradoxically enough, was able to follow popular opinion more closely than a full Western democracy. The only two countries in the world where I have known every single man to praise and thank the government were both Arab states with autocratic or semi-autocratic rulers.

The Mamlook system in Egypt seems to us at first sight one of the most abominable imaginable. A régime headed by former slaves, many of whom came to power by murdering their predecessors and under which the sultan imprisoned, tortured or executed his enemies without legal trial, may appear to have been as evil as any in history. Yet in fact the same pressures of public opinion operated then also. If a certain sultan ascended the throne but proved incapable, he was removed in a short time by some means or other. But when a really capable ruler emerged, he reigned uncontested until his death.

The Mamlook system, indeed, differed from those which we have been considering because the public opinion which made and unmade sultans was not primarily that of the Egyptian people but of the Mamlook ruling class. It is impossible, at this distance, to state with confidence how much influence was exerted by the opinion of the actual Egyptian public, but it was probably considerable. It may be significant that, as we shall see, Malik al Nasir Muhammad, who was extremely popular with the Egyptian masses, twice lost his throne but was re-instated and ultimately reigned for forty-one years. The Egyptians, at this stage, were the educated part of the population, and their influence behind the scenes may well have been stronger than it appeared on the surface.

NOTABLE DATES

Ala al Deen Khalji becomes Sultan of Delhi	1296
Jagatai invasions of India	1299–1306
Defeat of the Mongols at Marj al Suffar	20th April, 1303
Death of Ghazan Khan	17th May, 1304
Oljaitu elected Il Khan	21st July, 1304
Death of Ala al Deen Khalji All India united under Muslim rule	1316
Death of Il Khan Oljaitu	19th December, 1316
Election of Abu Saeed as Il Khan	April 1317
Accession of Ghiyath al Deen Tughluq, Sultan of Delhi	1320
Murder of Ghiyath al Deen Accession of Muhammad Tughluq	1325
Death of Il Khan Abu Saeed Disappearance of the Il Khanate	1334
Period of disintegration in Persia. Emergence of the Jalair dynasty in Baghdad, the Muzaffarids in Fars and the Kerts in Herat	1334–1384
Death of Muhammad Tughluq Disintegration of Muslim hegemony of all India	1351
Expulsion of the descendants of Qubilai from China Rise of the Chinese Ming dynasty	1370
Emergence of White Sheep Turkmans in the Jezira Emergence of the Black Sheep Turkmans in Van	1378
Death of Firuz Shah Tughluq Anarchy in the Kingdom of Delhi	1388

PERSONALITIES

Il Khans of Persia	
Ghazan	1295–1304
Oljaitu	1304–1316
Abu Saeed	1317–1334
Successors of the Il Khans	
Shaikh Hasan Buzurg (Jalair)	1336–1356
Muhammad Muzaffar	1313–1357
Muizz al Deen Kert	1331–1370
The Great Sultans of Delhi	
Mamlooks	
Iltutmish	1211–1236
Balban	1266–1287
Khaljis	
Ala al Deen Muhammad Khalji (United all India)	1296–1316
Tughluqs	
Ghiyath al Deen Tughluq	1320–1325
Muhammad Tughluq (lost southern India)	1325–1351

XVIII

The Victorious King
1303–1341

The long reign of Nasir was a golden age . . . He owed his long tenure of the precarious throne partly to his personal qualities. This self-possessed iron-willed man—absolutely despotic, ruling alone—physically insignificant, small of stature, lame of a foot, and with a cataract in the eye, with his plain dress and strict morals, his keen intellect and unwearied energy, his enlightened tastes and interests, his shrewd diplomacy degenerating into fruitless deceit, his unsleeping suspicion and cruel vengefulness, his superb court, his magnificent buildings—is one of the most remarkable characters of the Middle Ages. His reign was certainly the climax of Egyptian culture and civilization. STANLEY LANE POOLE, *The Story of Cairo*

Egypt, from 1260 to 1341, enjoyed . . . not only power and prestige, but also a high degree of prosperity. This was due to three things. Baybers I, Qalaun and al Malik al Nasir, were exceedingly capable and far-sighted rulers. In the second place the bureaucratic administration which Egypt had inherited from its Byzantine and Fatimid governors was in all probability the most efficient instrument which existed in the Middle Ages. Thirdly Egypt enjoyed almost a monopoly of the Indian trade. Under these circumstances the Mamluk sultans were able to maintain their authority against the Mongols in Syria and to extend it into Nubia and Anatolia.
H. A. R. GIBB, *Introduction to the Travels of Ibn Battuta* (abbreviated)

XVIII

WE left Egypt on 19th June, 1303, when the young Sultan Al Nasir made his triumphal entry into Cairo after the defeat of the Mongols at Marj al Suffar. All authority continued to be vested in the two regents, Salar and Baybers. The young sultan, however, was becoming increasingly resentful of this state of affairs. The regents never spoke to him of public business and, moreover, allowed him scarcely any pocket money.

In 1308, when Al Nasir was already twenty-two years old, he planned a *coup d'état* in which Salar and Baybers were to be arrested. But the regents were informed of the plot, which they forestalled by placing troops outside the sultan's apartments on the morning chosen for the *coup*. Al Nasir was popular with the Egyptian inhabitants of Cairo. A rumour having spread that he was being murdered by the regents, the shops closed and a large crowd collected shouting "O Nasir! O Victorious!" Eventually the crowd was calmed and persuaded to disperse. As soon as order was restored, the regents arrested a number of the sultan's intimates, depriving him of friends and advisers.

Soon afterwards, in the spring of 1309, Nasir announced his desire to perform a pilgrimage to Mecca. The regents agreed, thinking to dispose of the remainder of his adherents during his absence. In March 1309, he left for Mecca, the people lining the road to bid him farewell, weeping and praying to God for his safe return. The convoy proceeded to Kerak where it was to join the pilgrimage coming from Damascus. No sooner was Nasir inside the impregnable castle of Kerak than he sent a letter to Salar and Baybers informing them that he had abdicated and begging to be allowed to live in Kerak in peace. The letter produced alarm and anxiety in Cairo. Salar and Baybers had long been jealous of one another but as long as Al Nasir remained as titular sultan, they had maintained a precarious balance of power. Now a struggle became inevitable.

On 5th April, 1309, the principal Mamlook ameers assembled in Cairo and summoned the khalif and the religious qadhis to assist at the election of a new sultan. The majority of the ameers expressed their support for Salar, who was considered the more prudent and diplomatic of the two. It will be remembered that Sultan Qalaun had instituted the Tower Mamlooks, quartered in the citadel and largely recruited from Circassians, to offset the power of the River Mamlooks, who were predominantly Turks. Baybers the Jashnekeer was a

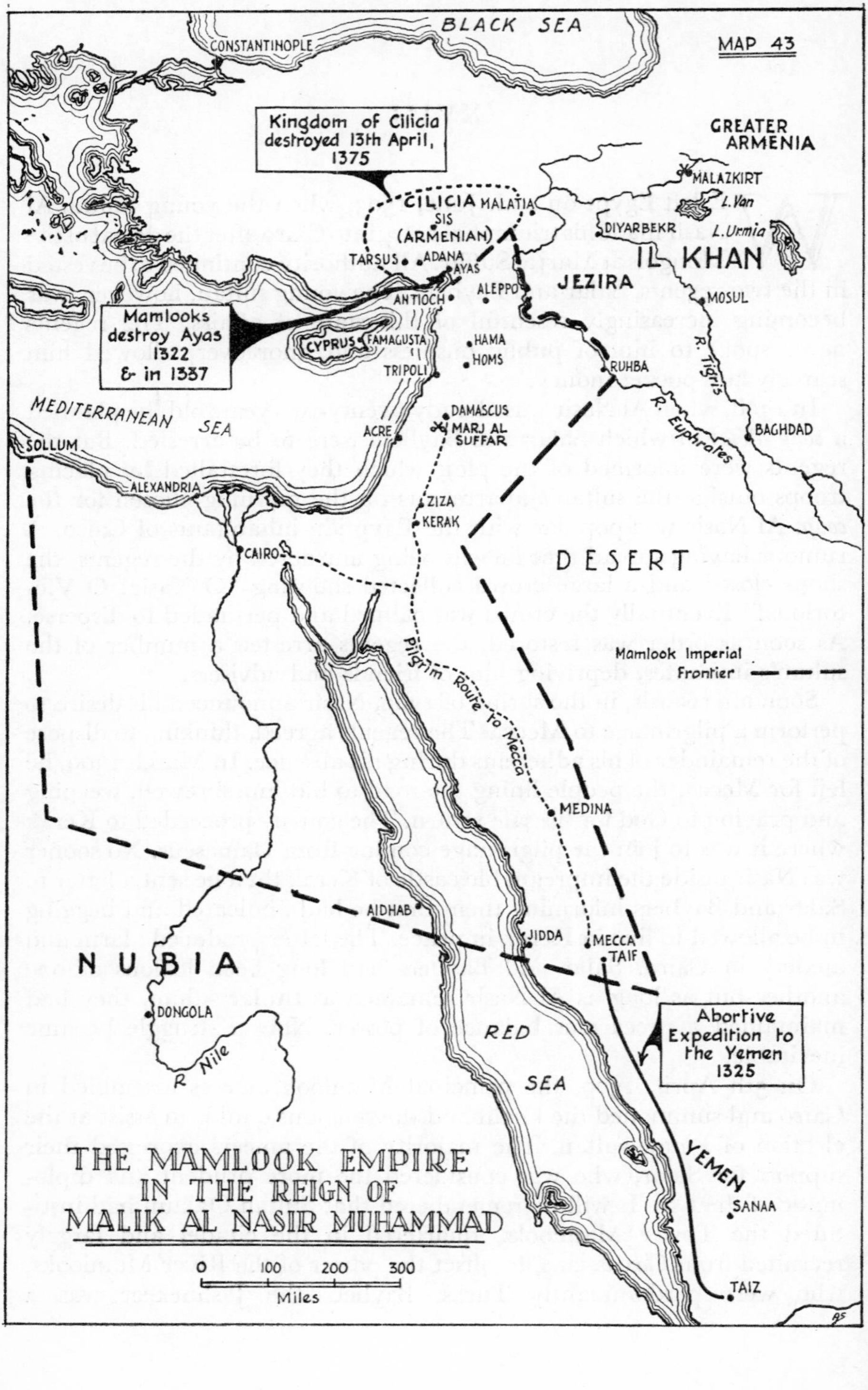
MAP 43
BLACK SEA
CONSTANTINOPLE
Kingdom of Cilicia destroyed 13th April, 1375
GREATER ARMENIA
MALAZKIRT
L. Van
L. Urmia
CILICIA
(ARMENIAN)
MALATIA
SIS
DIYARBEKR
IL KHAN
TARSUS
ADANA
AYAS
JEZIRA
ANTIOCH
ALEPPO
MOSUL
Mamlooks destroy Ayas 1322 & in 1337
CYPRUS
FAMAGUSTA
HAMA
HOMS
TRIPOLI
RUHBA
R. Tigris
MEDITERRANEAN
SEA
DAMASCUS
MARJ AL SUFFAR
R. Euphrates
BAGHDAD
SOLLUM
ACRE
ALEXANDRIA
ZIZA
KERAK
CAIRO
DESERT
Pilgrim Route to Mecca
Mamlook Imperial Frontier
MEDINA
AIDHAB
JIDDA
MECCA
TAIF
NUBIA
Abortive Expedition to the Yemen 1325
DONGOLA
RED
R. Nile
SEA
YEMEN
SANAA
0 100 200 300
Miles
TAIZ

THE MAMLOOK EMPIRE IN THE REIGN OF MALIK AL NASIR MUHAMMAD

Circassian, and the Tower Mamlooks had packed the hall to support his candidature. When the majority declared for Salar, the latter rose and said, "By God, gentlemen, I am not worthy of the throne. My brother here"—indicating Baybers—"is more capable of ruling."

It is not clear whether these words were a diplomatic expression of modesty or whether Salar was afraid of the Tower Mamlooks. In any case, no sooner were the words spoken than the Tower Mamlooks began to shout, "The ameer has spoken the truth." Then raising Baybers to his feet, they began cheering and calling his name. Mounting him hastily on a horse, they threw the coronation robes over his shoulders, girded him with the two ceremonial swords of state and set out in procession through the city. Salar, the ameers and the qadhis had no alternative but to fall in behind them. After riding through the city in state, Baybers mounted the throne and accepted the oaths of allegiance of the ameers.

In the autumn the Nile failed to rise, food prices soared and famine threatened. The common people attributed the public misfortunes to Divine displeasure at the unjust treatment suffered by Al Nasir. Baybers as a result became jealous and suspicious and sent emissaries to Kerak to deprive him of his money, weapons and horses. Al Nasir wrote to his friends to complain of the persecution to which he was subjected. In December 1309, sixty mamlooks deserted from Cairo and joined Al Nasir in Kerak, followed by a further hundred and twenty. Cairo was tense and Baybers made three hundred arrests. Then Al Nasir left Kerak and camped on the reservoir at Ziza on the road to Damascus, whence he wrote letters to the governors of the cities of Syria.

In early 1310, Al Nasir left Ziza for Damascus. The commanders of the garrison came out to meet him bringing with them the royal regalia, the parasol and the military standards. Amid wild enthusiasm, the youthful ex-sultan made his state entry into the gaily decorated streets of Damascus. On the 5th March, 1310, Al Nasir entered Cairo in a triumphal procession. Baybers had fled but was caught and executed. Shortly afterwards Salar also was arrested and starved to death in prison.

Salar was a typical Mongol, short, thick-set and of yellow complexion. He had been taken prisoner and brought to Cairo by Qalaun—another commentary on this extraordinary Mamlook system which raised its own ostensible enemies to the highest rank. Though he came to Cairo as a prisoner-of-war, Salar when he died was found to be the possessor of thirty million dinars in cash and an indescribable quantity of jewels, gold and silver plate, clothing, animals and slaves. Those who today consider race to be an essential barrier between men may note that in the fourteenth century it seemed to have scarcely any importance. Al Nasir was twenty-four years old when he commenced his third reign in March 1310. Having disposed of Salar and Baybers, he ordered the arrest of many officers who previously supported them. The Viceroy of Aleppo, Qara Sonqor, and a number of officers in Syria, fearing arrest like their comrades in Egypt, deserted to the Mongols.

In 1315, Al Nasir sent a party to Sultaniya to murder Qara Sonqor but the plot was revealed to the authorities and most of the would-be assassins were caught and executed. The incident, however, caused much alarm in Sultaniya where it was rumoured that assassins had also been sent to murder the Il Khan Abu Saeed and his wazeer, Ali Shah. In 1319, the sultan again sent assassins to Adharbaijan to murder the Mamlook ameers who had deserted to the Mongols, but once again the plot came to light.

Sultan Al Nasir was genuinely interested in administration and in 1315 ordered a survey of all agricultural land in Egypt. The work was carried out by a committee accompanied by judges, who took sworn statements from all witnesses regarding the ownership of each plot and its productivity. The land was measured with ropes.[1]

The survey was undertaken because in Egypt fiefs of lands were allotted to the Mamlooks for their maintenance. It was therefore essential for the government to know the value of each fief. The system was extremely oppressive on the Egyptian cultivators or fellaheen, who were serfs bound to the soil and unable to leave their villages. The ameer, his agent and the officials took nearly all the produce and the fellaheen were always in debt. The ameer would then advance them loans at interest, impoverishing them yet further. When we contrast the grinding taxes with the immense wealth possessed by the sultan and the Mamlook ameers, we can judge something of the oppression practised by the régime. At this stage of his life, however, the young sultan seemed anxious to lighten these burdens.

When the survey was completed, a new allotment of fiefs was made to the Mamlooks. The sultan is alleged to have interviewed every soldier personally and to have asked him his name, country of origin, service and the battles and sieges in which he had shared. When one fine young man came before him, with a long scar across his face, the sultan handed him the title-deeds to a valuable farm.

As the lad was moving away, the sultan called after him, "In what battle did you get that sword-cut across the face?"

"O King," replied the young man frankly, "I did not get that in a battle. I fell off a ladder."

The treasury officer at the sultan's elbow quickly pointed out that the boy did not deserve so good a farm. "Let him go," replied Al Nasir, "he

[1] From 1926 to 1928, I was myself employed in Iraq in measuring crops with ropes in the same manner.

told the truth. Nobody could have contradicted him if he had named a battle."

* * *

To us Jenghis Khan and his Mongols appear to have been hordes of blood-thirsty savages but in the fourteenth century the extent of their conquests inspired profound veneration. As a result, Al Nasir in 1316 sent a deputation to Sarai on the Volga, the capital of the Golden Horde, to ask for a bride from the family of Jenghis Khan. The request created a sensation among the Mongols. "Never before," they exclaimed, "had any monarch in the world ventured to proffer such a request."

It was eventually decided to agree but to ask a dowry of a million dinars, a million horses, weapons, suits of armour and other impossible demands. However, two years later, in 1319, a great-granddaughter of Jenghis Khan landed at Alexandria without any request for a dowry. She travelled to Cairo amid much public rejoicing. Unfortunately Al Nasir did not like her and the day after the wedding he left on a hunting trip.

The sultan had gone on pilgrimage in 1313 and had returned riding a camel and wearing an Arab cloak and head-dress, as Maqrizi specifically reports. In 1319, he left again for Mecca. As the way lay largely through desert, containers filled with earth had been slung on camels and sown with vegetables and herbs. Gardeners accompanied the convoy and each evening picked what was needed for the sultan's dinner, which was served on vessels of silver and gold. A kitchen garden on camelback seems to us as exotic as the hanging gardens of Babylon. In Mecca Al Nasir refused to have the courtyard of the Kaaba cleared for his benefit but mingled incognito with the jostling crowds of pilgrims. To gain further religious merit, he washed the Kaaba with his own hands.

In the course of this pilgrimage, the Sultan encountered many Arab desert tribes such as Beni Lam, Beni Mehedi and Al Fadhl. The courtiers were horrified at the familiarity of the tribesmen in approaching the sultan. "They behaved like Arabs without any politeness," says the Egyptian historian Maqrizi contemptuously. The sultan, however, took it all in good part, even when a small son of the shaikh of the Fadhl grasped his beard.

"May God cut off your hand, you brat," shouted the chief qadhi, "what do you mean by putting your hand on the sultan?" Al Nasir smiled and said that such was the custom of the Arabs. The qadhi rose and left the tent in a rage, shouting, "Miserable wretches! And their customs, by God, are even more wretched than they." This vivid scene depicted by Maqrizi six hundred years ago could well be repeated today, if any distinguished Egyptian were to visit the tribes of Arabia.

Al Nasir was all his life sympathetic to the bedouin tribes, perhaps because as a boy he spent several years in exile in Kerak, on the verge of the desert. Nevertheless Al Nasir's affection for bedouins is of interest, for he was of course not an Egyptian but a descendant of the peoples of the steppes of southern Russia. The "romantic" attraction felt for Arab tribes by northern races who, like Al Nasir, delight in dressing up in Arab clothes, was likewise experienced by the Crusaders and survives to this day as does also the antipathy of the Egyptians to them.

* * *

The position of the Armenian Kingdom of Cilicia was now desperate. Originally constituted by Armenian immigrants coming from Greater Armenia after the Battle of Malazkirt in 1071, it had survived two stormy centuries. When the First Crusade arrived in 1097, the Armenians had allied themselves with the Franks, but with the extinction of Outremer the Cilician Armenians found themselves a small Christian state entirely surrounded by Muslims.

The appearance of the Mongols seemed to offer the Armenians a ray of hope and, in 1254, Haithum I, King of Cilicia, had visited the Khaqan Mangu and become his vassal. In 1260, when Hulagu invaded Syria, Haithum I marched with him, but when Hulagu withdrew, the Armenians were left alone to face Mamlook vengeance. In 1266, Baybers the Bunduqdari had laid waste the whole of Cilicia.

When Ghazan had taken Damascus in 1300, hope dawned once more, but his withdrawal, like that of Hulagu, only drew down further retribution. In 1302, a Mamlook army plundered and burned the whole country. The Mongols invariably called on the Armenians to join in their invasions of Syria, but did little to defend their vassals from subsequent Egyptian reprisals. The reign of the Armenian King Oshin, from 1308 to 1320, nevertheless passed comparatively peacefully, as the Il Khans Oljaitu and Abu Saeed did not stir up trouble by invading Syria. Oshin, who had been married to Isabella, the daughter of Hugh III, King of Cyprus, died in 1320, and was succeeded by his son Leo V, who was thus half a Lusignan.

Emphasis has already been frequently laid in these pages on the immense value of the Oriental trade. While the Franks held Syria, much of this commerce passed through Acre, Tripoli and Antioch. With the elimination of the Franks, the Armenians developed a port at Ayas or Lajazzo on the Gulf of Alexandretta. In view of the close relations existing between Cyprus and the Armenian Kingdom, many Frankish merchants conducted their business between Famagusta and Ayas, the only remaining port not in Mamlook hands.

THE HAITHUMIAN ARMENIAN KINGS OF CILICIA

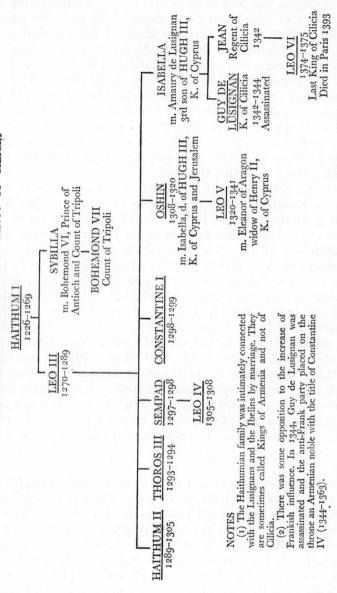

- HAITHUM I, 1226–1269
  - LEO III, 1270–1289
    - HAITHUM II, 1289–1305
    - THOROS III, 1293–1294
    - SEMPAD, 1297–1298
      - LEO IV, 1305–1308
    - CONSTANTINE I, 1298–1299
    - OSHIN, 1308–1320, m. Isabella, d. of HUGH III, K. of Cyprus and Jerusalem
      - LEO V, 1320–1341, m. Eleanor of Aragon widow of Henry II, K. of Cyprus
    - ISABELLA, m. Amaury de Lusignan 3rd son of HUGH III, K. of Cyprus
      - GUY DE LUSIGNAN, K. of Cilicia 1342–1344, Assassinated
      - JEAN, Regent of Cilicia 1342
        - LEO VI, 1374–1375, Last King of Cilicia, Died in Paris 1393
  - SYBILLA, m. Bohemond VI, Prince of Antioch and Count of Tripoli
    - BOHEMOND VII, Count of Tripoli

NOTES

(1) The Haithumian family was intimately connected with the Lusignans and the Ibelins by marriage. They are sometimes called Kings of Armenia and not of Cilicia.

(2) There was some opposition to the increase of Frankish influence. In 1344, Guy de Lusignan was assassinated and the anti-Frank party placed on the throne an Armenian noble with the title of Constantine IV (1344–1363).

In 1322, a Mamlook army invaded Cilicia without any apparent cause, destroyed the port of Ayas and laid waste the whole kingdom. Leo V, King of Cilicia, wrote to implore the pope for help but the sovereign pontiff replied that the kings of Christendom were fully employed in fighting one another. Al Nasir, hearing that Leo had written to the pope, sent a second expedition which razed the town of Adana. The pope seems to have been genuinely distressed by the fate of the Armenians and wrote to the Il Khan Abu Saeed, urging him to protect his vassals. The letter was dated from Avignon on 13th July, 1322. In 1323, however, peace was signed between the Il Khan Abu Saeed and Sultan Nasir (one condition of which was that Nasir cease sending assassins to Persia). Shortly afterwards, the Armenians also obtained a truce from the Mamlooks.

It may be convenient at this place to relate the final end of the Armenian Kingdom, even if to do so means departing from strict chronology in the history of Egypt. The Mamlooks destroyed Ayas once again in 1337, thereby finally securing for Egyptian Alexandria a complete monopoly of the oriental trade. On 25th May, 1347, the Mamlooks again took Ayas and incorporated it in their empire. In 1359, they likewise annexed Adana and Tarsus and the Armenian Kingdom was reduced to a small area round the town of Sis in the Taurus Mountains.

It will be remembered that the Armenian dynasty of Haithum had intermarried with the Lusignans of Cyprus. The male line having failed, the last King of Cilicia was a Lusignan, connected to the Haithumians through the female side. Leo VI de Lusignan was crowned in Sis on 14th September, 1374. Almost immediately afterwards he was besieged in his capital by a Mamlook army. After a heroic defence, Sis surrendered on 13th April, 1375, and Leo VI was taken as a prisoner to Cairo. After seven years in captivity, he was released and died in Paris on 29th November, 1393. The Kingdom of Cilicia had ceased to exist.

* * *

After this digression we must go back once more to Egypt, which we left in 1320, when Sultan Al Nasir returned from the pilgrimage. On a certain Friday in 1320, as the Muslim crowds were leaving the mosques after the midday prayers, the worshippers in the main cities of Egypt suddenly attacked and demolished all the Christian churches. This widespread plot had been most efficiently organized and some sixty churches were razed to the ground before the authorities could intervene. A few days later fires broke out mysteriously in different parts of Cairo and spread rapidly. In spite of the efforts of troops and gangs of workmen, the fire could not be arrested. At length three Christians were apprehended who confessed under torture that they had started the fires in revenge for the destruction of their churches. Six monks were burnt alive in retaliation and an intense persecution of Christians ensued. Al Nasir was indignant at the continuation of the disturbances and sent troops to restore order but the crowds merely grew more violent. Eventually, seeing that the fanaticism of the mob only increased, the sultan withdrew the troops and the crowds were left free to attack and rob all Christians indiscriminately.

Mecca was now entirely under Egyptian domination. On 22nd May, 1325, a Mamlook army left the Holy City for the Yemen at the request of the king of that country whose subjects were in rebellion. When the column approached the frontier, however, the rebels became reconciled to their king, who was thenceforward anxious only to get rid of the Mamlooks. The column camped in the vicinity of Taiz. The Yemenis, half-naked and armed only with swords and spears, looked with astonishment at the lavish clothing, equipment and weapons of the Egyptian army. They cut off water supplies from the camp, stole the camels and horses sent out to graze and killed stragglers. When the troops endeavoured to chase them, they ran up the steep mountain sides and bombarded their pursuers with stones. A complete deadlock ensued until eventually the army turned back, reaching Mecca on 24th August, 1325.

* * *

Early in May 1332, the sultan's eldest son was married to the daughter of the Ameer Bektimeer, one of the most powerful Mamlook officers. In the evening the sultan seated himself in state at the gate of the palace, in front of which three thousand candles or torches had been lit. Then the senior ameers presented themselves one by one, each carrying a candle and followed by their private mamlooks, likewise carrying candles. Every officer came up in order of seniority and kissed the ground before the sultan, so that the ceremony lasted well into the night.

The sultan then moved to the women's apartments where the wives of the ameers were assembled. Each wife kissed the ground before the sultan at the same time offering some priceless wedding gift. Nasir then gave permission for the women to dance, an orchestra played, slave girls sang and gold and silver coins were scattered. When these entertainments were over, the bride was carried in procession. Even today the procedure for state weddings in Arab countries has changed little since the fourteenth century.[2]

After the wedding the sultan decided to go once more on pilgrimage. He was accompanied by the Ameer Bektimeer, whose daughter had

[2] Regarding the custom of holding weddings at night, see the parable of the Wise Virgins. "And at midnight there was a cry made, Behold the bridegroom cometh." Matthew XXV, 6.

just married his son. But Bektimeer had become too great, his wealth was immense, his retinue as splendid as that of the sultan. As the pilgrimage was about to set out, an informer warned Al Nasir that Bektimeer intended to murder him on the pilgrimage. The sultan was greatly alarmed. He changed his sleeping place several times each night and by day rode knee to knee with Bektimeer himself. After performing the pilgrimage, Al Nasir succeeded in killing both Bektimeer and his son by poison on the way home, an incident which sheds a remarkable light on Mamlook morals.

Many wild rumours had been circulating in Cairo and when the sultan's cavalcade approached the city, the whole population turned out to greet him. The route to be taken by the procession had been carpeted with silk and cloth of gold. When the sultan entered the streets packed with dense crowds, he was wearing an Arab head-dress drawn across his face. The crowd was in an agony of doubt and cries of "It is he! It is not he!" could be heard on all sides. At length a shout was raised, "Undo your kerchief! Let's see your face!" When Al Nasir uncovered his face, a mighty roar rose from the crowd, "Praise be to God for your safety," and the people went wild with shouting and laughter. When we are inclined to denounce the Mamlooks as a blood-thirsty crew, we should perhaps remember that roar of welcome from the crowds of Cairo.

To a great extent the sultan's popularity was deserved, for he was a serious and conscientious ruler. He watched the government revenue and expenditure carefully, calling for frequent financial statements. The situation was, however, almost impossible to control. Senior government posts such as that of Viceroy of Egypt, Damascus or Aleppo were held by Mamlook ameers unable to supervise the administration. Indeed the Viceroy of Egypt at this time could not even speak Arabic. The officials who actually did the administrative work, collected the taxes and staffed the treasury, were Egyptians or Syrians, some of them Christians or Copts. In the absence of adequate supervision or audit, many revenue officials became extremely rich.

A further difficulty arose from the fact that the Mamlooks were paid by the award of fiefs of land. The sultan was strong enough to prevent the fiefs becoming hereditary and when an officer was promoted he often surrendered his fief and was awarded a better one, thereby giving him the equivalent of a rise of pay. The system had the disadvantage that the Egyptian officials were afraid to take action against a Mamlook ameer who defrauded the treasury. An additional drawback was that the Mamlooks took little interest in fiefs which the sultan could at any time withdraw and thus nothing was done to improve these estates.

In 1335, owing to a failure of the Nile, prices of foodstuffs rose rapidly.

Many Mamlook ameers refused to sell their grain in the hopes of a further increase in prices, though the people were already suffering from hunger. When the situation was explained to Al Nasir he was speechless with rage and had the bailiff of one of the ameers flogged in his presence for refusing to sell his master's grain. Seeing the sultan in such a fury, the other ameers hastened to put their grain on the market and prices fell rapidly.

At this stage, Al Nasir took into his service a certain Saif al Deen Neshu, a Christian clerk who had been converted to Islam and who was an extremely capable revenue official. By using as spies the women and slave-girls employed in wealthy families, he discovered how much each possessed and what means were used to defraud the treasury. His method was then to arrest the accused and apply flogging or torture until an arbitrarily assessed amount of unpaid taxes was produced.

In some cases, doubtless, the information lodged was correct, but in others the victims were reported to have sold all their possessions before they could escape from the clutches of the treasury. A few, either from their obstinacy or their innocence, died under torture without producing any money at all. None dared to complain to the sultan who supported Neshu in all he did.

Al Nasir, however, seems to have enjoyed his popularity with the Egyptian public. At last, in 1340, he was persuaded that the methods used by Neshu were alienating the affection of the public and he gave his consent to a search of his house. Neshu had extorted vast sums of money for the treasury but had often assured the sultan that he himself was a poor man who was frequently obliged to borrow money to pay the expenses of his family. Unhappily for Neshu, the search of his house revealed immense sums of money, not to mention quantities of jewels, clothing, textiles and foodstuffs. The sultan was furious and gave orders that Neshu and his brother be tortured to death. His end was horrible, but he had often inflicted the same torments on others to extract their money.

This gruesome mediaeval story is not without interest in our own times. Al Nasir, the descendant of a northern race, a man who prided himself on his morality and his benevolence, was completely hoodwinked by an Egyptian clerk, a process often repeated in the experience of most Europeans who have worked in the Middle East in our own times. For the fact is that members of northern races are, in general, simple-minded and gullible and readily fall victims to the plausible cleverness of the peoples of the Eastern Mediterranean, a point emphasized by another fourteenth-century historian, whom we shall encounter in subsequent pages.[3]

[3] Abu al Mahasin ibn Taghri Birdi.

We have already seen that Al Nasir had himself poisoned the Ameer Bektimeer, who had grown too powerful. The following year the sultan likewise became suspicious of the Ameer Tinkiz who had for twenty-eight years been Viceroy of Damascus. For many years it appeared that Nasir could never do enough for Tinkiz who, like Bektimeer, had married his daughter to one of the sultan's sons. Tinkiz had governed Syria well, but after too long a retention of power he grew tyrannical and ceased to treat the sultan himself with sufficient respect. In 1341, he was suddenly arrested, carried to Cairo in chains and executed. He was found to have accumulated great wealth. To take one item alone, a thousand satin robes were found in his wardrobe.[4]

These incidents reveal certain curious inconsistencies in the character of Al Nasir or perhaps in Mamlook morality as a whole. On the one hand, the sultan was a sincerely religious man. He several times performed the pilgrimage to Mecca and was, on the whole, anxious to ensure the welfare of the people. He was, however, by no means fanatical and was indignant at the persecution of his Christian subjects. He disapproved of sexual immorality and of drunkenness and any young man in Cairo accused of indulgence in women or wine might find himself banished overnight to a distant outpost in Syria. He was also extremely severe against bribery.

On the other hand, he several times sent assassins to Persia and he murdered Bektimeer and his son, if not Tinkiz, who in theory was executed for disloyalty. Although he eventually expressed indignation at the methods employed by Neshu, it was the lavish expenditure of the court which made it necessary to extort money by such means. On the whole, however, if we recognize murder as a routine political expedient employed by mediaeval sovereigns, we must admit that the sultan was, in most respects, a careful and conscientious ruler.

Compared to his predecessors, Al Nasir was fortunate in that the decline and final collapse of the Il Khanate saved him from the fear of Mongol invasion. The crusading spirit had also weakened in Europe and the Mamlooks found themselves without a major enemy. As a result, the sultan was free to devote himself to minor wars to expand his empire.

Mecca and Medina, previously ruled independently by descendants of the Prophet Muhammad's family, were reduced to the status of Egyptian satellites. Several vain attempts were made to conquer Nubia, now the Sudan. The expedition to the Yemen, as we have seen, nearly

[4] The Mamlook ameers—the men of the sword as they were called—were dressed with extraordinary magnificence in brightly coloured silk and satin robes, heavily embroidered with gold lace. Egyptian and Syrian administrative and religious officials—the men of the pen—also received handsome robes but of a different and more sober cut. Dress was controlled by strict protocol, the richness of the costume being in exact proportion to rank.

ended in disaster. The frequent invasions of Cilicia produced great quantities of loot but the Armenian Kingdom was not to be finally destroyed for a further forty years, as already mentioned.

Early in June 1341, Al Nasir was attacked by a severe dysentery and died on the seventh of the month at the age of fifty-seven years, leaving fifteen sons and eleven daughters. Eight of his sons were to be sultans.

* * *

Al Nasir had first been made sultan in December 1293 at the age of nine. In November 1294, however, he was deposed by Kitbugha and sent into exile in Kerak, where he remained until his recall to the throne in February 1299 after the assassination of Lajeen. He remained under the regency of Salar and Baybers the Taster until 1309, when he abdicated and withdrew to Kerak. His third reign began in 1310 and thereafter he governed Egypt autocratically for a further thirty-two years.

The sultan ruled two entirely distinct communities. Of these the first was the Mamlook class, a turbulent Foreign Legion which had already murdered many of his predecessors. It speaks volumes for his personality that the senior ameers were so afraid of him that they scarcely dared to speak in his presence. The people of Egypt, whose lot in life was to toil and moil for their masters, formed the second group of his subjects. His popularity with the people of Cairo, at any rate in his youth, bears witness to his character and may be partly accounted for by the fact that he was the first great sultan to be born in an Arab country, and, it seems, the first to speak Arabic. Aibek, Qutuz, Baybers the Bunduqdari and Qalaun had all been reared on the steppes.

Nasir spent large sums of money on the purchase of young Mamlooks. The chief source of these boys was the Qipchaq country, but his agents were always active in buying both boys and girls in Persia, Iraq, Asia Minor and elsewhere. A regular routine had been established under former sultans whereby new boys were given to the care of eunuchs for training. The boys of each nation were educated together and taught the Muslim religion, social manners and deportment, archery, horsemanship and the use of lance and sword. While under training they wore plain cotton clothes and were kept under rigid discipline for several years. Al Nasir changed all this. From the moment of arrival of a new slave boy, he was given gorgeous clothing, splendid horses and many rich gifts. "A boy who is suddenly overwhelmed with riches of which he had never dreamt," the sultan used to say, "immediately forgets his native country and becomes entirely devoted to his new master." Whether this method was calculated to produce good soldiers is extremely doubtful.

Nasir was passionately fond of horses. He would only buy thoroughbred

Arabs from the tribes of Arabia, but for these he would pay almost any money, with the result that the bedouin tribes became rich. Their women, formerly clad in ragged cotton dresses, now flaunted silks and satins and rode in camel litters, it was said, decorated with gold and jewels.[5]

Maqrizi has left us a vivid picture of one occasion when a bedouin arrived in Cairo leading a grey mare and bearing a message from Mahenna ibn Isa, shaikh of the Fadhl tribe. "If this mare can beat anything you have in Egypt," wrote the shaikh, "you can keep her. But if you can beat her, send her back to me in disgrace." He stipulated, however, that she be ridden by the bedouin who had brought her.

The sultan was only too anxious to take up the challenge and sent for his best horses and those of the ameers. On the great day, all rode out to the racecourse outside Cairo and the sultan, with a large group of ameers, took up his position by the finish. The atmosphere was tense as the horses went down to the start. Then they were off and could be seen coming on in a compact group to the gradually increasing thunder of hoofs until amid wild excitement, the grey mare, ridden by the bedouin clad only in a long white shirt and riding barebacked, pounded past the post several lengths ahead of the field.

The sultan kept a stud farm on which at his death there were four thousand mares. There was a staff of clerks on the farm, who kept the stud book with folios for every horse giving full details of breed, price, date of birth and veterinary notes.

The sultan was extremely polite in conversation and had never been heard to use obscene or vulgar language. Though his court was magnificent, he himself always dressed plainly, often in cotton clothes without gold or jewels. His memory was exceptional and he knew every one of his personal Mamlooks by name, together with his life's history. It was said that he also knew all the officials in the government offices in Cairo and what appointment was held by each. He never forgot even one of his mares and would say, "Bring me that chestnut mare, Flana, the one we bought four years ago from Ibn Isa for fifty thousand dirhems." Having been born in Syria and lived in exile for several years in Kerak, he was much more arabicized than previous Mamlook sultans.

Al Nasir was strongly opposed to drink and issued frequent orders for the closure of wine shops and the confiscation of alcohol. He was, however, fond of slave girls and paid high prices for the most beautiful obtainable. Unlike most Mamlooks he disliked war and preferred to achieve his political ends by bribery or by sending assassins to dispose of his enemies.

[5] Although Al Nasir had a sympathy for bedouins, the latter maintained their reputation for periodical rebellions and disorders, sometimes even intriguing with the Tatars.

His was a great age for the building of mosques, colleges and palaces. More than forty splendid mosques and colleges were built in Cairo between 1320 and 1360.[6] It was a period famous also for artistic furniture, silver, gold lamps, fabrics and *objets d'art*. He was interested in public works and used himself to superintend the digging of canals and the construction of irrigation works. As a result, the revenues of Egypt increased during his reign, in spite of the fact that he abolished a number of vexatious taxes.

In appearance Al Nasir was short in stature and slightly lame but he was always calm, self-possessed and strong-willed. As a young man, he had been a comparatively just, generous and benevolent ruler, but he encouraged great magnificence in the court and the army, thereby giving rise to a constant need for money, resulting in the extortions practised by Neshu and his like. Al Nasir himself grew somewhat tyrannical in later life as a result of too long an enjoyment of despotic power. Maqrizi who, however, as an Egyptian, was inclined to be critical of Mamlook high-handedness, says that "some people he killed by starvation and thirst, some by strangling, some he drowned, some he banished and some he imprisoned."

Al Malik al Nasir Muhammad, the son of Qalaun, was the *roi soleil* of the Mamlook régime and one of the great rulers of history. The Mamlooks had seized power in Egypt in 1250 and under Al Nasir they attained their Golden Age. The stern years of war against the Mongols and the Crusaders were passed and were succeeded by the high noon of wealth, glory and peace, with Egypt in the first rank of the Great Powers of the world. With the death of the victorious king, the Mamlook government fell into confusion and the glories of his long reign were never again to be revived.

NOTABLE DATES

Battle of Marj al Suffar, Mongols defeated	20th April, 1303
Abdication of Al Nasir. Baybers the Jashnekeer becomes sultan	1309
Commencement of Al Nasir's third reign	1310
Destruction of Ayas in Cilicia	1322
Abortive campaign in the Yemen	1325
Death of Sultan Al Nasir	1341

PERSONALITIES

Salar Baybers the Jashnekeer.	Regents

[6] Stanley Lane Poole, *The Story of Cairo*.

Malik al Nasir Muhammad	Mamlook Sultan
Saif al Deen Neshu	Fraudulent Collector of Taxes

The Great Bahri Sultans

Aibek and Spray of Pearls	1250–1257
Ali, son of Aibek	1257–1259
Qutuz	1259–1260
Baybers the Bunduqdari	1260–1277
Baraka, son of Baybers	1277–1279
Salamish, son of Baybers	1279
Qalaun	1279–1290
Khalil, son of Qalaun	1290–1293
Malik al Nasir Muhammad. First reign	1293–1294
Kitbugha	1294–1296
Lajeen	1296–1299
Malik al Nasir Muhammad. Second reign	1299–1309
Baybers the Jashnekeer	1309–1310
Malik al Nasir Muhammad. Third reign	1310–1341

XIX

The Rise of the Othmanlis
1340–1403

The Othmanli tribe of Turks were one of these independent communities of flock-owners. They had moved west, where they were in direct contact with the Greeks. The East and West began to fuse and create something which proved of value to posterity. Through the Greeks, the Turks came in contact with the art and culture of the ancient world. The two great civilizations of this period were the Arab and the Byzantine. The Arab was ruined by the Mongol invasion, the Byzantine was ruined by the Latin occupation. It was the Turkish rôle in history to pick up what survived of Hellenic civilization and incorporate it into the system they were now to create.

M. PHILIPS PRICE, *A History of Turkey*

XIX

WITH the death of Al Nasir in 1341, the glory departed from the régime of the River Mamlooks and indeed to a great extent from Egypt as a whole. In the ensuing forty years of confusion, twelve of Nasir's descendants mounted the throne, eight sons, two grandsons and two great-grandsons.[1] The great Mamlook ameers remained rich but the state finances, owing to the absence of strong central rule, fell to the verge of bankruptcy.

In 1348 and 1349, the Black Death added to Egypt's misfortunes, some ten to twenty thousand people dying in Cairo alone in one day. It was fortunate indeed that the Mamlooks, during these forty years, were free of major external enemies. The Il Khans had disappeared and Tamerlane had not yet gained power.

It will be remembered that the destruction of Acre and subsequently that of Ayas in Cilicia, had given Alexandria a complete monopoly of the eastern trade. The Frankish merchants of Venice, Pisa, Genoa and Marseilles had established themselves in this great port, where they owned wealthy offices and warehouses. The Egyptian government likewise obtained large sums from customs and transit charges.

Peter I de Lusignan,[2] who succeeded to the throne of Cyprus in 1359, was young, brave, chivalrous and intensely pious. When twenty years of age, in the Monastery of the Holy Cross near Larnaca, he believed that Christ Himself had ordered him to lead a crusade. On 24th October, 1362, he sailed for the West to enlist support and visited Venice, Genoa, the papal court at Avignon, Flanders, Germany and Paris. Crossing to England, he was entertained by Edward III, who held a great tournament at Smithfield in his honour. Returning through Aquitaine, he called upon the Black Prince. He sailed from Venice for Cyprus on 27th June, 1365. Many volunteers followed him but none of the monarchs he had visited took the cross in person.

The crusade sailed from Cyprus at the end of September 1365. To ensure surprise, King Peter had not revealed his objective and it was only when the fleet was at sea that he told the officers of his intention to attack Alexandria. The fleet came in sight of the great Egyptian city on 9th October, 1365.

Alexandria was one of the richest cities in the world. The defences were considered impregnable but there was scarcely any garrison. The government of Egypt was in some confusion, the nominal sultan being Shaaban, a boy of eleven years of age, but the real power rested in the

[1] A list of these ephemeral rulers will be found at the end of this chapter.

[2] Genealogical tree, page 204.

hands of a Mamlook Ameer, Yalbugha al Khassiki. The Nile was in flood, rendering it difficult to despatch reinforcements to Alexandria.

On the morning of 10th October, the fleet entered the Old Harbour, the troops landed and attempted an immediate assault on the western end of the city walls. The small garrison hastily concentrated on this sector and repulsed the attack. Meanwhile, however, a few Franks had wandered along to the shore of the new harbour where they noticed that the walls were not manned. Ladders were brought and a party of Franks mounted the wall unopposed. By the morning of 11th October, the Crusaders were in unopposed possession of the city.

King Peter proposed to hold Alexandria until the sultan came to terms, a plan similar to that of Jean de Brienne at Damietta. The majority of the Franks, however, were not inspired by religious motives. Seeing the immense wealth of Alexandria, they insisted on looting and then evacuating the city. Already they were sacking the warehouses, mosques and palaces, bearing their treasures to the ships. King Peter ordered and protested in vain. After seven days Alexandria had been stripped bare and the ships could carry no more. The city was then set on fire and the fleet sailed back to Cyprus.

The crusade of King Peter was a tragedy for all concerned. For many years the wealthy eastern trade was arrested to the mutual loss of Muslims and Christians alike. Religious hatred was fanned into flame and the Egyptian government retaliated with a persecution of the native Christians. Finally, sixty years later, the Mamlooks were to obtain their revenge.

* * *

On 26th November, 1382, seventeen years after the tragedy of Alexandria, the last descendant of Al Nasir, Malik al Salih Hajji, was removed from the throne of Egypt. With him ended the rule of the River Mamlooks. It will be remembered that Sultan Qalaun had founded the Burji or Tower Mamlooks to offset the power of the River Mamlooks. The Burjis were recruited from Circassians, a race inhabiting the Caucasus and in no way connected with the Turks of the steppes.

The new sultan was Malik al Dhahir Barqooq, a Circassian born in the Caucasus and sold as a slave boy in Egypt to Yalbugha al Khassiki, at that time dictator of the country. Barqooq played an active part in the *coups d'état* which marked the last years of the puppet descendants of Al Nasir, until in 1382 he himself seized power and Egypt once again acknowledged a single master.

Barqooq's position was at first by no means secure, even the Khalif Mutawakkil being involved in a plot to kill him. Finally, in February 1389, when he had been on the throne for seven years, Yalbugha al

Nasiri, the Viceroy of Aleppo, rose in open revolt, seized Damascus and marched on Egypt. There may have been some opposition among Turkish mamlooks against a Circassian sultan, in addition to the hostility of the mamlooks of the dynasty of Qalaun.

When the rebels neared Cairo, Barqooq blockaded himself in the citadel instead of marching out to give battle. His apparent timidity undermined the morale of his supporters. On 29th May, 1389, Yalbugha's troops entered the city, which for forty-eight hours was given over to plunder. Then Hajji, the child sultan, whom Barqooq had previously dethroned, was proclaimed sultan once again, Yalbugha al Nasiri was made regent and Barqooq was sent to prison in Kerak.

One of the principal drawbacks of military *coups d'état* is that they tend to recur. Yalbugha had overthrown Barqooq and now Mintash, another senior officer, rose against Yalbugha. Mintash seized the mosque of Sultan Hasan in Cairo, while Yalbugha held the citadel. Both erected siege engines, and soon rocks, arrows and every form of projectile were flying backwards and forwards, while heavy street fighting developed between the two factions.

This battle is of particular interest because the descriptions left of it by two contemporary historians, Maqrizi and Ibn Taghri Birdi, seem to refer to the employment of cannon. Accounts of the introduction of guns into the Mamlook armies are difficult to follow, owing to the confusion in technical terms. The weapons formerly used for throwing Greek fire were called by the Arabs "naphtha guns". In the accounts of this street battle in Cairo we are told that "a stone fired by the naphtha guns pierced the dome of the mosque."[3] It would appear possible that all guns continued to be called naphtha guns, even after they had ceased to throw liquid fire and had begun to throw cannon balls.

Guns using gunpowder as a propellant were introduced in Europe between 1325 and 1350 and it is thus almost certain that they would have appeared in Egypt by 1389. It is of interest to note that, about the middle of the fourteenth century, we find Europe overtaking and passing the Muslim world in certain branches of technology.[4]

Eventually on 12th August, 1389, Yalbugha was defeated and Mintash occupied the citadel and was appointed regent and commander-in-chief. In Egypt people were already regretting the "good old days" of Sultan Barqooq. In the autumn of 1389, Barqooq escaped from prison in Kerak and reached Damascus. Mintash marched to fight him and, on 2nd and 3rd January, 1390, two days of heavy fighting at Shaqhab sixteen miles south of Damascus resulted in a victory for Barqooq. On 1st February, 1390, he re-entered Cairo in triumph amid wild popular

[3] Maqrizi, *Kitab al Suluk*.
[4] For a fuller discussion, see D. Ayalon, *Gunpowder and Firearms in the Mamlook Kingdom*.

enthusiasm, eight months of confusion having disillusioned the public. Barqooq, on the whole, behaved with tact and generosity. A few of the rebels, however, were cut in half at the waist, including a number of ameers. This was an innovation, as ameers had until then enjoyed the privilege of being strangled with a bowstring.

Three years later, in August 1393, ambassadors arrived from the Prince of Mardin in the Jezira to report that Tamerlane[5] had taken Tabriz. On 30th August, Tamerlane seized Baghdad, the ruler of which, Ahmed ibn Uwais of the Jalair, arrived in Cairo as a fugitive and was regally welcomed. In February 1394, the Viceroy of Aleppo reported a skirmish with the advanced guard of Tamerlane's army. Shortly afterwards a long letter, full of Qoranic quotations, was received from Tamerlane, demanding instant submission or alternatively threatening the destruction of Syria and Egypt. An equally lengthy reply was sent, no less full of verses from the Qoran, pronouncing defiance. Mobilization was ordered and, on 12th February, 1394, outside Cairo the sultan reviewed the Mamlook army, magnificently armed, equipped and mounted.

On 23rd March, Barqooq reached Damascus and in September the army advanced to Aleppo. Ambassadors were received from Toqtamish, Khan of the Golden Horde, and from Bayazid, the Ottoman Sultan,[6] proposing an alliance against Tamerlane, who, however, had meanwhile marched away to Samarqand. On 13th December, 1394, Barqooq was back in Cairo.

Barqooq was now firmly established on the throne. The critical years were past during which he was threatened by the Mamlooks of his predecessors and he had now installed his own men in every important position in the government. A list of the principal officers of state in the Mamlook Empire at this time may be of interest.

In Cairo

Grand Ameer and Commander-in-Chief
Ameer of Arms
Ameer of the Council
Ameer of the Horse
Grand Chamberlain
Grand Secretary
Commander of the Guards[7]

These senior ameers constituted an advisory council for the sultan.

[5] The career of Tamerlane will be related in the next chapter.

[6] See later in this chapter.

[7] The precise duties of some of these officers are not clear. The Mamlooks introduced into Egyptian Arabic a mixed jargon of Turkish, Persian and other words, the meanings of some of which are doubtful.

There were in the army twenty-four ameers of the first class, who might perhaps be compared to the generals in a modern army.

The khalif was in theory the supreme religious authority but in fact was allowed no power whatever. The qadhis and religious shaikhs were appointed and removed by the sultan's orders. Unlike the ameers, the qadhis were Syrians and Egyptians.

In the time of Barqooq, there were in Egypt Viceroys of Alexandria and of upper and lower Egypt. Syria was governed by seven viceroys, Damascus, Aleppo, Tripoli, Hama, Safad, Gaza and Kerak. All viceroys were directly responsible to the sultan. Although the Viceroy of Damascus was the senior governor in Syria, he did not exercise any authority over the others. In 1397, all these key positions were held by Barqooq's Mamlooks, of whom Taghri Birdi, the father of our historian, was Viceroy of Aleppo.[8]

The governorships of Mecca and Medina were held by sherifs, descendants of the family of the Prophet. These august personages, however, did not always set an edifying example to the faithful, being frequently engaged in fighting one another.

In December 1397, reports were received that Tamerlane was in India and the threat of a Tatar invasion of Syria ceased to cause alarm.

On 10th June, 1399, Barqooq fell ill and by the 19th of the month he was dying. In the presence of the khalif, the qadhis and the Mamlook ameers, he appointed his ten-year-old son Faraj as his successor. Aitemish al Bajasi, the commander-in-chief, and Taghri Birdi, the Viceroy of Aleppo, were made regents.

Barqooq died on 20th June, 1399. He was believed to be more than sixty years old. He had ruled as sultan for nearly seventeen years although during this period he had been deposed for eight months. His reign had, on the whole, been a period of peace and security and his death was deeply mourned. He was wise, brave and energetic and it is difficult to account for his apparent panic during the revolt of Yalbugha in 1389. He was of vigorous intellect, sometimes cruel, but diligent and painstaking in the administration of justice. He thought out every problem carefully, and frequently sought advice before taking a decision. He was a competent, if not a great, ruler.

* * *

We have been following the rivalries of the Mongols and the Mamlooks from the conquests of Jenghis Khan in 1220 until the death of Barqooq in 1399—a period of nearly two centuries. During this time a great new Muslim Empire had appeared in Asia Minor, the rise of which it is now our task to trace.

[8] Abu al Mahasin ibn Taghri Birdi, *Al Nujoom al Zahira*.

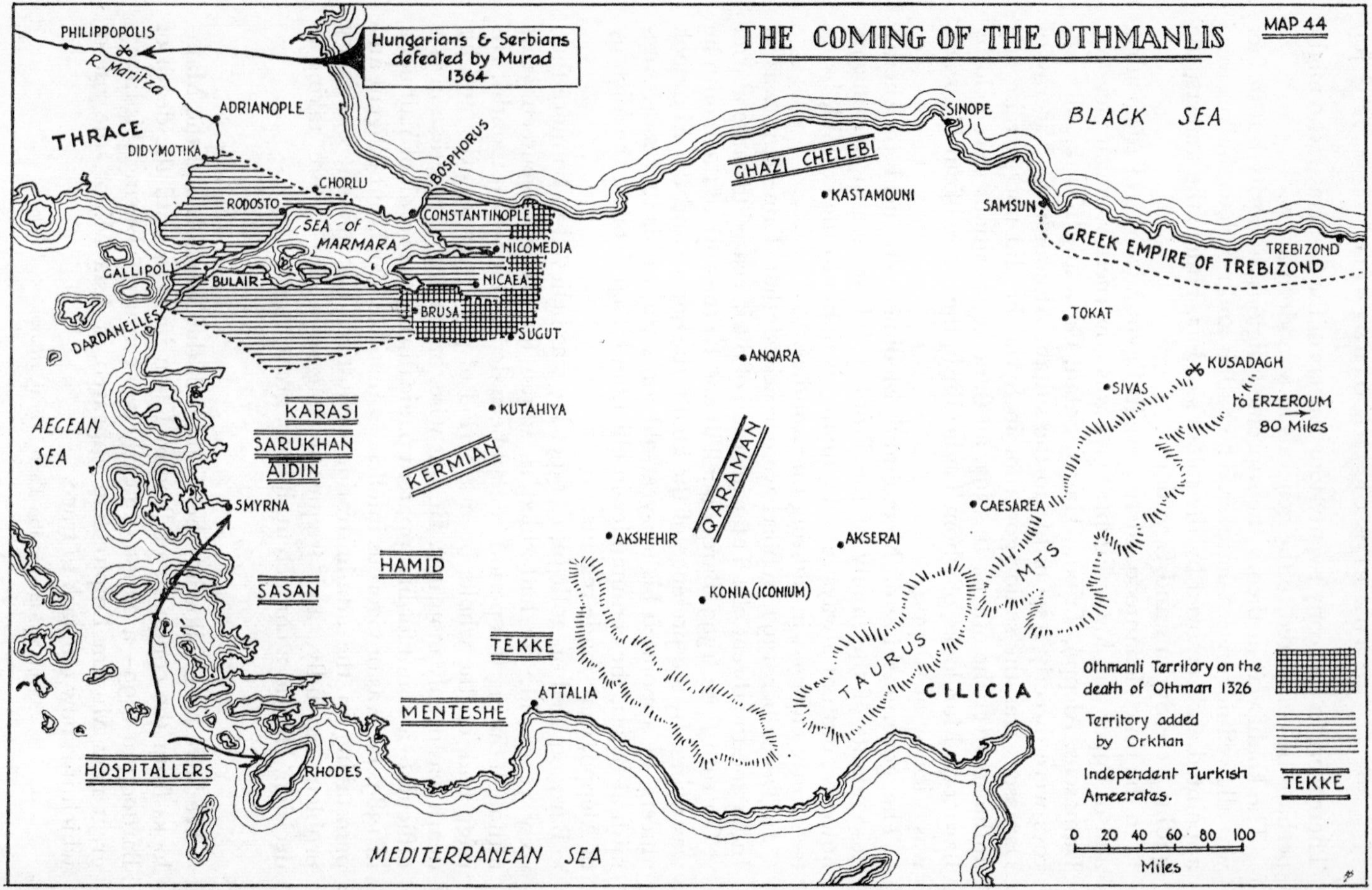
THE COMING OF THE OTHMANLIS
MAP 44
Hungarians & Serbians defeated by Murad 1364
PHILIPPOPOLIS
R Maritza
ADRIANOPLE
THRACE
DIDYMOTIKA
CHORLU
RODOSTO
BOSPHORUS
CONSTANTINOPLE
SEA of MARMARA
NICOMEDIA
GALLIPOLI
BULAIR
NICAEA
BRUSA
SUGUT
DARDANELLES
BLACK SEA
SINOPE
GHAZI CHELEBI
KASTAMOUNI
SAMSUN
GREEK EMPIRE OF TREBIZOND
TREBIZOND
TOKAT
ANQARA
KUSADAGH
SIVAS
To ERZEROUM 80 Miles
KARASI
KUTAHIYA
AEGEAN SEA
SARUKHAN
AIDIN
KERMIAN
QARAMAN
SMYRNA
CAESAREA
AKSHEHIR
AKSERAI
HAMID
MTS
SASAN
KONIA (ICONIUM)
TEKKE
TAURUS
CILICIA
ATTALIA
MENTESHE
HOSPITALLERS
RHODES
MEDITERRANEAN SEA
Othmanli Territory on the death of Othman 1326
Territory added by Orkhan
Independent Turkish Ameerates.
TEKKE
0 20 40 60 80 100
Miles

In the years following 1220, there had been a considerable influx of refugees into Asia Minor, fleeing from Jenghis Khan. Of these we have already noted[9] a small tribe of Turkmans which escaped from Khurasan in 1221 and reached Erzeroum. The majority returned from there to the east on the news of the death of Jenghis Khan but a small group of perhaps some four hundred families continued westwards, entering the dominions of the Seljuq Sultan Ala al Deen Kai Qobad I. Somewhat mistrustful of these easterners, the sultan moved them farther to the west and settled them on the borders of Byzantine territory, in the little town of Sugut, near the Sea of Marmora. The Turkman leader, Ertoghrul, accepted the land as a fief in return for military service.

In 1243, however, the Mongols invaded Asia Minor.[10] The Seljuq Sultan Ghiyath al Deen Kai Khosrou II[11] was defeated by them at Kusadagh and died in 1245. His sons fought one another for the succession and Hulagu divided the Seljuq dominions between them, as we have seen. Thereafter the Seljuqs lost their power and the dynasty came to an end in 1300.

The last great Il Khan, Ghazan, died on 17th May, 1304, and thereafter Mongol power was remote and ineffective. The Byzantines were too weak to profit by the power vacuum and between 1330 and 1350 there appeared no less than twenty-six independent Turkish ameerates in Asia Minor. Byzantium still held Nicaea, Nicomedia, Brusa and a strip of coast on the Sea of Marmora. In the north-east, the Greek Empire of Trebizond, established during the Latin régime in Constantinople, still survived. On the south, Cilicia remained an Armenian Kingdom until its extinction by the Mamlooks in 1375.

Ertoghrul had died in 1288 and had been succeeded by his son Othman. Ertoghrul was probably a heathen but Othman was converted to Islam. Curiously enough, Othman was born in 1258, the year of Hulagu's destruction of Baghdad and the virtual end of the Abbasid khalifate, at a moment when Islam seemed to be threatened with extinction. The progeny of Othman were to restore Islam as a conquering empire and were themselves to assume the office of khalif.

At Sugut, the neighbours of Othman were nearly all Christians. With the enthusiasm of the convert, he began to encroach on the Christians in the vicinity. Between 1290 and 1300, his armed followers increased from four hundred to four thousand men. Othman was one of the twenty-six independent Turkish chiefs in Asia Minor, who followed the collapse of the Seljuq dynasty, but he was one of the smallest. The most powerful was the Qaramanli Ameer with his capital at Konia.

Othman extended his territory slowly by infiltration, by cutting the roads and by making life difficult for the Greek villagers. The Byzantines

[9] Page 183. [10] Page 247. [11] Genealogical tree, page 168.

THE OTHMANLI DYNASTY

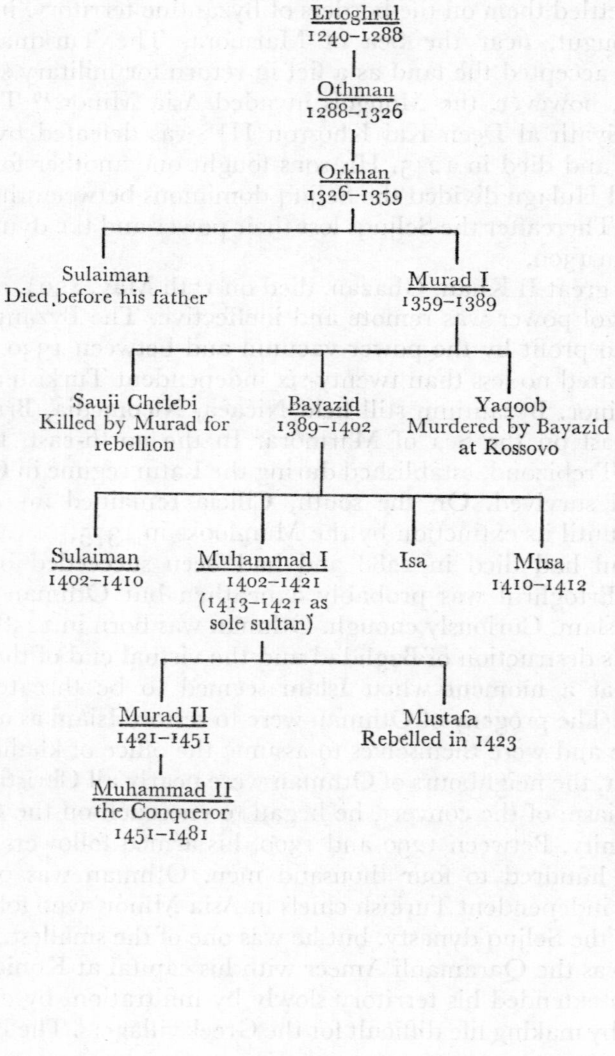

Ertoghrul
1240–1288
Othman
1288–1326
Orkhan
1326–1359
Sulaiman
Died before his father
Murad I
1359–1389
Sauji Chelebi
Killed by Murad for rebellion
Bayazid
1389–1402
Yaqoob
Murdered by Bayazid at Kossovo
Sulaiman
1402–1410
Muhammad I
1402–1421
(1413–1421 as sole sultan)
Isa
Musa
1410–1412
Murad II
1421–1451
Mustafa
Rebelled in 1423
Muhammad II
the Conqueror
1451–1481

were despairing and defeatist, Othman was pushing and energetic. There were no great battles or massacres. In 1308, the followers of Othman, who had bypassed Nicomedia, appeared on the shores of the Bosphorus. In general, they controlled the open country but could not take the walled cities. Early in 1326, Brusa surrendered, the governor and many of the citizens professing Islam. They resented the fact that the Byzantines had not attempted to help them, although Brusa was only fifty miles from Constantinople.

Soon after the fall of Brusa, Othman died. In thirty-eight years, he had extended his little patrimony by about seventy miles to the north and west. This insignificant village headman was to bequeath his name to one of the world's great empires, the Othmanli, a word corrupted in Europe to the Ottoman.

Orkhan, the son of Othman, continued to employ his father's slow and cautious methods, making Brusa his capital. In 1329, Nicaea surrendered. In 1333, Orkhan extended his boundaries south-westwards as far as the Asian shore opposite Gallipoli. When Nicomedia surrendered in 1337, the Othmanli state became a small compact area which included three towns. There was religious toleration but only Muslims were employed as soldiers, the Christians paying a poll-tax in lieu of service.

If they had persecuted the Christians, the Othmanlis would have provoked retaliation and perhaps revivified the life of the Orthodox Church. There was nothing dramatic or even noteworthy about their expansion—nothing to arouse opposition. The Byzantine Greeks surrendered to them from sheer weariness and discouragement and out of disgust with their own government. The limitation of military service to Muslims was a means of promoting conversions, for all the men of influence in the little state were soldiers. Thus an ambitious Greek was tempted to become a Muslim and join the warrior class, as indeed many of them did.

Orkhan laid the foundation of a regular army by employing a few paid mercenaries, the remainder of his force being feudal levies. His little territory was divided into small holdings for which only Muslims were eligible and which carried an obligation of military service. He was a man of restless energy, always on the move round his tiny state and he must have been personally known to all his subjects—a valuable asset in a small country. Neither Othman nor Orkhan fought any battles worth mentioning. Like all enduring empires, the Ottoman just happened, naturally, slowly and unperceived.

* * *

The utter decadence of the Byzantines was a principal factor in the rise of the Othmanlis. Andronicus II Palaeologus, who reigned from

1282 to 1328 and was thus a contemporary of Othman, had associated his son Michael IX with himself as co-emperor. But Michael died in 1320, leaving a son also called Andronicus, who had once been the darling of his grandfather Andronicus II, surnamed the Old. But Andronicus the Young took to debauchery and gambling and fell into debt. In 1321 Andronicus the Young fled to Adrianople, and declared war on his grandfather. In the ensuing thirty-four years, the tiny remnant of the Byzantine Empire was to be torn by no less than twenty-one civil wars.

In 1328, Andronicus the Young seized Constantinople, imprisoned his grandfather and assumed the purple with the title of Andronicus III. He struggled to restore order but died on 15th June, 1341, leaving an infant son, John V. (1341 was also the year of the death of Al Nasir of Egypt.) John Cantacuzene, a member of the nobility, was made regent and, in 1343, proclaimed himself co-emperor with his ward, under the title of John VI. A new civil war broke out immediately.

Byzantine anarchy was Ottoman opportunity. In 1345, Cantacuzene traded the hand of his daughter Theodora for the loan of six thousand Othmanlis to fight in the Greek civil war. For the first time the Othmanlis crossed to Europe at the invitation of a Byzantine pretender. (In 1072, the Seljuq Turks had overrun Asia Minor as a result of Byzantine civil wars in precisely the same manner.)[12] In 1347, John VI Cantacuzene, assisted by the Othmanlis, captured Constantinople.

The Serbians had profited by the Byzantine civil wars to occupy Macedonia. Cantacuzene was fain to ask Orkhan to send ten thousand Othmanlis to drive out the Serbians. At the same time he wrote to the pope begging him to organize a crusade in the West to drive out of Europe the Othmanlis whom he himself had brought in. He repeated the appeal in 1349, 1350 and 1353.

Three accidental factors favoured Orkhan. The first was the arrival of the Black Death which spread in the West in 1348 and which for some years almost cut off Europe from the East and made a crusade unthinkable. Moreover, in Thrace itself the plague, being due to rats and fleas, was much more severe in towns, where most of the Greeks lived, than in the open country where the Othmanlis camped.

The second factor which favoured Orkhan was the bitter hostility between Genoa and Venice. Both possessed powerful fleets and, if they had united, could easily have prevented the Muslims from crossing at Gallipoli. Instead, however, the Genoese allied themselves to Orkhan, ferried his troops across the Dardanelles and sunk the Byzantine fleet.

Thirdly, civil war broke out again in 1351 between John V Palaeologus and John VI Cantacuzene. In 1352, the Venetians and the Bulgarians declared for Palaeologus and Cantacuzene begged Orkhan to

[12] *The Course of Empire.*

THE DYNASTY OF THE PALAEOLOGI

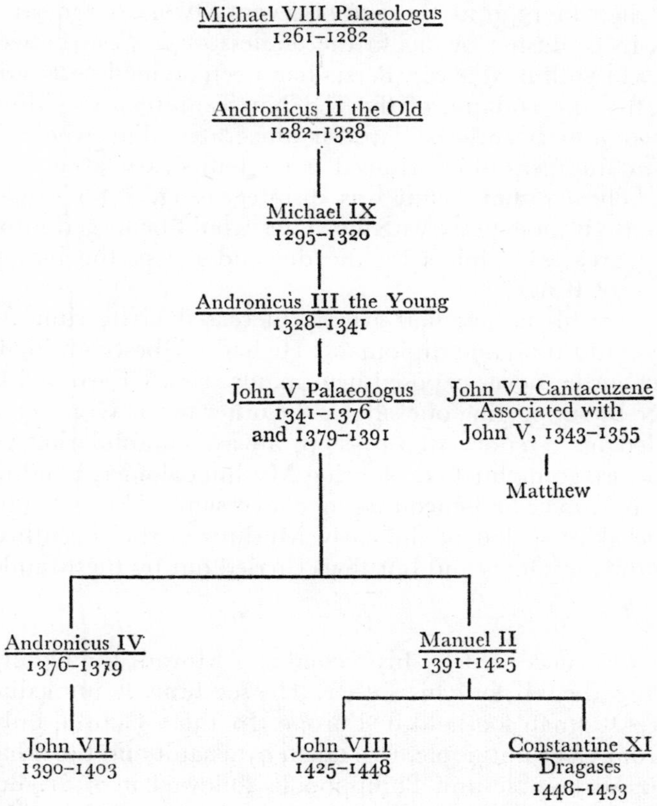
Michael VIII Palaeologus
1261–1282
Andronicus II the Old
1282–1328
Michael IX
1295–1320
Andronicus III the Young
1328–1341
John V Palaeologus
1341–1376
and 1379–1391
John VI Cantacuzene
Associated with
John V, 1343–1355
Matthew
Andronicus IV
1376–1379
Manuel II
1391–1425
John VII
1390–1403
John VIII
1425–1448
Constantine XI
Dragases
1448–1453

send twenty thousand Muslims to Thrace. Soon the Othmanlis were firmly established in Thrace and, in 1356, they occupied Gallipoli, Bulair and Rodosto on their own account. The Greeks laid the blame on Cantacuzene, who was obliged to abdicate, leaving John V Palaeologus as sole emperor. Unable to evict the Othmanlis, he signed a treaty with Orkhan, ceding him an area in Thrace on condition he would not annex any more. Orkhan immediately brought over Muslim settlers and established them on the land.

Orkhan died in 1359 at the age of seventy-two. At the same time Egypt was in confusion owing to the endless *coups d'état* between the descendants of Sultan Al Nasir. Persia had been divided between minor dynasties after the collapse of the Il Khan Empire. Asia Minor had disintegrated into twenty-six Turkish ameerates. The whole Middle East was in fragmentation. Indeed a contemporary observer might well have believed that Islam was disintegrating. Who would have dreamed that all these petty warring states would be forged into one of the world's greatest empires by the descendants of the insignificant tribal ameer of Brusa?

Orkhan, like his father, had greatly increased his territory, not by war but by infiltration and diplomacy. He had the best fighting force in the Levant but he never exposed it to major risks. He worked his way into Thrace by supporting one side or the other in the Greek civil wars. He extended his territory step-by-step, always consolidating what he had won before going further, planting Muslim colonies, building forts, winning people over and encouraging conversions. This procedure was much more akin to that of the early Muslims of the seventh century than were the massacres and burnings carried out by the Mamlooks.

* * *

Orkhan was succeeded by his second son Murad, the eldest, Sulaiman, having died before his father. He set himself immediately to extend the Ottoman foothold in Europe. In 1360, Chorlu, only forty-six miles from Constantinople, was taken by assault and the inhabitants massacred. Adrianople and Philippopolis followed in 1361. But Pope Urban V was now thoroughly alarmed and urged King Louis of Hungary to drive the Muslims from Europe. In 1364 a combined army of Hungarians, Serbians and Bosnians marched on Adrianople but was completely defeated by Murad in a surprise night attack on the River Maritza. All the territory south of the Balkan mountains was annexed by Murad and John V Palaeologus became an Othmanli vassal. In 1366, Murad moved his capital from Brusa in Asia to Adrianople and the Ottomans became a European power.

These fresh conquests enabled the Ottoman settlers to acquire great

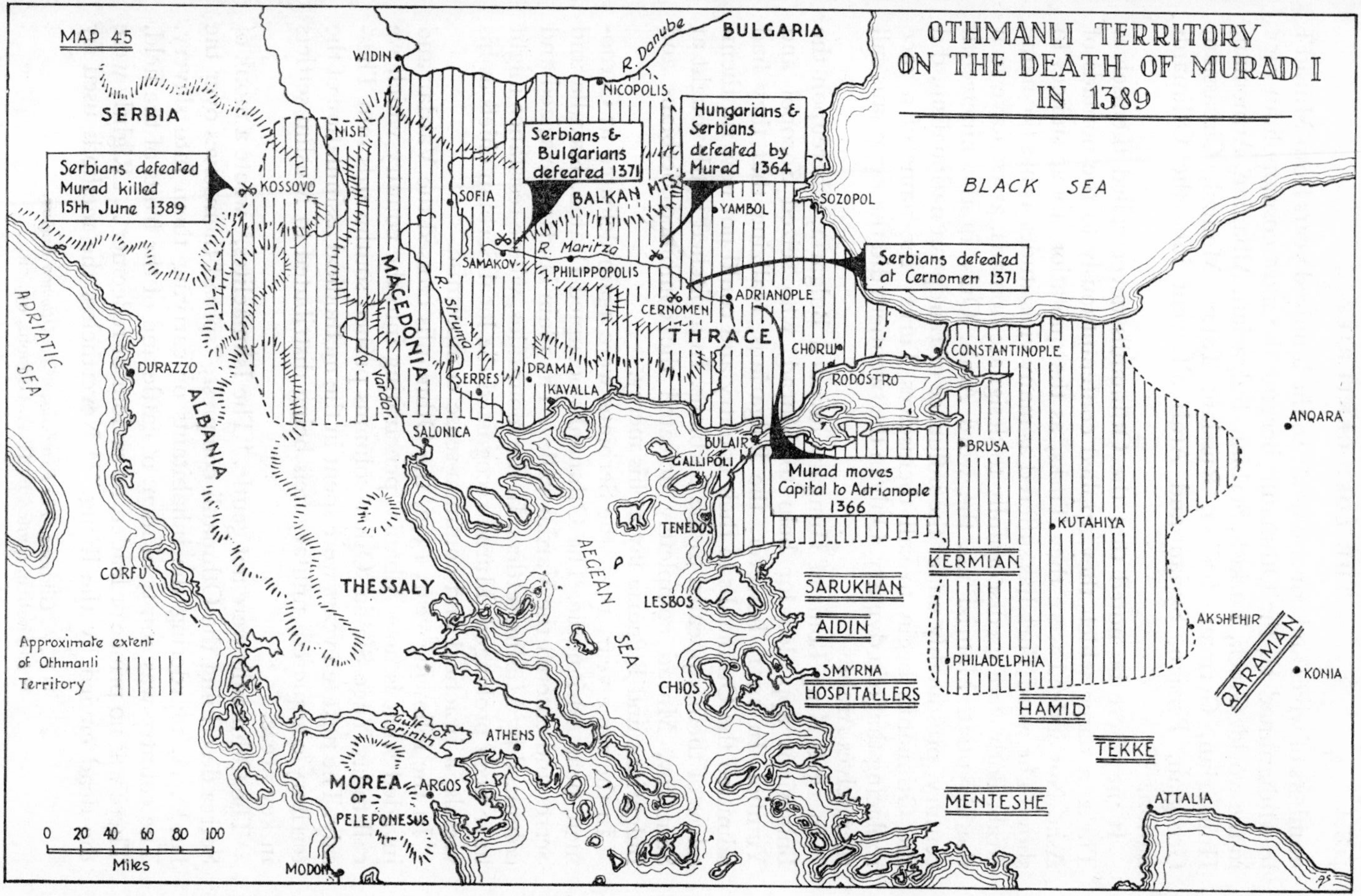
MAP 45
OTHMANLI TERRITORY ON THE DEATH OF MURAD I IN 1389
BLACK SEA
BULGARIA
R. Danube
WIDIN
NICOPOLIS
SERBIA
NISH
Serbians defeated Murad killed 15th June 1389
KOSSOVO
Serbians & Bulgarians defeated 1371
Hungarians & Serbians defeated by Murad 1364
SOFIA
BALKAN MTS
YAMBOL
SOZOPOL
SAMAKOV
R. Maritza
PHILIPPOPOLIS
Serbians defeated at Cernomen 1371
CERNOMEN
ADRIANOPLE
THRACE
MACEDONIA
R. Struma
R. Vardar
CHORU
CONSTANTINOPLE
RODOSTRO
SERRES
DRAMA
KAVALLA
SALONICA
BULAIR
GALLIPOLI
Murad moves Capital to Adrianople 1366
BRUSA
ANQARA
KUTAHIYA
TENEDOS
AEGEAN SEA
KERMIAN
SARUKHAN
AIDIN
LESBOS
AKSHEHIR
QARAMAN
KONIA
PHILADELPHIA
SMYRNA
HOSPITALLERS
CHIOS
HAMID
TEKKE
MENTESHE
ATTALIA
ADRIATIC SEA
DURAZZO
ALBANIA
CORFU
THESSALY
Gulf of Corinth
ATHENS
MOREA or PELEPONESUS
ARGOS
MODON
Approximate extent of Othmanli Territory
0 20 40 60 80 100
Miles

numbers of wives and concubines. "In the hundred years from Murad I to Muhammad II, the Othmanlis became the most cosmopolitan race in the world. Greek, Turkish, Serbian, Bulgarian, Albanian, Armenian, Hungarian, German, Italian, Russian, Tatar, Mongol, Circassian, Georgian, Persian, Syrian and Arab all went into the Othmanli nation."[13]

It may here be noted that the Othmanlis never called themselves Turks, a name which they applied contemptuously to the nomads of Asia. Nor indeed were they Turks, as the quotation above suffices to show. The word Turk has suffered as many vicissitudes as has the name Arab. Both were used scornfully to designate nomads, as we have seen the Egyptian Maqrizi use the word Arab. Only in the nineteenth century, presumably under the influence of European nationalism, did the Othmanlis begin to call themselves Turks—the name of a race replacing that of a dynasty. Only in the twentieth did the Egyptians call themselves Arabs.

In 1366 King Louis of Hungary invaded Bulgaria, whereupon the Bulgarians appealed for help to Murad, who seized Sozopol and Yambol. In 1371, however, the Bulgarians, realizing that they had admitted the Othmanlis to their country and could not now rid themselves of them, appealed to the Serbians. In a pitched battle fought at Samakov, Murad completely defeated the combined Serbians and Bulgarians and Bulgaria lay at his mercy.

In the same year, 1371, the Serbians were again defeated at Cernomen, near Adrianople. The Othmanlis occupied Drama, Kavalla and Serres and entered the Vardar valley. The plain lands were seized and colonized by Muslim settlers. In the mountains, where resistance might have been prolonged, Murad recognized the local Serbian chiefs as his vassals, a practical and common-sense compromise.

In the following year, 1372, the Othmanlis crossed the Vardar and invaded what is now Albania, penetrating into the country which we call today Yugo-Slavia. Other columns pushed southwards into Thessaly. The next ten years were spent in the methodical assimilation of the territory conquered, military fiefs being distributed to Muslim settlers in key areas.

The Othmanlis were not gentle. "The Ishmaelites," wrote a monk of Serres describing the Othmanli conquest, "spread themselves over the land . . . murdering the inhabitants or carrying them into slavery. The country was empty of men, of cattle and of the fruits of the field. There was no prince or leader, no saviour or redeemer . . . Rightly were the dead envied by the living."[14] Nevertheless the methods used by

[13] H. A. Gibbons, *The Foundation of the Ottoman Empire.*
[14] Miklositch, quoted by H. A. Gibbons, op. cit.

Murad were in striking contrast to those of Jenghis Khan. Murad advanced step by step, pausing to consolidate, planting settlers, organizing an administration, even endeavouring to win the loyalty of the conquered.

The papacy seems at this time to have conceived the hope that the disastrous situation of Constantinople might be used to persuade the Orthodox Church to submit to Rome. In 1369, John V Palaeologus went to Rome to solicit help from the West. On 19th October, before the High Altar of St. Peter's, he abjured the "heresies" of the Orthodox Communion and, in return, received letters from the pope to the princes of Western Christendom, who, however, replied only with polite excuses. When John returned to Constantinople the Greek clergy and people loudly rejected his declaration of submission to Rome.

In 1373, as though the times were not already precarious enough for the Byzantines, John Palaeologus decided to disinherit his eldest son Andronicus IV and to associate his second son Manuel with himself as co-emperor. Curiously enough the eldest son of Murad, Sauji Chelebi, was also estranged from his father. The two boys rebelled together against their two fathers. Murad made short work of his son whose eyes were torn out and then his head cut off. Murad ordered John V to inflict the same penalty on his son but the operation was done half-heartedly, Andronicus recovered his sight and lived soon to rebel again.

In 1375, two years later, John Palaeologus sold the island of Tenedos to Venice. The Genoese, mad with jealousy, offered to make Andronicus emperor if he would give Tenedos to them. On 12th August, 1376, they seized Constantinople, John V Palaeologus and his son Manuel were thrown into prison, Andronicus IV was crowned emperor and the Venetians had to flee for their lives. Three years later, on 1st July, 1379, the Venetians retaliated by releasing John V and Manuel, who took refuge with Murad. These insane hatreds between so-called Christians had placed all the cards in the hands of the Muslims. Murad intervened and re-appointed John and Manuel as co-emperors on condition of an annual tribute of thirty thousand pieces of gold, the maintenance of twelve thousand soldiers to fight in the Ottoman army and the cession of Philadelphia, the last Greek city in Asia Minor.

Being now firmly established in Europe, Murad turned to Asia Minor, proceeding with his usual prudence. The Ameer of Kermian found it advisable to give his daughter in marriage to Murad's son Bayazid with the city of Kutahiya as her dowry. In 1377, Murad bought the important city of Akshehir from its ameer, thereby making his frontier march with that of the Qaramanli Ameer, the most powerful prince in Asia Minor. Murad thus considerably extended his territory without a fight.

In 1385, the Othmanlis occupied Sofia and the following year Nish. In 1387, Murad crossed once more to Asia and fought a bitter but indecisive battle against the Qaramanli Ameer near Konia. This was the first battle he had fought against Muslims. For a hundred years all Othmanli wars had been against Christians.

In 1388, however, there was a rising in Serbia where a column of twenty thousand Ottomans was almost exterminated. The Serbians, in great exultation, invited the Albanians and the Bosnians, to join them in the final expulsion of the Muslims. Murad took the reverse calmly and, in fact, sent off a column to Bulgaria and annexed the whole country up to the Danube, as far north as Widin and Nicopolis. Only in 1389 did he concentrate a large force to deal with the rebellious Serbians. The two armies confronted one another on 15th June, 1389, on the Plain of Kossovo—the Plain of Blackbirds. The fate of the Balkan Peninsula for five hundred years hung in the balance.

The fighting was long and desperate and when noon had passed neither side had as yet gained a decisive advantage, when Vuko Brankovitch, a nephew of the Serbian King Lazarus, withdrew with his troops from the field. He had quarrelled with other members of the royal family and chose this moment to give way to his resentment. The Othmanlis once more pressed the attack and the Serbians collapsed. The victory was complete and the Christian army was virtually destroyed.

According to the Othmanli version, Murad was inspecting the battlefield after the victory when he was suddenly attacked and murdered by a wounded Serbian soldier An alternative account alleges that a Serbian noble, Miloch Obranovitch, entered the Ottoman camp before the battle, saying that he had important information to give to Murad. When introduced into his presence, he stabbed him with a dagger.

Murad had led the Othmanlis for thirty years with extraordinary wisdom and patience. He was not merely a successful fighter, however, but a leader, an organizer, an administrator and a politician. He exploited with skill the family quarrels of the Palaeologi, and the mutual jealousies of the Serbians and Bulgarians, and of Venice and Genoa.

His handling of the Christians was remarkable and throughout his reign large contingents of Orthodox Christians fought in the Ottoman army. He was also the founder of the Janissaries, or new troops, later to become world famous. The Othmanlis took selected Christian boys, converted them to Islam and trained them up as the sultan's household troops. Forbidden to raise families, their whole lives were inspired by the *esprit-de-corps* of their units.

Murad was careful to show respect for the Christian Church, yet he encouraged conversion to Islam by every means in his power.

Nationality soon became identified with religion. Any Christian who adopted Islam became an Othmanli, just as, in the eighth century, all who became Muslims were regarded as Arabs.

"A majority of the conquered Byzantines must have become Othmanlis," writes Professor Gibbons, "and the same could probably be said of many Serbians, Bulgarians and Albanians. Thus the Othmanlis of the fourteenth century were in reality a new race of which the ruling family was of Turkman origin but of which the people were a mixture of Turk and European with the European probably predominating. Moreover, the Othmanli nation grew up in Constantinople and the Balkans amid ancient, cultured peoples, long permeated by the traditions of Greece and Rome."[15]

* * *

Two of Murad's sons had been at the Battle of Kossovo, Bayazid and Yaqoob. No sooner did Bayazid hear of his father's death than he immediately sent some men to strangle his brother in his tent. Fratricide was always to be a characteristic of the family of Othman.

When Genoese and Venetian representatives tendered their congratulations to Bayazid on his accession, he boasted arrogantly that one day he would stable his horses in St. Peter's in Rome. Murad had been careful not to be offensive to Christians but Bayazid made no secret of his hatred. The Serbians, however, constituted an exception and he became a personal friend of Stephen, the son of Lazarus, the Serbian prince, whose sister he married. The Serbians as a result fought gallantly for the Othmanlis as long as he was alive. Although Bayazid was scarcely an ideal husband, he always remained genuinely fond of Despina.

Murad, it will be remembered, had skilfully extended his boundaries in Asia Minor at the price of only one indecisive battle with the Qaramanlis. Bayazid was less circumspect. In 1390, he overran and annexed the ameerates of Aidin, Sarukhan, Hamid and others, leaving only Smyrna which had been annexed by the Knights Hospitallers in 1344.

In 1391, Bayazid fought a drawn battle with Ala al Deen Qaraman who, however, surrendered some territory as the price of peace. But when Bayazid returned to Adrianople in 1392, Ala al Deen re-occupied the area ceded and marched on Brusa. Bayazid instantly called in all his vassal contingents, Serbians, Bulgarians and Byzantines, crossed at Gallipoli and marched against the enemy. The speed of his action earned for him the nickname of Yilderim or Lightning. In a battle near Kutahiya, Ala al Deen was taken prisoner and hanged on the battlefield. The Othmanlis took Akshehir, Akserai and Konia and then also

15 H. A. Gibbons, *The Foundation of the Ottoman Empire.*

Caesarea and Kastamouni. In 1393, Bayazid occupied Tokat, Samsun and Sinope.[16] In two years, he had annexed almost all Asia Minor.

* * *

In 1395, the Othmanlis established a close blockade of Constantinople. John V Palaeologus had died in 1391 and his son Manuel II was now emperor. Bayazid decided to continue his father's policy of sowing discord. A young nephew of Manuel II, John, the son of Andronicus IV, was encouraged to make trouble. The heirs of the Caesars were made to cringe before the haughty barbarian. The abject humiliations inflicted on a once great and noble nation make painful reading.

When King Louis the Great of Hungary died in 1382, one of his daughters married Sigismond of Luxemburg, thereby making him King of Hungary. Sigismond was the only Western ruler who appreciated the Ottoman danger. In the West the great schism between rival popes had made a united Christian effort impossible. Urban VI and Boniface IX were popes in Rome while, in 1394, Benedict XIII was crowned in Avignon. The Venetians, with their usual perfidy, were simultaneously assuring Sigismond and Bayazid of their support. The business of Venice was business.

In 1395, however, an appeal by Sigismond to the court of France met with unexpected success. For a brief moment Europe was at peace and many volunteers flocked to Sigismond's standard. The French contingent numbered a thousand knights and six thousand men-at-arms, commanded by Jean de Nevers, the twenty-four-year-old son of the Duke of Burgundy. There was a German party under Frederick of Hohenzollern and England, Flanders, Lombardy and Savoy were also represented. The Knights Hospitallers were led by their Grand Master from Rhodes, Philibert de Naillac. The total Frank contingent may have been two thousand knights and eight thousand men.

In the spring of 1396, the Crusaders left Buda. Widin surrendered and in September the army reached Nicopolis, while the Othmanlis had concentrated at Philippopolis. So bitter was the feeling between the Orthodox and the Roman churches that the Byzantines, the Serbians and the Bulgarians were ready to fight for the Muslims against the Latins. Crossing the Balkan Mountains, while the Franks still thought him to be far away, "Lightning" Bayazid reached a point four miles south of Nicopolis on 25th September, 1396.

Bayazid prepared quickly for battle. The two armies were about equally matched in numbers.[17] The Ottoman position was on high

[16] Map 44, page 410.

[17] Each side is alleged to have had about 100,000 men but the figure may be exaggerated. A. S. Atiya, *The Crusade in the Later Middle Ages*.

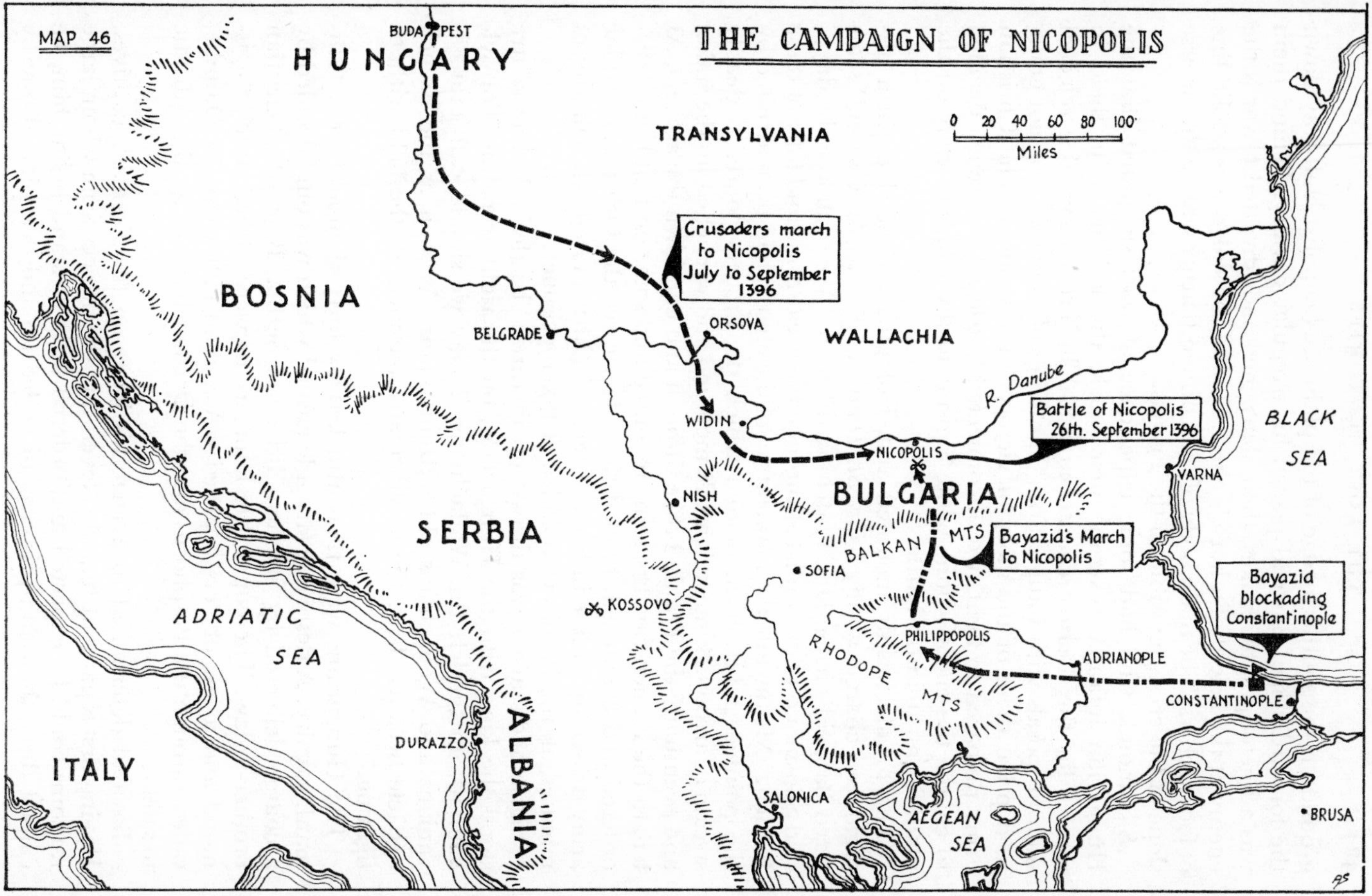
MAP 46
THE CAMPAIGN OF NICOPOLIS
0 20 40 60 80 100
Miles
BUDA PEST
HUNGARY
TRANSYLVANIA
Crusaders march to Nicopolis July to September 1396
BOSNIA
BELGRADE
ORSOVA
WALLACHIA
R. Danube
WIDIN
NICOPOLIS
Battle of Nicopolis 26th. September 1396
BLACK SEA
VARNA
BULGARIA
NISH
SERBIA
BALKAN MTS
Bayazid's March to Nicopolis
SOFIA
KOSSOVO
Bayazid blockading Constantinople
ADRIATIC SEA
PHILIPPOPOLIS
RHODOPE MTS
ADRIANOPLE
CONSTANTINOPLE
DURAZZO
ALBANIA
ITALY
SALONICA
AEGEAN SEA
BRUSA

ground on the southern edge of the plain of Nicopolis. Half-way down the forward slope, Bayazid placed his irregular cavalry. Behind them was a line of pointed stakes, their sharpened ends directed towards the enemy at the height of a horse's chest. Behind the stakes was a solid line of foot archers. The main body of the Othmanli army was on the reverse slope of the crest, invisible to the Franks.

Sigismond, who had some experience of war, suggested that the Hungarian infantry take the first shock, the knights being held in reserve for the decisive counter-attack. The French chivalry rejected such proposals with indignation. The King of Hungary was not going to deprive them of the glory of victory, they shouted. The Christian army prepared to fight two unconnected battles. The French decided to charge the enemy alone while Sigismond drew up his army on the plain for an infantry battle.

The Franks hastily mounted and, galloping up the slope in a disorganized charge, crying "*Vive St. Denis*" and "*Vive St. Georges*," scattered Bayazid's irregulars. Watching them go, "We shall lose the day," said Sigismond to de Naillac, "through the great pride and folly of these French." Meanwhile the momentum of the charge had been arrested by the pointed stakes, from behind which the archers poured a deadly stream of arrows. Some knights dismounted and wrenched up the stakes and eventually the Franks broke through and cut down the archers. At length the French cavalry, some mounted and some on foot but all disordered and exhausted, topped the ridge to see the Othmanli regular army drawn up in line in front of them. In little more than a matter of minutes, all the Franks were killed or taken prisoner.

Sigismond's army was drawn up in three "battles". In the centre stood the king with the Hungarians, on the right were the Transylvanians, on the left the Wallachians. Today we should call Transylvanians and Wallachians alike Roumanians. As soon as the French débâcle became clear, the Wallachians marched off the field without fighting.

The Hungarians were then attacked by forty thousand fresh Othmanli cavalry. A desperate struggle ensued which was only decided by a charge delivered by Stephen, Prince of Serbia, Bayazid's Christian brother-in-law. Thereupon the Hungarians were exterminated. Sigismond and a few officers boarded a Venetian galley on the Danube, sailed through the Bosphorus and the Dardanelles and up the Adriatic to safety.

Bayazid determined to avenge his losses on the Frankish captives. Having first separated Jean de Nevers and the princes from whom large ransoms could be expected and ordered them to stand beside him, he caused three thousand prisoners to be led up and decapitated one by

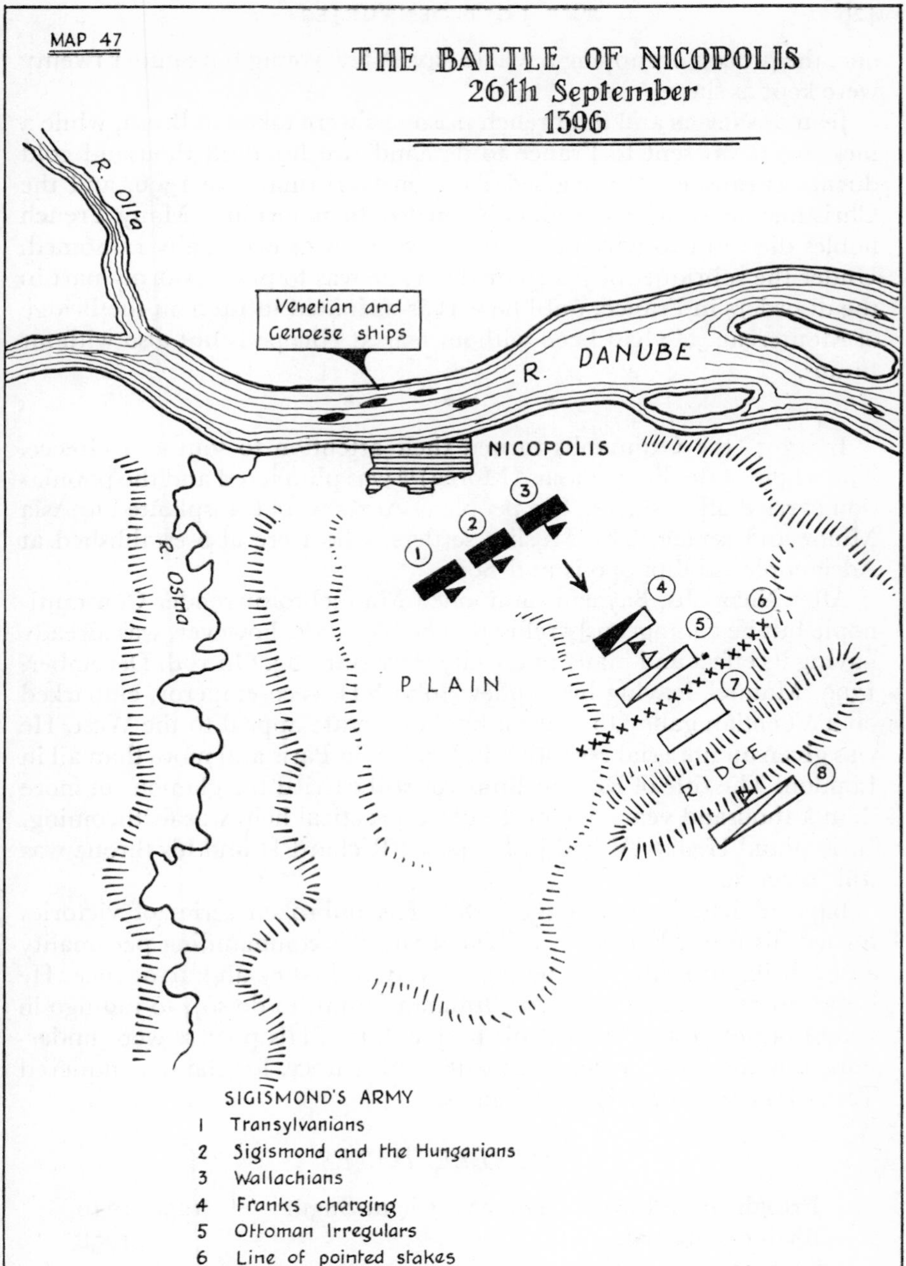
MAP 47
THE BATTLE OF NICOPOLIS
26th September
1396
R. Olta
Venetian and
Genoese ships
R. DANUBE
NICOPOLIS
R. Osma
PLAIN
RIDGE
1
2
3
4
5
6
7
8
SIGISMOND'S ARMY
1 Transylvanians
2 Sigismond and the Hungarians
3 Wallachians
4 Franks charging
5 Ottoman Irregulars
6 Line of pointed stakes
7 Ottoman Archers
8 Ottoman regular cavalry and Serbian cavalry
With acknowledgements to Prof. A.S. Atiya

one, the process occupying a whole day. A few young boys under twenty were kept as slaves.

Jean de Nevers and the French prisoners were taken to Brusa, while a messenger was sent to France to demand two hundred thousand gold ducats as ransom. He reached Paris on Christmas Eve 1396, and the Christmas feasting was suddenly turned to mourning. Many French nobles died in captivity but Jean de Nevers was eventually ransomed. Under the sobriquet of Jean-sans-Peur, he was to play a stormy part in the disorders in France, until he was assassinated in 1420 on the Bridge of Montereau. He had been without fear at Nicopolis but also without brains.

* * *

In 1397, the Othmanlis turned their attention to southern Greece. The whole of the Peleponesus (Morea)[18] was plundered and the population carried off as slaves. The people of Argos were transplanted to Asia Minor and replaced by Muslim settlers, who were also established at Adrianople, Philippopolis and Sofia.

After Nicopolis, Bayazid summoned Manuel to surrender Constantinople but he courageously refused. The blockade, however, was already having its effect and many in the city were starving. On 10th December, 1399, Manuel, leaving his nephew John VII as co-emperor, embarked on a Venetian galley to make a final desperate appeal to the West. He was given an imperial reception in Venice, in Paris and more than all in London. The title of Roman Emperor still carried the glamour of more than a thousand years of glory. But no practical help was forthcoming. In England Henry IV had just deposed Richard II and his throne was still insecure.

Bayazid had been too successful. His unbroken series of victories turned his head. Formerly a diligent ruler, a commanding personality and a brilliant soldier, he now gave way to luxury and arrogance. He began to drink wine (the first Ottoman Sultan to do so), to indulge in sexual orgies and to neglect his public duties. His powers were undermined at the most critical moment of his career, for the unconquered Tamerlane was already at the gates.

NOTABLE DATES

Ertoghrul and his Turkmans settle at Sugut	1230–1240
Birth of Othman	1258
Surrender of Brusa Death of Othman Orkhan becomes ameer	1326

[18] Map 45, page 417.

Surrender of Nicaea	1329
Death of Sultan Al Nasir of Egypt	June 1341
Mamlook Empire in confusion	1341–1382
Othmanlis cross to Thrace at invitation of John Cantacuzene	1345
Black Death in Europe	1348
Othmanlis occupy all Thrace	1360–1361
Serbians and Hungarians defeated on the Maritza	1364
King Peter of Cyprus sacks Alexandria	10th to 17th October, 1365
Adrianople made the Othmanli capital	1366
Serbians and Bulgarians defeated at Samakov	1371
Barqooq becomes Sultan of Egypt	26th November, 1382
Serbians defeated at Kossovo Murad killed Accession of Bayazid	15th June, 1389
Battle of Nicopolis	26th September, 1396
Death of Barqooq	20th June, 1399

PERSONALITIES

Hungary

Louis The Great	1342–1382
Mary, daughter of Louis, married Sigismond of Luxemburg, who became Sigismond, King of Hungary	1386–1410

Puppet Sultans of Egypt after Al Nasir

Death of Malik al Nasir Muhammad	1341
Al Ashraf	1341
Al Nasir Ahmed	1342
Al Salih Ismail	1342
Al Kamil Shaaban	1344
Al Mudhaffar Hajji	1346
Al Nasir Hasan (1st reign)	1347
Al Salih Salih	1351
Al Nasir Hasan (2nd reign)	1354
Al Mansoor Muhammad	1361
Al Ashraf Shaaban	1363
Al Mansoor Ali	1377
Al Salih Hajji (1st reign)	1381
Al Dhahir Barqooq	1382

Al Mansoor Hajji (2nd reign)	1389
Al Dhahir Barqooq	1389–1399

Notes

(1) Hajji was called Malik al Salih during his first reign but was renamed Malik al Mansoor during the eight months of his second reign.

(2) An examination of the dates reveals the frequency with which these helpless sultans were raised and then dismissed.

XX

The Lame Genocide
1336–1405

Unhappy Persia—that in former age
Hast been the seat of mighty conquerors
That, in their power and their policies,
Have triumphed over Africa and the bounds
Of Europe, where the sun dares scarce appear.
Now Turks and Tartars shake their swords at thee,
Meaning to mangle all thy provinces.

CHRISTOPHER MARLOWE, *Tamburlaine The Great*

Timur was lofty in stature as though he belonged to the remnants of the Amalekites, robust in body, brave and fearless like a hard rock . . . He was called the unconquered lord of the seven climes, ruler by land and sea, conqueror of kings and sultans.

AHMAD IBN ARABSHAH, *Timur, The Great Prince*

This man, comparatively cultivated, a lover of Persian art and literature, sharing in one of the most refined civilizations of the old world, behaved like a gang leader, plundering for plundering's sake, massacring and destroying as if incapable of understanding cultural values.

GROUSSET, *L'Empire des Steppes*

XX

TAMERLANE was born at Kish in Trans-Oxiana on 8th April, 1336. His name was Timur, meaning iron, a name common among Turks and Mongols. His father was the chief of the unimportant Barlas tribe of Turkic origin, settled in that area.

The magic of the personalities of great men cannot be caught by the historian, but we may note the peculiarly favourable circumstances which enabled Timur to be a conqueror. In the mid-fourteenth century, four great military powers lay within reach of Trans-Oxiana, the Mamlooks of Egypt, the Il Khans of Persia, the Sultanate of Delhi and the Othmanlis. The Seljuq Empire of Konia (Iconium) had ended in 1300.

In 1334, the Il Khanate broke up. In 1341, five years after the birth of Tamerlane, the great Mamlook Sultan Al Nasir died in Cairo and Egypt suffered a period of weakness and instability. In India, the Sultanate of Delhi, which a few years before had controlled the whole subcontinent, had shrunk to a small state when Muhammad ibn Tughluq died in 1351. When Firuz Shah Tughluq died in 1388, even the little state of Delhi fell into confusion. All these countries continued unstable, weak and divided throughout the life of Tamerlane.

A wind of change was blowing in the East and the old régimes were in dissolution. From the resulting anarchy, the Safavid Empire of Persia and the Ottoman Empire were to emerge. Tamerlane's intervention did not help to build the new order but merely added to the miseries of the age of transition.

* * *

In 1359, Tughluq Timur, the Jagatai Khan, who lived as a nomad on the steppes, invaded the settled area of Trans-Oxiana to reassert his suzerainty. Tamerlane first served Tughluq Timur but then rebelled against him and joined a local chief called Ameer Husain. It was at this period of disorder that he received an arrow-wound in the leg, as a result of which he was nicknamed Timur i Lenk or Timur the Lame, corrupted in the West to Tamerlane.

In 1366, the nomad Jagatai were driven out but, in 1370, Tamerlane killed Ameer Husain, thereby becoming himself the dictator of Trans-Oxiana. Still presumably uncertain of his position, he discovered a mild and retiring descendant of Jenghis Khan and caused him to be acclaimed as khan. Then, marrying a woman from the Golden Family, he assumed the title of Gurgan, or son-in-law of the Great Khan. These

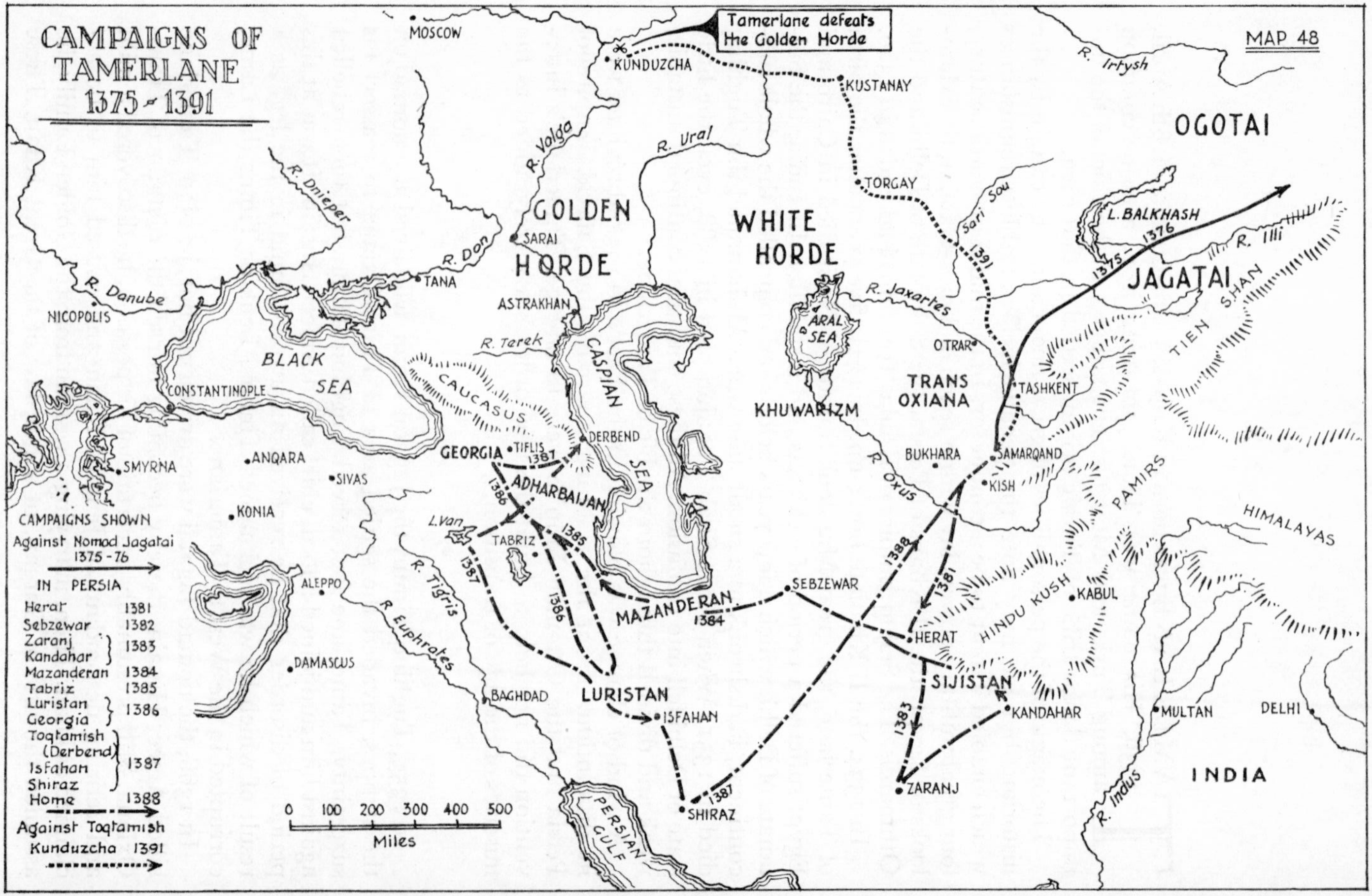
CAMPAIGNS OF TAMERLANE 1375 - 1391
MAP 48
Tamerlane defeats the Golden Horde
MOSCOW
KUNDUZCHA
KUSTANAY
R. Irtysh
OGOTAI
R. Volga
R. Ural
TORGAY
R. Dnieper
GOLDEN HORDE
WHITE HORDE
Sari Sou
L. BALKHASH
1375 - 1376
R. Illi
JAGATAI
TIEN SHAN
SARAI
R. Don
TANA
1391
R. Danube
NICOPOLIS
ASTRAKHAN
R. Jaxartes
ARAL SEA
OTRAR
R. Terek
BLACK SEA
CAUCASUS
CASPIAN SEA
TRANS OXIANA
TASHKENT
CONSTANTINOPLE
KHUWARIZM
DERBEND
GEORGIA
TIFLIS
BUKHARA
SAMARQAND
SMYRNA
ANQARA
SIVAS
ADHARBAIJAN
R. Oxus
KISH
PAMIRS
KONIA
L. Van
TABRIZ
HIMALAYAS
ALEPPO
R. Tigris
R. Euphrates
SEBZEWAR
KABUL
HINDU KUSH
MAZANDERAN
HERAT
DAMASCUS
SIJISTAN
BAGHDAD
LURISTAN
ISFAHAN
KANDAHAR
MULTAN
DELHI
INDIA
ZARANJ
R. Indus
SHIRAZ
PERSIAN GULF
1381
1383
1384
1385
1386
1387
1388
0 100 200 300 400 500
Miles
CAMPAIGNS SHOWN
Against Nomad Jagatai 1375 - 76
IN PERSIA
Herat 1381
Sebzewar 1382
Zaranj, Kandahar 1383
Mazanderan 1384
Tabriz 1385
Luristan, Georgia 1386
Toqtamish (Derbend), Isfahan, Shiraz 1387
Home 1388
Against Toqtamish Kunduzcha 1391

efforts to associate himself with the family are yet another tribute to the overwhelming prestige of Jenghis Khan. Having thus acquired social status, Tamerlane set himself to organize an army.

The territory of Khuwarizm had been seized by an independent Turkish chief. In 1371, Tamerlane invaded Khuwarizm and annexed it to Trans-Oxania, though it was not finally subdued until 1379. In 1375 and 1376, he invaded the Illi valley and pursued the nomad Jagatai tribes east of the Tien Shan.

In comparing Tamerlane with Jenghis Khan, one remarkable contrast confronts us. Jenghis Khan was never obliged to conquer the same country twice. Thus between his major campaigns against China or Persia, for example, he was able to spend two or three years virtually at rest. Although Tamerlane was no less ruthless a killer, the countries which he conquered rebelled again as soon as he withdrew. As a result, all his life was filled with an endless succession of campaigns, returning again and again to repress revolts in areas already conquered.

In April 1381, Tamerlane captured Herat from the Kert dynasty already mentioned[1] but, in 1382, the city revolted and was captured a second time by Miran Shah, the third son of Tamerlane. A general massacre followed, the heads of the victims being built into towers of skulls. All the members of the ruling family were killed. The Kerts had been Princes of Herat for a hundred and thirty years.

From Herat, Tamerlane moved on to Sebzewar, where the ruler, Ali al Muaiyid, did homage. The following winter, however, Sebzewar revolted, with the result that it suffered a fearful destruction. As a refinement of cruelty, two thousand living human beings were covered with mortar and built alive into a tower.

In 1383, Tamerlane overran Sijistan. In the capital, Zaranj, every soul was killed "from old men of a hundred years to children at the breast". The soldiers built mountains of dead bodies, the heads being cut off and used for the erection of special towers. All the elaborate irrigation works of the province were destroyed, the main dam on the Hilmend River, on which the irrigation of the area depended, being laboriously removed stone by stone until no trace of it remained. Sijistan, once a fertile and smiling countryside, has remained a semi-desert ever since. From Sijistan Tamerlane took Kandahar, then, turning back northwards, in 1384 he overran Mazanderan, all the inhabitants of the capital being killed.

Mention has already been made of the Jalair, a family of Mongol origin, which at this time ruled a state which extended from Baghdad to Adharbaijan.[2] In 1385, Tamerlane took Tabriz, the Jalair ruler, Ahmad ibn Uwais, withdrawing to Baghdad. Thence early in 1386,

[1] Map 41, page 371. [2] Map 41, page 371.

Luristan was raided, the inhabitants being killed by being pushed over the cliffs in the mountains. In the summer of 1386, Tamerlane was back in Tabriz and, the same autumn, invaded the Christian Kingdom of Georgia.

* * *

It will be remembered that Juji, the eldest son of Jenghis Khan, had inherited the steppes of the Lower Volga and that his dominion had come to be known as the Altun Ordu or the Golden Horde. Juji was succeeded by his second son Batu, whom we have seen conquering Russia and eastern Europe in his campaigns of 1236 to 1240. The eldest son of Juji was called Orda and was a somewhat self-effacing character. While Batu became Khan of the Golden Horde, Orda was given an appanage to live on, extending from the right bank of the Jaxartes—or Sir Darya—to the Sari Sou. (See tree, page 440.)

This division in the heritage of Juji became permanent, the descendants of Batu ruling the Golden Horde while the appanage of Orda became known as the White Horde. The Golden and White Hordes remained independent of one another. In 1359, the Golden Horde, which had already been a good deal weakened by family disputes, fell into anarchy on the death of Birdibeg.

The White Horde was meanwhile ruled by Ourous Khan, a lineal descendant of Orda, against whom his nephew Toqtamish rebelled but was driven out. Thereupon he appealed for help to Tamerlane, who was flattered at receiving a descendant of Jenghis Khan as a suppliant. In 1378, Ourous Khan having died, Toqtamish with the help of Tamerlane became Khan of the White Horde. In 1380, he attacked and defeated the Golden Horde, which was in some confusion, and was acclaimed at Sarai as emperor of the Golden and White Hordes, the reunited posterity of Juji. Toqtamish then marched against the Russians, who had revolted, carried fire and sword through Russia, and razed Moscow to the ground on 13th August, 1382.

* * *

We left Tamerlane in 1386 in Adharbaijan. Meanwhile Toqtamish, who owed his original rise to Tamerlane, had conquered a vast empire, bigger than that of Tamerlane, his benefactor. Moreover, Toqtamish was no upstart Turk of doubtful origin but a direct descendant of Jenghis Khan. Tamerlane spent the winter of 1386 to 1387 in Adharbaijan where, to his surprise, in early 1387, he found himself attacked by his former protégé, Toqtamish. After heavy fighting, the latter was driven back through the pass of Derbend.

In the summer of 1387, Tamerlane marched against Van, the capital of the Black Sheep Turkmans whom he put to flight, the citizens of Van being killed by being thrown over the mountain precipices. In October 1387, he moved southwards against the Muzaffarids. Isfahan surrendered without a fight but the citizens were nevertheless all butchered, seventy thousand severed heads being built into towers outside the city. He then took Shiraz where the most beautiful women in the city were obliged to serve him wine in golden cups at a grand banquet. The artisans, the men of letters and the scientists of Shiraz were sent to Samarqand to grace the Conqueror's court.

Hafiz, one of the most famous Persian poets of all time, was a resident of Shiraz. In one of his poems he had written these lines:

> "If that fair maid of Shiraz would give me love,
> I would give Samarqand and Bukhara for the mole upon her cheek."

Tamerlane sent for the poet and said to him fiercely that he had conquered a great part of the world and sent its spoils to Bukhara and Samarqand, while an insignificant little creature like Hafiz had dared to give away both cities for the mole on the cheek of a girl. Hafiz bowed to the ground and replied, "Alas, O Prince, it is this prodigality which is the cause of the poverty in which you see me." Tamerlane was delighted at the poet's repartee and loaded him with gifts.

From Shiraz, Tamerlane was suddenly obliged to hasten back to Trans-Oxiana, where the impenitent Toqtamish was ravaging the country. When Tamerlane reached Samarqand in February 1388, Toqtamish had withdrawn but he was back again in 1389. It became evident to Tamerlane that he would be unable any further to press his conquests of the rich countries to the west, south and south-east, as long as Toqtamish hung about the steppes, ready to invade and devastate Persia whenever Tamerlane's back was turned. He decided that he must eliminate Toqtamish before any other campaigns could be undertaken.

On 19th January, 1391, Tamerlane left Tashkent for the Sari Sou, but as fast as he advanced Toqtamish retired before him. Soon the army of Tamerlane was exhausted and short of food in the immensity of the empty steppes. If Toqtamish had continued to retire northwards, Tamerlane might, in 1391, have met his 1812. But fortunately for him, the Golden Horde gave battle on 19th June, 1391, at Kunduzcha. After a long day of fierce fighting, Toqtamish was defeated. Tamerlane celebrated his success with six weeks of debauchery, women and drink on the banks of the Volga. He endeavoured to neutralize the hostility of Toqtamish by recognizing Timur Qutlugh, the grandson of Ourous Khan, as chief in his place, hoping thereby to promote a civil war. In fact, however, Toqtamish quickly re-asserted his authority as soon as Tamerlane withdrew.

In 1392, Tamerlane set out for northern Persia on what became known as the Five Years War, 1392 to 1396. He first overran Mazanderan, then marched southwards to Fars, where he was opposed by the Muzaffarid, Shah Mansoor. A furious battle took place outside Shiraz, where Tamerlane's army of thirty thousand was suddenly charged by Shah Mansoor at the head of four thousand horsemen. So reckless was the charge that it burst right through the enemy's ranks, whereupon Shah Mansoor wheeled round and charged back again. By sheer courage, he hacked his way through the ranks until he reached Tamerlane, whom he twice struck on the helmet with his sword before he was himself cut down by Shah Rukh, Tamerlane's son. All the members of the Muzaffarid family were put to death.

From Fars the Conqueror, in June 1393, returned to Hamadan and in October entered Baghdad unopposed, the ruler, Ahmad ibn Uwais, having fled to Sultan Barqooq in Cairo. Tamerlane spent three months in Baghdad in feasting and pleasure while his army plundered and massacred up and down lower Iraq. "The Tatar troops," sings the Zafar Nama, "swarmed over Iraq like ants and locusts, covering the whole countryside, plundering and ravaging." This is not an accusation made by Tamerlane's enemies, but the boast of his court historian.

Thence he moved up the Tigris and, in March 1394, captured Mardin. Then on northwards, he took Van for the second time and ravaged Georgia in the late autumn. While he had been in Iraq, Toqtamish, recovered from his defeat, had again invaded Adharbaijan by way of Derbend. As a result of this continued aggression Tamerlane decided to destroy the Golden Horde once and for all. In the spring of 1395, the Conqueror passed through the Derbend Gates and on 15th April, 1395, he defeated Toqtamish on the River Terek. Thence he marched northwards as far as Yeletz, presumably in pursuit of the defeated remnants of the Golden Horde.

Turning southwards, on 26th August, 1395, he captured Tana on the Sea of Azov, a rich commercial city where many Genoese and Venetians did business, which included the export of Turkish slave boys to Egypt. All the Europeans were killed and their warehouses and churches demolished. In the winter of 1395–1396, the great cities of Astrakhan and Sarai were utterly destroyed, the inhabitants being first tortured and then butchered.

The destruction of Sarai and Astrakhan, the sources of the wealth of the Golden Horde, ruined the eastern caravan trade which had brought prosperity to Persia, the Russian steppes and eastern Europe. Toqtamish struggled on until 1406 when he was killed by his rivals, the

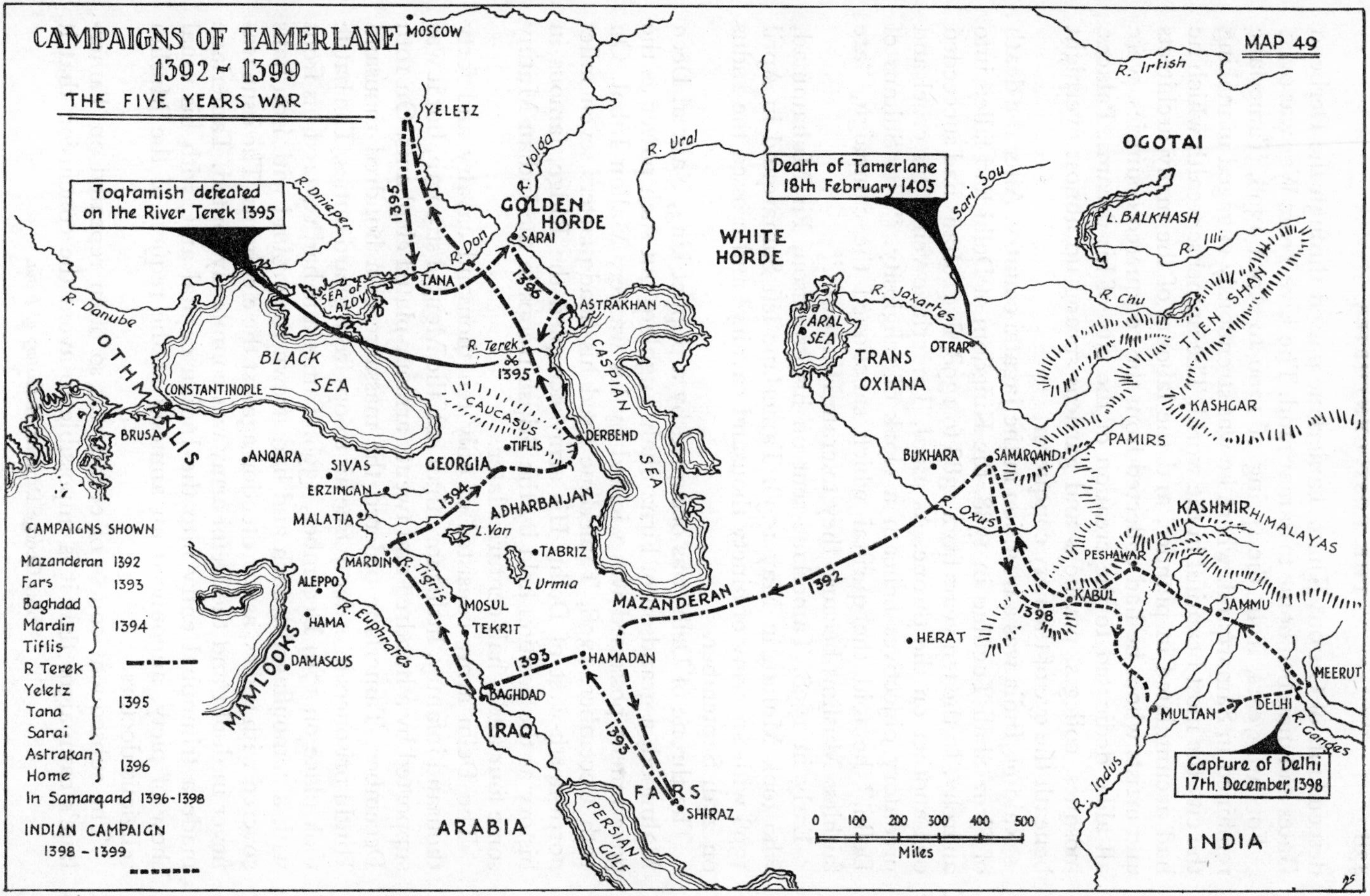
CAMPAIGNS OF TAMERLANE
1392 ~ 1399
THE FIVE YEARS WAR
MAP 49
Toqtamish defeated on the River Terek 1395
Death of Tamerlane 18th February 1405
Capture of Delhi 17th. December, 1398
CAMPAIGNS SHOWN
Mazanderan 1392
Fars 1393
Baghdad
Mardin
Tiflis
1394
R Terek
Yeletz
Tana
Sarai
1395
Astrakan
Home
1396
In Samarqand 1396-1398
INDIAN CAMPAIGN
1398 - 1399
MOSCOW
YELETZ
R. Dnieper
R. Danube
GOLDEN HORDE
R. Volga
R. Don
SARAI
TANA
SEA of AZOV
ASTRAKHAN
R. Ural
WHITE HORDE
R. Irtish
OGOTAI
L. BALKHASH
R. Ili
R. Chu
TIEN SHAN
Sari Sou
R. Jaxartes
OTRAR
ARAL SEA
TRANS OXIANA
KASHGAR
PAMIRS
OTHMANLIS
BLACK SEA
CONSTANTINOPLE
BRUSA
R. Terek
CAUCASUS
CASPIAN SEA
DERBEND
TIFLIS
GEORGIA
ANQARA
SIVAS
ERZINGAN
MALATIA
ADHARBAIJAN
L. Van
TABRIZ
L. Urmia
MARDIN
R. Tigris
ALEPPO
HAMA
R. Euphrates
DAMASCUS
MAMLOOKS
MOSUL
TEKRIT
BAGHDAD
IRAQ
ARABIA
HAMADAN
MAZANDERAN
FARS
SHIRAZ
PERSIAN GULF
BUKHARA
SAMARQAND
R. Oxus
HERAT
KASHMIR
HIMALAYAS
PESHAWAR
KABUL
JAMMU
MULTAN
DELHI
MEERUT
R. Ganges
R. Indus
INDIA
1392
1393
1394
1395
1396
1398
0 100 200 300 400 500
Miles

descendants of Ourous Khan. Tamerlane passed through the Derbend Gates and marched home to Samarqand. The Five Years War was over.

For two years, from the spring of 1396 to April 1398, Tamerlane remained in Samarqand, where he was strenuously engaged in making the city the most beautiful in the world. The immense wealth which he had accumulated in plunder, and the labours of the many architects and artists whom he had collected from the conquered countries, were all alike dedicated to the creation of the city of his dreams. Palaces, mosques, colleges, pavilions and gardens sprang up almost overnight beneath the eye of the fiery conqueror.

Raiding India was a tradition in the Jagatai country. After the death of Firuz Shah Tughluq in 1388, the Kingdom of Delhi had fallen into anarchy. In the ten years from 1388 to 1398, five sultans had succeeded one another on the throne. As usual, Tamerlane veiled his cruel and predatory objectives beneath a cloak of religiosity. "The Sultans of Delhi," he told the quriltai which sanctioned the campaign, "are faithless Muslims because they tolerate Hinduism."

Early in 1398, Tamerlane sent on his grandson, Pir Muhammad, who took Multan in May 1398. Tamerlane left Samarqand in April 1398 with an army of ninety thousand cavalry[3] and crossed the Indus on 24th September.

The throne of Delhi was occupied by a puppet king, Nasir al Deen Mahmood, a grandson of Firuz Shah Tughluq, but such power as the government possessed was wielded by his wazeer, Mallou Iqbal. On 10th December, 1398, Tamerlane fixed his headquarters seven miles north-north-west of Delhi. His army occupied the Ridge, famous in history as the position held by the British troops in the Indian Mutiny some four and a half centuries later.

The Delhi army consisted of only ten thousand cavalry and forty thousand infantry, little more than half the Mongol strength, but it was supported by a hundred and twenty armour-plated elephants. On 10th December, Tamerlane ordered the massacre of a hundred thousand Hindu prisoners in order to free his troops from guard duties. The battle took place on 17th December, 1398. Tamerlane had covered his front with a camouflaged trench and had strewn the ground with iron balls covered with spikes, as a protection against the elephants. The issue was never in doubt and the Delhi army was completely routed. Tamerlane made a triumphal entry into the Indian capital and, with his usual show of piety, announced an amnesty at the request of the Muslim religious doctors.

The subsequent course of events was so often repeated on Tamerlane's campaigns that it is impossible to avoid the conclusion that it

[3] Sir George Dunbar, *A History of India*.

was a carefully planned technique. Thousands of Tatar soldiers swarmed into the city and proceeded to seize provisions and commit endless outrages. Sooner or later, as was doubtless intended, some of the inhabitants resisted, a Mongol soldier was killed, the population were accused of a breach of the conditions of the amnesty and general massacre and plunder were ordered "in retaliation".

The sack of Delhi lasted five days and was accompanied by the usual wholesale raping and butchery. The customary towers of severed heads were then erected. The plunder was immense, for Delhi had for two centuries been the capital where the Muslims had accumulated the vast treasures which they had extracted from the sub-continent. Tamerlane spent only fifteen days in Delhi, during which he sat on the throne of the sultans and held a march past of the well-trained Indian war elephants, who all bowed and trumpeted together as they passed the saluting base.

On 1st January, 1399, Tamerlane set out for home, leaving Delhi a city of the dead. The six hundred miles' march from the capital through Meerut and along the foothills of the Himalayas occupied two months. Everything encountered was destroyed, the countryside was laid waste, the inhabitants were raped, tortured and butchered. The Muslim ruler of Kashmir escaped the devastation of his country by sending tribute and submission or perhaps owing to the lateness of the season, for the Tatars always feared the hot weather in India. The Hindu Raja of Jammu was less fortunate for, having been taken prisoner, he was "converted" and obliged to eat beef.

Before leaving Samarqand, the Conqueror had as usual announced that he was undertaking a holy war against the Hindu infidels. In practice, however, the Sultan of Delhi and nearly all the other rulers overthrown had been Muslims. However, to justify his claim to be engaged in a holy war, Tamerlane ordered that all Hindus be flayed or burned alive. As true believers, Muslims enjoyed the preferential treatment of having their throats cut.

Tamerlane recrossed the Indus on 19th March, 1399. Before doing so, he appointed Khidhr Khan, a descendant of the Prophet, to be Sultan of Delhi. Apart from this "appointment", he made no provision for the future government of India. Leaving behind him the ruins of a Muslim empire, a trail of plundered and gutted towns and villages and a countryside strewn with rotting corpses, the conqueror climbed the passes into Afghanistan on the homeward march to Samarqand.

It will be remembered that, after destroying Sarai and Astrakhan, Tamerlane had "recognized" the sons of Ourous Khan as chiefs of the Golden Horde, thereby plunging the steppes into a ten-year civil war between them and Toqtamish. His action in India was exactly similar.

THE DESCENDANT[S OF ...]
GO[LDEN HORDE ...]

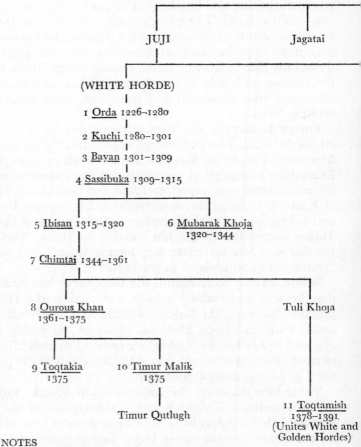

JUJI

Jagatai

(WHITE HORDE)

1 Orda 1226–1280

2 Kuchi 1280–1301

3 Bayan 1301–1309

4 Sassibuka 1309–1315

5 Ibisan 1315–1320

6 Mubarak Khoja 1320–1344

7 Chimtai 1344–1361

8 Ourous Khan 1361–1375

9 Toqtakia 1375

10 Timur Malik 1375

Timur Qutlugh

Tuli Khoja

11 Toqtamish 1378–1391 (Unites White and Golden Hordes)

NOTES

(1) Sometimes Batu's descendants were called the Blue Horde, and the name Golden Horde was used for both hordes combined.

(2) Baraka was the first to become a Muslim.

, KHANS OF THE
:DE

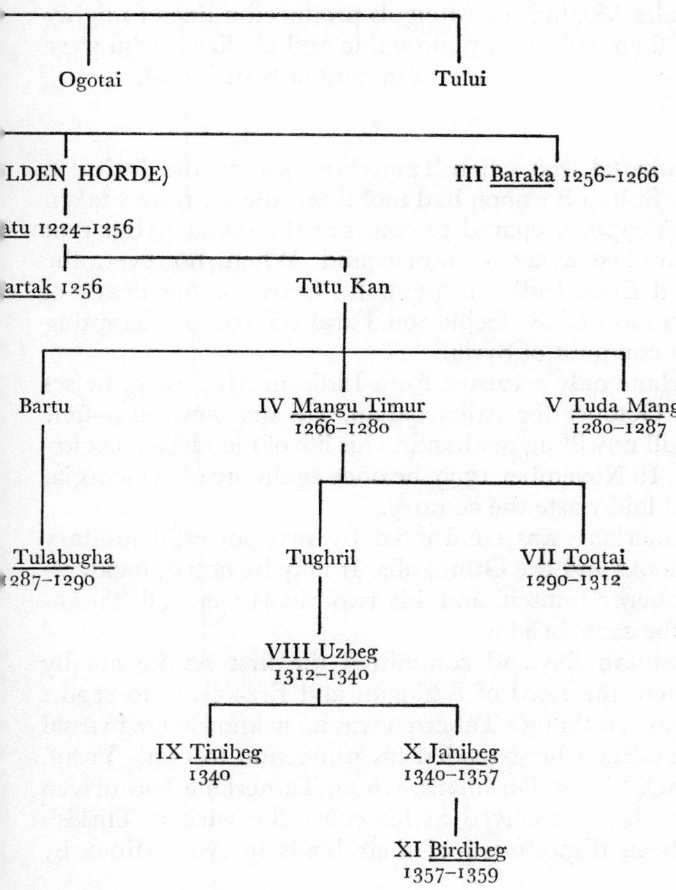

After Janibeg the Golden Horde fell into con-
and was united to the White Horde by Toqtamish
It was Uzbeg (No. VIII) who sent a bride to
al Nasir, Sultan of Egypt.

By "recognizing" Khidhr Khan as sultan, he provoked a civil war between him and Nasir al Deen Mahmood, the previous sultan. After fifteen years of bloodshed, Khidhr Khan at length mounted the throne of Delhi, of which his descendants were to maintain a precarious hold until 1451.

Ironically enough it was a lineal descendant of Tamerlane, Babar, who ultimately in 1526 became the first Muslim to establish a stable dynasty in India. The Moghuls or Mongols produced a line of mighty emperors, many of them cultured, philosophic and civilized, who were only eventually superseded by the establishment of British rule.

* * *

It will be remembered that when Tamerlane was in the Jezira in 1394, the Mamlook Sultan Barqooq had mobilized the army and taken up his position at Aleppo, prepared to confront the invader, but that Tamerlane had marched away to Samarqand. When, however, the Conqueror returned from India in 1399, he heard of the death of Barqooq. The succession of his feeble son Faraj offered the tempting prospect of an easy conquest of Syria.

Although Tamerlane only returned from India in May 1399, he set out once again in October for Adharbaijan. He was now sixty-four years old but was still unwilling to abandon his life of bloodshed, excitement and conquest. In November 1399, he once again invaded Georgia, destroyed Tiflis and laid waste the country.

In the west, Tamerlane was confronted by two powerful military empires, the Mamlooks and the Othmanlis. It may be noted, incidentally, that the conqueror himself and his two rivals were all Turko-Mongols of much the same origin.

The Othmanli Sultan Bayazid committed the first hostile act by summoning Taherten, the Lord of Erzingan and Erzeroum, to report to him and do homage, although Taherten was an acknowledged vassal of Tamerlane. In addition he extended his protection to Qara Yusuf, the chief of the Black Sheep Turkmans, whom Tamerlane had driven out. Conversely the latter received at his court the various Turkish ameers who had been dispossessed of their lands in Asia Minor by Bayazid.

Tamerlane sent a letter to Bayazid, protesting against his attempt to compel Taherten to do him homage. Bayazid, however, replied arrogantly that he would chase Tamerlane back to Tabriz. On receipt of this answer, the Conqueror, in August 1400, marched on Sivas, a city recently annexed by the Othmanlis, and attacked it with a massive bombardment and energetic mining beneath the walls. After twenty days, Sivas surrendered on terms. To lend colour to his rôle of the hero

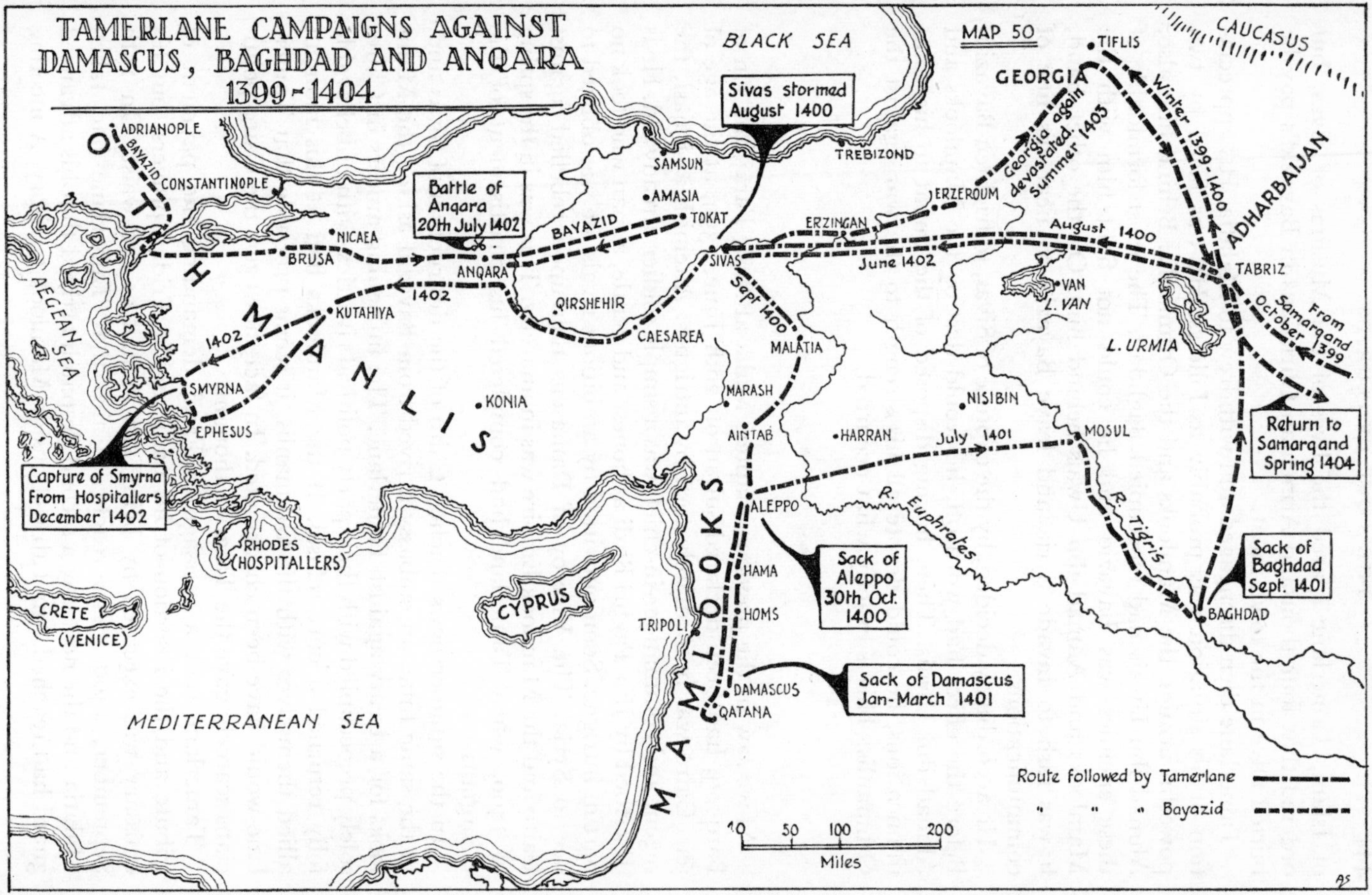

TAMERLANE CAMPAIGNS AGAINST
DAMASCUS, BAGHDAD AND ANQARA
1399 - 1404
MAP 50
BLACK SEA
CAUCASUS
TIFLIS
GEORGIA
Winter 1399-1400
Georgia again devastated Summer 1403
ADHARBAIJAN
Sivas stormed
August 1400
ADRIANOPLE
BAYAZID
CONSTANTINOPLE
SAMSUN
TREBIZOND
ERZEROUM
AMASIA
TOKAT
Battle of
Anqara
20th July 1402
NICAEA
BAYAZID
ERZINGAN
August 1400
TABRIZ
BRUSA
ANQARA
SIVAS
June 1402
VAN
L. VAN
From Samarqand October 1399
1402
QIRSHEHIR
Sept 1400
KUTAHIYA
CAESAREA
MALATIA
L. URMIA
AEGEAN SEA
1402
OTHMANLIS
SMYRNA
KONIA
MARASH
NISIBIN
EPHESUS
AINTAB
HARRAN
July 1401
MOSUL
Return to
Samarqand
Spring 1404
Capture of Smyrna
From Hospitallers
December 1402
ALEPPO
R. Euphrates
R. Tigris
RHODES
(HOSPITALLERS)
MAMLOOKS
Sack of
Aleppo
30th Oct.
1400
HAMA
Sack of
Baghdad
Sept. 1401
CRETE
(VENICE)
CYPRUS
HOMS
BAGHDAD
TRIPOLI
Sack of Damascus
Jan-March 1401
DAMASCUS
QATANA
MEDITERRANEAN SEA
Route followed by Tamerlane
" " " Bayazid
10 50 100 200
Miles

of Islam, Tamerlane spared the lives of the Muslims of Sivas, but ordered that four thousand Armenian Christians in Bayazid's pay be buried alive in the town moat.

Tamerlane then disengaged and withdrew to Malatia. His appreciation of his situation was probably as follows. He was faced by two powerful armies, the Mamlooks and the Othmanlis. Behind him also, Ahmad ibn Uwais had reoccupied Baghdad. The most formidable of these enemies was Bayazid and he could not fight him with the Mamlooks and Ahmad ibn Uwais behind him. On the other hand, it was rash to invade Syria and leave Bayazid so near his line of communications.

He accordingly decided, by the capture of Sivas, to frighten Bayazid. Before the effect had worn off, he would destroy the Mamlooks and Ahmad ibn Uwais. Then, having disposed of the threat to his communications, he could devote all his strength to the war against the Othmanlis. This is exactly what occurred.

* * *

As we saw in the previous chapter, Malik al Nasir Faraj, the son of Barqooq, had been declared sultan on 20th June, 1399, at the age of ten. Cairo was immediately torn by intrigues. Aitemish al Bajasi, the regent and commander-in-chief, was a simple soldier already old. He is described by Ibn Taghri Birdi as honest and gentle, a man who took no part in intrigue. Soon outwitted by ambitious rivals, he was obliged to flee to Syria. The Viceroy of Damascus thereupon rebelled against Cairo and the Mamlook Empire was in anarchy. This was in the spring of 1400, when Tamerlane had completed his chastisement of the Georgians.

In the summer news reached Cairo of the destruction of Sivas and, at the same time, an embassy arrived from Bayazid asking the Mamlooks for a treaty against Tamerlane. The intriguing ameers in Cairo, solely preoccupied with their party political rivalries, with unbelievable folly returned a curt refusal. If the Mamlooks had at this moment allied themselves with the Othmanlis, it seems probable that Tamerlane would have been checkmated. In fact, however, the Cairo politicians scarcely gave the Tatars a thought.

Tamerlane sent a message to Faraj demanding the payment of tribute and the insertion of his name in the Friday prayers, but his emissary was executed by being cut in half at the waist. On 15th September, 1400, news reached Cairo that Tamerlane had taken Malatia and the next day a second despatch arrived that his advanced guard had reached Ain Tab well inside Mamlook territory. A meeting was called in Cairo to consider action but everyone spoke at once, no decisions were reached and the situation was left to drift.

In October 1400, Tamerlane marched on Aleppo. Syria was in panic, especially as Egypt gave no signs of activity. The army of Syria was concentrated at Aleppo, but the lack of news of reinforcements from Cairo was undermining morale. On 28th October, Tamerlane surrounded Aleppo and on 30th, the Mamlook army of Syria marched out to give battle. A general engagement ensued in which Tamerlane made use of the war elephants which he had brought from India. The Mamlook army was completely defeated and Aleppo was carried by assault in the *sauve qui peut* after the battle.

The sack of Aleppo lasted four days. All men and children were butchered but the women were collected for the amusement of the troops. According to Ibn Taghri Birdi, they were stripped naked, even in the mosques, and were raped again and again. The streets were littered with corpses, the heads of which had been severed to be built into the usual towers of skulls. While this carnage was raging, Tamerlane, assuming his air of piety, caused the Muslim religious qadhis to be collected and engaged with them in a theological debate.

Miran Shah, a son of Tamerlane, was meanwhile sent on ahead and summoned Hama to surrender, promising to spare the people's lives. As soon, however, as his troops had entered the city, he claimed that the terms agreed upon had been violated—the usual trick—and Hama also was sacked and the inhabitants massacred.

The news of the sack of Aleppo reached Cairo on 8th November, 1400. At last, on 8th December, the army of Egypt, accompanied by the child Sultan Faraj, left Cairo, reaching Damascus on 23rd December. In the city all was confusion with rival ameers quarrelling with one another. Three days later, Tamerlane's advanced guard arrived. The invaders by-passed the city and camped at Qatana, fourteen miles to the south-west, cutting the road from Damascus to Egypt.

The Mamlook army marched out to confront the Tatars and an indecisive action took place, after which Tamerlane requested an armistice which was refused. Ibn Taghri Birdi thinks that Tamerlane was afraid, but it seems more likely that the request was a trick intended to reduce the vigilance of the Mamlooks.

The two armies remained confronting one another until 8th January, 1401, when a rumour reached the Mamlook camp that another group of ameers was planning a *coup d'état* in Cairo. The senior officers were much more concerned with their political positions in Egypt than with the defence of Syria. Taking the young sultan with them, they left the army secretly by night and rode for Cairo. When it became known in the morning that the sultan and the army commanders had deserted, many Mamlook soldiers did the same, while the remainder withdrew within the walls of Damascus, the citizens of which, seeing themselves abandoned, prepared to resist with the courage of despair.

Tamerlane, however, had no wish to embark on a long and costly siege. He sent for a delegation from the city. When they arrived, he assumed his religious manner and, fingering his rosary, declared piously that he would spare Damascus "for the sake of the Companions of the Prophet who had dwelt there". The city delegates, immensely relieved, agreed to open the gates.

No sooner, however, were the Tatars in possession of the city than the Conqueror changed his tune. Damascus was given over to the soldiery as Delhi had been, and the usual butchery resulted. All women were collected and raped in public before large crowds. Excruciating tortures were inflicted on the inhabitants with sadistic refinement. According to Ibn Taghri Birdi, some of the victims were torn limb from limb, others were burned alive. The killing, torturing and raping lasted for nineteen days. Finally the survivors were driven off as slaves, among them Ahmad ibn Arabshah, a twelve-year-old Damascene boy carried off to Samarqand, whose account of his adventures is still in our hands.

Before leaving, the Tatars set fire to the city. As a day of strong wind was chosen, the greater part of Damascus was soon a raging furnace, including the great mosque of which the roof and the walls collapsed. Tamerlane marched away from Damascus on 19th March, 1401. As it was considered that small children would be a nuisance on the march, infants under five were left behind unattended when the older children and adults were led off to slavery. The babies, abandoned in this city of the dead, themselves died within a few days. The Conqueror did not annex Syria or make any arrangements for its government.

It will be remembered that Tamerlane had taken Baghdad in 1393, but that subsequently Ahmad ibn Uwais of the Jalair had reoccupied the city while the Conqueror was in India. From Aleppo he descended once more on Baghdad, which he reached in July 1401. Ahmad ibn Uwais had fled to the Othmanlis in Asia Minor but his men and the people of Baghdad decided to resist. The whole Tatar army was concentrated around the city and, for six weeks, an intense bombardment was maintained, but the defenders with frenzied energy repaired every breach as soon as it was made. Beneath the scorching August sun of Iraq, the desperate struggle dragged on until at last Baghdad was carried by assault.

The obstinacy of the defence had infuriated the Conqueror. Every soldier, according to Ibn Arabshah, was ordered to hand in two severed heads. The same author gives the killed as ninety thousand, excluding those who died in the siege before the assault. Ibn Taghri

Birdi gives the number as a hundred thousand. Maqrizi as ninety thousand. One hundred and twenty towers were built with the severed heads.

* * *

Tamerlane had now terrorized both the Mamlooks and Ahmad ibn Uwais and his communications would be safe if he invaded Asia Minor. He spent the winter of 1401–1402 in Adharbaijan to rest his troops, graze his horses and call up fresh reinforcements. Bayazid was similarly employed. In the spring of 1402, every Othmanli soldier available was collected from Europe, including all the Christian vassal contingents, and was transported to Asia Minor. During Tamerlane's absence in Syria and Iraq, Bayazid had given further proof of his intransigence by capturing Erzingan, the capital of Taherten, Tamerlane's vassal concerning whom the two rulers had already exchanged violently worded letters.

It was not until June 1402 that the Lame Conqueror was ready to advance. He began by retaking Erzingan and then held a grand review of his whole army in the plain outside Sivas. We are perhaps inclined to visualize the Tatar hordes of Jenghis Khan and Tamerlane as mobs of savage tribesmen, massacring and plundering without order or discipline. The truth appears to have been very different. On the plain of Sivas, we are told, some of the regiments wore red breastplates, their saddles, quivers, sashes, lance-pennants, shields and banners being of the same colour. Other regiments were dressed in yellow, in white or in other colours. The equipment of all the men within each unit was identical.

All through history, the most successful armies have indulged in splendour, in bright colours, flashing metal, waving banners and stirring music. There seems here to be some deep psychological urge which modern rationalists, who allege such display to be a waste of time and money, would do well to consider.

Tamerlane had conquered an immense extent of territory without ever meeting a large well-trained regular army, capably led and accustomed to victory. Bayazid, equally fortunate, had extended his dominions in every direction owing to the weakness and futility of his rivals. Neither of the two conquerors had ever been defeated. Now both had at last found an opponent worthy of his steel.

It was already past midsummer and the ripe crops were ready for cutting. Bayazid, presumably anxious to prevent the destruction of the countryside at harvest time, marched rapidly through Anqara to Tokat, hoping to engage Tamerlane east of Sivas. Many of the Turkish ameers who had been dispossessed by Bayazid were accompanying the Tatars and must have been of great service in providing intelligence. Having heard that Bayazid had left Anqara for Tokat, the Conqueror left Sivas and marched in six days to Caesarea, where a four-day halt was made and the horses were allowed to graze the standing crops.

From Caesarea the Tatars covered the remaining distance to Anqara in seventeen days, with ample water and grazing all the way. Not till they reached Qir Shehir was contact made with any Othmanli troops. Bayazid with his army was near Tokat. Anqara was the crossroads and centre of communications for all Asia Minor. Tamerlane had placed himself squarely across Bayazid's communications. He immediately laid siege to Anqara with his siege engines and his sappers.

As soon as he heard that he had been outmanoeuvred, Bayazid turned round and hastened back to Anqara by forced marches. Tamerlane's army consisted almost entirely of cavalry, whereas Bayazid's included many infantry, who suffered intensely from the scorching July sun and from lack of water. It was two hundred miles of semi-desert country from Anqara to Sivas and the Othmanlis covered most of the distance twice. Meanwhile Tamerlane was resting his horses and men in the fertile plains round Anqara and was preparing the position on which he proposed to fight. When Bayazid's exhausted infantry arrived back at Anqara, they could not even slake their thirst, for Tamerlane had carefully occupied all the water points.

Bayazid, whose "lightning" genius seemed to have deserted him, continued to make every possible mistake. His infantry, the backbone of his army, was thirsty and exhausted. He could have stood on the defensive, a form of tactics at which the Ottomans to this day have always been invincible. Instead he attacked the Tatars who were all cavalry and thoroughly rested.

Bayazid's army was half Muslim and half Christian. On his right were the Serbians and the Balkan Christians, on the left the men of Asia Minor under his eldest son, Sulaiman Chelebi. Bayazid was in the centre with the reserves. Historians differ widely in their estimates of the numbers involved. It is possible that each side had some two hundred thousand men, but probably less.

While waiting for Bayazid, Tamerlane had fortified his position with palisades, ditches and pointed stakes driven into the ground. His Indian elephants were also ranged in his front line. If his military dispositions were efficient, his political preparations had been no less thorough. A considerable part of Bayazid's army—one report says a quarter—consisted of Qipchaqs, Turkmans and perhaps even Mongols. For several months, unknown to Bayazid, Tamerlane's agents had been sowing disloyalty among these steppe nomads, claimed as kinsmen by the Conqueror's emissaries.

The Battle of Anqara was fought on 20th July, 1402, but some accounts say 28th July. According to his usual practice, Bayazid first sent forward his light cavalry, recruited from the tribes of the steppes, who immediately went over in a body to the Tatars. He then ordered his son Sulaiman to attack the Tatar right flank but he was so vigorously repulsed that he could not rally his men, who streamed off the field. Sulaiman's troops consisted largely of the subjects of those Turkish ameers whom Bayazid had dethroned and who were fighting beside Tamerlane. The existence of so much disloyalty in the Othmanli ranks can be attributed to the arrogant conduct of Bayazid, which contrasted so unfavourably with the patient wisdom of Othman, Orkhan and Murad.

After the desertion of the light cavalry and the repulse of the Ottoman flank attack, Tamerlane gradually worked his flanks forward. The Othmanli centre and right were still intact and fighting fiercely but this encircling movement forced them back inch by inch on to one another. After the initial reverses, the honours for this desperate all-day-long resistance go to the Ottoman regulars in the centre and the Serbians on the right. The battle lasted from early morning until sunset when, seeing defeat to be inevitable, the Serbians withdrew in good order and marched for home. Bayazid, with the Janissaries and a few reserve units, was left surrounded. At last, fighting with great courage in the front rank and wielding his battle axe with deadly effect, he decided to break out, but his horse was shot under him and he was taken prisoner.

Tamerlane was playing chess in his tent with his son Shah Rukh when his adversary was brought before him with his hands tied. The Conqueror at first greeted him courteously but later on, owing to rumours that he wished to escape, he was placed in irons at night. By day he was carried in a litter apparently enclosed in a grille or in iron bars. He died in captivity, perhaps largely of mortification, on 9th March, 1403, eight months after his defeat.

Despina, the sister of Prince Stephen of Serbia, the wife of whom Bayazid had been really fond, was taken prisoner with the other inmates of the haram, all of whom were made to serve wine to the Conqueror at his banquets. Some alleged that Bayazid's women were made to wait naked at Tamerlane's feast but the meaning may be only unveiled. By a refinement of cruelty, Bayazid was made to attend the banquet. In any case the humiliation of princesses waiting at the Conqueror's table was bitter enough. It is not surprising that Bayazid died.

After the Battle of Anqara the Tatars swept over the whole of Asia Minor. Sulaiman Chelebi, the eldest son of Bayazid, escaped from one gate of Brusa as the enemy entered by another, and crossed to Europe.

The Tatars took Brusa unopposed, stabled their horses in the mosques, raped all the women and then set fire to the city. Tamerlane set up his headquarters in Kutahiya, whither all the women of the Othmanli royal family were sent to him. Muhammad Sultan, a grandson of Tamerlane, was married to a daughter of Bayazid. All the cities in the vicinity were plundered including Nicaea.

The numerous Turkish ameers of Asia Minor, driven out by Bayazid, were reinstated by Tamerlane, including the most powerful of them, the Qaramanli Ameer. Forty thousand Ottoman troops reached the Asian shore opposite Gallipoli but were unable to cross. If Christendom had wished to drive the Muslims from Europe, the task could now have been easily accomplished and five centuries of war in south-east Europe might have been avoided. But cash was a more convincing argument than Christian solidarity and the Genoese and Venetians ferried the remains of the Ottoman army over the Dardanelles in return for exorbitant payments.

Sulaiman Chelebi established his capital in Adrianople, where he received a diploma from Tamerlane, appointing him his vassal as ruler of the Ottoman territories in Europe. At the same time, however, the Conqueror encouraged each of Bayazid's remaining sons, Isa, Musa and Muhammad, to hope for the throne, thereby leaving the seeds of a ten-year civil war between them. When Tamerlane left Asia Minor, he made no arrangements for its future government except to ensure the continuance of confusion and civil war, precisely as he had done in the Golden Horde and in India.

Bayazid had never been able to take Smyrna which was held by the Knights Hospitallers. From Kutahiya, Tamerlane marched, in December 1402, to besiege the town, which was built on a promontory jutting out into the sea. With his usual fiery energy, he bombarded the fortress, undermined the walls and built causeways out into the sea. After two weeks, when the walls collapsed, some of the knights fought their way down to the harbour, embarked on their galleys and put to sea, which must have been a remarkably skilful Dunkirk. Many of the knights, however, were captured and decapitated and their heads built into a tower. When Tamerlane moved to Ephesus after taking Smyrna, the children of the city came out to meet him singing, in the hope of winning his favour to spare Ephesus from pillage. Annoyed at the noise, the Conqueror ordered his cavalry to ride them down, and the children were trampled to death beneath the hoofs of the horses.

After Anqara, a despatch had been sent to Cairo, demanding instant submission. The boy Sultan Faraj and his intriguing ameers hastened to comply. The names and titles of Tamerlane were inserted in the Friday prayers, coins were minted in his name and a humble embassy was sent from Cairo, laden with priceless gifts and a promise to pay tribute.

Tamerlane, still apparently as energetic as ever, though he was now sixty-seven years old, spent the summer again ravaging Georgia, an unimportant country but one which, being Christian, enabled the Conqueror to claim another holy war. The winter of 1403–1404 was passed in the grazing grounds of Adharbaijan. In the spring of 1404, the army set out for Samarqand. The summer and autumn of 1404 were spent in the capital in feasting and pleasure, in vigorous activities for the beautification of Samarqand and in preparation for the next campaign.

When Tamerlane began his conquests, four great military empires had dominated his world—the Othmanlis in the west, the Mamlooks in Egypt, the Sultans of Delhi in India and the Ming Emperor of China. Only the last remained unconquered. Though now nearly seventy years old, Tamerlane made up his mind to destroy China. The army collected for this purpose was probably some two hundred thousand strong.

The distance from Samarqand to Peking was in the neighbourhood of three thousand five hundred miles, most of it desert or thinly populated steppe. The amount of administrative preparation required for such a march was enormous, both in the way of storing provisions and equipment along the route and in the collection of sufficient transport to accompany the troops. In addition, an army of two hundred thousand men had to be equipped with weapons, armour, clothing, saddlery, tools, siege trains, tents and every form of gear. Historians are inevitably inclined to record stirring details of battles and sieges but few, at any rate in the Middle Ages, trouble to describe the immense labour expended in administrative preparation. Tamerlane's army, as we have noted, was not a mob of primitive tribesmen each bringing his own food and weapons, but a uniformly equipped regular army.

The army set out in December in spite of the intense cold. The Jaxartes was crossed on the ice. Tamerlane reached Otrar in the middle of January. But the old campaigner had at last overtaxed his strength. He fell ill and, after declaring his grandson Pir Muhammad to be his heir, the Emperor of the World passed away on 18th February, 1405, on the steppes east of Otrar.

The apparently paradoxical character of Tamerlane has often puzzled historians. Jenghis Khan and his immediate successors can be dismissed as savages. When his descendants became civilized, they produced such comparatively humane rulers as Qubilai and Ghazan. All this is in the usual tradition. But Tamerlane, pretending to be civilized, interested in philosophy, history, literature and art, above all endlessly quoting the Qoran and appealing for divine aid, was as cruel—perhaps more cruel—than Jenghis Khan. Moreover, while he claimed that all his campaigns were Muslim holy wars, his victims were nearly all Muslims.

First of all, it may assist us to remember that everything that Tamerlane did was in the Jenghis Khan tradition. His favourite title was that of Gurgan or son-in-law of Jenghis Khan, owing to his having married a princess of the Golden Family. All his life he carried about with him a Jagatai prince, whom he alleged to be the khaqan. There is an amusing incident described by the great North African historian, Ibn Khaldun, who had several audiences with Tamerlane at the time of his capture of Damascus.

Discussing other famous conquerors such as Caesar and Alexander, the Conqueror remarked that Nebuchadnezzar was only a military commander. "I also," he added, "am in the same position, being only the representative of my sovereign. The real king is here"—and he looked round at a group of men standing behind his throne but could not see the person he sought. Some of those present then told him that the man in question had gone home.[4]

We may therefore perhaps find some keys to Tamerlane's conduct by studying Jenghis Khan and his immediate family. Even Jenghis Khan was devoted to his friends, enjoyed discussions with religious leaders and philosophers and, while ordering the wholesale massacre of men, women and children, was ready to discuss God and His service. Similarly the monk Plan Carpin, who visited Batu, the grandson of Jenghis Khan and the conqueror of eastern Europe, described him as "gentle, affable and benign towards his own people, but extremely cruel in war".[5] We may perhaps deduce the same qualities in the utter devotion of Kitbugha for Hulagu, whom we otherwise believe to have been a monster of cruelty. We know also that Hulagu had a Christian wife to whom he was deeply attached.

The ambassador, Ruy Gonzalez de Clavijo, who visited Tamerlane at Samarqand in 1404 on a mission from the King of Castile, gives a not unattractive picture of the lame, white-haired old Conqueror, surrounded by his many wives, children and grandchildren, and of his benevolent and patriarchal manner. The old man even got slightly drunk at a wedding banquet and performed a little dance of his own, in spite of his lame leg. We may perhaps, therefore, sense, as the explanation of the Conqueror's simultaneous benevolence and cruelty, the old Mongol tradition of patriarchal kindness to his own people, combined with almost incredibly sadistic cruelty to those outside. We may note, however, that his own people were not a racial or national group but his faithful, personal retainers, of many differing ethnic origins.

[4] Ibn Khaldun. Trans. by Walter J. Fischel.
[5] Plan Carpin, quoted by René Grousset in *L'Empire des Steppes*.

The repeated acts of treachery of which Tamerlane was guilty were likewise entirely in the Mongol tradition, for it will be remembered that, in the days of Jenghis Khan, guile was admired as an essential quality of a soldier. The regularity with which Tamerlane pledged himself to spare besieged cities and then, on some trumped-up excuse, ordered a general massacre seems undoubtedly to have been calculated policy.

On the subject of religion it is necessary to be even more cautious. The human mind is so skilled at justifying its own conduct and blaming that of others, that we must exercise caution before condemning any man as a conscious hypocrite. Throughout the whole of his career, Tamerlane claimed incessantly to be a pious Muslim. His letters were full of quotations from the Qoran and the name of God was always on his lips. Yet almost all his campaigns were against his fellow Muslims. In the east, the Sultan of Delhi was a Muslim fighting against Hindus, in the west the Ottoman Sultan was battling with Christians. Tamerlane stabbed them both in the back.

The use of intoxicating drinks is not to Muslims a deadly sin but it is regarded as a detestable vice. Certainly no really pious Muslim can encourage inebriation. Yet Clavijo, the Castilian envoy, who attended many feasts in Samarqand in 1404, declares that no feast or celebration could take place at Tamerlane's court without all the men present becoming drunk. Clavijo himself was a total abstainer and experienced the greatest difficulty in resisting the attempts of the Tatars to make him drink.

Although Tamerlane's tribe were not steppe nomads but at least half settled, he spent nearly all his life in tents. When in Samarqand, he lived chiefly in the surrounding gardens, where were pitched groups of tents, made of silk and cloth of gold, supported on poles covered with gold and held up by many-coloured silk ropes. Many of these groups of tents in the gardens were surrounded by walls of brick work or sham walls made of embroidered textiles. The "walls" were pierced by gates and archways, often decorated with mosaics. Yet each such garden encampment would be used for only a few days of feasting, after which the Conqueror would move to another.

According to the Archbishop of Sultaniya, who was in Tamerlane's confidence and was the bearer of his letters to Charles VI, King of France, the Conqueror spent most of his life in tents because his army was so large that no city could accommodate the troops. The military camps, however, were extremely well ordered. Clavijo reports that he saw the troops pitch a camp of twenty thousand tents. Everyone knew exactly where his tent should go, the organization was perfect and there was no noise or fuss. The camp when pitched included streets of shops, butchers, greengrocers, bakers and every other trade. Moreover, in every military camp there were bathing establishments where soldiers could obtain a hot bath. This indeed was a departure from the practice of Jenghis Khan in whose days, it will be remembered, the Mongols did not wash.

In brief, we must not consider the troops of Tamerlane to have consisted of wild mobs of savages. On the contrary, the army was, from the military angle, extremely professional, well disciplined and very efficiently administered.

NOTABLE DATES

Birth of Tamerlane	8th April, 1336
Death of Sultan Al Nasir of Egypt	1341
Confusion in Egypt	1341–1382
(In France, Battle of Crécy	1346)
Tamerlane ruler of Trans-Oxiana	1370
Toqtamish becomes chief of the Golden Horde	1378
Capture of Herat by Tamerlane	1381
Accession of Barqooq in Cairo	1382
Capture of Tabriz by Tamerlane	1385
Capture of Isfahan and Shiraz	November 1387
Death of Firuz Shah Tughluq	1388
Serbians defeated by Othmanlis at Kossovo Sultan Murad killed	1389
Tamerlane occupies Baghdad	October 1393
Tamerlane's second campaign against Toqtamish	1395–1396
Battle of Nicopolis	1396
Tamerlane's invasion of India	1398–1399
Death of Barqooq	20th June, 1399
Defeat of Mamlook army of Syria Destruction of Aleppo	30th October, 1400
Sack of Damascus	March 1401
Destruction of Baghdad	August 1401
Battle of Anqara	20th July, 1402
Death of Tamerlane	18th February, 1405

PERSONALITIES

Tamerlane (Timur i Lenk), The Conqueror

Umar Shaikh Miran Shah Shah Rukh	sons of Tamerlane

Muhammad Sultan Pir Muhammad	grandsons of Tamerlane

Ahmad ibn Uwais, Jalair ruler of Iraq and Adharbaijan
Toqtamish, Khan of the White and Golden Hordes
Shah Mansoor, the Muzaffarid
Nasir al Deen Mahmood, the Sultan of Delhi
Faraj ibn Barqooq, Mamlook Sultan of Egypt
Qara Yusuf, chief of the Black Sheep Turkmans
Bayazid Yilderim (Lightning), Othmanli Sultan

Sulaiman Chelebi Isa Musa Muhammad	sons of Bayazid

Stephen, Prince of Serbia
Despina, his sister, married to Bayazid

XXI

A Roman Death

Western Europe, with ancestral memories of jealousy of Byzantine civilization, with its spiritual advisers denouncing the Orthodox as sinful schismatics and with a haunting sense of guilt that it had failed the city at the end, chose to forget about Byzantium . . . In the villages men knew better . . . There their spirits kindled and their courage rose as they told of the last Christian Emperor standing in the breach, abandoned by his Western allies, holding the infidels at bay till their numbers overpowered him and he died, with the Empire as his winding-sheet.

STEVEN RUNCIMAN, *The Fall of Constantinople*

For nine centuries . . . Constantinople preserved Christendom, industry, the machinery of government and civilization from successive torrents of barbarians. For seven centuries it protected Europe from the premature invasions of the Crescent; giving very much to the East, receiving much from the East and acting as the intellectual . . . clearing-house between Europe and Asia.

FREDERIC HARRISON, *Byzantine History in the Early Middle Ages*

The distress and fall of the last Constantine are more glorious than the long prosperity of the Byzantine Caesars.

GIBBON, *Decline and Fall of the Roman Empire*

XXI

WHEN Faraj the son of Barqooq came of age he assumed the rule of the Mamlook Empire, but Syria remained in continual rebellion. It is significant that, during the whole Mamlook period, nearly every rebellion began in Damascus. It is true that both sides were Mamlooks, not Syrians and Egyptians, yet it would seem as if the spirit of Damascus inspired its successive viceroys to revolt against the dictators of Cairo.

Faraj, who since his accession at the age of ten had been surrounded by fear and treachery, became increasingly cruel and suspicious. He particularly mistrusted his father's Mamlooks, causing many to be executed. In the spring of 1412, Syria being in anarchy, the sultan led his army to Damascus, where the viceroy, Taghri Birdi, the father of our historian, begged him to behave affably to his Mamlooks and to cease his constant executions.

Faraj, who was becoming more and more addicted to drink, marched against the rebels but was defeated in a confused battle in which he himself led the charge in a state of intoxication. Deserted by his army, he shut himself in the citadel of Damascus, but on 1st June, 1412, he surrendered and was assassinated three days later. He was twenty-four years old and had reigned for thirteen years of anarchy and humiliation, including his abject submission to Tamerlane. The administration had been neglected, irrigation works had fallen into disrepair, the revenues of Egypt had been reduced, heavier taxes were imposed and the currency was debased. According to Ibn Taghri Birdi, two-thirds of the population of Egypt died in his reign, from plague and from want. Thereafter Mamlook rule suffered constantly from financial stringency until its ultimate collapse in 1517.

Faraj was succeeded in 1412 by Shaikh al Mahmoodi, a Mamlook who had been brought up in the Caucasus and bought by Barqooq, to whom at one time he had been cup-bearer. Faced with the inevitable rebellion in Syria after his elevation, he not only suppressed it but marched on to Malatia and Abulistan. At the head of a large army, he proved that the Sultan of Egypt was once more a power in the land.

Conditions were still bad in Egypt in 1415 and there was yet another visitation of the plague. Shaikh, however, was a competent and diligent administrator, and arranged for the importation of wheat to reduce the cost of living. In 1417, he again led an army northwards across Syria, to impress the Qaramanli Ameer who, restored by Tamerlane, was gaining strength and prestige. Qara Yusuf and the Black Sheep Turkmans were also a threat to peace and required intimidation.

On his return the sultan made a triumphant entry into Cairo on 25th November, 1417. The city had been lavishly decorated, the shops were illuminated with lamps and candles while, on the flat roofs of the houses, sat troupes of girls, singing and beating time on their tambourines. The ameers were in full dress of silk, satin and cloth of gold and rode on golden saddles studded with jewels. In the drab dullness of our industrial civilization, we perhaps forget the moral effect produced by splendid state ceremonies.

In July 1420, the Nile failed to rise and special prayers were offered on an open space outside Cairo. The sultan attended, dressed in a coarse penitential garment and wept during the prayers. He returned to Cairo without an escort amid a large crowd of people, many of them in tears. The next day the Nile rose in flood.

Ibn Taghri Birdi, himself at this time a government servant, gives a note on the Mamlook army in 1418. He divides it into three categories:

(1) Soldiers of the sultan's guard, to each of whom a fief in Egypt was allotted for his maintenance. These were presumably those previously referred to as royal Mamlooks, and composed the main regular army.[1]

(2) Ibn Taghri Birdi calls the second group sultan's Mamlooks, "who did not receive fiefs but pay, rations and clothing from the sultan's bureau". Possibly these were the Khassikiya or the sultan's intimate Mamlooks or members of the royal household.

(3) Thirdly he mentions the ameers' Mamlooks.

The officer structure of the regular army appears to have been unchanged from Ayoubid days. Under this organization, every thousand men of the regular army were commanded by a first-class ameer or ameer of one hundred. This designation signified that such an ameer owned a hundred personal Mamlooks. Thus an ameer of one hundred was the owner of a hundred personal Mamlooks and the commander of a thousand Mamlooks of the regular army.

To assist him to command his regiment, each first-class ameer had, as his second-in-command, a second-class ameer, also called an ameer of drums, who had forty personal Mamlooks. There were also in the regiment one third-class and one fourth-class ameer, with twenty and ten personal Mamlooks respectively.

Ibn Taghri Birdi explains this organization in order to denounce the abuses which had crept in since the Circassians took over. The Turkish sultans were stricter soldiers than their successors. In 1418, our historian tells us, it had become common for the same man to be entered as an ameer's Mamlook and also as a member of the regular army to whom a

[1] Page 314.

fief was allotted. Sometimes one man was entered in all three categories, thereby enjoying three salaries. As a result, the actual strength of the army was only about a half of what appeared on paper. Sultan Shaikh al Mahmoodi endeavoured, apparently with only partial success, to put an end to these abuses.

Shaikh died on 13th January, 1421, in his fifties. After the humiliations of the reign of Faraj, he had in eight years restored something of the prestige of Egypt. He insisted that every officer be thoroughly efficient and gave his young Mamlooks a good education. He bequeathed the throne to his son Ahmad, who was one year old. However, the Ameer Tatar, appointed regent, married the widow of Shaikh and was accepted as sultan on 29th August, 1421. Tatar was a Circassian born in the Caucasus and bought by Barqooq, who caused him to be educated until he was well-versed in law, in Arabic and in the Qoran. This was indeed a new type of sultan.

Tatar was wise, patient, capable and generous and might have been a great ruler, but he died of illness on 30th November, 1421, after a reign of only ninety-four days, leaving the throne to his ten-year-old son, Malik al Salih Muhammad. It had become almost a convention for a dying sultan to bequeath the throne to an infant. No one expected the child to reign for long, but the system enabled the government to continue until the new sultan emerged after the usual struggle for power. Muhammad the son of Tatar reigned in this manner from 30th November, 1421, until 1st April, 1422. He was then deposed in favour of Malik al Ashraf Barsbai. The new sultan had been born in the Caucasus and had been a Mamlook of Barqooq. Barsbai abolished the custom of kissing the ground before the sultan, a ritual introduced by the first Fatimid Khalif Muizz, four hundred years earlier.

* * *

Cyprus had fallen on evil days since the reign of Peter I, the crusader king who had seized Alexandria. The island, immensely rich, was a depôt for European merchants, most prominent of whom were as usual the Venetians and the Genoese. On 12th October, 1372, a riot took place in Famagusta,[2] in which the Genoese were defeated by the Venetians. A year later, in October 1373, a Genoese squadron of forty galleys landed fourteen thousand troops who seized Famagusta, plundered Nicosia, arrested King Peter II and later imprisoned James de Lusignan, the uncle of the king, in Genoa. An indemnity of more than two million gold crowns was demanded and, pending payment, the Genoese retained Famagusta, where they collected the customs dues on their own account, thereby further impoverishing the island government.

[2] Map 21, page 198.

In 1383, they also occupied Kyrenia. Although the king remained on his throne, Cyprus, financially at least, became little more than a Genoese colony.

The once powerful Egyptian fleet had long been neglected with the result that the eastern Mediterranean had become a happy hunting ground for pirates. Many of these were Italians and based themselves on Cyprus while robbing Muslim ships off Syria and Egypt. In retaliation a Muslim fleet was sent, in October 1424, to raid Limassol.

Encouraged by the success of this raid, the government of Egypt sent a larger fleet in July 1425 and plundered Famagusta. An even more powerful expedition was prepared for 1426. The force landed at Limassol in the first week of July. After destroying the town, the army marched up the east coast towards Larnaca, the fleet keeping abreast offshore. At Choirokoitia, a pitched battle was fought with the Cypriot army, which was utterly defeated, Janus de Lusignan, King of Cyprus, being taken prisoner with many of his men. A Muslim unit sent by the Qaramanli ameer was found fighting for the Cypriots. The Muslims remained only two days to plunder Nicosia and set fire to the city and, on 18th July, 1426, they set sail after a stay of only seventeen days on the island. They took with them the king, many thousands of prisoners and an immense booty.

When Barsbai heard of this staggering victory, he and his entourage burst into tears of joy and emotion. Military bands were sent to play in Cairo and the public went mad with enthusiasm. On 11th August, 1426, the returned expeditionary force camped on Cairo racecourse. The next day, it made a victory march through the gaily decorated city. Dense crowds lined the streets and were packed in the windows and on the roofs, the women trilling their shrill undulating cries, the men chanting, "God is most great", "There is no god but God."

The expedition had consisted only partly of Mamlooks assisted by contingents from the desert tribes and by volunteers. First in the procession came the great ameers, then the regular Mamlooks, followed by the volunteers and after them the tribesmen. Next came camels, horses, mules and asses laden with the plunder, the golden crown of Cyprus being carried on the head of a porter.

Behind the plunder followed the Cypriot banners, their staffs broken, dragged inverted in the dust and then several thousand prisoners, men, women and children, led away to slavery. Last of all came King Janus, in chains, barefoot and bareheaded and riding bareback on a mule.

Barsbai, surrounded by a glittering retinue of ameers and foreign diplomats, received King Janus in a pavilion in the citadel. He was obliged to kiss the ground repeatedly before the sultan and to rub his face in the dust. The consuls of Genoa and Venice interceded for the unhappy king, as well they might, for it was largely their greed which had reduced Cyprus to such straits. Eventually the king was released after promising to pay a huge ransom and an annual tribute. He returned to Nicosia a broken man and it is said that he never smiled again.

The fact that the Cyprus expedition included local troops, bedouins and volunteers under only a few Mamlooks, illustrates the limitations of Egypt's rulers. The nomads of the steppes prided themselves on being the world's finest horsemen, invincible with sword, lance and bow. But, by corollary, they were completely uninterested in other forms of war. They never consented to serve as infantry or at sea and when such units were required other and despised troops had to be employed. This intense passion for cavalry alone was to result in the destruction of the Mamlook Empire when the introduction of firearms made infantry and artillery essential.

* * *

Although the sultan and the great ameers were still former slave boys born in the Caucasus or on the steppes, the Mamlook community was becoming civilized. Ibn Taghri Birdi, for example, who was born in Egypt, the son of a Mamlook of Barqooq, wrote a great historical work in Arabic. Referring to a contemporary ameer, he writes, "Baktamur was endowed with every perfection, a scholar and a soldier, brave, wise, gentle and strong, intelligent, modest and refined." But this transformation of the bloodstained Mamlooks into cultured gentlemen resulted in a relaxation of army discipline. The sultans no longer exercised themselves daily on the parade ground with bow, sword and lance, while we hear increasingly often of army indiscipline and of soldiers molesting civilians.

* * *

When Tamerlane died on 18th February, 1405, he had named his grandson Pir Muhammad as his sole heir, but Khalil Sultan, son of Miran Shah, disputed his right. After four years of some confusion, however, Shah Rukh, the fourth son of Tamerlane, became sole sultan and was to rule from 1409 until 1447. He made his capital in Herat, while his son Ulugh Beg ruled in Samarqand.[3]

Unlike his father, Shah Rukh was a man of peace who devoted most of his long reign to repairing the devastation and ruin caused by Tamerlane and the Mongols. The courts of Herat and Samarqand were famous for their magnificence and both Shah Rukh and his son encouraged scientists, poets and men of learning.

[3] Map 48, page 432.

THE DESCENDANTS OF TAMERLANE

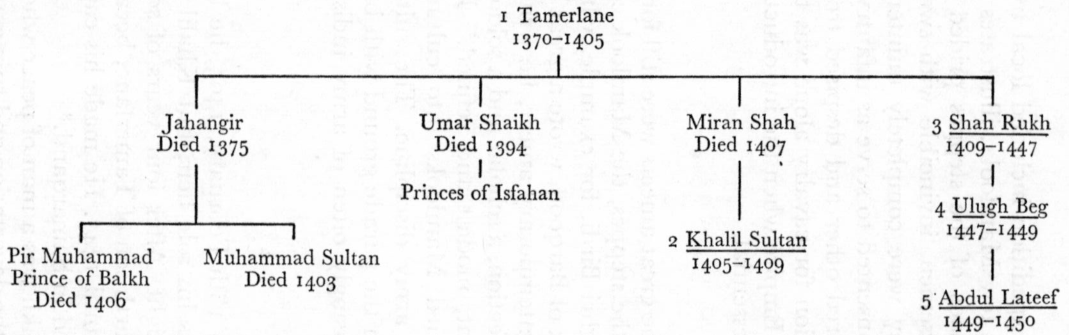

NOTES

(1) Tamerlane had nominated Pir Muhammad to succeed him but he was defeated by Khalil Sultan.

(2) After 1450, the dynasty split up into many small princedoms.

(3) Babar, the first Moghul Emperor of India, was descended from Miran Shah. He conquered India in 1525.

It will be remembered that the Jalair ruler, Ahmad ibn Uwais, had been driven from Adharbaijan and then from Baghdad by Tamerlane and had been obliged to seek refuge in Egypt. In 1410, he recovered Baghdad but when trying also to win back Adharbaijan he was defeated by the Black Sheep Turkmans, who themselves thereby became masters of Iraq. Qara Yusuf, however, was defeated by Shah Rukh, whose suzerainty Iskander, the son of Qara Yusuf, was obliged to acknowledge.

Since the death of Tamerlane in 1405, the Black Sheep and the White Sheep Turkmans had been constantly plundering Iraq and the Jezira. In July 1429 the White Sheep took Edessa. The Mamlook army of Syria was sent against them, using guns against the citadel of Edessa. The Turkmans surrendered on terms, but the Mamlook soldiers refused to observe the conditions, sacked the city and committed many atrocities. Maqrizi, a civilized Egyptian, bewails the incident. "Egypt," he writes, "had always reproved such deeds and now we commit this horrible and shameful crime." A few massacres or breaches of faith would have produced little comment in the days of Baybers the Bunduqdari.

In 1429, Iskander, the son of Qara Yusuf, seized Sultaniya. As a result Shah Rukh, the son of Tamerlane, marched against and defeated him. Shah Rukh destroyed Tabriz, creating more devastation than Tamerlane, according to Ibn Taghri Birdi. Meanwhile Iraq was laid waste by Muhammad, another son of Qara Yusuf. "The very word civilization was no longer applied to Baghdad," laments Ibn Taghri Birdi.

When I first went to Iraq in 1920, I remember being told that the country had been rich in the time of the ancient Persians but that it had been ruined by the Arabs. In fact, during the Arab golden age of the Abbasids, Iraq had been one of the richest countries in the world. It was first the Ghuzz Turkmans in 1050,[4] but even more Hulagu, Tamerlane and the Black Sheep Turkmans who destroyed the accumulated culture and wealth of past centuries.

In 1435, an ambassador from Shah Rukh arrived in Cairo and was given a state reception. The letter which he brought was read in public at a royal levée when, to the consternation of all present, it proved to contain an arrogant summons to insert the name of Shah Rukh in the public prayers. The ambassador endeavoured to give Barsbai a robe of honour of the type normally presented to provincial governors.

Barsbai was almost speechless with rage and ordered that the ambassador be immediately stripped and flogged. He was then dragged to the royal stables, thrown into the horse-pond and ducked frequently till he

[4] *The Course of Empire.*

was nearly drowned. (In the fifteenth century, a diplomatic career involved a number of occupational hazards.) Ibn Taghri Birdi was frankly delighted. "A great rise in the prestige of Egypt and in that of the sultan resulted," he exclaims.

In the autumn of 1437, Barsbai was ailing. His complexion turned yellow and he felt tired and ill. He struggled on with his public duties until he died on 7th June, 1438. He had ruled for seventeen years in peace and security with very few wars or seditions. He had been a great sultan, wise, capable and intelligent, always courteous, and somewhat given to piety. In figure he was tall and slender, fair-haired and handsome. (Many Circassians have fair hair and blue eyes.) He was somewhat weak with his Mamlooks and in his time the general discipline of the army deteriorated disastrously.

Barsbai was succeeded by his fourteen-year-old son Yusuf. The commander-in-chief, Jaqmaq al Alai, became regent, and after three months' political manoeuvring, was accepted as sultan and Yusuf was dethroned. Jaqmaq had been brought up in the Caucasus and had been a personal Mamlook of Barqooq. Under Faraj he became cupbearer and an ameer of ten. The viceroys of Aleppo and Damascus rebelled but were defeated and executed. In these operations brass cannon were used against the citadel of Aleppo.

Jaqmaq ruled the Mamlook Empire for fifteen years, during which there were no wars. The potential enemies of Egypt were otherwise engaged, Shah Rukh in the arts of peace and the Othmanlis in rebuilding their empire shattered by Tamerlane. Sultan Jaqmaq died on 13th February, 1453, being about eighty years old. He was pious, modest, and studious and his personal morals were irreproachable, once again a contrast to the River Mamlook Sultans of earlier times.

* * *

Before leaving the Mamlooks, a few words on their extraordinary system may be of interest. Firstly, in an age like ours perhaps oversupplied with political theorists, we may note that the Mamlooks were extremely capable and practical men, whose methods were entirely empirical. Their system grew as a result of experiment. Nobody could ever have thought out such extraordinary institutions. Yet they made Egypt a greater power than she had ever been before. Themselves strangers, in most cases ignorant of the language, they performed this miracle by themselves doing all the fighting, while at the same time benefiting by the commerce, industry, culture and highly developed administrative services of one of the world's oldest civilizations. The Mongols with less perspicacity had destroyed the culture and wealth of Persia in the process of conquering it.

In spite of these advantages, however, there is no doubt that, if succession to the throne had been hereditary, the Mamlooks would have lasted for three or four generations and then collapsed. Many sultans did indeed pass the throne to their sons but the violence and the jealousies of the Mamlooks nearly always ended in their overthrow. These methods led to the perpetuation of the régime by ensuring the succession of powerful rulers, probably unequalled by any legitimate dynasty.

Although so fantastic a system as dictatorship by foreign ex-slaves seems to us to be almost incredible, the choice of a new leader by trial by *coup d'état* is still perhaps the most widely practised method today. Although abhorrent to the law-abiding peoples of north-west Europe and North America, it must be admitted that it is unlikely to produce a nonentity. The value of the test is, of course, in proportion to the danger. When unsuccessful claimants are normally strangled with a bowstring or halved at the waist, the winner will be a man of real courage and resolution.

In spite, however, of the constant importation of fresh blood, the Mamlook régime began at length to show signs of decadence. The rough military customs of the River Mamlooks gave way to refinement and then to intellectualism. Indiscipline, which may perhaps be another sign of decadence, was increasingly apparent after 1400. The early sultans never left the citadel except when "properly dressed" and surrounded by a cortège in brilliant uniforms, even if they were only going to play polo. Often, if not always, they were accompanied by a band of drums and trumpets. The degenerate Faraj was the first sultan to go out in casual clothes. It would be interesting to investigate the possible connection of decadence with slovenly dress.

Ibn Taghri Birdi makes some interesting remarks concerning Turks and Arabs which are as true today as they were in 1450. He emphasizes the contrast between the intellectual subtlety of the Syrians and Egyptians and the simple gullibility of the Turks, and his words could equally well be applied to relations between Arabs and North Europeans. Historical research might well reveal that races originating from cold climates are more slow-witted than those of the Mediterranean, and more readily accept information at its face value, whereas peoples from warmer climates tend to seek a subtle motive concealed beneath what appears to northerners to be a plain statement of fact.

The lack of mental subtlety among northern races has not proved entirely a disadvantage. It seems to have made them more successful in war and even in government—activities requiring a grasp of the main objective and its pursuit with courage, perseverance and stability. But in the subtleties of politics, subversion and propaganda, Europeans and

Turks still lag behind the peoples of the eastern Mediterranean seaboard. Moreover, it is extremely remarkable that the Ottomans never achieved distinction in science or culture as the Arabs had done. The Ottomans were courageous and brutal, but practical and simple-minded as the Mamlooks had been. The Arabs were less brutal but more subtle, intellectual and poetic.

* * *

The Battle of Anqara might well have changed the history of the world but, in practice, its effect was short-lived. Tamerlane marched away and the Ottoman Empire recovered from the shock, largely owing to the sound foundations laid by Othman, Orkhan and Murad I.

Sulaiman, Bayazid's eldest son, hastened from the battlefield to Adrianople where he caused himself to be proclaimed sultan. His brothers refused to recognize him, Isa declared himself independent in Brusa while Muhammad, the youngest, set himself up at Amasia, north of Sivas.[5]

The first fratricidal civil war occurred in Asia Minor between Isa and Muhammad. Isa was defeated and took refuge with Sulaiman in Adrianople. Meanwhile, however, Tamerlane, who always tried to sow civil war in the countries he had conquered, released the fourth brother Musa, who had been captured at Anqara, and urged him to claim the throne.

The war between the sons of Bayazid was now two against two, Sulaiman and Isa in Thrace facing Musa and Muhammad in Asia. The first two assumed the offensive and crossed to Asia, where Muhammad was soon hard pressed, when Musa crossed to Europe and raised a revolt in Adrianople.

Sulaiman hastened back toward the capital but was assassinated on the way in 1410, whereupon Musa[6] proclaimed himself sultan, and threatened Constantinople. Manuel II appealed for help to Muhammad, who crossed to Europe in response to his call. Musa was defeated and killed and, in 1413, Muhammad I was proclaimed Othmanli Sultan in Adrianople.

Ten years of fratricidal anarchy had followed the Battle of Anqara. Realizing that the empire needed a breathing-space to recover its strength, the new sultan laboured constantly to avoid wars. He made peace with Manuel, treated his Christian subjects with fairness and ruled with justice and moderation. In Asia Minor, he compelled the Qaramanlis and the ameers reinstalled by Tamerlane to acknowledge his suzerainty. His high moral standards earned him the respect of his people, though it is true that he killed the son of his elder brother Sulaiman and blinded a brother of his own. He died in 1421 at the age

[5] Map 50, page 443. [6] Genealogical tree, page 412.

of forty-seven, leaving a renovated and consolidated empire, and was suceeded by his son Murad II.

Constantinople had enjoyed eight years of peace in the reign of Muhammad I but old Manuel II, with incredible folly, encouraged a rival claimant to oppose Murad II. The pretender was easily defeated and the sultan turned to revenge himself on Manuel. The walls of the imperial city were for the first time bombarded with cannon but a diversion obliged Murad to abandon the attack. Mustafa, a younger brother of his, rebelled in Asia Minor supported by the Qaramanli ameer. He was defeated but meanwhile Manuel II had died and Murad agreed to make peace with his successor, John VIII. Salonica had hitherto acknowledged the suzerainty of Constantinople but the emperor sold the great seaport to Venice. In 1430, Murad attacked and captured the city by assault in spite of a vigorous Venetian defence.[7]

The most serious wars of Murad's reign, however, were against John Hunyadi, an illegitimate son of Sigismond and a Hungarian hero. Sigismond, of Nicopolis fame, had been elected Holy Roman Emperor in 1410. Hunyadi was a splendid leader who repeatedly defeated Ottoman armies. In 1442, he drove the Ottomans out of Serbia. On 3rd November, 1443, at the head of an army of Serbians and Hungarians, he defeated the Othmanlis again between Sofia and Nish, captured Sofia, crossed the Balkan Mountains in the depth of winter and gained another victory north of Adrianople.

Murad was anxious for peace, negotiations were opened and, in June 1444, a ten-year peace was signed at Szegeddin, in which Murad recognized Serbian independence. Ladislaus, King of Hungary, swore on the Gospels to observe its terms, while Murad took a similar oath on the Qoran. Ladislaus and Hunyadi made a triumphal entry into Buda, followed by thirteen captive pashas, nine Othmanli war standards and four thousand prisoners. As soon as the treaty was signed, Murad abdicated in favour of his fourteen-year-old son Muhammad and retired to Asia Minor.

Scarcely had the treaty been signed than the Christians decided to break it, the papal legate having persuaded King Ladislaus to commit perjury. "History," says Sir Edwin Pears, "furnishes few examples of equally bad faith."[8] Skanderbeg of Albania and George Brankovitch, King of Serbia, refused to break their oaths. Thus the Hungarians had not only broken their faith but had also mismanaged the whole affair and were obliged to fight without allies.

Hunyadi and King Ladislaus nevertheless marched on Varna with only twenty thousand men. Murad immediately cancelled his abdication, returned to Thrace and led his army against the Hungarians. On

[7] Map 45, page 417. [8] Sir Edwin Pears, *The Destruction of the Greek Empire.*

11th November, 1444, a desperate battle was fought near Varna, the Christians being outnumbered by more than two to one. For a time, Hunyadi seemed to be winning, but the Janissaries stood firm round the sultan who had planted a lance in front of his position with the broken treaty on its point. Finally, in a rash charge, King Ladislaus was unhorsed and captured. He was forthwith decapitated and his head raised on a lance in full view of the Hungarian army, which thereupon broke and fled. In the crisis of the battle, Murad is alleged to have prayed, "O Christ, if Thou art really God, punish the perfidy of Thy followers."

Murad II abdicated for the second time after this victory but was again recalled, this time by a mutiny of the Janissaries. His return was greeted by a great ovation from the army and the Janissaries immediately returned to discipline. On 18th October, 1448, Murad II again defeated Hunyadi on the same field of Kossovo where, in 1389, Murad I had overthrown the Serbians and met his own death. In spite of this victory, however, the Albanians, fighting in their own mountains under Skanderbeg, their national hero, proved to be unconquerable.

On 13th February, 1451, Murad II died of a stroke after a reign of thirty years. He had been a wise, just and capable ruler of his own subjects. Although most of his life was spent in war, he was in fact always desirous of peace and most of his campaigns were forced upon him. Ironically enough, the Serbians and Hungarians had done nothing after the Battle of Anqara when the Othmanlis could easily have been evicted from Europe, but offered them bitter opposition when they had recovered their strength.

Murad was officially a devoted Muslim, founded a number of colleges and hospitals and encouraged conversions to Islam, even by force. In private life, however, he was a voluptuary, addicted to wine, luxury and sexual indulgence and, in later life, grew very fat. In appearance he was short and thickset, with a large hooked nose.

* * *

Muhammad II, who had twice already been proclaimed sultan when Murad II abdicated, eventually succeeded his father in 1451 at the age of twenty-one. His first action was to kill his younger brother who was still a child. From the moment of his accession, Muhammad determined to take Constantinople. When a child, he had been neglected by his father and had grown up lonely and unloved until the death of his elder brothers made him heir to the throne. He was inclined to be reserved and secretive but was well educated and of an energetic and determined character.

His first actions appeared pacific. He made a truce with the Hungarians and welcomed embassies from Venice and other Christian

States. He began work early in 1451 to build a fort at Roumeli Hisar on the Bosphorus opposite one built by Bayazid at Anadolu Hisar on the Asian shore. The fleets of Venice, Genoa and Byzantium had hitherto been able to sail unchallenged through the Bosphorous and the Dardanelles. By their artillery fire, the two Othmanli castles could now close the Bosphorus, an evident indication of the sultan's intention to blockade Constantinople.

During the winter of 1452–1453, preparations for the attack on Constantinople were energetically pushed forward. For a thousand years the walls of the city had withstood every attack but Muhammad's clear intellect had realized that the new artillery would spell the end of masonry walls, and he personally superintended the casting of great numbers of cannon. In their previous attacks, the Ottomans had been handicapped by their lack of a fleet. As a result, the sultan ordered the immediate construction of large numbers of galleys. Muhammad himself was everywhere, consulting, inspecting, reproving, encouraging. Early in 1453, an army of a hundred and fifty thousand men was assembled before the walls of the city.

* * *

Constantine XI Dragases had succeeded to the imperial title on 31st October, 1448, on the death of his brother John VIII.[9] The Palaeologi, by their family feuds, had often done their country more harm than good, but Constantine XI, the last Byzantine Emperor, was by his heroism to atone for the sins of his forebears. On 10th November, 1452, ominous event, two Venetian ships bringing wheat from the Black Sea to Constantinople were sunk in the Bosphorus by the New Turkish forts. The Venetian sailors captured were halved at the waist.

In the vain hope of obtaining help from the West, Constantine XI agreed to the reunion of the Latin and Orthodox churches. On 12th December, 1452, a solemn service of reunion was held in Santa Sophia in the presence of the papal legate and the emperor. But these efforts created division rather than union. The Byzantines were split into bitterly hostile factions, one favouring, the other opposing reunion with Rome.

As a last resort, Constantine XI again sent ambassadors to the West. The King of France expressed his sympathy, the Emperor Frederick III sent a note of protest to the sultan, the Venetian senate debated whether or not to send troops, Pope Nicholas V resolved to send a fleet but failed to act on his resolution. "Byzantium knew that she was lost but at least she knew how to die a worthy death."[10]

On 28th January, 1453, John Giustiniani, a Genoese, arrived in

[9] Genealogical tree, page 415. [10] Louis Bréhier, *Vie et Mort de Byzance*.

Constantinople with two ships and seven hundred men. The Byzantines numbered some five thousand men with perhaps two or three thousand more foreigners, giving a total of perhaps a little over seven thousand. These numbers, however, included monks and volunteers without military training. Constantinople in its heyday had been one of the greatest cities in the world with probably more than a million inhabitants, but long years of troubles, blockade and loss of trade had reduced the population in 1453 to not more than a hundred thousand.

Constantine was as short of money as he was of men, and was unable to buy weapons. Many of the defenders were armed only with swords and the Byzantines had only a few small iron cannon to oppose to the large force of Othmanli artillery. Moreover, both powder and ammunition were in short supply, and it was difficult to use the guns from the walls for fear of loosening the masonry.

The city was defended on three sides by water, the Sea of Marmora, the Bosphorus and the Golden Horn. Only on the west was there a land front, covered by a ditch and triple walls four miles long. The two inner walls were massive, with towers at intervals of only a hundred and fifty feet. Including the waterfronts, however, the perimeter was nearly fourteen miles, far too long for seven thousand men to hold, especially if the enemy had a fleet.

The Othmanli army camped outside the walls was said to be one hundred and fifty thousand strong, of whom perhaps only half were regulars. The professional Ottoman troops may have numbered about eighty thousand, of whom twelve thousand were Janissaries, perhaps at that time the finest troops in the world.

But however good their cavalry and infantry, it was the Ottoman artillery which was to take the city. The Greek historian Phrantzes speaks of fourteen batteries of four guns each. Never in the history of war had artillery been used in such masses, which, moreover, included the biggest guns ever cast. The heaviest cannon were made by a Hungarian called Urban, who had first offered his services to Constantine but had refused the meagre pay which was all the emperor could afford. It is interesting once again to note the early examples of the employment of Western technicians by Muslims, marking the fact that the West was now overtaking the East in technology. On the other hand, it was the genius of Muhammad II which grasped the immense power of more and bigger guns, a conception in which he was in advance of Europe.

The Ottoman army concentrated outside the city in the first week in April 1453. It immediately covered its whole front with a ditch and breastwork, extending from the Golden Horn to the Sea of Marmora. A detachment was sent north of the Golden Horn to blockade the Genoese

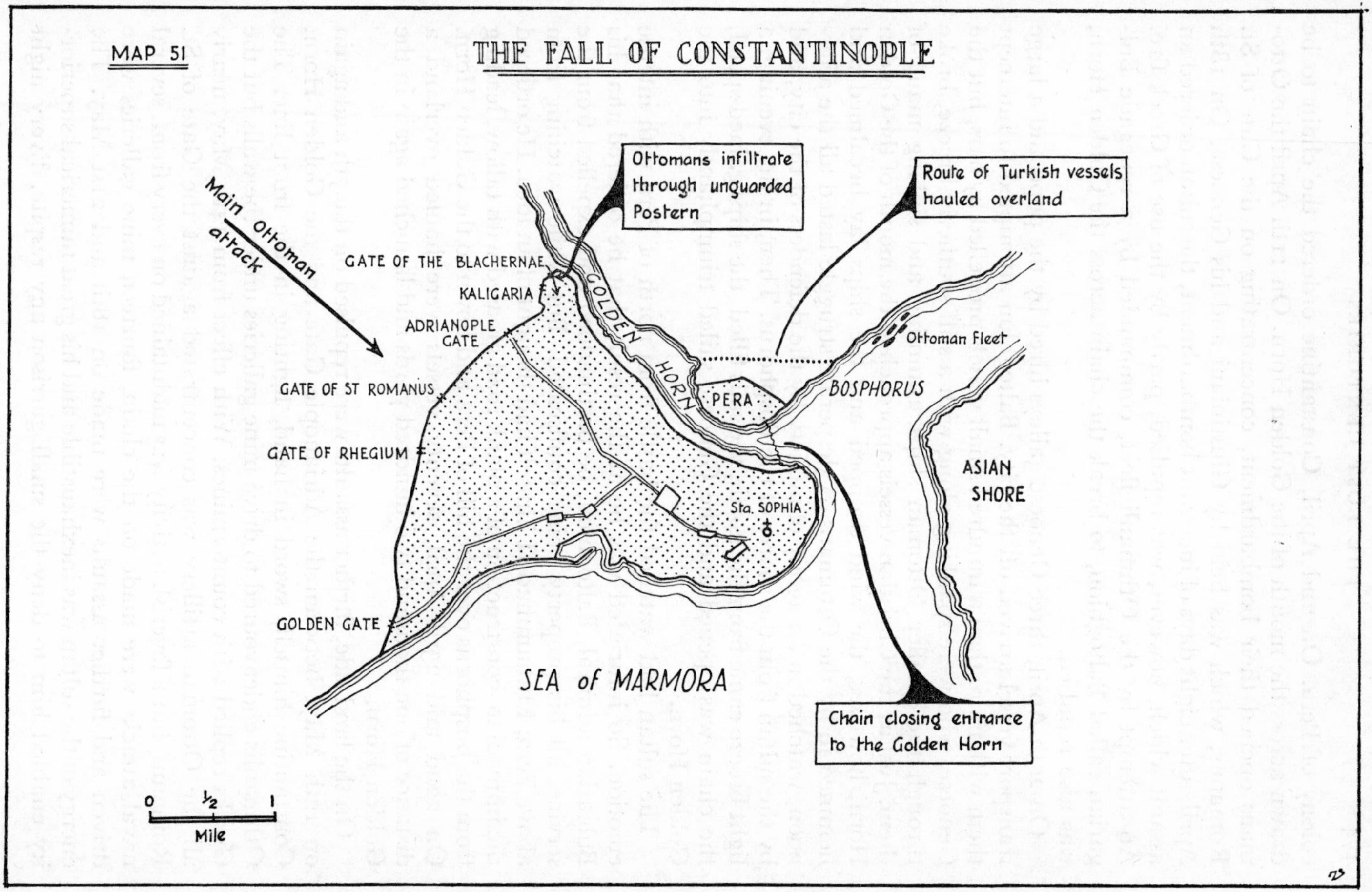
MAP 51
THE FALL OF CONSTANTINOPLE
Ottomans infiltrate through unguarded Postern
Route of Turkish vessels hauled overland
Main Ottoman attack
GATE OF THE BLACHERNAE
KALIGARIA
ADRIANOPLE GATE
GATE OF ST ROMANUS
GATE OF RHEGIUM
GOLDEN GATE
GOLDEN HORN
PERA
Ottoman Fleet
BOSPHORUS
ASIAN SHORE
Sta. SOPHIA
SEA of MARMORA
Chain closing entrance to the Golden Horn
0
½
1
Mile

colony of Pera. On 2nd April, Constantine ordered the chain to be drawn across the mouth of the Golden Horn. On 11th April the Ottomans opened their bombardment, concentrating on the Gate of St. Romanus, which was held by Giustiniani and his Genoese. On 18th April, after eight days of incessant bombardment, the sultan ordered an assault which, however, was repulsed, partly by the use of Greek fire. An attempt by the Othmanli fleet, commanded by a renegade Bulgarian called Baltoghlou, to break the chain across the Golden Horn, was also repulsed.

On 20th April, three Genoese galleys hired by the pope and a large transport vessel arrived off the city. Baltoghlou attempted to intercept them with more than a hundred small vessels propelled by oars, but the Genoese, who were spanking along with a stiff southerly breeze, broke through the smaller Ottoman ships, ramming and sinking many of them. Just as the Christian vessels approached the mouth of the Golden Horn, however, the wind dropped and the ships lay becalmed and hemmed in by the Ottomans. A desperate struggle lasted all the afternoon, watched in an agony of anxiety by the defenders of the city, and by the sultan from the shores of the Bosphorus. Then, in the evening, a light breeze came from the north, the sails filled, the ships gained speed, the chain was opened and the Genoese sailed triumphantly into the Golden Horn.

The sultan had watched the battle from north of Pera with intense emotion. So infuriated was he at the result that he ordered that his Bulgarian admiral, Baltoghlou, be bastinadoed and expelled from the service, all his property being confiscated. But while watching from above Pera, Muhammad II himself had thought of an idea. He ordered the immediate construction of a plank road greased with tallow, leading from the Bosphorus over the hill of Pera and down to the Golden Horn. On 22nd and 23rd April, seventy vessels were hauled overland a distance of one thousand two hundred yards and launched again in the Golden Horn.

On the land side, further assaults were repulsed on the 7th and again on 12th May, between the Adrianople Gate and the Golden Horn, Constantine himself, sword in hand, fighting in the front line. The Othmanlis endeavoured to drive mine galleries under the walls but the Greeks replied with countermines. With effect from 14th May, nearly all the Ottoman artillery was concentrated against the Gate of St. Romanus, but a feverish activity was maintained on every front, several naval attacks were made on the chain, fourteen mine galleries were driven and further assaults were made on 18th and 21st May. The energy of the sultan was inexhaustible and his great numerical superiority enabled him to deny the small garrison any respite. Every night parties of citizens and even women toiled to repair the crumbling walls and to block the breaches with wooden beams and barrels filled with earth.

Throughout all the long and tragic days of the siege, the Genoese colony at Pera had remained neutral and done nothing to assist the city. No help appeared from the West. There were even Christian Serbians fighting for the sultan. The emperor's advisers urged him to escape from the city and raise help in Europe or in southern Greece, but Constantine replied heroically that he would die with his people.

Three practicable breaches had now been made in the walls and some reports allege that the sultan summoned the emperor for the last time to surrender, offering to make Constantine ruler of the Peloponesus under Ottoman suzerainty but threatening otherwise to massacre the whole population. Constantine replied in dignified terms that he and his people were ready to die. After the abject humiliations to which the Palaeologi had submitted in the past, it is bracing to find the last emperor speaking out boldly in heroic words.

On 26th May, the sultan held a council of war at which it was decided to launch a general assault. On 27th, Muhammad inspected all the troops and issued final operation orders. The soldiers were promised that all the wealth in this splendid city would be theirs, including great numbers of beautiful women and girls and that the sultan desired nothing for himself.

In the city, the defenders were working feverishly to block the breaches in the walls, erecting barricades with sacks of earth, wooden beams, bales of cotton and any material available. The Othmanlis made no attempt to conceal the imminence of the great assault. Huge fires were lit in their camps, the ships lying off the city were illuminated and military bands, trumpets and drums played all night.

On 28th May, 1453, Constantine ordered religious processions and solemn litanies and the holy icons were carried through the streets. Then the emperor, his ministers and his army commanders received the Holy Eucharist, the last Christian service to be held in the splendid cathedral of Santa Sophia. Greeks and Italians alike swore to give their lives and embraced one another for the last time as men about to die. All of them returned to their posts on the walls, fully aware that they had but a few hours left to live.

The defenders took up their position between the second and the inner wall, the outer wall or breastwork having long ago disappeared and the moat being virtually filled in. All doors leading through the inner wall into the city were locked, so that none of the defenders could escape. Literally with their backs to the wall, they awaited the moment of death.

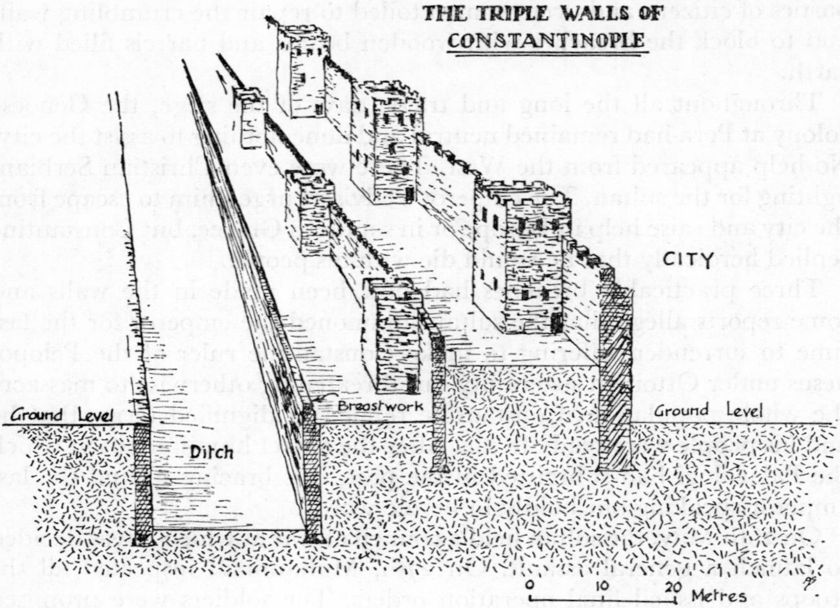

The young sultan had planned the attack with care. All the walls of the city were to be attacked simultaneously, by land and by sea, across the Golden Horn and by landing-parties from the ships on the Sea of Marmora. The main attack, however, was to be on the sector from the Gate of St. Romanus to that of the Kaligaria. Only two thousand men could be spared by the defence to hold this sector.

With his immensely superior numbers, the sultan was determined to deliver successive attacks until the defenders were exhausted. The assault began at a half past one in the morning of 29th May, 1453, accompanied by a terrifying din of drums, trumpets and pipes and the screams of the attackers. The first assault was delivered by clouds of irregulars, some of them Christian adventurers, some carrying ladders, supported by archers who poured streams of arrows into the defenders. The engagement lasted for two hours, after which the attackers fell back. The sultan had not expected the irregulars to take the city. Their rôle was to exhaust the defenders.

At 3.30 a.m. the second attack was delivered without allowing the Christians a moment's rest. It consisted of regular, trained infantry, mostly recruited in Asia Minor. These attacked the breaches strongly but after half an hour's desperate hand-to-hand fighting, they too fell back. A brief lull ensued during which the Othmanlis brought up their artillery to point-blank range and carried out a short and intense bombardment of the breaches. On the completion of this "softening-up", the infantry attacked again but were again repulsed.

The sun had now risen and all the defences were still holding. The guns again carried out a brief but intense bombardment of the breaches. The sultan, who was personally directing the attack, decided to commit the Janissaries. As soon as the guns stopped firing and before the dust and smoke had cleared, the Janissaries moved forward in steady, perfect ranks with loud shouts. Muhammad accompanied them himself up to the edge of the moat. In a minute the troops were across the ruined ditch and mounting the breach.

The noise was deafening and in the city all the church bells were ringing. The defenders who had already been fighting continuously for four hours were almost exhausted. The most intense fighting developed at the Gate of St. Romanus, which was held by Giustiniani and his Genoese. At this moment of supreme crisis, Giustiniani was severely wounded and left the front. Some Greek writers later accused him of cowardice, but he had until then been the heart and soul of the defence and he died of his wound three days later.

The departure of Giustiniani caused some confusion among the defenders, which was noticed by the sultan who was standing close by on the other side of the ditch. The Janissaries had been fighting hand-to-hand for an hour and were themselves weakening when the sultan called out that the defenders were in confusion and ordered a fresh attack. The Janissaries pressed forward up the breach once again and mingled with the defenders in a bitter contest.

Meanwhile the Ottomans had found a postern gate open in the wall near the Blachernae and had already infiltrated into the city. Constantine, seeing that the defence was now hopeless, threw off his imperial mantle and insignia and, sword in hand, plunged into the mêlée in the breach. He was never seen again. By this time the attackers were everywhere swarming into the city, killing all they met regardless of age or sex. In the afternoon, Muhammad II, thereafter to be known as the Conqueror, rode in state into the city. Proceeding directly to Santa Sophia, he mounted to the sanctuary, threw down the altar and trampled upon it.

The Byzantines had always claimed to be Romans. For a thousand years they had held the eastern gateway of Europe. Many have criticized them for their intrigues, their revolutions, their assassinations and their superstitions. But whether or not these accusations were justified, the Byzantine Empire had lived longer than any other empire in history. Then, when at last her end did come, she died heroically in face of overwhelming odds and abandoned by the Europe she had so long defended—an ancient Roman death—with her emperor at her head.

NOTABLE DATES

Battle of Anqara	20th July, 1402
Ottoman Civil Wars	1402–1413
Accession of Shah Rukh, son of Tamerlane	1409
Death of Faraj son of Barqooq Accession of Shaikh al Mahmoodi in Cairo	1412
Accession of Muhammad I, Othmanli Sultan	1413
Death of Mamlook Sultan Shaikh	13th January, 1421
Death of Muhammad I Accession of Othmanli Sultan Murad II	1421
Accession of Sultan Barsbai in Cairo	1st April, 1422
Mamlook raid on Cyprus Defeat and capture of King Janus	July 1426
Death of Barsbai Accession of Sultan Jaqmaq al Alai	1438
Treaty of Szegeddin between Hungarians and Murad II First abdication of Murad	1444
Hungarians break treaty Murad defeats them at Varna	1444
Second Battle of Kossovo	1448
Death of John VIII Palaeologus Accession of Constantine XI Dragases	31st October, 1448
Death of Murad II Accession of Muhammad II	13th February, 1451
Death of Mamlook Sultan Jaqmaq al Alai	13th February, 1453
Opening of the Othmanli attack on Constantinople	11th April, 1453
Fall of Constantinople	29th May, 1453

PERSONALITIES

Egyptian Sultans

Sultan Faraj, son of Barqooq	1399–1412
Sultan Shaikh al Mahmoodi	1412–1421
Sultan Tatar	1421
Sultan Barsbai	1422–1438
Sultan Jaqmaq al Alai	1438–1453

Byzantine Emperors

Manuel II Palaeologus	1391–1425

John VIII	1425–1448
Constantine XI Dragases	1448–1453

Othmanli Sultans

Civil wars between sons of Bayazid	1402–1413
Sultan Muhammad I	1413–1421
Sultan Murad II	1421–1451
Sultan Muhammad II, the Conqueror	1451–1481

XXII

The Lost Centuries

What seems clear is that all history is one history . . . The story is a greater and a more moving one than any one man can tell; and there is nothing better than that a man read it for himself, wherever he may find it, and see what it means for himself.

T. R. GLOVER, *The Ancient World*

If the future is hidden, yet you should guess it from the past.

AHMAD IBN ARABSHAH

The entire story of man on earth has no meaning at all except a religious meaning. There is no hope except in a vast increase of spiritual religion.

ARNOLD TOYNBEE

The fear of the Lord is the beginning of wisdom: a good understanding have all they that do his commandments. *Psalm CXI*, 10

Nature's great secret let me now rehearse—
Long have I pondered o'er the wondrous tale,
How Love immortal fills the universe,
Tarrying till mortals shall His Presence hail:
When will ye cast the veil of sense aside,
Content in finding Love to lose all else beside.

JALAL AL DEEN RUMI (Trans. E. H. PALMER)

XXII

OUR attempt to fill the long gap between the fall of Rome and the rise of Europe is completed. When we began in the sixth century, the Mediterranean world still felt a homogeneity inherited from Roman imperial days. In the seventh century, half the Roman world was conquered by the Arabs and the feeling of community was restricted to a limited area of southern Europe called Christendom. This area itself, cut off from world trade by the Arab Empire extending from the Atlantic to China, relapsed into the ignorance and the poverty of the Dark Ages.

Muslim civilization and power dominated the world for five or six centuries, the period which has been omitted from our history books. The theory that these were ages of barbarism can no longer be maintained. We have seen that the Arabs and their successors invented algebra, trigonometry and logarithms, and introduced modern mathematics and the use of zero to Europe. In chemistry, astronomy, medicine, surgery and ophthalmology their works were standard text-books in the West for centuries. By bringing to Europe the manufacture of paper, they immensely facilitated the spread of knowledge. They had measured the circumference of the earth six hundred years before Europe admitted it to be round.

In poetry they invented rhyme and in the fields of imagination, fairy tales, romance and chivalry, we owe them an immense debt. It is a sobering thought that the very existence of such a civilization, in its time as powerful and as brilliant as is our own today, has been almost entirely forgotten. The peoples of Europe and North America believe themselves to be the *élite* of the human race through all the ages. The Romans and the Arabs likewise, each in their time, considered their world supremacy to be both natural and eternal, yet their Ages of Gold have passed into semi- or total oblivion.

* * *

Politically we see the Muslim states, throughout their long centuries of leadership, constantly torn by civil wars between rival claimants to rule. This factor is further emphasized because we, in our own experience, see them once again frequently the scene of internal upheavals and of army seizures of power, precisely as they were eight hundred years ago. Our supercilious attitude in face of this internal instability is somewhat weakened when we realize that European nationalism, which in the eleventh and twelfth centuries broke up the "Roman" solidarity of Christendom, has given rise to much more misery in Europe than internal instability has caused in Muslim states. If men must fight, *coups d'état* are infinitely preferable to wars between nations. In the same manner, European armies are trained only to fight other nations. Throughout history, Muslim armies have been employed in internal struggles more often than in external wars. It is most sincerely to be hoped that Muslim nations will not absorb the spirit of nationalism which has ruined Europe. A few periodical *coups d'état* are harmless in comparison.

We see in Muslim countries the same rise and decline of nations, dynasties and empires as in the West at similar intervals of time. One contrast, however, may be indicated. We are accustomed in the West to trace the histories of countries from primitive tribal democracy, through aristocracy and monarchy to democracy, demagogy and then anarchy, terminated by the establishment of dictatorship to restore order. Throughout the whole process the centre of gravity of power is constantly changing from tribal anarchy to robber barons, despotic kings, balanced democracy, demagogic confusion and back to the autocratic dictator.

The history of the Muslim nations shows much less marked changes in the pattern of power. Great empires arise, endure about the same length of time as they do in the West, are followed by a break up into small states and then by another great empire, but the democratic and demagogic phases are much less pronounced, if indeed they appear at all. This feature coincides with a remarkable difference between the natures of north-western Europeans and Arabs. North-west Europeans and North Americans are inspired with stronger communal loyalties and a greater capacity for devotion to vague conceptions such as democracy or communism. In periods of greatness, their communal loyalties produce the noble conception of duty, in decadent times that of the all-powerful state, destroying the individuality of the citizen.

Muslim peoples normally have far warmer personal emotions. They are passionate lovers and haters, not of ideologies but of individuals. Their real loyalties are not to an intellectual conception like socialism but to a national hero. These profoundly important psychological differences seem never to have been analysed. I suspect that climate has much to do with them, for it is interesting to notice that nearly all the Muslims in the world live between the tenth and the fortieth parallels of north latitude. The Central American countries, which exhibit certain similar characteristics, lie within the same belt.

The Lost Centuries shed new light for us on the falsity of modern ideas in two other directions. The first of these is that "imperialism" is a modern European vice, directed to the "exploitation" of weaker peoples. Our narratives have shown us many races of Asia and Africa conquering empires, sometimes at the expense of Europeans. Moreover, empires have by no means been limited to exploitation but have often been the means of carrying civilization, learning and prosperity to races lagging behind.

The second fallacy which the Lost Centuries expose is the idea that the political system of western Europe and North America today is the perfect form of government for all nations for all time. To begin with, "Western Democracy" itself is changing rapidly from balanced democracy to demagogic anarchy, probably to be followed by dictatorship. It is virtually impossible to imitate a system which is itself changing so quickly. Secondly, changes from autocracy to democracy and back to autocracy have happened in Europe in the past but, as we have seen, politics have not followed the same course between the tenth and fortieth parallels of latitude. The assumption that political systems acceptable in the North are equally applicable in Muslim countries is not confirmed by history.

* * *

One of the most remarkable phenomena of the period covered by the present volume is the regularity with which conquering dynasties rise and fall. In the case of barbarian conquerors, the degeneracy of the ruling dynasty was normally sufficient to induce collapse after one hundred to a hundred and fifty years.

In *The Course of Empire* we saw that great national empires like the Arab, the Spanish or the British often seemed to collapse after two hundred and thirty or two hundred and fifty years. In the case of such great empires, the whole nation was involved in their rise and fall. For an entire people to absorb the idea that their wealth and power were automatic and that effort was not necessary, required a long period of time. Thus a truly national rise and fall might occupy some two hundred and fifty years. But when that fall came, it was utter and irrevocable, for the whole people had been involved both in the struggle to rise and in the decadence and fall.

It is to be noted that this rise and fall had no connection with the political institutions of the imperial nation. Every now and again in history, some race or other experiences an extraordinary outburst of energy and overruns a large part of the world. The government may or may not be authoritarian but every man of the nation seems to be inspired with a new spirit. The Arab expansion was one of the most truly popular and national of any of the great historical expansions, for when it began the Arabs had no government, no army and no trained military commanders. But in the case of the Spanish Empire, also despotically ruled, the exploits of the Conquistadors were only slightly less miraculous.

The rise and fall of barbarian conquering dynasties seem to fall in a different category. The conquests of the Arabs by the Seljuqs or the Ayoubids, for example, were rather the result of the outstanding qualities of a small number of individual leaders and were not accompanied by a great outburst of national enthusiasm and expansion. A despotic and victorious dynasty would naturally acquire the idea that its position was unassailable more quickly than would a whole nation. As we have seen, about a hundred and twenty years normally sufficed for their downfall, half the time needed for a nation-wide rise and collapse. But in such cases the fall of the dynasty did not involve the ruin of the whole country as was the case with the popular national breakdowns.

* * *

The reasons for the decadence and collapse of nations are, however, of more importance to us than the period of duration of their power. All human affairs are so immensely complicated by the great number of factors involved that generalizations cannot fail to be dangerous. Yet if we are mindful of these limitations, a considerable amount of light can be shed on our modern problems by a careful consideration of history.

The causes of decadence are doubtless numerous and differ in some respects in each case. Yet the results produced seem to be so strikingly uniform that the basic explanations are probably the same in every instance. When any community has for several generations enjoyed a high degree of power and wealth, further effort seems to be unnecessary. In addition, in the case of a really extensive empire, many of the boldest and most enterprising citizens have gone abroad and lost their lives or settled in distant countries. Any dominating race will have lost a large proportion of its bravest men killed in war.

The weaker and the less enterprising will have remained at home to breed future generations. Moreover, the wealth of the imperial homeland will have attracted many foreign immigrants, whose loyalty to the state will often be less single-minded than that of the original citizens. In this manner the quality of the imperial race will slowly deteriorate. At the same time, however, the inhabitants of the homeland will gradually assume their wealth and power to be automatic and natural and will see no need for further effort to maintain their pre-eminence. It will not occur to them that the splendid position achieved for them by their predecessors can only be retained by a continuance of that heroism and self-sacrifice which originally won it.

It is tempting to imagine that the fall of great nations could be prevented by a more careful and widespread study of history. The general public might be persuaded by the examples of the fall of the empires of the past to appreciate the need for action to avoid a similar fate. Unfortunately, however, human beings are swayed more strongly by emotion than by logic. It is for this cause that reason has always failed to control human conduct where religion has often succeeded. Enlightened self-interest, the hope of the Victorians, has proved a broken reed.

In popular estimation, decadence conveys a suggestion of moral laxity, not only lethargy and weakness but also of sexual license, drunkenness and idleness. It is true that these vices are often conspicuous under the circumstances but they are probably secondary results, produced by the belief that wealth and power are the natural right of the nation concerned, without effort or obligation. Conceit of this kind breeds self-indulgence, frivolity, selfishness and a refusal to acknowledge any obligation to serve the public interest. Such a spirit inevitably leads to the downfall of the state which can only be maintained by the devoted service of its members.

Thus degeneracy may originate in a mistaken idea of our own superiority, which, however, gives rise to a moral landslide, inevitably terminating in collapse. No amount of intellectual cleverness can make up for the moral bankruptcy of a nation. In this manner, our problem today has become a moral one. We need prophets not politicians.

* * *

Another conclusion to which the narrative contained in this book seems to point is that periods of decadence are accompanied by internal struggles. It might have been expected that the obviously precarious position of a nation in decline would cause the people to rally round the government in a desperate effort to save the country. In fact, the reverse seemed always to result—the more catastrophic the situation, the more bitter were the internal feuds.

Once again, the course of events was unconnected with the form of government. Where the régime was autocratic, innumerable rival princes fought one another for the throne until all were swept away by a new conqueror, as occurred in the case of the Muwahhids, the Ayoubids and the Seljuqids. But when the Kingdom of Jerusalem disintegrated, Acre was governed by a commune, and Tripoli likewise. The political factions fought one another until all was lost. The internal schisms of the disintegrating Byzantine Empire similarly endured up to the moment of the siege of Constantinople by Muhammad the Conqueror.

It is true, however, that rising young states also are sometimes torn by civil wars as in the case of Castile until the time of Ferdinand and Isabella. A reasonably satisfactory generalization may perhaps be found by putting the problem another way. When a great nation is at the height of its glory and power, all its citizens feel a pride in the national achievement and are willing to make personal sacrifices to maintain it. Before greatness has been achieved, there is nothing of which to be proud. In the same manner, when the decline has set in, the glory which inspired an earlier generation to heroism has faded, and men turn once again to their petty selfish interests. There may even at this stage be a reaction of resentment against those ancestors whose achievements the new generation have failed to maintain.

Thus the last generations, secretly frustrated by their humiliating failure to maintain their heritage, may even appear hostile to their own nation. Feeling that they have failed their country, they denounce it, claim that they do not *want* to maintain it and even assist outside enemies to demolish it. In some such manner, the Greeks, disgusted with the Byzantine Empire, joined the Ottomans, became Muslims and helped to destroy their own heritage.

* * *

An interesting aspect of the question of decadence is to know whether it arises principally from a deterioration in the quality of individuals or whether it is the system which has grown out of date. For example, would a citizen of a "decadent" nation who moved to the country of a "rising" state find himself inferior to his neighbours? The rise of the Ottoman Empire might have interesting lessons to teach us in this connection. We saw how this young and energetic new state absorbed great numbers of persons who were previously citizens of the decadent Byzantine Empire. In our own times, the United States is a Great Power at the height of its prosperity, recruited almost entirely from immigrants from old races. Have these people been rejuvenated by absorption into a new community?

Decadence may, however, be partly due to the out-of-date organization of the community or to slavish adherence to old traditions. The Mamlook refusal to use artillery might be a case in point or, a more modern example, the possible resistance of factory workers to automation.

Yet if only the institutions were out of date and the individuals were as good as ever, a revolution should be able to renew the "youth" of a nation. In 1789, the French revolution seemed to be a complete departure from tradition and was indeed succeeded by a great outburst of energy. Yet, once this had subsided, the slow decline in the power of France was resumed as if no upheaval had occurred.

In fact, no epoch-making event in history is ever due to a single cause. Many factors doubtless contribute to decadence, of which the assumption that the superiority of the nation is natural and lasting is probably the chief. Certain it is that, for reasons difficult to diagnose, the heroic age of courage, energy and devotion which occasionally raises a nation to international pre-eminence can never be recaptured.

* * *

History is a tantalizing subject because it presents so many situations similar to our own and announces so many principles which are still true in our own experience. Two thousand three hundred years ago, for example, Thucydides remarked that democracies cannot rule empires, and we have seen the truth of his words in our own lifetime. Yet, given these unchanging principles, the remarkable fact is that in no past age have men ever been able correctly to foretell the future. With the advantage of our knowledge of what actually occurred, it seems obvious to us now that in the thirteenth century Europe was overtaking and passing Islam and would soon dominate the world but, as far as we can tell, neither Europeans nor Asians at the time foresaw this outcome.

Similarly, in the middle of the nineteenth century, the peoples of the West thought that great wars were a thing of the past and that the human race would achieve a glorious future of ever-increasing wealth, comfort, peace and culture. We know how different events proved to be.

I remember, in the early 1920s, talking to an old Arab policeman on the Euphrates above Anah. The country was mostly semi-desert, inhabited by tribes of nomadic graziers. The winter had been disastrous, the country was dry and burnt, no rain had fallen, the flocks had died and the tribes were faced with starvation.

"I suppose the tribesmen must be nearly desperate," I said. "No doubt you police will have a bad year trying to control their crime."

"On the contrary," replied the old policeman, "there will be very few crimes this year. People do not commit crimes when they are starving but when they are affluent."

Victorian sociologists were convinced that crime was due to the grinding poverty of the workers. If only all men could have an assured livelihood, they believed, crime would disappear. Now that the dream has been realized and that destitution in Britain is a thing of the past, our crime statistics have gone up tenfold. It would seem that that old Arab gendarme knew more about human nature than the sociologists. Whatever the future holds for us, historical precedent suggests that it will be something entirely unforeseen and quite probably the opposite of what is predicted for us by those who consider themselves our wisest thinkers.

* * *

Finally, it is unreasonable to close the history of the centuries in which almost all wars were ostensibly fought for religion without mentioning the motive which, in theory at least, inspired them. I have, as far as possible, avoided the word Christians in my account of the Crusades and have used Franks or Crusaders, because it does not seem to me that, in their capacity of Crusaders, such people need have been Christians at all. For Christians are not persons who happen to have been born in countries of which the official religion is classified as Christianity, but rather are such individuals as sincerely endeavour to model their lives on that of Christ. "Now if any man have not the spirit of Christ, he is none of His."[1] It is not necessary to be a believing Christian in order to realize that many of the actions of the Crusaders were not in accordance with the teaching of Christ.

The position of those Crusaders who were indeed conscientious Christians seems to us rather pathetic, for they were at times exhorted by their religious leaders to behave in a manner apparently contrary to their religion. Neither the early Christian Church nor the Orthodox Eastern Church has ever advocated religious wars. How was it then that the Western Church began to do so?

The Prophet Muhammad, who had a somewhat inadequate conception of Christianity, bore for many years with exemplary patience the vituperation and persecution directed against him in Mecca. But after his move to Medina he decided to use force against his opponents —not against the Christians but against his unbelieving fellow-Meccans. All through history, the use of force has appeared to the passionate reformer as a tempting short cut.

This change of policy suited the warlike Arab tribes perfectly. After the Prophet's death, his followers conquered a great part of the known world. As a result, Syria, Palestine, Egypt, North Africa and Spain, all Christian countries, were lost to Christendom and became Muslim. It must have seemed to the surviving Christians that their religion would have been eliminated from the face of the earth if Charles Martel had not defeated the Arabs in battle at Tours in 732.

Given these facts, it was but a short step to the belief that the millions who, as a result of war, had abandoned Christianity for Islam could be regained by the same process. The omission of all mention of the Arab and other Muslim Empires from our history books has induced many Europeans to believe that religious wars originated with the Crusaders,

[1] Romans VIII, 9.

who were guilty of an act of unprovoked aggression against the Muslims. As soon, however, as we realize that from the seventh to the twelfth centuries Europe had lived in constant fear of Arab imperialism, we may argue that the Crusades were wars of liberation from Muslim domination.

In actual fact, the great Muslim conquests were partly national and the Arabs became for two centuries the dominant race. Their wars, however, were waged in the name of religion and their enemies were not another nation as such but Christians, Hindus and heathen. It was therefore natural that the European reaction when it came should also be in the name of religion. Spaniards, French and Italians may actually have feared foreign racial domination. As, however, the invasions of their countries were made in the name of religion, their counter-attack likewise assumed a religious colour.

The religious wars waged between Christians in the Middle Ages have frequently been held up as proof of the ineffectiveness of Christianity. It would be interesting to explore much more deeply the extent to which Islam gave rise to the whole idea of religious wars, which were alien to the spirit of antiquity as well as to that of Christianity. We certainly cannot imagine Christ organizing a massacre of His Jewish enemies or of the Roman garrison. His system was based on love, not on force.

There would thus appear to be much to be said for a theory that Islam originated the idea of religious wars, which in their turn suggested to the papacy the policy of preaching Crusades against Christian heretics, like the Albigensians in Provence. The whole of this question provides an excellent example of how in history one thing leads to another. By arbitrarily omitting from our curricula the six centuries of Muslim predominance, we have thrown away the key to the comprehension of our own religious and historical movements in the Middle Ages.

In reality the use of violence to settle religious differences is an extraordinary example of the presumptuous arrogance of men. If God be a spirit who created the whole universe, how supremely ridiculous it is to suppose that men—unimaginably tiny animalculae on a world which is itself no more than a speck of dust in space—can understand their Creator so completely that they are justified in massacring those who do not agree in every detail with their ideas. If God could be understood by such as we, He would not be God.

* * *

It is interesting to note that the ancient world was conscious of the endlessly revolving rise and fall of empires, seemingly hopeless and purposeless. It was the advent of Christ which originated the idea of progress and thence of hope. If a loving and fatherly God were really interested in men, then the whole of human development must be following a plan and was not meaningless. Thus, although our civilization may or may not be declining as so many others have done before it, we need no longer despair of the world as a whole, as the ancients did.

There can surely be no more absorbing subject than that of the slow upward struggle of the human race, although the manner in which we learn history in short snippets here and there, conceals from us the majestic rhythm of the millennia. But if we wish to explore these mighty processes, we must study them with all the humble impartiality at our command. We can no longer afford to suppress periods which do not flatter our petty prejudices and vanities, as we have hitherto done in the case of The Lost Centuries.

Bibliography

Abdul Dhahir, Muhi al Deen ibn, *Tashrif al Ayyam wa al Asur*
Abulfeda *Al Mukhtasir fi akhbar al beshr* (Fr. trans. de Slane. Paris 1872)
— *Taqwim al Buldan*
Abu Shama *Kitab al Raudhatain fi akhbar al daulatain* (Fr. trans. in Historiens Arabes des Croisades)
Ambroise *Estoire de la Guerre Sainte* (Eng. trans. M. J. Hubert "The Crusade of Richard Lion Heart")
Ameer Ali *A short history of The Saracens*
Arabshah, Ahmad ibn *Timur, the Great Prince* (Eng. trans. J. H. Sanders)
Arberry, A. J. *The Doctrine of the Sufis*
— *The Holy Qoran*
Arnold, T. W. *The Preaching of Islam*
Athir, ibn al *Al Kamil fi al Tarikh*
— *History of the Atabegs*
Atiya, A. S. *Crusade, Commerce and Culture*
— *The Crusade in The Later Middle Ages*
Ayalon, D. *Gunpowder and firearms in The Mamluk Kingdom*
Baha al Deen ibn Sheddad *Al Nuwadir as Sultaniya wa al Mahasin al Yusufiya* (Eng. trans. Palestine Exploration Society)
Bailly, Auguste *Byzance*
Baladhuri, al *Futuh al buldan*
Bar Hebraeus *The Chronography of Gregory abu al Faraj, commonly known as Bar Hebraeus* (Eng. trans. E. A. Wallis Budge)
Barthold *Turkestan down to the Mongol invasion*
Basri, al *Futuh ash Sham*
Battuta, ibn *Travels* (Eng. trans. H. A. R. Gibb)
Baybers al Mansoori *Zibdat al Fikra*
Bekri, al *Description de l'Afrique septentrionale* (Fr. trans. de Slane)
Belloc, Hilaire *The Crusade*
— *The Battle Ground*
Benjamin of Tudela In *Early Travels in Palestine* (ed. T. Wright)
Bertrand, Louis *Histoire D'Espagne*
Bertrandon de la Brocquière In *Early Travels in Palestine* (London, Bohn, 1848)
Boyle, J. A. *History of The World Conqueror* by Ala al Deen Ata al Juwaini (q.v.) (Cambridge 1957)
Bréhier, Louis *Vie et Mort de Byzance*
Brion, Marcel *Tamerlan*

Brockelmann, C. *A History of the Islamic peoples*
— *A History of Arabic Literature*
Browne, E. G. *A literary history of Persia*
— *A Persian Anthology*
Burke, E. *A History of Archery*
Bury, J. B. *A History of the Later Roman Empire*
— *A History of the Eastern Roman Empire*
Butler, A. J. *The Arab conquest of Egypt*
Cambridge Mediaeval History
Cambridge History of India
Caussin de Perceval *Historie des Arabes avant l'Islamisme*
Chabot, J. B. See Michel le Syrien
Chalandon, F. *Les Comnènes*
Conder, C. R. *The Latin Kingdom of Jerusalem*
Creasy, S. E. S. *History of the Ottoman Turks*
Creswell, K. A. C. *Muslim architecture in Egypt*
Czaplicka, M. A. *The Turks of Central Asia*
Davis, E. J. *The Invasion of Egypt by Louis IX*
Dermengheen, E. *The Life of Muhammad*
De Slane *Résumé de l'histoire des Croisades* (Fr. trans. of Abulfeda)
Devizes, Richard of *Concerning The Deeds of Richard I, King of England*
Dhahabi, Shams al Din al *Duwal al Islam*
Dozy, R. *The Moslems in Spain*
— *Essai sur l'Histoire de l'Islamisme*
Dunbar, Sir George *A History of India*
Duri, A. K. *Al asr al abbasi al awwal*
Encyclopedia of Islam
Eversley, Lord *The Turkish Empire, its Growth and Decay*
Extraits des historiens Arabes des Croisades (*Journal Asiatique* 1849)
Fagnan, E. *Histoire des Almohades* (Fr. trans. of Marakishi) (q.v.)
Finlay, G. *History of the Byzantine Empire*
Fisher, H. A. L. *A History of Europe*
Fox, R. *Genghis Khan*
Freeman, E. A. *History and Conquests of the Saracens*
Gaudefroye-Demombynes *Fr. Trans. of Umari* (q.v.)
— *La Syrie à l'Epoque des Mamelouks* (Fr. trans. of Al Qalqashandi)
Gaudefroye-Demombynes et Platonov *Le monde musulman et Byzantin jusqu'aux Croisades*
Gibbon, E. *Decline and Fall of The Roman Empire*
Gibbons, H. A. *The Foundation of The Ottoman Empire*
Gibb, H. A. R. *The Arabs*
— *The Arab Conquests in Central Asia*
— *The Damascus Chronicle* (see also Qalanisi)

Gilman, A. *The Saracens*
Grousset, René *Histoire des Croisades* (3 vols)
— *L'Empire des Steppes*
— *L'Empire du Levant*
— *Le Bilan de l'Histoire*
Grunebaum, von *Mediaeval Islam*
Guillaume, A. *A Life of Muhammad* (Trans. of Ibn Ishaq)
Hallam, H. *Europe during the Middle Ages*
Harrison, F. *Byzantine History in the Early Middle Ages*
Harvey, J. *The Plantagenets*
Hauqal, ibn. *Al masalik wa al mamalik* (Fr. trans. de Slane. *Journal Asiatique*)
Haywood, R. M. *The Myth of Rome's Fall*
Hell, Joseph *The Arab Civilization* (Eng. trans. S. Khuda Bukhsh. Cambridge 1926)
Heritage, The Arab (Ed. Nabih Amin Faris)
Hill, Sir George *A History of Cyprus* (Cambridge 1948)
Hisham, ibn *Sirat Rasulillah* (Edition of Ibn Ishaq)
Hitti, P. K. *History of the Arabs*
— *An Arab Gentleman in the Period of the Crusades* (Eng. trans. of Usama ibn Munqidh)
— *The Near East in History* (New York 1961)
Hookham, H. *Tamburlaine The Great*
Houdas et Marçais *Les Traditions Islamiques*
Howorth, Sir Henry *History of The Mongols*
Huart *Histoire des Arabes*
Hughes *Dictionary of Islam*
Idrisi, al *Description of Africa and Spain*
Isfahani, Imad al Deen al *Al fath al qussi*
— Abu al Faraj al *Kitab al Aghani*
Ishaq, ibn *Sirat Rasulillah* (Life of Muhammad) (See also Guillaume)
Joinville, Jean, Sieur de *Memoirs of Louis IX, King of France* (Eng. trans. "Chronicles of the Crusades", London 1848)
Jubair, ibn *Travels* (Eng. trans. R. J. C. Broadhurst)
Julien, C. A. *Histoire de l'Afrique du Nord*
Juwaini, al *Tarikh i Jahan Gushai* (See Boyle)
Kelly, A. *Eleanor of Aquitaine*
Khaldun, ibn *Kitab al Ibar*
— *Histoire des Berbères* (Fr. trans. de Slane)
Khalliqan, ibn *Biographical Dictionary*
Kharraz, Abu Said al *Kitab al Sidq* (Eng. trans. A. J. Arberry, *The Book of Truthfulness*)
Khatib, ibn al *Al ihatah fi akhbar Gharnatah*

Kremer, von *The Orient under the Caliphs*
Lamb, H. *The Crusades—Iron Men and Saints*
— *The Crusades—The Flame of Islam*
— *The March of the Barbarians*
Lammens *L'Islam*
Landon, Lionel *Itinerary of Richard I* (London, Pipe Roll Society, 1935)
Lane-Poole, S. *The Story of Cairo*
— *A History of Egypt in The Middle Ages*
— *The Moors in Spain*
— *The Muhammadan dynasties*
— *Saladin*
Larousse *Encyclopedia of Ancient and Mediaeval History*
Legacy of Islam (Anthology)
Lewis, Bernard *The Arabs in History*
Lévi-Provençal, E. *Islam d'Occident*
— *La Civilization Arabe en Espagne*
— *Poésie Arabe d'Espagne et Poésie d'Europe Mediaevale*
— *Le Rôle Spirituel de l'Espagne Musulmane*
Lindsay, J. *Byzantium into Europe*
Lot, Ferdinand *L'art Militaire et les Armées au Moyen Age*
Luke, Sir Harry *Cyprus*
Machiavelli, Nicolo *The Art of War*
— *The Prince*
Makkari, al *Fragments from the History of the Arabs of Spain*
Maqrizi, al *Kitab al Suluk fi Maarifat al duwal wa al muluk*
— *Ittiadh al Hunafa*
Marakishi, Abdul Wahid ibn Ali al *Al Majib fi talkhis akhbar al Maghrib*
Margoliouth *Muhammad and the Rise of Islam*
Masoodi, al *Muruj al Dhahab* (Meadows of Gold)
Maundeville, Sir John, The Book of (In *Early Travellers in Palestine*, London, Bohn 1848)
Mayer *Saracenic Heraldry*
Mazahéri, Aly *La Vie Quotidienne des Musulmans au Moyen Age*
Mercier, Louis *La parure des Chevaliers et l'insigne des preux* (Fr. trans. of Ibn Hulayl, Hilyat al fursan)
Mez, Adam *The Renaissance of Islam*
Michel le Syrien, Chronique de. (Fr. trans. J. B. Chabot)
Montgomery-Watt, W. *Muhammad at Mecca*
Muhammad Ali *The Living Thoughts of The Prophet Muhammad*
— *The Holy Qoran*
Muir, Sir William *The Caliphate, its rise, decline and fall*
— *Annals of the Early Caliphate*
— *Life of Muhammad*

— *The Mameluke Slave Dynasty of Egypt*
Muqdasi, Al *A Description of The Muslim Empire*
Nasir i Khusrau *Diary of a Journey Through Syria and Palestine* (Eng. trans. Guy le Strange)
Nicholson, R. A. *A Literary History of The Arabs*
— *Translations of Eastern Poetry and Prose*
Nidham al Mulk *Siyasat nama*
Noldeke *Sketches from Eastern History*
Novara, Philip de *The Wars between Frederick II and the Ibelins*
Nuwairi, al *Al Ilman*
— *Nihayat al arab fi funun al adab* (Fr. trans. de Slane in *Journal Asiatique*)
Ockley, Simon *History of the Saracens*
Ohsson, Baron d' *Histoire des Mongols*
Okey, Thomas *Venice*
O'Leary, de Lacy *Arabia before Muhammad*
Oman, Sir Charles *The Art of War in The Middle Ages*
Osborn, R. D. *Islam under the Arabs*
Pears, Sir Edwin *The Destruction of The Greek Empire*
Pernoud, R. *The Crusade*
Pidal, R. M. *The Cid and his Spain*
Pirenne, Henri *A History of Europe*
— *Muhammad and Charlemagne*
Poliak, A. N. *Feudalism in Egypt, Syria, Palestine and Lebanon*
Prescott, H. F. M. *Jerusalem Journey*
Prescott, W. H. *Ferdinand and Isabella*
Price, M. Philips *A History of Turkey*
Popper, William *A History of Egypt, 1382–1469* (Eng. trans. of Ibn Taghri Birdi)
Qalanisi, al *The Damascus Chronicle of the Crusades* (Eng. trans. H. A. R. Gibb)
— *Subh al A'sha*
Quatremère *Histoire des Mongols de Perse* (Fr. trans. of Rasheed al Deen)
— *Histoire des Sultans Mamlouks de l'Egypte* (Fr. trans. of Maqrizi, Kitab al Suluk)
Ramsay, Sir William *The Intermixture of Races in Asia Minor*
Rasheed al Deen, Fadhlullah *Histoire des Mongols de Perse* (Fr. trans. Quatremère)
Revue de l'Orient Latin *Collection of Historians of The Crusades*
Robertson-Smith, W. *Kinship and Marriage in Early Arabia*
Runciman, Steven *A History of the Crusades* (3 vols)
— *Byzantine Civilization*
— *The Fall of Constantinople*
Sayyid Faiz Mahmud *A Short History of Islam*

Scott, S. P. *The Moorish Empire in Europe*
Setton, K. M. (ed) *History of The Crusades*
Shama, abu *See Abu*
Sibt ibn al Jozi (Yusuf ibn Qazaughli) *Mirat al Zaman fi tarikh al ayan*
Sirdar Iqbal Ali Shah *The Book of Oriental Literature*
Stevenson, W. B. *The Crusaders in The East*
Smail, R. C. *Crusading Warfare*
Strange, Guy le *Baghdad during The Abbasid Caliphate*
— *Palestine under The Moslems*
— *Lands of The Eastern Caliphate*
Suyuti, al *Tarikh al Khulafa*
Sykes, P. M. *A History of Persia*
Tabari, al *Tarikh al Rusul wa al muluk*
Taghri Birdi, ibn *Al Nujoom al Zahira fi tarikh Misr wa al Qahira*
Tisdall *Sources of The Qoran*
Trevor-Roper, H. *The Rise of Christian Europe*
Tyre, William of *A History of Deeds done beyond the Seas* (Eng. trans. Babcock & Krey N.Y. 1943)
Umar ibn Ibrahim al Ansari *Tafrij al kurub fi tadbir al hurub*
Umari, Ahmed ibn Fadhullah al *Masalik al absar fi mamalik al amsar*
Usama ibn Munqidh *An Arab Gentleman in The Period of The Crusade* (Eng. trans. P. K. Hitti)
Utbi, al *Tarikh al Yamini*
Vinsauf, Geoffrey de *Chronicle of Richard The First's Crusade*
Waqidi, al *Al mughazi*
Wellhausen, J. *The Arab Kingdom and its Fall*
— *Muhammad in Medina*
Wells, H. G. *The Outline of History*
Wiegler, Paul *The Infidel Emperor*
Wilkinson, C. *Richard Coeur de Lion*
Wittek, P. *The Rise of The Ottoman Empire*
Yacubi *Kitab al Buldan*
Yule, Sir Henry *Travels of Marco Polo*
Zaki, Abdul Rahman *Cahiers d'Histoire Egyptienne*

Index